THE MIDDLE SEA

The Normans in the South
The Kingdom in the Sun
Mount Athos (with Reresby Sitwell)
Sahara
A History of Venice
Byzantium: The Early Centuries
Byzantium: The Apogee
Byzantium: The Decline and Fall
The Architecture of Southern England
Fifty Years of Glyndebourne
Shakespeare's Kings
Paradise of Cities
The Twelve Days of Christmas
Christmas Crackers, 1970–79
More *Christmas Crackers, 1980–89*
Still More *Christmas Crackers, 1990–99*

THE MIDDLE SEA

A History of the Mediterranean

JOHN JULIUS NORWICH

Doubleday

NEW YORK   LONDON   TORONTO   SYDNEY   AUCKLAND

PUBLISHED BY DOUBLEDAY

Copyright © 2006 by John Julius Norwich

Published simultaneously in the U.K. by Chatto & Windus, London. This edition published
by arrangement with Chatto & Windus.

Published in the United States by Doubleday, an imprint of The Doubleday Broadway
Publishing Group, a division of Random House, Inc., New York.
www.doubleday.com

DOUBLEDAY and the portrayal of an anchor with a dolphin are registered trademarks
of Random House, Inc.

Library of Congress Cataloging-in-Publication Data
Norwich, John Julius, 1929–
The Middle Sea : a history of the Mediterranean / John Julius Norwich.—1st ed.
p. cm.
Includes bibliographical references and index.
1. Mediterranean Region—History. I. Title.
DE80.N67 2007
909'.09822—dc22   2006026071

ISBN-13: 978-0-385-51023-3
ISBN-10: 0-385-51023-3

PRINTED IN THE UNITED STATES OF AMERICA

1   3   5   7   9   10   8   6   4   2

First U.S. Edition

Contents

List of Maps

Maps by Reginald Piggott

List of Illustrations

Introduction

When, some five or six years ago, it was first suggested to me that I should write a history of the Mediterranean, my heart sank. The subject seemed so huge, the time span so vast; how could the whole thing possibly be compressed into a single volume? Where should it begin? Where should it end? And how – since it would obviously have to be mercilessly selective – would the selecting be done?

Somewhat to my surprise, these questions – together with many others that arose along the way – answered themselves. I had at one moment considered an introductory chapter that would deal with the formation of the Middle Sea, that majestic moment when the waters of the Atlantic crashed through the barriers at what are now the Straits of Gibraltar and flooded the immense basin which they have occupied ever since. It would have gone on to describe the seismic upheaval, almost equally dramatic, which split Europe from Asia in the northeastern corner, linking the Mediterranean with its neighbour – so close in physical terms, but so immeasurably distant in character – the Black Sea. But I am no geologist, and rather than launch my story some six million years ago I decided to begin, not with rocks and water, but with people.

And not the first people, either – simply because the first people were prehistoric, and I have always found prehistory a bore. (If an author tries to write about a subject that bores him, you can be perfectly certain that his readers will be bored too.) How much more sensible, I thought, to start with ancient Egypt, a culture which has fascinated the West ever since it was first effectively discovered by Napoleon's expedition in 1798–99. From there we have easy stepping stones leading via Crete, Mycenae and the Trojan War to ancient Greece and Rome – and then we are away.

The other vital question was where to stop. This was a problem that I had never had to face before. In the past I have written histories of a kingdom, a republic and an empire, each of which came eventually to its appointed end. Since, however, the Mediterranean can be confidently expected to continue for several million more years at least, it was clear that I should have to choose an arbitrary cut-off point; and after long hesitation, I chose the end of the First World War. One could argue forever over whether this changed the Western world more radically than did the Second; my own feeling is that it did, bringing down three mighty empires and, incidentally, making its successor inevitable. But there was another, more practical consideration too. Had I continued the story through the interwar years and on to 1945, this book would have had to be at least half as long again, and had I taken it even further – perhaps to the creation of the state of Israel in 1948 – history would have started to merge into current affairs. In such an event what I hope will prove a smooth and happy voyage might well have ended in shipwreck.

Throughout the thirty-three chapters that follow, I have done my best to keep the centre of attention on the Mediterranean itself. Once again I have as far as possible avoided physical geography. Let no one think that I underestimate the importance of tides, winds, currents and other oceanographical and meteorological phenomena; these things have shaped the whole art of navigation, they have dictated trade routes and they have decided the outcome of many a naval battle. But they have no place in these pages. All I have tried to do here is to trace the main political fortunes of the lands of the Middle Sea, insofar as their history was affected by their positions around it. This in turn means a number of perhaps surprising changes of emphasis. France, for example, is unquestionably a Mediterranean country, but its political centre is far away to the north; the French Revolution consequently receives only a passing mention, and you will find no references at all to Joan of Arc or the Massacre of St Bartholomew. The county of Provence, with the great city of Marseille and the magnificent port of Toulon, matters to us far more than does Paris.

Spain is something of a special case. Ferdinand and Isabella are of huge importance for a number of reasons: their destruction of the Kingdom of Granada, their wholesale expulsions of Muslims and Jews which profoundly affected the demography of western Europe, and not least their sponsorship of Columbus – the first step in the downgrading of the Mediterranean to the comparative backwater which it was to become in the sixteenth and seventeenth centuries. Later Spanish dynastic problems are also all too relevant to our story, throwing as they did much of the continent into confusion. The Peninsular War, on the other hand, principally centred as it was on northwest Spain and Portugal, I deemed to be no concern of ours.

There was no doubt about Constantinople. The city itself may command only the Bosphorus and the Sea of Marmara, but the two successive empires of which it was the capital, the Byzantine and the Ottoman, occupied at various times well over half the shoreline of the Mediterranean. Each, therefore, constitutes an integral part of our story. And we have only to think of the great historic islands: Sicily, Cyprus, Malta and Crete. The first was part of the Byzantine Empire for several centuries (and, for one brief moment, its capital);[1] the other three all suffered appalling sieges by the Ottoman Turks, two of which were successful. Only Malta survived unconquered until the time of Napoleon.

The two Mediterranean countries *par excellence* are Italy and Greece. No reader of this book will be surprised at the prominence given to the former – the more so since before the second half of the nineteenth century Italy was merely, in Metternich's words, 'a geographical expression'. Between Savoy in the north and Sicily in the south, the peninsula was, for some fourteen centuries, a constantly shifting kaleidoscope of kingdoms, principalities, duchies, republics and city-states, all liable to major or minor invasions by their Italian neighbours or by others: the French, the Spanish, and even – if we count Nelson's fleet as invaders – the British. I have tried, in the Italian chapters, to keep the issues as simple as possible; but history is a cruel and remorseless taskmaster, and if an occasional paragraph has to be read twice I can only plead *force majeure*. It was with immense relief that I finally reached the Risorgimento and the unification of Italy – a goal for which I personally had longed every bit as much as Mazzini. By then my work was almost done.

Greece, by contrast, makes only four major appearances in this book: in Chapters II, VIII, XVIII and XXV. The reason is not far to seek: for some five centuries it lay, like the rest of eastern Europe, under Turkish rule. Thus, from the time of the Ottoman conquest of the mainland (and most of the islands) in the late fourteenth century, it was condemned to a state of near stagnation; not until the first years of the nineteenth did the Greek spirit revive. The ensuing fight for independence was not, perhaps, the epic of uninterrupted heroism that is sometimes depicted, but it succeeded; and the capture of Salonica in 1912 gave us, in all its essentials, the Greece that we have today.

We are left with North Africa – or most of it. Egypt is of course a special case, thanks very largely to the river Nile. Had there been other,

---

[1] See Chapter VI, p.88.

parallel streams to the west, the history of the entire region would have been radically different; as there are not, the countries bordering the Mediterranean on its southern side consist very largely of desert, apart from the cities and towns ranged along a fairly narrow coastal strip. It is, of course, with this strip that we are chiefly concerned. In the days of antiquity it managed to have a remarkably distinguished history. As early as the sixth century BC, in what is now Cyrenaica in eastern Libya, several Greek cities were already flourishing; Cyrene, with its port of Apollonia, was one of the most prosperous in the Greek world. A hundred years later, Carthage – in what is now Tunisia – dominated well over half the North African coast and was soon to constitute a major threat to Rome, while by the third century AD Roman Africa extended from the Atlantic coast to Tripolitania – whose capital, Leptis Magna, was the birthplace of Septimius Severus, one of the most distinguished of the later Roman Emperors.

Further to the west, Algeria and Morocco have, I fear, received comparatively short shrift. Algerian history was much as might have been expected: Roman – as part of what the Romans called Mauretania Caesariensis – then Vandal, Byzantine, Umayyad, Almoravid, Almohad and Ottoman until the arrival of the French in 1830. In Morocco the situation was much the same in the earlier centuries; in the later, there was one crucial difference: this was the only country in North Africa that never suffered Turkish domination, keeping its own native rulers until the nineteenth century. This simple fact has had an extraordinary effect on the character of the country which – though it extends further to the west than anywhere in mainland Europe and is indeed far more an Atlantic country than a Mediterranean one – is somehow infused with an oriental exoticism unique in the modern Islamic world.

I feel a little guilty, too, about one indisputably Mediterranean country which I have most unjustly overlooked. The principality of Monaco may measure only one square mile, but it can claim to have been an independent nation since the fifteenth century, with a reigning royal house, that of the Grimaldis, going back even earlier, to 1297 – the oldest in Europe. It certainly deserves a mention, and it has not had one. I thought at one moment of introducing a few light-hearted pages about the growth of the Riviera, in which I should certainly have given the principality its due, but I realised that they would have settled only very uneasily into their surroundings and regretfully gave up the idea. I hope at least that this paragraph will reassure the Monegasques that they have not been entirely forgotten.

A word about proper names. In a book of this kind there can be no rules; far too much, it seems to me, can be sacrificed on the altar of consistency. I have therefore allowed myself to be guided by familiarity alone. Greek names have tended to be Latinised (Comnenus rather than Komnenos), Christian names to be Anglicised (William of Sicily rather than Guglielmo) and Arabic names where possible simplified (Saladin). To avoid confusion, on the other hand, I have made countless exceptions: thus you will find Lewis, Louis and Ludwig; Francis, François and Franz; Isabella and Isabel, Peter and Pedro, Caterina and Catherine. Where places have an English name I have normally used it (though I draw the line at Leghorn); where the names changed, as it were, in midstream (Adrianople to Edirne, Zante to Zakynthos) I have changed with them, but where necessary have given the older name in brackets. This is all very unscholarly, but as I have pointed out in almost every book I have ever written, I am no scholar.

There is a special problem about Constantinople. In theory, after the Turkish conquest of 1453, it should be called by its Turkish name, Istanbul. In fact, however, it was invariably referred to as Constantinople by the British government – and fairly generally in this country – until well after the Second World War. I have therefore used whichever name seemed most suitable in the context.

I cannot hope to thank all those who have helped me to write the pages that follow, but one debt in particular cannot go unrecorded. Soon after I started work, my wife and I were invited to dinner at the Spanish Embassy. I told the Ambassador, my dear friend Santiago de Tamarón, that while I was fairly familiar with the eastern Mediterranean (having written a history of Byzantium) and with the central (having written one of Venice) I was shamefully ignorant of the western, knowing little of Spanish history and speaking no Spanish. 'Oh,' he said, 'I think we might be able to do something about that.' A few weeks later there came an invitation for my wife and me to spend ten days in Spain as guests of the Fundación Carolina, going wherever we wanted. Those days – for which we are both more than grateful – proved of immense value; even though my lack of Spanish scholarship will still, I fear, be all too apparent, I trust that thanks to them I have not actually disgraced myself.

My daughter Allegra Huston copy-edited this book from New Mexico and put me through a grilling such as I have never suffered before. I am hugely grateful to her, as to Penny Hoare and Lily Richards at Chatto. Virtually every word in the pages that follow – and in nearly all my previous books, for that matter – has been written in the Reading Room of the London Library. My thanks go, as always, to all members of its staff for their unfailing helpfulness and courtesy. What would I do without them?

John Julius Norwich

CHAPTER I

Beginnings

The Mediterranean is a miracle. Seeing it on the map for the millionth time, we tend to take it for granted; but if we try to look at it objectively we suddenly realise that here is something utterly unique, a body of water that might have been deliberately designed, like no other on the surface of the globe, as a cradle of cultures. Almost enclosed by its surrounding lands, it is saved from stagnation by the Straits of Gibraltar, those ancient Pillars of Hercules which protect it from the worst of the Atlantic storms and keep its waters fresh and – at least until recent years – unpolluted. It links three of the world's six continents; its climate for much of the year is among the most benevolent to be found anywhere.

Small wonder, then, that the Middle Sea should not only have nurtured three of the most dazzling civilisations of antiquity, and witnessed the birth or blossoming of three of our greatest religions; it also provided the principal means of communication. Roads in ancient times were virtually nonexistent; the only effective method of transport was by water, which had the added advantage of being able to support immense weights immovable by any other means. The art of navigation may have been still in its infancy, but early sailors were greatly assisted by the fact that throughout much of the eastern Mediterranean it was possible to sail from port to port without ever losing sight of land; even in the western, a moderately straight course was all that was necessary to ensure an arrival on some probably friendly coast before many days had passed.[1] To be sure, life at sea was never without its dangers. The *mistral* that screams down the Rhône valley and lashes the Gulf of Lyons to a frenzy, the *bora* in the Adriatic that can make it almost impossible for the people of Trieste to walk unassisted down the street, the *gregale* in the Ionian that has ruined many a winter cruise – all these could spell death for the inexperienced or unwary. Even the mild *meltemi* in the Aegean, usually a blessing to ships under sail, can transform itself within an hour into a raging monster and drive them on to the rocks. True, there are no Atlantic hurricanes or Pacific

---

[1] Unless of course one was Odysseus; ten years between Troy and Ithaca must, even in his day, have been something of a record.

typhoons, and for most of the time – given a modicum of care – the going is easy enough; still, there was no point in taking unnecessary risks, so the earliest Mediterranean seafarers kept their journeys as short as possible.

When possible, too, they kept to the northern shore. To most of us today, the map of the Mediterranean is so familiar that we can no longer look at it objectively. If, however, we were to see it for the first time, we should be struck by the contrast between the littorals to the north and south. That to the north is full of incident, with the Italian and Balkan peninsulas flanked by three seas – Tyrrhenian, Adriatic and Aegean – and then that extraordinary conformation of the extreme northeast corner, where the Dardanelles lead up to the little inland Sea of Marmara, from the eastern end of which the city of Istanbul commands the entrance to the Bosphorus and ultimately to the Black Sea. The southern coast, by contrast, is comparatively featureless, with few indentations; there one is always conscious, even in the major cities, that the desert is never far away.

One of the many unsolved questions of ancient history is why, after countless millennia of caveman existence, the first glimmerings of civilisation should have made their appearance in widely separated areas at much the same time. Around the Mediterranean that time is, very roughly, about 3000 BC. It is true that Byblos (the modern Jbeil, some fifteen miles north of Beirut), which gave its name to the Bible – the word actually means papyrus – was settled in palaeolithic times and is believed by many to be considerably older still; indeed, it may well be the oldest continuously inhabited site in the world. But the remains of a few one-room huts and a crude idol or two can hardly be considered civilisation, and there as elsewhere nothing much really happens until the coming of the Bronze Age at the beginning of the third millennium BC. Then at last things start to move. There are some extraordinary monolithic tombs in Malta dating from about this time, and others in Sicily and Sardinia, but of the people who built them we know next to nothing. The three great cultures that now emerge have their origins a good deal further east: in Egypt, Palestine and Crete.

Of the traditional Seven Wonders of the Ancient World, only the oldest, the Pyramids of Egypt, survives today; and there is little doubt that they will still be standing five thousand years hence. The most venerable of all, the step pyramid at Saqqara, is said to date from 2686 BC; the grandest and noblest, that of the Pharaoh Khufu – known to Herodotus and so, normally, to us as Cheops – from a century later.

Their longevity should cause us no surprise; their shape alone is almost enough to confer immortality. No buildings in the world are less top-heavy. Not even an earthquake could seriously shake them. Gazing up at them, one is dumbfounded by the sheer magnitude of the achievement, and of the underlying ambition: that a man, nearly five thousand years ago, should take it upon himself to build a mountain, and succeed in doing so. Only twenty-five years later, Cheops's son Chefren built another, connected to a monumental hall of alabaster and red granite, along the walls of which were twenty-three seated statues of himself. Finally, he commissioned the Sphinx. It may well be his portrait; it can certainly claim to be the oldest piece of monumental sculpture – it is actually carved from an outcrop of rock – known to man.

Egypt, having started so early, was always slow to change. Cheops and Chefren belonged to the Fourth Dynasty; of the first three we know nothing but the names of some of the rulers. The last dynasty was the Thirty-First, which ended in 335 BC with the conquest of the country by the Persians; three years later they in their turn were thrown out by Alexander the Great. Alexander did not linger – he never did – but marched on to Mesopotamia and the further east. After his death in 323 Egypt passed to his former general, Ptolemy, whose line, more Greek than Egyptian, continued for another three centuries. Thus, from the shadowy beginnings with the First Dynasty until the death of Cleopatra in 30 BC, there extended a period of more than three thousand years; yet the untutored eye, balefully staring at relief carvings on the walls of tombs or at endless columns of hieroglyphics, finds it hard to distinguish the art of one millennium from that of the next.

Nonetheless, a few other great names imprint themselves on the memory: Queen Hatshepsut (1490–69 BC), for example, who, though technically only regent for her stepson and nephew Thutmose III, completed the temple at Karnak – erecting two obelisks there to commemorate the fact – and decorated the awe-inspiring pink granite temple of Deir el-Bahri at Thebes, on the walls of which she is represented as a man; Thutmose himself, who on her death in 1469, in what seems to have been a paroxysm of vindictive spite, ordered every portrait of her to be defaced and every inscription bearing her name chiselled away, but who later extended the bounds of his kingdom to the upper reaches of the Euphrates and proved himself – by his talents as general, lawgiver, builder and patron of the arts – one of the greatest of the pharaohs; Amenhotep IV, better known as Akhnaton (1367–50 BC) – instantly recognisable by his long, narrow, pointed face, stooping body and huge thighs – a religious fanatic who forbade the worship of the Theban sun god Amon, instituting instead that of the solar disc Aton, its rays as depicted ending in tiny hands outstretched to bless (or curse); his son-in-law and second successor the boy king Tutankhamun (1347–39 BC), who reverted to the old religion but would be obscure enough today were it not for Howard Carter's discovery on 5 November 1922 of his tomb, the sarcophagus almost invisible beneath the higgledy-piggledy piles of golden treasure – treasure which is to this day the chief glory of the Cairo Museum; and Rameses II, the Great (1290–24 BC), the megalomaniac who erected statues of himself all over Egypt and Nubia and may well have been the Pharaoh of the Exodus – though scholars are still arguing about this, and will continue to do so for many years to come. Finally we must make special mention of Akhnaton's queen, Nefertiti, whose bust – found in the excavated studio of an ancient craftsman in her husband's capital of Tell-el-Amarna and now in Berlin – suggests that she was one of the most ravishingly beautiful women who ever lived.[1] Neither the Greeks nor the Romans, nor even the greatest sculptors of the Italian Renaissance, were ever to portray her equal. If ancient Egypt had produced no other work of art than this, those three millennia would still have been worth while.

Another reason for the strange timelessness of Egypt is its astonishing geography. Seen from the air, it looks exactly like a map of itself: vast expanses of yellow, with a thin blue-green line snaking up from the south, and a narrow border of green along each side before the yellow takes over again. To Egypt, the Nile is like the sun: a necessity to continuing national life in a way that no other river could ever be, as essential as a breathing tube to a deep-sea diver. In such conditions there is little opportunity for change; outside Cairo, Alexandria and one or two of the larger towns, life in most of Egypt carries on very much as it always has. There are few greater travelling pleasures than to board the night sleeper from Cairo to Luxor, and to awake early the next morning to find oneself moving at about ten miles an hour along the riverbank, while just outside the train window, golden in the early sunlight, there passes scene after scene straight out of a Victorian child's geography book.

From earliest times the Egyptians were a single, coherent state; their

---

[1] Though I wish someone would do something about her left eye.

Phoenician contemporaries seem to have made no attempt ever to create one. Though they were compulsive travellers, their home was Palestine. The Old Testament refers to the people of Tyre and Sidon, of Byblos and Arwad (this last situated further up the coast, roughly opposite the southern shore of Cyprus). All four communities sprang up around 1550 BC, and all four were ports, the Phoenicians being essentially a maritime people. We read in the First Book of Kings how Hiram, King of Tyre, sent King Solomon timber and skilled craftsmen for the building of the Temple in Jerusalem, but for the most part he and his subjects stuck to the narrow coastal strip between the mountains of Lebanon and the sea. They had developed one memorable home industry: gathering the shells of the murex, a form of mollusc which secreted a rich purple dye, worth far more than its weight in gold.[1] But their principal interest lay always in the lands to the west – with whom, however, they traded more as a loose confederation of merchant communities than as anything resembling a nation.

Today we remember the Phoenicians above all as seafarers, a people who sailed to every corner of the Mediterranean and quite often beyond. Herodotus tells us that in about 600 BC, at the behest of Pharaoh Necho, they circumnavigated the continent of Africa. If he was right (or nearly so), this was an achievement which would not be repeated for more than two thousand years. (If, on the other hand, he was wrong, how did he know – or even believe – that it was circumnavigable?) There is little doubt, in any case, that Hiram and Solomon participated in occasional voyages from Ezion-Geber (near the modern Eilat) to the fabled Ophir, which – though nobody seems quite sure – was probably on the Sudanese or Somali coast. At other times Phoenician merchants established trading colonies at Mozia in Sicily, Ibiza in the Balearic Islands and along the shores of North Africa. They then passed through the Straits of Gibraltar to explore the Atlantic ports of both Spain and Morocco; they certainly had an outpost on the promontory of Cadiz, protected by its surrounding marshes. We are told that a certain Himilco even crossed the English Channel, landing on the south coast of Britain (probably Cornwall) in quest of tin.

---

[1] In Roman times the Emperor Nero was to pass an edict restricting the wearing of this purple to himself alone. It remained an imperial colour – certain emperors were said to have been 'born in the purple' – until the fall of the Byzantine Empire in 1453, and even today retains something of its old prestige. The principal drawback of the murex industry was the appalling smell that it created; the piles of broken shells were always sited downwind of the town.

The Phoenicians remained an important economic force in the Mediterranean until the end of the eighth century BC, when they were overshadowed first by the growing might of Assyria, and then by that of the Greeks.

Thanks above all to the luxury goods which they provided, they were also a force for civilisation. From their Levantine home, as well as from Cyprus, Egypt, Anatolia and Mesopotamia, they would bring ivory and rare woods, superb drinking vessels of gold and silver, flasks of glass and alabaster, seals and scarabs of precious and semiprecious stone. But their greatest gift to posterity was unconnected to trade or navigation; it was they, almost certainly, who first evolved an alphabet. Hieroglyphics in the Egyptian manner were all very well, but they were slow to write, frequently ambiguous to read and incapable of expressing subtle shades of meaning. The invention of a system whereby any spoken word could be represented by a small group of letters drawn from a repertoire of a couple of dozen was an immeasurably great step forward, and there is little doubt that this step was first taken by a group of Semitic-speaking people on the eastern shore of the Mediterranean. The earliest clearly readable alphabetic inscription, found at Byblos, probably dates from the eleventh century BC, but primitive versions of the alphabet – consisting entirely of consonants – were in use several centuries before that; if we date the original invention to somewhere between 1700 and 1500 BC we shall not be very far wrong. In due course this alphabet was first adopted, then adapted by the Greeks; it can thus be seen as the rude forefather of our own.

As the pyramids were being built in Egypt, the people of Crete were also beginning to stir. Men there were working in copper and bronze, but more interesting are the early knives made of obsidian – that strange volcanic glass, usually coal-black, which when chipped produces an edge like a razor – because obsidian had to be imported, probably from Anatolia, and imports mean trade. Archaeologists have found objects from still further afield – ivory, rock crystal and semiprecious stones – of only slightly later dates. By 2000 BC Crete seems to have become the commercial crossroads of the eastern Mediterranean – we have it from no less an authority than Odysseus himself[1] that during the spring and summer the winds in the Aegean made it possible to cross from Crete to

---

[1] *Odyssey*, Book X.

Egypt in only five days – and the island's two greatest palaces, at Knossos and Phaestos, were rapidly taking shape.

Crete's Windsor Castle is the palace of Knossos, where the first excavations by Sir Arthur Evans began in 1899. Small, swarthy and immensely strong, Evans gave the best years of his life to the palace, and very remarkable it is: it covers a vast area, well over 10,000 square metres; parts of it were three or even four storeys high; and the plumbing seems to have been better than anything known in Europe before the nineteenth century. The trouble is that in Evans's day archaeology was still in its infancy, and he was able to indulge his artistic imagination to a degree that leaves the modern visitor aghast. King Minos, entering the palace today, might find vaguely familiar some of the architecture and furnishings that have survived – the gypsum throne, for example (on which one is still allowed to sit), and those curious columns in the Hall of the Palace that taper downwards – but would he recognise Sir Arthur's attempts to reproduce his interior decoration: the blazing vermilions, the rich butter-yellows, the unmistakable suggestions of art nouveau, or, most astonishing of all, the murals? The most famous of these is based, so far as one can see, on what appears to be a large piece of toffee in one corner, bearing a few barely identifiable traces of colour. From this Evans has extrapolated a wildly exuberant design of leaping dolphins – pleasing, perhaps, but far, far from authentic.

Did King Minos – the question has to be asked – really exist? According to Homer, he was the son of Zeus and Europa, but Diodorus Siculus, writing in Agrigento during the first century BC, gives him a rather less elevated lineage and relates how, in a contest for the kingship of Crete, he prayed to Poseidon to send him a bull from the sea for sacrifice. The god obliged, but the bull was so beautiful that Minos could not bear to sacrifice it and kept it for himself. In revenge Poseidon caused Minos's wife, Pasiphae, to fall in love with the animal, and it was their most unnatural union that engendered the Minotaur, half man and half bull, whom the King kept in a Daedalus-designed labyrinth. None of this, admittedly, suggests a historical personage; on the other hand Thucydides, a historian who normally keeps his feet firmly on the ground, credits Minos with having assembled the first great navy in the Mediterranean, subjugating the Cyclades, largely clearing the sea of pirates and establishing governors on certain islands of the Aegean. As for the labyrinth, there is no better description of the palace of Knossos; the unwary visitor without a guide may well envy

7

Theseus, who, leaving the Minotaur dead behind him, had the advantage of Ariadne's thread to lead him back to freedom. Finally, the bull. He is seen, or at least suggested, everywhere throughout the palace; there is a fascinating fresco – perhaps a degree or two more authentic than most – showing a charging animal with an intrepid little athlete somersaulting clear over his horns. In the life as well as the religion of the Minoans the bull clearly played a key role; one would love to know more about him.

This extraordinary civilisation – talented, cultivated and extremely rich – ruled an empire covering most of the islands of the Aegean and until around 1400 BC exercised a powerful influence over the whole eastern Mediterranean, leaving traces as far afield as Transylvania and on the Danube, as well as in Sardinia and the Aeolian Islands just off the northeast coast of Sicily. It must have been fun to be a Minoan. The objects that they left behind them give the impression of a happy, peaceful, carefree people, secure enough to leave their cities unwalled; the invention of the potter's wheel provided them with drinking vessels, jugs and storage jars in astonishingly sophisticated shapes, which they decorated with swirling abstract patterns or designs of birds, flowers and fish. Their clothes were elaborate – sometimes almost fantastical – with a good deal of toplessness, their jewellery of dazzling golden filigree. They enjoyed a degree of luxury unprecedented in history and not to be equalled until the dissipated days of the Roman Empire. Their life was easy, their climate delectable. They mistrusted all things military. They made love, not war.

But then disaster struck, as sooner or later it always does. Just what happened is unclear. An invasion by a powerful and vindictive enemy has been suggested; in such a case that enemy would most probably have been Mycenae. A likelier explanation – though it does not necessarily rule out the other – lies in the tremendous volcanic eruption which occurred around 1470 BC on Santorini (the modern Thira), some sixty miles to the north. Knossos was simultaneously shattered by a series of violent earthquakes, while an immense tidal wave swept against the north coast of Crete, flooding every harbour along it. The eruption also threw up a vast cloud of ash similar to that which was to bury Pompeii thirteen centuries later. (Some of this ash has been identified as far away as Israel and Anatolia.) The island, depopulated and defenceless, would have been an easy prey to foreign invaders. Minoan civilisation was over.

*

Exactly how the civilisation of Greek Mycenae became the heir and successor to that of Crete is not altogether clear. There had been people living in this little mountain stronghold since the sixth millennium BC, but not until the middle of the second did they distinguish themselves in any particular way. Then, from one generation to the next around 1500 BC, they became very much richer and more sophisticated, their shaft graves on the acropolis filled with ornaments and accoutrements of gold. Curiously enough, none of these show any Minoan influence. Did the Mycenaeans, perhaps, hire themselves out as mercenaries to the pharaohs of the Eighteenth Dynasty, bringing back with them the Egyptian belief in life after death, the custom of packing their graves with necessities for that afterlife, and the fashion for golden death masks – one of which was to cause Heinrich Schliemann, while digging at Mycenae, to cable to the King of Prussia: 'I have gazed upon the face of Agamemnon!'? It would be pleasant to think that they did; alas, we shall never know.

Very soon after this, however – and still well before the eruption and earthquake – Minoan ideas took hold. Here, suddenly, all over Mycenae, are the bulls, the double axes, the horns of consecration and all the insignia of Knossos. Were they the result of one or more important dynastic marriages? Probably: it is hard to think of any other convincing explanation. At all events, Mycenae underwent a rapid education, and when the Minoans suffered their mysterious eclipse their successors were ready. By about 1400 BC their cultural influence had spread all over the Peloponnese, with commercial links extending yet further afield. In Italy, which they seem to have reached towards the end of the fifteenth century BC, there were Mycenaean settlements along the southern coast of the Adriatic, the Gulf of Taranto and even as far as Sardinia, Ischia and the Bay of Naples. In Mycenae itself the Cyclopean walls surrounding the acropolis, with their famous Lion Gate in the northwest corner, went up around 1300 BC; there was gold and bronze in abundance, with craftsmanship sufficiently developed to produce the massive chariots for which the city had long been famous. Mycenae, then at the height of its power, was ready for the Trojan War.

Troy stands at the northwestern corner of Asia Minor. The city today – or what remains of it – seems a small enough settlement, and indeed the war itself, which is nowadays usually ascribed to some time in the middle of the thirteenth century BC, may well have been of no great historical significance. Culturally, on the other hand, it was one of the most important wars ever fought, since it supplied the subject for

9

the world's first great epic poems. Homer's *Iliad*, written in the eighth century BC, tells the story of the ten-year siege of Troy; its successor, the *Odyssey*, follows the wanderings of the war's hero Odysseus before he eventually returns to his own kingdom of Ithaca. Here is the beginning of poetry – and perhaps of history too – as we know it today.

The story is familiar to us all. Paris, the son of King Priam of Troy, abducts Helen, who is not only the wife of Menelaus, King of Sparta, but is also – having been hatched out of an egg laid by Leda after her adventure with Zeus in the guise of a swan – the most beautiful woman in the world. In revenge, a league of Greek cities declares war on Troy and sends against it a huge fleet, carrying an army under the command of Menelaus's brother Agamemnon, King of Mycenae. For ten years the Greeks besiege the city; finally, by means of the wooden horse, they capture it. The horse can safely be ascribed to legend; so, too, can the beauty of Helen, 'the face that launched a thousand ships'; so, very probably, can Helen herself. But the *Iliad* is by no means all myth. When Heinrich Schliemann first visited the site of Troy in 1868, there was a substantial body of opinion which held that the city had never existed at all, and the majority of those who did believe in it favoured a completely different location, a place called Bunarbashi; it was Schliemann who first identified Hisarlik, some six miles away to the north, as the true site, entirely on the basis of the geographical evidence given in the *Iliad*. One of the reasons for his rejection of Bunarbashi was that it was three hours' journey from the coast: Homer specifically states that the Greeks were able to go back and forth several times a day between their ships and the beleaguered city. Another was the steepness of the slope:

> I left my guide with the horse at the top and I went down the precipice, which inclines at first at an angle of 45 degrees and then at an angle of about 65 degrees so that I was forced to go down on all fours. It took me almost fifteen minutes to get down and I came away convinced that no mortal, not even a goat, was ever able to run down a slope of 65 degrees and that Homer, always so precise in his topography, could not have wanted us to believe that Hector and Achilles ran down this impossible slope three times.

At Hisarlik the situation was very different:

> The slopes which one has to cross in going around the city are so gentle that they can be traversed at running speed without risk of falling. In running three times around the city Hector and Achilles thus covered fifteen kilometres.

Unfortunately, Homer clearly states in the *Iliad* that there were two springs at Troy, one hot and one cold; none could be found at Hisarlik. At Bunarbashi, on the other hand, the situation was even less as he describes: Schliemann found no fewer than thirty-four – all, according to his pocket thermometer, of precisely equal temperature – and was later told that there were six more that he had missed. He got over the difficulty by assuming that the underground watercourses had been changed by subsequent earthquakes, which indeed they very probably had.

There also exists historical evidence for the Trojan War, or for something very like it. Records left by the Hittites of Anatolia[1] indicate a large-scale Mycenaean military expedition to Asia Minor during the thirteenth century BC; moreover, the city that is revealed in the sixth of the nine archaeological layers discovered on the site at Hisarlik – which is now generally accepted to be that of the Homeric Troy – shows every sign of having come to a violent end. We shall have to be content with that – not, of course, that Schliemann was. He had burrowed right down to the second layer when suddenly, on the penultimate day of the dig, he came upon a quantity of golden treasure and later proclaimed to the world that he had found the jewels of Helen of Troy; he even had a photograph taken of his beautiful Greek wife – whom he had previously sent for, sight unseen, by mail order from Athens – bedecked with them. We now know, however, that that treasure belonged to a period almost a thousand years earlier than the days of King Priam. Poor Schliemann: he never knew how wrong he was.[2]

The three or four centuries following the Trojan War were marked by no outstanding civilisation of the kind we have been discussing. This was a period of change and transition, with invasions of Dorian tribes from the north and consequent shifts of population which involved considerable new Greek settlements in Asia Minor. It was not until about 800 BC that things finally settled down again, with the lands bordering the Aegean finally united by a single language and culture. Even then, among the countless isolated feudal communities which made up the Greek world, we find no single town or city rising to the

---

[1] Barely heard of before the end of the nineteenth century, the Hittites are now known to have created a powerful kingdom during the second millennium BC; their civilisation was related, however, more to the Anatolian uplands than to the Mediterranean.

[2] The treasure was looted by the Russian army from the Berlin Museum during the Second World War. For many years it was thought to have gone forever – possibly melted down by some Russian soldier. Only recently have the Russians announced that they have it in safe keeping.

top or in any way standing out from the rest; but trade and communications had been restored, and – more important still – the alphabet had been revived and improved, above all by the introduction of vowels. The stage was thus set for the beginnings of literature, and promptly on cue, probably around 750 BC, Homer made his appearance. Had he been born any earlier, his two great epics might never have existed; the language would not have been ready for him and he himself would almost certainly have been illiterate. (Several scholars have indeed argued that he was; both works betray signs of oral composition and transmission, and both contain occasional inconsistencies where the poet seems to contradict himself.[1]) Even if they were originally written, we know for a fact that it was only under the rule of Peisistratus, around 540 BC, that they were first transcribed in what must pass for an authentic edition.

However his work was composed, Homer sang of a golden age, an age of gods and heroes that had absolutely nothing in common with the humdrum world of his own day. But to him that age, however different, would not have seemed so very distant. He was, after all, writing only some five hundred years after the events he described, a period rather less than that which separates us from the Wars of the Roses. And if, as is now generally agreed, he was an Ionian – born probably in either Smyrna (now Izmir) or Chios – Troy itself was not impossibly far away.

We know of only one other major poet who seems to have been a rough contemporary of Homer. Hesiod tells us that his family, too, was of Ionian stock, though his father had settled in Boeotia shortly before he was born. His most celebrated work is probably the *Theogony*, or the 'Birth of the Gods'. In it he tells of the events that led to the birth and kingship of Zeus: the castration of Uranus by Cronus, and the overthrow of Cronus and the Titans by the gods of Olympus. He left several other long poems which we possess in whole or in part, of which the most important is his *Works and Days* – a work as unlike the *Theogony* as can possibly be imagined. It is more like a sermon than anything else, written perhaps by a slightly cantankerous upper-class English vicar in the late seventeenth century, extolling the virtues of honest toil and denouncing dishonesty and idleness; there is also practical advice on such subjects as agriculture, religious observance and good behaviour. Not many people read Hesiod today, and that is

---

[1] Self-contradiction, it must be said, is not unknown in modern literature either. All it proves is that Homer had a poor copy-editor.

hardly surprising. His poems are not without interest, and it is remarkable that at that date they should have been written at all; but he has none of Homer's drive, none of his raciness, none of his wild imagination. Hesiod is a pale, silver moon; Homer is the sun in all its golden splendour.

It was probably only some ten or fifteen years after the Trojan War – though it may have been earlier – that there occurred one of the most important migrations in all history: that of the Hebrews under Moses, who led his people out of Egypt and into the land of Canaan, known to us more familiarly as Palestine. Whether the relatively short distance they travelled – some 400 miles at the most – really took them forty years as the Bible tells us, is open to doubt; a good deal more certain is the fact that their presence was resented by the Philistines and others who already inhabited what the people of Israel regarded as their promised land. Their original twelve tribes were therefore compelled to unite, and to elect sovereigns around whose thrones they could lead a more coherent national life. The first of these kings was Saul, who reigned from 1025 to 1010 BC, but it was under his successor, David, and David's son Solomon that the kingdom rose to its apogee. David it was who annihilated the Philistines and subdued all the other neighbouring tribes, choosing the little hill town of Jerusalem as his capital. There Solomon built a splendid palace and – still more magnificent – the first Temple. He also developed the port of Ezion-Geber on the Red Sea, giving the kingdom a new and direct link with Africa.

But it was all too good to last. After Solomon's death his realm split, into the Kingdom of Israel in the north and that of Judah in the south; the constant discord between the two rivals weakened them both and made them an easy prey to their enemies. Around the middle of the eighth century BC the Assyrians invaded, and in 722 BC the Kingdom of Israel was destroyed. Judah, under its king Hezekiah, remained for the moment inviolate, but only for another twenty-odd years. As the century ended, the Assyrian king Sennacherib swept down, in Byron's words, 'like a wolf on the fold', to the walls of Jerusalem and called for the city's surrender. Hezekiah, encouraged by the prophet Isaiah, defied him. At this point Assyrian records suggest that Sennacherib had to hurry home to deal with domestic troubles; Isaiah, on the other hand – supported to some extent by Herodotus – claims that a miraculous plague descended on the invading army. Somehow, in any case, Jerusalem was spared.

But not for long. A century later, in 586 BC, Nebuchadnezzar, King of Babylon, destroyed the city utterly, blinding King Zedekiah – having first obliged him to witness the death of his sons – and carrying him off, together with 10,000 of his leading subjects including the prophet Ezekiel, to their Babylonian captivity. Only in 538 BC, with the capture of Babylon by Cyrus the Great of Persia, were the exiles – or the Jews, as we may now call them – permitted to return. They founded a new Hebrew state, restored the Temple and re-established the old ritual as prescribed in the books of Leviticus and Numbers. Their troubles were, for the moment, over.

CHAPTER II

Ancient Greece

The centuries following Homer saw the collapse of what one might call the palace-based civilisations of the late Bronze Age and their replacement by far more open, more numerous and comparatively more democratic regimes. One of the first and most powerful was that of the city of Corinth, which rapidly grew to be the leading naval power in Greece. The Corinthians boasted a superb geographical position astride the isthmus which bears their city's name, and which gave them access to both the Ionian Sea and the Aegean; they established control of the trade routes to Italy, and founded colonies as far away as Syracuse in Sicily, Apollonia in present-day Libya and, after the first naval battle recorded in Greek history – it was fought in about 670 BC and was won largely by Corinth's new secret weapon, the trireme – the island of Corfu. But Corinthian supremacy was relatively short; by the sixth century BC the star of Athens was rising fast.

By this time the Greeks had colonised the entire eastern Mediterranean as far west as Sicily. (One group, from the city of Phocaea in Asia Minor, went even further and founded a colony at Emporion, now Empuries, on the coast of Catalonia, the only Greek colony in Spain of which we have firm evidence.) They had civilised it too – with their art and architecture, their literature and philosophy, their science and mathematics and their manufacturing skills. We should also be grateful to them for their introduction of fine wine, and with it its associated rites and social practices, the most important of which was the feast, or symposium. But the Greeks were never an empire in the sense that Rome was to be. Politically, they were simply a large quantity of small city-states, often at war among themselves, occasionally forming temporary leagues and alliances but essentially independent. Athens was in those days in no sense a capital, any more than, for example, Halicarnassus in Asia Minor where Herodotus was born, or Syracuse in Sicily which was the birthplace of Archimedes, or the island of Samos, home of Pythagoras. St Paul was to boast that he was a Roman citizen; such a thing could never have been said about Greece, which – not unlike Judaism today – was a concept rather than a nationality. There was no precise definition. If you felt you were Greek and spoke the Greek language, then Greek is what you were.

One consequence of this broad diaspora is that there are as many magnificent Greek sites in Italy, Sicily and around the west and south coasts of Asia Minor as there are in mainland Greece, and they are often even more rewarding to the visitor. The Parthenon, it goes without saying, is in a class by itself;[1] the same could be said, perhaps, for the architectural masterpieces at Olympia and Bassae. But then one thinks of the great temples of Paestum south of Naples, or of those at Segesta and Agrigento in Sicily; or, beyond the Aegean, of the immense Greek theatre at Ephesus, of the smaller ones overlooking the sea at Side and Kaş or of the almost unbearably evocative ruins of Priene, one of the relatively few Greek cities of the coast to have escaped romanisation, with its lovely little *bouleterion* where the chosen representatives of the people would meet under the sky and conduct the business of the city. All this may not be Greece as we think of the country today, but it is the Greek world, which is far more important.

There were also a number of petty kingdoms in Asia Minor which, though increasingly influenced by Greek culture until they were almost completely hellenised, had their origins in those far-off days before the Greeks were ever heard of: Pergamum, for example, whose shrine to Aesculapius, the god of healing, had made it a place of pilgrimage for many centuries before it acquired something approaching political supremacy in the second and first centuries BC; or Phrygia, whose celebrated King Midas – he of the fabled golden touch – reigned in the eighth century BC;[2] or Lydia, ruled in the sixth century BC by the still richer King Croesus, where coinage and gambling were both invented – perhaps simultaneously? – and of whose inhabitants Herodotus was to write: 'Except for the fact that they prostitute their daughters, the manners of the Lydians are much like our own.'

This lack of political unity was entirely beneficial to the development of Greek art, culture and thought. It encouraged diversity and gave rise to a good deal of healthy competition. But it proved a serious weakness

---

[1] Although the architect Harry Goodhart-Rendel, seeing it after the Second World War for the first time, remarked to Osbert Lancaster, 'Well, I don't think we can call it a *complete* success.'

[2] It was in the Phrygian capital, Gordium, that Alexander was confronted with the Gordian knot, said to have been tied by Gordius, founder of the dynasty, to attach the yoke to the shaft of an ancient farm wagon. According to long tradition, whoever succeeded in unravelling it would become master of Asia. Alexander solved the problem by drawing his sword and slicing it down the middle.

in the face of a formidable imperial power which, through most of the sixth century BC, was steadily increasing in strength. The Persian Empire was essentially the creation of Cyrus the Great, who during his thirty-year reign from 559 to 529 BC welded a number of disparate tribes into a single nation, and made that nation the mightiest on earth. The Persians were superb soldiers and magnificent bowmen, who would again and again overwhelm their enemies under hails of arrows: thanks to them and to his equally fine cavalry Cyrus defeated Croesus in 546 BC, subsequently extending his authority along the Anatolian coast to Caria and Lycia. At a stroke, Persia had become a Mediterranean power.

Under Darius the Great – who came to the throne in 522 BC, having murdered Cyrus's son Cambyses – it very nearly became a European one. Darius launched his first major expedition against the Greeks in 490 BC, when he sent a huge fleet and at least 15,000 men under his nephew Datis across the Aegean in an all-out assault on Athens. The Greek general Miltiades quickly rallied some 10,000 Athenian citizen-soldiers and another 1,000 from the little town of Plataea, ranging them in a long line across the plain of Marathon some twenty-two miles from the city. A reluctant Spartan army failed to turn up in time, and Miltiades did not wait for it. The battle was over quite quickly. The strongly reinforced Greek wings penetrated their Persian opposites and then wheeled inwards to envelop the centre. Datis's army turned and fled, with the Greeks in hot pursuit. Persian losses amounted to 6,400; the Athenians lost 192, and captured five Persian ships into the bargain.[1]

Athens had won a battle, but she had not won the war. All she had gained was breathing space in which to prepare for the next onslaught. Her leader Themistocles, who had been elected archon – titular head of state – in 493 BC, was convinced that her best hope lay in sea power and set about building a navy. By an extraordinary stroke of good luck a rich new vein of silver had just been discovered in the mines at nearby Laurium, so finance was not a serious problem. Fortunately too the Persians were heavily engaged in putting down a rebellion in Egypt, and the death of Darius in 486 BC delayed them still further. Finally, however, in the spring of 481 BC, a new expedition of 100,000 men under Darius's son and successor, Xerxes, crossed the Hellespont (Dandanelles) on a

---

[1] Our modern marathon race of 26 miles, 385 yards is based on the story of the messenger Pheidippides, who is said to have run that distance to carry news of the victory to Athens, but this story is in turn based on a misconception. Herodotus – our only authoritative source - tells us that Pheidippides in fact ran the 140 miles from Athens to Sparta, to seek its help. He is said to have covered the distance in two days.

bridge of boats and marched through Thrace into Thessaly; it was said to be so huge a horde that the men and pack animals together drank the rivers dry. The anxious Athenians consulted the oracle at Delphi and were told to put their faith in their wooden walls; but as nobody knew whether this was meant to refer to the fortifications of the Acropolis or the new ships, it did not help much. At any rate, they ignored the advice and – accompanied this time by a fair-sized contingent from Sparta, under the Spartan King Leonidas – marched north to meet the enemy.

They decided to make their stand at the pass of Thermopylae, the gateway to Boeotia and Attica. Spartans and Athenians fought valiantly side by side for three days, but then a local guide showed Xerxes a narrow path through the mountains by which he could fall upon the Spartans from behind. While the main body of Greeks retired to the south, Leonidas and 300 picked troops fought a desperate rearguard action – and were killed to the last man. Now the way to Athens lay open. Themistocles evacuated the city and established a new headquarters on the neighbouring island of Salamis, summoning all his available ships – they amounted, we are told, to 378 vessels – to assemble in the Saronic Gulf. They did so, only to find themselves almost immediately bottled up by the Persian fleet of nearly 600. But then, instead of trying to burst through the blockade, they craftily withdrew into the narrow waters behind Salamis, luring the Persians in after them. Fighting at close quarters, the Greek triremes proved far nimbler and more manoeuvrable than the heavy Persian war galleys, which they rammed mercilessly while the increasingly furious Xerxes, seated on a silver-footed throne under a golden umbrella, watched the progress of the engagement from the Attic shore. By the time the battle was over, the Greeks had sunk almost half his ships, at a cost of forty of their own. He returned to his capital at Susa, and never set foot in Greece again. In Thessaly he left an army of some 30,000 men under a general named Mardonius; this was defeated at the battle of Plataea the following year, and – traditionally on the same day – a last naval engagement off Cape Mycale in Asia Minor did for the few Persian ships remaining. The war was won.

Inevitably, the outcome of the Persian War was seen as a victory of western liberty over eastern autocracy and absolutism: the Great King, with all his huge and lumbering war machine, had been unable to destroy a mere handful of Greek city-states. But why, it may be asked, only a handful? Athens and Plataea, Sparta and the few other cities that made up the Spartan-led Peloponnesian League had distinguished themselves nobly; what about the rest? The truth is that the vast majority of Greek states had not lifted a finger. Some, doubtless, had collaborated with the Persians out of fear; others had simply accepted life under a probably tolerant and undemanding satrap[1] with a shrug: after all, the great cities of the Ionian coast – Pergamum and Ephesus, Miletus and Priene – had lived under the banner of the Great King for the past forty years without complaint. Finally, there were many upper-class, conservative Greeks all over the Aegean who shuddered at the radical steps towards popular democracy that had been taken over the past century – above all in Athens, by reformers like Solon and Cleisthenes – and frankly preferred the *ancien régime*. Having no real nationality themselves, they saw no objection to a mildly benevolent foreign domination.

Halicarnassus (the modern Bodrum) was also under Persian domination when Herodotus was born there in 484 BC. At the age of about twenty, however, he opposed the tyranny of the Persian satrap Lygdamis and narrowly escaped a death sentence. Expelled from the empire, he settled in Samos, which was to remain his principal base until, in 444 BC, he was involved in the Athenian colonisation of Thurii in southern Italy. Throughout his life he seems to have been constantly on the move. He certainly spent some time in Athens – where he became a close friend of Sophocles – and travelled all over Greece and Asia Minor, the Lebanon and Palestine. Other journeys took him to Cyrene in Libya, to Babylon in Mesopotamia and up the Nile to Aswan in Upper Egypt. Wherever he went he asked questions, not only about history but about geography, mythology, social customs and anything else that occurred to him.

His history – the first important European literary work to be written in prose – was mostly composed towards the end of his life and was divided after his death into nine books, each named after one of the Muses. Although written nearly two and a half millennia ago, it remains today quite astonishingly readable, enlivened as it is with countless digressions, anecdotes and snatches of curious information

---

[1] It was one of these satraps, Mausolus, governor of the province of Caria from 377 to 353 BC, whose sister-wife Artemisia built him the great tomb at Halicarnassus – the Mausoleum that was one of the Seven Wonders of the World. Its remains were removed in the early fifteenth century by the Knights of St John, to make room for the castle which still dominates the bay, but the great statue of Mausolus survived – more or less – and is now in the British Museum. The stepped tower on which the statue stood inspired Nicholas Hawksmoor when he designed the neighbouring church of St George's, Bloomsbury (now magnificently restored); here, however, the statue is – rather less appropriately – of George I.

picked up on the author's travels. The whole thing is infused with an irresistible sense of curiosity, of wonder, of sheer fascination with the beauty and diversity of the world around him. Herodotus is thus thoroughly, magnificently Greek. He embodies the Greek spirit as completely as the great tragedians of the fifth century, or even as Homer himself.

We have all been brought up to see the fifth century BC in Athens as a Golden Age: an age which not only saw an unprecedented advance in the arts and sciences as well as in philosophy and political theory, but which in many cases attained in these same fields a level of perfection that has never since been surpassed. This, it need hardly be said, is a generalisation. We can see the beginnings of the phenomenon almost a hundred years earlier, and those responsible for it were by no means only Athenians. It was in Ionia that Thales of Miletus – who was considered by Aristotle to be the first natural philosopher – correctly predicted a solar eclipse as early as 585 BC, and that his colleague Anaximander produced the first map of the inhabited world. Half a century later on the island of Samos, Pythagoras produced his famous theorem about right-angled triangles. But it was in Athens that Peisistratus began the Temple of Olympian Zeus in 540 BC, by which time the art of black-figure pottery was at its height; and it was again in Athens that, after the end of the Persian War, all this creativity, versatility and brilliance seemed to come together in a single con-centration of genius, bringing with it a huge wave of confidence and optimism. Man, it seemed, had freed himself from the primitive superstitions of former times; at last he was beginning to understand the universe about him, and to understand it was surely to control it. Simultaneously, he was discovering the basic truths of political philosophy, which taught him how to live in the society into which he had been born. With such a combination of power and knowledge he would not simply enjoy his Golden Age; he would make it go on forever.

The presiding spirit over all this was Pericles. He dominated Athens from 461 BC, when he was thirty-four, until his death in 429 BC of plague, and everything he did or said was inspired by a passionate love for his native city. He did his best to adorn it in every way possible – by restoring the temples destroyed by the Persians and organising the construction of new ones, particularly on the Acropolis, where he was directly responsible for the Propylaea, the Odeon, the Erechtheum and the Parthenon itself. But he was also a war leader and an incorrigible imperialist – for it should never be assumed that the fifth century in Athens was a time of peace. On the contrary, there was almost constant fighting with Sparta, as also with many other Greek states who resented and resisted Athenian expansionist policies, the pressures steadily building up until in 431 BC they exploded in the Peloponnesian War. That war – one of the chief reasons for which was the determination of each side to control the trade routes linking Greece to the Adriatic – lasted for just over a quarter of the glorious fifth century. Anyone wanting to know the full story can read Thucydides; here it need only be said that it ended with a winter-long siege of Athens (405–04 BC), during which the city was starved into surrender. So much, it might be thought, for the Golden Age. But the Golden Age was never about politics; it was about art and thought. In the field of literature – and in particular that of Greece's greatest strength, the drama – the first great name was that of Aeschylus. Having been born in 525 BC, he had certainly fought at Marathon, and probably also at Salamis and Plataea. During his long life he wrote over eighty plays, of which seven have survived, including the only extant Greek trilogy, the *Oresteia*. Aeschylus was in many ways a pioneer. His tragedies were the first to explore human personality, and the first also to use a second actor, thus reducing to some degree the importance of the chorus. He made two prolonged visits to Sicily – at that time still an integral part of the Greek world – and it was there, in 456 BC, that he died – killed, according to a venerable tradition, by an eagle which mistook his bald head for a rock and dropped a tortoise on to it in order to crack the shell.

Sophocles, some thirty years younger than Aeschylus, was still more prolific, with 123 plays to his credit; once again, seven tragedies have come down to us, including three which deal with the Oedipus legend. Apart from these – *Oedipus Rex, Antigone* and *Oedipus at Colonus* – his masterpiece is unquestionably *Electra*, which tells the story of the murder by Electra and her brother Orestes of their mother, Clytemnestra – wife of Agamemnon – and her lover, Aegisthus. Sophocles too was an innovator. Aristotle tells us that he added a third actor, and he also introduced the art of scene-painting. On top of all this, he somehow found the time to distinguish himself in Athenian public life. Treasurer of the Delian League, he served twice on the military council of ten generals; he was also a priest of Halon, another, lesser god of healing. He died in 406 BC, at the age of ninety. Some time before his death his sons took him to court on the grounds that he had grown senile and was no longer competent to manage his affairs. He replied by reciting from memory a long extract from his most recent play, *Oedipus at Colonus* – and won his case.

Third and last of the great tragedians was Euripides. Born in 484 BC, he was twelve years younger than Sophocles and died a few months before him in 406 BC. (At the festival of Dionysus in that year, Sophocles dressed the chorus and actors in black in his memory.) In a later age, Euripides would have been hailed as a Renaissance man. As well as a playwright he was a fine painter and a skilled musician; his library was one of the best in Athens. He is believed to have written ninety-two plays, nineteen of which have survived. They include *Andromache, Hippolytus, Medea* and *The Trojan Women*: the same old myths used by his predecessors, but usually given an unexpected – often contemporary – twist.

The only other dramatist of the day who deserves to be mentioned in the same breath as these three was a writer not of tragedies but of comedies, and highly satirical ones at that. Aristophanes, who was born around 445 BC, was a generation younger than Euripides and – as might be expected – still more down to earth. He wrote some fifty-four plays, of which we have eleven in their entirety; in them he mercilessly caricatured the leading figures of Athenian political, cultural and social life, including Socrates (in *The Clouds*), Cleon (in *The Knights*) and Lamachus, one of the leading Athenian generals during the Peloponnesian War (in *The Acharnians*). In *The Frogs* Dionysus, god of the theatre, goes down to Hades to fetch back Euripides, but after a mock trial scene brings back Aeschylus instead. Most famous of all, perhaps, is *Lysistrata*, in which the women of the Greek cities withhold their favours from their husbands until peace is restored.

Of the great Athenian philosophers, only Socrates – who lived from 469 to 399 BC – properly belongs to the fifth century. He wrote nothing, simply because he claimed to know nothing – nor, he believed, did anybody else – and so he did not feel justified in teaching. Instead, he discussed – anything and everything: good, evil, truth, justice, virtue, religion. This last subject proved to be his downfall. In the early spring of 399 BC he was accused of impiety, having, it was said, introduced strange new gods whom the state did not recognise; moreover, though he had a wife, Xanthippe, and two sons, he was also accused of having habitually seduced young men. These two charges together were enough to have him found guilty by a jury of 501 citizens and sentenced to death. His friends offered to bribe the prison authorities to let him escape; he refused on moral grounds. A month later he publicly drained a cup of hemlock and died.

Plato, who was to immortalise him, was twenty-eight when he attended the trial of Socrates and was deeply shaken by his death, after which he spent some years travelling in Egypt, Italy and Sicily. Unlike his friend, he wrote copiously, often expounding his philosophical theories in the form of dramatic dialogues in which Socrates plays a prominent part. He himself remains in the background and – though he argues with consummate brilliance – never quite commits himself to any particular doctrine of his own. Some time in the 380s BC he founded a school just outside Athens, in a grove sacred to the hero Academus. It consequently became known as the Academy, a word later adopted by nearly all the languages of Europe.

Plato's star pupil – whom he described as 'the mind of the school' – was a young Ionian Greek from Thrace by the name of Aristotle, born at Stagira near Thessalonica in 384 BC. Aristotle remained at the Academy until Plato's death in 347 BC, when he settled at Assos in Asia Minor and opened a school. In 342 BC he received an invitation from Philip II of Macedon to be private tutor to the King's fourteen-year-old son, Alexander, a post he held for two years. His charge then became regent for Philip, at which point Aristotle returned to Athens to found another school of his own – this time in a grove sacred to Apollo Lykeios, which earned it the name Lyceum. Aristotle was more than a philosopher; his surviving oeuvre also contains works on ethics, history, science, politics, literary and dramatic criticism, nature, meteorology, dreams and – a particular interest of his – zoology. He was, in short, a polymath – perhaps the first in history. And he left behind him the first true library, a vast collection of manuscripts and maps which was the prototype for Pergamum, Alexandria and all the other great public libraries of antiquity.

For some years after the end of the Peloponnesian War, Sparta ruled the Greek roost; but early in the next century the spotlight shifted to a place both unexpected and unfamiliar. In those days of antiquity, Macedonia must have seemed rather like Scotland appeared to medieval Englishmen: a land of wild and uncouth barbarians divided into endlessly warring clans, their almost total lack of culture and *politesse* rivalled only by a prodigious capacity for alcohol. All this was certainly true of the Macedonian highlands; but the lowlands included the city of Pella from which, for a century already, a dynasty known as the Argeads had held sway – at least in theory – over the entire country.

For our purposes the story begins with King Philip II, who succeeded to the throne on the death of his brother in 359 BC. The country he inherited was poor and disorganised; he immediately established a professional army, which he subjected to intensive training and kept mobilised not just in summer, as was the usual practice, but all the year round. In twenty years he made Macedonia the most powerful state in eastern Europe, dramatically upsetting the balance of power throughout the Greek world. In 338 BC he led his army southward, forcing the city-states of southern Greece – led by Athens and Thebes – to make a hasty alliance. They despatched an army to meet him, and the opposing forces met on 4 August at Chaeronea in Boeotia. The result was a resounding victory for Philip. To this day, by the roadside just to the east of the modern village, a stone lion marks the common tomb of the Theban 'Sacred Band', a body 300 strong which was traditionally composed of 150 pairs of male lovers; 254 skeletons have been found nearby.

Among the ambassadors sent by Philip to Athens to offer terms for a settlement was his son Alexander. Though still only eighteen, the young prince had fought with distinction at Chaeronea, leading the cavalry on the left wing. From childhood he had been brought up as his father's eventual successor; his tutor Aristotle – one of the most reactionary intellectuals that ever lived – had given him a strong sense of his divine right to rule, and gone so far as to advise him 'to be a leader to the Greeks and a despot to the barbarians, to look after the former as after friends and relatives, and to deal with the latter as with beasts or plants'. The boy was consumed with ambition, and so impatient to assume the reins of kingship that Philip soon began to suspect a conspiracy against him. He may well have been right: in 336 BC, in the course of festivities to celebrate the alarmingly incestuous marriage of his wife's brother with her own daughter, the King was assassinated by a member of his own bodyguard.

Was Alexander implicated in the murder? Nothing was ever proved, but what evidence there is points fairly convincingly to him and to his mother, Olympias, whom Philip had recently divorced. It certainly came at a providential moment. With the unanimous consent of the army, Alexander at once assumed his father's command. Then, pausing only to institute a swift campaign against Thebes – of which he left not one stone standing on another – in the spring of 334 BC he crossed the

Hellespont and started off on the great expedition that was to occupy the remainder of his short but astonishing life: an expedition launched with the dual purpose of freeing the Greek cities of Asia Minor from Persian domination and then forging a great empire of his own in eastern lands. While still on Mediterranean territory he won two historic battles over the Persian king Darius III, the first on the river Granicus (now the Çan Çayı) about thirty miles east of Troy, the second in the following year on the plain of Issus, between Alexandretta and Antioch (now Iskenderun and Antakya respectively). After this there was little opposition as he led his army south along the coast of Palestine and across the north of the Sinai peninsula into Egypt, where he spent the winter of 332–31 BC. With the coming of spring he struck east again, first to Tyre and then over the mountains to Damascus. And so he passes out of our story.

Alexander died in Babylon on 13 June 323 BC aged thirty-two, leaving chaos behind him. His only surviving son, Heracles, was a bastard; his wife, Roxane, was pregnant at the time of his death, but the baby might well have proved to be a girl and nobody was prepared to wait another six weeks to see. Fierce infighting broke out among his generals and the noble Macedonians who formed his court. This soon spread to the Mediterranean, and before long the entire Greek world was being torn apart by ambition and avarice. It was, in its way, inevitable. Alexander's empire could never have lasted. It was too large, too unwieldy, too quickly conquered. A victim of his own ambition, the young adventurer had thought only of advance, never of consolidation. And the almost random fragmentation of the empire after his death made its further dissolution inevitable.

Infinitely more important than Alexander's short-lived empire was the cultural legacy that he left behind him. The eastward extension of Greek culture as far as Afghanistan and the Indus valley, and its fusion with that of Persia, both fall outside the scope of this book; but the Hellenistic period[1] also had a huge impact throughout the eastern Mediterranean. There as elsewhere Greek-style cities sprang up, with temples and agoras, theatres and gymnasia, but the vast majority were no longer independent city-states as they had been in the past. They were now part of a larger polity, richer and stronger, able to launch

---

[1] *Hellenistic* is the word normally applied to the period immediately following the death of Alexander.

programmes of shipbuilding on a scale which would have been unthinkable in previous centuries. Moreover, they were eventually to provide a fertile field for the spread of a new religion, which was to develop out of Judaism while professing none of the latter's exclusiveness: Christianity, as preached and developed by St Paul.

When at last the smoke from Alexander's dying empire cleared away – and it was to take the best part of twenty years – three major powers emerged from the ashes. One was the old Kingdom of Macedonia, no longer master of western Asia but still dominating northern Greece and a considerable force throughout the Greek world. The second was the empire built up by Alexander's general Seleucus – formerly leader of the Shield-Bearers, his own personal guard of honour – who, beginning in Babylonia, soon imposed his authority over Mesopotamia and Syria until his domains extended from his capital at Antioch to the eastern end of the Persian Gulf. The line of Seleucid kings that he established was to continue for nearly four centuries, until it was eventually wiped out by Rome in 72 AD.

The third power was Egypt, where in 305 BC Alexander's oldest friend, a soldier-historian named Ptolemy, proclaimed himself king. He proved a remarkable success. Ruling from Alexander's new foundation of Alexandria – home of the greatest library in the ancient world, a city in which the large Jewish community would regularly read the Torah not in Hebrew but in Greek – and from another city which he himself founded called Ptolemais in Upper Egypt, this bluff Macedonian assumed the character – as well as the power – of the ancient pharaohs, and during a forty-year reign extended his dominions to Palestine and southern Syria, Cyprus, Asia Minor and the Cyclades. He also engendered a line of no less than fifteen rulers of Egypt: a remarkable number for a single dynasty, but more remarkable still by reason of the fact that almost every one of them married his own sister, half-sister or niece. It was Ptolemy XIV, coming to the throne in 47 BC, who took as his bride his twenty-one-year-old sister, Cleopatra.

Greek the Ptolemies may have been; the world they lived in, however, at least where later generations were concerned, was Roman. The time has now come to retrace our steps a century or two and to inquire how it was that a small and inconsequential Italian town made itself, in a remarkably short space of time, master of the civilised world.

CHAPTER III

Rome: The Republic

The rise of Rome was due, more than anything else, to the character and qualities of the Romans themselves. They were a simple, straight-forward, law-abiding people with a strong sense of family values, willing to accept discipline when required to do so – as they certainly had been in 510 BC when they expelled the Tarquins, that line of Etruscan kings who had ruled them for the previous century,[1] and established a republic of their own. Their city, they claimed, predated the Etruscans by many centuries; it had originally been founded by the Trojan prince Aeneas, who had made his way to Italy after the Greeks' destruction of his city. Rome was thus the successor to ancient Troy.

In 280 BC, an ambitious ruler of a Hellenistic state in northwestern Greece, King Pyrrhus of Epirus, landed with an army estimated at 20,000 at Tarentum (the modern Taranto). The Roman army met him near Heraclea, where it was narrowly beaten, Pyrrhus's losses being almost as great as the Romans': thus the concept of a Pyrrhic victory was born. For the next five years the King continued to make trouble, but with less and less success; finally, in 275 BC, having lost some two-thirds of his army, he returned to Epirus. Rome, a still obscure republic in central Italy, had defeated a Hellenistic king. The subsequent triumphal procession in the capital featured Pyrrhus's captured elephants – the first to make their appearance in Italy.[2]

But Rome's greatest enemy was Carthage, originally a colony of the Phoenicians, which occupied part of the site of the modern city of Tunis. The Carthaginians were a thorn in the Roman flesh for well over a hundred years, from 264 to 146 BC, during which the Romans were obliged to fight two separate Punic Wars[3] before they were able to

---

[1]According to Herodotus, the Etruscans had arrived in Italy from Lydia in Asia Minor towards the end of the ninth century BC. Their language, which is not even Indo-European, has recently been largely deciphered, but the few Etruscan documents that remain give us all too little information. Much weightier evidence is provided by their surviving works of art - their sculptures (particularly on their tombs), paintings and exquisite jewellery. They were certainly far more gifted artistically than the Romans who expelled them.

[2] These elephants – and Hannibal's after them – were presumably African; and African elephants, unlike the Indian variety, are always said to be untamable. Did Pyrrhus and Hannibal know something that we don't?

[3] 'Punic' comes from the Latin *poeni*, which has the same root as 'Phoenician'.

eliminate it forever. It was these two wars that brought Rome to the centre of the Mediterranean stage and – since it soon became clear that Carthage could never be defeated on land alone – made her a leading sea power. The first, which ended in 241 BC, had one extremely happy result for Rome: the acquisition of the greater part of Sicily, which would henceforth constitute her principal granary. (Corsica and Sardinia were to follow three years later.) She had greater cause for concern, however, during the twenty-three-year interval that elapsed before the beginning of the second, because during that period Carthage succeeded in establishing a whole new empire – this time in Spain.

The Phoenicians had first reached the Iberian peninsula around 1100 BC, when they founded the port of Cadiz. It was in those days an island and it set the pattern for subsequent Phoenician colonies, all of which tended to be positioned on promontories or offshore islands, often at a river mouth, presumably – since, like all merchants, they were a peaceful lot – in order not to encroach more than necessary on the natives. Of these last the most advanced were the Iberians, a mysterious people whose two languages are, like the Etruscan, not Indo-European and, unlike the Etruscan, continue to baffle us. The Iberians traded enthusiastically with the Phoenicians, with whom they seem to have existed on friendly terms. Some centuries later they were to develop a remarkable civilisation of their own, notable above all for its statuary: the so-called *Dama de Elche*, dating from the fourth century BC and now in the Archaeological Museum in Madrid, is one of the most beautiful – and most haunting – ancient sculptures to be seen anywhere.

In about 237 BC Hamilcar Barca, Carthage's most distinguished general – or admiral, since he seems to have been equally at home on land and at sea – set off for the Iberian peninsula, taking with him his little son Hannibal, aged nine. Here, over the space of just eight years, he built up all the infrastructure of a prosperous state, with a sizable army to defend it. Accidentally drowned in 229 BC, he was succeeded by his son-in-law Hasdrubal, who established the permanent capital of Carthaginian Spain at what the Romans called New Carthage and we call Cartagena. He also did much to develop the art of mining: a single mine, Baebelo, was said to produce 300 pounds of silver a day. When Hasdrubal was assassinated by an Iberian slave in 221 BC, his place was taken by Hannibal, now twenty-six.

Hannibal was to prove the greatest military leader the world had seen since Alexander; indeed, he may well have been one of the greatest of all time. According to tradition, his father had made him swear eternal hatred of Rome; he was determined from the moment of his accession to avenge his country's defeat of twenty years before, and confident that the new Spanish dominion, with all its vast resources of wealth and manpower, would enable him to do so. He left Spain in the spring of 218 BC with an army of some 40,000 men, taking the land route along the south coast of France, up the Rhône valley, then east to Briançon and the pass at Mont-Genèvre. His infantry was mostly Spanish, though officered by Carthaginians, his cavalry drawn from Spain and North Africa; it included thirty-seven elephants. His famous crossing of the Alps took place in the early autumn and was followed by two victorious battles in quick succession; by the end of the year he controlled virtually the whole of northern Italy. But then the momentum began to fail. He had counted on a general rising of the Italian cities, uneasy as they were at the growing power of Rome, but he was disappointed; even a third victory in April 217 BC, when he trapped the Roman army in a defile between Lake Trasimene and the surrounding hills, proved ultimately ineffective. It was no use his marching on Rome; the city possessed formidable defensive walls, and he had no siege engines worth speaking of. He therefore swung round to Apulia and Calabria, where the largely Greek populations had no love for the Romans and might well, he thought, defect to his side.

Once again he was wrong. Instead of the sympathetic allies for which he had hoped, he soon found himself faced by yet another Roman army, far larger and better equipped than his own, which had followed him southward; and on 3 August 216 BC, at Cannae (beside the Ofanto river, some ten miles southwest of the modern Barletta) battle was joined. The result was another victory for Hannibal, perhaps the greatest of his life, and for the Romans the most devastating defeat in their history. Thanks to his superb generalship, the legionaries found themselves surrounded and were cut to pieces where they stood. By the end of the day over 50,000 of them lay dead on the field. Hannibal's casualties amounted to just 5,700.

Hannibal had now destroyed all Rome's fighting forces apart from those kept within the capital for its defence; but he was no nearer his ultimate objective, the destruction of the Republic. His strongest weapon, that magnificent Spanish and North African cavalry – by now strictly equine, since the elephants had all succumbed to the cold and damp – was powerless against the city walls. He was encouraged, on the other hand, by the hope that his brother – another Hasdrubal –

might be raising a second army, this time with proper siege engines, and joining him as soon as it was ready. Then, to his surprise, he found in Campania – that province of Italy south of Rome of which Naples is the centre – just that degree of popular support that seemed to be lacking elsewhere in the peninsula. Marching his army across the mountains to Capua, at that time Italy's second largest city, he established his headquarters there and settled down to wait.

He waited a very long time, for Hasdrubal had problems of his own. The Romans, swift to take advantage of Hannibal's absence, had within months of his departure invaded Spain, with a force of two legions and some 15,000 allied troops under a young general named Gnaeus Cornelius Scipio, who was soon joined by his brother Publius. The immediate consequence of this invasion was a long struggle between Roman and Carthaginian forces, with the local Iberians fighting on both sides; the eventual result was a Roman presence in the peninsula which lasted over six centuries. After the death of the two Scipios in 211 BC they were replaced by a kinsman, also called Publius, who took Cartagena after a short siege. With the capture of their capital the Carthaginians swiftly lost heart, and by 206 BC the last of them had left the peninsula.

While there had been a hope of victory over the Romans in Spain, Hasdrubal had had no chance of organising a relief expedition to help his brother. Not until 206 BC, when he knew he was beaten, could he begin to consider such an enterprise, and when in 205 he in turn led his men across southern France and across the Alps, he was marching to disaster: on the Metaurus river, just outside Ancona, he encountered a Roman army and his force was cut to pieces. Hannibal learned the news only when his brother's severed head was delivered to his Capuan camp. He remained in Italy for another four years, but he would have been wiser to return; elsewhere in the Mediterranean, young Publius Cornelius Scipio had by now taken the offensive.

In 204 BC Publius and his army landed on the North African coast at Utica, less than twenty miles west of Carthage, where they routed 20,000 local troops and established a position on the Bay of Tunis threatening the city itself. In the spring of 203 Hannibal, now seriously alarmed, hurried back to Carthage and in the following year led an army of 37,000 men and eighty elephants against the Roman invaders. The two sides eventually met near the village of Zama where, after a long and hard-fought battle, Hannibal suffered the only major defeat of his extraordinary career. It was at Zama, we are told, that the

Romans finally discovered how to deal with the Carthaginians' favourite tactical weapon, their elephants. First a sudden blast of trumpets would terrify them, to the point where their riders lost control; the Romans would then open their ranks, and the panic-stricken animals would charge between them, out of what they thought to be harm's way. The Roman victory was complete. The Second Punic War was over. Rome's prize for her victory was Spain. All the carefully built-up Carthaginian military and civil administration had already been dismantled – the Scipios had seen to that – and now it remained only for Carthage formally to cede the peninsula to her conquerors. Hannibal himself – who had narrowly escaped death at Zama – lived on until 183 BC, when he took poison to avoid being captured by the enemy he so hated. As for the victorious Scipio, he was rewarded with the title of 'Africanus', which he richly deserved. He, more than any other of his compatriots, had ensured that it was Rome, not Carthage, which would be mistress of the Mediterranean in the centuries that followed.

But the Punic Wars had had a traumatic effect. They had brought the Roman Republic several times to the brink of disaster and had in all claimed the lives of perhaps two or three hundred thousand of her men. And yet there, across the narrow sea, the city of Carthage still stood – its population of some 750,000 unharmed, industrious and enterprising, recovering from its recent defeat with almost frightening speed: to every patriotic Roman a reminder, a reproach and a continuing threat. Clearly, its survival could not be tolerated. *'Delenda est Carthago'* ('Carthage is to be deleted'): these words were spoken by the elder Cato at the end of every speech he made in the Senate until they eventually became a watchword; the only question was how the job was to be done. At last, in 151 BC, an excuse was found when the Carthaginians presumed to defend their city from the depredations of a local chieftain. Rome treated this very natural reaction as a *casus belli*, and in 149 BC once again sent out an invading army. This time the Carthaginians surrendered unconditionally – until they heard the Roman peace terms, which were that their city should be utterly destroyed and that its inhabitants should not be permitted to rebuild their homes anywhere within ten miles of the sea. Appalled, they decided after all to resist. The result was a terrible two-year siege, after which, in 146 BC, the threatened destruction took place, not one stone being left on another. Cato was obeyed: Carthage was deleted.

*

31

The Kingdom of Pontus – a hitherto somewhat insignificant state lying along the southern shore of the Black Sea – should have no place in a history of the Mediterranean. Nor would it have had but for its young king Mithridates VI, who for twenty-five years was the principal thorn in the flesh of the Roman Republic. Although by race he and his subjects were Persian, he always liked to think of himself as a Greek, a proud champion of Hellenism who would inspire all the Greek cities to rise up against their Latin oppressors. In 88 BC he invaded the Roman province of Asia[1] and engineered a mass uprising which ended in a massacre of some 80,000 Italian residents; then, emboldened by this success, he crossed the Aegean and occupied Athens. Several other Greek cities fell to him in their turn.

Clearly, Rome had to act; and the Roman Senate chose as supreme commander of its expeditionary force a fifty-year-old patrician by the name of Lucius Cornelius Sulla, possessed of a fine military record and a first-hand knowledge of Asia. Just as he was about to embark, however, the democratic faction in the Senate successfully moved that he be replaced by an old and somewhat decayed general under whom he had once served, Gaius Marius. It was a disastrous decision, and Sulla categorically refused to accept it. With his army behind him to a man, he marched on Rome, liquidated his enemies and, without more ado, set off for Greece. He stormed Athens, destroyed its port of Piraeus, won two decisive victories in the field and eventually concluded a peace treaty with Mithridates – though on what to many seemed surprisingly easy terms. All this, however, he had achieved without any semblance of authority from the government in Rome – where, in his absence, the Marian party had returned to power.

Hastening back to the capital, Sulla routed them for the second time and assumed the role of dictator, unhesitatingly ordering the mass murder of nearly 10,000 of his political enemies, including forty senators and some 1,600 *equites*, or knights. He then passed a series of highly reactionary laws which had the effect of putting back the clock by at least half a century. Finally, with this work successfully completed, he abdicated and returned to his home in Campania. Here he led an extremely dissolute life, terrorising his many slaves. From time to time – *pour encourager les autres*, perhaps – he would sentence one or two of them to death, usually taking care to be present when the sentence was carried out; but one day in 78 BC, while he was watching

---

[1] This area of western Asia Minor had been bequeathed to Rome in 133 BC by King Attalus III of Pergamum.

a strangulation, the excitement became too much for him. He suffered a sudden seizure and died soon afterwards.

The next forty years were dominated by the three military men who, even more than Sulla before them, were to put their indelible mark on republican Rome. They were Gnaeus Pompeius Magnus (better known to us as Pompey), Marcus Licinius Crassus and Gaius Julius Caesar. Pompey had won victories for Sulla – to whose stepdaughter he was married – in Sicily and North Africa, for which services he had been grudgingly granted the rare privilege of a Triumph.[1] Unlike most noble Romans of his day he had little interest in money, and politics bored him stiff. What he liked was power. He was a soldier through and through, and a highly ambitious one.

Crassus, the second of the three giants, could hardly have been more different. Born rich, he had made himself still richer by clever if unscrupulous wheeling and dealing in the Roman property market. He too was a first-rate general when he wanted to be, but while Pompey was forever seeking means to enhance his already formidable military reputation Crassus preferred to stay in Rome, intriguing behind the scenes for his own political and financial ends. His one major military achievement was in putting down a slave revolt which broke out in 73 BC. Having first pursued its leader, Spartacus, through Calabria, he finally caught up with him in Apulia, where he executed him on the spot. Six thousand rebel slaves were subsequently crucified, their crosses lining the Appian Way.

Pompey, who had been absent in Spain – where he founded the city of Pamplona and named it after himself – returned just in time for the crucifixions, in which he participated with enthusiasm; characteristically, he then attempted to take the credit for the entire operation. As can be readily understood, Crassus was furious. Each had an army behind him, and for a moment it looked as if the Republic was once again to be plunged into civil war; fortunately the rivals came to a last-minute understanding: the two would present themselves for election to the consulship in the year 70 BC. Strictly speaking, neither of them was eligible, neither having disbanded his army as consular candidates were required to do. Pompey, moreover – who was still only thirty-six – had

---

[1] A Triumph was in essence a formal procession of a victorious Roman general to the temple of Jupiter on the Capitol. It depended on a special vote of the people, with the additional advice of the Senate. The *triumphator* rode in a four-horse chariot; he was followed by eminent captives (probably destined for execution), freed Roman prisoners of war, the major spoils captured, the army and finally animals for sacrifice.

not even taken his seat as a senator. But the Senate had not the courage to stand up against two such men, and they were duly elected. They spent their year of office meticulously undoing all Sulla's legislation.

In the years that followed, while Crassus remained busy in Rome – occupied with an interminable quarrel with the Senate over tax collections in Asia – Pompey went from strength to strength. In 67 BC, with 120,000 men and 500 ships and in only sixty days, he virtually eliminated the pirates who had long plagued the Mediterranean, thus making the seas safe for the best part of a thousand years. He was then despatched to the east, where the King of Pontus was up to his old tricks. Unfortunately for Pompey, Mithridates committed suicide before battle could be joined, but there was plenty of other work to be done in eastern lands before he returned home. Without bothering to consult the Senate, he rapidly annexed Pontus; moving south to Syria, he expelled the last Seleucid king and made this too a province, thereby acquiring for Rome the great city of Antioch. Finally he pressed on to Judaea, where he captured Jerusalem – sensibly allowing the reigning king to remain on his throne as a 'client' of Rome. All this he accomplished in just four years, during which it is not too much to say that he changed the face of the Near East more radically than at any other time until the coming of Islam.

When Pompey returned to Rome in 62 BC it was as a conquering hero. He was granted a second Triumph, far more splendid than the first. Many Romans trembled, remembering the return of Sulla just twenty years before, but the *triumphator* disbanded his troops, asking nothing but the ratification of all that he had done in the east and a grant of land on which his veteran soldiers could settle. Both requests seemed reasonable enough; with regard to the first, he had indeed acted without authority, but the slowness of communications in those days had left him no alternative. In any case Rome's gains had been immense; the Romans had little cause to complain.

Complain, however, they did. One of the principal critics of Pompey's actions was Crassus, clearly motivated by personal jealousy of his old rival. The two most powerful men in Rome were now at loggerheads, both with the government and with each other.

The third and greatest member of this astonishing triumvirate[1] now appears on the scene. In 62 BC Gaius Julius Caesar was thirty-eight, and

---

[1] I use the word loosely and with a small 't'; though the three have often been dubbed 'the First Triumvirate', they were never so described at the time.

married to Sulla's granddaughter Pompeia (he was to divorce her in the following year).[1] His reputation in Rome was that of a cultivated intellectual and a formidable orator in the Senate, a provider of lavish entertainments who was consequently always in debt, and a sexual profligate, whose affairs – with both men and women – were legion but who had nevertheless been elected Pontifex Maximus, chief of the priesthood of the Roman state: talented, fascinating, but basically unreliable. In 60 BC he returned from Spain, where he had been serving as governor and where, after a few insignificant victories, he too had been promised a Triumph. But now there arose a difficulty. He was determined to gain the consulship; to announce his candidature, however, he would be obliged to appear in Rome long before the Triumph could be arranged, and by doing so he would forfeit his right to the ceremony. He tried to solve the problem by formally requesting that the announcement be made by proxy; when this was refused, he hesitated no longer. Plans for the Triumph were put aside. He came straight to Rome. Power was more important than glory.

But now there came a further blow. It had long been the custom in Rome to allocate to its prospective consuls, even before they took office, the provinces which they would be sent to govern at the end of their term; the Senate, knowing that it could not hope to prevent Caesar's election but determined at least to cut him down to size, allotted to him no provinces worthy of the name, but simply 'the forests and cattle-runs of Italy'. This was certainly a deliberate snub; and Caesar certainly took it as such.

The Senate had now succeeded in antagonising the three most powerful men in Rome, and since Caesar remained on excellent terms with Pompey and Crassus it was hardly surprising that he should have approached the two men with a proposal for a coalition. In return for their support he would give both what they wanted, so long as neither raised an objection and on condition that they refrained also from squabbling with each other. He was as good as his word. His fellow consul, a colourless figure laughably named Bibulus, withdrew to his house 'to watch the sky for omens'; Caesar simply ignored him. He rewarded Pompey's veterans with the land they wanted and ensured the

---

[1] Pompeia had been in charge of the rites of the *Bona Dea*. This goddess was worshipped in an annual service held at night, from which men were strictly excluded. In December 62 BC, one Publius Clodius Pulcher slipped in disguised as a woman – it was said in order to approach Pompeia in her husband's absence. Caesar, who liked Clodius, stoutly proclaimed the innocence of both, but divorced Pompeia anyway on the grounds that she 'must be above suspicion'.

ratification of his achievements in the east, and was delighted when Pompey – who had by now divorced his first wife – asked for the hand of his daughter Julia. Where Crassus was concerned, the little matter of the tax-gathering was also quickly settled. Meanwhile, with the help of his new allies, Caesar had personally allocated to himself two real provinces to govern when his consulate was over: Cisalpine Gaul (northern Italy) and Illyricum (Dalmatia). As it happened, the news arrived at that moment of the sudden death of the governor of Transalpine Gaul, which covered most of modern France. Here was an opportunity indeed: he took that over as well.

After his consulship Caesar left at once for Gaul, where he was to remain for the next eight years; by the time he returned to Rome he had conquered the entire country. Plutarch estimates that a million Gauls lost their lives, with another million enslaved; far more important to Caesar himself, he had built up a military reputation which put even Pompey in the shade, showing himself to be one of the supreme commanders of all time. His mind worked like lightning and could adapt instantly to a changing situation; his timing was faultless. Physically too, he possessed almost incredible energy and powers of endurance, often travelling a hundred miles in a light carriage in a single day, in spite of appalling weather and execrable roads.

Back in Rome, although Pompey and Crassus were still in charge, their authority was rapidly weakening thanks to the intrigues and machinations of Publius Clodius Pulcher – he who had infiltrated the *Bona Dea* ceremony. Clodius had by now revealed himself as a dangerously radical demagogue, whose activities were becoming a serious threat to the state. Determined that their triumvirate should be preserved, the three met in 56 BC at Lucca, a city just inside Cisalpine Gaul – Caesar being aware that a number of irregularities during his consulship might well render him liable to prosecution if he set foot on Roman territory. There, by dividing the Roman world into three separate spheres of influence – east to Crassus, centre to Caesar, west to Pompey – they decided how best their several ambitions could be fulfilled. Pompey and Crassus would stand for the consulship for the second time in the following year; after that Crassus – who was beginning to feel overshadowed by the other two and was determined to prove himself in battle – would lead an expedition beyond the Euphrates against the Parthian Empire, now the only substantial nation confronting Rome anywhere in the world. Pompey would take over a five-year responsibility for Spain – governing it, however, for most of the time through subordinates so that he could remain in Rome as effective head of the administration. As for Caesar, he would have his Gallic command extended for another five years so that he could extend and consolidate his conquests.[1]

But the partnership's inevitable stresses and strains were beginning to tell. In 54 BC Julia died in childbirth; she had done much to hold her father and husband together, and with her death they drifted apart. Then, in 53 BC, away in the east, the army of Crassus suffered an overwhelming defeat by Parthian mounted archers at Carrhae (the modern Harran, in southeast Turkey). Of the 6,000 Roman legionaries engaged, 5,500 were killed, and when Crassus went to negotiate peace terms he was killed too. Pompey and Caesar were left alone, each becoming more and more aware of the fact that Rome was not big enough for both of them, and when Pompey rejected Caesar's suggestion of another marriage tie between their two families, taking instead as his third wife the daughter of Caesar's enemy Metellus Scipio, whom he then made his fellow consul, it was clear that matters were coming to a head. Pompey, moreover, had the distinct advantage: he was in Rome.

But Rome was fast declining into anarchy. Although Pompey enjoyed more authority than anyone else, he had almost as many enemies in high places as Caesar, and he was increasingly unable to control the rival gangs of Clodius and his principal adversary, Milo, who divided the streets between them. Then in 52 BC Clodius was murdered and Pompey was made sole consul, with special emergency powers to enable him to restore order in the city; two years later it was moved in the Senate that Caesar should be relieved of his command. The motion was blocked by an energetic young tribune named Curio, one of Caesar's most ardent supporters, but the stalemate continued. Curio then proposed that both Caesar and Pompey should simultaneously resign their posts, and it was when this proposal too was rejected that one of the consuls then in office called on Pompey to take command of all the forces of the Republic – effectively assuming dictatorial powers. Pompey accepted – on condition, as he put it, that no better way could be found – and immediately took over two legions that happened to be in the capital.

Curio set off at once with the news to Caesar's headquarters at Ravenna, then returned to Rome – completing the 140-mile journey in

---

[1] It was in the following year, and again in 54 BC, that he invaded Britain, staying there for eighteen days and three months respectively. He achieved little, however, except a show of strength; Britain was to have almost a century's grace before the Romans returned.

three days – with a letter in which Caesar detailed his immense services to the state and insisted that if he must indeed relinquish his command, Pompey must do the same. The Senate, however, could hardly be persuaded even to have it read; instead they supported a motion by Metellus Scipio (now Pompey's father-in-law) that Caesar must resign unilaterally or be declared a public enemy. The die, as Caesar himself declared, was cast; and on the night of 10 January 49 BC he and the single legion he had taken with him crossed the little river Rubicon,[1] which constituted the southeastern border of Cisalpine Gaul. In doing so he deliberately flouted the Roman law which forbade a governor to lead an army outside his province, thereby incurring a charge of treason. Henceforth it would be a trial of strength: a civil war.

That war was to be fought on several fronts. In Italy Caesar encountered little opposition. Town after town opened its gates to him without a struggle; when he was called upon to fight, his battle-hardened troops were more than a match for any that might be ranged against them. Only two months after the Rubicon crossing the two consuls fled to Dalmatia, where they were shortly joined by Pompey himself. Caesar did not pursue them at once, since they remained in control of the Adriatic; instead he set off by land to Spain, the heartland of Pompey's power in the west. On the way he stopped briefly at the free city of Massilia (Marseille) and, finding the population loyal to Pompey, placed it under siege, finally crossing the Pyrenees with an army of 40,000 men. Against him were not less than 70,000, commanded by three of Pompey's leading generals, but he effortlessly outmanoeuvred them until, finding themselves encircled, they capitulated without further resistance. By the time he returned to Massilia that city too had surrendered. Now at last he was ready for the final round of the struggle.

With his enemies satisfactorily scattered, Caesar had no difficulty in having himself elected consul once again in 48 BC. He then pursued Pompey, who had by this time gone on to Greece. An attempt to blockade Pompey's key base and bridgehead at Dyrrachium (now Durrës in Albania) was a failure, but 200 miles away to the southwest, on 9 August 48 BC on the sweltering plain of Pharsalus in Thessaly, the two armies met at last. Caesar – aided by the young tribune Mark

---

[1] Surprisingly, this stream has never been certainly identified. The modern river Pisciatello is the most likely candidate.

Antony, who commanded his left wing – once again won an easy victory. Pompey, we are told, was one of the first to retreat. He escaped to the coast and thence to Egypt, whose boy king Ptolemy XIII had been his staunch supporter, supplying him with ships and provisions; but Ptolemy was anxious to be on the winning side, and when Caesar, in hot pursuit of his enemy, arrived in turn at Alexandria it was to find that Pompey had been assassinated.

Caesar's journey, on the other hand, had not been in vain; Ptolemy had recently banished his twenty-one-year-old half-sister, wife and co-ruler, Cleopatra, and arbitration was urgently needed. In this case it took a somewhat unusual form: Cleopatra returned secretly to Egypt to plead her case, whereupon Caesar – now fifty-two – instantly seduced her and took her into his palace as his mistress. Ptolemy, furious, laid the palace under siege, but a Roman relief force soon came to the rescue and in March 47 BC defeated the Egyptians in battle. Ptolemy fled and was drowned, appropriately enough, in the Nile; Caesar established Cleopatra on the throne with her younger brother, Ptolemy XIV, as her co-ruler, Egypt becoming a client state of Rome. He himself had one further task before he returned to the capital: the proper chastisement of Pharnaces, son of that old troublemaker Mithridates of Pontus, who was showing every sign of taking after his father. With seven legions he marched quickly northwards through Syria and Anatolia. The expedition was very nearly a disaster. At Zela (the modern Zile) in central Anatolia, on 2 August, just as the Roman army was pitching its camp, Pharnaces attacked. The legions were taken by surprise; only their discipline and experience won the day. It was then, Plutarch tells us, that Caesar reported his victory back to Rome with the words which used to be known to every English schoolboy: *veni, vidi, vici* – 'I came, I saw, I conquered.'[1]

Pompey was dead, but his two sons remained undefeated and there were two more campaigns to be fought – the first in North Africa, the second in Spain – before the civil war could be considered properly at an end. As always, Caesar now faced the problem of finding land on which to settle the legionaries who had served him so well. He established several colonies in Italy, and – since there was not enough territory available in the peninsula to accommodate all his men – well over forty others in provinces overseas, Corinth and Carthage among

---

[1] According to Suetonius, Caesar was so pleased with this remark that he had it emblazoned on a banner for his subsequent Triumph in Rome.

them. Nor were these colonies intended for war veterans alone; some 80,000 of the Roman unemployed were sent to join them. Thus were the seeds sown for the long-term Romanisation of the Mediterranean coastline, so much of which bears the Roman stamp to this day.

Julius Caesar was now supreme. He had packed the Senate with 900 of his own creatures, many of whom were obliged to him for favours received and all of whom he could trust to give him their support. Through them he controlled the state; through the state, the civilised world. Meanwhile, a cult of personality – the first Rome had known – was growing up around him. Portrait busts were widely distributed, both in Italy and abroad; his image even appeared on coins, an unheard-of innovation. None of this, however, added to his popularity. With all the power gathered into his own hands, the way was blocked to ambitious young politicians, who grew more and more to resent his arrogance, his capriciousness and – not least – his immense wealth. They also resented his frequent long absences on campaign, which they considered unnecessary and irresponsible. He was after all fifty-six years old, and known to be epileptic; future wars should surely be left to his generals. The truth was that Caesar hated the capital, with its perpetual petty lobbyings and intrigues; he was only really happy when out on campaign with his legionaries, who worshipped him and gave him their unfaltering loyalty. It was probably for this reason more than any other that, at the beginning of 44 BC, he announced a new expedition to the east, to avenge the death of Crassus and to teach the Parthians a lesson. He would be commanding it in person, and would leave on 18 March.

For the Roman patricians, to be ruled by a dictator was bad enough; the prospect of being ordered about by his secretaries for the next two years or more was intolerable. And so the great conspiracy took shape. It was instigated and led by Gaius Cassius Longinus, who had supported Pompey until Pharsalus but whom Caesar had subsequently pardoned. With Cassius was his brother-in-law Marcus Brutus. Brutus had been a special protégé of Caesar, who had made him governor of Cisalpine Gaul, but he could never forget his putative descent from the early hero Junius Brutus, who had driven the Etruscan king Tarquin from Rome – in revenge for the rape and subsequent suicide of Lucretia Collatina – and was thus considered the architect of republican liberty. When in February 44 BC Caesar was nominated *dictator in perpetuo*, Brutus seems to have felt that it was time for another blow to be struck in the same cause. Together, he and Cassius collected some sixty fellow conspirators, and on 15 March they were ready.

On that day, just three days before Caesar was to leave for the east, he attended a meeting of the Senate in the large hall that adjoined the Theatre of Pompey. As he approached, a Greek who had formerly been a member of Brutus's household slipped into his hand a note of warning, but Caesar, not troubling to read it, walked on. The conspirators had ensured that his principal lieutenant, Mark Antony – who was not only utterly loyal to his master but was also possessed of huge physical strength – should be detained in conversation by one of their number. They had also carefully stationed nearby a band of gladiators to be ready in the event of a free fight, but the precaution proved unnecessary. Publius Casca seems to have been the first to attack, his dagger striking the dictator in the throat; within moments Caesar was surrounded by the conspirators, all of them frenziedly stabbing, pushing their fellows aside the better to plunge their own blades into whatever part of his body they could reach. Their victim defended himself as best he could, but he had no chance. Covering his bleeding head with his toga, he fell against the plinth of Pompey's statue.

Seeing him dead, those present were seized by a sudden panic; they fled from the building, leaving the body alone where it lay. It was some time before three slaves arrived with a litter and carried it back to his home – one of the arms, we are told, dragging along the ground. Later, when doctors examined it, they counted twenty-three wounds – only one of which, however, they believed to have been fatal.

Just six months before his death, on 13 September 45 BC, Julius Caesar had formally adopted his great-nephew, Gaius Octavius, as his son. Although still only nineteen, Octavian (as he is generally known in his pre-imperial years) had long been groomed for stardom. Already at the age of sixteen he had been appointed Pontifex Maximus; since then he had fought with distinction with Caesar in Spain. Thus, despite his youth, on the death of his great-uncle he might have expected to assume power; but Mark Antony, Caesar's chief lieutenant, moved fast and – not hesitating to falsify certain of his dead master's papers – seized control of the state. Octavian fought back, and thanks largely to the championing of Cicero – one of the greatest orators in all history, who loathed autocrats in general and Antony in particular and made a series of dazzling speeches against him – gradually won a majority in the Senate.

Rome was once again polarised and on the brink of civil war. There was even a small battle at Modena, which ended in a victory for

Octavian. But by November 43 BC the two had effected an uneasy reconciliation and, with another of Caesar's generals, Marcus Aemilius Lepidus, formed an official five-year triumvirate entrusted with the task of setting the government back on its feet. Their first priority was to track down the two men chiefly responsible for Caesar's murder. Brutus and Cassius had fled with their loyal soldiers across the Adriatic; leaving Lepidus in charge in Rome, Octavian and Antony pursued them to Philippi in Macedonia where, in two successive battles three weeks apart, the rebel army was defeated, its two leaders both falling on their swords. By mutual agreement, Lepidus was firmly relegated to a back seat. The victors now divided up the Roman world between them, Antony taking the eastern half, Octavian the west.

The little town of Tarsus in Cilicia is perhaps best known today for having been the birthplace of St Paul; some forty years before his birth, however, it was the scene of another event which had a still greater effect on the world as we know it. It was at Tarsus, some time in the summer of 41 BC, that Mark Antony first set eyes on Queen Cleopatra VII. Six years before, Julius Caesar had established her on the throne of Egypt, together with the man who was both her brother and her brother-in-law, Ptolemy XIV. Before long, according to the curious tradition of the Ptolemys, he also became her husband; even this triple relationship, however, failed to endear him to her and in 44 BC she had him murdered. She now reigned alone, but she needed another Roman protector and she had come to Tarsus knowing that it was there that she would find him.

Despite the testimony of Shakespeare – and Pascal's famous remark that, if her nose had been a little shorter, the whole history of the world would have been changed – Cleopatra seems to have been attractive rather than classically beautiful. She nevertheless had little difficulty in ensnaring Mark Antony just as she had Caesar himself, even persuading him to arrange for the death of her sister Arsinoë, whom she had never forgiven for once having established a rival regime in Alexandria. (Arsinoë was the last of her five siblings to die a violent death, at least two of them having perished on Cleopatra's personal initiative.) Antony was delighted to oblige, and as a reward was invited to Alexandria for the winter; the result was twins. After that the two did not see each other again for three years, but in 37 BC he invited her to join him in his eastern capital of Antioch and they formed a permanent liaison, another son being born the following year.

Theirs was an idyll; but, regularly punctuated as it was by Antony's military campaigns, it could not last. In Rome his fellow triumvir Octavian – whose sister Octavia Antony had recently married – was outraged by his brother-in-law's behaviour and grew more and more resentful of Cleopatra's obvious power over him; in 32 BC, after Antony had formally divorced Octavia, her brother declared war on Egypt. On 2 September 31 BC the rival fleets met off Actium, just off the northern tip of the island of Leucas. Octavian scored a decisive victory, pursuing the defeated couple back to Alexandria; it was almost another year, however, before the final scene of the drama was enacted. Not until 1 August 30 BC did Octavian enter the city, where he gave orders that Egypt should in future be a province of Rome, remaining under his direct personal control. Cleopatra barricaded herself in her private mausoleum and gave it out that she had committed suicide; hearing the news, Antony in his turn fell on his sword, but immediately afterwards learned that the report was false. He was carried into her presence, and according to Plutarch the two had a last conversation together; then he died.

The manner of Cleopatra's death is less certain. She certainly poisoned herself, but how? Plutarch tells the story of the asp much as Shakespeare wrote it, but adds that 'the real truth nobody knows'. Nonetheless, the arguments for the snake-bite theory are strong. The Egyptian cobra – which represented Amon-Ra, the sun god – had been a royal symbol since the days of the earliest pharaohs, who wore its image as a diadem on their crowns; a more regal manner of death could scarcely have been imagined. More conclusive still, Suetonius tells us that Octavian later let it be known that the moment he heard of Cleopatra's suicide he had summoned the snake-charmers and had ordered them to suck the poison from the wound. But if they came at all, they came too late.

> Dost thou not see the baby at my breast,
> That sucks the nurse asleep?

CHAPTER IV

Rome: The Early Empire

The Battle of Actium had two tremendous results. First of all, it ensured that the political spotlight remained firmly focused on Italy and the west. The largely Greek-speaking lands of the eastern Mediterranean had been the territory of Mark Antony, according to the agreement that he had reached with Octavian after Philippi, and if Antony had been victorious he would have almost certainly continued to favour them in any way he could. Under Octavian Rome was still supreme, and would remain so for the next three centuries until Constantine the Great deserted it in 330 for his new capital of Constantinople. The second consequence of the battle was that it established Octavian, at the age of thirty-two, as the most powerful man who had ever lived, the undisputed master of the known world. The problem for him now was how best to consolidate his position. The Republic was effectively dead, so much was plain; but Julius Caesar's open autocracy had proved fatal to him, and his great-nephew was determined not to make the same mistake. For some time yet, at least in appearance, the old republican forms had to be observed. Every year from 31 to 23 BC Octavian held the consulship, using this as the constitutional basis of his power; but his assumption, on 16 January 27 BC, of the new title of Augustus was a clear enough indication of the way things were going.

It is thus impossible to put a definite date to the establishment of the Roman Empire. It was a gradual process – but perhaps it was better that way. In his youth Augustus was certainly hungry for power; once he had gained it, however, he mellowed and became a statesman. His other achievements are harder to quantify. He reorganised the administration and the army; he established permanent naval bases on the North African coast and even in the Black Sea. Rome was now the unchallenged mistress of the Mediterranean – in which, between 200 BC and 200 AD, there was a greater density of commercial traffic than at any time in the next thousand years.[1] In 26–25 BC he personally pacified the rebellious tribes of northern Spain, establishing no less than

---

[1] It is hardly surprising that the most common Latin name for the Mediterranean was *mare nostrum*, 'our sea'. No previous power had ever been in a position to make such a claim; nor has any been able to do so since.

44

twenty-two colonies, their inhabitants all Roman citizens; later he – or, more accurately, his generals – doubled the extent of the Roman dominions. More important than any of this, he moulded the old Republic into the new shape that its vast expansion had made necessary, and somehow reconciled to it all classes of Roman society, rallying them to the support of his new regime. It was said of him that he found Rome a city of brick and left it a city of marble, but he did more: he found it a republic and left it an empire.

That empire included the Roman province of Syria, acquired during the wars with King Mithridates early in the first century BC. It was not considered particularly important by its administrators, but it was there, during the reign of Augustus – perhaps in BC 5 or 6[1] – that there was born into a humble but deeply pious Jewish family the man who was probably to reshape the world more radically than any other before or since. This is not the place to consider either the personal impact that Jesus Christ had on his contemporaries; even the long-term effects of the religion which he founded might have been very different had not Pontius Pilate, Procurator of Judaea from 26 to 36 AD, reluctantly yielded to the clamourings of the populace and given his authority for the crucifixion. Yield, however, he did. Within thirty years St Paul, the first and arguably the greatest Christian missionary, had carried the new message throughout the eastern Mediterranean. Within three hundred years, as we shall shortly see, the faith that he preached was to be adopted by the Empire itself.

What, in the 500-odd years of its existence, had the Roman Republic achieved? The first thing to remember is that the Romans always saw themselves as heirs of the Greeks. Since the second century BC in the eastern Mediterranean the two civilisations had existed side by side, and though politically they might take very different forms, culturally the Romans liked to think that they were continuing the Greek tradition. In literature, for example, the two greatest Roman writers, Virgil and Horace – both of them, incidentally, personal friends of Octavian – openly acknowledged their debt to their Greek predecessors. Virgil's tremendous epic, the *Aeneid*, is clearly inspired by Homer (though the style and language are more sophisticated) and embodies the all-important myth of the city's connection with Troy – through the Trojan hero Aeneas, who escaped at the time of the Greek

---

[1] King Herod is known to have died in 4 BC.

conquest and after many wanderings made his way to Italy, where his descendants, Romulus and Remus, founded Rome. The *Eclogues* and *Georgics* too, even if they cannot be traced directly back as far as Hesiod, follow a venerable Greek bucolic tradition. Horace, born in 65 BC (five years after Virgil), had actually studied in the Academy of Athens before fighting on the side of Brutus and Cassius at Philippi. His family property in Apulia had been confiscated by the victorious Triumvirate, but his friend Maecenas (to whom he had been introduced by Virgil), a patron of almost legendary wealth and generosity, brought about his reconciliation with Octavian and gave him the farm in the Sabine hills where he settled happily for the rest of his life. It was there that he wrote his celebrated Odes,[1] which he proudly claimed to have modelled on early Greek lyric poets like Alcaeus, Pindar and Sappho. Prose writers were restricted by the fact that the novel had not yet been invented, but there were brilliant letter-writers like Pliny, orators like Cicero, and above all the great historians: Livy, Tacitus and – by no means least – Julius Caesar himself.

In the visual arts the same influences are clearly traceable. Such was the Roman admiration for Greek sculpture that the Emperors and nobles filled their palaces and gardens with copies of statues by Phidias and Praxiteles; many famous Greek works of art are nowadays known only by their Roman copies. Original Roman sculpture, splendid as it could often be, admittedly never quite succeeded in capturing the spirit of the Greek: there is no Roman equivalent of the Elgin Marbles, let alone of the greatest piece of classical sculpture in existence, the so-called Alexander Sarcophagus in the Archaeological Museum of Istanbul.[2] In the art of painting a fair comparison is a good deal harder, if only because – apart from those on vases – so few Greek examples have survived. Of Roman paintings – if Roman they can be considered – by far the most astonishing are those funerary portraits, mostly dating from the first and second centuries AD, found in the region of Fayum, some eighty miles southwest of Cairo. Together, these portraits constitute the most outstanding body of painting to have come down to us from the ancient world.

But the Roman achievement extended well beyond the field of the

---

[1] The English title is misleading. The Latin one, *Carmina* ('Songs'), is a much better description of what are essentially lyrics.
[2] This sublime work, found in 1887 in the necropolis of Sidon, is thought to have been intended for the body of the city's last king, Abdalonymous, who was appointed by Alexander in 332 BC. On its sides are representations of Alexander himself, in peace and at war.

arts. The Romans were legists, scientists, architects, engineers and of course soldiers. It was in these last two capacities that they built up their astonishing network of roads the length and breadth of Europe, with the primary object of getting an army to its destination in the shortest possible time; if these were to be passable in all weathers it was essential that they should be properly paved, and it was self-evident that they should run, wherever possible, in a dead straight line. The first stretch of the Appian Way was finished as early as 312 BC, and the year 147 BC saw the completion of the Via Postumia, running from sea to sea – from Genoa on the Tyrrhenian to Aquileia on the Adriatic. Such communities as these, and countless others like them which in the early days of the Republic had been little more than settlements, were now prosperous cities, with temples and public buildings conceived on a size and scale unimaginable in former times.

All this had been made possible by perhaps the single most important discovery in the history of architecture. To the ancient Greeks, the arch was unknown. All their buildings were based on the simple principle of a horizontal lintel laid across vertical columns; although they were able to use this principle to create buildings of surpassing beauty, such buildings were severely limited, both in their height and in their ability to carry weight. With the invention of the arch and its extension, the vault, vast new possibilities were opened up; we have only to think of the Colosseum, or those mighty constructions like the Pont du Gard near Nîmes, or the tremendous 119-arch aqueduct at Segovia in Spain, to understand the size and scale of the architecture of which the Romans were now capable.

Thoughts of the Colosseum, however, evoke other, less happy associations. The Romans were talented, efficient and industrious; they produced fine artists and writers; they spread their remarkable civilisation across much of the known world. Why, then, did they display such a passion for violence? Why did they flock, in their tens of thousands, to witness gladiatorial contests which were invariably fatal to at least one of the participants, to cheer while innocent and defenceless men, women and children were torn to pieces by wild animals, or as those animals in their turn were subjected to slow and hideous deaths? Has any European people ever, before or since, publicly demonstrated such a degree of brutality and sadism? Nor are we speaking exclusively of the mob; the Emperors themselves, over at least the first two centuries of the Roman Empire, again and again descended to levels of depravity which may occasionally have been matched elsewhere, but have certainly never been surpassed. The historian Suetonius tells us gleefully of the pederasty of Tiberius who, during his years of retirement in Capri, trained young boys to swim around him and nibble his most sensitive areas under the water; of the gluttony of Vitellius, who according to Gibbon 'consumed in mere eating, at least six millions of our money in about seven months';[1] of the brutality of Caligula – his nickname means 'little boot' – who, not content with incest with one of his sisters, regularly offered the other two 'to be abused by his own stale catamites',[2] set up a public brothel in the imperial palace and had innocent men sawn in half to entertain him at lunch.

But there were good Emperors too. The golden age of the Roman Empire extended from 98 to 180 AD, when 'the empire of Rome comprehended the fairest part of the earth, and the most civilised portion of mankind.'[3] It began with Trajan, who broadened the frontiers of the Empire to cover Dacia (embracing roughly the present territory of Romania) and Arabia Petraea, which extended from Phoenicia in the north down to the shores of the Red Sea. He also enriched his capital with some of its most magnificent buildings, and governed his vast empire with decency, firmness and humanity – qualities all too seldom seen in first- and third-century Rome. It continued with his successor and fellow-Spaniard Hadrian,[4] perhaps the most capable Emperor ever to occupy the throne, who spent much of his twenty-one-year reign visiting every corner of his vast empire – including Britain, where in 122 he ordered the construction of the great wall from the Solway to the Tyne which still bears his name. Then, with Hadrian's death, came the Antonines: first Antoninus Pius, whose long, peaceful reign gave the Romans a welcome breathing space after the endless exertions of his two predecessors, and finally the philosopher-emperor Marcus Aurelius, whose *Meditations* – written in Greek, probably during his long campaigns against rebellious German tribes – is the only work in existence which allows us an insight into the mind of an ancient ruler.[5] But alas, that golden age ended as suddenly as it had begun, with the succession of Marcus Aurelius's son Commodus who, with his harem of women and boys – 300 of each – returned Rome to the worst days of imperial degeneracy.

---

[1] 'It is not easy,' he adds, 'to express his vices with dignity, or even decency.'
[2] Such is the inspired phrase of Philemon Holland, translating Suetonius in 1606.
[3] Gibbon again: from the first sentence of *The Decline and Fall*.
[4] All his life Hadrian was mocked for his Spanish accent.
[5] It is said to have been an inspiration to – of all people – Cecil Rhodes.

The story of the Roman Empire in the third century makes unedifying reading. Historians tell of the blood-lust of Caracalla – declared Caesar at the age of eight – who in 215 ordered on a whim a general massacre in Alexandria in which many thousand innocent citizens perished, and of the sexual ambivalence of his successor, Elagabalus, who took his name from the Syrian sun god (with whom he identified) and who in 219 made his ceremonial entry into Rome rouged, bejewelled and dressed in purple and gold. He it was of whom Gibbon wrote:

> A long train of concubines, and a rapid succession of wives, among whom was a vestal virgin, ravished by force from her sacred asylum, were insufficient to satisfy the impotence of his passions. The master of the Roman world affected to copy the dress and manners of the female sex, preferred the distaff to the sceptre, and dishonoured the principal dignities of the empire by distributing them among his numerous lovers; one of whom was publicly invested with the title and authority of the emperor's, or as he more properly styled himself, of the empress's husband.

With rulers like these, the corruption inevitably spread downwards through Roman society, to the point at which law and order broke down almost completely and the government was in chaos. It is a sobering fact that the Emperor Septimius Severus, expiring at York in 211, was the last Roman Emperor for eighty years to die in his bed.

Just ninety-five years later, that same city of York was the scene of another imperial death, the consequences of which were considerably more important to world history. The reigning Emperor at the time was Diocletian, who had soon found his empire too unwieldy, his enemies too widespread and his lines of communication too long to be properly governable by any single monarch. He therefore decided to split the imperial power into four. There would be two Augusti – himself and an old and beloved comrade-in-arms named Maximian – and two rulers with the slightly inferior title of Caesar, who would exercise supreme authority in their allotted territories and would ultimately become Augusti in their turn. The supremacy in northwestern Europe – with special responsibility for the reimposition of Roman rule in rebellious Britain – he entrusted to one of his most successful generals, Constantius Chlorus, who became one of the first two Caesars. The other Caesar was Galerius, a rough, brutal professional soldier from Thrace, who was given charge of the Balkans.

Then, in 305, there occurred an event unparalleled in the history of the Roman Empire: the voluntary abdication of an Emperor. Diocletian decided that he had had enough. He retired to the enormous palace he had built for himself at Salona (the modern Split) on the Dalmatian coast, and forced an intensely unwilling Maximian to abdicate with him. Overnight, Constantius Chlorus found himself the senior Augustus, but he was not to enjoy his inheritance for long. A few months later, on 25 July 306, he died at York, his son Constantine at his bedside. Scarcely had the breath left his body than his friend and ally, the delightfully named King Crocus of the Alemanni, acclaimed young Constantine as Augustus in his father's stead. The local legions instantly took up the cry, clasped the imperial purple toga round his shoulders, raised him on their shields and cheered him to the echo.

At this time Constantine was in his early thirties. On his father's side his lineage could scarcely have been more distinguished; his mother, Helena, on the other hand, far from being – as the twelfth-century Geoffrey of Monmouth (and, more recently, Evelyn Waugh) would have us believe – the daughter of Coel, mythical founder of Colchester and the Old King Cole of the nursery rhyme, was almost certainly the offspring of a humble innkeeper in Bithynia.[1] (Other, less reputable historians have gone so far as to suggest that as a girl she had been one of the supplementary amenities of her father's establishment, regularly available to his clients at a small extra charge.) Only later in her life, when her son had acceded to the supreme power, did she become the most venerated woman in the Empire; in 327, when she was already over seventy, this passionate Christian convert made her celebrated pilgrimage to the Holy Land, there miraculously to unearth the True Cross and thus to gain an honoured place in the calendar of saints.

But let us return to Constantine. The first thing to be said is that no ruler in all history – not Alexander nor Alfred, not Charles nor Catherine, not Frederick nor even Gregory – has ever more fully merited his title of 'the Great'; for within the short space of some fifteen years he took two decisions, either of which, alone, would have changed the future of the civilised world. The first was to adopt Christianity – the object, only a generation previously, of persecutions under Diocletian more brutal than any that it has suffered before or since – as the official religion of the Roman Empire. The second was to

---

[1] A Byzantine province extending from the Asiatic shore of the Bosphorus along the southern coast of the Black Sea.

transfer the capital of that empire from Rome to the new city which he was building on the site of the old Greek settlement of Byzantium and which was to be known, for the next sixteen centuries, by his own name: the city of Constantine, Constantinople. Together, these two decisions and their consequences have given him a serious claim to be considered – excepting only Jesus Christ, the Prophet Mohammed and the Buddha – the most influential man who ever lived.

Immediately after his acclamation, Constantine had naturally sent word to his co-Augustus Galerius, now ruling from Nicomedia (the modern Izmit) across the Bosphorus; but Galerius, while very reluctantly agreeing to acknowledge him as a Caesar, refused point-blank to recognise him as an Augustus, having already appointed a certain Valerius Licinianus, called Licinius, one of his old drinking companions. Constantine did not seem particularly worried. Perhaps he did not yet feel ready for the supreme power; at all events, he remained in Gaul and Britain for another six years, governing the two provinces on the whole wisely and well. Only after the death of Galerius in 311 did he begin preparations to assert his claim, and not until the summer of 312 did he move across the Alps against the first and most immediately dangerous of his rivals, his brother-in-law Maxentius, son of Diocletian's old colleague the Emperor Maximian.[1]

The two armies met on 28 October 312 on the Via Flaminia, some seven or eight miles northeast of Rome where the Tiber is crossed by the old Ponte Milvio.[2] This Battle of the Milvian Bridge is principally remembered now for the legend related by Constantine's contemporary, Bishop Eusebius of Caesarea – who claims to have heard it from the Emperor himself – according to which

> at about midday, just as the sun was beginning to decline, he saw with his own eyes the trophy of a cross of light in the heavens, above the sun, and bearing the inscription 'Conquer by This' [hoc vince]. At this sight he himself was struck with amazement, and his whole army also.[3]

Inspired, it is said, by this vision, Constantine soundly defeated the army of his brother-in-law and put it to flight, driving it southward towards the old bridge. This was extremely narrow, and Maxentius

---

[1] In 307 Constantine had put away his first wife to marry Maximian's daughter Faustina.
[2] The old bridge still stands. It has been restored many times, but much of its original second-century fabric remains.
[3] *De Vita Constantini*, I, 28. The story is not quite as straightforward as it sounds; another version by the scholar Lactantius raises a number of intriguing points. I have gone into the matter a good deal more fully in *Byzantium: The Early Centuries*, pp. 38–43.

had somewhat pessimistically constructed next to it another, broader one on pontoons, on which he could if necessary make an orderly retreat and which could then be broken in the middle to prevent pursuit. Over this the remains of his shattered army stampeded, and all might yet have been well had not the engineers in charge of the bridge lost their heads and drawn the bolts too soon. Suddenly the whole structure collapsed, hurling hundreds of men into the fast-flowing water. Those who had not yet crossed made wildly for the old stone bridge, but this too proved fatal. Such was its narrowness that many were crushed to death, others were trampled underfoot, still others flung down by their own comrades into the river below. Among the last was Maxentius himself, whose body was later found washed up on the bank. His severed head, impaled on a lance, was carried aloft before Constantine as he entered Rome the following day.

His victory at the Milvian Bridge made Constantine absolute master of the western world from the Atlantic to the Adriatic, from Hadrian's Wall to the Atlas Mountains. Whether it also achieved his conversion to Christianity is unclear; it certainly marked the point at which he set himself up as protector and active patron of his Christian subjects. On his return to Rome he immediately subsidised from his private purse twenty-five already existing churches and several new ones; he presented the newly elected Pope Melchiades with the old house of the Laterani family on the Coelian hill, which was to remain a papal palace for another thousand years; and next to it he ordered the building, once again at his own expense, of the first of Rome's great Constantinian basilicas, St John Lateran, still today the cathedral church of the city. It is all the more surprising to find his coins for another twelve years associating him not with Christianity but with the then popular cult of *Sol Invictus*, the Unconquered Sun, and refusing to accept Christian baptism, which he was to continue to postpone until he was on his deathbed a quarter of a century later.

This same note of caution is evident in the Edict of Milan, which Constantine promulgated jointly with his fellow Augustus (and by now another brother-in-law)[1] Licinius in 313, describing its purpose as that of

> securing respect and reverence for the Deity; namely by the grant, both to the Christians and to all others, of the right freely to follow whatever form of worship might please them, to the intent that *whatsoever Divinity*

---

[1] Licinius was married to Constantine's half-sister Constantia.

dwells in heaven [my italics] might be favourable to us and to all those living under our authority.

The two Augusti might have spoken with one voice on religious toleration, but they agreed on little else, and another ten years of civil war were necessary before Constantine could finally eliminate his last rival. Not until 323 was he able to establish peace throughout the Empire, under his rule alone.

Constantine by now seems to have been a Christian in all but name, but at this point the Christian Church was split by the first great schism in its history. This was the work of a certain Arius, presbyter of Alexandria, who held that Jesus Christ was not co-eternal and of one substance with God the Father, but had been created by Him at a certain time as His instrument for the salvation of the world. Thus, although a perfect man, the Son must always be subordinate to the Father, his nature being human rather than divine. The ensuing dispute quickly became a *cause célèbre*, which Constantine resolved to settle. He did so by summoning the first universal Council of the Church, which was held between 20 May and 19 June 325 at Nicaea (the modern Iznik), with some 300 bishops taking part. The proceedings were opened by the Emperor himself, and it was he who proposed the insertion, into the draft statement of belief, of the key word *homoousios* – meaning consubstantial, 'of one substance' – to describe the relation of the Son to the Father. Its inclusion was almost tantamount to a condemnation of Arianism, and such were the Emperor's powers of persuasion that by the close of the conference only seventeen of the assembled bishops maintained their opposition – a number that the threat of exile and possible excommunication subsequently reduced to two.

But Arius fought on. It was not until 336, during a final investigation of his beliefs, that

> made bold by the protection of his followers, engaged in a light-hearted and foolish conversation, he was suddenly compelled by a call of nature to retire; and immediately, as it is written, 'falling headlong, he burst asunder in the midst, and all his bowels gushed out'.[1]

This story, it must be admitted, comes from the pen of Arius's leading opponent, Archbishop Athanasius of Alexandria, but the unattractive circumstances of his demise are too well attested by

---

[1] Acts, i, 18.

contemporary writers to be open to serious question. Inevitably, they were attributed to divine retribution: the archbishop's biblical reference is to the somewhat similar fate which befell Judas Iscariot.

Constantine's dream of spiritual harmony throughout Christendom was not to be achieved in his lifetime; indeed, we are still awaiting it today.

When Constantine first set eyes on Byzantium, the city was already nearly a thousand years old. According to tradition, it was founded in 658 BC by a certain Byzas as a colony of Megara; there can, at any rate, be little doubt that a small Greek settlement was flourishing on the site by the beginning of the sixth century BC, and none at all that the Emperor was right to choose it for his new capital. Rome had long been a backwater; none of Diocletian's four tetrarchs had dreamed of living there. The principal dangers to imperial security were now concentrated on the eastern frontier: the Sarmatians around the lower Danube, the Ostrogoths to the north of the Black Sea and – most menacing of all – the Persians, whose great Sassanian Empire now extended from the former Roman provinces of Armenia and Mesopotamia as far as the Hindu Kush. But the reasons for the move were not only strategic. The whole focus of civilisation had shifted irrevocably eastward. Intellectually and culturally, Rome was growing more and more out of touch with the new and progressive thinking of the Hellenistic world; the Roman academies and libraries were no longer any match for those of Alexandria, Pergamum or Antioch. Economically, too, the agricultural and mineral wealth of what was known as the *pars orientalis* was a far greater attraction than the Italian peninsula, where malaria was spreading fast and populations were dwindling. Finally, the old Roman republican and pagan traditions had no place in Constantine's new Christian empire. It was time to start afresh.

The advantages of Byzantium as a strategic site over any of its oriental neighbours were also self-evident. Standing as it did on the very threshold of Asia and occupying the easternmost tip of a broad, roughly triangular promontory, its south side washed by the Propontis (which we call the Sea of Marmara) and its northeast by that broad, deep and navigable inlet, some five miles long, known since remotest antiquity as the Golden Horn, it had been moulded by nature at once into a magnificent harbour and a well-nigh impregnable stronghold, needing major fortification only on its western side. Even an attack from the sea would be difficult enough, the Marmara itself being protected by two long and narrow straits: the Bosphorus to the east and the Hellespont (or Dardanelles) to the west. No wonder that the people of Chalcedon, who only seventeen years earlier had founded their city on the flat and featureless shore opposite, became proverbial for their blindness.

Constantine spared no pains to make his new capital worthy of its name. Tens of thousands of artisans and labourers worked day and night. On a site on the old acropolis – formerly occupied by a shrine of Aphrodite – rose the first great church of the city, St Irene, dedicated not to any saint or martyr but to the Holy Peace of God. A few years later it was to be joined – and overshadowed – by its larger and still more splendid neighbour St Sophia, the Church of the Holy Wisdom. A quarter of a mile away towards the Marmara stood the immense Hippodrome, the Emperor's box having direct access to the imperial palace behind it. All the leading cities of Europe and Asia, including Rome itself, were plundered of their finest statues, trophies and works of art for the embellishment and enrichment of Constantinople. At last all was ready, and on Monday, 11 May 330, the Emperor attended a mass in St Irene, at which he formally dedicated the city to the Virgin. On that day the Byzantine Empire was born.

And yet in fact there had been no real change. To its subjects it was still the Roman Empire, that of Augustus and Trajan and Hadrian. And they were still Romans. Their capital had been moved, that was all; nothing else was affected. Over the centuries, surrounded as they were by the Greek world, it was inevitable that they should gradually abandon the Latin language in favour of the Greek, but that made no difference either. It was as Romans that they proudly described themselves for as long as the empire lasted, and when, 1,123 years after its foundation, that empire finally fell, it was as Romans that they died.

Of those years, Constantine himself was to live for another seven. Then, in the spring of 337, already a sick man, he travelled to Helenopolis, a city that he had had rebuilt in memory of his mother, where the hot medicinal baths might, he hoped, effect a cure. Alas, they failed to do so, and on the way home to the capital he grew rapidly worse until it was plain that he would be unable to complete the journey. It was therefore not in Constantinople but in Nicomedia that this extraordinary man, who had for years been a self-styled bishop of the Christian Church, finally received his baptism. When the ceremony was done, Eusebius tells us, 'he arrayed himself in imperial vestments white and radiant as light, and laid himself down on a couch of the purest white, refusing ever to clothe himself in purple again.'

Why, it may be asked, did he delay this baptism for so long? The most probable answer is also the simplest: that this sacrament conferred complete absolution from all sins, but unfortunately could be celebrated only once. It stood to reason, therefore, that the longer it was deferred the less opportunity there would be of falling once again into the ways of iniquity. This last supreme example of brinkmanship was perhaps a fitting conclusion to Constantine's reign of thirty-one years – the longest of any Roman Emperor since Augustus – which ended at noon on Whit Sunday, 22 May 337. He was buried in his newly-completed Church of the Holy Apostles. By virtue of this dedication 'he caused twelve sarcophagi to be set up in this church, like sacred pillars, in honour and memory of the number of the Apostles, in the centre of which was placed his own, having six of theirs on either side of it.'

Constantine's undivided rule did not last long. On the death of the Emperor Theodosius the Great in 395 the Empire split again and, although the supreme authority was firmly rooted in Constantinople, a series of semi-puppet emperors reigned in Italy (mostly in Ravenna) for the best part of another century. During this period, however, the Italian peninsula – and indeed much of western Europe – was transformed.

Those who transformed it were the people contemptuously known to the citizens of the Empire as the barbarians. Of their many and various tribes, two only are of interest to us at this point in our story: the Goths and the Huns. They could hardly have been more different. By the end of the fourth century the Goths were a relatively civilised people, the majority of them Arian Christians. Although the western branch, that of the Visigoths, was still ruled by local chieftains, the Ostrogoths of the east had already evolved into a united and prosperous central European kingdom. The Huns, on the other hand, were savages: an undisciplined, heathen horde, Mongolian in origin, which had swept down from the central Asian steppe, laying waste everything in its path. Both tribes, at different times, posed major threats to the Empire. Surprisingly, perhaps, it was the Goths who attacked first.

During the last years of the fourth century, the Visigothic chieftain Alaric had spread terror from the walls of Constantinople to the southern Peloponnese; in 401 he invaded Italy. The Empire somehow managed to hold him at bay, and for several years more it continued to do so; but it suffered from two huge misconceptions. The first was that all barbarians were alike: undisciplined hordes of skin-clad savages who would be no match for the highly trained imperial army. This delusion did not last long. The second – that Alaric was bent on the Empire's overthrow – unfortunately lasted a good deal longer. The truth was quite the contrary: he was fighting not to destroy the Empire but to establish a permanent home for his people within it, in such a way that they might enjoy their own autonomy while he, as their chieftain, would be granted high imperial rank. If only the Western Emperor Honorius – away in Ravenna – and the Roman Senate could have understood this simple fact, they might well have averted the final catastrophe. By their lack of comprehension they made it inevitable.

Three times between 408 and 410 Alaric besieged Rome. The first siege starved it out; the Romans were obliged to pay an enormous ransom, which included 5,000 pounds of gold and 30,000 of silver. The second ended when they agreed to depose the Emperor; the third, which had begun when Honorius, safely entrenched in Ravenna, refused to go, resulted in the sack of the city. Even then, it could have been worse: Alaric, devout Christian that he was, ordered that no churches or religious buildings were to be touched and that the right of asylum was everywhere to be respected. A sack, nevertheless, remains a sack; and the Goths, Christians though they may have been, were very far from being saints. When the traditional three days allowed for pillage and plunder were over, Alaric moved on to the south, but he had got no further than Cosenza when he fell victim to a violent fever – most probably malaria – and within a few days he was dead. He was only forty. His followers carried his body to the river Busento, which they dammed and temporarily deflected from its usual channel. There, in the stream's bed, they buried their leader; then they broke the dam, and the waters came surging back and covered him.

The Huns – who, unlike the Goths, were barbarians in more than name – had first smashed their way into Europe in 376 and destroyed the Ostrogothic kingdom; their first contact with the civilised world, however, had had little effect upon them. The vast majority still lived and slept in the open, disdaining all agriculture and even cooked food – though they liked to soften raw meat by putting it between their own thighs and their horses' flanks as they rode. For clothing they favoured tunics made from the skins of field mice crudely stitched together. These they wore continuously, without ever removing them, until they dropped off of their own accord. Their home was the saddle; they seldom dismounted, not even to eat or to sleep. Attila himself was typical of his race: short, swarthy and snub-nosed, with beady eyes set in a head too big for his body and a thin, straggling beard. Within a very few years of his accession he had become known throughout Europe as 'the scourge of God': more feared, perhaps, than any other single man – with the possible exception of Napoleon – before or since.

Not until 452 did he launch his army upon Italy. All the great cities of the Veneto were put to the torch; Pavia and Milan were ruthlessly sacked. Then he turned south towards Rome – and suddenly, unaccountably, stopped. Why he did so remains a mystery. Traditionally, the credit has always been given to Pope Leo the Great, who travelled from Rome to meet him on the banks of the Mincio – probably somewhere near Peschiera, where the river issues from Lake Garda – and persuaded him to advance no further.[1] But it seems hardly likely that the pagan Hun should have obeyed the Pope out of respect for his office alone. He would surely have demanded a substantial tribute in return. Quite different possibilities have also been suggested. There is reason to believe that his followers, having devastated all the surrounding country, were running seriously short of food, and that disease had broken out in their ranks. Meanwhile, troops were beginning to arrive from Constantinople to swell the local imperial forces. Finally, since Attila is known to have been incorrigibly superstitious, could it not be that Leo reminded him of how Alaric had died within weeks of his sack of Rome, and suggested that a similar fate befell every invader who raised his hand against the holy city? We can never be sure. All we know is that if the King of the Huns thought by sparing Rome to ensure his own survival, he was mistaken. A year later, during the night following his marriage to yet another of his already innumerable wives, his exertions brought on a sudden haemorrhage. As his lifeblood flowed away, all Europe breathed again – although not, as it soon became clear, for long.

By comparison with the Goths and the Huns, the Vandals – the last of the great barbarian peoples to have cast its shadow over the unhappy fifth century – had little direct influence on the Empire, but their effect on the Mediterranean was greater than that of the other two put together. These Germanic tribesmen, their creed fanatically Arian, had

---

[1] The scene is most enjoyably portrayed in Verdi's opera *Attila* – despite the fact that Pope Leo is disguised – as was required by the censorship – as 'an old Roman'.

fled westward from the Huns some half a century before and in 409, after invading and laying waste a large area of Gaul, had settled in Spain. There they had remained until 428, when the newly crowned King Gaiseric led his entire people – probably some 180,000 men, women and children – across the sea to North Africa. Just eleven years later he captured Carthage,[1] the last imperial stronghold on the coast, which he effectively made into a centre for piracy. By now he had built himself a formidable fleet – the only barbarian ruler to do so – and, particularly after his conquest of Sicily in around 470, was the undisputed master of the western Mediterranean.

In the early summer of 455, Gaiseric launched his most fateful expedition – against Rome itself. The reaction there was one of panic. The elderly Emperor Petronius Maximus, cowering in his palace, issued a proclamation – not, as might have been expected, calling upon all able-bodied men to rally to the defence of the Empire, but announcing that anyone who wished to leave was free to do so. His subjects had not awaited this permission. Already the terrified Romans were sending their wives and daughters away to safety, and the roads to the north and east were choked with carts as the more well-to-do families poured out of the city with all the objects of value that they wished to save from Vandal clutches. On 31 May the palace guard mutinied, killing and dismembering Petronius and throwing the pieces into the Tiber. For the fourth time in less than half a century – and but for Pope Leo it would have been the fifth – a barbarian army stood at the gates of Rome.

Once again, the long-suffering Pope did what he could. He was unable to stop Gaiseric altogether, but he did manage to extract a promise that there would be no wanton killing and no destruction of buildings, public or private. On this understanding the gates of the city were opened, and the barbarians passed into an unresisting city. For fourteen relentless days they systematically stripped it of its wealth: the gold and silver ornaments from the churches, the statues from the palaces, the sacred vessels from the Jewish synagogue, even the gilded copper roof – or half of it – from the Temple of Jupiter Capitolinus. Everything was carted down to Ostia, loaded into the waiting ships and carried away to Carthage. True to their word, however, they had left the people and the buildings unharmed. They had behaved like brigands, certainly, but not, on this occasion, like Vandals.

*

---

[1] After its destruction in 146 BC, Carthage had remained virtually deserted for over a century, until in 29 BC Augustus made it the capital of his Roman province of Africa.

After the sack of Rome, one might have thought that the Vandals would have been satisfied. One would have been wrong. Over the next few years they systematically ravaged Campania and occupied the Balearic Islands, Corsica and Sardinia. Then it was the turn of Sicily, after which, for good measure, they sacked the western shores of Greece. As this unedifying story shows all too clearly, the Roman Empire of the West was by now sick unto death, and the abdication in 476 of its last Emperor, the pathetic child Romulus Augustulus – his very name a double diminutive – need cause us no surprise. He was toppled by another Germanic barbarian named Odoacer,[1] who refused to accept the old plurality of emperors, recognising only the authority of the Emperor Zeno in Constantinople. All he asked of Zeno was the title of Patrician, in which capacity he proposed to rule Italy in the Emperor's name.

Five years before, in 471, a boy of about seventeen named Theodoric had succeeded his father as paramount leader of the eastern Goths. Although he had received little or no formal education during the ten years of his childhood spent as a hostage in Constantinople – he is said to have signed his name all his life by stencilling it through a perforated gold plate – he had acquired an instinctive understanding of the Byzantines and their ways which was to serve him in good stead in the years to come. His main objective on his accession, like that of so many barbarian leaders before him, was to find and secure a permanent home for his people. To this end he was to devote the better part of the next twenty years: fighting sometimes for and sometimes against the Empire, arguing, bargaining, threatening and cajoling by turns, until, some time in 487, he and Zeno made an agreement. Theodoric would lead his entire people into Italy, overthrow Odoacer and rule the land as an Ostrogothic kingdom under imperial sovereignty. And so, early in 488, the great exodus took place: men, women and children, with their horses and their pack animals, their cattle and their sheep, lumbering slowly across the plains of central Europe in search of greener and more peaceful pastures.

Odoacer fought back, but his army was no match for that of the Goths. He withdrew to Ravenna, where Theodoric blockaded him for more than two years until the local bishop arranged an armistice. It was then agreed that Italy was to be ruled by the two of them jointly, both

---

[1] Sometimes known as Odovacar. He was a Scyrian, member of an obscure Germanic tribe which will not trouble us again.

sharing the imperial palace. In the circumstances this solution seemed remarkably generous on the part of Theodoric, but it soon became clear that he wished only to lull his rival into a false sense of security; he had not the faintest intention of keeping his word. On 15 March 493 he invited Odoacer, his brother, his son and his senior officers to a banquet. There, as his guest took his place in the seat of honour, Theodoric stepped forward and, with one tremendous stroke of his sword, clove through the body of Odoacer from collarbone to thigh. The other guests were similarly dealt with by the surrounding guards. Odoacer's wife was thrown into prison, where she died of starvation; his son, whom he had surrendered to the Ostrogoths as a hostage, was sent off to Gaul and executed. Finally Theodoric laid aside the skins and furs that were the traditional clothing of his race, robed himself – as Odoacer had never done – in the imperial purple and settled down to rule in Italy.

He was to do so, quietly and efficiently, for the next thirty-three years, and the extraordinary mausoleum which he built for himself – and which still stands in the northeastern suburbs of Ravenna – perfectly symbolises, in its half-classical, half-barbaric architectural strength, a colossus who himself bestrode two civilisations. No other Germanic ruler, setting up his throne on the ruins of the Western Empire, possessed a fraction of Theodoric's statesmanship and political vision. When he died, on 30 August 526, Italy lost the greatest of her early medieval rulers, unequalled until the days of Charlemagne.

The scene is now set for the appearance of perhaps the greatest of all the Byzantine Emperors – and Empresses – after Constantine himself. Justinian was born in 482 in a small Thracian village. He came from humble stock, and was already thirty-six when in 518 his uncle Justin, a rough, barely literate soldier who had somehow risen to command one of the crack palace regiments, succeeded the eighty-seven-year-old Emperor Anastasius on the throne of Constantinople. Precisely how he managed to do so remains unknown; there was almost certainly a coup of some kind, and it is more than likely that his nephew had a hand in it.

Justinian must have come to Constantinople as a child; he would not otherwise have been known as a man of wide education and culture, of a kind that he could not possibly have acquired outside the capital. His uncle was consequently only too happy to defer to Justinian's infinitely superior intelligence and to allow him, as his *éminence grise*, effectively to govern the Empire. He had been doing so with consummate ability for two or three years when he met his future wife, Theodora. She was not, to put it mildly, an ideal match. Her father had been a bear-keeper at the Hippodrome, her mother a performer in the circus, and she herself had done little to improve her acceptability into polite society. The descriptions of her depravity given by her contemporary Procopius in his *Secret History* can – one hopes – be taken with more than a pinch of salt;[1] but there can be little doubt that at least in her youth, as our grandparents would have put it, she was no better than she should have been.

By the time she caught the eye of Justinian, however, she was in her middle thirties – beautiful and intelligent as ever, but with all the wisdom and maturity that had been so noticeably absent in earlier years. Such obstacles to the marriage as presented themselves were quickly overcome, and in 525 the Patriarch[2] declared Justinian and Theodora man and wife. Only two years later, on the death of Justin, they found themselves the sole and supreme rulers of the Roman Empire. The plural is important. Theodora was to be no Empress Consort. At her husband's insistence she was to reign at his side, taking decisions in his name and participating in the highest affairs of state. Her future appearances on the public stage were to be very different from those of the past.

Justinian is probably best remembered today for the sublime monument he left behind him: the third Church of St Sophia – the first two having been destroyed by fire – which he built in five years between 532 and 537.[3] Almost as astonishing was his complete recodification of Roman law: removing all contradictions, ensuring that there was nothing incompatible with Christian doctrine, substituting clarity and concision for confusion and chaos. For our purposes, however, his greatest achievement was his recovery of the Empire of the West. To

---

[1] To take but one example: 'Often in the theatre . . . she would spread herself out and lie on her back on the ground. And certain slaves whose special task it was would sprinkle grains of barley over her private parts; and geese trained for the purpose would pick them off one by one with their beaks and swallow them . . .'

[2] From the early sixth century, the title of Patriarch was accorded to the bishops of the five chief sees of Christendom: Rome, Alexandria, Antioch, Constantinople and Jerusalem. (The Bishop of Rome, being Pope, seldom if ever used it.) In more recent times the title has also been given to the heads of certain autocephalous Orthodox Churches (Russia, Serbia, Romania, Bulgaria and Georgia) and also – in view of the city's historical associations with Byzantium – to the Bishop of Venice.

[3] He had by then already built the ravishingly beautiful little church of St Sergius and St Bacchus, just below the southern end of the Hippodrome, which was to provide the model for his magnificent S. Vitale in Ravenna. It is now a mosque known as Little St Sophia – *Küçük Ayasofya Camii*.

him it was clear that a Roman Empire without Rome was an absurdity, and he was fortunate in having as his instrument the most brilliant general in all Byzantine history, a Romanised Thracian like himself named Belisarius.

The first territory to be singled out for reconquest was the Vandal kingdom in North Africa. Belisarius was given his orders, and on or about Midsummer Day 533 the expedition set sail: 5,000 cavalry and 10,000 infantry – at least half of them barbarian mercenaries, mostly Huns – travelling in 500 transports, escorted by ninety-two *dromons*.[1] The Vandal king Gelimer and his men put up a spirited resistance, but the Hun cavalry – hideous, savage and implacable – was too much for them. In two separate battles, that cavalry charged; on both occasions the Vandals turned and fled; and on Sunday, 15 September 533, Belisarius made his formal entry into Carthage. Gelimer himself did not surrender at once. For three months in the depths of winter he wandered in the mountains; in January 534, knowing that he was surrounded, he sent a request for a sponge, a loaf of bread and a lyre, his messenger explaining that he needed the first for a sore eye, and the second to satisfy a craving for real bread after weeks of unleavened peasant dough. As for the third, it appeared that he had devoted his time in hiding to the composition of a dirge bewailing his recent misfortunes, and was eager to try it out. Not until March did he give himself up.

Now it was the turn of Ostrogothic Italy. With an army surprisingly reduced in size – some 7,500 men altogether, though once again containing a large contingent of Huns – Belisarius sailed straight to Sicily, which he took without a struggle. Then, in the late spring of 536, he crossed the Straits of Messina and pressed onward up the peninsula, meeting no resistance until he reached Naples – which, on its eventual surrender, paid a heavy price for its heroism. The murder, rapine and pillage which followed was appalling even by the standards of the time, the pagan Huns in particular having no compunction in burning down the churches in which their intended victims had taken refuge. The news soon spread to Rome, where Pope Silverius hastily invited Belisarius to occupy the city, and on 9 December 536 the Byzantine army marched in through the Porta Asinaria near St John Lateran, while the Goths hurried out through the Porta Flaminia.

---

[22] The smallest type of Byzantine warship, designed for lightness and speed, with a crew of about twenty oarsmen.

But if Silverius had hoped to spare Rome yet another siege, he was disappointed. Belisarius himself knew perfectly well that the Goths would be back and immediately began defence preparations; it was just as well that he did, because in March 537 the Gothic army took up its positions around the walls. The ensuing siege – which began with the cutting of all the aqueducts, thus dealing Rome a blow from which it was not to recover for a thousand years – lasted for a year and nine days. It might well have continued even longer had not substantial reinforcements arrived just in time from Constantinople. Even then the struggle was not over. The Goths refused absolutely to give in, and for another three years the peninsula was to be fought over, ravaged and laid waste from one end to the other.

The end came in a manner which, in the minds of many, reflects little credit on Belisarius. He had slowly closed in on Ravenna – now the Gothic capital, just as it had been the Byzantine one – and by the spring of 540 he had the city surrounded, by his army on land and by the imperial fleet at sea. One night a secret emissary arrived from the Gothic court with an extraordinary proposal: they would deliver up the crown to Belisarius on the understanding that he should proclaim himself Emperor of the West. Many an imperial general would have seized such an opportunity; the bulk of his army would probably have supported him, and with the Goths at his back he would have been more than capable of dealing with any punitive expedition from Constantinople. Belisarius's loyalty never wavered, but he suddenly saw a means of bringing the war to a quick and victorious end. He immediately signified that the offer had been accepted, and the imperial army marched into the city.

As the chief Gothic nobles were carried off into captivity they must have reflected bitterly on the perfidy of the general who had betrayed them. Belisarius, on the other hand, was unmoved. The Goths' proposal had been in itself perfidious; were they not all of them rebels against the imperial authority? War was war, and by occupying Ravenna as he had done he had saved untold bloodshed on both sides. In May 540 he took ship for the Bosphorus feeling, we may be sure, nothing but satisfaction with a job well done. After his recovery of North Africa the Emperor had awarded him a splendid Triumph; what might he not expect this time, having delivered the whole Italian peninsula, including Ravenna and even Rome itself, into Justinian's hands?

Alas, there was no feeling of victory in the air when he returned to Constantinople. Neither Justinian nor his subjects were in any mood for celebration. In June 540, only a few weeks after the fall of Ravenna, the troops of the Persian King Chosroes had invaded the Empire and destroyed Antioch, massacring most of its inhabitants and sending the rest into slavery. The general's presence was urgently required – not in the Hippodrome but on the eastern front.

Fortunately it turned out that Chosroes had been out for plunder rather than conquest; in return for 5,000 pounds of gold and the promise of another 500 each succeeding year he turned happily back to Persia. Even so, Belisarius never received his reward. He was unlucky enough to fall foul of the Empress Theodora, and in 542, while Justinian – stricken by plague – lay between life and death, she relieved the general of his eastern command, disbanded his magnificent household and confiscated all his accumulated treasure. In the following year, when the Emperor was sufficiently recovered to reassert his authority, Belisarius was pardoned and restored to favour, up to a point; but it was a sadder and wiser man – though he was still under forty – who returned in May 544 to Italy.

He found all his work there undone. Justinian had obviously been informed of the Goths' offer of the throne to Belisarius, and was terrified lest any of the Commander's successors should succumb to the same temptation. Accordingly he had entrusted Italy to no less than five subordinate generals, giving no single one of them authority over the rest; left to themselves, they had simply divided up the territory between them and settled down to plunder it. Within weeks the demoralisation of the Byzantine army in Italy was complete, and the way was clear for the rise of by far the most attractive – and, after Theodoric, the greatest – of all the Gothic rulers. His name, according to the evidence of every one of his coins, was Baduila, but even in his lifetime he seems to have been universally known as Totila, and it is thus that he has gone down in history.

On Totila's accession to the Gothic throne in 541 he was still in his early twenties, but wise before his time. He never forgot that the majority of his subjects were not Goths, but Italians. In the days of Theodoric and his successors, relations between Italian and Goth had been close and cordial; since the victories of Belisarius, however, the Italian aristocracy had thrown in its lot with the Empire. It was therefore to the humbler echelons of Italian society – the middle class, the urban proletariat and the peasantry – that the young ruler made his appeal. He promised them an end to Byzantine oppression. The slaves would be liberated, the great estates broken up, the land redistributed; no longer would their taxes be used to maintain a huge and corrupt court, to build vast palaces a thousand miles away or to pay protection money to distant barbarian tribes of whom no Italian had ever heard. He struck an immediate chord. Within three years virtually the entire peninsula was under his control, and in January 544 the Byzantine generals in their various redoubts simply gave up. Respectfully they informed the Emperor that they could no longer defend the imperial cause in Italy. It was their letter, almost certainly, that decided Justinian to send back Belisarius.

Belisarius did what he could. Almost at once, however, he saw several defections by imperial troops – many of whom had received no pay for well over a year – and realised that it was no longer just the Goths who were actively hostile to the Empire; it was the vast majority of the population. With the forces at his command he might just succeed in maintaining an imperial presence in Italy, but he could not hope to reconquer the whole peninsula. In May 545 he wrote personally to the Emperor:

> Sire, you must be plainly told that the greatest part of your army has enlisted and is now serving under the enemy's standards. If the mere sending of Belisarius to Italy were all that were necessary, your preparations for war would be perfect; but if you would overcome your enemies you must do something more than this, for a general is nothing without his officers. First and foremost you must send me my own guards, both cavalry and foot-soldiers; secondly, a large number of Huns and other barbarians; and thirdly, the money with which they may all be paid.

But from Constantinople there came no response. The following year, after yet another long siege, Totila captured Rome. Immediately he sent ambassadors to the Emperor offering peace on the basis of the old dispensation as it had been under Theodoric, but Justinian refused to listen. To have done so would have meant writing off ten years' campaigning, and admitting the defeat not only of his armies but of his most cherished ambitions. Nor, on the other hand, would he give his general the support he needed.[1] And so the situation in Italy deteriorated into a stalemate, and early in 549 Belisarius, frustrated and disillusioned, was ordered home.

---

[1] The Emperor's attitude towards Belisarius was always ambivalent. Jealousy obviously played its part, but so did suspicion. Despite countless proofs of loyalty given by the general, Justinian never quite trusted him. Robert Graves's novel *Count Belisarius* – which is well worth reading for its insight into their two lives – is particularly interesting in this connection.

He found the Emperor deeply depressed. Theodora had died of cancer some months before; her husband was to mourn her for the rest of his life. He also had a major theological crisis on his hands – of the kind that arose in Byzantium with distressing frequency – and while he was still determined on the reconquest of Italy he was for the moment incapable of giving the matter the attention it deserved. Not until 551 did news from the peninsula finally sting him into action. Totila had staged a full-scale revival of the traditional Games in the Circus Maximus, and had personally presided over them from the imperial box. Meanwhile his fleet was ravaging both Italy and Sicily, and had recently returned to Rome loaded to the gunwales with plunder. This double insult was too much. At last Justinian decided on an all-out effort. Whether he offered Belisarius command of a third expedition is uncertain; such an offer is nowhere recorded, but would probably anyway have been refused. Belisarius had had enough. The Emperor's choice was his own first cousin, Germanus, but Germanus died of a fever before even setting sail. His second was even more surprising: a septuagenarian Armenian eunuch called Narses.

Narses was no soldier. Most of his life had been spent in the Palace, where he had risen to be commander of the imperial bodyguard, but this was more a domestic appointment than a military one. Justinian had, however, sent him to Italy in 538, ostensibly in command of a body of troops to swell the Byzantine army during the Goths' siege of Rome but in fact to keep an eye on Belisarius, whose youth, brilliance and unconcealed ambition were already making the Emperor uneasy. There Narses had shown himself to be a superb organiser, strong-willed and determined; thirteen years later he had lost none of his energy or his decisiveness. He also knew his Emperor better than any man alive, and easily persuaded him to make available a far greater army than he had intended for Germanus: at least 35,000 men, most of them barbarians but also including a number of Persians captured during the recent war with Chosroes.

Not until the early summer of 552 did Narses begin his march into Italy. Still lacking the ships to transport his army, he was obliged to take the land route, advancing round the head of the Adriatic to Ravenna, where he provided what was left of the local troops with their long overdue arrears of pay. He then headed south across the Apennines and down the Via Flaminia towards Rome, Totila marching northward up the same road to block his path. They met near the little village of Taginae, for what was to prove the decisive encounter of the entire war. The Gothic army was progressively outflanked and out-fought and finally, as the sun was sinking, took flight. Totila himself, mortally wounded, fled with the rest but died a few hours later.

For the Goths all hope was now lost, but they did not surrender. Unanimously they acclaimed Teia, one of the bravest of Totila's generals, as his successor and continued the struggle. Narses meanwhile pursued his journey south, city after city opening its gates to the conquerors. Rome itself fell after a brief siege – changing hands for the fifth time since the beginning of Justinian's reign – but still the old eunuch marched on. Totila, he had learned, had deposited vast reserves of treasure and bullion at Cumae on the Bay of Naples; Narses was determined to lay his hands on it before it was spirited away. Teia was equally determined to stop him, and at the end of October, in the Sarno valley just a mile or two from the already long-forgotten Pompeii, the two armies met for the last time. Teia was felled by a well-aimed javelin, but even after his head had been impaled on a lance and raised aloft for all to see, there was to be no retreat: his men battled on until the evening of the following day. By the terms of the subsequent treaty, the Goths undertook to leave Italy and to engage in no further warfare against the Empire. Justinian's grandest ambition was realised at last.

History offers few examples of a campaign as swift and decisive as that of Narses being successfully concluded by a general in his mid-seventies – nor, surely, any more persuasive argument in favour of castration. Almost unbelievably, however, just as the ancient Armenian was marching his men into Italy in the spring of 552, another, smaller Byzantine expeditionary force had landed in Spain under the command of a general older still. His name was Liberius, and he is recorded as having been Praetorian Prefect of Italy sixty years before, in the days of Theodoric. At the time of which we are speaking, therefore, he cannot possibly have been less than eighty-five.

By now Spain was firmly in the hands of the Visigoths, who had first arrived there – in the wake of several other barbarian tribes – in 416, and who in 418 had made a pact with Rome by the terms of which they agreed to recognise the sovereignty of the Empire. The position was thus very much the same as it had been in Italy under Theodoric, with a Roman landowning aristocracy living comfortably on its estates, perfectly satisfied with the status quo and doubtless grateful that the immense distance separating them from Constantinople reduced imperial interference to the point of imperceptibility. For them and their Visigothic masters, the first warning of the approaching storm came with Belisarius's recovery of North Africa from the Vandals in 533, and his eviction of a Visigothic garrison from the port of Septem (now Ceuta) the following year. An attempt by the Visigothic king Theodis to seize it back in 547 ended in disaster; his protests that the Romans had cheated by attacking on a Sunday while he was in church did not alter the fact that his army had been annihilated, and he himself met his death shortly afterwards at the hands of an assassin.

Then, in 551, Theodis's second successor, King Agila, found himself faced with a rebellion led by his own kinsman, Athenagild, who appealed to the Emperor for help. Here was precisely the opportunity Justinian had been waiting for. He ordered that a small force – perhaps a thousand or two at the most – should be detached from Narses's army and sent under Liberius to Spain. It met with little resistance: the Visigothic army was split down the middle. Before long Liberius effectively controlled the whole area south of a line drawn from Valencia to Cadiz, including Cordoba. In 555 Agila was murdered by his own troops and Athenagild assumed the throne without opposition.

Had the new king agreed to rule as an imperial vassal, all would have been well; such, however, had never been his intention, and he made it clear to Liberius that he expected him and his army to withdraw as soon as they conveniently could. The old man – who was clearly every bit as good a diplomat as he was a general – agreed in principle, but gradually persuaded Athenagild to negotiate; finally the two reached an understanding whereby the Empire kept much of the territory it had conquered. But there were nowhere near enough soldiers available for adequate garrisoning, and the lines of communication were dangerously long: Justinian was soon forced to acknowledge that a good 80 percent of the Iberian peninsula lay beyond his control. On the other hand he retained the Balearic Islands – which, together with Corsica and Sardinia (reconquered respectively by Belisarius and Narses) gave him a firm base in the western Mediterranean – and he could boast that his empire now once again extended from the Black Sea to the Atlantic Ocean.

So, technically, it did; but the Visigoths continued to flourish. Ruling now from Toledo, Athenagild and his successors in a series of highly successful campaigns managed to extend their authority over more and more of the country, until finally in the early seventh century the last imperial enclave, centred on Cartagena, was liquidated. By the end of that same century the two separate communities, Roman and Gothic, that had characterised Spain for the past three hundred years had similarly ceased to exist. In the year 700 it was thus a relatively united Gothic people that inhabited the Iberian peninsula, but only a single decade of the new century was to pass before that people was called upon to face a new and terrible enemy.

Justinian is believed to have been the last Byzantine Emperor to have spoken Latin more easily than he did Greek – though he was fluent in both. Two centuries after Constantine the Great had transplanted his empire into the Greek world, the hellenisation of the Empire was almost complete. From its foundation by Augustus it had always embraced both the Latin and the Greek civilisations, and with the passage of time these had continued to diverge, developing in their own very different ways. The Greeks, for example, having been spared the worst of the barbarian invasions, had rapidly outclassed the Latins in learning as well as in general sophistication, and felt themselves to be immeasurably superior. Their passion for disputation, however, kept the Eastern Church in almost continual ferment and led to the development of several serious heresies; and succeeding Patriarchs, if they recognised the supremacy of the Pope at all, did so with increasing reluctance. Excepting only the Papacy, the Byzantine Empire was almost certainly the most religiously orientated state in the history of Christendom. Already in the fourth century St Gregory of Nyssa had written:

> If you ask a man for change, he will give you a piece of philosophy concerning the Begotten and the Unbegotten; if you enquire the price of a loaf, he replies: 'The Father is greater and the Son inferior'; or if you ask whether the bath is ready, the answer you receive is that the Son was made out of nothing.

In later centuries this tendency showed no sign of diminishing; indeed, it is arguable that without it the Byzantines would never have developed the most deeply spiritual art that the Mediterranean world has ever known. Their artists were instructed to depict the Spirit of God: a tall order perhaps, but one which, in their icons, mosaics and frescos, they fulfilled again and again.

The Mediterranean world as it existed under Justinian was very different from the one known to the Emperors of the first and second centuries; Constantine the Great and the barbarian invasions had seen to that. However much the Byzantines might protest to the contrary, their Roman Empire had little in common with that of Augustus and his successors. From Rome itself power and authority had long since departed; and Constantinople, by virtue of its geographical position alone, could never dominate the western Mediterranean as Rome had done. No longer were the Middle Sea and the lands surrounding it subject to a single power; no longer could it be described as a Roman lake, still less – even after Justinian's reconquest of Italy – as *mare nostrum*. Even such tenuous claims in that direction as could be made in the sixth century were, all too soon, to be dramatically revised.

CHAPTER V

Islam

Until the second quarter of the seventh century, the land of Arabia was terra incognita to the Christian world. Remote and inhospitable, productive of nothing to tempt the sophisticated merchants of the west, it had made no contribution to civilisation and seemed unlikely ever to do so. Its people, insofar as anyone knew anything about them, were presumed to be little better than savages, periodically slaughtering each other in violent outbreaks of tribal warfare, falling mercilessly upon any traveller foolhardy enough to venture among them, making not the slightest attempt towards unity or even stable government. Apart from a few scattered Jewish colonies around the coast and in Medina, and a small Christian community in the Yemen, the overwhelming majority practised a sort of primitive polytheism which, in the city of Mecca – their commercial centre – appeared to be somehow focused on the huge black stone, the Kaaba, that stood in their principal temple. Where the outside world was concerned they showed no interest, made no impact and certainly posed no threat.

Then, in the twinkling of an eye, all was changed. In September 622 the Prophet Mohammed had taken flight with a few followers from the hostile city of Mecca to friendly Medina, thus marking the starting point for the whole Muslim era; just five years afterwards, in 633, showing a discipline and singleness of purpose of which they had previously given no sign and which therefore took their victims totally by surprise, his followers suddenly burst out of Arabia. A year later, an Arab army had crossed the desert and defeated the Byzantine Emperor Heraclius on the banks of the Yarmuk river; after three years they had taken Damascus; after five, Jerusalem; after eight, they controlled all Syria, Palestine and Egypt. Within twenty years, the whole Persian Empire as far as the Oxus had fallen to the Arab sword; within thirty, Afghanistan and most of the Punjab. Then, after a brief interval for consolidation, the conquerors turned their attention to the west. The Byzantine Empire having proved too tough a nut to crack – they had made no headway at all in Asia Minor – they took the longer but easier route along the southern shore of the Mediterranean. The conquest of Egypt took just two years, from 639 to 641, after which the pace slowed, owing partly to the fact that the post-conquest Egyptian administration presented so many problems; without the help and experience of the natives – the Copts and the Jews, the Samaritans and the Greeks – the still unsophisticated Arabs would have been quite unable to impose their authority.

Thus it was not before the end of the century that they reached the Atlantic, and not until 711 that they were ready to cross the Straits of Gibraltar into Spain. But by 732, still less than a century after their eruption from their desert homeland, they had made their way over the Pyrenees and, according to tradition, pressed on to Tours – where, only 150 miles from Paris, they were checked at last by the Frankish king Charles Martel in an engagement which inspired Gibbon to one of his most celebrated flights of fancy:

> A victorious line of march had been prolonged above a thousand miles from the Rock of Gibraltar to the banks of the Loire; the repetition of an equal space would have carried the Saracens to the confines of Poland and the Highlands of Scotland; the Rhine is not more impassable than the Nile or the Euphrates, and the Arabian fleet might have sailed without a naval combat into the mouth of the Thames. Perhaps the interpretation of the Koran would now be taught in the schools of Oxford, and her pupils might demonstrate to a circumcised people the sanctity and truth of the Revelation of Mahomet.

Modern historians are quick to point out that the battle of Tours is scarcely mentioned by contemporary or near-contemporary Arab historians, and then only as a comparatively insignificant episode. The evidence of these writers strongly suggests that the Arabs encountered by Charles Martel were simply a raiding party that had ventured perhaps hundreds of miles in advance of the main army, and that the so-called battle was in fact little more than a protracted skirmish. In any case, a glance at the map will show that the real Muslim threat to Europe would come from the east, a far shorter and easier route for an army that had already mopped up the Levant. It was not to Charles and his Franks, but to the stalwart defenders of Constantinople under Constantine IV in 674–78 and Leo III in 717–18, that we owe the preservation of both Eastern and Western Christendom.

History provides, nevertheless, few parallels for so dramatic a saga of conquest, or for the establishment, in the space of less than a hundred years, of an empire stretching from the Himalayas to the Pyrenees. For this phenomenon the usual explanation is that the Arabs were carried forward on a great surge of religious enthusiasm; and so in a way they were. It is worth remembering, however, that this enthusiasm was almost untouched by missionary zeal. The Muslim leaders never saw themselves as having been divinely appointed to conquer the world in the name of Islam. The Koran permitted warfare in self-defence but did not sanctify it for its own sake; moreover, it stated clearly that where Jews and Christians were concerned there should be no coercion in matters of faith. They too were monotheists – 'peoples of the Book' – who had received perfectly valid revelations of their own.

What the new religion provided was above all a sense of brotherhood and unity. In the past the various Arab tribes had been constantly at war with one another; now, all fellow-servants of Allah, they were as one. This in turn imbued them with almost limitless self-confidence. They were utterly convinced that their God was with them; even if it were His will that they should fall in battle, they would receive their immediate reward in paradise – and a most agreeably sensual paradise at that, whose promised delights were, it must be admitted, a good deal more alluring than those of its Christian counterpart. In this world, on the other hand, they were only too willing to adopt a disciplined austerity that they had never known before, together with an unquestioning obedience whose outward manifestations were abstinence from wine and strong drink, periodic fasting and the five-times-daily ritual of prayer.

The founder of their religion was himself never to lead them on campaign. Born of humble origins some time around 570, orphaned in early childhood and finally married to a rich widow considerably older than himself, Mohammed was that rare combination of a visionary mystic and an astute, far-sighted statesman. In the former capacity he preached, first, the singleness of God and second, the importance to mankind of total submission (*islam*) to His will. This was not a particularly original creed – both Jews and Christians, inside Arabia as well as out, had maintained it for centuries – but it seemed so to most of those who now heard it for the first time; it was Mohammed's skill to present it in a new, homespun form, clothed in proverbs, fragments of desert lore and passages of almost musical eloquence, all of which were combined in the posthumous collection of his revelations which we know as the Koran. He was clever, too, in the way in which – though he almost certainly considered himself a reformer rather than a revolutionary – he managed to identify his own name and person with the doctrine he preached: not by ascribing any divinity to himself, as

Jesus Christ had done, but by putting himself forward as the last and greatest of the prophets, among whom all his predecessors – including Jesus – were subsumed.

To be a prophet, however, was not to be a theologian; and perhaps the most striking difference between Mohammed and the Christians whose lands his followers were so soon to overrun was his indifference to theological speculation. It was, he maintained, useless to argue over abstruse dogmas (as the Greeks loved to do), the more so since their truth or falsehood could never be proved. Islam, as E. M. Forster put it, 'threw them all down as unnecessary lumber that do but distract the true believer from his God'. Far more important was the way one lived in society, upholding justice and compassion for one's fellow men and maintaining a fair and reasonable distribution of wealth. Spiritual fervour he possessed in abundance, but he was never a fanatic; like Jesus, he had come not to destroy but to fulfil. He perfectly understood the people among whom he lived, and was always careful not to push them further than they would willingly go. He knew, for example, that they would never abandon polygamy; he therefore accepted it, and indeed himself took several more wives after the death of his first. Slavery was another integral part of Arabian life; this too he tolerated. He was even prepared to come to terms with the old animist religion; as early as 624 he decreed that the faithful should turn towards the Kaaba in Mecca when praying, rather than towards Jerusalem as he had previously enjoined. He never ceased to stress, on the other hand, one entirely new and distinctly unpalatable aspect of his creed – the inevitability of divine judgement after death; often, it seemed, he described the torments of hell even more vividly than the joys of paradise. This fear of retribution may well have proved useful when he came to weld his followers into a political state.

Mohammed died of a fever in Mecca – to which he had triumphantly returned – on 8 June 632. The leadership, both religious and political, of his people passed to his oldest friend and most trusted lieutenant, Abu-Bakr, who assumed the title of Caliph – literally, representative – of the Prophet. In the year following, the Muslim armies marched. But Abu-Bakr was already growing old; he in turn died in 634 – according to tradition during the month of August, on the very day of the capture of Damascus – and it was under the second Caliph, Omar, that the initial series of historic victories was won. In one respect in particular, luck was on the side of the Arabs; the indigenous Christian peoples of Egypt and North Africa, Syria and Palestine felt no real loyalty towards the Emperor in Constantinople, who represented an alien Graeco-Roman culture and whose lack of sympathy for their several heresies had periodically led to active persecution. To many of them the Muslim tide, composed as it was of Semites like themselves, professing a rigid monotheism not unlike their own and promising toleration for every variety of Christian belief, must have seemed infinitely preferable to the regime it had swept away.

Before the Muslim conquest, North Africa had formed part of the Byzantine Empire and was protected by the Byzantine navy. To the Arabs it was consequently enemy territory, which they were determined to appropriate. Egypt offered little resistance. The Arab leader Amr ibn al-As[1] had only 4,000 men when he invaded the country in the early spring of 640; two and a half years later, the great city of Alexandria – the most venerable in the entire Mediterranean, founded by Alexander of Macedon and for some six centuries the seat of one of the four patriarchates of Eastern Christendom – was voluntarily surrendered by the Empire. It was never to recover its former glory.[2] Returning southward from the delta, Amr then founded the garrison city of al-Fustat, the germ of modern Cairo. His other achievement was to clear the canal that ran eastward from the Nile to the former Byzantine port of Klysma, about a mile from the modern Suez, opening the way to the passage of vessels laden with grain from the Nile valley to the Red Sea and Arabia.

During their first advance the Muslims had no fleet – few of them, indeed, had ever seen the sea – but it soon became clear that if they were to maintain their impetus they would have to master the arts of seamanship and navigation. Just as the Romans had whenever possible used Greeks to man their vessels, so the Arabs found experienced shipbuilders and seamen in the Christians of Egypt and Syria; with their help they were gradually able to construct dockyards, and so to build up a formidable fleet both of war galleys and of merchantmen until they were able to challenge the naval supremacy of Byzantium itself. By 655

---

[1] E. M. Forster tells us that Amr was 'an administrator, a delightful companion, and a poet – one of the ablest and most charming men that Islam ever produced'. He goes on to tell a lovely story of how, when Amr lay on his deathbed, 'a friend said to him: "You have often remarked that you would like to find an intelligent man at the point of death, and to ask him what his feelings were. Now I ask *you* that question." Amr replied, "I feel as if the heaven lay close upon the earth and I between the two, breathing through the eye of a needle."'

[2] The theory, however, that the Muslims were responsible for the destruction of the great library is almost certainly without foundation. Everything we know about Amr suggests that he would have treated it with immense respect.

they had launched raids on Cyprus, Crete, Rhodes and Sicily; after the Muslim annihilation of the main Byzantine fleet, commanded by the Emperor Constans II in person, off the coast of Lycia in that same year, it must have seemed uncertain whether the balance of naval power in the Mediterranean would ever be the same again. Fortunately the Byzantines had already developed their most effective secret weapon, 'Greek fire', shot in great tongues of flame from their ships' prows. It was thanks to this alone that the Empire was able to maintain some degree of control.

There was another reason too for the slowness of the Arab advance after the conquest of Egypt. As anyone who has driven the 600-odd miles between Benghazi and Tripoli knows all too well, the desert terrain is featureless and the road apparently interminable; it certainly offered no chance of booty or plunder to make it remotely attractive to the Arab army. The area was also a hotbed of hostile tribes. Sooner or later the task of pacification and conquest would clearly have to be undertaken, but political crises in Medina delayed the fateful decision; and the foundation of the Umayyad Empire,[1] with the consequent removal of the seat of government to Damascus in 661, caused still further delays. Not until 667 did the great march begin, and three years later its leader, Okba ibn Nafi, established the great fortress of Kairouan in what is now Tunisia. Further west, however, he encountered heavy resistance from both the Byzantines and the Christian Berber tribesmen; only in 692, after another army of 40,000 had been despatched by Caliph Abdul-Malik, could progress be resumed. In 693 Carthage fell, despite a Berber uprising led by a mysterious queen-priestess named al-Kahina – a figure straight out of Rider Haggard – and an amphibious assault by a Byzantine army. Both were eventually beaten back, though al-Kahina continued to fight a guerrilla war until 701. The Arabs did not make Carthage their capital; its harbour was too vulnerable to attack from the sea. Instead they built a great fortress at Tunis, connecting an inland lake to the coast. Here was a formidable new springboard from which to harass Sardinia, Sicily, Cyprus and the Balearic Islands. Raids on all these – often ending in temporary occupation – continued until around 750, when Byzantine resistance suddenly grew stronger and when, as we shall shortly see, the Muslim world found that it had other things to think about.

---

[1] The first of the two great Arab empires of the Middle Ages: the Umayyad, based in Damascus, which lasted from 661 to 750, and the Abbasid, based in Baghdad, which continued until its destruction by the Mongols in 1258.

From Carthage the westward advance speeded up again until at last, with the entire coast from Egypt to the Atlantic in their hands, the Muslims could think seriously about Spain: a land infinitely richer and more fertile than the vast territories that they had fought so long and hard to conquer, and one that promised huge rewards. At that very moment, too, the old Visigothic kingdom was crumbling. Its monarchy was theoretically elective, always a certain recipe for disputes over the succession and an open invitation for ambitious noblemen. After years of persecution, the large Jewish community was on the point of revolt. The economy was in ruins. The Spanish fruit, in short, was ripe and ready for the plucking. In 710 an Arab officer named Tarif, with a reconnaissance party of 500 men, slipped across the straits and occupied the southernmost tip of the Iberian peninsula, where the city of Tarifa still bears his name. The ships returned laden with spoils, and Muslim minds were made up. The following year a certain Tariq ibn Zaid sailed from Tangier with an army of 9,000 Berbers, landing this time in the shade of an immense rock, by which his name too is now immortalised.[1]

After Tariq's landing, one battle near the Guadalete river – even though it is said to have lasted an entire week – was enough to destroy Visigothic resistance. Sending out small detachments to receive the submissions of Malaga, Murcia and Cordoba, Tariq himself set out for the capital, Toledo, which he found abandoned by all but its Jewish population. Here still more plunder awaited him, including – if we are to believe the Arab chronicler Ibn Idhari – the Table of Solomon, set with concentric circles of pearls, sapphires, and chrysolite, the jewels of Alexander the Great, the staff of Moses and the robes of the Gothic kings. Leaving the Jews to administer the territories he had conquered, he then continued northward to Castile, Asturias and Leon. The speed of his advance would have been remarkable were it not for the fact that the Moorish army was generally welcomed, the vast majority of the local Christian populations being only too happy to accept the domination of such tolerant conquerors, whom many of them saw as a considerable improvement on their Visigothic predecessors.

Word of Tariq's successes soon got back to his superior, one Musa ibn Nusair, who arrived in the peninsula in June or July 712 with some 18,000 men, this time mostly Arabs. Deliberately following a different

---

[1] The rock was known to the Arabs as Jebel al-Tariq (Mount Tariq), whence comes its modern name of Gibraltar.

route from that of his predecessor, he landed at Algeciras and took Huelva and Seville before meeting up with Tariq at Toledo. The following year was largely spent in consolidation; then, in 714, the combined force captured Barcelona and crossed the Pyrenees, advancing into the Rhône valley as far as Avignon and Lyon. There they halted. Musa's original ambition had been to press eastward to Damascus via Constantinople, but this, he now realised, was out of the question. Resistance was increasing; lines of communication were growing perilously long. There was nothing for it but to return to Spain – and thence, since he was determined to make his personal report to the Caliph, to Africa. That same winter he transferred the responsibility for the conquered territories to his son Abdul-Aziz in Seville, while he and Tariq, accompanied by a huge retinue including a large number of captive Visigoths and countless slaves – to say nothing of vast quantities of gold, silver and precious stones – marched slowly and with great pomp back along the North African coast, through Egypt and Palestine and finally to Damascus. Unfortunately for them, Caliph al-Walid, who had approved of the Spanish expeditions, died almost as soon as they arrived; his successor Süleyman was disappointingly unimpressed.

The Muslim armies invaded France three times – in 716, 721 and 726 – but they never took root. Basically, their work was done; and under its Arabic name of al-Andalus, Spain – or much of it – became part of the Umayyad Empire. Never would it be the same again. Henceforth the land would harbour three totally separate peoples: Arabs, Jews and Christians, different in race and in religion, in language and in culture. Inevitably, over the 750-odd years of Muslim occupation, they would influence and cross-fertilise each other in a thousand ways, to the ultimate advantage of all three. For most (though not all) of that time, they coexisted amicably enough – sometimes very amicably indeed.

Such difficulties as did arise came principally from within the Muslim ranks. Musa's son Abdul-Aziz had made the cardinal mistake of marrying the daughter of Rodrigo, the principal general of the Visigoths, and under her influence had been induced to wear a crown in the Christian manner. This had infuriated his Arab followers to the point where they had murdered him; thereafter confusion reigned, and over the next forty years al-Andalus was ruled by no less than twenty-one successive governors. It might well have disintegrated altogether but for a spectacular *coup d'état* which no one could possibly have foreseen. In 750 the Umayyad Caliphate was overturned: the last Caliph of the line, Marwan II, was executed; almost his entire family was massacred at a banquet, reminiscent of that at which Theodoric the Ostrogoth had dealt with the family of Odoacer two and a half centuries before; and a new dynasty, the Abbasids, established itself in Baghdad. Only one of the Umayyad princes, the nineteen-year-old Abdul-Rahman, managed to escape. After wandering incognito for five years through Palestine, Egypt and North Africa, in 755 he landed in Spain and, finding the entire country in chaos, had little difficulty in establishing himself as its ruler. In the following year, when still only twenty-six, he was formally proclaimed Emir of al-Andalus. The dynasty that he founded was to rule in Muslim Spain for nearly three hundred years.

Abdul-Rahman was not, however, universally welcomed. There were several revolts in Spain, and one still more serious crisis when in 778 the Frankish King Charles the Great – Charlemagne – was persuaded by a group of Spanish rebels to march against him. Charles quickly occupied Pamplona and had just begun a siege of Saragossa when – fortunately for the Emir – he changed his mind. For some reason he seems to have decided that the game was not after all worth the candle and, on the pretext of pressing problems at home, gave the order to return. It was on 15 August, on his way back across the Pyrenees, that his rearguard, commanded by Roland, Marquis of Brittany, was surprised by a combined force of Muslims and Basques in the narrow pass of Roncesvalles. Not a man escaped. Only the name of Roland has survived, as the hero of one of the first epic poems of western European literature.

Abdul-Rahman's later years were a good deal more tranquil. He never succeeded in imposing political unity on Spain, but he was a wise and merciful ruler and a deeply cultivated man. His capital city of Cordoba he transformed, endowing it with a magnificent palace, a famously beautiful garden and – most important of all – with the Mezquita, its great mosque, begun in 785 on the site of the early Christian cathedral, which when completed was the most sumptuous mosque in the world and still stands today.[1] He was also a celebrated

---

[1] It was disgracefully vandalised in the early sixteenth century when a Christian chapel – now the cathedral – was erected in its centre. The Emperor Charles V, seeing it in 1526, made no secret of his feelings. 'You have built here,' he said to the assembled chapter, 'what you or anyone might have built anywhere else, but you have destroyed what was unique in the world.'

poet, who wrote sensitively and nostalgically about the Syrian homeland that he would never see again. His love of culture was fully inherited by his great-grandson and third successor, Abdul-Rahman II, who – reigning for nearly half a century from 912 to 961 – filled his court with poets, musicians and scholars, as well as enlarging his great-grandfather's mosque and building others in Jaén and Seville. He also imported vast quantities of luxury goods from the east, together with numbers of foreign artists and craftsmen; he is said to have introduced the art of embroidery into the country, and was the first Emir to strike his own coins. During his reign, Cordoba was probably the most cultivated city in Europe. In 940 came the final accolade: a diplomatic mission from Constantinople, bearing gifts of great price and proposing an alliance against their common enemy, the Abbasids.

But the Abbasids were far away. In transferring their capital and court from Damascus to Baghdad, they had radically changed the nature of the Caliphate. No longer was it essentially a Mediterranean empire; with its centre now in the heartland of Asia, it took little or no interest in the affairs of Europe or of the Middle Sea. For the next seven centuries – until the capture of Constantinople in 1453 – it was to have relatively little impact in the west, where the Muslims of North Africa and Spain were left largely to their own devices. The former in particular steadily developed their navy until, by the first half of the ninth century, they were probably the leading sea power in the Mediterranean – even though the Byzantines maintained a stout opposition, and certainly did not let them have things all their own way. Indeed, after the accession of the Emperor Basil I in 867, the tables were conclusively turned: the forces of Islam were once again very much on the defensive.

In 929 Abdul-Rahman II adopted the title of caliph. Thenceforth Muslim Spain, with a perfectly good caliphate of its own, no longer paid even lip service to Abbasid Baghdad. Politically this caliphate was called upon to face more than its fair share of problems; artistically and culturally, on the other hand, it shone, and its surviving monuments continue to dazzle us today. The first Abdul-Rahman's great mosque of Cordoba was enlarged and beautified by successive rulers in the ninth and tenth centuries; in 950 Abdul-Rahman III endowed it with a new minaret 240 feet high. In Seville there is the Alcazar, the lovely twelfth-century building which in 1353 was to become the palace of Pedro the Cruel, and the 300-foot-high Giralda, built between 1172 and 1195 both as a minaret and an observatory. And in Granada that astounding complex of palaces known as the Alhambra, with the summer palace and glorious gardens of the Generalife on the hill above it, still has the power to catch the breath. Here, surely – with the Cordoba mosque – is the ultimate tour de force of all Spanish Islam.[1]

Perhaps it was to some extent the splendour of the architecture that gave rise to the countless recorded conversions. The Jews, of course, hardly ever renounced their ancient heritage, and rare indeed was the Muslim who sought Christian baptism; but throughout the Arab occupation – and particularly in the cities and towns between about the middle of the ninth and the beginning of the eleventh century – tens of thousands of Christians voluntarily embraced the faith of their conquerors. Still more of them, while retaining their religion, adopted Arabic as the language of their daily life. To this day modern Spanish has retained a remarkable number of Arabic words, and visitors to Spain cannot fail to be struck by the quantity of Arabic place names which still abound. Islamic culture, too, spread widely across the land. Al-Andalus maintained a vast commercial network with North Africa and the Near East, and even as far as India and Persia; to it came not only silks and spices (particularly pepper and ginger), rice and sugar-cane, citrus fruits and figs, aubergines and bananas, but works on architecture, ceramics, calligraphy, music, mathematics, astronomy and medicine.

This extensive new knowledge did not by any means confine itself to the Muslim world. Many Christians, superficially Islamicised as they might be, sooner or later found their way to the Christian lands to the north and northeast – to Galicia and Asturias, Catalonia and Navarre – bringing their culture with them. These Mozarabs, as they were called, had a lasting impact on the Christian north on both sides of the Pyrenees – above all in the field of mathematics, of which early medieval Christendom was still lamentably ignorant. It was they who are believed to have introduced Arabic numerals into northern Europe, together with the abacus, a device which had an impact on commercial life comparable to that of the computer in our own day.

Politically, relations between the Christians of the north and the Muslims of the south were somewhat less clear-cut. The caliphate came to an end in 1031 and was succeeded by a number of small states known

---

[1] It is often suggested that flamenco, the traditional music of Andalusia, is another legacy of the Muslim occupation. It may well contain Arabic elements, but it seems essentially to be the creation of the gypsies who began to settle in the area in the later fifteenth century.

as *taifas*, normally consisting of a central town with the countryside immediately surrounding it, not altogether unlike the city-states growing up in northern Italy at much the same time. Like the Italians they too tended to squabble among themselves, allowing the larger and stronger Christian kingdoms of Aragon and Castile either to play them off one against another or to institute what were in effect glorified protection rackets, offering military support in return for substantial tribute. Here was fertile ground for the many soldiers of fortune, freelance mercenaries similar to the Italian *condottieri*, who cheerfully sold their swords to the highest bidder regardless of his faith. By far the most celebrated of these was the eleventh-century Castilian aristocrat actually named Rodrigo Diaz de Vivar but better known by his Spanish sobriquet of El Cid, literally 'the boss'. Later legend has turned him into the supreme Spanish patriot, who devoted his life to driving the infidel from his native land and indeed continued to do so after his death, when his corpse was propped upright on his horse, Babieca, to lead his army into battle. The same authority[1] maintains that the corpse remained so perfectly preserved that it sat for ten years immediately to the right of the altar in the church of the monastery of San Pedro de Cardena near Burgos. The truth, alas, is somewhat less romantic. Rodrigo was in fact a military adventurer like many another, who after an outstandingly successful and profitable career, ended up as ruling prince of the state of Valencia on the shores of the Mediterranean.

Had El Cid been born fifty years later than he was – in 1190 rather than about 1140 – such a career would have been impossible. Some time around the middle of the eleventh century in what is now southern Morocco, what had begun as a loose confederation of Berbers developed, in the space of a very few years, into a fundamentalist movement preaching the strictest Islamic doctrines. Calling themselves *al-Murabitun* – to us, the Almoravids – they founded the great city of Marrakesh, conquered northern Morocco and much of western Algeria and then turned their attention to Spain. In 1086 they crossed the straits, defeated King Alfonso VI of Leon-Castile at Sagrajas near Badajoz and quickly mopped up all the Muslim *taifas*, together with many towns reconquered by the Christians only a few years previously. Before the end of the century al-Andalus was once again reunited, but now for the first time linked with North Africa under a regime both deeply uncivilised and fanatically intolerant.

---

[1] *Estoria del Cid*, trans. P. E. Russell.

Fortunately for all concerned, the Almoravids' rule was short. They suffered from one great weakness: as a small Berber minority at the head of a now considerable Spanish–African empire, they could inspire no real loyalty. They tried to hold Spain with their own troops and North Africa with a guard composed very largely of Christians, but after the fall of Saragossa to King Alfonso I of Aragon in 1118 the tide began to turn, and only seven years later a fiercer and still more bigoted fundamentalist sect, the Almohads, had arisen in the Atlas Mountains and broke out in open rebellion. The civil war that followed lasted for nearly a quarter of a century; it ended only with the fall of Marrakesh in 1147, after which Almoravid authority quickly crumbled.

The victorious Almohads crossed the straits, and by the end of the twelfth century their grip on the country from their capital at Seville was just as firm as that of their predecessors. Before long, however, they too found their power waning to the point where they were forced into retreat; this time the enemy was not an Islamic religious sect but an alliance of the three main Christian kingdoms of the Iberian peninsula: Castile, Aragon and Portugal. In 1212 King Alfonso VIII of Castile won a major victory at Las Navas de Tolosa, which effectively secured the preponderance of the Christian cause in Spain; his grandson Ferdinand III continued his work, in his thirty-five-year reign regaining much of Andalusia, including the port of Cartagena, and on occasion – as at Seville in 1248 – actually expelling entire Muslim populations.[1] By mid-century Muslim Spain had been reduced to a single emirate: that of Granada. The Reconquista was well under way.

The intolerance of the Almohads had had one beneficial effect: many Jewish and Mozarabic communities, finding life under them intolerable, had fled into Christian Castile and Aragon where they had received a warm welcome. They included philosophers and physicians like Maimonides and Averroes, whose influence was to spread through the whole western world, together with any number of lesser intellectuals who set themselves up as professional translators from the Arabic, making available a considerable corpus of Arab scholarship hitherto unknown in the west. Many of these settled in Toledo – reconquered in 1085 amid scenes of great rejoicing – where they enjoyed the personal patronage and encouragement of the king.

The Emirate of Granada was to survive for well over two centuries, until 1492, but this seems an appropriate moment to try to assess the

---

[1] His contemporary James I of Aragon had done the same at Valencia ten years before.

effects, first of Islam on Spain and, second, of Muslim Spain on the rest of western Europe. Culturally, there is no doubt that the country was immeasurably enriched. Close contact with Islam could not have failed to broaden the Spanish mind. It also brought European intellectuals to Spain; Gerbert of Aurillac – the future Pope Sylvester II – was not the only medieval scholar to be drawn across the Pyrenees by thirst for a knowledge that could be obtained nowhere else on the continent. Mathematics and medicine, geography and astronomy and the physical sciences were still deeply mistrusted in the Christian world; in that of Islam, they had been developed to a point unequalled since the days of ancient Greece. Any serious student in these disciplines would feel the attraction of al-Andalus; once there, since translations of the seminal scientific works were few and inaccurate, he might even set himself the formidable task of learning Arabic. One who succeeded in doing so was the great English scholar Adelard of Bath, who was in Spain at the beginning of the twelfth century disguised as a Muslim student, and who in 1120 or thereabouts produced the first Latin version of Euclid, which he had translated from an Arabic version of the original Greek.

In other ways, however, the coexistence of three radically different faiths in the same land was a source of continued suffering. Much unnecessary bloodshed had been involved in the original Arab conquest, and more still in the long, painful struggle of the Reconquista. Moreover, though they all got on well enough on a daily basis, in neither the Christian nor the Muslim states were the subject peoples invariably treated with due consideration. The Prophet's injunction that Christians and Jews, as 'peoples of the Book', were to be treated by all good Muslims as their brothers was by no means always observed in practice. In 1066 there was a massacre of Jews in Granada, in 1126 a mass deportation of Christians to slavery in Morocco. The Christian communities were never (so far as we know) guilty of atrocities on quite the level of these, but there can be no doubt that both the Jews and the mudejars – the name given to Muslims living under Christian rule – were looked down upon as second-class citizens and were regularly the objects, if not of persecution, then at least of discrimination.

When we consider how much Muslim Spain had to offer, it is surprising that it did not have a greater impact on the Christian west. There would seem to be several reasons. The first is confessional: medieval Christendom loathed all manifestations of what it considered to be paganism. It accepted the Jews – up to a point – largely because they had always been there and they came in useful, and also because, lacking a nation of their own, they normally spoke the language of those around them. The Muslims of al-Andalus were different. They were little known and even less understood; their language, both written and spoken, was incomprehensible; and they inhabited the remotest corner of Europe – remoter far, in those days, than the lands of the eastern Mediterranean, where Byzantium acted as a huge cultural and commercial magnet, attracting not only scholars from one continent, but merchants, statesmen and diplomatists from three. After those early days when men feared that Islam was on course to conquer the world, and once the Muslims had withdrawn behind their relatively modest frontier, it seemed wiser and more prudent to leave them to their own peaceable and unthreatening devices. They were after all steeped in error and so, to the contemporary Christian mind, of no real interest anyway.

CHAPTER VI

Medieval Italy

Justinian's war with the Goths had ushered in a dark age. His local governors – to whom he gave the title of exarch – did their best to restore prosperity, but they had little success. Italy was a desolation; Milan in the north and Rome in the south lay in ruins. And now, within a few years of the Goths' departure, a new Germanic horde appeared on the scene: the Lombards, crossing the Alps in 568, spreading relentlessly over northern Italy and the great plain that still bears their name, finally establishing their capital at Pavia. Within five years they had captured Milan, Verona and Florence; Byzantine rule over North Italy, won at such a cost by Justinian, Belisarius and Narses, was ended almost as soon as it had begun. The Lombards' line of advance was finally checked by Rome and the Exarchate of Ravenna, but two spearheads pressed through to set up the great southern duchies of Spoleto and Benevento. From here they might have gone on to conquer the rest of the south, but they never managed to unite quite firmly enough to do so. Apulia, Calabria and Sicily remained under Byzantine control – as, surprisingly, did much of the Italian coastline. Unlike the Vandals, the Lombards showed little interest in the sea; they never really became a Mediterranean people.

That Rome itself did not succumb to the Lombard tide was a miracle hardly less extraordinary than that which had saved her from Attila in the preceding century. Once again it was wrought by a Pope – this time one of Rome's most outstanding medieval statesmen, Gregory the Great, who succeeded to the throne of St Peter in 590 and occupied it for the next fourteen years. Finding that the Exarch of Ravenna had insufficient forces to give him the support he needed, he assumed personal control of the militia, repaired the walls and aqueducts and fed the starving populace from the granaries of the Church. Having first bought off the Lombard King Agilulf, in 598 he concluded an independent peace with him; he was then able to set to work to make the Papacy a formidable political and social power. (It was he, incidentally, who sent Augustine, prior of the Benedictine abbey which he himself had founded on the Coelian hill in Rome, to convert the heathen English.) Gregory was no intellectual – like most churchmen of his day, he cherished a deep suspicion of secular learning – but he was autocratic and utterly fearless, and through these troubled times it was he alone who preserved the prestige of the city.

Yet even Gregory recognised the Emperor at Constantinople – where he had once served as papal ambassador – as his temporal overlord, and Rome under his successors became steadily more Byzantinized as the seventh century took its course. Greek refugees from the Middle East and Africa poured into Italy as first the Persians and then the Arabs overran their lands. In 663 there was an unusually distinguished Byzantine immigrant: the Emperor Constans II, determined to shift his capital back again to the west. Rome he found as uncongenial as Constantinople, but hellenistic Sicily proved more to his taste and he reigned for five years in Syracuse until one day a dissatisfied chamberlain, in an access of nostalgia, surprised him in his bath and felled him with the soapdish.

The court returned to the Bosphorus and Italy to her own problems. Of these the most serious remained the Lombards, who, as they increased in numbers and strength, were casting ever more covetous eyes over neighbouring territory. Their actual progress was slow, the Exarchate constituting a moderately effective bulwark, but pressure on the frontiers was never relaxed. This uneasy equilibrium lasted over the turn of the century; then, in 726, came crisis, when the Emperor Leo III[1] ordered the destruction of all icons and holy images throughout his dominions on the grounds that they were idolatrous.

The Emperor was being puritanical, but in no sense revolutionary. Neither Judaism nor Islam permitted the use of pictures or images, and in more recent centuries England alone has seen two serious outbreaks of iconoclasm, under Edward VI in the sixteenth century and again during the Commonwealth. Nonetheless, the effect of his decree was immediate and shattering. Men rose everywhere in wrath; the monasteries, in particular, were outraged. In the eastern provinces, where the cult of icons had reached such proportions that they were worshipped in their own right and frequently served as godparents at baptisms, Leo found some measure of support; but in the more moderate west, which had done nothing to deserve them, the new laws could not be tolerated. Italy, under energetic papal leadership, refused absolutely to comply, Pope Gregory III going so far as to excommunicate all iconoclasts. Paul, Exarch of Ravenna, was assassinated, his provincial governors put to

---

[1] Not, of course, to be confused with the Pope of the same name.

flight. Throughout the Exarchate the rebellious garrisons – all of which had been recruited locally – chose their own commanders and asserted their independence. In the communities gathered around the Venetian lagoon, their choice fell on a certain Ursus, or Orso, from Heraclea, who was given the title of *dux*. There was nothing especially remarkable about this; the same thing was happening almost simultaneously in many other insurgent towns. What distinguishes Venice from the rest is that Orso's appointment inaugurated a tradition which was to continue unbroken for more than a thousand years; his title, transformed by the rough Venetian dialect into 'doge', was to pass down through 117 successors until the end of the Venetian Republic in 1797.

The main beneficiaries of the iconoclast dispute in Italy were the Lombards. Playing Rome and Byzantium off against each other, they steadily gained ground until at last, in 751, they captured Ravenna. It was the end of the Exarchate. Such Byzantine lands as remained in Italy were cut off by the Lombard duchies of the south and were thus powerless to help. Rome was left naked to her enemies.

Not, however, for long. Before the end of the year, beyond the Alps to the west, the Frankish leader Pepin the Short had obtained papal approval for the deposition of the Merovingian[1] figurehead King Childeric III and his own coronation. He could not now ignore the Church's appeal. In 754 Pope Stephen II travelled to St Denis, where he confirmed and anointed Pepin, with his two sons Charles and Carloman, as Kings of the Franks; two years later, in response to a letter said to have been miraculously penned by St Peter himself, Frankish troops swept into Italy and brought the Lombards to their knees. Pepin now established the Pope as the head of an independent state, snaking across central Italy to embrace Rome, Perugia and Ravenna – roughly the lands of the defunct Exarchate. He may have been basing his action on the so-called Donation of Constantine, by which Constantine the Great was supposed to have granted to the Papacy temporal rule over 'Italy and all the western regions'; if so, he was seriously misled. The Donation was later shown to be a forgery, shamelessly concocted in the curia; but the Papal States which it brought into being, however shaky their legal foundations, were to last for over a thousand years, until 1870.

Rome was saved; but warfare continued, and for the next forty years Pepin and his son Charles found themselves the chief protectors of the

---

[1] The dynasty of Merovius, which ruled over the Franks from the sixth to the eighth century.

Papacy against all its foes. Although Charles – better known to us as Charlemagne – has already made one appearance in these pages, he cannot conceivably be considered a Mediterranean figure. His impact, however, was felt all the way across Christian Europe. He became sole ruler of the Franks in 771; three years later, he captured Pavia and proclaimed himself King of the Lombards. This was effectively the end of Lombard power north of Rome. To the south, however, the great Lombard duchy of Benevento, while technically now under Frankish suzerainty, remained effectively an independent state with its capital at Salerno.

Returning to Germany, Charles next subdued the heathen Saxons and converted them en masse to Christianity before going on to annex the already Christian Bavaria. His invasion of Spain was, as we know, less successful, but his subsequent campaign against the Avars in Hungary and Upper Austria resulted in the destruction of their kingdom as an independent state and its incorporation within his own dominions. Thus, in little more than a single generation, he raised the Kingdom of the Franks from being just one of the many semi-tribal European states to a single political unit of vast extent, unparalleled since the days of imperial Rome.

When Charles returned to Italy a quarter of a century later – towards the end of the year 800 – there was serious business to be done. Pope Leo III, ever since his accession four years before, had been the victim of incessant intrigue on the part of a body of young Roman noblemen who were determined to remove him. On 25 April he had actually been set upon in the street and beaten unconscious; only by the greatest good fortune had he been rescued by friends and removed for safety to Charles's court at Paderborn. Under the protection of Frankish agents he had ventured back to Rome a few months later, only to find himself facing a number of serious charges fabricated by his enemies, including simony, perjury and adultery.

By whom, however, could he be tried? Who was qualified to pass judgement on the Vicar of Christ? In normal circumstances, the only possible answer to that question would have been the Emperor at Constantinople, but the imperial throne at that time was occupied by a woman, the Empress Irene. The fact that she was notorious for having blinded and murdered her own son was, in the minds of both Leo and Charles, almost immaterial; it was enough that she was female. By the old Salic Law, women were debarred from ruling; thus, as far as western Europe was concerned, the throne of the Emperors was vacant.

Now Charles was fully aware, when he arrived in Rome, that he had no more authority than Irene to sit in judgement at St Peter's; but he also knew that while the accusations remained unrefuted Christendom lacked not only an Emperor but effectively a Pope as well, and he was determined to do all he could to clear Leo's name. As to the precise nature of his testimony we can only guess, but on 23 December, at the high altar, the Pope swore a solemn oath on the Gospels that he was innocent of all the charges levelled against him – and the assembled synod accepted his word. Two days later, as Charles rose from his knees at the conclusion of the Christmas Mass, Leo laid the imperial crown upon his head while the congregation cheered him to the echo. He had received, as his enemies were quick to point out, only a title; the crown brought with it not a single new subject or soldier, nor an acre of new territory. But that title was of more lasting significance than any number of conquests; it meant that the Holy Roman Empire was born and, after more than three hundred years, there was once again an Emperor in western Europe.

If Leo conferred a great honour on Charles that Christmas morning, he bestowed a still greater one on himself: the right to appoint, and to invest with crown and sceptre, the Emperor of the Romans. Here was something new, perhaps even revolutionary. No pontiff had ever before claimed for himself such a privilege: not only establishing the imperial crown as his own personal gift but simultaneously granting himself implicit superiority over the Emperor whom he had created. Meanwhile, the reaction in Constantinople to the news of Charles's coronation can easily be imagined. To any right-thinking Byzantine, it was an act not only of quite breathtaking arrogance, but also of sacrilege. The Empire, as everyone knew, was built on a dual foundation: on the one hand the Roman power, on the other the Christian faith. The two had first come together in the person of Constantine the Great, Emperor of Rome and Equal of the Apostles, and this mystical union had continued through all his legitimate successors. It followed inevitably that, just as there was only one God in heaven, so there could be but one supreme ruler on earth; all other claimants to such a title were impostors, and blasphemers as well.

Despite Irene's reputation, it was not perhaps altogether surprising that Charles's thoughts should have turned to the possibility of marriage. Here, after all, was an opportunity that would never be repeated: if he could persuade the Empress to become his wife, all the imperial territories of east and west would be reunited under a single crown – his own. When, in 802, his ambassadors arrived in Constantinople with their proposal, they found Irene disposed to accept. Loathed and despised by her subjects, her exchequer exhausted, she was well aware that a *coup* would not be long in coming, in which event her life would be in danger. It mattered little to her that her suitor was a rival Emperor, an adventurer and effectively a heretic, nor that he was to all intents and purposes illiterate. (Charles could in fact read a bit, but made no secret of his inability to write.) Her chief consideration was that by marrying him she would preserve the unity of the Empire and – far more important – save her own skin.

But it was not to be. Her subjects had no intention of allowing the throne to be taken over by this boorish Frank, with his outlandish linen tunic and his ridiculously cross-gartered scarlet leggings, speaking an incomprehensible language and unable even to sign his own name. On the last day of October 802 a group of high-ranking officials summoned an assembly in the Hippodrome and declared their empress deposed. She escaped, however, the fate that she had so greatly feared. She was sent into exile, first to the Princes' Islands in the Marmara and afterwards – not very appropriately – to Lesbos. A year later she was dead.

Charlemagne always maintained, probably truthfully, that his imperial coronation had taken him by surprise; according to his friend and first biographer, Einhard, he was so angry that he left St Peter's at once. Not only did he deeply resent the suggestion that as Emperor he was the creation of the Pope; he knew that Leo's action was devoid of any legal basis. On the other hand, the old order was becoming more and more of a contradiction. Constantinople may have been the theoretical repository of Roman law, civilisation and imperial traditions, but in spirit it was now entirely Greek. Rome, shattered by the barbarians, demoralised by centuries of near-anarchy, was still the focal point of Latin culture, and it was Charlemagne, not his Byzantine counterparts, who upheld the *Pax Romana* in the west. For the chaotic Europe of the middle ages, one Emperor was no longer enough. Perhaps, subconsciously, the Byzantines suspected as much, for it took Charlemagne only twelve years to obtain their official recognition. The price he paid was Venice.

It had been four hundred years since the first refugees from Attila had sought shelter in the northwestern corner of the Adriatic, among that cluster of little islands which lay protected by sandbanks and shoals, inaccessible to all but their own native boatmen. Successive barbarian invasions had overrun the rest of Italy, but here the natural defences had always held; and thus Venice, alone among the north Italian towns, had managed to escape Teutonic contamination. She had been a largely autonomous republic ever since the election of her first Doge in 726, and after the fall of the Exarchate found herself the only power left in north Italy which still remained loyal to Byzantium. She was already rich, her trade was fast developing, her navy was by now the best in the Mediterranean. Charlemagne immediately saw both her strategic importance and her value as a diplomatic pawn. His first attempt at conquest was repelled by a Venetian–Byzantine fleet. A second, by his son Pepin in 810, partially succeeded, but though most outlying districts fell into Frankish hands the islands of the Rialto continued their resistance until Pepin, dying of fever, was forced to withdraw. Venetian national pride later transformed his retreat into a historic victory, but the Byzantines, less starry-eyed, were ready to negotiate. Thus Charles received the recognition he needed, and Constantinople retained its old links with Venice while allowing her, in gratitude for her loyalty, still more privileges than before.

It might have been thought that Charlemagne, whether possessed of the Byzantine Empire or not, would continue to see himself as the natural champion of Christendom against the rising tide of Islam. In fact, after that one brief and ineffectual foray into Spain in his youth – which was anyway conducted for political rather than religious reasons – he never again rode against a Muslim army. The Anglo-Saxon churchman Alcuin, who was director of the palace school in Aachen before becoming Abbot of Tours, might well aver that it was the Emperor's duty 'to defend the Church of Christ in all places from the incursions of pagans and the ravages of infidels, and to secure inward recognition of the Catholic faith', but Charles was no Crusader. He even maintained excellent relations – so far as the state of communications allowed in those days – with the Abbasid Caliph Haroun al-Rashid in Baghdad.

In achievement as in physical stature, Charlemagne was well over life-size; but that achievement was short-lived. This extraordinary figure – illiterate, immoral, more than half barbarian – kept his newly forged empire together by the strength of his personality alone; after his death in 814 its story is one of steady decline, with virtual disintegration following the extinction of his family in 888. North Italy became once again a battleground of faceless princelings, squabbling over a meaningless crown, dragging their land ever deeper into chaos. In the south, also, new dangers arose. First Corsica, then in 826 Crete fell into Muslim hands, this latter conquest radically transforming the entire strategic situation in the area: for 130-odd years, until it was reconquered by the Byzantine Emperor Nicephorus II Phocas, Crete was to be both a nest of pirates and the centre of the Mediterranean slave trade. Then, in 827, the Arabs of North Africa invaded Sicily in strength at the invitation of the Byzantine governor Euthymius, who was rebelling against Constantinople in an effort to avoid the consequences of having eloped with a local nun. Four years later they took Palermo. Henceforth the Italian peninsula was in constant danger. Brindisi fell, then Taranto and Bari – which for thirty years was the seat of an emirate – and in 846 it was the turn of Rome itself. A Saracen[1] fleet sailed up the Tiber, sacked the Borgo and plundered St Peter's, even wrenching the silver plate from the doors of the basilica. Again the city was saved by its Pope. In 849, summoning the combined navies of his three maritime neighbours – Naples, Gaeta and Amalfi – and himself assuming the supreme command, Leo IV destroyed the fleet off Ostia. The hundreds of captives were set to work building an immense rampart around the Vatican and down as far as the Castel Sant' Angelo: the Leonine Wall, considerable sections of which remain today. Fortunately, as the century entered its last quarter, Muslim pressure relaxed. In 871 Bari fell to the Western Emperor Lewis II, and on his death the city passed to Byzantium, becoming the capital of Byzantine Italy for the next two hundred years.

At this time too there was a constant threat to the south coast of France. Around 890 a band of Andalusian corsairs landed at Saint-Tropez and dug themselves in on a nearby hilltop nowadays known as La Garde Freinet. From there they raided west to Marseille, north to Vienne and even to the abbey of St Gall in Switzerland. Not until 972 were they finally expelled. The number of wrecks of tenth-century Muslim ships found off the coast of Provence suggests considerable traffic with the rest of the Muslim world.

Leo IV and his second successor, Nicholas I, were the last two outstanding Popes to occupy the throne for a century and a half – unless we include the Englishwoman Pope Joan, who apparently managed to conceal her sex throughout her three-year pontificate until,

---

[1] The word 'Saracen' was applied by medieval writers to all Arabs.

by some unhappy miscalculation, she gave birth to a baby on the steps of the Lateran. Joan belongs, alas, to legend, but her story is symptomatic of the decadence and chaos of a period in which many of the historical Popes seems scarcely less fantastic: John VIII for example, hammered to death by his jealous relations; Formosus, whose dead body was exhumed, brought to trial before a synod of bishops, stripped, mutilated and cast into the Tiber, then miraculously recovered, rehabilitated and reinterred in its former tomb; John X, strangled in the Castel Sant' Angelo by his mistress's daughter so that she could instal her own bastard son by Pope Sergius III on the papal throne; or John XII, during whose reign, according to Gibbon, 'we learn with some surprise . . . that the Lateran palace was turned into a school for prostitution; and that his rapes of virgins and widows had deterred the female pilgrims from visiting the tomb of St Peter, lest, in the devout act, they should be violated by his successor.'

But if John XII marked the nadir of the papal pornocracy, he was also responsible for Italy's deliverance. In 962, powerless against the Italian 'King' Berengar II,[1] he appealed for help to Otto, Duke of Saxony, who had recently married the widow of Berengar's predecessor and was by now the strongest power in north Italy. Otto hurried to Rome, where John hastily crowned him Emperor. (This act was the Pope's undoing. His debauchery was bad enough, but when two years later he also proved insubordinate to the Emperor he had created, Otto summoned a synod and had him deposed, obtaining a promise from the bishops that they should henceforth obtain prior imperial approval for any Pope they elected.) Berengar soon surrendered, leaving Otto supreme, and the Empire of the West was reborn, to continue virtually uninterrupted until the age of Napoleon.

Otto's title of 'the Great' was not undeserved. He had but one ambition – to restore his empire to the power and prosperity it had enjoyed under Charlemagne – and he came close to achieving it. In the eleven years of his reign, spent largely in Italy, he brought to the north a measure of peace unparalleled in living memory. Rome was more of a problem. In the heat generated by constant papal intrigue flashpoint was never very far off, and in 966 the Emperor was faced with serious riots, which he was able to quell only after he had hanged the prefect of the city by his hair from the equestrian statue of Marcus Aurelius in

---

[1] After the death of the last of the Carolingian line, Charles the Fat, in 888, the Empire of the West was dismembered and Berengar of Friuli was elected King of Italy; but he was in no sense a national ruler.

front of the Lateran.[1] It was in the south, however, that Otto found himself in real difficulties. He knew that he could never control the peninsula while Apulia and Calabria remained in Byzantine hands, but the Greeks' hold on their Italian provinces was too strong for him. When war failed he tried diplomacy, marrying his son and heir to the lovely Byzantine princess Theophano; her dowry was generous, but it did not include south Italy. Otto died a disappointed man. His former allies, the Lombard duchies, were left more powerful than ever, while Apulia and Calabria remained as Greek as ever they had been.

Like his hero Charlemagne, Otto the Great was unfortunate in his successors. His son Otto II did his best, but after a hair's-breadth escape from a Saracen expeditionary force which had trounced his army in Calabria he was struck down in 983, at the age of twenty-eight, after an overdose of aloes following a fever. (He is the only Roman Emperor to be buried in St Peter's.) His son by Theophano, Otto III, proved a strange contrast to his forebears, combining the ambitions of his line with a romantic mysticism clearly derived from his mother and forever dreaming of a great Byzantinesque theocracy that would embrace Germans, Italians, Greeks and Slavs, with God at its head and Pope and Emperor His twin viceroys. This extraordinary youth had hardly left Rome after his imperial coronation when the city rose once again in revolt, but two years later he returned in strength, re-established order, restored the young German visionary Gregory V to the Papacy and built himself a magnificent palace on the Aventine. Here he passed the remaining years of his life in a curious combination of splendour and asceticism, surrounded by a court stiff with Byzantine ceremonial, eating in solitude off gold plate, occasionally shedding his purple dalmatic in favour of a pilgrim's cloak and trudging barefoot to some distant shrine. In 999 he elevated his old tutor Gerbert of Aurillac to the Papacy under the name of Sylvester II. Gerbert was not only a distinguished theologian; he was also the most learned scientist and mathematician of his time, and is generally credited with having popularised Arabic numerals and the use of the astrolabe in the Christian west. For a Pope of such calibre the Romans should have been grateful to their Emperor, but Otto tried their patience too hard and in 1001 they expelled him from the city. He died the following year, leaving, as might have been expected, no issue. He was twenty-two.

---

[1] The statue was subsequently moved by Michelangelo to his newly-designed Campidoglio, and has more recently been transferred to the Capitoline Museum.

*

In Italy at the end of the first millennium, we find certain patterns already formed, others slowly taking shape. First and most important is the interrelationship of Italy, the Papacy and the Empire of the West. Italy was once again an integral part of the Empire, united with Germany under a single ruler, but subordinate in that she had no say in his election. That ruler was thus always a German prince, never an Italian. On the other hand, though titular King of the Romans, he could assume the dignity of Emperor only after his coronation by the Pope in Rome; and the imperial claim to the right of papal appointment was not generally accepted in Italy – least of all by the curia and the Roman aristocracy. Even the journey to Rome through Lombardy, Tuscany and the Papal States could be made difficult for an unpopular candidate.

Meanwhile, the free towns of north Italy were growing steadily stronger and more self-willed. The chaos of the ninth and early tenth centuries had given them a taste for independence, and the peace which they had known under the Ottos had favoured their commercial development and already made many of them rich – particularly Milan, the first great crossroads south of the Alpine passes, and the swelling sea republics of Genoa, Pisa and Venice. This was a characteristically Italian phenomenon. All over western Europe, the revival of trade and the beginnings of organised industry had set in motion that slow drift from the country to the towns which still continues today; but in Italy, where there was no embryonic concept of nationhood to override that of municipal solidarity, the process was quicker and more self-conscious than elsewhere. For most of the north Italian towns the Emperor was too remote, his local representative too weak or irresponsible, to constitute a serious brake on their independent development. The result was that the towns continued to take advantage of the growing discord between Empire and Papacy, some using papal support to sever their allegiance to the Emperor, others pledging him, in return for an imperial charter, their constant steadfastness against papal blandishments. Thus during the eleventh and twelfth centuries were born the city-states of Italy, self-governing according to a communal system often consciously based on the Roman model, strong enough both to defend their independence against all comers – including each other – and to exert an increasing gravitational pull on the local landed aristocracy. And thus, simultaneously, were sown the seeds of that grim conflict, later associated with the names of the papalist Guelf and the imperialist Ghibelline, which was to lacerate northern and central Italy for centuries to come.

In Rome and the Papal States the old mixture of turbulence and turpitude still prevailed, as the great rival families – the Crescenti, the Counts of Tusculum and the rest – circled ceaselessly round the throne of St Peter. Yet even here and within the curia itself a new spirit was beginning to appear, an awakening consciousness of the Church's need, if she were to survive, to shake off the shame of the past century and somehow to regain her intellectual and moral ascendancy. This was the spirit of Cluny, the great French mother abbey of reform. A Cluniac dependency had existed in Rome for the past fifty years; at the outset it had had little influence, but now at last its example and teachings were beginning to take effect.

Thus, so far as north and central Italy were concerned, the overriding tendency which was to shape the course of events in the eleventh century – the quickening of the struggle between an arrogant Empire and a resurgent Papacy, with the increasingly self-reliant Lombard and Tuscan cities playing off one against the other – was already discernible as the century opened. In the south, on the other hand, the situation in 1000 AD gave no clue to the momentous developments which lay in store. Of the four tenth-century protagonists in the region, two had now withdrawn: the Western Empire had shown no further interest since Otto II's debacle, while the Saracens, though continuing their pirate raids from Sicily, seemed to have renounced the idea of establishing permanent settlements on the mainland. This led to a polarisation between the two remaining parties, Lombard and Byzantine, whose desultory fighting might have been expected to drag on interminably had they been left to themselves. In the event, however, they were now joined by a race of newcomers from the north, superior alike in courage, energy and intelligence, by whom they were outclassed and, in little more than fifty years, overthrown.

The story of the Normans in south Italy begins around 1015 with a group of about forty young Norman pilgrims at the shrine of the Archangel Michael on Monte Gargano, that curious rocky excrescence which juts out from what might be called the calf of Italy into the Adriatic. Seeing in this underpopulated, unruly land both an opportunity and a challenge, they were easily persuaded by certain Lombard leaders to remain in Italy as mercenaries with the object of driving the Byzantines from the peninsula. Word soon got back to Normandy, and the initial trickle of adventurous, footloose younger sons swelled into a steady immigration. Fighting indiscriminately for the highest bidder, they soon began to exact payment in land for their services. In 1030 Duke Sergius of Naples, grateful for their support, invested their leader, Rainulf, with the County of Aversa. Thenceforth their progress was fast, and in 1053, when Pope Leo IX raised a vastly superior army and led it personally against them, they defeated him on the field of Civitate and took him prisoner.

By this time the supremacy among the Norman chiefs had been assumed by the family of Tancred de Hauteville, an obscure Norman knight from the Cotentin peninsula, of whose twelve sons eight had settled in Italy and five were to become leaders of the first rank. After Civitate papal policy changed; and in 1059 Robert de Hauteville, nicknamed Guiscard – the Crafty – was invested by Pope Nicholas II with the dukedoms of Apulia, Calabria and Sicily. Of these territories much of Apulia and most of Calabria remained Greek, while Sicily was largely in Saracen hands; but Robert, fortified by his new legitimacy, could not be checked for long. Two years later he and his youngest brother Roger crossed the Straits of Messina, and for the next decade were able to maintain constant pressure on the Saracens, both in Sicily and on the mainland. Bari fell in 1071, and with it the last remnants of Byzantine power in Italy. Early the next year Palermo followed, and the Muslim hold on Sicily was broken for ever. In 1075 came the collapse of Salerno, the last Lombard principality. By the end of the century the Normans had annihilated foreign opposition. In all Italy south of the Garigliano river they reigned supreme, while in Sicily they were well on their way to establishing the most brilliant and cultivated court of the Middle Ages.

The Western Emperors of the eleventh century were less preoccupied with Italy than the Ottos had been. Neither Henry II 'the Holy' nor Conrad II left an appreciable imprint on the peninsula; nor, in all probability, would Conrad's successor, Henry III, have done so had not the situation in Rome deteriorated to such a point that in 1045 no less than three rival Popes were squabbling over the papal crown. Henry hurried to Rome and firmly deposed all three, but his two successive nominees lasted less than a year between them – the second, Damasus II, expiring after only twenty-three days in circumstances that strongly suggested poison – and it was not until December 1048 that a great council of Bishops assembled at Worms voted unanimously for the Emperor's second cousin, Bishop Bruno of Toul.

With Bruno, who took the name of Leo IX, the Church recovered its self-respect. The dreadful spell that had so long degraded Rome was broken, and though the Pope died after only six years – it was he whom the Normans captured at Civitate, and he never really recovered from the humiliation – he had already laid the foundations for a reformed and revitalised Papacy. In this task, however, he had the whole-hearted support of his Emperor – an advantage which his own successors were never to enjoy for, with his death in 1054 and Henry's two years later, the fleeting era of harmonious cooperation between Emperor and Pope was at an end. It was the irony of Henry's life that, in striving to build the Papacy into an ally, he succeeded only in creating a rival. The Church, having regained her virtue, now began to seek power as well – a quest that was bound to bring her into conflict with imperial interests, especially when pursued with the inflexible determination of prelates such as Archdeacon Hildebrand.

For nearly thirty years before his election as Pope Gregory VII in 1073, Hildebrand had played a leading part in ecclesiastical affairs. Throughout his career, he had but one object in view: to impose upon all Christendom, from the Emperor down, an unwavering obedience to the Church. Sooner or later, therefore, a clash was inevitable; it came, unexpectedly, in Milan. In 1073, during a dispute over the vacant archbishopric, Henry's son Henry IV had aggravated matters by giving formal investiture to one candidate while fully aware that Pope Gregory's predecessor, Alexander II, had already approved the canonical appointment of another. Here was an act of open defiance which the Church could not ignore and in 1075 Gregory categorically condemned all ecclesiastical investiture by laymen, on pain of anathema, whereupon the furious Henry immediately invested two more German bishops with Italian sees, adding for good measure a further Archbishop of Milan, although his former nominee was still alive. Refusing a papal summons to Rome to account for his actions, he then called a general council of all German bishops and, on 24 January 1076, formally deposed Gregory from the Papacy.

He had badly overplayed his hand. The Pope's answering deposition, accompanied by Henry's excommunication and the release of all his subjects from their allegiance, led to revolts throughout Germany which brought the Emperor literally to his knees. Crossing the Alps in midwinter with his wife and baby son, he found Gregory in January 1077 at the castle of Canossa and there, after three days of abject humiliation, he at length received the absolution he needed.

The story of Canossa, often enlivened by an illustration of the Emperor, barefoot and in sackcloth, shivering in the snow before the locked doors of the castle, has been a perennial favourite with German writers of children's history books, in which it is apt to appear as an improving object lesson in the vanity of temporal ambitions. In fact, Gregory's triumph was empty and ephemeral, and Henry knew it. He had no intention of keeping his promises of submission, and in 1081 he crossed into Italy once again – this time at the head of an army. At first Rome held firm, but after two years Henry managed to break through its defences. A few half-hearted attempts at negotiation were soon abandoned, and on Easter Day 1084 he had himself crowned Emperor by his own nominee, the antipope Clement III.

Even now Gregory, entrenched in the Castel Sant' Angelo, refused to surrender. He had one more card to play. The Normans, to whom he had always appealed when in trouble, had this time been slow to respond, Robert Guiscard being fully occupied with a Balkan campaign against the Eastern Empire; but in May 1084 Robert suddenly appeared with an army of 36,000 at the walls of Rome. Henry, hopelessly outnumbered, withdrew just in time. The Normans broke through the Porta Flaminia, and for three days the city was given over to an orgy of pillage and slaughter. When at last peace was restored, the whole district between the Colosseum and the Lateran had been burned to the ground. Rome had suffered more from the champions of the Pope than she had ever had to endure from Goth or Vandal. Robert, not daring to leave the unhappy Gregory to the mercy of the populace, escorted him south to Salerno, where he died the following year. The Pope's last words, ironical and self-pitying, have come down to us: 'I have loved righteousness and hated iniquity, therefore I die in exile.'

It was a bitter valediction, but Gregory's achievement had been greater than he knew. He had finally established papal supremacy over the church hierarchy – the practice of lay investitures, already losing ground, was to die out altogether early in the following century – and even if he had not won a similar victory over the Empire, he had at least asserted his claims in such a way that they could never again be ignored. The Church had shown her teeth; future Emperors would defy her at their peril.

The events of the eleventh century, and in particular the weakening of the imperial hold on Italy as the investiture struggle gained momentum, provided the perfect climate for the development of the Lombard and Tuscan city-states; but while these fissile and republican tendencies were shaping the destinies of north Italy, the south was developing on opposite lines. Here too there existed trading cities such as Naples, Salerno and Amalfi, with long histories of independence. Outside these, however, the energy of the Normans had welded the land together for the first time in five centuries, imposing on it an autocratic feudalism stricter than anything the north had ever known. Robert Guiscard died in 1085 on an expedition against Constantinople,[1] leaving his mainland dominion to his son but effective control in Sicily to his brother – now the Great Count Roger – who had been largely responsible for its conquest. It was a fortunate decision, since it enabled Roger to consolidate the Norman hold on the island, where in certain areas Saracen resistance was still strong. In the sixteen years that he was to survive his brother, he laid the foundations of a secure and brilliantly organised state – foundations on which his son was triumphantly to build.

In Roger II Europe saw one of the greatest and most colourful rulers of the Middle Ages. Born of an Italian mother, raised in Sicily where – thanks to his father's principles of total religious toleration – Greek and Saracen mingled on equal footing with Norman and Latin, in appearance a southerner, in temperament an oriental, he had yet inherited all the ambition and energy of his Norman forebears and combined them with a gift for civil administration entirely his own. In 1127 he acquired the Norman mainland from an incapable and feckless cousin, thus becoming in his own right one of the leading rulers of Europe. Only one qualification was lacking before he could compete as an equal with his fellow princes: he desperately needed a crown.

His opportunity came in February 1130, in the all too familiar guise of a dispute over the papal succession. Pope Honorius II was dying. His obvious successor was Cardinal Pietro Pierleoni, former papal legate to Henry I of England, a cleric of outstanding ability and irreproachable Cluniac background – who, however, being a member of a rich and influential family of Jewish origins, was unacceptable to the extreme reformist section of the curia. While the majority acclaimed Pierleoni as Pope Anacletus II, this group elected its own candidate, who took the name of Innocent II. Within a few days, Innocent's position became so

---

[1] It is fascinating to speculate on how history would have been changed if he had survived, and if his expedition had been successful.

dangerous that he was forced to leave Rome – but his departure proved his salvation. Once over the Alps, his cause championed by one of the most disastrous and most disruptive political influences of the age, St Bernard of Clairvaux, he rapidly gathered support from all Christian Europe. Anacletus was left with only Rome – and Roger. Roger's terms were simple: Norman support in return for a crown. Instantly the Pope agreed, and so it was that on Christmas Day 1130, in conditions of unprecedented splendour, Roger was crowned King of Sicily and Italy in the cathedral of Palermo.

His troubles, however, were not over. Anacletus died in 1138 and in the following year Innocent, at last secure on his throne, himself led an army against the new kingdom. It was always a mistake for Popes to meet Normans on the battlefield; Innocent was captured at the Garigliano river just as Leo IX had been at Civitate, and received his liberty only on formally recognising Roger's title to the crown. But the King was too dangerous a threat to the southern frontier of the Papal States to allow of any real reconciliation. Neither were his relations with the two empires any happier. Both saw him as a challenge to their own sovereignty, and in 1146 even Roger's superbly tortuous diplomacy failed to prevent an entente of all three powers against him. He was saved only by the Second Crusade, that humilating fiasco which was the price the princes of Europe paid for allowing St Bernard to meddle in their affairs.

And yet, with all his problems, foreign and domestic – for the powerful vassals in Apulia maintained a state of almost constant insurrection during much of his reign – Roger's power continued to grow, as did the magnificence of his court. The navy that he created under his brilliant admiral[1] George of Antioch soon became, despite the hostility of the Italian sea republics, paramount in the Mediterranean. Malta he conquered, and the North African coast from Tripoli to Tunis;[2] Constantinople itself was raided; so were Corinth and Thebes, the latter the centre of the Byzantine silk-weaving industry, whence captive artisans were brought back to staff the royal workshops in Palermo. Here, in his palaces and pavilions among the orange groves, Roger spent the last ten years of his life, working with his polyglot chancery – Latin, Greek and Arabic were all official languages of the

---

[1] The word 'admiral' is derived from the Arabic *emir al-bahr*, 'lord of the sea'. It comes down to us directly from Norman Sicily, where the title was first used.
[2] Sicily did not, however, keep her African conquests long; all were lost by 1160.

kingdom – discussing science and philosophy with the foremost international scholars of the time (for Sicily was now the main channel through which both Greek and Arabic learning passed into Europe), or taking his ease like any oriental potentate in his splendidly stocked harem.

His supreme monument is the Palatine Chapel, which he built during the 1130s and 1140s on the first floor of the royal palace of Palermo. In plan it is on the traditional Latin model, with a central nave flanked by two aisles, and steps leading up into an apsed sanctuary. The floor and lower walls are Latin too, though of astonishing opulence and sumptuousness, their creamy white marble inlaid with gold leaf and polychrome *opus alexandrinum*. Every square inch of the upper walls, on the other hand, is completely covered with Byzantine mosaics, nearly all of the same date and of superb quality,[1] clearly the work of Greek mosaicists expressly imported from Constantinople. These alone would be enough to mark the chapel as a jewel, rare and utterly unique, but they are not alone. Soaring above them is a painted stalactite roof of purest Arabic workmanship – a roof that would do credit to Cordoba or Damascus. Roger's most astonishing political achievement was to weld together the three great civilisations of the Mediterranean – Latin, Greek and Arab – so that they worked together in peace and harmony, and to do so in a century in which they were everywhere else at each other's throats: the century of the Crusades, and less than a hundred years after the Great Schism between the Eastern and Western Churches. Here, in this one small building, we find that same achievement expressed quite spectacularly in visual terms. We see it too in the King's other great foundation at Cefalù. There the Arabic influence may be rather less evident, but the wholly Byzantine mosaic of Christ Pantocrator – the Ruler of All – in the high eastern apse is surely the greatest portrait of the Redeemer in all Christian art.

Meanwhile, the wind of change, having already swept through northern Italy, was moving slowly south to Rome. In 1143 a civil insurrection broke out in the city and a Senate was once again established. The Papacy fought back – in 1145 Pope Lucius II actually died of wounds sustained while storming the Capitol – but the communal

---

[1] Alas, there are one or two more recent replacements, including an appalling representation of the Virgin in the centre of the apse that should be removed at once.

movement steadily gained ground, particularly after the arrival of a certain Arnold of Brescia, a fiery young monk in whom an extreme asceticism was buttressed by a new approach to religious thinking: scholastic philosophy. This had grown up during the past century in France, under theologians such as Arnold's old master Peter Abelard, and it was now taking root in Italy. Essentially a trend away from the old mysticism towards a spirit of logical, rationalistic enquiry in spiritual matters, it was one of the two dominant influences in Arnold's life. The other was the revived interest in Roman law now being expounded at the University of Bologna. From these two influences he had developed his theory, which he preached tirelessly through the streets and piazzas of Rome, that the Church should subject itself entirely in all things temporal to the civil authority of the state, renouncing all worldly power and reverting to the pure and uncompromising poverty of the early fathers. Here was dangerous stuff; to St Bernard, who preached diametrically opposite views with equal force and who had already condemned Abelard and Arnold together at the great Council of Sens in 1140, it was anathema. But not even Bernard could loosen Arnold's hold on Rome. This was to be the joint achievement of two other towering figures of their century, the Emperor Frederick Barbarossa and Nicholas Breakspear who, as Pope Adrian (or Hadrian) IV, was the only Englishman ever to occupy the throne of St Peter.

Adrian made it clear from the outset that he intended to take orders from no one. When, therefore, he found that the Roman commune, supported by Arnold, was barring him access to the Lateran, his reply was swift. Early in 1155 all Rome was placed under an interdict, to continue until Arnold had been expelled from the city. No Pope had ever dared to take such a step before, but it proved triumphantly successful. Holy Week was approaching; a godless Easter was unthinkable; and popular feeling rose sharply against the commune. Suddenly Arnold disappeared, and Adrian at last found himself free once more. On Easter Day he presided, as planned, at High Mass in the Lateran.

Frederick of Hohenstaufen, King of the Romans and thus Emperor-elect[1] since 1152, kept the feast at Pavia. He had recently received the iron crown of Lombardy – in a ceremony even more symbolic than usual since several of the Lombard towns, led by Milan, were now in

---

[1] See above, p.97

open opposition to the Empire – and was heading south to his imperial coronation in Rome. Near Siena he was met by papal legates with an urgent request: his assistance in capturing Arnold of Brescia, who had taken refuge in a neighbouring castle. For Frederick's army this presented no difficulty. Arnold soon gave himself up and was returned to Rome. Condemned by the prefect of the city, he was first hanged, then burned; finally his ashes were cast into the Tiber.

Still, the prospect of Frederick's imminent arrival in Rome was beginning to cause concern in the curia. Not without difficulty – for neither party trusted the other an inch – a meeting was arranged between King and Pope near Sutri. It nearly ended in fiasco when for two days Barbarossa refused to perform the symbolic act of holding Adrian's bridle and stirrup as he dismounted, but at last agreement was reached and the two rode on to Rome together. They were soon intercepted by some tight-lipped envoys from the commune; if Frederick wished to enter the city he would have to pay tribute and guarantee all the citizens their civic liberties. The King refused point-blank and the envoys sullenly returned; but Adrian, scenting trouble, quickly despatched a heavy advance force to take over the Leonine City. The next morning at first light he and Frederick secretly slipped into Rome, and a few hours later the new Emperor had been crowned. The news reached the commune while it was meeting to discuss how best to prevent the coronation. Furious at having been tricked, mob and militia together attacked the Vatican. All day the fighting went on, with heavy slaughter on both sides, but by evening the imperial forces had prevailed and the remaining attackers withdrew across the river.

Frederick, having got what he wanted, now returned to Germany. For Adrian, however, it had been an empty victory. Without the Emperor's troops to protect him he could not remain in Rome, and he had failed utterly to mobilise Frederick's support against King William I 'the Bad' of Sicily, Roger II's son and successor, whom he still refused to recognise. His best hope of achieving the downfall of the Sicilian kingdom now lay with the Apulian barons, once again in revolt and this time supported by a Byzantine army. But his luck had deserted him. William did not deserve his nickname, which seems to have been due more to his swarthy and sinister appearance and his Herculean physical strength than to any serious defects of character. True, he was lazier and still more pleasure-loving than his father, but he had retained the Hauteville gift of galvanising himself and all those around him when faced with a crisis. He now swept up from Sicily at the head of his

Saracen shock-troops, smashed the Greeks and the Apulian insurgents at Brindisi and then went on to besiege Adrian at Benevento. For the third time the Normans had a great Pope at their mercy. In June 1156, forced to capitulate, Adrian confirmed William in his Sicilian kingdom.

Humiliating as it was, the Pope soon had cause to be glad of his action, for Barbarossa was proving more of a menace to the Papacy than William had ever been. During the summer of 1158 he returned to Italy in strength, and at the Diet of Roncaglia left the Italian cities in no doubt as to his own concept of imperial sovereignty, as four celebrated savants from Bologna – a university to which he had always shown especial favour – demolished all their beloved ideals of municipal independence, showing them to be totally devoid of legal foundation. Henceforth, he declared, every city would be subjected, through a foreign governor (*podestà*), to complete imperial control. Throughout Lombardy the effect was electric; but Frederick had come prepared for trouble. In 1159, at Crema, he tied fifty hostages, including children, to his siege engines to prevent the defenders from counter-attacking; in 1162 he at last brought the Milanese to their knees and destroyed their city so completely that for the next five years it lay deserted and in ruins. But he only stiffened the cities' resistance. Past rivalries now forgotten, they formed the great Lombard League to defend their liberties.

Pope Adrian had died in 1159. Clearly, from Frederick's point of view, much depended on the choice of his successor, and he was well aware that by far the most likely candidate was Cardinal Roland Bandinelli, who was, like Adrian, strongly opposed to his claims. To what degree he was responsible for what followed is uncertain; it can only be said that the investiture which was held two days after Roland's election in St Peter's on 7 September was the most grotesquely undignified in papal history. The scarlet mantle of the Papacy was produced and the new Pope, after the customary display of reluctance, bent his head to receive it. At that moment Cardinal Octavian of S. Cecilia suddenly dived at him, snatched the mantle and tried to don it himself. A scuffle ensued, during which he lost it again, but his chaplain instantly brought forward another – having presumably foreseen just such an eventuality – which Octavian this time managed to put on, unfortunately back to front, before anyone could stop him.

There followed a scene of scarcely believable confusion. Wrenching himself free from the furious supporters of Roland who were trying to tear the mantle forcibly from his back, Octavian – whose frantic efforts to turn it right way round had succeeded only in getting the fringes tangled round his neck – made a dash for the papal throne, sat on it and proclaimed himself Pope Victor IV. He then charged off through the basilica until he found a group of minor clergy, whom he ordered to give him their acclamation – which, seeing the doors burst open and a band of armed cut-throats swarming into the church, they obediently did. For the moment at least, the opposition was silenced; Roland and his adherents slipped out while they could and took refuge in the fortified tower of St Peter's. Meanwhile, with the cut-throats looking on, Octavian was enthroned a little more formally than on the previous occasion and escorted in triumph into the Lateran – having, we are told, been at some pains to adjust his dress before leaving.

However undignified its execution, the coup could now be seen to have been meticulously planned in advance, and on a scale that left no doubt that the Empire must have been actively implicated. Octavian had long been known as an imperial sympathiser, and his 'election' was immediately recognised by Frederick's two ambassadors in Rome, who at the same time launched a vigorous campaign against Roland. This proved unsuccessful; before long public opinion in Rome swung firmly behind the rightful Pope, who, on 20 September at the little town of Ninfa, at last received his formal consecration as Pope Alexander III. The Church remained effectively in schism, but gradually Octavian lost his support. He died in 1164 in Lucca, where he had been keeping alive on the proceeds of not very successful brigandage and where the local hierarchy would not even allow him burial within the walls.

Venice, Sicily and – as soon as he was able – Pope Alexander lent their active support to the Lombard League, and soon Frederick began to feel, for the first time, the full weight of Italian opposition. Soon, too, his luck began to turn. In 1167 a march on Rome was brought to nothing when plague broke out in the imperial army; the Emperor was obliged to retreat, almost defenceless, through hostile Lombardy, and barely managed to drag his pale survivors back over the Alps. In 1174 he returned, but the momentum had gone; on 29 May 1176 his German knights were routed at Legnano by the forces of the League. It was the end of Frederick's ambitions in Lombardy. At the Congress of Venice in the following year he publicly kissed Pope Alexander's foot at the entrance to St Mark's[1] and in 1183, at Constance, the Venetian truce

---

[1] A small lozenge of black marble set in the pavement beneath the central doorway of the Basilica marks the precise place at which he did so.

became a treaty. Though imperial suzerainty was technically preserved, the cities of Lombardy (and to some extent Tuscany also) were henceforth free to manage their own affairs. It was hardly the solution Frederick had foreseen at Roncaglia, but consolation was soon at hand. The Empire, which had fought so vainly and so long for control over Lombardy, was now to acquire Sicily with hardly a struggle.

Roger II, who died in 1154, was unfortunate in his descendants. His son, William the Bad, despite his triumph over the Pope, had a basically undistinguished reign of only twelve years, after which he was succeeded in turn by his son, William II. Genetically, the new king was a throwback; unlike his father, who was described as a huge ogre of a man, 'whose thick black beard lent him a savage and terrible aspect which filled many people with fear', the younger William was fair-haired and outstandingly handsome. It was somehow inevitable that he should be called William the Good, though in fact as a ruler he turned out to be rather worse than his father: weak and ineffectual, always striving after effect but hardly ever achieving it. His only true inheritance from Roger was a passion for building, and his immense cathedral of Monreale in the hills above Palermo, the vast expanse of its interior walls a blaze of dazzling mosaic, stands as an unforgettable monument to Sicily's last legitimate Norman king.

For when William the Good died, aged thirty-six, on 18 November 1189, the Hauteville line died out. His wife, Joanna – she was the daughter of Henry II of England[1] – had borne him no children, and the throne passed to, of all people, his aunt: Constance, the posthumous daughter of Roger II – she was in fact a year younger than her nephew the King – who, nearly four years before, had been given in marriage to Henry, son and heir of Frederick Barbarossa. Why William and his advisers had ever contemplated such an idea for a moment will never be understood, since it meant that were the King to die childless Sicily would fall into the Emperor's lap, its separate existence at an end. Admittedly, there was plenty of time yet for Joanna to conceive; in 1186 she was still only twenty, her husband thirty-two. But life in the twelfth century was a good deal more uncertain than it is today, infant

---

[1] Which is presumably why we see, among the mosaic saints depicted in the apse of Monreale cathedral, the somewhat surprising figure of St Thomas of Canterbury. He must have been included at the Queen's specific request, as further atonement for his murder. As a child, she would have known him well; it seems likely, therefore, that she would have described him to the artist and that the portrait is a fairly accurate likeness.

mortality was high, and to take such a risk before the succession was properly assured was, by any standards, an act of almost criminal folly.

There were, it need hardly be said, many Norman barons bitterly opposed to Constance and determined to fight, if necessary, for the kingdom's continued independence. Early in 1190, with the encouragement of Pope Clement III, the Archbishop of Palermo laid the crown of Sicily on the head of Roger II's illegitimate grandson, Tancred, Count of Lecce.[1] Tancred was small and villainously ugly, and his illegitimacy should technically have debarred him from the throne; but he was able and energetic, and had he lived a normal lifespan and managed to find just one strong ally apart from the Pope there is just a chance that he might have saved his country from extinction. Sadly, he had half the Norman barons against him and was faced from the start with widespread rebellion. Moreover, he was to die in early middle age. His son and successor, still a child, was powerless when Henry – now the Emperor Henry VI – arrived in 1194 to claim his crown; he too was to die in mysterious circumstances soon afterwards. Henry's coronation took place in Palermo on Christmas Day 1194, and brought the most dazzling realm of the middle ages all too prematurely to its end.

Sixty-four years is a short life for a kingdom, and indeed Sicily might have survived had William II – his sobriquet is better forgotten – shown himself either sensible or fertile. Instead, he made a present of it to its oldest and most persistent enemy – who, on the pretext of a suspected conspiracy, was to massacre virtually all the Sicilian and south Italian noblemen who had opposed him just four days after his coronation, instituting a reign of terror that was to last for the rest of his life. The Norman Kingdom of Sicily was never defeated; it was thrown away.

For one more generation, however, its spirit lived on. Queen Constance had not been present when her husband was crowned in Palermo. Pregnant for the first time at the age of forty, she was determined on two things: first, that her child should be born safely; second, that it should be seen to be unquestionably hers. She did not put off her journey to Sicily, but travelled more slowly and in her own time; she had got no further than the little town of Jesi, some twenty miles west of Ancona, when she felt the pains of childbirth upon her. There, on the day after the coronation, in a tent erected in the main square to which free entry was allowed to any matron of the town who

---

[1] He was actually the bastard son of Roger II's eldest son, Duke Roger of Apulia, who had died before his father.

cared to witness the birth, she brought forth her only son – whom, a day or two later, she presented in that same square to the assembled inhabitants, proudly suckling the baby at her breast. Of that son, Frederick – later to be nicknamed *Stupor Mundi*, 'the Astonishment of the World' – we shall hear more, much more, as our story continues.

CHAPTER VII

The Christian Counter-Attack

After the Muslims had conquered Spain in the eighth century and the greater part of Sicily in the ninth, they made no further permanent territorial acquisitions. To the Christian lands surrounding the Mediterranean, however, they seemed a more horrible threat than ever. Their unofficial colonies in the south of Italy and in southern France were the terror of their Christian neighbours; no area of the Middle Sea was safe from the danger of their pirate fleets, and there were few coastal towns or cities that did not live in fear of a surprise onslaught. Venice almost alone, secure in her shallow lagoon, had no need for vigilance. Rome itself, as we have seen, had been sacked in 846, and in the following century Genoa and Pisa suffered similar fates.

Nor was the Muslim menace confined to piracy. Egypt was also becoming increasingly dangerous. A Turkish soldier of fortune, Ahmed ibn Tulun, became governor in 868 and extended his authority through much of the Levant as far as Cilicia, in the southeastern corner of the coast of Asia Minor. Finally, in the last years of the century, the Abbasid Caliph sent a punitive fleet to Egypt and Tulunid rule ended in 905.[1] Three decades of confusion followed, after which another considerably more distinguished and longer-lasting dynasty took the stage – the Fatimids, Shias of the Ismaili sect, who traced their descent to the Prophet's daughter Fatima. First coming into prominence in Tunisia, they conquered Egypt in 969 and built themselves a new capital which they named al-Qahira, 'the Victorious', known to us today as Cairo. By this time the Abbasid Caliphate was on its last legs, and unable to prevent the Fatimid conquest not only of Palestine and Syria but also of the Arabian heartland, the Hejaz.

In theory, from the ninth century onward, it was the Western Emperor who bore the ultimate responsibility for defending his empire from infidel attack; but the Emperor was powerless. Aachen, the imperial capital, was several weeks' march from the Mediterranean: even when an army ventured south it was perforce confined to the land,

---

[1] They left behind them in Cairo the ninth-century mosque of Ibn Tulun, perhaps the loveliest in the city.

since the few vessels that constituted the imperial navy normally found themselves in the Baltic. Poor Otto II was a case in point: in December 980 he had decided to free south Italy once and for all from the Saracen scourge. To begin with, his campaign had gone well enough, but in the summer of 982, as he was advancing into Calabria, he had been surprised by an Arab force near Stilo. His army had been cut to pieces, and he himself had escaped only by swimming to a passing ship, concealing his identity and later, as the vessel approached Rossano, jumping overboard again and striking out for the shore. His defeat was the clearest possible illustration of imperial powerlessness in the face of Islamic pressure.

Yet even then – though still almost imperceptibly – the pendulum had begun its backward swing. From the late tenth century onward we see a slow increase in Christian resistance. The Muslim settlers in the south of France were expelled by 975. Genoa and Pisa were building up navies of their own; already by 1016 these enabled them to band together to drive the Saracens from the island of Sardinia, which since 721 had suffered at least nine major raids – often accompanied by massacres of the local population. Not many years later the Arabs of North Africa were given a taste of their own medicine, as Italian ships began in their turn to threaten the coastal towns. By the end of the fifty-year rule of the Byzantine Emperor Basil II the Bulgar-Slayer in 1025, his empire had regained control of virtually the entire Balkan peninsula, all Asia Minor, Apulia, Crete and Cyprus. The grand climacteric came in 1087, when Genoa and Pisa made another joint expedition, this time against Mahdia – the Arab capital, in what is now Tunisia – capturing the town, burning the ships in its harbour and imposing peace terms on its ruler. Four years later the Great Count Roger I completed his conquest of Sicily, and in 1092 and 1093 further expeditions from Italy and southern France joined a substantial force of Normans to reconquer much of northern Spain. On every side the Muslim world was breaking up. Politically, the Mediterranean was once again becoming a Christian sea.

But there was bad news too. In 1055 the first wave of Turkish invaders, the Seljuks, had captured Baghdad; in 1071 they had burst into Asia Minor. The Byzantine Emperor Romanus IV Diogenes had personally led an army against them, but on 26 August he had been soundly defeated and taken prisoner at the battle of Manzikert. The Seljuk leader, Alp Arslan – whose moustaches, we are told, were so long that he had to have them tied behind his back when hunting – had treated the Emperor handsomely and sent him back with an escort to Constantinople, but the damage was done. In the years that followed the Turks spread all over central Anatolia, leaving only parts of the coast in Byzantine hands. Fourteen years after the battle, in 1085, they captured Antioch, the third of the five patriarchates of the Eastern Church – after Alexandria and Jerusalem – to fall to the Muslims. Only Rome and Constantinople remained.

The story of this first wave of Turkish expansion in Anatolia had one important and quite unexpected consequence. The Seljuk conquest of Armenia – far to the northeast, centred on Mount Ararat – led to a huge southward exodus on the part of its people, and in 1080 a certain Roupen, a relative of the last King of Ani, founded a small principality in the heart of the Taurus in Cilicia. Gradually – though it was the best part of a thousand miles from the Armenian heartland – this grew in strength and importance until in 1199 it was to become the Kingdom of Lesser Armenia. The Armenians have always prided themselves on being the first nation in the world to adopt Christianity, which they did in about 300 AD; here, suddenly, was a Christian kingdom, virtually surrounded by Muslim states, hostile to Byzantium but shortly to give invaluable support to the Crusaders – above all those of the First Crusade – on their way through Cilicia to the Holy Land.[1]

In the immediate aftermath of Manzikert it was all the more to be expected that Western Christendom should turn its attention to the Muslim east. The Italian coastal cities were attracted by the obvious commercial possibilities; the Normans were as always impelled by their deep-seated urge for conquest and adventure; but militant Christians, wherever they might be, were determined somehow to stem the Muslim tide. Thus, when Pope Urban II addressed the Council of Clermont on 27 November 1095 and concluded his speech with an impassioned appeal for a Crusade, he was preaching to the already half-converted, providing religious justification for an enterprise which might well have been launched without him. The continued occupation of the Holy Places – and above all of Jerusalem itself – by the infidel was, he declared, an affront to Christendom; Christian pilgrims were now being subjected to every kind of humiliation and indignity. It was the duty of all good Christians to take up arms against those who had desecrated the ground upon which Christ had trod and to recover it for their own true faith.

---

[1] It was to last a total of 176 years – until 1375, when Turks and Egyptian Mamelukes together drove out the last Armenian king, Leo VI, who ended his life an exile in Paris.

In the months that followed, Urban's words were carried by the Pope himself through France and Italy and by a whole army of preachers to every corner of western Europe. The response was tremendous; from as far afield as Scotland, men hastened to take the Cross. Neither the Emperor Henry IV nor King Philip I of France[1] – who had recently been excommunicated for adultery – were on sufficiently good terms with Rome to join the Crusade, but this was perhaps just as well; Urban was determined that the great enterprise should be under ecclesiastical control, and nominated as leader and his official legate one of the relatively few churchmen to have already made a pilgrimage to Jerusalem, Bishop Adhemar of Le Puy. The bishop was to be accompanied, however, by several powerful magnates: Raymond of Saint-Gilles, Count of Toulouse, the oldest, richest and most distinguished of them all; the French king's brother Count Hugh of Vermandois, who arrived severely shaken after a disastrous shipwreck in the Adriatic; Count Robert II of Flanders; Duke Robert of Normandy (son of William the Conqueror) and his cousin Count Stephen of Blois, and Godfrey of Bouillon, Duke of Lower Lorraine. With Godfrey came his brother Baldwin of Boulogne – who, as a younger son without a patrimony, had brought along his wife and children and was determined to carve out a kingdom for himself in the east. From south Italy came Bohemund, Prince of Taranto, son of Robert Guiscard, who cherished similar ambitions. True Norman that he was, he cared little for the Holy Places but looked on the Crusade as the greatest adventure of his life.

One of the most popular leaders, however, was not a nobleman at all but an elderly itinerant monk called Peter, nicknamed 'the Hermit' for the hermit's cape that, so far as could be seen, he never removed. He stank to high heaven and was said to look almost exactly like the donkey that he always rode, but his personal magnetism was undeniable. According to the historian Guibert of Nogent, 'whatever he said or did seemed like something half-divine'. He had preached the Crusade all over France and in much of Germany, and by the time his particular expedition set out he may have had a following of over 40,000. Many of these, doubtless, were sincere, God-fearing men eager

---

[1] It is now possible to speak of France as a political entity. The breakdown of Charlemagne's empire had led to the formation of a number of minor principalities, one of which, centred on the Paris–Orleans axis, was later known as the Ile-de-France. Here there arose the Capetian dynasty of kings, the first of whom, Hugues Capet, came to the throne in 987. This was the nucleus of the France we know today, though it was to be another 300 years before it covered even approximately the same amount of territory.

to fight for the sacred cause, but there were also large numbers of sick and lame – including women and children – who hoped for miraculous cures, while the vast majority seem to have been footloose riffraff attracted only by the possibility of plunder and by the promise, to all who completed the journey, of a place in paradise.

Inevitably, considering the numbers involved and their many different points of departure, the Crusaders left at various times and took various routes to their first gathering point, Constantinople. Urban seems to have genuinely believed that they would receive a warm welcome from the Byzantine Emperor Alexius I Comnenus; had Alexius not himself appealed to the West for military assistance against the Turks? What the Pope failed to understand was that there is a vast difference between a regiment or two of trained mercenaries coming to swell a defence force and putting themselves unconditionally under its commanders, and a number of full-scale armies, many of them totally undisciplined, expecting to be fed and lodged but unprepared to take orders from anyone except themselves. In the short time at his disposal, Alexius coped magnificently; he organised huge supplies of provisions in all the cities through which the Crusaders were to pass, with military detachments to meet each army as it crossed the imperial frontier and to escort it to the capital. Once there, the rank and file were provided with lodgings outside the walls; visitors were allowed into the capital only in small and manageable groups of perhaps half a dozen at a time, to see the sights and worship at the principal shrines.

The Crusading armies arrived in Constantinople between October 1096 and May 1097. Before they could continue on their way, however, there was serious diplomatic work to be done. First of all, Alexius insisted that each leader should swear to him an oath of allegiance, with an acknowledgement – almost certainly in writing – of imperial claims in Asia Minor and Syria. These were given, with varying degrees of reluctance, by all but one: Raymond of Toulouse. Raymond had arrived in the middle of April, and was still intriguing to get himself recognised as commander-in-chief. If, he declared, the Emperor were to put himself at the head of the Crusade, he would be his loyal follower; if not, he would accept no suzerain other than God. His fellow-princes, fearing that his attitude might imperil the success of the whole expedition, begged him to relent, and he finally agreed to a compromise, swearing – by a form of oath common in his native Languedoc – to respect the life and honour of the Emperor and to see that nothing would be done to his detriment. Alexius, realising that this was the best he could hope for, very sensibly accepted. He made his displeasure felt only by witholding from Raymond those magnificent presents – of food, horses and sumptuous silken robes – that he showered on all the other leaders.

The Emperor's relief, as he watched the last of the Crusaders board the vessels that were to carry them over to Asia, may well be imagined. Even he can have had no clear idea of how many men, women and children had crossed his territory in the previous nine months: the total, ranging from the rabble of Peter the Hermit – which had been predictably massacred by the Turks the previous October, having got no further than Nicaea – to the great feudal lords, cannot have been far short of 100,000. Thanks to his meticulous preparations and precautions, the Crusading armies had caused less trouble than he had feared, and all the commanders except one had sworn him their allegiance; but he had no delusions about them. Foreign armies, however friendly they might be in theory, were never welcome guests, and these dirty and ill-mannered barbarians were surely worse than most. They had ravaged the land, ravished the women, plundered the towns and villages, and yet they still seemed to take all this as their right, expecting to be treated as heroes and deliverers rather than as the ruffians they were. Their departure occasioned much rejoicing, and it was a further consolation to know that, if and when they returned, they would be considerably fewer in number than on the outward journey.

Contrary to the expectations of many, the First Crusade turned out to be a resounding, if undeserved, success. On 1 July 1097 the Seljuk army was smashed at Dorylaeum (now Eskisehir) in Anatolia; on 3 June 1098 the Crusaders recovered Antioch; and finally, on Friday, 15 July 1099, amid scenes of hideous carnage, the soldiers of Christ battered their way into Jerusalem, where they celebrated their victory by slaughtering all the Muslims in the city and burning all the Jews alive in the main synagogue. Two of their former leaders were not, however, by then among them: Baldwin of Boulogne had made himself Count of Edessa (now Urfa) on the middle Euphrates, while Bohemund of Taranto – after a bitter quarrel with Raymond of Toulouse – had established himself as Prince of Antioch.

In Jerusalem itself, an election was held to decide upon its future ruler. Raymond was the obvious candidate, but he refused. He was too unpopular, and he knew it; he would never be able to count on his colleagues for their obedience and support. The choice eventually fell on Godfrey of Bouillon, less for his military or diplomatic abilities than for his genuine piety and irreproachable private life. He accepted, declining only – in the city where Christ had worn the crown of thorns – to bear the title of king. Instead, he took that of *Advocatus Sancti Sepulchri*, Defender of the Holy Sepulchre, and was always addressed as *dux* or *princeps*, never as *rex*. But Godfrey lived for only a year after the capture of the city, and his successors were less punctilious; they were crowned as kings, of the Latin Kingdom of Jerusalem.

That kingdom was to endure for eighty-eight years, during which time it would vary in size; at its largest extent, it reached from the head of the Gulf of Aqaba in the south to the Dog river, a few miles beyond Beirut, in the north. Its eastern frontier was the Jordan valley, its western the Mediterranean. To the Emperor Alexius, as a devout Christian, the news of its foundation could only have been welcome; the city had been in infidel hands for the best part of four centuries, and was anyway too far from Constantinople to be of major strategic importance. The situation in Antioch, on the other hand, caused him acute anxiety. This ancient city and patriarchate had also had a chequered history: it had been sacked by the Persians in the sixth century and occupied by them for nearly twenty years in the early seventh, before falling to the Arabs in 637; in 969 it had been reconquered by the Empire, of which it had remained an integral part until 1078. Its inhabitants were overwhelmingly Greek-speaking and Orthodox; in the eyes of Alexius and all his right-thinking subjects, it was a Byzantine city through and through. Now it had been seized by a Norman adventurer who, despite his oath of allegiance, clearly had no intention of surrendering it and was no longer making any secret of his hostility. He had even gone so far as to expel the Greek Patriarch and to replace him with a Roman Catholic. There was but one source of comfort: Bohemund was every bit as unwelcome to his neighbours to the north, the Danishmend Turks,[1] and Alexius's satisfaction can well be imagined when he heard, in the summer of 1100, that the Prince of Antioch was their prisoner. He was to remain a captive for three long

---

[1] A Turkoman dynasty whose founder, the Emir Danishmend, had appeared in Asia Minor some fifteen years before and ruled in Cappadocia and the regions round Sebasteia (now Sivas) and Melitene. Over the next century the Danishmends were to play a significant part in the history of the area, but after the Seljuk capture of Melitene in 1178 they vanished as suddenly as they had appeared.

years until he was finally ransomed by Baldwin, who had succeeded his brother Godfrey on the throne of Jerusalem.

During these first years following the Crusaders' triumph, it became ever more clear that Bohemund was not alone in his attitude to Byzantium. After the capture of Jerusalem, the genuine pilgrims – many of them sickened by the atrocities they had seen committed in Christ's name – had begun to trickle home; the Franks who remained in Outremer (as the Crusader lands in the Middle East had come to be called) were the military adventurers who, having taken the Holy City, were now out for what they could get. Of all the leaders of the First Crusade, only Raymond of Toulouse – who, ironically, had alone refused to swear the oath of allegiance at Constantinople – had acted in good faith and had returned to the Emperor certain conquests of what had formerly been imperial territory. The rest were proving little better than the Saracens they had supplanted. Worst of all was Bohemund. In 1104, a year after his release by the Danishmends, he sailed for Apulia, where there was work to be done on his long-neglected estates. Then in September 1105 he moved on to Rome, where he effortlessly convinced Pope Paschal II that the arch-enemy of the Crusader states of Outremer was neither the Arab nor the Turk, but Alexius Comnenus himself. So enthusiastically did Paschal accept his arguments that, when the time came for Bohemund to go on to France, he found himself accompanied by a papal legate with instructions to preach a holy war against Byzantium. Alexius and his subjects saw their worst suspicions confirmed. The entire Crusade was now revealed as having been nothing more than a monstrous exercise in hypocrisy, in which the religious motive had been used merely as the thinnest of disguises for unashamed imperialism.

The Crusader county of Edessa, in southern Anatolia not far from the Syrian border, is nearly 150 miles from the Mediterranean. Its fall on Christmas Day 1144 to the forces of Imad ed-Din Zengi, Atabeg of Mosul, after a siege of twenty-five days and amid scenes of hideous butchery, would not therefore greatly concern us but for its direct consequence: the Second Crusade. The dreadful news had horrified the whole of Christendom. To the peoples of the west, who had seen the success of the First Crusade as a sign of divine favour, it called into question all their comfortably held opinions. How, after less than half a century, had the Cross once again given way to the Crescent? Travellers to the east had for some time been returning with reports of widespread degeneracy among the Franks of Outremer. Could it be, perhaps, that they were no longer worthy in the eyes of the Almighty to serve as guardians of the Holy Places?

The Franks knew better. The problem was, quite simply, that the vast majority of the original Crusaders had returned to their homes; the only permanent standing army – if it could be called such – was formed by the two military orders, the Knights of St John and the Templars, and they alone could not hope to hold out against a concerted offensive. The only hope was another Crusade. But Pope Eugenius III was no Urban; moreover, he had recently been obliged to flee the usual turmoil of medieval Rome and had taken refuge in Viterbo. The burden of leadership consequently fell on King Louis VII of France. Though still only twenty-four, Louis had already assumed an aura of lugubrious piety that made him look much older – and irritated to distraction his beautiful and high-spirited young wife, Eleanor of Aquitaine. He was one of nature's pilgrims; the Crusade was his duty as a Christian; and there were family reasons too, since Eleanor was the niece of Raymond, Prince of Antioch.[1] At Christmas 1145 he announced his intention of taking the Cross; then, in order that the hearts of all his subjects should be filled like his own with crusading fire, he sent for Bernard, Abbot of Clairvaux.

St Bernard, now fifty-five, was far and away the most powerful spiritual force in Europe. Tall and haggard, his features clouded by the constant pain that resulted from a lifetime of exaggerated physical austerities, he was consumed by a blazing religious zeal that left no room for tolerance or moderation. For the past thirty years he had been constantly on the move, preaching, arguing, debating, writing innumerable letters and compulsively plunging into the thick of every controversy, religious or political. The proposed Crusade was a venture after his own heart. On Palm Sunday, 31 March 1146, at Vézelay in Burgundy, he made the most fateful speech of his life, King Louis standing at his side. The King was wearing on his breast the cross sent him by the Pope in token of his decision, and as Bernard spoke all those who heard him – and there were many thousands – began to cry out for crosses of their own. Bundles of these, cut from rough cloth, had already been prepared for distribution; when the supply was exhausted, the Abbot flung off his own robe and began to tear it into strips to make

---

[1] Bohemund's son, Prince Bohemund II of Antioch, had been killed in 1130, leaving his principality to his two-year-old daughter, Constance. She had been married off at the age of eight to Raymond of Poitiers, younger son of Duke William IX of Aquitaine.

more. Others followed his example, and he and his helpers were still stitching as night fell.

It was an astonishing achievement. No one else in Europe could have done it. And yet, as events were soon to tell, it were better had it not been done.

Away in Constantinople, Manuel I Comnenus fully understood the extent of the nightmare that the First Crusade had caused his grandfather Alexius half a century before. He had no wish to see it repeated. He made it clear at the outset that he would provide food and supplies for the armies, but that everything would have to be paid for. Moreover, all the leaders would be required once again to swear an oath of fealty to him as they passed through his dominions. The German army of about 20,000 which was the first to arrive, proved to be the most irresponsible yet. Many of its leaders, too, set a poor example to their men: although Conrad, King of the Romans[1] – who had at first refused to have anything to do with the Crusade but had repented after a public castigation by Bernard – behaved with his usual dignity, his nephew and second-in-command, the young Duke Frederick of Swabia – better known in history by his later nickname of Barbarossa – burned down an entire monastery at Adrianople (the modern Edirne) in reprisal for an attack by local brigands, massacring a large number of perfectly innocent monks. Conrad indignantly rejected Manuel's suggestion that his army should cross to Asia by the Hellespont – thereby avoiding Constantinople altogether – and when in mid-September 1147 the Crusaders at last pitched their camp outside the walls of the capital, relations between German and Greek could hardly have been worse.

The French army, arriving a few weeks later, was smaller and on the whole more seemly. Discipline was a little better, and the presence of many distinguished ladies, including Queen Eleanor herself, accompanying their husbands doubtless exercised a further moderating influence. Even then, however, progress was not altogether smooth. Not surprisingly, German excesses had made the Balkan peasants frankly hostile: they were now asking ridiculous prices for what little food they had left to sell. Mistrust soon became mutual and led to sharp practices on both sides. Thus, long before they reached Constantinople,

---

[1] He was effectively the Holy Roman Emperor, but since he was never crowned in Rome he could not claim the title.

the French had begun to feel considerable resentment against Germans and Byzantines alike.

Manuel flattered his chief guests with the usual round of entertainments and banquets, but even as he did so he feared the worst. Having recently returned from a campaign of his own in Anatolia, he knew that these shambling forces, already as lacking in morale as in discipline, would stand no chance against the Seljuk cavalry. He had furnished them with provisions and guides; he had warned them about the scarcity of water; and he had advised them not to take the direct route through the hinterland but to keep to the coast, most of which was still under Byzantine control. He could do no more. If, after all these precautions, they insisted on getting slaughtered, they would have only themselves to blame. He for his part would be sorry – but not, perhaps, inconsolable.

It cannot have been more than a few days after the Emperor had bidden the German army farewell that he received news that it had been taken by surprise by the Turks and virtually annihilated. Conrad himself and Frederick of Swabia had escaped and had returned to join the French, who were still at Nicaea, but nine-tenths of their men now lay dead and dying amid the wreckage of their camp. It was a bad start, and there was worse to follow. Conrad had continued only as far as Ephesus when he fell gravely ill. Manuel had immediately sailed down from Constantinople and brought him safely back to the palace. He prided himself on his medical skills, and personally nursed Conrad back to health. Finally, when Conrad was well enough to continue his journey, an imperial squadron was put at his disposal to carry him on to Palestine.

The French, meanwhile, had an agonising passage through Anatolia, where they suffered heavily at Turkish hands. Although this was entirely the fault of King Louis, who had ignored the Emperor's warnings to keep to the coast, he persisted in attributing every encounter with the enemy to Byzantine carelessness or treachery or both, and rapidly developed an almost psychopathic resentment against the Greeks. At last in despair he, his household and as much of his cavalry as could be accommodated took ship from Attaleia (modern Antalya), leaving the rest of the army and the pilgrims to struggle on as best they might. It was late in the spring of 1148 before the sad remnants of the once great host dragged themselves into Antioch.

And that was only the beginning. The mighty Zengi was dead, but his mantle had passed to his still greater son-in-law Nur ed-Din, whose stronghold at Aleppo had now become the focus of Muslim opposition to the Franks. Aleppo should thus have been the Crusaders' first objective, and Louis found himself under heavy pressure from Raymond of Antioch to mount an immediate attack on the city. He refused, on the ludicrous grounds that he must first pray at the Holy Sepulchre; whereat Queen Eleanor, whose affection for her husband had not been increased by the dangers and discomforts of the journey – and whose relations with Raymond were already suspected of going somewhat beyond those normally recommended between uncle and niece – announced her intention of remaining at Antioch and suing for divorce. She and her husband were distant cousins; the question of consanguinity had been conveniently overlooked at the time of their marriage, but if resurrected could still prove troublesome – and Eleanor knew it.

Louis, for all his moroseness, was not without spirit in moments of crisis. He ignored his wife's protests and dragged her off to Jerusalem; he antagonised Raymond to the point where the Prince of Antioch refused to play any further part in the Crusade; and in May he arrived, his tight-lipped queen in tow, in the Holy City. There he remained until 24 June, when a meeting of all the leading Crusaders was held at Acre to decide on a plan of campaign. Why they chose at this moment to attack Damascus remains a mystery. The only major Arab state to continue hostile to Nur ed-Din, it could – and should – have been an invaluable ally. By attacking it, they drove it against its will into the Emir's Muslim confederation – and they made their own destruction sure. They arrived to find Damascus strong, its defenders determined. On the second day, by yet another of those disastrous decisions that characterised the whole Crusade, they moved their camp to an area along the southeastern section of the walls devoid alike of shade and water. Louis and Conrad soon realised that to continue the siege would mean the almost certain destruction of their whole army. On 28 July, just five days after the opening of the campaign, they decided on retreat.

There is no part of the Syrian desert more shattering to the spirit than that dark grey, featureless expanse of sand and basalt that lies between Damascus and Tiberias. Retreating across it in the height of summer, the remorseless sun and scorching desert wind full in their faces, harried incessantly by mounted Arab archers and leaving a stinking trail of dead men and horses in their wake, the Crusaders must have felt despair heavy upon them. This, they knew, was the end. Their losses had been immense, but still worse was the shame. Their once glorious army that had purported to enshrine every ideal of the Christian west had given up the entire enterprise after four days' fighting, having regained not one inch of Muslim territory. Here was the ultimate humiliation – which neither they nor their enemies would forget.

'The failure of the Second Crusade,' wrote Sir Steven Runciman, 'marked a turning point in the story of Outremer.' The Kingdom of Jerusalem was to endure for another thirty-nine years but, to any dispassionate observer after 1148, the eventual fall of the city to the Saracens must have seemed inevitable. On the Muslim side there was already one leader of genius: Nur ed-Din, whose capture of Damascus in April 1154 made him master of Muslim Syria. And there was soon to be another: Salah ed-Din – better known as Saladin – the greatest Muslim hero of the Middle Ages. Born in 1137 into a prominent Kurdish family, at the age of thirty-one he was appointed both commander of the Syrian troops in Egypt and Vizir of the Fatimid Caliph. By 1171 he had grown sufficiently strong to abolish the moribund Shia Caliphate and reintroduce Sunni Islam; he was thenceforth Egypt's sole ruler. Just three years later, on the death of Nur ed-Din, he had quickly moved his small but strictly disciplined army into Syria and had devoted himself to the task of uniting, under his own standard, all the Muslim lands of Egypt, Syria, northern Mesopotamia and Palestine.

Against these two giants the Kings of Jerusalem stood little chance. Baldwin III and his successor, Amalric I, might conceivably have saved the situation had they lived; but they died, at thirty-two and thirty-eight respectively. The next king, Baldwin IV, was a leper, who succumbed to the disease in 1185 when he was only twenty-four, leaving the throne to his nephew, Baldwin V, who succeeded as a child of eight and was dead before he was nine. In the circumstances, his death might have been considered a blessing in disguise, but the opportunity of finding a true leader was thrown away and the throne passed to his stepfather, Guy of Lusignan, a weak, querulous figure with a record of incapacity which fully merited the scorn in which he was held by most of his compatriots. Jerusalem was thus in a state bordering on civil war when, in May 1187, Saladin declared his long-awaited jihad and crossed the Jordan into Frankish territory. Under the miserable Guy, the Christian defeat was a foregone conclusion. On 3 July he led the largest army his kingdom had ever assembled across the mountains of Galilee towards Tiberias, where Saladin was besieging the castle. After a long day's march in the hottest season of the year this army was obliged to pitch camp on a waterless plateau; the next day, exhausted by the heat and half-mad with thirst, beneath a little double-summited hill known as the Horns of Hattin, it was surrounded by the Muslim forces and cut to pieces.

It remained only for the Saracens to mop up the isolated Christian fortresses one by one. Tiberias fell the day after the battle; Acre, Nablus, Jaffa, Sidon and Beirut capitulated in swift succession. Wheeling south, Saladin took Ascalon by storm; Gaza surrendered without a struggle. Now he was ready for Jerusalem. The defenders of the Holy City held out heroically for twelve days; but on 2 October, with the walls already undermined by Muslim sappers, they knew that the end was near. Their leader, Balian of Ibelin – King Guy having been taken prisoner after Hattin – went personally to Saladin to discuss terms for surrender.

Saladin, neither bloodthirsty nor vindictive, agreed that every Christian in Jerusalem should be allowed to redeem himself by payment of a suitable ransom. That same day he led his army into the city, and for the first time in eighty-eight years, on the anniversary of the day on which the Prophet had been carried in his sleep from Jerusalem to paradise, his green banners fluttered over the Temple area from which he had been gathered up, and the sacred imprint of his foot was once again exposed to the adoration of the faithful. Everywhere, order was preserved. There was no murder, no bloodshed, no looting. Of the 20,000 poor who had no means of raising the ransom, 7,000 were freed on payment of a lump sum by the various Christian authorities; Saladin's brother and chief lieutenant, al-Adil, asked for 1,000 of the remainder as a reward for his services and immediately set them free. Another 700 were given to the Patriarch, and 500 to Balian; then Saladin himself spontaneously liberated all the old, all the husbands whose wives had been ransomed and finally all the widows and children. Few Christians ultimately found their way to slavery. Saladin's restraint was all the more remarkable in that he could not have forgotten the massacre that had followed the arrival of the first Crusaders in 1099. The Christians had not forgotten it either, and they could not have failed to be struck by the contrast.

When the news of the fall of Jerusalem reached the west, Pope Urban III died of shock; his successor Gregory VIII lost no time in calling upon Christendom to take up arms for its recovery. Plans were quickly laid.

Leading this Third Crusade would be the Emperor Frederick Barbarossa, who had succeeded his uncle Conrad in 1152. Also taking the Cross were three other western sovereigns: Richard Coeur-de-Lion of England, Philip Augustus of France, and William the Good of Sicily. The Byzantine Emperor, Isaac II Angelus, was spared many of the appalling logistical problems with which his predecessors Alexius and Manuel had had to contend, since Barbarossa, who was taking the land route, had agreed to cross into Asia by the Hellespont rather than the Bosphorus, while the three kings had all elected to travel by sea. William's unexpected death necessitated one or two minor changes to their arrangements, but the basic plan that all three fleets should gather at Messina for the last stage of their journey remained unaltered, and in September 1190 Richard and Philip Augustus arrived, within ten days of each other, in Sicily.

Richard was in a black and dangerous mood. He bore a deep grudge against the Sicilian King Tancred. Though William the Good had died intestate, he seems at some stage to have promised his father-in-law, Henry II of England, an important legacy that included a twelve-foot golden table, a silken tent big enough to hold 200 men, a quantity of gold plate and several additional ships, fully provisioned, for the Crusade. Now, with William and Henry both dead, Tancred was refusing to honour that promise. There was also the problem of Richard's sister, Queen Joanna: he had heard that Tancred was keeping her under distraint and wrongfully withholding from her certain revenues which she had received as part of her marriage settlement. It may be, too, that he saw Sicily as a potential new jewel in his own crown. Tancred was after all illegitimate, while Constance, thanks to her marriage to the Emperor's heir, spelt death to the kingdom. Perhaps he too, as the late king's brother-in-law, might be entitled to stake his claim.

Tancred had too much on his plate already to risk hostilities in yet another quarter. Clearly he must get his unwelcome guest away from the island as soon as possible, and if that meant making concessions, then concessions there would have to be. Five days after Richard's arrival he was joined by Joanna herself, now at complete liberty and having received generous compensation for her other losses. But the Lion-Heart was not to be bought off so easily. On 30 September he set off furiously across the Straits of Messina to occupy the inoffensive little town of Bagnara on the Calabrian coast. There, in an abbey founded by Count Roger a century before, he settled his sister under the protection of a strong garrison. Returning to Messina, he fell upon the city's own most venerable religious foundation, the Basilian monastery of the Saviour, magnificently sited across the harbour. The monks were evicted, and Richard's army moved into its new barracks.

The predominantly Greek population of Messina had already been scandalised by the conduct of the English soldiery, in particular by their free and easy ways with the local women. The occupation of the monastery was the last straw. On 3 October serious rioting broke out, and on the following day Richard's army burst into the city, ravaging and plundering as it went. Within hours, the whole town was in flames. Philip Augustus, who had tried hard to mediate between Richard and Tancred, was horrified when he saw Richard's standard floating above the walls; he immediately sent an urgent message to Tancred, advising him of the gravity of the situation and offering the support of his own army if Richard were to press his claims any further. Tancred needed no such warning; but he had the long-term future to consider, and he knew that Henry of Hohenstaufen was a greater menace than Richard would ever be. Sooner or later Henry would invade; when he did so Tancred would need allies, and for this purpose the English, for all their faults, would be far preferable to the French. Richard hated the Hohenstaufen; the French king, on the other hand, was on excellent terms with Frederick Barbarossa. If the Germans were to invade now, while the Crusaders were still in Sicily, French sympathies would be to say the least uncertain. Tancred thanked Philip and sent him some suitably lavish presents; meanwhile, he sent a trusted envoy to negotiate with Richard at Messina.

The terms he offered were more than Richard could resist: 20,000 ounces of gold for his sister and the same amount for himself. In return he promised to give Tancred full military assistance for as long as he and his army remained in the kingdom, and undertook to restore to its rightful owners all the plunder that had been taken during the recent disturbances. On 11 November the resulting treaty was signed at Messina. It was sealed by an exchange of gifts; Richard's present to Tancred purported to be King Arthur's famous sword Excalibur, recently unearthed at Glastonbury. Not surprisingly, relations between Richard and Philip Augustus grew even chillier than before, but the French king – unlike the English – knew how to keep his temper under control. Somehow they all got through the winter without coming to any more blows, and on 30 March Philip and his army sailed for Palestine.

A few days later a ship arrived with Richard's mother, the seventy-year-old Eleanor of Aquitaine,[1] bringing with her his betrothed, the Princess Berengaria of Navarre. The original plan had probably been that the two should marry in Sicily, but marriages were forbidden during Lent and Richard – whose tastes in any case did not lie in this direction – was in no hurry for matrimony. It was therefore resolved that Berengaria should sail with him to the Holy Land. Eleanor, who retained unpleasant memories of her last visit, had no wish to return; the young bride would be escorted by Queen Joanna, and a special ship was put at their disposal. On 10 April 1191, Richard – whose immense fleet, we are told, consisted of at least 200 vessels – set sail for Palestine.

On the third day out of Messina the English ships ran into one of those terrible spring storms for which the eastern Mediterranean is famous. Most of them managed to stick together – the King kept a lamp burning at his masthead as a guide to the rest – but several vessels were blown disastrously off course and a number were completely wrecked. For some time the ship carrying Berengaria and Joanna was feared lost, but it was eventually found with two others just outside the port of Limassol in Cyprus.

Apart from its brief periods of Arab occupation, Cyprus had always been part of the Byzantine Empire; just five years previously a certain Isaac Ducas Comnenus had arrived bearing documents appointing him governor of the island. These were subsequently found to be forgeries, but not before Isaac had gained control of all the principal strongholds. He then declared himself an independent ruler, assumed the title of emperor and – in order to strengthen his position against the legitimate Emperor in Constantinople – concluded a treaty with Saladin. In such circumstances, there could be no question of his giving assistance, or even shelter, to the Crusading fleet; the survivors of the shipwrecks had been stripped of everything they possessed and thrown into prison. On being told of the arrival of the two distinguished ladies, he invited them ashore; but Joanna – who had heard about his prisoners – did not trust him an inch. Her suspicions were confirmed when he refused the ships' request for water and began to muster troops along the shore.

Word was sent quickly back to Richard, who sailed at once for

---

[1] Eleanor's marriage to Louis VII had been duly annulled in 1152. Just two months later, she had married Henry Plantagenet, Count of Anjou and Duke of Normandy, the future Henry II. The relationship was stormy – she was released from prison only on her husband's death – but she nevertheless bore him five sons and three daughters. Richard was her third son.

Limassol and gave orders for an immediate attack. Isaac had done everything he could to fortify the beach, but his men were no match for the English archers and soon took to their heels. By evening the town was in Richard's hands. That same night Isaac's camp was surrounded. He himself managed to escape, but left everything behind: arms, horses, treasure – and, not least, his imperial standard, which Richard later presented to the Abbey of Bury St Edmunds. He had given the King a perfect *casus belli*, and Richard was not one to miss his opportunity. All Cyprus, he had now decided, should be his. There was one prior formality to be gone through: on Sunday, 11 May, in the Chapel of St George in the castle, he and Berengaria were married by the Bishop of Evreux, who went straight on to perform the bride's coronation.[1] Then he settled down to prepare for war.

The conquest of Cyprus did not take long. Richard had been joined by Guy of Lusignan, titular King of Jerusalem but now stripped of his kingdom. He entrusted Guy with part of his army, with instructions to pursue Isaac and capture him; the rest, under his own command, would circumnavigate the island – half of them sailing in each direction – capturing the coastal towns and castles and any ships they might encounter on the way. He returned to find that Guy had failed – predictably – to locate Isaac, who had taken refuge in one of the string of virtually impregnable mountain castles along the northern coast. His plan was presumably to remain there until the Crusaders had left the island; it might even have succeeded had not the fortress of Kyrenia, in which he had left his wife and little daughter, fallen to Guy's men. After this Isaac lost heart and agreed to give himself up, stipulating only that he should not be put in irons. Richard willingly gave his promise – and had fetters specially forged in silver. By 1 June the King of England was also master of Cyprus. Two Englishmen were appointed governors to administer the island in his name, and all Cypriot men were ordered to shave off their beards as a sign of loyalty to the new regime.

On 5 June the King set sail from Famagusta, taking Isaac Comnenus with him and leaving him a prisoner in the great fortress of Margat (now Qalaat Marqab in Syria) – the blackest, grimmest and most sombre of all the Crusader castles – which had been acquired by the Knights of St John five years before. He then continued southward along the coast to Acre, being fortunate enough on the way to

---

[1] The castle, which now houses the Medieval Museum, was rebuilt by the Templars in the thirteenth century. There is, however, some reason to believe that the altar in the present east chapel may be the one used for the double ceremony.

encounter and destroy a Saracen ship flying the French colours and bent on penetrating the Frankish blockade. (According to a widespread rumour among the Franks, this vessel was found to be carrying a cargo of some 200 particularly venomous snakes, which were destined for release in the Christian camp.) On their arrival he and his fleet were given a predictably warm welcome, but Richard immediately found himself embroiled in a diplomatic crisis that seriously threatened what remained of the Christian alliance.

Eleven months after the battle of Hattin, Guy of Lusignan had been released by Saladin on condition that he would take no further part in the fighting. Guy had agreed, but everyone knew that promises made to infidels could be safely ignored – particularly since it now emerged that he was henceforth going to have something more than just the Holy Places to fight for: his own throne was at stake. During his imprisonment a new leader had appeared: a certain Conrad of Montferrat, who had heroically defended Tyre against a Saracen attack and was now holding on to the city despite the fact that it was an integral part of the Kingdom of Jerusalem. Guy, deprived of Tyre, determined to show his mettle and, desperate for a city to rule from, had marched down with hardly more than a handful of men to Acre, where he started a siege. He was not, it was generally agreed, over-endowed with intelligence, but here was an act bordering on the insane. Acre was the largest town in the kingdom, larger even than Jerusalem; Guy's army was pathetically small; there was nothing to stop Saladin bringing up a relief force and surrounding him in his turn – which indeed he did. Yet somehow Guy maintained his position until the arrival of Richard Coeur-de-Lion in the early summer of 1191.

On 12 July of that same year the Muslim garrison in Acre capitulated, and the Crusaders took possession of the city. Six weeks later Richard gave orders for the massacre of all his Saracen prisoners – 2,700 of them, together with their wives and children – before leaving Acre in the hands of Guy of Lusignan. Guy's difficulties should then have been over – but for Conrad of Montferrat, whose eyes were now firmly on the throne of Jerusalem. Guy had succeeded to it only through his wife, Sibylla, but Sibylla and her two little daughters had died of an epidemic in the autumn of 1190; did her husband still have a valid claim? Whatever the legal position might be, most of the surviving barons of Outremer saw the perfect opportunity for getting rid of a weak and generally unreliable ruler. Their own candidate for the throne was Conrad. Admittedly he had no legal title to it, but to this problem there was a simple solution: marriage to the Princess Isabella, daughter of King Amalric I. It was perhaps a minor disadvantage that she was already married, to Humphrey, Lord of Toron; but Humphrey, though a man of considerable culture and an impressive Arabic scholar, was also famously homosexual. With every semblance of relief, he unhesitatingly agreed to a divorce. On 24 November 1190 Conrad and Isabella were pronounced man and wife.

A royal marriage, however, is not a coronation; the rivalry between Guy of Lusignan and Conrad of Montferrat dragged on for another eighteen months, and might well have continued for substantially longer had not King Richard – whose power and prestige in the Holy Land were far greater than theirs – received news from England that persuaded him to return at once if his own crown were to be saved. Before his departure he called a council of all the knights and barons of Outremer and told them that the question of the kingship must now be decided once and for all; whom would they choose to rule over them, Guy or Conrad? Unanimously, they chose Conrad. Guy was sent by Richard to Cyprus where – for a consideration – he was allowed to rule the island as he liked. He assumed the title of king and founded a dynasty that was to reign in Cyprus for nearly three hundred years.

On 10 June 1190, after a long and exhausting journey through the Taurus mountains in southern Anatolia, Frederick Barbarossa led his troops out on to the flat coastal plain. The heat was savage, and the little river Calycadnus (nowadays known, rather less euphoniously, as the Göksu) that ran past Seleucia (the modern Silifke) to the sea must have been a welcome sight. Frederick, who was riding alone a short distance ahead of his army, spurred his horse towards it. He was never seen alive again. Whether he dismounted to drink and was swept off his feet by the current, whether his horse slipped in the mud and threw him, whether the shock of falling into the icy mountain water was too much for his tired old body – he was nearing seventy – we shall never know. He was rescued, but too late. Most of his followers reached the river to find their Emperor lying dead on the bank.

Almost immediately his army began to disintegrate. Many of the German princelings returned to Europe; others took ship for Tyre, then the only major port in Outremer still in Christian hands; the rump, carrying the Emperor's body preserved – not very successfully – in vinegar, marched grimly on, though it lost many more of its men in an ambush as it entered Syria. The survivors who finally limped into

Antioch had no more fight left in them. By this time, too, what was left of Frederick had gone the same way as his army; his rapidly decomposing remains were hastily buried in the cathedral, where they were to rest for another seventy-eight years – until a Mameluke army under the Sultan Baibars[1] burned the whole building, together with most of the city, to the ground.

Fortunately for Outremer, Richard and Philip Augustus arrived with their armies essentially intact; it was thanks to them that the Third Crusade – although, since it failed to recover Jerusalem, it can hardly be accounted a success – was at least somewhat less humiliating than the Second. Acre became the capital of the kingdom; but that kingdom, now reduced to the short coastal strip between Tyre and Jaffa, was a pale shadow of what Crusader Palestine had once been. It would struggle on for another century, and when it finally fell to Baibars in 1291 the only surprise was that it had lasted so long.

In all the history of Christendom, there is no more unedifying chapter than that which relates the story of the Crusades. The First, though militarily successful, was marked by a degree of barbarity and brutality which even by medieval standards has seldom been surpassed; the Second was a fiasco, due in large measure to the idiocy of its leadership; the Third, though somewhat less shaming than its predecessor, was a lacklustre affair that also failed hopelessly in its object. None of the three, however, apart from the amount of pointless bloodshed they involved, had much long-term historical impact; arguably by the end of the twelfth century and unquestionably by the end of the thirteenth, the Muslim Near East was little different from what it had been when Pope Urban sounded his great rallying cry at Clermont. The Fourth Crusade was to be quite unlike these. Its participants virtually destroyed the one mighty Christian bastion that they should have given their lives to uphold, Europe's only strong defence against the Muslim tide. In doing so they changed the course of history.

The end of the twelfth century found Europe in confusion. On 8 April 1195, the Byzantine Emperor Isaac II Angelus had fallen victim to a coup engineered by his brother Alexius, who deposed and blinded him and had himself declared emperor in his stead. Isaac had indeed been a disaster; it could only be said that Alexius was a good deal worse. Then, on 28 September 1197, just as he was preparing a new

---

[1] See Chapter X.

Crusade, the Western Emperor Henry VI died of a fever at Messina. Germany was torn apart by civil war over the imperial succession, and both England and France were similarly – though less violently – occupied with inheritance problems following the death of Richard Coeur-de-Lion in 1199. Norman Sicily was gone, never to return. Of all the luminaries of Christendom, one only was firmly in control: Pope Innocent III.

Under Innocent, the medieval Papacy attained the height of its power and prestige. He had ascended the papal throne in 1198, and during the nineteen years of his pontificate he presided over two separate Crusades. One of them – if we are to be strictly chronological, it was in fact the later – was of relatively little international importance, being largely confined to southwestern France. Its objective was to stamp out the Albigensian heretics, otherwise known as the Cathars, who professed the Manichaean belief that the two opposing principles of good and evil are constantly struggling for supremacy. The material world is evil; man's task is to free his spirit, which is by its nature good, and to restore it to communion with God. This could be achieved only by a life of extreme austerity, avoiding all worldliness and corruption as exemplified by the Catholic Church.

Clearly, such a doctrine struck right to the heart of orthodox Christianity and of the political and pastoral institutions of Christendom, and Innocent moved vigorously against it. In 1209 he ordered the Cistercians to preach a Crusade. It continued throughout the century, though the Cathars never recovered from the capture in 1244 of their great stronghold of Montségur in the foothills of the Pyrenees, after which they were forced underground. By the time the heresy was at last stamped out, Provence, the Languedoc and much of the southwest had been ravaged, many of the inhabitants massacred in cold blood, and the brilliant Provençal civilisation of the troubadours destroyed.

The other Crusade was that which we know as the Fourth. The lack of crowned heads to lead it worried the Pope not a jot; previous experience had shown that kings and princes, stirring up as they invariably did national rivalries and endless questions of precedence and protocol, tended to be more trouble than they were worth. Far more serious were the problems of logistics. Coeur-de-Lion, before leaving Palestine, had given it as his opinion that the weakest point of the Muslim east was Egypt, to which any future expeditions should therefore be directed. It followed that the new army would have to travel by sea, and would need transport in a quantity that could be obtained from one source only: the Republic of Venice.

Thus it was that during the first week of Lent in the year 1201, a party of six knights led by Geoffrey de Villehardouin, Marshal of Champagne, arrived in Venice. They made their request at a special meeting of the *Maggior Consiglio*, and a week later received their answer. The Republic would provide transport for 4,500 knights with their horses, 9,000 squires and 20,000 infantry, with food for nine months. In addition Venice would provide fifty fully-equipped galleys at her own expense, on condition that she received one-half of the territories conquered. The price would be 84,000 silver marks.

This reply was conveyed to Geoffrey and his colleagues by the Doge, Enrico Dandolo. In all Venetian history there is no more astonishing figure. We cannot be sure of his age when, on 1 January 1193, he was raised to the ducal throne; the story goes that he was eighty-five and already stone-blind, though this seems hardly credible when we read of his energy – indeed, his heroism – a decade later on the walls of Constantinople. But even if he was only in his middle seventies, at the time of the Fourth Crusade he would have been an octogenarian of several years' standing. He carefully glossed over the fact that his ambassadors were at that very moment in Cairo negotiating a highly profitable trade agreement, as part of which they had almost certainly undertaken not to be party to any attack on Egyptian territory; it was agreed simply that the Crusaders should meet in Venice on the feast of St John, 24 June 1202, when the fleet would be ready for them.

On that day, the number gathered on the Lido under their new leader, the Marquis Boniface of Montferrat, numbered less than a third of what had been expected. In some, their enthusiasm for the cause had simply evaporated; others, doubtless, had yielded to family pressures; yet others had heard of the true destination of the Crusade and, seeing Jerusalem as the only legitimate goal, had declined to waste their time anywhere else. With their numbers so drastically reduced, the Crusaders could not hope to pay the Venetians the money they had promised. They did what they could, but there was a shortfall of 34,000 marks. As soon as Dandolo had satisfied himself that there was no more to be got, he came forward with an offer. Zara (the modern Zadar, on the Dalmatian coast) had recently fallen into the hands of the King of Hungary. If the Crusaders would help Venice to recapture it, settlement of the debt might be postponed.

And so, on 8 November 1202, the army of the Fourth Crusade set sail from Venice – 480 ships, led by the galley of the Doge himself, which, according to the French Crusader and chronicler Rober of Clary, was 'painted vermilion, with a silken vermilion awning spread above, cymbals clashing and four trumpeters sounding from the bows'. A week later, Zara was taken and sacked. Fighting broke out almost at once between the Franks and the Venetians over the division of the spoils, and when order was finally restored the two groups settled in different quarters of the city for the winter. Before long news of what had happened reached the Pope; outraged, he excommunicated the entire expedition.

Worse was to follow. Early in the new year a messenger arrived with a letter to Boniface from Philip of Swabia, youngest son of Frederick Barbarossa. Philip had married the daughter of the unfortunate Emperor Isaac, who had been dethroned by Alexius III. Isaac's young son, however – confusingly, he was also called Alexius – had escaped from the prison in which he and his father were being held and had taken refuge with Philip. Philip's proposal was simple enough: if the Crusade would escort the young Alexius to Constantinople and enthrone him there in the place of his usurper uncle, Alexius for his part would finance the subsequent conquest of Egypt, supplying in addition 10,000 soldiers of his own and afterwards maintaining 500 knights in the Holy Land at his own expense. He would also submit the Church of Constantinople to the authority of Rome.

To both Boniface and Doge Dandolo, the scheme had much to recommend it; most of their followers, too, were only too happy to lend themselves to a plan which promised to strengthen and enrich the Crusade – enabling it, incidentally, to pay off the debt to Venice – while also restoring the unity of Christendom. So it was that on 24 June 1203, a year to the day after the rendezvous in Venice, the Crusader fleet dropped anchor off Constantinople. Geoffrey de Villehardouin, who wrote a highly readable account of the whole affair, reported:

> You may imagine how they gazed, all those who had never before seen Constantinople. For when they saw those high ramparts and the strong towers with which it was completely encircled, and the splendid palaces and soaring churches – so many that but for the evidence of their own eyes they would never have believed it – and the length and the breadth of that city which of all others is sovereign, they never thought that there could be so rich and powerful a place on earth. And mark you that there was not a man so bold that he did not tremble at the sight; nor was this any wonder, for never since the creation of the world was there so great an enterprise.

To begin with, the Crusaders met with remarkably little opposition. On 5 July they landed below Galata, on the northeastern side of the Golden Horn. Being a commercial settlement largely occupied by foreign merchants, Galata was unwalled; its only major fortification was a single round tower. This was, however, of vital importance, because in it stood the huge windlass for the raising and lowering of the great iron chain that was used in emergencies to block the entrance to the Horn. The Byzantine garrison put up a spirited defence, but after twenty-four hours the Venetian sailors were able to unshackle the windlass, and the chain subsided thunderously into the water. The fleet swept in, quickly destroying such few seaworthy Byzantine vessels as it found in the inner harbour. The naval victory was complete.

Constantinople, however, was not yet taken. The walls that ran along the shore of the Golden Horn could not compare with the tremendous land ramparts on the western side, but they could still be staunchly defended. The Crusaders directed their attack against the weakest point, where these two defences met, at the extreme northwest corner of the city near the imperial palace of Blachernae. The first attempt – by the Franks – to make a landing was driven back; it was the Venetians who decided the day – and, to a considerable degree, Enrico Dandolo in person. The story of his courage is told by Geoffrey himself:

> And here was an extraordinary feat of boldness. For the Duke of Venice, who was an old man and stone-blind, stood fully armed on the prow of his galley, with the banner of St Mark before him, and cried out to his men to drive the ship ashore if they valued their skins. And so they did, and ran the galley ashore, and he and they leaped down and planted the banner before him in the ground. And when the other Venetians saw the standard of St Mark and the Doge's galley beached before their own, they were ashamed, and followed him ashore.

Before long, Byzantine resistance crumbled: the Crusaders poured through the breaches in the walls into the city itself, setting fire to the wooden houses until the whole quarter of Blachernae was ablaze. That evening Alexius III fled secretly from the city, leaving his wife and all his children – except a favourite daughter – to face the future as best they might.

Byzantium, at this gravest crisis in its history, could not long be left without an emperor: old Isaac Angelus was hastily fetched from his prison and replaced on the throne. But this was by no means the end of the affair. Thanks to his brother's ministrations he was even blinder than the old Doge, and had already shown himself to be hopelessly incompetent; and there remained the undertakings made by his son Alexius to Boniface and Dandolo. Only when Isaac had made Alexius co-emperor with him – as Alexius IV – did the Crusaders accord him their formal recognition. They then withdrew to Galata to await their promised rewards.

These rewards, however, were not forthcoming. The imperial treasury was found to be empty; the clergy, already scandalised when Alexius began to seize and melt down their church plate, were incandescent with rage when they heard of his plans to subordinate them to Rome. The continued presence of the Franks, who had no intention of leaving until the Emperor fulfilled his promises, increased the tension still further. One night a group of them came upon a little mosque in the Saracen quarter behind the church of St Irene, pillaged it and burned it to ashes. The flames spread, and for the next two days Constantinople was engulfed in the worst fire since the days of Justinian, nearly seven centuries before. This disaster brought the already fraught situation to breaking point, and when a few days later the Emperor admitted to a delegation of Franks and Venetians that there was absolutely no prospect of their ever receiving the sum owed to them, the result was war.

Ironically enough, neither the Greeks nor the Franks wanted it. The former wished only to be rid of these uncivilised thugs once and for all; the latter had not forgotten the reason why they had left their homes, and increasingly resented their enforced stay among what they considered an effete and heretical people when they should have been getting to grips with the infidel. Even if the promised money were paid in full, they themselves would not benefit; it would only enable them to settle their own outstanding account with the Venetians. The key to the whole impossible affair lay, in short, with Venice – or, more accurately, with Enrico Dandolo. It was open to him at any moment to give his fleet the order to sail. Had he done so, the Crusaders would have been relieved and the Byzantines overjoyed. The fact that he did not was no longer anything to do with the Frankish debt. His mind had turned to greater things: the overthrow of the Byzantine Empire and the establishment of a Venetian puppet on the throne of Constantinople.

And so Dandolo's advice to his Frankish allies took on a different tone. Nothing more, he pointed out, could be expected of the two hopeless co-emperors. If the Crusaders were ever to obtain their due, they would have to take Constantinople by force. Once inside the city, with one of their own leaders installed on the throne, they could pay Venice what they owed almost without noticing it and still have more than enough to finance the Crusade. This was their opportunity; they should seize it now, for it would not recur. It was a cogent argument, and it gained still greater strength when, on 25 January 1204, Alexius IV was deposed and shortly afterwards murdered, his old father following him with suspicious promptness to the grave. His murderer, a nobleman named Alexius Ducas – nicknamed Murzuphlus on account of his eyebrows, which were black and shaggy and met in the middle – was then crowned in St Sophia as Alexius V, and immediately began to show the qualities of leadership that the Empire had lacked for so long. Regiments of workmen were set to work, day and night, strengthening the defences and raising them ever higher. An all-out attempt on the city, if it were to be made at all, must clearly be made at once; now that the new Emperor had not only usurped the throne but had revealed himself as a murderer, the Crusaders were morally in an even stronger position than if they had moved against his predecessor, who had been at least legitimate as well as their erstwhile ally.

The attack began on Friday morning, 9 April 1204. Murzuphlus led a desperate resistance, but in vain. He in turn fled, and on the 12th the Franks and Venetians finally broke through the walls. The carnage was dreadful; even Villehardouin was appalled. Not for nothing had the army waited so long outside the world's richest capital; now that it was theirs and the customary three days' looting was allowed them, they fell on it like locusts. Never since the barbarian invasions had Europe witnessed such an orgy of vandalism and brutality; never in history had so much beauty, so much superb craftsmanship, been so wantonly destroyed in so short a space of time. A Greek eye-witness, Nicetas Choniates, wrote:

> They smashed the holy images and hurled the sacred relics of the Martyrs into places I am ashamed to mention, scattering everywhere the body and blood of the Saviour . . . As for their profanation of the Great Church, it cannot be thought of without horror. They destroyed the high altar, a work of art admired by the entire world, and shared out the pieces among themselves . . . And they brought horses and mules into the Church, the better to carry off the holy vessels and the engraved silver and gold that they had torn from the throne, and the pulpit, and the doors, and the furniture wherever it was to be found; and when some of these beasts slipped and fell, they ran them through with their swords, fouling the Church with their blood and ordure.

A common harlot was enthroned in the Patriarch's chair, to hurl insults at Jesus Christ; and she sang bawdy songs, and danced immodestly in the holy place . . . nor was there mercy shown to virtuous matrons, innocent maids or even virgins consecrated to God . . . In the streets, houses and churches there could be heard only cries and lamentations.

And these men, he continues, carried the Cross on their shoulders, the Cross on which they had sworn to pass through Christian lands without bloodshed, to take arms only against the heathen and to abstain from the pleasures of the flesh until their holy task was done.

After three days of terror, order was restored and the Crusaders applied themselves to their next task: the election of a new Emperor. Boniface of Montferrat would have been the obvious candidate, but his association with the deposed Alexius IV had been too close, and he now found himself to some degree discredited. Besides, he had secret links with the Genoese, and Dandolo knew it. The old Doge had no difficulty in steering the electoral commission – half of which was made up of Venetians – towards Count Baldwin of Flanders and Hainault, who was duly crowned on 16 May in St Sophia. But the dominions over which he was to reign were to be dramatically reduced. Already in March the Venetians and the Franks together had agreed that he should retain only a quarter of the city and the Empire, the remaining three-quarters to be divided equally between Venice and the Crusading knights. Dandolo consequently appropriated for the Republic the entire district surrounding St Sophia, down to the Golden Horn; for the rest, he took all those regions that promised to strengthen Venice's mastery of the Mediterranean and to give her an unbroken chain of trading colonies and ports from the Lagoon to the Black Sea. They included Ragusa (now Dubrovnik) and Durazzo (now Dürres); the western coast of the Greek mainland and the Ionian Islands; all the Peloponnese; the islands of Naxos and Andros, and two cities of Euboea; the chief ports on the Hellespont and the Marmara, Gallipoli, Rhaedestum and Heraclea; the Thracian seaboard, the city of Adrianople and finally – after a brief negotiation with Boniface – the all-important island of Crete. For all this the Doge was specifically absolved from doing the Emperor homage. The harbours and islands would belong to Venice absolutely, but where mainland Greece was concerned, Dandolo made it clear that as a mercantile republic Venice had no interest in occupying more than the key ports.

Thus it emerges beyond all doubt that it was the Venetians who were the real beneficiaries of the Fourth Crusade, and that their success was due, almost exclusively, to Enrico Dandolo. Refusing the Byzantine crown for himself – to have accepted it would have created insuperable constitutional problems in Venice and might even have brought down the Republic – he had ensured the success of his own candidate. Finally, while encouraging the Franks to feudalise the Empire – a step which he knew could not fail to create fragmentation and disunity and would prevent its ever becoming strong enough to obstruct Venetian expansion – he had kept Venice outside the feudal framework, holding her new dominions not as an imperial fief but by her own right of conquest. For a blind man not far short of ninety it was a remarkable achievement.

Enrico Dandolo – who now proudly styled himself 'Lord of a Quarter and Half a Quarter of the Roman Empire' – had deserved well of his city; but in the wider context of world events he was a disaster. The Fourth Crusade – if indeed it can be so described, for it never entered Muslim territory – surpassed even its predecessors in faithlessness and duplicity, in brutality and greed. Constantinople in the twelfth century was the most intellectually and artistically cultivated metropolis of the world, and the chief repository of Europe's classical heritage, both Greek and Roman. By its sack, Western civilisation suffered a loss far greater than the sack of Rome by the barbarians in the fifth century – perhaps the most catastrophic single loss in all history.

Politically, too, the damage done was incalculable. Although Frankish rule on the Bosphorus was to last less than sixty years, the Byzantine Empire never recovered its strength, or any considerable part of its lost dominions. It was left economically crippled, territorially truncated, powerless to defend itself against the Ottoman tide. There are few greater ironies in history than the fact that the fate of Europe should have been sealed – and half Christian Europe condemned to some five centuries of Ottoman rule – by men who fought under the banner of the Cross. Those men were transported, inspired, encouraged and ultimately led by Enrico Dandolo in the name of the Venetian Republic; and just as Venice derived the major advantage from the tragedy, so she and her magnificent old Doge must accept the major responsibility for the havoc that they wrought upon the world.

CHAPTER VIII

The Two Diasporas

The Fourth Crusade had not only come near to destroying Constantinople; it had stirred up the entire eastern Mediterranean. The upheaval affected Greeks and Latins alike. Virtually all the noble Byzantines had fled the city – or left it in disgust – rather than submit to Frankish rule, and had gravitated to one or other of the successor states in which the Byzantine spirit and the Orthodox faith were still faithfully preserved. One of these states, the so-called Empire of Trebizond, need not concern us here, confined as it was to a narrow strip of coastline on the Black Sea. The second, the so-called Despotate of Epirus, was founded soon after the Latin conquest by a certain Michael Comnenus Ducas, an illegitimate great-grandson of Alexius I Comnenus. From his capital at Arta, Michael gradually established control over the northwestern coast of Greece and part of Thessaly. The last state to be established – but from our point of view by far the most important – was the Empire of Nicaea, of which Alexius III's son-in-law Theodore Lascaris was recognised as emperor in 1206, being crowned there two years later. It occupied the northwestern extremity of Anatolia, extending all the way from the Black Sea to the Aegean. To the north lay the Latin Empire of Constantinople; to the south and east, the Seljuk sultanate. Although the official capital was Nicaea (Iznik), Theodore's successor John III Vatatzes was to establish his chief residence at Nymphaeum (now Kemalpaşa, just a few miles from Izmir); for most of the fifty-seven-year period of exile from Constantinople it was from here, as a Mediterranean state, that the Empire of Nicaea was effectively governed.

Even that, however, might have been little more than a footnote to our story had it not been for the Bulgarian Tsar Kalojan, to whom the Greeks of Thrace had promised the imperial crown if he could drive the Latins from Constantinople. On 14 April 1205 Kalojan virtually annihilated the Frankish army. He failed to capture the city, but he succeeded in taking prisoner the Emperor Baldwin himself, who never regained his freedom and died soon afterwards. Just six weeks later, on 1 June, old Doge Dandolo – who, despite his ninety-odd years, had fought determinedly at Baldwin's side – followed him to the grave. His body, rather surprisingly, was not returned to Venice but was buried in St Sophia. The sarcophagus did not survive the later Turkish conquest but, embedded in the floor of the gallery above the south aisle, his tombstone may still be seen.

Thus, just a year after the capture of the capital, the power of the Latins was broken. They remained in Constantinople; in all Asia Minor, however, only the little town of Pegae (now Karabiga) on the southern shore of the Sea of Marmara remained in Frankish hands. Now at last Theodore Lascaris could concentrate on forging his new state – following the old Byzantine pattern in every detail, since he never doubted that his countrymen would be back, sooner or later, where they belonged. Thanks to him, there were now effectively two Emperors in the east and two Patriarchs, the Latin in Constantinople and the Greek in Nicaea. Clearly there was no question of their living in harmony; each party was determined to destroy the other, but neither was sufficiently strong to do so unaided. Thus it was that Baldwin's successor, Henry of Hainault, introduced into the equation a most unlikely new agent: Kaikosru, the Seljuk Sultan of Konya.

In the long and melancholy history of the Crusades, Christian had all too frequently fought Christian. To recruit a Muslim ally against a Christian enemy, however, was something altogether new. The Seljuk Turks were by now masters of several hundred miles of Mediterranean coastline. They had come a long way since their Central Asian beginnings. In the eleventh century they had spread rapidly through Persia, Armenia and Mesopotamia – where they had made themselves masters of Baghdad, ruling in the name of the Abbasid Caliphs – and their conquests had taught them much. After their invasion of Anatolia and their victory in 1071 over the Byzantines at Manzikert,[1] they had established their capital at Konya (Iconium), and by their twelfth-century heyday they had created a remarkable state. The Sultanate of Rum, as they proudly called it – for had it not been part of the Roman Empire? – embraced at its fullest extent virtually all Asia Minor, some 250,000 square miles, with a mixed population of Turks, Greeks and Armenians. The Seljuks did not last long – their power was destroyed by the Mongols towards the end of the century – but they left behind them an extraordinary architectural heritage, much of which still survives today: superb mosques, their façades normally

---

[1] See Chapter VII, p. 113.

flanked by twin minarets and intricately carved, often with superbly ornate calligraphic inscriptions; bridges of soaring grace and elegance; fortifications and a shipyard at their summer capital of Alanya; and magnificent caravanserais – one every twenty miles along the main caravan routes – each with its own mosque, living accommodation, stabling for horses and camels and a resident cobbler who would repair shoes without charge.

It is interesting to speculate what would have happened if the Emperor in Constantinople and the Sultan in Iconium had cemented their alliance with an overwhelming victory, but they failed to do so. There were several hard-fought battles, all but one of them indecisive; during the last, in the spring of 1210 near Antioch on the Meander, Kaikosru was unhorsed and killed – if Greek sources are to be believed, by the Emperor Theodore himself, in single combat. His successor immediately came to terms, leaving Theodore free to concentrate his forces against the Franks; the situation was finally resolved only in late 1214, when the two Emperors concluded a treaty of peace at Nymphaeum. Henry, it was agreed, would keep the northwest coast of Asia Minor; all the rest, as far as the Seljuk frontier, would go to Theodore. This treaty marked the beginning of Nicaean prosperity. At last, the young empire had obtained formal recognition by its Latin rival of its right to exist.

'I shall not pursue,' wrote Edward Gibbon, 'the obscure and various dynasties that rose and fell on the continent or in the isles.' As a historian of the Roman Empire, there is no particular reason why he should have, but for chroniclers of the Mediterranean such tasks cannot be shuffled off so easily. No one travelling through central Greece and the Peloponnese can fail to be struck by the quantity of medieval castles that crown, it sometimes seems, almost every peak and ridge of that mountainously spectacular land. For those anxious to know more, some explanation is surely required; yet few indeed, even nowadays, are the books that relate their history.

This is largely because that history is so diabolically complicated. The simple fact is that the Greek diaspora which followed the catastrophe of the Fourth Crusade was matched by a still more dramatic territorial expansion on the part of the Latins. The Frankish barons who had sailed to the Crusade – together with a good many others who had not, but who had heard tell of the resulting spoils and were determined not to be left out – roamed over Greece, seizing all the land they could, carving out fiefs for themselves much on the lines of those they had known in the west, but doing so in a country where the feudal system as they understood it was virtually unknown. In western lands that system was based on a pyramid of wealth and power, with the king at its head. In the east, the Latin Empire of Constantinople was far too weak to exert any real control, and a picture therefore emerges of countless independent city-states, more often than not at war with one another, constantly intriguing and jockeying for position. In the Aegean, where the influence of Venice was paramount, the sheer quantity of islands rendered the situation more complex still. No wonder that many a would-be historian of the place and period has recoiled with a shudder and turned his attentions elsewhere.

The story of this Latin diaspora begins essentially with the Marquis Boniface of Montferrat. Already furious at having been passed over as Emperor, he had been further enraged by Baldwin's offer of a large estate in Anatolia; instead, pointing out that his brother, on his marriage to the daughter of Manuel I Comnenus a quarter of a century before, had been given the courtesy title of King of Thessalonica, he laid formal claim to that city. Now it was Baldwin's turn to object, and it was only thanks to the mediation of Doge Dandolo and several of the Frankish leaders – above all, the young Burgundian nobleman Otho de la Roche – that open warfare was avoided. Eventually the Emperor was forced to give his grudging consent, on the understanding that Boniface did homage to him for his still notional realm and held it as an imperial fief.

The Marquis's next task was to conquer his new kingdom, and with this object in view he set out in the autumn of 1204 on a prolonged campaign through northern and central Greece. With him went a motley assortment of Crusaders: Frenchmen and Germans, Flemings and Lombards, all determined to carve out fiefs of their own. They included – to name but four – the Frenchman William of Champlitte, grandson of the Count of Champagne; Otho de la Roche, the Burgundian; the Fleming Jacques d'Avesnes; and the young Italian Marquis Guido Pallavicini. Moving south through Thessaly, they advanced to the pass of Thermopylae, where Leonidas of Sparta had made his heroic stand nearly seventeen centuries before. On this occasion they were unopposed; but Boniface, realising the immense strategic importance of the place, there and then invested Pallavicini with the marquisate of Boudonitza to cover its southern approaches. This, with the neighbouring barony of Salona, was to last another two hundred years, and to play an important part in the history of Frankish Greece.[1]

Boeotia surrendered without a struggle, as did Attica – including Athens itself, where Boniface immediately established a garrison on the Acropolis. At that time the Parthenon was serving as the city's cathedral, but the Frankish soldiers, it need hardly be said, showed the building scant respect. It was the same story, though on a smaller scale, as in St Sophia: the treasury looted, the gold and silver vessels melted down, the library dispersed and destroyed. The two provinces together were bestowed on Otho de la Roche, probably as a reward for his mediation during Boniface's quarrel with the Emperor Baldwin. At first Otho styled himself, with relative modesty, *Sire d'Athènes*, a title which his Greek subjects magnified into 'Great Lord' or *megas kyr*. Not until 1260, well after his death, was Athens formally constituted a duchy.

Jacques d'Avesnes, meanwhile, the Flemish soldier of fortune, had left the main body of the army and strayed off to the east, where he had received the submission of the island of Euboea. (This had been allotted to Venice during the partition, but the Venetians had not yet had time to do anything about it.) He stayed there, however, only long enough to build a small fortress in the middle of the Euripos – that mysterious channel[2] which separates the island from mainland Greece – and to leave a small garrison. Then, eager to participate in the coming conquest of the Peloponnese – and, presumably, the benefits arising therefrom – he hurried back to Boniface. The Marquis, however, had gone on to besiege Nauplia, so Jacques – with Otho de la Roche, who had joined him en route – launched a concerted attack on Corinth. With some difficulty they managed to take the lower town; the high fortress of Acrocorinth, on the other hand, proved impregnable, and its siege was still in progress when one night the defenders made a sudden sortie and inflicted serious damage on the Frankish camp, d'Avesnes himself being gravely wounded.

But the Peloponnese was doomed; and its effective conqueror was to be neither Boniface of Montferrat – who was anyway soon obliged to return to Thessalonica to face the Bulgar army of Tsar Kalojan – nor

---

[1] The descendants of the Lords of Boudonitza still survive in the distinguished Zorzi family of Venice. At Salona, the ruins of Thomas de Stromoncourt's castle constitute the most majestic Frankish remains in the country.

[2] Mysterious because of its unique geographical character. At its narrowest only some thirty yards across, its currents change direction six or seven times a day, sometimes more. The cause is still not fully understood; Aristotle is said to have been so frustrated at his failure to solve the problem that he flung himself in.

Jacques d'Avesnes, nor even Otho de la Roche. It was Geoffrey de Villehardouin, nephew and namesake of the chronicler of the Fourth Crusade. A year or two previously this young man had himself set out on a pilgrimage to Palestine, and having heard while in Syria of the Franks' capture of Constantinople had immediately re-embarked to join them. Soon after his departure, however, his ship had been driven seriously off course by a violent Mediterranean storm and forced to take shelter in the harbour of Modone (Methoni) in the southwestern Peloponnese; and he was still there when he heard of Boniface's siege of Nauplia. Less than a week later he was in the latter's presence. The Morea,[1] he told the Marquis, may technically have been Venetian, but it was a fruit ripe for the plucking. Given a few hundred men at most, the whole land could be theirs. Boniface was unimpressed, preferring to stick to his own plan of campaign, but Geoffrey found a new ally in the camp in the shape of his old friend William of Champlitte. William agreed to join him, provided only that Geoffrey recognise him as his liege lord in respect of any conquests that the two might make. As grandson of the Count of Champagne he could hardly have done otherwise, and Geoffrey made no objection. Boniface gave the expedition his blessing, and with 100 knights and perhaps 500 men-at-arms the two friends rode off into the unknown.

From the start they carried all before them. The city and castle of Patras were the first to fall. They then headed south, meeting practically no resistance until they reached the neighbourhood of Kalamata in the province of Messenia. By this time the Greeks had amassed their own army of some four or five thousand, which included a considerable force under Michael Ducas, Despot of Epirus; and in 1205, among the olive groves of Koundoura in the northeastern corner of the province, the two armies stood face to face. The Greeks, fully aware of their overwhelming superiority in numbers, were supremely confident of victory; but they were also disastrously inexperienced, and the Franks went through them like butter. From that day on, the Peloponnese was effectively Frankish territory. Greek folklore is full of stories of local heroism: of the great warrior Doxapatres, for example, whose mace no man could lift and whose cuirass weighed more than 150 pounds; and of his daughter, who hurled herself from the castle tower rather than submit to the lust of the conquerors. And indeed there were several

---

[1] This medieval word for the Peloponnese is unknown before the early twelfth century. It is thought to have derived from the Greek word for a mulberry tree, either because of its shape or because of the number of mulberry trees that grow there.

pockets of resistance still remaining, among them Acrocorinth, Nauplia (whose siege Boniface had been forced to abandon), the great rock of Monemvasia, and the dark fortresses of the Taygetus in the Mani. But as early as 19 November 1205 a letter from Pope Innocent III already describes William de Champlitte as 'Prince of all Achaia'[1] – and so, to all intents and purposes, he was.

Thus it came about that, within three years of the Latin conquest of Constantinople, the Frankish Crusaders had effectively and almost effortlessly mopped up nine-tenths of continental Greece and the Peloponnese. Their success had been due less to their own courage than to the pusillanimity of the local populations, who had seldom put up more than a token show of resistance. In Macedonia, on the other hand, it had been a different story. The Emperor Baldwin, as we have seen, had been captured by the Bulgarian Tsar and disappeared into a prison from which he was never again to emerge. Boniface, on hearing the news, had abandoned the siege of Nauplia to defend his northern dominions, and had been killed in a minor skirmish some weeks later. After his death his head was cut off and sent as a present to the Tsar. Just when firm and confident leadership was needed, his throne passed to his infant son, but the situation was saved when soon afterwards Kalojan was murdered in his turn (at the instigation of his wife) and the power of Bulgaria was effectively broken.

So much for the successes and failures of the Franks. What, it may be asked, about the Venetians? Thanks to the negotiating skills of old Dandolo, they had won the lion's share of the spoils; they had soon realised, however, that that share was far too large to be easily digested, and were accordingly a good deal slower than their Frankish allies to occupy their new territories – a delay that had already cost them the Peloponnese. There was also a difference in their two philosophies. The Franks, raised as they had been in the feudal system, saw their new dominions as fiefs, their tenants as vassals. But the feudal system was based on the ownership of land – a commodity which Venice, being a sea republic, had never possessed. The Venetians were merchants and traders, and for them foreign colonies were of use only insofar as they advanced their own commercial interests. It was for this reason that Dandolo had limited his claims, apart from the Peloponnese, to coastal areas and islands; even then, his eyes – such as they were – had been too

---

[1] Essentially, the northwestern Peloponnese.

big for his stomach. He did not lift a finger when Jacques d'Avesnes moved into Euboea, or when Champlitte and Villehardouin forged their Principality of Achaia; all he really cared about were the twin ports of Modone and Corone at the southern tip of the Peloponnese, and in 1206 he sent his son with a small fleet to recover them for the Republic. The job was quickly done, and the two ports were to remain Venetian for several centuries to come.

As for the quantities of Aegean islands – including all the Cyclades – that had fallen to them, the Venetians were once again obliged to admit to themselves that, despite the considerable resources of the Serenissima, the task of administering them all directly was unmanageable. It was therefore agreed that the majority of the islands should be occupied and governed, in the name of Venice, by numbers of her private citizens. As it turned out, the Venetian contingent to the Crusade had included Doge Dandolo's nephew, a certain Marco Sanudo, and on hearing the news he had lost no time. Equipping eight vessels at his own expense, he had quickly assembled a group of like-minded young Venetians with a taste for adventure and had sailed with them to stake their several claims. There, on Naxos, Andros, Paros and Antiparos, Melos, Ios, Amorgos, Santorini and a dozen other islands, they would carve out their individual domains, holding them in fief to Sanudo as Duke of the Archipelago.[1] With Corfu and the other Ionian Islands off the Adriatic coast, similar arrangements were made.

There remained only Crete, the largest and most important of all the Greek islands, for which Dandolo had had to drive a bargain with Boniface. Once again, however, the problem was Genoa. Even before the Venetians got possession of the island the Genoese had established a trading colony there, and it was plain from the outset that they would not give it up without a fight. Venice accordingly despatched a sizable fleet, which succeeded in temporarily driving out the dashing Genoese corsair commander Enrico Pescatore, Count of Malta; he, however, appealed to Pope Innocent, and the struggle was to continue for another five years until 1212, when he and his compatriots were at last compelled to withdraw. Thenceforth and for the next four and a half centuries the island was ruled by a Venetian governor bearing the title of Doge – a clear indication of the importance attached to it by the Serenissima.

---

[1] The various fates of all the individual islands of the Aegean would be, for the general reader, hard going indeed. Those seeking further information should refer to W. Miller, *The Latins in the Levant*, pp. 40–45.

*

With the death of Henry of Hainault in 1216 at the age of forty, the Frankish Empire embarked on its long decline. Henry had been a remarkable ruler. The only Latin Emperor to have shown genuine statesmanship, he had inherited what seemed already to be a lost cause and within barely a decade had transformed it into a going concern. Had his successors possessed a fraction of his ability, there might never again have been a Greek ruler on the throne of Constantinople; but once his hand was no longer on the helm, it was plain that the eventual recovery of the Empire's true capital would be only a matter of time. The Empire of Nicaea, meanwhile, under Lascaris's son-in-law John Vatatzes, went from strength to strength. By 1246 his dominions extended over most of the Balkan peninsula and much of the Aegean, his rivals were crippled or annihilated, and he stood poised to achieve at last the purpose to which he had dedicated his life.

It was John Vatatzes who deserved more than anyone else to lead a Byzantine army in triumph into Constantinople. Alas, his health had long been giving cause for concern. He was an epileptic, and as he grew older the fits became increasingly frequent and severe, at times seriously affecting his mental stability – and, in particular, making him insanely jealous of his leading general, Michael Palaeologus. More tragic still, he passed the disease on to his son and successor, Theodore II, in an even more acute form; and when in August 1258 Theodore died at the age of thirty-six after a reign of just four years, leaving only a small child to succeed him, a palace revolution bestowed the throne on Palaeologus. Though still only thirty-four, the young general had already had a somewhat chequered career. He had been obliged, first of all, to cope with a hostile Emperor, who in 1252 had even had him excommunicated and imprisoned; and his problems continued after his accession, when he was called upon to face an alliance comprising the Despotate of Epirus, the Crusader Principality of Achaia in the Peloponnese and young Manfred of Sicily, the bastard son of the Western Emperor Frederick II. Here was a formidable enemy indeed; but when the two armies met at Pelagonia (now Bitolj) in the early summer of 1259, the coalition simply disintegrated.

Determined to keep up his momentum, early in 1260 Michael marched on Constantinople. At this first attempt he failed. A secret agent inside the city was unable to open a gate as arranged, and an alternative plan to attack Galata on the further side of the Golden Horn proved equally unsuccessful. That winter, however, Michael scored a diplomatic triumph: on 13 March 1261 he signed a treaty with Genoa, by the terms of which, in return for their help in the struggle to come, the Genoese were promised all the concessions in Constantinople hitherto enjoyed by the Venetians, including their own quarter in both the city and the other principal ports of the Empire, and free access to those of the Black Sea. For Genoa this was a historic agreement, laying as it did the foundations for her commercial empire in the east; for Byzantium it was ultimately to prove a disaster, since the two Italian sea republics would gradually usurp all that remained of her naval power and pursue their centuries-old rivalry over her helpless body. But that was in the future. In the spring of 1261, the Genoese alliance must have seemed to Michael Palaeologus and his subjects like a gift from heaven.

The eventual recovery of Constantinople came about almost by accident. In the high summer of 1261, Michael had sent one of his generals, Alexius Strategopulus, with a small army to Thrace. When he reached Selymbria (the modern Silivri), some forty miles from Constantinople, Alexius learned that the capital's Latin garrison was absent, having been summoned by the Venetians to attack the Nicaean island of Daphnusia, which controlled the entrance to the Bosphorus from the Black Sea. He was also told of a postern gate in the land walls, through which armed men might easily pass into the city. That night a small detachment put this information to the test. Slipping in unobserved, they took the few Frankish guards by surprise and threw them from the ramparts. Then they quietly opened one of the city gates. At dawn on Monday, 25 July 1261, the rest of the army poured into Constantinople, meeting scarcely any opposition.

The Emperor Baldwin II, asleep in his palace, was awakened by the tumult and fled for his life, finally chancing upon a Venetian merchantman on which he escaped to Euboea. Meanwhile, Alexius Strategopulus and his men set fire to the entire Venetian quarter of the city so that the sailors on their return from Daphnusia, finding their houses destroyed and their terrified families huddled homeless on the quayside, would have no spirit for a counter-attack and no choice but to sail disconsolately back to their lagoon. Among the remaining Franks there was widespread panic, gleefully described in the Greek chronicles. But they need not have worried; the expected massacre never occurred. Soon they emerged from their various hiding places, gathered up all the possessions that they could carry and staggered down to the harbour, where some thirty Venetian ships were waiting. The moment they were all aboard, this fleet too left for Euboea – not, apparently, even pausing to take on sufficient provisions, since it is recorded that many of the refugees died of hunger before reaching their destination.

Two hundred miles away in his camp at Meteorum in Asia Minor, the Emperor Michael was also sleeping when the great news arrived. His elder sister Eulogia – who when he was a child had regularly lulled him to sleep by singing of how he would one day become Emperor and enter Constantinople through the Golden Gate – woke him (according to one authority, by tickling his toes) and told him the news. At first he refused to believe it; only when he was handed the crown and sceptre that Baldwin had left behind in the palace was he finally convinced. Three weeks later, on 15 August, he duly passed through the Golden Gate and proceeded on foot the length of the city to St Sophia. There a second coronation ceremony was performed by the Patriarch for both himself and his wife Theodora, their baby son Andronicus being proclaimed heir presumptive.

From the start, the Latin Empire of Constantinople had been a monstrosity. The miserable offspring of treachery and greed, in the fifty-seven years of its existence it achieved nothing, contributed nothing, enjoyed not a single moment of distinction or glory. After 1204 it made no territorial conquests, and before long had shrunk to the immediate surroundings of the city that had been ruined and ravaged in giving it birth. Of its seven rulers only one, Henry of Hainault, rose above the mediocre; none of them seem to have made the slightest attempt to understand their Greek subjects or to adopt their customs, let alone to learn their language. And the empire's fall was, if anything, even more ignominious than its beginning – overpowered in a single night by a handful of soldiers on the spur of the moment.

If this pathetic travesty could only have confined its misdeeds to itself, we might have passed it over with little more than a pitying glance. Alas, it did not. The dark legacy that it left behind affected not only Byzantium but all Christendom. The Greek Empire never recovered from the damage it sustained during those fateful years, damage that was spiritual as well as material. Nor, bereft of much of the territory that had remained to it after the disaster of Manzikert, with many of its loveliest buildings reduced to rubble and its finest works of art destroyed or carried off to the west, did it ever succeed in recovering its former morale. And it had been robbed of something else also. Before the Latin conquest it had been one and indivisible, under a single ruler standing halfway to heaven, Equal of the Apostles. Now that unity too was gone. True, the Empire of Nicaea was no more, subsumed – as it had always longed to be – in that of Constantinople. But there were the Emperors of Trebizond, still stubbornly independent in their tiny Byzantine microcosm on the rainswept shore of the Black Sea, and there were the Despots of Epirus, forever struggling to recapture their early years of power, always ready to welcome the enemies of Constantinople and to provide a focus of opposition. How, fragmented as it was, could the Greek Empire continue to perform the function that it had fulfilled for so long – that of the last grand eastern bulwark of Christendom against the Islamic tide?

But Christendom too had been changed by the Fourth Crusade. Long divided, it was now polarised. For centuries before and after the Great Schism of 1054, relations between the Eastern and Western Churches had fluctuated between the politely distant and the bitterly acrimonious; their differences, however, had been essentially theological. After the sack of Constantinopole by the Western Crusaders, this was no longer true. In the eyes of the Greeks, these barbarians who had desecrated their altars, plundered their homes and violated their women could no longer be considered, in any real sense of the word, Christians at all. How now could they ever agree to the idea of union with Rome? 'Better the Sultan's turban than the cardinal's hat,' they used to say; and they meant it.

CHAPTER IX

Stupor Mundi

A few days after the Empress Constance had given birth in the village of Jesi on the day after Christmas 1194,[1] she and her son continued their journey to the south. It was in Palermo, on the premature death of his father just four years later, that the child – named Frederick Roger, after his two grandfathers – was in his turn crowned King of Sicily.

There it was that he spent his childhood, receiving an education as far removed from that normally given to German princes as could possibly be imagined. Latin, Greek and Arabic were all official languages of Norman Sicily; to these Frederick was to add German, Italian and French. Ever since the days of his grandfather Roger II, the court had been the most cultivated in Europe, the meeting place of scholars and geographers, scientists and mathematicians, Christian, Jewish and Muslim. His personal tutor was very possibly Michael Scot, translator of Aristotle and Averroes, who is known to have spent several years in Palermo and was to become his close friend. It was impossible to find a subject which did not interest him. He would spend hours not only in study but in long disputations on religion, philosophy or mathematics. Often, too, he would withdraw to one of the parks and palaces that, we are told, ringed the city like a necklace, watching the birds and animals that were to be a constant passion. Many years later he was to write a book on falconry, *De Arte Venandi cum Avibus*,[2] which became a classic, displaying a knowledge and understanding of wildlife rare indeed in the thirteenth century.

The physical energy fully matched the intellectual. A contemporary, who clearly knew him well, wrote:

> He is never idle, but passes the whole day in some occupation or other, and so that his vigour may increase with practice he strengthens his agile body with every kind of exercise and practice of arms. He either employs his weapons or carries them, drawing his shortsword, in whose use he is expert; he makes play of defending himself from attack. He is

---

[1] See Chapter VI, p. 110.
[2] *On the Art of Hunting with Birds.*

a good shot with the bow and often practises archery. He loves fast thoroughbred horses; and I believe that no one knows better than he how to curb them with the bridle and then set them at full gallop. This is how he spends his days from morn to eve, and then begins afresh the following day.

To this is added a regal majesty and majestic features and mien, to which are united a kindly and gracious air, a serene brow, brilliant eyes and expressive face, a burning spirit and a ready wit. Nevertheless his actions are sometimes odd and vulgar, though this is not due to nature but to contact with rough company . . . However he has virtue in advance of his age, and though not adult he is well versed in knowledge and has the gift of wisdom, which usually comes only with the passage of years. In him, then, the number of years does not count; nor is there need to await maturity, because as a man he is full of knowledge, and as a ruler of majesty.

This description was written in 1208, when Frederick was thirteen. He came of age on his fourteenth birthday, 26 December, and nine months later was married to Constance, daughter of Alfonso II of Aragon, ten years older than he and already a widow, her first husband having been King Imre of Hungary. She was the choice of Pope Innocent III, and at least in the early days of the marriage Frederick does not seem to have altogether shared the papal enthusiasm for her; but she brought 500 armed knights in her train, and in view of the continuing unrest throughout the kingdom, he needed all the help he could get. She also introduced, with her knights and ladies and troubadours, an element of worldly sophistication which had hitherto been lacking in Palermo. To Frederick, always alive to every new stimulus, there now opened up a whole new world, the world of courtly love. The marriage itself remained one of political convenience – though Constance duly presented her husband with a son, Henry, a year or two later – but it removed the rough edges; long before he was twenty, Frederick had acquired the social graces and the polished charm for which he would be famous for the rest of his life.

Early in January 1212 an embassy arrived in Palermo with a message from beyond the Alps. Once again, western Europe had been shown the perils of an elective monarchy; since the death of Henry VI, Germany had been torn apart by a civil war among the various claimants to the imperial title. One of these, Otto the Welf, Duke of Brunswick, had actually been crowned Emperor by Pope Innocent in 1209, and two years later had taken possession of south Italy, the entire mainland part of Frederick's kingdom. Unfortunately for him, however, he went too far: his invasion of the papal province of Tuscany led to his instant excommunication, and in September 1211 a council of the leading German princes met at Nuremberg and declared him deposed. They it was who had despatched the ambassadors, with an invitation to Frederick to assume the vacant throne.

This invitation came as a complete surprise, and created a considerable stir in the Sicilian court. Frederick's principal councillors strongly advised against acceptance; so too did his wife. He had no ties of his own with Germany; indeed he had never set foot on German soil. His hold on his own kingdom was still far from secure; it was scarcely a year since the Duke of Brunswick had been threatening him from across the Straits of Messina. Was this really a moment to absent himself from Sicily for a period of several months at least, for the sake of an honour which, however great, might yet prove illusory? On the other hand a refusal would, he knew, be seen by the German princes as a deliberate snub, and could not fail to strengthen the position of his chief rival. Both in Italy and in Germany, the Duke of Brunswick still had plenty of support. Having renounced none of his long-term ambitions, he was fully capable of launching a new campaign – and he would not make the same mistake next time. Here, on the other hand, was an opportunity to deal him a knockout blow. It was not to be missed.

Pope Innocent, after some hesitation, gave his approval. Frederick's election would admittedly tighten the imperial grip to the north and south of the Papal States, and it was in order to emphasise the independence – at least in theory – of the Kingdom of Sicily from the Empire that the Pope insisted on Frederick's renunciation of the Sicilian throne in favour of his newborn son, with Queen Constance acting as regent. Once these formalities – and a few others of lesser importance – had been settled, Frederick's way was clear. At the end of February he sailed with a few trusted companions from Messina. His immediate destination, however, was not Germany but Rome; and there, on Easter Sunday, 25 March 1212, he knelt before the Pope and performed the act of feudal homage to him – technically on behalf of his son the King – for the Sicilian Kingdom. From Rome he sailed on to Genoa in a Genoese galley, somehow eluding the fleet which the Pisans (staunch supporters of the Duke of Brunswick) had sent to intercept him. The Genoese, unlike their Pisan rivals, were enthusiastically Ghibelline,[1] none more so than their leading family, the

Dorias, who put their principal palace at the disposal of the Emperor-elect until such time as the Alpine passes were once again open to enable him to complete his journey. Meanwhile, an agreement was reached, to the benefit of both sides, by the terms of which Frederick promised – in return for a substantial subsidy – to confirm on his accession as Emperor all the privileges granted to Genoa by his predecessors.

Even then his path to Germany was not clear. On 28 July he was given a warm welcome in Pavia; but the Lombard plain was being constantly patrolled by bands of pro-Guelf Milanese, and it was one of these bands that surprised the imperial party as they were leaving the town the next morning. Frederick was lucky indeed to be able to leap on to one of the horses and, fording the river Lambro bareback, to make his way to friendly Cremona. By which route he finally crossed the Alps is not recorded; it was certainly not the Brenner, for we know that the Duke of Brunswick and his army were at Trento. By the beginning of autumn Frederick was safely in Germany.

On 25 July 1215, in the cathedral at Aachen upon the throne of Charlemagne, the Archbishop of Mainz crowned Frederick King of the Romans, the traditional title of the Emperor-elect. He was just twenty-one. All that he now needed for the full imperial title was a further coronation by the Pope in Rome. Almost exactly a year before, on 27 July 1214, the army of Philip Augustus of France had defeated that of Otto of Brunswick and King John of England on the field of Bouvines, near Lille, effectively destroying all Otto's hopes of opposing him. From that day his supremacy was unquestioned, and it was now – perhaps as a thank-offering to God, perhaps as a way of winning further papal approval – that he announced his intention of taking the Cross.

Few acts in Frederick's life are to us today more incomprehensible. He had never been particularly pious; moreover, he had been brought up among Muslim scientists and scholars, whose religion he respected and whose language he spoke. Nor at this time was he under pressure from the Pope or anyone else. Indeed, there is plenty of reason to believe that he soon regretted his promise; he certainly showed no

---

[1] The political factions of Guelf and Ghibelline, which were to dominate Italian politics for almost two centuries, derived their names from those of the two great German clans, the house of Welf and that of Waiblingen (or Staufen). As time went on they came to be associated with the papal and imperial houses respectively.

eagerness to fulfil it. He was in fact to remain in Germany for another four years, spent largely in ensuring the imperial succession of his son Henry, who in 1217 arrived with Queen Constance from Sicily. In the late summer of 1220 his parents made their way back to Italy, leaving their disconsolate little eight-year-old behind them. There followed a solemn progress through Italy, during which Frederick dispensed royal grants and diplomas with his usual largesse. In mid-November he arrived in Rome, and on the 22nd Pope Honorius III laid the imperial crown on his head.

Just sixty-five years before, his grandfather Barbarossa had been obliged to undergo a hole-and-corner coronation which had been followed by something not far short of a massacre.[1] Those days, however, were long past; this time Rome was at peace – Frederick's boundless generosity had seen to that – and the ceremony was perhaps the most splendid that had ever been seen in the basilica. When it was completed, and Pope and Emperor emerged into the winter sunshine, it was noted that the Emperor – unlike Barbarossa – unhesitatingly grasped the Pope's stirrup as he mounted his horse, which he then led by the bridle for a few paces before mounting himself. Such gestures meant little to him. Not only was the Empire his own; he had also extracted from the Pope an undertaking which he valued very nearly as much – the restoration to him of his Sicilian realm. After eight years in Germany he longed to return to Palermo.

Those years had brought him the greatest secular title the world could bestow, but they had also showed him that he was at heart a man of the south, a Sicilian. Germany had been good to him, but he had never really liked the country or felt at home there. Of his thirty-eight years as Emperor, only nine were to be spent north of the Alps; throughout his reign he was to do all he could – though without conspicuous success – to shift the focus of the Empire to Italy, and it was in Italy that the main body of his life's work was to be done. He began it in late December 1220 even before he had crossed the Straits of Messina, in the first important city within his northern frontier: the city of Capua.

About the state of Sicily he was under no illusions: for over thirty years – ever since the death of William the Good in 1189 – it had been in chaos. His father's reign of terror had only increased the unruliness and dissatisfaction; then there had been his own minority – his mother

---

[1] See Chapter VI, p. 106.

as regent had barely succeeded in holding things together – followed by his long absence in Germany, during which the state had survived more in name than anything else. As the most urgent priority, order must be restored; it was with what are known as the Assizes of Capua that Frederick took the first steps in doing so, promulgating – in no less than twenty chapters – a series of laws that he must have pondered for many months before, laws which laid down the foundations for the national regeneration that was to continue for the rest of his reign. Essentially, they involved a return to the status quo existing at the time of William's death, and a recentralisation of power under the Crown. The most far-reaching law of all was the *de resignandis privilegiis*, which decreed that all privileges, however small or seemingly insignificant, granted to any person or institution since that time should be submitted to the Royal Chancery for confirmation before the spring of 1221. Obviously, this edict fell hardest on the chief recipients of such privileges, who also constituted the most serious threat to the supremacy of the Crown: the nobility and the Church. For the nobility, moreover, there were two additional blows. No holder of a fief was permitted to marry, nor his children to inherit, without the consent of his sovereign. And all castles built anywhere in the kingdom since King William's death were automatically forfeit to the Crown.

The proceedings at Capua were repeated, if on a slightly more modest scale, in the following months at Messina, Catania and Palermo; the Emperor then moved on to Syracuse, where he had serious business with the Genoese. Genoa had always been his friend, but as long ago as 1204 Genoese merchants had virtually taken possession of the city, from which they had spread their influence all over the island. One of the chief causes of the decline of Sicilian trade over the previous thirty years had been the fact that most of it had fallen into the hands of foreigners; there was no chance of a return to prosperity while outsiders remained in control. And so, despite the help that he had received from the Genoese on his journey to Germany, Frederick acted with characteristic firmness. He threw them out. His new laws gave him all the authority he needed. All the concessions that had been granted to Genoa, not only in Syracuse but in Palermo, Messina, Trapani and other trading centres across the island were summarily withdrawn, all Genoese depots and warehouses declared confiscate, with their contents, to the Sicilian Crown. Similar action was taken against Pisa, although the Pisan presence in Sicily was insignificant and her losses were relatively small.

But alas, there was another, far greater enemy than Genoa to be faced: the Muslims of western Sicily. Three-quarters of a century before, in the days of King Roger, the Arab community had been an integral and respected part of the kingdom. It had staffed the entire treasury and had provided most of the physicians, astronomers and other men of science who had earned Norman Sicily its outstanding reputation in the field of scholarship. But those days were long gone. Already during the reign of William the Good much of the semi-autonomous Arab region had been granted to the Abbey of Monreale; with the final collapse of Norman power, the Arabs had found that they were no longer appreciated or even respected. They had consequently been forced back, entrenching themselves in the wild and mountainous west, where Arab brigands and freebooters now constantly terrorised the local Christian communities. Frederick's first campaign against them, in the summer of 1221, proved inconclusive; not until the following year did his troops capture the Saracen fortress of Iato, and with it the Muslim leader Ibn Abbad, who soon afterwards ended his days on the scaffold.

Not even his execution, however, marked the final solution to the problem. This came about only between 1222 and 1226, when Frederick adopted a still more drastic measure. He decided to remove the entire Muslim population of the rebellious western region – perhaps fifteen or twenty thousand people – altogether from the island, and to resettle them at the other end of his kingdom: at Lucera in northern Apulia, which became effectively a Muslim town, virtually every one of its Christian churches being replaced by a mosque. This was not, it must be emphasised, in any sense a penal colony. Its citizens enjoyed complete liberty and the free exercise of their religion, and Frederick, who had been brought up with Muslims from his cradle, ultimately built his own palace there – a building in distinctly oriental style which was to become one of his favourite residences.

The Saracens of Lucera, for their part, showed their new loyalty by providing him with his personal bodyguard. They also manned his principal weapons factory, their swordsmiths producing blades of damascened steel that only Toledo could equal, their carpenters constructing those vast engines of war – catapults, trebuchets, mangonels and the like – without which effective siege operations were impossible. Meanwhile, their women provided the Emperor with his harem: the Saracen dancing-girls who lived in considerable luxury in a wing of the palace, with their own staff of female servants and a body of eunuchs to see that they came to no harm. A number of these girls would

accompany the Emperor on his constant travels, and although it was always maintained that they existed only to provide innocent entertainment for the imperial court there can be little doubt – as Gibbon remarks on the similar establishment kept by the Emperor Gordian – that they were in fact intended for use rather than ostentation.

At the time of his imperial coronation in November 1220, Frederick had confirmed to Pope Honorius the promise that he had made after his coronation as King of the Romans: that he would personally lead a new Crusade to Palestine, to recover the Holy Places for Christendom. He could hardly have reneged upon it; yet the confirmation remains surprising, since an expedition gathered by the Pope from various sources had in fact sailed for the east some two years before. It had initially been led by the sixty-eight-year-old John of Brienne, titular King of Jerusalem, but on the arrival – four months late – of the papal contingent under the Spanish Cardinal Pelagius of St Lucia, Pelagius had insisted on assuming the overall command.

This so-called Fifth Crusade[1] had had as its object the capture of the Egyptian city of Damietta, which it was hoped to exchange later for the Holy City itself. The siege of Damietta had been a good deal harder than expected. It lasted in all for seventeen months, and just before its end the Egyptian Sultan al-Kamil in desperation offered the whole Kingdom of Jerusalem west of the Jordan in return for the Crusaders' departure; idiotically, as it turned out, this offer was refused by Cardinal Pelagius, who was determined to conquer Cairo and the whole of Egypt. Damietta duly fell on 5 November 1219, but the war dragged on for nearly two more years, and would have continued even longer had not the Crusading army been trapped by Nile floods – from which it extricated itself only by surrender. The Crusade, so nearly a success, proved a disaster, thanks entirely to the pigheadedness of its leader.

With its failure, the Emperor found himself under still greater pressure to initiate another – and also to take another wife. The Empress Constance had died in June 1221, and a year later the Grand Master of the Teutonic Knights, Hermann of Salza, Duke of Swabia, arrived from the Pope with a proposal that Frederick should now marry Yolande de Brienne, the hereditary Queen of Jerusalem, now twelve years old.[2] Her title came from her mother, Maria, the

---

[1] The Albigensian Crusade (Chapter VII, p. 133.)
[2] She is also known as Isabella; in this book, however, she will be Yolande, if only to prevent confusion with Frederick's third wife, Isabella of England.

granddaughter of King Amalric I, who at the age of seventeen had married the sexagenarian John of Brienne. John had promptly assumed the title of king. After his wife's early death a year or two later his claim to it was clearly questionable, but he had continued to govern the country as regent for his little daughter Yolande – and, as we have seen, had led the disastrous Fifth Crusade.

Frederick was not at first enthusiastic. His proposed bride was penniless, and little more than a child; he was more than twice her age. As for her title, few were emptier: Jerusalem had now been in Saracen hands for half a century. There was, on the other hand, at least one strong argument in favour of the idea. The kingship, purely titular as it might be, would greatly strengthen his claim to the city when he eventually left on his long-postponed Crusade. And so, after some deliberation, he agreed to the match. He agreed too, in the course of further discussions with the Pope, that his Crusade – to which the marriage was indissolubly linked – would set out on Ascension Day, 15 August 1227; any further delay, Honorius made clear, would result in his excommunication.

It was in August 1225 that fourteen galleys of the imperial fleet arrived in Acre – the last surviving outpost of Crusader Outremer – to conduct Yolande to Sicily. Even before her departure she was married to the Emperor by proxy; next, at Tyre, being now deemed to have come of age, she received her coronation as Queen of Jerusalem. Only then did she embark on the journey which was to take her to a new life, accompanied by a suite which included a female cousin several years her senior. Frederick, together with her father, was waiting for her at Brindisi, where a second marriage took place in the cathedral on 9 November. It was, alas, ill-fated. On the following day the Emperor left the city with his bride and without previously warning his father-in-law; by the time John caught up with them he was informed by his tearful daughter that her husband had already seduced her cousin. When Frederick and Yolande reached Palermo the poor girl was immediately packed off to his harem. Her father, meanwhile, had been coldly informed that he was no longer regent. Still less did he have any further right to the title of king.[1]

---

[1] Even then, however, his career was not over. In 1224, when he was in his middle seventies, he became regent once again – in the Latin Empire of Constantinople, where the child Emperor Baldwin II had married John's four-year-old daughter Maria. This time the old ruffian assumed the title of emperor rather than king – a title which he was to retain until his death in 1237.

Whether John's fury was principally due to the Emperor's treatment of his daughter or to the loss of his titular kingdom is not clear; at any rate, he went at once to Rome, where Pope Honorius predictably took his side and refused to recognise Frederick's assumption of the royal title. This could hardly have failed to exacerbate the strain in imperial–papal relations, already at an abysmal level owing to Frederick's continued dilatoriness over the long-delayed Crusade – originally promised eleven years before – and to his refusal to acknowledge the Pope's authority over north and central Italy. The quarrel took a further downward plunge when Honorius died in 1227 and was succeeded by Cardinal Hugo of Ostia, who took the name of Gregory IX.[1] Already an old man, Gregory started as he meant to go on. 'Take heed,' he wrote to Frederick soon after his accession, 'that you do not place your intellect, which you have in common with the angels, below your senses, which you have in common with brutes and plants.' To the Emperor, whose debauches were rapidly becoming legendary, it was an effective shot across the bows.

By this time the Crusade was gathering its forces. A constant stream of young German knights was crossing the Alps and pouring down the pilgrim roads of Italy to join the Emperor in Apulia, where the army was to take ship for the Holy Land. But then, in the savage heat of an Apulian August, an epidemic broke out. It may have been typhoid; it may have been cholera; but it swept relentlessly through the Crusader camps. Frederick had taken the now pregnant Yolande first to Otranto and then to the little offshore island of Sant' Andrea for safety, but now he too succumbed to the dread virus. So too did the Landgrave of Thuringia, who had brought with him several hundred cavalry. The two sick men embarked nonetheless and sailed from Brindisi in September, but a day or two later the Landgrave was dead, and Frederick realised that he himself was too ill to continue. He sent the surviving Crusaders ahead, with instructions to make what preparations they could; he himself would follow when sufficiently recovered, at the latest by May 1228. Ambassadors were simultaneously despatched to Rome, to explain the situation to the Pope.

Gregory, however, refused to receive them. Instead, in a blistering encyclical, he accused the Emperor of having blatantly disregarded his Crusading vows. Had he not, after repeated postponements, himself set

---

[1] This was already an ominous sign: it was Gregory VII – the formidable Cardinal Hildebrand – who had brought Frederick's great-great-great-uncle Henry IV to his knees at Canossa exactly 150 years before.

a new date for his departure? Had he not agreed to his own excommunication if he did not fulfil his pledge? Had he not foreseen that, with thousands of soldiers and pilgrims crowded together in the summer heat, an epidemic was inevitable? Had he not therefore been responsible for that epidemic, and for all the consequent deaths that it had caused, including that of the Landgrave? And who was to say that he himself had really contracted the disease? Was this not just a further attempt to wriggle out of his obligations? On 29 September he declared Frederick excommunicate.

In doing so, however, he created for himself a new problem. It was self-evident that excommunicates could not lead Crusades, and as the weeks passed it became increasingly clear that this was precisely what Frederick intended to do. Another awkward fact, too, was beginning to emerge: the Pope had badly overplayed his hand. Frederick had replied with an open letter addressed to all those who had taken the Cross, explaining his position quietly and reasonably, appealing for under- standing and conciliation – setting, in short, an example to the Holy Father of the tone which he would have been well advised to adopt himself. The letter had its effect. When, on Easter Sunday 1228, Pope Gregory launched into a furious sermon against the Emperor, his Roman congregation rioted; hounded from the city, he was obliged to seek refuge in Viterbo. From there he continued his campaign, but whereas only a few months before he had been urgently calling Frederick to leave on the Crusade, he was now in the ludicrous position of preaching equally urgently against it, knowing as he did that were the Emperor to return victorious, papal prestige would sustain a blow from which it would take long indeed to recover.

On Wednesday, 28 June 1228, the Emperor Frederick II sailed from Brindisi with a fleet of about sixty ships, bound for Palestine. He was now fully restored to health, but his relations with Pope Gregory had not sustained a similar improvement; indeed, on discovering that he really was preparing for departure, the Pope had fired off another excommunication on 23 March. (Yet another was to follow on 30 August.) Frederick, meanwhile, had once again become a father. Two months earlier, the sixteen-year-old Yolande had given birth to a boy, Conrad, only to die of puerperal fever a few days later. Poor girl: she had never wanted to be Empress, and had wept copiously when she had had to leave Palestine. Intellectually she had nothing to offer to her dazzling polymath of a husband, and he in turn had shown little enough consideration for her, at least until he knew that she was carrying his child. She seems to have spent the thirty sad months of her marriage pining for Outremer; would Frederick have allowed her to accompany him there, had she lived? Did he grieve for her at all? We shall never know. His mind was probably more occupied with the fact that her death had seriously weakened his claim to the Kingdom of Jerusalem, for he was now in precisely the same position as old John of Brienne: if, as he had so stoutly maintained, John had held the title only as a consort of the rightful queen, then so had he; with her death it should properly pass to her son, the baby Conrad.

Conrad, however, was hardly likely to question his father's claim in the foreseeable future, and the Emperor had more pressing diplomatic problems to consider. Saladin's empire was at that time controlled by three brothers of his own tribe, the house of Ayub: al-Kamil, Sultan of Egypt; al-Ashraf, generally known as the Sultan of Babylon, with his seat in Baghdad; and al-Mu'azzam, governor of Damascus, with direct authority over Jerusalem and the Holy Land. Al-Mu'azzam, who suspected (with good reason) that his brothers were planning to unite against him, had recently allied himself with the Khwarazmian Turks and besieged al-Ashraf in his capital; al-Kamil in Cairo, fearing that he might be next on the list, had secretly appealed to Frederick: if the Emperor would drive al-Mu'azzam from Damascus, he himself would be in a position to restore to him the lost territory of the Kingdom of Jerusalem. Frederick had replied sympathetically; it was obviously in his interest to encourage as much division as possible in the Muslim east, and as one who had spent his youth in a partially Muslim environment, understanding the Arab mentality and speaking the Arabic language, he was in an excellent position to do so. Just as he was leaving on the Crusade, however, word reached him of al-Mu'azzam's death; it looked in consequence as though al-Kamil's enthusiasm for an alliance was likely to fade.

A little over three weeks later, on 21 July, the imperial fleet dropped anchor in the harbour of Limassol in Cyprus. Richard Coeur-de-Lion, having captured it in 1191, had subsequently tried to sell it to the Knights Templar, but on finding that they could not pay for it had passed it on to Guy of Lusignan, the dispossessed King of Jerusalem.[1] Guy had founded a feudal monarchy which – surprisingly perhaps – was to last until the end of the Middle Ages. Technically, there can be

---

[1] See Chapter VII, p. 131.

little doubt that this monarchy was a fief of the Holy Roman Empire: Guy's brother and successor, Almeric, had done homage for it to Frederick's father Henry VI. But there were complications, among them the fact that the present king was a minor and that the effective regent, John of Ibelin, was also Lord of Beirut and one of the richest and most powerful magnates of Outremer. Several other members of the Cypriot nobility also possessed considerable estates in Palestine and Syria, and it was important that they should not be antagonised.

Frederick, however, could hardly have handled them worse. At first he was all kindness and consideration, inviting John of Ibelin with the young King and the local lords and barons to a great banquet in the castle of Limassol. It began quietly enough, then suddenly a body of soldiers with drawn swords entered the hall and took up positions round the walls. In the hush that followed, the Emperor rose to his feet and, in a voice of thunder, informed John of Ibelin that he required two things of him. John replied that he would happily comply, so long as he deemed it right. Frederick then demanded, first, the city of Beirut, to which he claimed that John had no title, and second, all the revenues of Cyprus received since the accession of the young King. These demands were unreasonable enough; the arrogance with which they were pronounced, the obvious attempts at intimidation while all concerned were – or should have been – protected by the laws of common hospitality, made the effect far, far worse. John replied, giving as good as he got. He held Beirut from the King of Jerusalem. It had no connection with Cyprus; though he readily acknowledged the Emperor's authority over the island, he could not admit similar suzerainty over Syria and Palestine. As for the Cyprus revenues, they were regularly and correctly handed over to the King's mother, Queen Alice, in her capacity as regent.

Frederick was angry, but he did not insist. The legal position where the mainland was concerned was indeed far from clear. The Kingdom of Jerusalem had been seriously truncated – one might almost say decapitated – by Saladin's conquest of the Holy City, and had been further weakened by a series of disastrous minorities; several of the barons, including the Ibelin family, were now considerably richer and more powerful than their king and very often acted accordingly. He could not afford to get involved too deeply in such matters. Besides, he was in a hurry. He was well aware that the Pope had his eye on the Sicilian Kingdom, and that if he were to prolong his stay in the east an invasion would not be long in coming. His only hope was to move fast, strike his blow and return home as soon as possible. He therefore had no choice but to continue his journey – taking the young King of Cyprus with him.

He landed in Tyre towards the end of 1228. Impressive detachments of Templars and Hospitallers were there to greet him, still further swelling the ranks of what was already a considerable army; but Frederick had no intention of fighting if his purposes could be achieved by peaceful diplomacy. An embassy was despatched to Sultan al-Kamil, who was gradually gaining possession of his dead brother's lands and deeply regretting his former offer. It pointed out that the Emperor had come only on the Sultan's invitation, but that the world now knew that he was here; how then could he leave empty-handed? The resulting loss of prestige might well prove fatal, and al-Kamil would never be able to find himself another Christian ally. As for Jerusalem, it was nowadays a relatively insignificant city, defenceless and largely depopulated, even from the religious point of view far less important to Islam than it was to Christendom. Would its surrender not be a small price to pay for peaceful relations between Muslim and Christian – and, incidentally, for his own immediate departure?

There were no threats – none, at least, outwardly expressed. But the imperial army was on the spot, and its strength was considerable. The Sultan was in an impossible position. The Emperor was there on his very doorstep, waiting to collect what had been promised and unlikely to leave until he had got it. Meanwhile, the situation in Syria, where al-Kamil's continued attempts to capture Damascus were having no effect, was once again causing him increasing alarm. Perhaps an alliance would be no bad thing after all. Finally the Sultan capitulated, agreeing to a ten-year treaty – on certain conditions. First, Jerusalem must remain undefended. The Temple Mount, with the Dome of the Rock and the al-Aqsa Mosque opposite it, might be visited by Christians but must remain in Muslim hands, together with Hebron. The Christians could have their other principal shrines of Bethlehem and Nazareth, on the understanding that they would be linked to the Christian cities of the coast only by a narrow corridor running through what would continue to be Muslim territory.

On Saturday, 17 March 1229, Frederick – still under sentence of excommunication – entered Jerusalem and formally took possession of the city. On the following day, in open defiance of the papal ban, he attended Mass in the Church of the Holy Sepulchre, deliberately wearing his imperial crown. He had effectively achieved everything he had set out to achieve, and had done so without the shedding of a drop of Christian – or Muslim – blood. Among the Christian community, a degree of rejoicing might have been expected; instead, the reaction was one of fury. Frederick, while still under the ban of the Church, had dared to set foot in the most sacred shrine of Christendom, which he had won with the collusion of the Sultan of Egypt. The Patriarch of Jerusalem, who had studiously ignored the Emperor ever since his arrival, now showed his displeasure by putting the entire city under an interdict. Church services were forbidden; pilgrims visiting the Holy Places could no longer count on the remission of their sins. The local barons were outraged that they had not been consulted, and more furious still when they found that the newly restored lands in Galilee were being mostly bestowed on the Teutonic Knights[1] in the Emperor's suite, rather than on their traditional family owners. How anyway, they asked themselves, were they expected to retain all these territories that Frederick had so dubiously acquired, once the imperial army had returned to the west?

The last straw, to priests and laymen alike, was the Emperor's obvious interest in – and admiration for – both the Muslim faith and Islamic civilisation as a whole. He insisted, for example, on visiting the Dome of the Rock – of whose architecture he made a detailed study[2] – and the al-Aqsa Mosque, where he is said to have expressed bitter disappointment at not having heard the call to prayer. (The Sultan had ordered the muezzins to be silent as a sign of respect.) As always, he questioned every educated Muslim he met – about his faith, his calling, his way of life or anything else that occurred to him. To the Christians of Outremer, such an attitude was profoundly shocking; even the Emperor's fluent Arabic was held against him. With every day that he remained in Jerusalem his unpopularity grew, and when he moved on to Acre – narrowly escaping an ambush by the Templars on the way – he found it on the verge of open rebellion.

By this time he too was in a dangerous mood, shocked by the apparent ingratitude of his fellow Christians and ready to give as good as he got. He ordered his troops to surround Acre, allowing no one to enter or leave. Churchmen who preached sermons against him were

---

[1] Of the three great military orders – Templars, Hospitallers and Teutonic Knights – the last was the most recent, having been instituted only at the time of the Third Crusade. It too began with a hospital in the Holy Land, but from about 1230 onwards it was involved principally with the conquest of Prussia and the Baltic territories.

[2] It has been plausibly suggested that its octagonal shape may have been the model for Frederick's magnificent hunting lodge, Castel del Monte in Apulia.

bastinadoed. Nor was his temper improved by reports of the invasion of his Italian realm by a papal army under old John of Brienne – yet another reason to leave this ungrateful land as soon as possible. He ordered his fleet to be made ready to sail on 1 May. Soon after dawn on that day, as he passed through the butchers' quarter to the waiting ships, he was pelted with offal. Only with some difficulty did John of Ibelin, who had come down to the quayside to bid him farewell, manage to restore order.

Stopping only very briefly in Cyprus, the Emperor reached Brindisi on 10 June. He found his kingdom in a state of helpless confusion. His old enemy Gregory IX had taken advantage of his absence to launch what almost amounted to a Crusade against him, writing to the princes and churches of Western Europe demanding men and money for an all-out attack on Frederick's position both in Germany and in Italy. In Germany the Pope's attempts to establish a rival Emperor in the person of Otto of Brunswick had had little effect. In Italy, on the other hand, he had organised an armed invasion with the object of driving Frederick out of the south once and for all, so that the whole territory could be ruled directly from Rome. Furious fighting was at that moment in progress in the Abruzzi and around Capua, while several cities of Apulia, believing the rumours – deliberately circulated by papal agents – of Frederick's death, were in open revolt. To encourage others to follow their example, Gregory had recently published an edict releasing all the Emperor's subjects from their oaths of allegiance.

The situation could hardly have been more serious, yet from the moment of Frederick's arrival the tide began to turn. Here was the Emperor, once again among his people, not dead but triumphant, having recovered without bloodshed the Holy Places for Christendom. His achievement may not have impressed the Christian communities of Outremer, but to the people of south Italy and Sicily it appeared in a very different light. Moreover, with his return to his kingdom, Frederick himself instantly became a changed man. Gone were the anger, the bluster, the insecurity, the lack of understanding; he was back now in a land he knew, and deeply loved; once again, he was in control. All that summer he spent tirelessly on campaign, and by the end of October the papal army was broken.

Gregory IX, however, was not, and the final reconciliation between the two was a long, difficult and painful process. In the months that followed Frederick made concession after concession, knowing as he did that the obstinate old Pope still retained his most damaging weapon. He was still excommunicated: a serious embarrassment, a permanent reproach and a potentially dangerous diplomatic liability. As a Christian, too – insofar as he was one – Frederick would have had no wish to die under the ban of the Church. But still Gregory prevaricated; it was not until July 1230 that, very reluctantly, he agreed to a peace treaty – signed at Ceprano at the end of August – and lifted his sentence. Two months later still, the two men dined together in the papal palace at Anagni. The dinner, one feels, must have been far from convivial, at least at first; but Frederick was capable of enormous charm when he wanted to use it, and the Pope seems to have been genuinely gratified that the Holy Roman Emperor should have taken the trouble to visit him, informally and without pomp. So ended yet another of those Herculean struggles between Emperor and Pope on which the history of medieval Europe so frequently seems to turn.

In 1231 Frederick was in a position to promulgate what came to be known as the Constitutions of Melfi – no less than a complete new codification of the law on a scale unattempted since the days of Justinian seven centuries before. The Emperor took full control of criminal justice, instituted a body of itinerant judges acting in his name, curtailed the liberties of the barons, the clergy and the towns, and laid the foundations of a system of firm government paralleled only in England, with similar representation of nobility, churchmen and citizens.

The truth was that, of all his dominions, the Regno (as the Kingdom of Sicily was generally known) was the least troublesome. He had been born there; he knew every inch of it; he understood its people. Things were very different in the two other great regions subject to his rule, north Italy and Germany, in which imperial power – having no solid basis of the kind which England and France, with their firmly hereditary monarchies, were rapidly building up – had declined dramatically over the previous hundred years. In north Italy in particular, the great Lombard cities and towns had been a perennial thorn in the flesh to successive Emperors – none of whom had suffered more than Frederick's own grandfather, Barbarossa, soundly defeated at Legnano little more than half a century before. To maintain their independence, their most successful policy had always been to play Pope and Emperor off against each other; news of the reconciliation of 1230 had consequently filled them with dismay. The Lombard League had been hastily revived, its members closing ranks against the coming danger.

They had been right to do so. Had Frederick been willing to divide his empire, allotting Germany to himself and entrusting Sicily to his son Henry – or even vice versa – north Italy might have been left to its own devices, but that was not his way. Determined as he was to rule both territories himself, he knew that a safe overland route between them was essential. And there was another reason too. For him, Italy was more important than Germany would ever be. This was after all the Holy Roman Empire, not the Holy German. Its capital belonged in Rome – and to Rome, one day, he hoped to transfer it.

As a first step towards this objective, the Emperor summoned his son Henry, all the principal German princes and the representatives of the great cities of north Italy to a council, to be held in Ravenna on All Saints' Day, 1 November 1231. He did everything he could to allay Lombard fears. He undertook to bring no military escort, only a small personal suite; the proceedings would be dedicated to 'the honour of God, the Church and the Empire, and the prosperity of Lombardy'. Doubtless he meant every word, but for the Lombard leaders the alarm signal was unmistakable. They did not want him; still less did they want a horde of truculent German barons. Instantly, they closed the Alpine passes. The measure was not entirely successful – a good many of the delegates managed to circumvent the blockade and make their way round by an eastern route through Friuli – but it delayed the conference by a good two months.

For all that, the delegates celebrated Christmas with a round of elaborate festivities and displays, including special exhibitions of the Emperor's famous menagerie, which accompanied him on all his travels and which included not only his unrivalled collection of falcons but lions, panthers, camels, apes and monkeys and even an elephant – whose effect on the local peasantry is not easy to imagine. Frederick was always good at putting on a show; he was conscious, however, that one delegate remained absent, and that delegate the most important of all: his son Henry, King of the Romans. Henry had sent no message of explanation – let alone of apology – and it soon became clear that he had made no effort to answer his father's summons.

The cause may well have been sheer embarrassment. This is not the place to discuss the imperial administration in Germany. Suffice it to say that Henry had been left by his father as titular sovereign at the age of eight; in consequence, when he came of age at eighteen, he felt little affection or loyalty towards a father of whom he had only vague childhood recollections. By adopting towards the German princes a confrontational policy diametrically opposite to that followed by Frederick he had already succeeded in dangerously antagonising them, and when matters came to a head in 1231 they had extracted from him a whole series of rights and privileges, thus seriously weakening imperial power in Germany.

Furious, Frederick called another council for the following summer in Aquileia, making it clear that his son would ignore the summons at his peril. This time Henry dared not disobey, and was forced to swear an oath that he would henceforth defend the rights and standing of the Emperor, dismissing those counsellors who had encouraged him in his disastrous policies. But if Frederick thought that with a submissive son and well-disposed princes he could subdue Lombardy, he was wrong. Most of the last nineteen years of his life were to be spent in warfare up and down the Italian peninsula, striving, as his grandfather had striven before him, to establish his authority. There was, however, an important difference between them. Frederick Barbarossa had been a German through and through; his empire was a German empire. For Frederick II, Italy always came first; despite the occasional temporary reconciliation this guaranteed the hostility of the Pope, uncomfortably squeezed as he was between the two nominally imperial territories, Lombardy and the Regno.

Over those last years, many of the leading characters would be replaced. Henry, King of the Romans, after further acts of disobedience, was dethroned in 1235 and was succeeded two years later by his half-brother Conrad. (That same year Frederick himself remarried, taking as his third wife Isabella, sister of King Henry III of England.) Pope Gregory, having excommunicated Frederick yet again in 1239, died in 1241. If his successor – the hopeless old Celestine IV – had lived, Frederick's worries might have been almost at an end, but after just seventeen days Celestine had followed Gregory to the grave. For the next year and a half the Emperor, while simultaneously preparing a huge fleet to sail against Genoa and Venice, did everything he could to influence the next election, but in vain; the Genoese Cardinal Sinibaldo dei Fieschi, who in June 1243 became Pope Innocent IV, proved if anything an even more determined adversary than Gregory had been. Only two years after his accession, at a General Council in Lyons, he declared the already excommunicated Frederick deposed, stripping him of all his dignities and titles.

But Emperors could not be thrown out so easily. The Hohenstaufen name retained immense prestige in Germany, while in the Regno Frederick's endless peregrinations had ensured him a consistently high profile, to the point where he seemed omnipresent, part of life itself. Loftily ignoring the papal pronouncement, he continued the struggle; it was still in progress when in December 1250 he was seized by a sudden violent attack of dysentery at Castel Fiorentino in Apulia. He died a few days later on Tuesday, 13 December, just thirteen days short of his fifty-sixth birthday. Inevitably there were rumours of poison, but no real evidence has ever been put forward. His body was taken to Palermo where, at his request, it was buried in the cathedral, in the magnificent porphyry sarcophagus that had been prepared for his grandfather Roger II at his own foundation of Cefalù but had till then remained unoccupied.

As his heir in Germany and the Regno Frederick had named Conrad, son of Yolande of Jerusalem, and during Conrad's absence in Germany he had entrusted the government of Italy and Sicily to Manfred, the favourite of his eleven illegitimate children. Manfred proved a worthy scion of his father. He recreated Frederick's brilliant court, founded the Apulian port of Manfredonia and married his own daughter Helena to Michael II, Despot of Epirus, an alliance which gained him the island of Corfu and a considerable stretch of the Albanian coast, including the historic city and port of Durazzo. Another daughter, Constance, became the wife of Peter, heir to the throne of Aragon (the second Constance of Aragon to rate a mention in this chapter).

Even after his half-brother Conrad died in 1254, Manfred did not – to the Pope's inexpressible relief – seek authority over northern or central Italy; nevertheless, his increasing power in the south could not but reawaken anxieties in Rome, and these became greater still when, in August 1258, he prevailed upon the Sicilian baronage to proclaim him king. Ever since Frederick's theoretical deposition in 1245, Pope Innocent had been seeking an 'athlete of Christ' who would rid south Italy once and for all of the house of Hohenstaufen and lead the army of the Church to victory in the peninsula. Richard Earl of Cornwall, the brother of King Henry III and the richest man in England – he had been elected King of the Romans in 1257 – had at one moment seemed a possibility, but Innocent had been unable to persuade him to take up the challenge. The Pope was still trying to find a suitable candidate when he died in 1261, to be succeeded by Urban IV, the first

Frenchman to occupy the papal throne. Urban's eye soon fell on a compatriot, Charles of Anjou.

The brother of King Louis IX, Charles was now thirty-five. In 1246 he had acquired through his wife the county of Provence, which had brought him untold wealth; he was also lord, *inter alia*, of the thriving port of Marseille. To this cold, cruel and vastly ambitious opportunist the Pope was now offering a chance not to be missed. The army which Charles was to lead against Manfred, and which began to assemble in north Italy in the autumn of 1265, was to be officially designated a Crusade – which meant that it would be as always something of a ragbag, with the usual admixture of adventurers hoping to secure fiefdoms in south Italy, pilgrims seeking the remission of their sins and ruffians simply out for plunder. With them, however, was an impressive number of knights from all over western Europe – French, German, Spanish, Italian and Provençal, with even a few Englishmen thrown in for good measure – who, Charles firmly believed, would be more than a match for anything that Manfred could fling against them.

On 6 January 1266 Pope Urban crowned Charles of Anjou with the crown of Sicily; less than a month afterwards, on 3 February, Charles's army crossed the frontier into the Regno. This time there was to be no long campaign. The two armies met on the 26th outside the old Roman city of Benevento, and it was all over quite quickly. Manfred, courageous as always, stood his ground and went down fighting, but his troops, hopelessly outnumbered, soon fled from the field. The battle had been decisive: the Crusade was over. And so – or very nearly – was the house of Hohenstaufen. Two years later King Conrad's son Conrad IV – better known as Conradin – and Prince Henry of Castile made a last desperate attempt to save the situation, leading an army of Germans, Italians and Spaniards into the Regno. Charles hurried up and met them at the border village of Tagliacozzo. This time the battle, which was fought on 23 August 1268, proved a good deal harder, resulting in hideous slaughter on both sides; eventually the Angevins once again won the day. Conradin escaped from the field, but was captured soon afterwards. There followed a show trial in Naples after which, on 29 October, the young prince – he was just sixteen – and several of his companions were taken down to the marketplace and beheaded on the spot.

Manfred and Conradin were both, in their own different ways, heroes. It was hardly their fault that they were overshadowed by their father and grandfather; so, after all, was much of the known world.

Fluency in six languages was an even rarer accomplishment in the thirteenth century than it is today; in addition, Frederick was a sensitive lyric poet at whose court the sonnet was invented,[1] a generous patron of the arts, a skilled general, a subtle statesman and the greatest naturalist of his time. A passionate intellectual curiosity gave him a more than passing knowledge of philosophy and astronomy, geometry and algebra, medicine and the physical sciences. Not the least remarkable of his qualities was his talent for showmanship. His force of character alone, the sheer dazzle of his personality, would always have ensured that he impressed himself on everyone with whom he came in contact, but he deliberately built up his image still further: with that extraordinary menagerie, with his personal regiment of Saracens, even with his harem. These last two attributes were regularly held against him by his enemies, but they too carried a clear message: the Emperor was not as other men. He was a giant, a demigod, to whom the accepted rules of conduct did not apply.

In a word, he had style – and style has always been, as it still is today, a speciality of the Italians. Frederick was probably one of the first men – and in all history there have been surprisingly few – to have had a foot in both worlds, the Italian and the German, and to feel equally at ease on either side of the Alps; but his heart remained in Italy where he spent most of his life, and it is as an Italian that he finds his place in this book. Culturally, he gave the country much. Had the Provençal troubadours, fleeing from the horrors of the Albigensian Crusade, not found a warm welcome at the court of Palermo and fired the local poets with their ideals of courtly love, Italian literature might have taken a diametrically different course and the *Divine Comedy* might never have been written. In the field of architecture, too, he was an innovator. The immense fortified gateway to his frontier city of Capua, built to defend its bridge across the Vulturno river and designed by the Emperor himself, no longer stands; but much of its sculpture is preserved in the local museum, from which it is clear that the Emperor drew liberally on the decorative language of ancient Rome, pre-echoing the Renaissance well over a century before its time. Classical pediments and pilasters appear even more remarkably in his magnificent hunting-box of Castel del Monte, a vast turreted octagon in limestone crowning a remote Apulian hilltop. But perhaps we are wrong to be surprised. Frederick

---

[1] Most probably by the Sicilian Giacomo da Lentini, at least twenty-five of whose sonnets have come down to us.

was after all a Roman Emperor, and he was determined that we should not forget it.

Politically, on the other hand, he was a failure. His dream had been to make Italy and Sicily a united kingdom within the Empire, with its capital at Rome; the overriding purpose of the Papacy, aided by the cities and towns of Lombardy, was to ensure that that dream should never be realised. It was unfortunate for the Emperor that he should have had to contend with two such able and determined men as Gregory and Innocent, but in the long run the struggle could have had no other outcome. The Empire, even in Germany, had lost its strength and cohesion; no longer could the loyalty of the German princes be relied upon, or even their deep concern. As for north and central Italy, the Lombard cities would never again submit to imperial bluster. Had Frederick only accepted this fact, the threat to the Papacy would have been removed and his beloved Regno might well have been preserved. Alas, he rejected it, and in doing so he not only lost Italy; he signed the death-warrant of his dynasty.

CHAPTER X

The End of Outremer

No two contemporary European rulers have been more different than the Emperor Frederick II and King Louis IX of France. Frederick was an intellectual and a free-thinker. He had little respect for religion; indeed, he spent a good deal of his life under the ban of the Church. He could, on occasion, take a strong line with heretics, particularly if they threatened the peace or security of the Empire; at the same time, having been raised in the court of Palermo among Arabs and Greeks, he had a deep respect and understanding both of Islam and of eastern Orthodoxy, and liked nothing better than to discuss the finer points of theology with scholars of the two faiths. As a statesman he was by no means without principle, but he was also a pragmatist, and he knew full well that if he and his empire were to survive he simply could not afford too delicate a conscience. In appearance he had never been handsome: broad and stocky, with thin reddish hair. Physically he was hard as nails.

King Louis IX, on the other hand, was a saint and looked it. A contemporary friar who saw him just before he left for the Holy Land describes him as 'thin, slender, lean and tall, with an angelic countenance and a gracious person'. At times his face beneath his fair hair was disfigured by angry-looking patches caused by the erysipelas to which he remained a martyr all his life; nevertheless, goodness seemed to shine out of him. 'Few human beings,' writes Sir Steven Runciman, 'have ever been so consciously and sincerely virtuous.' Yet, strangely enough, there was no trace of sanctimoniousness; on the contrary, Louis was energetic, brave in battle, when necessary stern and uncompromising. He spent much of his waking life in prayer, often prone on the ground and forgetting himself so completely as to emerge in a daze, uncertain where he was; but, as he himself confessed, he had no tears 'to water the aridity in his heart'. This may have been one reason for his regular physical mortification with fasts, scourges and hair shirts, and his personal tending of the sick – particularly those with seriously unpleasant diseases. As for sin, he could hardly bear to contemplate its existence. To the heretic and the infidel, however, he was pitiless; never could he have bloodlessly regained the Holy Places, as Frederick did so stylishly.

Desperately ill with malaria at the end of 1244, the thirty-year-old King Louis vowed that if he lived he would lead a Crusade. As always he was as good as his word, and immediately on his recovery he began his preparations. They took three years, but on 25 August 1248, leaving his mother Blanche of Castile[1] as regent, he set sail from the specially constructed port of Aigues-Mortes accompanied by his wife, Margaret of Provence,[2] and two of his three brothers, Robert of Artois and Charles of Anjou. On 18 September they landed at Limassol in Cyprus, the appointed rendezvous for the Crusading army, and Louis settled down to plan his campaign. Despite the disaster of the Fifth Crusade it had been generally agreed that the objective should once again be Egypt, the richest and at the same time the most exposed province of Saladin's empire. Unfortunately the year was already too far advanced for operations to be started at once – the hidden sand-banks in the approaches to the Nile delta could be negotiated only in calm weather – so the King was reluctantly persuaded to winter on the island. With the coming of spring there arose another difficulty: an acute shortage of ships. Louis had relied on the Italian maritime republics to furnish the number necessary, but when the moment came Pisa and Genoa were at war and in need of all the vessels they could get, while the Venetians – who disapproved of the whole Crusade – simply refused. Not until the end of May 1249 could the King muster the necessary transport, and even then the first part of the fleet to sail was scattered by a violent storm and was obliged to limp back to Limassol.

After that the situation improved, and at dawn on 5 June, in the teeth of heavy opposition, the Crusaders landed on the sands to the west of the delta. The fighting was long and fierce, but the superior discipline of the French knights won the day; as night fell the Egyptian army withdrew over the permanent bridge of boats to Damietta. On its arrival the order was given for a general evacuation, and all the Muslims obeyed. The Christian Copts who remained sent word that resistance was at an end, and the Crusaders marched triumphantly over the bridge – which had unaccountably remained intact – and into the city. All this made a refreshing contrast to the Fifth Crusade, which had achieved a similar result only after a seventeen-month siege. As in 1219, the great mosque was converted into a cathedral; the three military

---

[1] She was the granddaughter of Henry II of England, whose daughter Eleanor had married Alfonso IX of Castile. She had already acted as regent during her son's minority, when she had given ample proof of her statesmanship.
[2] Her sister Eleanor was married to the English King Henry III.

orders – Templars, Hospitallers and Teutonic Knights – were installed in suitable accommodation; the Genoese, Pisans and – rather more surprisingly – the Venetians were each allotted a street and a market; and Damietta became, briefly, the effective capital of Outremer.

All too soon, however, the cracks began to show. The annual flooding of the Nile was imminent. Mindful of the experience of the Fifth Crusade, Louis was determined not to advance until the waters subsided, which in turn meant his army having to sweat it out in forced inactivity through the grilling heat of the delta summer. Food supplies began to run short; dysentery and malaria made their appearance in the Crusader camp. Like his father before him, the Egyptian Sultan al-Ayub – who was himself dying of tuberculosis – proposed from his sick-bed an exchange of Damietta for Jerusalem, but his offer was rejected out of hand: King Louis refused to treat with an infidel. Instead, when the Nile went down at the end of October, he gave orders to march on Cairo.

His army had advanced about a third of the way to the capital when it found itself confronted by the Saracen army at Mansurah, a town built only a few years before by the Sultan al-Kamil on the site of his victory over the Fifth Crusade. Then came catastrophe – a catastrophe which was exclusively the fault of Count Robert of Artois. Defying his brother's strict instructions not to attack until he was ordered to do so, and followed only by the Templars and a small contingent from England, he charged into the Egyptian camp where he took its occupants by surprise, slaughtering a good many and putting the rest to flight. Had he halted there all might have been well, but the camp was about two miles outside Mansurah itself, and in his exhilaration Robert galloped on into the city. This time the Egyptians were ready for him. The gates were wide open, and he and his followers found their way clear right up to the walls of the citadel. Only then did the defenders appear, pouring in on them from the side streets. The gates clanged shut, and the result was a massacre. Robert himself was killed, with most of his knights, and so were virtually all the English; of the 290 Templar knights, only five survived.

This disaster did not quite mark the end of the Crusade. Not until the beginning of April 1250 – by which time dysentery and typhoid were doing far more damage than the Egyptians to his men – did Louis decide to return. Now it was he who proposed the exchange of Damietta for Jerusalem, but the Sultan Turanshah – who had succeeded his father al-Ayub some three months before – was not interested. For those still able to ride or walk, the journey back was a nightmare. The King's own conduct was beyond praise, especially as he too was now seriously ill. At last the commander of his bodyguard, seeing that he could go no further, took him into a nearby house; but he was soon found, captured and taken in chains to Mansurah, where he slowly recovered. His knights and soldiers surrendered en masse and were led away into captivity, but they, alas, were not so lucky. Seeing that they were far too many to be effectively guarded, the Egyptians soon executed all those too weak to march; the remainder they beheaded in the course of the following week, at the rate of 300 a day. They spared only the leading barons – in the hope, it need hardly be said, of a good ransom.

And they got one. As well as the return of Damietta itself, which paid for the freedom of the King, it was agreed that the Egyptians should receive the enormous sum of half a million *livres tournois*[1] for all the rest. It was a hard bargain, and even that would have been impossible but for Queen Margaret. In the last stages of pregnancy, she had remained at Damietta; there her child was safely delivered – with an octogenarian knight as midwife – just three days after she had received reports of the surrender. She named her little son John Tristan, 'the child of sorrow'. Now there came a double blow: the news that food supplies were running dangerously short, and that the Pisans and Genoese had begun to evacuate the city. Summoning their leaders to her bedside, she begged them to stay, pointing out that she could not hope to hold Damietta without them, and that if it were to fall she would have nothing with which to ransom her husband. Only when she offered to buy up all the food left in the city and make herself responsible for its distribution did they agree to remain. The cost was enormous, but Damietta was saved until the ransom could be arranged. It was eventually handed over on 6 May 1250, while the balance of the funds required was later disgorged, with considerable reluctance, by the Templars. A week later Louis and those of the barons who were still able to walk disembarked at Acre. Those who were too sick or badly wounded to travel were left behind at Damietta on the understanding that they would be properly looked after. Scarcely had the ships left port than the whole lot were massacred.

In the Islamic world, the failed Sixth Crusade caused a major

---

[1] The coinage struck at Tours, which in the thirteenth century was preferred to that struck in Paris.

upheaval. Much of the Muslim fighting force was composed of Mamelukes, a vast corps of soldiers, mostly Georgian or Circassian, who had been bought as boy slaves in the Caucasus and trained as crack cavalrymen. Their power and influence had steadily increased during the reign of the Sultan al-Ayub; after his death in November 1249, Turanshah had tried to cut them down to size. It proved a fatal mistake. On 2 May 1250 he gave a banquet for his emirs; just as he rose to depart a band of Mameluke soldiers burst in and attacked him. Badly wounded, he fled and plunged into the Nile, but a leading Mameluke general named Baibars followed him and finished him off. The Ayubid dynasty perished with him.

The Mamelukes were now supreme, but they did not get off to a good start. Their leader, Izzadin Aibek, married the widow of al-Ayub to legitimise his position and proclaimed himself sultan. The marriage, however, was unhappy from the outset, and in April 1257 the Sultana bribed his eunuchs to murder him in his bath – an action she had cause to regret when, just seventeen days later, she herself was clubbed to death. Aibek was succeeded by his fifteen-year-old son, who was in his turn dethroned in 1259 and replaced by one of his father's colleagues, Saifeddin Qutuz. He too was destined to reign for less than a year, but during that year, as we shall shortly see, he was to win one of the most decisive victories in the whole history of Islam – a victory which may well have saved the Muslim faith from extinction in the eastern Mediterranean.

By the third quarter of the thirteenth century the Christians of Outremer showed little enough evidence of that Crusading spirit that had given their kingdom its birth; no longer did many of them think seriously about regaining the Holy Places. But they still controlled nearly all the eastern coast of the Mediterranean, from Gaza in the south to Cilician Armenia in the north. Apart from the so-called Kingdom of Jerusalem itself – its capital now perforce at Acre – there was the Principality of Antioch and the County of Tripoli; all three were protected from the east by a chain of magnificent fortresses, many of which still stand today. Some sixty miles from the coast of Cilicia was the Christian Kingdom of Cyprus. Life in all these lands may have been pleasant enough: they enjoyed a superb climate and rich, fertile soil, while the great harbour of Acre – incomparably better than any other on the coast of Palestine or Syria – guaranteed them a steady commercial income. Everything, however, depended on the maintenance of good relations with their Muslim neighbours, and this was not always easy to achieve. Even if the Christians were prepared to compromise their Crusading ideals, the Muslims understandably resented the presence of aliens and infidels occupying lands they regarded as their own.

Another problem was presented by the Italian sea republics. Without the Venetian, Genoese and Pisan fleets, regular communications with the western Mediterranean would have been almost impossible to maintain, as would the all-important through-trade from the east; but the republics themselves were arrogant, faithless and consistently unreliable, withholding their assistance when it was vitally needed, and even on occasion providing the Muslims with essential war supplies. The Military Orders, too, could frequently prove additional thorns in the government's side; the Templars in particular, whose banking activities had earned them enormous wealth, were often only too happy to make huge loans to Muslim clients. For these and several other reasons, few dispassionate observers would have allowed Frankish Outremer a very long expectation of life, but its end may, surprisingly enough, have been appreciably delayed by a series of largely unforeseeable events which left all western Asia transformed: the arrival on the Mediterranean coast of the Golden Horde.

When the first of the great Mongol rulers, Jenghiz Khan, died in 1227 he left to his sons an empire extending from the China Sea to the banks of the Dnieper river. By the time of the death of his son Ogodai in 1241, that empire included most of modern Russia and Hungary and reached south into Persia. Just two years later, at the battle of Köse Dağ, a Mongol army had inflicted a crushing defeat over the Seljuk Turks, effectively putting an end to the independence of the Seljuk state.[1] The rulers of Europe had watched the advance of this formidable people with mounting anxiety. Louis IX went so far as to send an ambassador to the Mongol court at Karakorum; when the envoy arrived there in 1254 he found embassies from the Latin Emperor of Byzantium, from the Abbasid Caliph in Baghdad, from the Seljuk Sultan and from the King of Delhi, as well as from several Russian princes. (Another, from the King of Armenia, was shortly to follow.) The ambassador reported, interestingly enough, that among the Mongols there was absolutely no religious discrimination: the Great Khan – Jenghiz's son Kublai – though in theory shamanist, regularly attended Christian, Muslim and

---

[1] It continued to exist until the end of the century, but as little more than a Mongol puppet.

Buddhist ceremonies. There was, he believed, a single god; how precisely he was worshipped was a matter for the individual worshipper.

But religious toleration did not mean peace. In January 1256 Kublai's brother Hulagu led a huge army against the sect of the Assassins, whose terrorist activities were making the Persian lands they occupied ungovernable. By the end of 1257 few of its several thousand members were left alive. Hulagu was then free to concentrate on his next victim: al-Mustasim, the Abbasid Caliph in Baghdad. The city fell on 10 February 1258. The Caliph was put to death – after he had personally revealed to Hulagu the secret hiding place in which he had concealed his treasure – and so was the whole Muslim population of the city, probably some 80,000 men, women and children, excepting of course some of the prettier girls and boys who were kept as slaves. Only the Christians, who had taken refuge in their churches, were saved – on the personal initiative of Hulagu's chief wife Dokuz Khatun, a deeply committed Nestorian.[1] The Nestorian Patriarch was actually presented with one of the former royal palaces for use as his church and his official residence.

While the Christian communities throughout Asia rejoiced, the news of the fall of Baghdad rocked the whole Muslim world. The Abbasid Caliphate had been in existence for over five centuries, since 747. Its political power was long since gone, but it remained the focus and the uniting force of orthodox Islam. Without it, the faith lost its cohesion and was effectively up for grabs – a prize to be seized by any Muslim leader with sufficient ambition and determination. Hulagu, however, was not a Muslim leader; he now set his sights on Syria. The city of Mayyafaraqin was the first to fall, its captured ruler being forced to eat his own flesh until he died. Aleppo followed. Antioch owed its salvation only to its Prince, Bohemund VI, who travelled out to Hulagu's camp to pay him homage. Next it was the turn of Damascus, which surrendered without a struggle. The Mongol army under Hulagu's deputy, another Nestorian Christian named Kitbuqa, entered the city on 1 March, accompanied by Bohemund and his father-in-law the King of Armenia; in the words of Sir Steven Runciman, 'the citizens of the ancient capital of the Caliphate saw for the first time for six centuries three Christian potentates ride in triumph through their streets.'

---

[1] The Nestorians held that Christ had two separate persons, the human and the divine. (The Orthodox view is that He was a single person, at once God and man.) A relatively small number survives today, mostly in Iraq, where they are known as Assyrian Christians.

To many of the faithful, it must have seemed the death-knell of Islam in Asia, the more so in that the Mongol conquerors – many of whom, like Kitbuqa, were Christians themselves – openly favoured the local Christian communities. With Syria secured, they now turned their gaze towards Palestine. Avoiding Jerusalem, they advanced southward in a broad sweep through to Gaza, leaving Acre untouched but encircled by their own forces and the sea.

The speed of the conquest and the measure of its success had been alike astonishing, but the Mongol lines of communication were already alarmingly extended. Some time in the autumn of 1259 word reached the Mongol camp that the Great Khan had been killed while on campaign in China. The succession – as so often – was disputed, and it soon became plain to Hulagu that if he were to preserve his own position he must return immediately to the east. And so, early in 1260, he set forth with the bulk of his army on the 4,000-mile march to Karakorum, leaving Kitbuqa with a much-reduced force to govern the conquered lands as best he could.

Shortly before his departure Hulagu had sent an embassy to the Mameluke Sultan of Egypt demanding his submission. The Sultan, Saifeddin Qutuz, had not taken it well; he had had the ambassador executed and had at once begun to prepare for a military expedition against Syria. Now, with the sudden dramatic reduction of the Mongol host, he seized his opportunity. On 26 July the Mameluke army under Baibars crossed the frontier, captured Gaza virtually without a struggle and headed north into Palestine. It was some time in September – no one seems sure of the precise date – that the two armies met at Ain Jalud, the Pools of Goliath. The Sultan Qutuz was in overall command; the vanguard, as usual, was led by Baibars. The Mongols were quickly surrounded. They fought magnificently, but now it was they who were outnumbered. Kitbuqa was taken prisoner, bound and brought before the Sultan, who ordered his immediate execution.

This was effectively the end of the battle – today largely forgotten yet arguably one of the most decisive in history, since it saved Islam from the most dangerous threat that it has ever had to face. The three greatest cities of the Muslim world – Baghdad, Aleppo and Damascus – were in the hands of the Mongols; had Kitbuqa been victorious once again and pursued his enemy into Egypt, there would have been no Muslim state worthy of the name to the east of Morocco. The Muslim victory, on the other hand, gave the Mameluke Sultanate of Egypt supremacy in the Near East until the rise of the Ottoman Empire – and it sealed the fate of Outremer.

Within a week after the battle of Ain Jalud, Qutuz was in Damascus; within a month, Muslim forces had regained Aleppo. When the Sultan led his army in triumph back to Egypt, he seemed to be carrying all before him. But he was rapidly losing confidence in his brilliant second-in-command, Baibars, and when Baibars demanded the governorship of Aleppo – a position which would have given him the power to seize control of Syria – Qutuz refused him outright. In doing so, he badly underestimated his man. On 23 October 1260 he decided to spend a day hunting in the delta, taking his senior emirs with him; as soon as they were a safe distance from the camp, Baibars approached him silently from behind and ran him through with his sword. Although he now had the blood of two sultans on his hands, no one dared to question Baibars's right to succeed. He was to reign for the next seventeen years: physically a giant, cruel and treacherous, devoid of pity or any finer feelings, but by a very long way the ablest of all the Mameluke rulers.

Ain Jalud had not altogether put an end to Mongol power in the area. Hulagu returned to Syria as soon as he could and maintained a strong resistance in the northeast, but he died in 1265, leaving Baibars free to resume his active campaigning against the Christians. They too remained a force to be reckoned with: King Hethoum I of Armenia and Bohemund VI, Prince of Antioch and Count of Tripoli, were particularly dangerous adversaries. But Baibars kept up a relentless pressure. Four times he actually descended on Acre itself and was beaten back, but in 1267 he captured Caesarea and Toron and ravaged Cilicia, dealing the Armenian Kingdom what proved eventually to be its death-blow. The year following saw the fall of Jaffa and – worst of all, on 18 May – Antioch, one of the original patriarchal seats, the first Christian principality of Outremer, the most prosperous and well-endowed of all the Frankish cities. No mercy was shown by the conquerors. The vast accumulated treasures were doled out to the troops, most of the leading citizens and ecclesiastics massacred. The city never recovered. Through-out Eastern Christendom, the psychological effect was catastrophic.

The fall of Antioch was followed by a truce – welcome, one would imagine, to both sides and enabling them to take stock of events both in Europe and Asia which would have repercussions in Outremer: the execution of Conradin, for example, which meant the extinction of the legitimate line of the royal house of Jerusalem, and – more disturbing still – reports of the imminent arrival of King Louis of France, on his second and last Crusade.

It was now nearly twenty years since Louis had arrived at Acre after his disaster at Damietta. Awaiting him he had found an urgent appeal from his mother, the Queen Regent Blanche, imploring him to return at once to France, but his conscience had told him that to do so would be tantamount to an admission of defeat. His high ideals had so far achieved nothing; indeed, they had destroyed not only his own army but also virtually the whole fighting force of Outremer. Before he returned home, he felt, the situation must somehow be redeemed. Besides, were not some of his soldiers still imprisoned in Egypt? For their sake too it was clear that he must stay for some time longer in the east.

And so he had stayed, for another four years. Since his arrival in Outremer he had learned much. No longer could he afford to despise the infidels; if he were to recover his position and his prestige, he must treat them as equals, and thanks to the new division in the Muslim world – for Palestine and Syria remained staunchly loyal to the Ayubids – he was able to do so with considerable success. He had treated with the Ayubids and the Mamelukes; he had treated with the Assassins, shortly before their virtual destruction at the hands of Hulagu; and he had of course treated with the Mongols. Technically, as he well knew, he had no right to negotiate at all, for since 1250 the Crusader kingdom had belonged to Frederick's son Conrad; but Conrad was away in Germany and likely to remain there, and in Outremer Louis was accepted *de facto* as king. Thanks to him, such Frankish prisoners as had remained in Egypt had eventually been released, and the Mamelukes had promised that once they had occupied Syria and Palestine they would return to the Christians all the old Kingdom of Jerusalem as far east as the river Jordan.

But there could be no question of another military offensive; and when civil war broke out at home following the death of Queen Blanche in November 1252, Louis realised that he could postpone his departure no longer. On 24 April 1254 he set sail from Acre, and early in July landed at Hyères on the south coast of France, a sad and disappointed man. Of all the Crusaders, he was the most honourable, the most upright and by far the most pious, but his intervention in the Holy Land had been little short of catastrophic and had led to the loss of thousands of innocent men, a large proportion of them his own subjects. He was also bewildered; past defeats and reverses suffered by the Crusaders had been ascribed to their sinful lives, yet he – who spent hours a day in prayer and led a life of unimpeachable moral rectitude – had fared no better than they. Could it be that the whole concept of the Crusades was unpleasing in the sight of God?

He could not bring himself to believe so, and continued to dream of one more attempt – of one last journey to the Holy Land that would be crowned with success and wipe the stain of failure from his conscience. For sixteen years domestic troubles kept him occupied in France, but in 1270 he thought he saw his opportunity; though already fifty-six years old and in poor health, he made ready once again to embark for Palestine. Precisely what he meant to do when he got there is far from clear; to have recovered the Holy Places at such a time would have called for nothing less than a miracle. But whatever his intentions may have been, they were effectively set at naught by his brother Charles of Anjou, King of Sicily.

Charles's defeat of Manfred and his execution of Conradin – thus finally ridding Italy once and for all of the house of Hohenstaufen – had awoken in him even greater ambitions. These now encompassed the domination of all Italy, the reduction of the Pope to the status of a puppet, the reconquest yet again of Constantinople – now once more in Greek hands – its return to the Latin faith and, ultimately, the establishment of a Christian empire that would extend the length and breadth of the Mediterranean. His first thought, therefore, was to persuade Louis to march against Byzantium, but the King refused to consider an attack on his co-religionists, heretical or not, so Charles tried again. The Emir of Tunis, he pointed out, was said to be well disposed towards Christianity and could well be ready for conversion. If that were indeed so, the true faith might be spread all along the north African coast; even if it were not, the advantages of a permanent Christian foothold on that coast were surely not to be ignored.

It is one of the great ironies of history that sanctity is so seldom accompanied by intelligence. Why King Louis believed his brother for a moment – despite the urgent advice of most of his friends and counsellors – is almost impossible to understand. But believe him he did and, accompanied by his three surviving sons, he and his army embarked once again at Aigues-Mortes in the hottest season of the year and sailed for Tunis on 1 July.

Were any enquiries made before his departure as to the truth of Charles's claim? Was there a shred of evidence, however circumstantial, to suggest that the Emir had ever considered abandoning the faith of his fathers? Even if he had, did Louis honestly believe that an armed attack was the best way to make him do so? In fact, when the army landed on 18 July, it was immediately clear that nothing was further from the Emir's mind. He was already rallying his men, strengthening his city's defences and preparing to fight.

Fortunately for him, he did not need to lift a finger. The north African summer did it all for him. Hardly had the Crusading army pitched camp when its soldiers began to sicken and die; within a week disease was raging uncontrolled. King Louis was among the first of the victims. For the first few days he would struggle determinedly to his feet to hear Mass, but soon this became impossible and before long only a faint movement of his lips showed that he was still able to follow the ceremony. When, on 25 August, Charles of Anjou arrived with his army, he was told that his brother had died just a few hours before. The King's heir, his eldest son Philip, was also lying dangerously ill; he, however, survived, and was to reign as Philip III ('the Bold') for the next fifteen years. Louis's younger son, the twenty-one-year-old John Tristan who had been born at Damietta during the earlier campaign, was not so lucky.

Charles fought on for a few more weeks, finally coming to an arrangement with the Emir by which, in return for a considerable indemnity, he agreed to return with what was left of the army to Italy. Honour was saved, but very little else. The final nail had been hammered into the coffin of the Crusades, since – apart from what the *Encyclopedia Britannica* refers to as 'sundry disjointed epilogues' – those of St Louis were effectively the last. The great contest that had lasted for nearly two centuries between the Cross and the Crescent was finally over, and the Crescent was the victor.

It took, inevitably, a little time for the princes of Europe to accept the fact. One who notably failed to do so was Prince Edward, son and heir of King Henry III of England. Henry himself had formerly taken the Cross, but the civil wars that blighted his reign had allowed him no opportunity to fulfil his vow. Edward, at the age of thirty-two, had no such impediment, and reports of the fall of Antioch decided him to go, with about 1,000 men, in his father's place. The early stages of his journey had not been happy. Originally intending to join Louis at Aigues-Mortes, he had arrived there to find that the King had already left; when he followed him to Tunis it was to be informed that Louis was dead. In May 1271 he eventually arrived at Acre, where he was horrified. Morale everywhere was abysmally low. The Venetians and Genoese were hand in glove with the Sultan, trading most profitably in everything from weapons to slaves; no one, it seemed, had stomach for a fight. Allying himself with the Mongols, Edward scored a few minor successes against Mameluke garrisons, but certainly caused Baibars no sleepless nights. He was, on the other hand, just enough of an irritation to be worth eliminating, and the Sultan therefore arranged for a local Christian assassin to enter his chamber and stab him with a poisoned dagger. Edward made short work of his assailant, but not before sustaining an ugly wound in his arm, which soon turned dangerously septic. Thanks to primitive and painful surgery he survived,[1] took ship from Acre in September 1272 and returned to England to find himself King Edward I.

Five years later, if persistent rumours are to be believed, Baibars was involved in another attempt at assassination which went more calamitously wrong. It was said that he had prepared a bowl of poisoned *kumiss* – that fermented mare's milk so unaccountably popular with Turks and Mongols alike – for an enemy, and had then thoughtlessly drunk from it himself. He did not live to see the end of Outremer; Franks were still to be found in plenty in most of the principal cities. In his seventeen-year reign, however, he had eliminated most of the Christian dominions around the coast. The days of the survivors, as they themselves well knew, were numbered.

Then, halfway across the Mediterranean on Easter Monday 1282, there occurred a totally unexpected event which was to have an immense impact on virtually the whole of the Middle Sea. It has always been known, somewhat poetically, as the War of the Sicilian Vespers.

If Charles of Anjou was to accomplish his grand design, he needed a suitably subservient Pope. On the death of Clement IV in 1268 he had therefore used his considerable influence in the curia to keep the papal throne unoccupied for three years (conveniently covering the time when he was away on his brother's Crusade); the vacancy had ended only when the authorities at Viterbo – where the conclave was being held – actually removed the roof from the palace in which the cardinals

---

[1] The famous story of Edward's life being saved by his wife, Eleanor of Castile, who is said to have sucked out the poison from the wound, derives only from a single obscure Dominican chronicler, Ptolomaeus Lucensis. According to the old *Dictionary of National Biography*, it is 'utterly unworthy of credit'; the new (Oxford) *DNB* is equally dismissive. Eleanor, in fact, had not even accompanied him on the Crusade.

were deliberating. Their hasty choice had then fallen on Gregory X, who proved distinctly unhelpful, thwarting Charles's attempts to have his nephew Philip III of France elected Holy Roman Emperor and allying himself with Byzantium to the extent of actually effecting, at the Council of Lyons in 1274, a temporary reunion of the Eastern and Western Churches. Only in 1281, with the election of another Frenchman, Martin IV, did Charles get his way at last. Already master of Provence and the greater part of Italy, titular King of Jerusalem[1] and by a long way the most powerful – and dangerous – man in Europe, he was now free to realise his greatest ambition by marching against Constantinople, whose Emperor, Michael VIII Palaeologus, Pope Martin had obligingly redeclared schismatic. It was only twenty years since the Greeks had recovered their capital from the Franks; as 1282 opened, their chances of keeping it looked slim indeed.

They were saved by the people of Palermo. The French were already hated throughout the Regno, both for the severity of their taxation and for the arrogance of their conduct, and when, on the evening of 30 March, a drunken French sergeant began importuning a Sicilian woman outside the Church of Santo Spirito just as the bells were ringing for vespers, her countrymen's anger boiled over. The sergeant was set upon by her husband and killed; the murder led to a riot, the riot to a massacre. Two thousand Frenchmen were dead by morning. Palermo, and soon afterwards Messina also, was in rebel hands. The rising could not have been better timed. In its later stages it was led by a Salernitan nobleman named John of Procida, a friend of Frederick II and of Manfred. John had recently spent some time at the court of Peter III of Aragon, husband of Manfred's daughter Constance, and while there had encouraged Peter to make good his somewhat shadowy claim to the Sicilian crown. Here was the ideal opportunity to do so. Peter reached Palermo in September, and by the following month had captured Messina, where the French had made their last stand.

For Charles of Anjou, surrounded by his court in Naples, the loss of Sicily spelt disaster. He naturally refused to recognise his defeat, even going so far as to propose deciding the fate of Sicily by single combat with Peter, to take place under English protection at Bordeaux – several weeks' journey away. Peter rather surprisingly accepted, though in subsequent negotiations it was decided that since Charles was already

---

[1] He had bought the title in 1277 from Princess Maria of Antioch, granddaughter of King Amalric II of Jerusalem, and had immediately sent out to Acre a certain Roger of San Severino as his viceroy.

fifty-five – an old man by the standards of the time – and Peter only forty, it would be fairer if each monarch were accompanied by 100 carefully chosen knights to fight beside him. The date for the great contest was fixed for Tuesday 1 June 1283; unfortunately – or perhaps fortunately – the precise hour was not specified. King Peter and his knights arrived early in the morning, to find no sign of Charles; after his heralds had duly proclaimed his presence, Peter accordingly left the field and on his return announced that his was the victory, his cowardly opponent having failed to put in an appearance. Charles arrived a few hours later and did exactly the same. The two never met. The cost to both, in time as well as money, was considerable, but honour was saved on both sides.

And so the Regno was split down the middle, Charles reigning (as Charles I) in Naples and Peter in Sicily, each determined to expel the other and to reunify the country. But Charles's reputation was gone. His Mediterranean empire was seen to have been built on sand. He had ceased to be a world power. There could no longer be any question of an expedition against Byzantium. In Outremer his principal supporters, the Templars and the Venetians, fell away; soon he recalled his viceroy from Acre, leaving only a relatively junior officer in his place. Three years later – on 7 January 1285 – he died at Foggia. For twenty years he had dominated the Mediterranean, possessed by both an insatiable ambition and a driving energy that allowed him no rest. He was genuinely pious, but his piety brought him no humility, since he had always seen himself as God's chosen instrument. Nor did it bring him humanity, or mercy; his execution of the sixteen-year-old Conradin had shocked all Europe, and was held against him all his life. He might on occasion have been admired; never could he be loved.

The War of the Sicilian Vespers – for which Charles was largely responsible – was to continue well into the next century. It was not only Philip III 'the Bold' of France, and his son and successor Philip IV 'the Fair' after him, who were bound for reasons of family honour to recover the island so rudely wrenched away. There was also the fact that Sicily and the Regno had been granted to Charles by the Pope, so the Papacy too had to look to its prestige. Pope Martin IV had promptly proclaimed a Crusade against the Aragonese; King Philip, for his part, had begun to raise an army. But it took more than these two powers to overawe the house of Aragon and its faithful ally, the Republic of Genoa. From both sides of the dispute diplomatic missions criss-crossed Europe, until almost all the Mediterranean nations were to a greater or lesser degree involved.

The notable exception was, of course, the Mamelukes of Egypt. They had little interest in Sicily; their eyes were fixed on the lands of Outremer and the destruction of the Crusader states. Those states might have been saved, at least temporarily, if the Christian nations of the west had forgotten their other preoccupations and marched to the defence of their beleaguered co-religionists; but they did not do so. The first alarm was sounded, surprisingly enough, by the Mongols; in 1287 the Great Khan – now Hulagu's grandson Arghun – sent to the west a Christian ambassador, a certain Rabban Sauma. He first visited Constantinople, then went on to Naples, Genoa, Paris and Bordeaux, where King Edward I of England was in residence in his mainland capital.[1] He returned via Rome. Everywhere he was accorded a royal reception. In Paris, Philip IV personally showed him round the Sainte-Chapelle to admire the sacred relics that his grandfather St Louis had purchased from the Byzantine Emperor; in Bordeaux, Edward – who was after all an old Crusader himself – invited him to celebrate Mass with his court; in Rome, he received the sacrament from the hands of the newly elected Pope Nicholas IV. Everywhere he stressed the urgent necessity of an expedition to recover the Holy Places and to save Outremer. Everywhere he received a sympathetic hearing, but never once was he given a firm undertaking or a definite date. The old Crusading spirit was gone. It would not return.

The Great Khan found this difficult to believe. In the early summer of 1289 he despatched to Europe another ambassador, a Genoese by the name of Buscarel, with letters to the Pope and the French and English kings. (Their impact must have been somewhat reduced by the fact that they were written in Mongolian, but Buscarel was presumably able to translate.) This time Arghun went so far as to propose an alliance. He himself, he wrote, intended to lead an army of 20–30,000 horsemen that would reach Damascus in mid-February 1291. If the two kings were prepared to send armies of their own and the Holy Places were consequently recovered, he would be happy to hand them over. Alas, this initiative was no more successful than its predecessor. The Great Khan made one more attempt, but it too proved a failure, and by the time his envoys returned he was dead.

By this time, as if to confirm Arghun's worst fears, the Mameluke

---

[1] At this time the English kings still ruled over a considerable part of what is now France.

Sultan Qalawun had moved his entire army into Syria. His pretext was to prevent the Genoese from taking over the County of Tripoli, as they were admittedly threatening to do, though there seems little doubt that his long-term objective was more sinister. Towards the end of March 1289 he drew up his troops beneath the walls of Tripoli and on 26 April they swarmed into the city. Every Christian man they found was put to death, every woman and child carried off into slavery, every building burned to the ground. Now at last the west began to take notice. Thanks to the urgings of Pope Nicholas, the Venetians – who had been delighted to see the Genoese deprived of Tripoli but had now begun to fear for their own interests in Acre – sent twenty war galleys, which were joined by five from King James of Aragon. Unfortunately, however, this fleet was accompanied by a rabble of peasants and small-time adventurers from north Italy, all of them out for what they could get; from the day of their arrival in Acre they proved drunken and irresponsible, and one sweltering day in August 1290 they went on the rampage, charging through the streets and killing every Muslim they encountered.

Following the fall of Tripoli, Qalawun had agreed to a truce with the Christians; had all gone well, they might have been able to enjoy a few more years of independence. But after the massacre at Acre the truce had clearly ceased to exist, and there was no doubt left in the Sultan's mind: the Franks must be eliminated. On 6 March 1291, under his son and successor al-Ashraf Khalil, the great army once again set forth. Its size was given as 60,000 cavalry and a 160,000 infantry: a wild exaggeration, perhaps, but there could be little doubt that the Christians of Acre – with a total population of fewer than 40,000, some 800 knights and some 14,000 foot-soldiers, including Venetians, Pisans and the three Military Orders – would find themselves outnumbered many times over.

The siege began on 6 April. The defenders fought bravely, with both the Templars and the Hospitallers making sorties – alas unsuccessful – into the enemy camp. They still had command of the sea, so they were not short of food; but they lacked armaments, and above all the manpower adequately to protect the length of the landward wall, which extended for well over a mile. Morale received a considerable boost when King Henry II of Jerusalem,[1] twenty years old and an

---

[1] By this time the titular Kings of Jerusalem were also Kings of Cyprus, where they understandably preferred to live.

epileptic, arrived from Cyprus on 4 May with forty ships, 100 horse-men and 2,000 infantry; but, welcome as they were, these numbers could not hope to make much difference. It was only a fortnight later that the Sultan ordered the general assault.

A full account of the fall of Acre makes horrifying reading.[1] There was no surrender; the Sultan in any case would never have accepted it. All that the people could do was to die fighting, or to try to escape by sea. A few, including King Henry and his brother Amalric, succeeded in getting back to Cyprus, and a number of the women and children ended up in the harems or slave markets; but the vast majority perished. Meanwhile, Acre itself was systematically destroyed, and the remaining Frankish settlements – Tyre, Sidon, Tortosa and Beirut, together with a number of castles – soon suffered a similar fate. It was the end. Crusader Outremer had lasted for 192 years. From its beginnings a monument to intolerance and territorial ambition, its story had been one of steady physical and moral decline and monumental incom-petence. There were few people in western Europe who shed tears over its passing, or were sorry to see it go.

---

[1] The best is that of Sir Steven Runciman in *A History of the Crusades*, vol. III, pp. 412–23.

CHAPTER XI

The Close of the Middle Ages

The War of the Sicilian Vespers was not responsible for the fall of Outremer; since the rise of the Mamelukes in 1250 – perhaps even since the capture of Jerusalem by Saladin in 1187 – this had been only a matter of time. But it certainly preoccupied the princes of Europe to the point where they could not concentrate on the plight of their fellow Christians in the east. As it was, the war was to continue for another eleven years after the destruction of Acre. It was not until 1302, after an abortive attempt to place Philip the Fair's brother Charles of Valois on the throne of Sicily, that Pope Boniface VIII was reluctantly compelled to recognise King Peter's son Frederick as ruler of the island, with the title of King of Trinacria[1] – a necessary if somewhat precious appellation since the Angevins in Naples still technically retained the Sicilian crown. Even now, however, their triumph was not as complete as the Aragonese would have liked; by the terms of the agreement Frederick was to marry Leonora, daughter of Charles of Valois, and at his death the island would revert to the house of Anjou.

Pope Boniface had been elected in 1294, after the abdication – the only one in papal history – of the saintly but incapable hermit Celestine V, whose only qualification for the Papacy was that he had once, at the court of Gregory X, hung up his habit on a sunbeam. The new Pope was his antithesis in every respect. For him the great sanctions of the Church existed only to further his own temporal ends and to enrich his family, the Caetani. Foreign rulers he treated less as his subjects than as his menials, while the rival Ghibelline house of Colonna, of which he was bitterly jealous and whose power he feared, was excommunicated en masse, its lands at Palestrina seized and devastated in the name of a Crusade. Such conduct brought the Papacy to a point of debasement from which it took many years to recover, and it made Boniface hated and reviled throughout Europe. When the Colonna all fled to France, his principal enemies in Italy became the Fraticelli, the Spiritual Franciscans, who had rebelled against the increasing worldliness of

---

[1] 'The land of the three promontories' – a reference to Sicily's triangular shape. The Greeks identified it with Homer's *Thrinacia*, where Helios, the sun god, kept his sheep and cattle (*Odyssey*, XI, 121).

their order to return to their founder's principles of asceticism and poverty. Boniface they loathed, not only for his wealth and arrogance but because they held him responsible – rightly – for Celestine's abdication and his subsequent imprisonment and death.

Still more serious for Boniface was the hostility of Philip the Fair, whom he had excommunicated and threatened with deposition after Philip had forbidden his French clergy to obey a papal summons to Rome. In the spring of 1303 Philip retaliated by calling a General Council, at which he intended that the Pope himself should be arraigned. An army of 1,600 was despatched to Italy with orders to seize Boniface and to bring him, by force if necessary, to France. They found him at his native Anagni, where he was putting the finishing touches to a bull releasing Philip's subjects from their allegiance, and took him prisoner. Three days later a popular reaction in his favour obliged them to withdraw, but their mission had not been in vain. The old Pope's pride had suffered a mortal blow. His friends the Orsini escorted him back to Rome and there, a month later, he died.

Boniface and Philip were arch-enemies, but it was their combined efforts that finally broke the morale of the medieval Papacy and destroyed what was left of its prestige in Italy. When in 1305 another Frenchman was elected as Clement V, he had himself crowned at Lyons; there he was joined by his curia, and for the next seventy-two years there was no Pope in Rome. This was the period dubbed by Petrarch 'the Babylonian Captivity', but the phrase is misleading: the Popes were in no sense captive. Clement had gone to Lyons of his own free will and had no intention of becoming a cat's-paw of the French king. Four years later, after a quarrel with Philip, he even moved his court to Avignon, precisely because the city was not then in France but just inside the Provençal dominions of the Kingdom of Naples, where papal independence could be more easily preserved. Nor did he and his successors ever voluntarily loosen their hold on Italian affairs, or ever look upon Avignon as anything but a temporary residence until such time as they could safely – and comfortably – return to Italy.

For Italy had become not only unpleasant but dangerous. There had been no crowned Holy Roman Emperor since Frederick II in 1250, and the cities of Lombardy and Tuscany, untroubled by imperial incursions, had been left to develop in their own way. In most of them their hard-won communal government had given place to despotism, as one mighty family or another – the Visconti and Della Torre in Milan, the Montecchi (Shakespeare's Montagues) and later the Scaligeri in

Verona, the Gonzaga in Mantua – asserted its domination. This mass of petty but absolute dictatorships, superimposed on a tradition of internecine strife and undermined by the hostility of a commercially-minded bourgeoisie, led to a deep unrest which permeated all aspects of north Italian life. Sometimes, admittedly, it provided a stimulus for the new spirit of artistic enquiry which was already heralding the Renaissance – Giotto was born in the year Manfred died – but more often the story is one of tyranny and unremitting bloodshed. Of the great northern sea republics, Genoa and Pisa continued at each other's throats until Genoa's decisive victory off Meloria in 1284; only Venice remained relatively untouched by the prevailing chaos, thanks to her sea-girt isolation, her carefully preserved oligarchy, her freedom from faction and that delicate system of political checks and balances which was to make the government of the Most Serene Republic the wonder – and the terror – of Europe.

Another haven of comparative peace in the surrounding turmoil was Florence. At that time it was the most artistically creative of all the Italian city-states, and was still more remarkable in having evolved perhaps the only successful government by artists and craftsmen that the world has ever seen. Here the effective administrative control lay in the hands of six guild-masters, called Priors of the Arts; their powers were great, but held for only two months at a time. Florence could also look back on an entrenched Guelf tradition which might have preserved her from much of the feuding that so bedeviled less fortunate cities, but towards the end of the century a rift occurred among the Guelfs, and in 1302 – Pope Boniface having allied himself with the reactionary 'blacks' – the leaders of the more moderate 'white' party were driven into exile.

Among them was Dante Alighieri, whose *Divine Comedy*, the greatest single achievement in the Italian language, is among many other things a profound and bitter commentary in which the poet, purporting merely to meet the leading figures of his age as he progresses through the afterworld, in fact sits in awful judgement over them. The grandeur of the conception is as breathtaking as is the technical mastery of a still developing vernacular, but the political ideas within it sometimes seem more redolent of the eleventh century than of the fourteenth. These ideas, which Dante develops more fully in *De Monarchia*, are in essence a return to the old dream of a worldwide Christian empire, governed in harmonious tandem by Emperor and Pope.

Just how unworkable they had become was shown in 1310 when their most active exponent, Count Henry of Luxemburg, descended into Italy as Emperor-elect. Idealistic and painfully well-meaning, Henry received his first coronation in Milan with a replica of the iron crown of Lombardy (the real one was in pawn), still stressing his impartiality between papalist Guelf and imperialist Ghibelline; but the Guelf cities of Lombardy and Tuscany left him in no doubt of their feelings towards an outmoded imperialism, and he was Ghibelline enough by the time he reached Rome – to the point indeed where he was denied entry to St Peter's and was forced to accept the crown of empire from papal legates at the Lateran. Meanwhile in Avignon, Clement V under pressure from King Philip had turned against him, as had Charles of Anjou's reigning grandson, King Robert the Wise of Naples. Reluctantly the new Emperor resorted to war, but it got him nowhere. In 1313 he died of a fever, having incontrovertibly proved the vanity of Dante's hopes.

Dante had never liked King Robert, whom he describes as a 're da sermone', or 'king of talk'; in fact, Robert had the makings of a great ruler. He was a scholar, whose genuine love of literature made him a munificent patron of poets and writers – especially of Petrarch, of whom he was a personal friend and who admired him to the point where he expressed the hope that he might one day be lord of all Italy. In more peaceful times he might have raised the Regno out of the miasma in which it always seemed to be sunk; alas, he never had the chance. The endless warring with his Aragonese rivals drained his coffers, and even at home his life was a constant struggle with rebellious barons who allowed him no rest.

Robert died in 1343 to be succeeded by his granddaughter Joanna, the wife of Prince Andrew of Hungary, and for the next half-century the history of Naples becomes a nightmare. (The reader is not expected to follow the rest of this paragraph and its successor, briefly included only to illustrate the level to which Neapolitan politics had sunk.) In 1345 Andrew was assassinated, on the orders of his wife's great-aunt Catherine of Valois but not without suspicion of Joanna's own complicity. His brother King Lewis of Hungary, on the pretext of avenging the murder, then claimed the kingdom for himself. He expelled Joanna and her second husband, murdering her brother-in-law for good measure, but he soon returned to Hungary and the local barons recalled Joanna. Her cousin Charles of Durazzo then conquered the kingdom and imprisoned her. Soon afterwards she was murdered in her turn. On Charles's death a disputed succession caused another civil war, and the kingdom slipped back into its old anarchy.

By the beginning of the following century Charles's son Ladislas seemed to have won the struggle, and by 1410 – thanks to the continuing papal schism[1] – he had three times occupied Rome itself, which the rightful Pope Gregory XII had been unable to hold. On the last occasion he had fired and sacked the city. His death in 1414 was unlamented by his subjects – at least until his sister and successor, Joanna II, dragged the kingdom down to still lower depths of degradation. In 1415 she married James of Bourbon, who kept her in a state of semi-confinement, murdered her lover and imprisoned her chief captain, Sforza; but his arrogance drove the barons once more to rebellion and they expelled him. There followed a still worse tangle of intrigues between Joanna, Sforza, her new lover Giovanni Caracciolo, her adopted heir Alfonso of Aragon and Louis III of Anjou, whom we find pitted against each other in every possible combination. Though Joanna died in 1435, it was another eight years before Alfonso finally proved victorious and achieved papal recognition as King of Naples.

The Kingdom of Jerusalem had been annihilated by the Mameluke armies, but the three great Military Orders of knighthood lived on – if for rather differing periods of time. The youngest of them, the German Order of the Teutonic Knights, moved after 1291 for a few years to Venice and then in 1308 to Marienburg on the Vistula, where it disappears from our story. The Knights Templar and the Knights Hospitaller of St John of Jerusalem, on the other hand, continued to play their part in Mediterranean affairs – even though the former did not do so for very long.

Let us consider the Templars first. It is difficult for us nowadays to understand – even to believe – their influence in the later Middle Ages. Founded in the early twelfth century to protect the pilgrims flocking to the Holy Places after the First Crusade, they were within fifty years firmly established in almost every kingdom of Christendom, from Denmark to Spain, from Ireland to Armenia; within a century, 'the poor fellow-soldiers of Jesus Christ' were – despite their Benedictine vows of poverty, chastity and obedience – financing half Europe, the most powerful international bankers of the civilised world. By 1250 they were thought to possess some 9,000 landed properties; both in

---

[1] See Chapter XII, p. 221.

Paris and London, their houses were used as strongholds in which to preserve the royal treasure. From the English Templars Henry III borrowed the purchase money for the island of Oléron in 1235; from the French, Philip the Fair extracted the dowry of his daughter Isabella on her marriage to Edward II of England. For Louis IX they provided the greater part of his ransom, and to Edward I they advanced no less than 25,000 *livres tournois*, of which they were to remit four-fifths.

The Templars were most powerful of all in France, where they effectively constituted a state within a state; and as their influence steadily increased, it was not surprising that Philip the Fair should have become seriously concerned. But Philip also had another, less honourable reason for acting against them: he was in desperate need of money. He had already dispossessed and expelled the Jews and the Lombard bankers; similar treatment of the Templars – which promised to secure him all Templar wealth and property in his kingdom – would solve his financial problems once and for all. The Order would, he knew, prove a formidable adversary; fortunately, however, he had a weapon ready to hand. For many years there had been rumours circulating about the secret rites practised by the Knights at their midnight meetings. All he now needed to do was to institute an official enquiry; it would not be hard to find witnesses who – in return for a small consideration – would be prepared to give the evidence required. That evidence, when given, was more satisfactory than he had dared to hope. The Templars, it now appeared, were Satanists who at their initiation denied Christ and trampled on the crucifix. Sodomy was not only permitted but actively encouraged. Such illegitimate children as were nevertheless engendered were disposed of by being roasted alive.

On Friday, 13 October 1307, the Grand Master of the Temple, Jacques de Molay, was arrested in Paris with sixty of his leading brethren.[1] To force them to confess, they were first tortured by the palace authorities and then handed over to the official inquisitors to be tortured again. Over the next six weeks no less than 138 Knights were subjected to examination, of whom – not surprisingly – 123, including de Molay himself, finally confessed to at least some of the charges levelled against them. Philip, meanwhile, wrote to his fellow monarchs urging them to follow his example. Edward II of England – who probably felt on somewhat shaky ground himself – was initially inclined to cavil with his father-in-law, but when firm instructions

---

[1] This is believed to be the origin of the grim reputation of the date.

arrived from Pope Clement – who was only too willing to assist the French king in any way he could – he hesitated no longer. The English Master of the Order was taken into custody on 9 January 1308. All his Knights followed him soon afterwards.

The Templars had their champions. When de Molay was interrogated by three cardinals sent expressly to Paris by the Pope, he formally revoked his confession and bared his breast to show unmistakable signs of torture. At Clement's first consistory, no less than ten members of the Sacred College threatened to resign in protest against his policy, and early in February the Inquisition was ordered to suspend its activities against the Order. But it was impossible to reverse the tide. In August the Grand Master, examined yet again, renewed his former confessions.

The public trial of the Order opened on 11 April 1310, when it was announced that any of the accused who attempted to retract an earlier confession would be burned at the stake; on 12 May fifty-four Knights suffered this fate, and in the next two weeks nine others followed them. The whole contemptible affair dragged on for another four years, during which Pope and King continued to confer – a sure sign of the doubts that refused to go away – and to discuss the disposition of the Order's enormous wealth. Meanwhile Jacques de Molay languished in prison until his fate could be decided. Not until 14 March 1314 did the authorities bring him out on to a scaffold before the Cathedral of Notre-Dame to repeat his confession for the last time.

They had reason to regret their decision. As Grand Master, Jacques de Molay can hardly be said to have distinguished himself over the previous seven years. He had confessed, retracted and confessed again; he had shown no heroism, few qualities even of leadership. But now he was an old man, in his middle seventies and about to meet his God: he had nothing more to lose. And so, supported by his friend Geoffroy de Charnay, he spoke out loud and clear: as God was his witness, he and his Order were totally innocent of all the charges of which they had been accused. At once he and de Charnay were hurried away by the royal marshals, while messengers hastened to Philip. The King delayed his decision no longer. That same evening the two old knights were rowed out to a small island in the Seine, where the stake had been prepared.

It was later rumoured that, just before he died, de Molay had summoned both Pope Clement and King Philip to appear at the judgement seat of God before the year was out, and it did not pass unnoticed that the Pope was dead in little more than a month, and the King killed in a hunting accident towards the end of November.[1] The two men faced the flames with courage and died nobly. After night had fallen, the friars of the Augustinian monastery on the further shore came to collect their bones, to be revered as those of saints and martyrs.

Although the Knights Hospitaller of St John had played no part in the persecution and ultimate annihilation of the Templars – and it would be unkind even to suggest that they experienced even a touch of *Schadenfreude* – there is no doubt that they were far and away the greatest beneficiaries of their brothers' demise. By a bull dated 2 May 1312, Pope Clement had decreed that all the Templars' wealth and property – outside the kingdoms of Castile, Aragon, Portugal and Majorca, on which he deferred his decision – should devolve upon the Order of the Hospital; even though King Philip received most of his expected rewards, it was the Hospitallers who suddenly found themselves richer than they had ever dreamed.

In its origins, their order was older even than that of the Templars. An early hospice for pilgrims to Jerusalem had been established by Charlemagne, and had been active until 1010 when it was destroyed by the fanatically anti-Christian Caliph Hakim; the site was purchased in about 1023 by a group of merchants from Amalfi, who re-established it under the authority of the Benedictines. Soon afterwards it was dedicated to St John the Baptist, and by the time of the Latin conquest of Jerusalem in 1099 its director, Brother Gerard, had made it the centre of its own religious order with a single aim: that of tending, and if possible healing, the sick. It was Gerard's successor, a certain Raymond of Le Puy, who revised its rule and gave it its second purpose: the military protection of Christian pilgrims. From the 1130s onwards both the Templars and the Hospitallers were taking a regular part in the wars of the Cross. Both were religious orders, whose members took the usual monastic vows; but whereas the Templars were a purely military organisation, the Hospitallers never forgot that they were primarily a nursing brotherhood, whose duty it was to minister to 'our lords the sick'. When not actually fighting, they were constantly

---

[1] The French writer Maurice Druon, in his brilliant series of novels *Les Rois Maudits*, suggests that de Molay also cursed King Philip from the stake, and with some effect: Philip and his five immediate predecessors had reigned a total of 177 years, while the next six kings of France covered only sixty-six.

occupied with the building and furnishing of their hospitals, and their standard of medical treatment was the highest in the medieval world.

After the fall of Acre and the end of Frankish Outremer, the Knights of the Hospital first took refuge in Limassol, but they had no wish to subject themselves to the house of Lusignan and in 1306 their Grand Master Foulques de Villaret – with the willing permission of Pope Clement – came to an agreement with a Genoese pirate named Vignolo de' Vignoli for a concerted attack on the island of Rhodes, then part of the Byzantine Empire. It was, geographically, a perfect choice. The most easterly island of the Aegean, it lay only ten miles off the coast of Asia Minor, the intervening channel carrying much of the merchant shipping that plied between the ports of western Europe and those of the Levant. Its mountain ridge, rising to some 4,000 feet, offered several vantage points from which lookouts could keep a watch on both Asia Minor and the islands of the Dodecanese; on clear days even the outline of Mount Ida in Crete – well over 100 miles away to the southwest – was clearly visible. The fields were rich in orchards and vineyards, ensuring copious supplies of food and wine. Vast pine forests provided virtually limitless wood for shipbuilding. Moreover, the people boasted a seafaring tradition that went back to the days of antiquity. The Roman navy of the east had been largely staffed by Rhodians, as had successive Byzantine fleets. If the Knights, hitherto based firmly on land, were now to become men of the sea, they could not hope to find better instructors in shipbuilding, seamanship and navigation.

First, however, the island had to be conquered. Its people put up a stubborn resistance, and it was only after two years' hard fighting that the city of Rhodes itself, with its two magnificent harbours, eventually fell to the Knights. On 15 August 1309 it opened its gates, and a year later became the official headquarters of the Order. An agreement was quickly reached with the pirate Vignolo according to which, in return for one-third of their revenues, the Knights were to keep the whole island except two small villages, plus the neighbouring islands of Kos and Kalymnos and several others of the Dodecanese. It was an excellent bargain. After nineteen years, they once again had a permanent home – on an island which, by a subsequent papal decree, was their property absolutely. In these new circumstances they were not only an order of knighthood; they were a sovereign state. Now at last they were able to resume their continuing war against the infidel, with its avowed object of 'reducing to silence the enemies of Christ', but even as they did so they never forgot that they had another duty, more pressing still. One of their very first tasks on settling in Rhodes was to start work on their new infirmary. It was to become the best and most celebrated hospital in the world. The great ward – which remains today almost exactly as it was when the Order left it nearly five centuries ago – could accommodate no less than eighty-five patients, all tended by the Knights themselves.

They also established a completely new administrative structure. The head of state was the Grand Master; beneath him the Order was divided into eight *langues*, or tongues – those of France, Provence, Auvergne, England, Italy, Germany, Aragon and Castile – each of which enjoyed a considerable degree of independence. In order to bind together this motley collection of races and languages, it was decided that each tongue should assume responsibility for an individual task. Thus the Admiral was almost invariably an Italian, the Grand Commander a Provençal, the Marshal an Auvergnat and the Grand Bailiff a German. The English provided the Turcopolier, who was charged with the coastal defences of the island. Every Knight without exception was required to wear on his gown or cloak the characteristic eight-pointed cross, 'to put him in mind of bearing always in his heart the cross of Jesus Christ, adorned with the eight virtues that attend it'.

Within the tongues, the Knights were of three main classes. First were the Knights of Justice, who were recruited only from the aristocratic families of Europe and were required to give proof of their noble blood. Next in the hierarchy came the serving brothers, who were of slightly lower social status; some would be soldiers, some diplomats and civil servants, others would work in the hospital. The third category was formed by the chaplains who served in the churches and chapels. Each Knight was required to serve two initial years on probation, one of which would be spent in the galleys. Only then was he required to take the oath:

> You promise and vow under God, and unto our Lady, and unto our Lord St John Baptist to live and to die in obedience. You likewise promise to live without property of your own. There is also one other promise, made only by the Order: to be the serf and the slave of our lords the sick.

Many remained abroad for the best part of their lives, in the Order's local commanderies, but all without exception were bound to return instantly to Rhodes when summoned.

As the fourteenth century wore on, it is not altogether surprising that the Knights began to compromise on some of their early ideals. Although their hospital continued to flourish and to attract patients from all over the eastern Mediterranean, their own steadily increasing wealth – combined, perhaps, with the near-perfect climate in which they lived – led to a gradual relaxation of their once austere monastic habits. But they never neglected their military duties. They continued to police the narrow seas; their consuls in Egypt and Jerusalem watched over the interests of the Christian pilgrims; and they kept up the pressure against the Turks, substantially delaying their development as a first-rate naval power. In 1348, in alliance with Venice and Cyprus, they took Smyrna (Izmir), successfully defending it against a Turkish counter-attack ten years later; and in 1365 they participated in the last effort ever made to rescue the Holy Land from the infidel.

Their ally and inspiration on this occasion was King Peter I of Cyprus, the first monarch since St Louis to be fired with a genuine Crusading spirit. In 1362 he set out on an extended tour of the west to seek support for his plans. Pope Urban V in Avignon, the Emperor Charles IV in Prague, John II of France and Edward III of England all promised help, and there was a useful naval contribution from Venice. The expedition assembled in Rhodes in August 1365, with a navy estimated at some 165 ships, including 108 from Cyprus – by far the largest combined force since the Third Crusade. Only after the whole fleet had set sail was it announced that the first destination was Alexandria. The Crusaders landed there on 9 October; two days later the city was theirs.

What followed was a massacre – a massacre worse, if anything, than that by the soldiers of the First Crusade in Jerusalem in 1099 or that by the Franks in Constantinople in 1204. The slaughter was indiscriminate. The important Christian and Jewish communities suffered as much as the Muslim majority; churches and synagogues as well as mosques were put to the torch. Five thousand prisoners were captured and sold into slavery. King Peter, horrified at the turn events had taken, did his best to restore order and to hold what was left of the city, but the army, having possessed itself of all the plunder it could carry, was impatient to be off before an avenging Mameluke army arrived from Cairo. The King had no course but to order his fleet back to Cyprus. Even then he hoped to sail back on a second expedition to the east, but on arrival at Famagusta the entire army disintegrated, knights and foot-soldiers alike thinking only of returning home with their loot as quickly as possible.

This was the last Crusade, and the most shameful of them all; it set back the cause of progress in the Mediterranean by the best part of a century. When it took place, the Franks and the Mamelukes had been at peace for fifty years and more. Pilgrims were travelling freely to the Holy Places; trade was flourishing between the west and the Muslim world. Now, at a stroke, all the old enmities were revived: native Christian communities began once again to suffer persecution, and the Church of the Holy Sepulchre was once again closed to pilgrims. To the Mamelukes of Egypt, the Christian Kingdom of Cyprus was once again their arch-enemy. Sixty years later they were to have their revenge.

It would be unfair to attach too much of the blame for this catastrophe to the Knights of the Hospital. Their lives were, after all, dedicated to the saving of life rather than to the taking of it; their vow of poverty ruled out any form of looting; and they had lived long enough in the east to understand the principles of coexistence. There can be little doubt that they were as shocked as anyone by the behaviour of their allies, and they would certainly have done their best to exercise a moderating influence; their guilt, such as it was, was guilt by association only. Nonetheless, the massacre at Alexandria signals the low point of their history, and marks their record with its blackest stain. For the rest, idle and ineffectual as they frequently were, it remains a fact that throughout their 213-year residence in Rhodes and for much of their 268-year occupation of Malta which followed it, the Knights Hospitaller of St John of Jerusalem were to be a beneficial – and occasionally dramatically decisive – force in Mediterranean affairs.

The palace of the Alhambra at Granada is one of the most superb Islamic buildings remaining anywhere in Europe. No visitor can fail to be seduced by the grace of its architecture, the delicacy of its carving, the play of sunshine and shadow in its courts and gardens. The horseshoe arches, the swirling Arabic calligraphy, the stalactite vaulting, all radiate the spirit of Islam at its elegant best. Then, suddenly, there comes a surprise. In three of the alcoves of the Sala de los Reyes – it is sometimes known as the Sala de la Justicia – are some extraordinary ceiling paintings. They are painted on leather, which might be thought unusual enough, but what makes them more remarkable still is their subject. In the central alcove ten men of Moorish appearance are sitting at a council meeting, while to each side there are scenes of hunting, fighting, chess-playing and the making of courtly love, all in the manner of Christian Europe in the later Middle Ages. The style suggests the mid-fourteenth century, so they must be virtually contemporary with the palace itself, which was completed in about 1350; but how did they come to be painted? The tenets of Islam strongly discourage figurative art in any form, and particularly representations of the human figure;[1] and Muslim Granada still had a century and a half to go. We can only conclude that an Islamic ruler commissioned a Christian artist to provide them, which in turn suggests that at this time at least the two religions had achieved a happy and harmonious coexistence.

One reason for this is that by the third quarter of the thirteenth century the Reconquista had run out of steam. King Pedro III of Aragon was fully occupied with his Sicilian adventure, while his contemporary Alfonso X 'the Wise' of Castile, cultured and erudite as he may have been, was far more interested in negotiating for the crown of the Holy Roman Empire and establishing his dynastic claims to Gascony than he was in smiting the infidel. As for Alfonso's son Sancho IV and Sancho's grandson Alfonso XI – whose long minority led to civil war and thirteen years of chaos until the *cortes* of Castile declared him to be of age in 1325 – they had more than enough to do in repelling invasions by the Berbers of Morocco; their successes were welcomed rather than lamented by the Muslim rulers of Granada.

With the accession to the Castilian throne of Alfonso XI's son Pedro I – better known by his well-deserved appellation of Pedro the Cruel – in 1350, it looked for a moment as if Christian–Muslim coexistence might again be threatened. But Pedro was in the early part of his reign primarily concerned with his domestic life: imprisoning his unfortunate wife, Blanche of Bourbon, almost certainly murdering her (though only after contracting a bigamous marriage), and later being himself kept under restraint by his enemies in the palace. Free again in 1356, he perpetrated a whole series of further murders before in 1360 finding himself faced with a civil war led by his bastard half-brother, Enrique of Trastamara. In the efforts of both sides to acquire international support Castile was suddenly swept up into the Hundred Years War, with Pedro being backed by the English – notably Edward the Black Prince – and Enrique by the French. The English alliance did

---

[1] Contrary to popular belief, they do not absolutely forbid it; the Persians never felt inhibited, nor very often did the Ottoman Turks. But in North Africa and Muslim Spain such productions by a Muslim artist would have been unthinkable.

1. Sophia Schliemann, wearing the gold jewellery wrongly thought
by her husband to be that of Helen of Troy

2. Phoenician silver coin,
with ship and sea monster

3. The goddess of the serpents.
From the Palace of Knossos, Minoan,
c. BC 1500

4. Odysseus
and the Sirens.
Athenian,
c. BC 490

5. Carved ivory plaque of a lion. Assyrian, c. BC 800

6. The Alexander Sarcophagus: detail. Hellenistic, c. BC 320

8. Pericles: Roman copy
of Greek original, c. BC 440

7. Bronze figure, life-size: found in 1973
by a diver off the coast of Calabria.
Thought to be a votive statue from the
sanctuary at Delphi, possibly by Phidias,
c. BC 430

9. Julius Caesar. Marble, c. BC 50

10. Two portrait mummy cases. From Fayum, Egypt, c. 100 AD

11. Cameo commemorating the Battle of Actium. Sardonyx, c. BC 31

12. Constantine the Great:
colossal head. Stone, c. 320 AD

13. Mausoleum of Theodoric.
Ravenna, c. 530 AD

14.
Gladiator
fighting
a leopard.
Mosaic,
c. 320 AD

15. Byzantine capital: Istanbul,
Church of St Sophia, c. 535 AD

16. Moorish capital: Granada,
Palace of Generalife, c. 785 AD

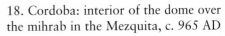

17. Cordoba: the Great Mosque
(Mezquita), c. 785 AD

18. Cordoba: interior of the dome over
the mihrab in the Mezquita, c. 965 AD

19. Cairo: Mosque of Ibn Tulun, 9th century AD

not last long; Edward, revolted by Pedro's faithlessness and brutality, soon afterwards returned to England, sick of the disease that was to kill him a short time later. Pedro, left on his own, was soon overpowered by Enrique and his ally, the famous French knight Bertrand du Guesclin. On 23 March 1369 Enrique stabbed Pedro to death in du Guesclin's tent, simultaneously becoming King Enrique II of Castile. As Pedro's successor, he could only be an improvement.

In 1371 there was forged one of Spain's few familial links with England, when Edward III's oldest surviving son, John of Gaunt, Duke of Lancaster, married Constance, Pedro's illegitimate daughter, and *in absentia* styled himself King of Castile. It was another fifteen years before he set foot in Spain to claim his inheritance; finally, on 7 July 1386, accompanied by his wife and two daughters, he sailed from Plymouth with an army of 20,000 men. A month later he landed at Corunna and soon made himself master of most of Galicia, in the northwest corner of the country. Then, in the spring of 1387, he joined forces with his son-in-law King John I of Portugal (now married to his daughter Philippa) for a joint invasion of Castile. The expedition was a failure: disease spread rapidly through the camp, the Duke himself was stricken, the conquered territories were lost again and the army was forced to retire across the Pyrenees. At last in 1389 Gaunt signed a treaty surrendering his claim to the throne in exchange for a payment of 200,000 crowns, a generous annual pension and the marriage of his daughter Catherine to the future Enrique III of Castile. Altogether, he had gained a good deal more than he deserved.

Throughout this time the Muslims of Granada lived happily and in comparative peace. The same could not, alas, be said for the Jews. Financially, Enrique relied on them as did everyone else, but during the civil war he had deliberately stirred up hatred against them, and as the century progressed so anti-Semitism intensified, finally bursting out in 1391 like a forest fire. It began in Seville on 6 June. Many of the Jewish population fled for their lives; many others, as synagogues were forcibly Christianised, submitted unwillingly to conversion. From Seville the flames spread quickly, first through Andalusia and thence to the rest of the peninsula, even beyond the Pyrenees as far as Perpignan. After a while, inevitably, there came a lull; but the fires continued to smoulder throughout the century that followed, until in 1492 Ferdinand and Isabella were to sign the fateful edict banishing all Jews from the territory of Spain.

*

At the beginning of Boccaccio's *Decameron*, ten young people flee Florence because of plague. That plague, better known as the Black Death, hangs like a baleful miasma over the second half of the fourteenth century. It had first appeared in Constantinople in the spring of 1347, brought almost certainly by ships escaping from the already plague-ridden Genoese trading colony of Caffa (now Feodosiya in the Crimea), which was then under siege by the Mongols. The city had suffered many similar visitations over the centuries, but never one so virulent or on such a scale. The fatal bacillus was – as we now know – introduced by fleas which were in turn usually (though not invariably) carried by the rats that infested all ships coming from the east. Curiously enough, these rats were themselves relatively new arrivals in Europe, the first of them having probably been brought in on ships carrying Crusaders back from Palestine; but they were rapid and indefatigable breeders, and by mid-century there were more than enough of them to propagate the disease throughout the European continent. We need not necessarily believe the anonymous contemporary chronicler from the Italian town of Este, who claims that in Constantinople plague accounted for eight-ninths of the entire population; to the Byzantines, however, it must have seemed the final proof of what they had suspected for so long: that the Holy Virgin, their patron and protectress, had after more than 1,000 years at last deserted them.

The Mediterranean proper had its first taste of the Black Death early in October 1347, when twelve Genoese galleys arrived in Messina. They too had probably come from Caffa; it was certainly from there that yet another Genoese fleet was to transmit the infection, in January 1348, to Genoa, Venice and Sicily. From there it spread north to Corsica and Sardinia, south to Tunis and North Africa, west to the Balearic Islands, and thence to Barcelona and Valencia on the Spanish coast, and, inevitably, across the straits to south Italy, whence its progress up the peninsula was swift.

Of all the Italian cities, Florence suffered most. Contemporary assessments are famously unreliable, but there is good evidence to show that out of a total Florentine population estimated at some 95,000, between 50,000 and 60,000 were dead within six months of the outbreak. Boccaccio himself provides us with an unforgettable description: the headlong flight of whole populations from the cities and towns, abandoning their houses and possessions; the way in which the sick – even sick children – were left to their fate, with no one daring to approach them; the mass burials in hurriedly dug trenches; the untended cattle wandering free through the countryside. In Venice, when the epidemic was at its height, 600 citizens a day were said to have perished; in Orvieto, out of every family of four, one of the parents and one of the children could statistically expect to die; in Siena – where the deaths were estimated at 50,000, two-thirds of the population – they were in the process of building the cathedral, which was to be one of the greatest in Christendom. The workmen all died; construction was abandoned, and although activity was resumed towards the end of the century the building has not to this day been completed as planned. As for Italy as a whole, to say that it lost a third, or slightly more, of its total population would probably not be very far wrong.

In France the story was much the same. The plague began, predictably enough, in Marseille. A few weeks later it had reached the Pyrenees, and by August 1348 it was raging through Bordeaux. To the east, it struck papal Avignon in March, killing at least half the population, including every single one of the English community of Austin Friars in the city. Pope Clement VI himself retired to his private apartments, where he received no one and spent the entire day and night roasting himself between two blazing fires. (The treatment proved successful; he survived.) Meanwhile, the pestilence sped up the Rhône valley to Lyons, and by June was working its way through Paris itself.

Wherever it struck, the more pious of the population withdrew to pray; particularly in the major cities of the north, however, the predominant reaction to imminent death seems to have been a feverish and frenetic gaiety. And why not? If God had deserted his people, why should his commandments be obeyed? If their lives were to be so cruelly cut short, let their last days be devoted to pleasure, whether that of the table, the bottle or the bed – or, ideally, all three. In Paris – where such delights have never been undervalued – there seems to have been what amounted to an almost complete breakdown in morality, both private and public.

Across the length and breadth of the Mediterranean, the story was much the same. In Cyprus, where the onset of the plague coincided with a severe earthquake and tidal wave, it led to a panic-stricken massacre by the landowners of all their Arab slaves, for fear that they might take advantage of the prevailing chaos by staging a revolt. On the Dalmatian coast, the citizens of Salona (Split) had a different hazard to endure: packs of ravening wolves, descending on the city from the mountains and attacking both sick and survivors alike. Such was the mortality that piles of unburied corpses were left in the streets for weeks at a time.

In Spain, having first appeared in the coastal cities, the plague moved slowly but persistently through the Kingdom of Aragon. Its king, Pedro IV, somehow survived; but he lost first a daughter, then a niece, and finally in October his second wife, Eleanor of Portugal. The scourge then spread, first to the Muslim lands and thence to the army of Castile, at that time engaged in a vigorous campaign of reconquest in the south under the leadership of King Alfonso XI himself. In 1344 he had taken Algeciras; he was now before Gibraltar. The besiegers of the Rock – unlike its defenders – remained unaffected throughout the summer of 1349, but early in March 1350 the dread sickness struck. Alfonso's generals implored him to withdraw into isolation until it should have run its course, but he refused to leave his men. He died on Good Friday, 26 March, the only ruling monarch to fall victim to the Black Death. Joanna, daughter of Edward III of England, died at Bordeaux on the way to her wedding with Alfonso's son, Pedro the Cruel. The territory of Castile itself, though it did not escape entirely, certainly got off lightly – thanks, it was widely believed at the time, to the eagerness of the landowning classes to make over their property to the Church. When the emergency was past, it was found that they had done so on such a scale as seriously to upset the economic balance of the country; in 1351 King Pedro I was obliged to order the ecclesiastical authorities to make full restitution of all that they had received.

The Black Death took a greater toll of life than any known war or epidemic in previous history. Its effect on international trade was dramatic, but relatively short-lived; more lasting was the alarming reduction of the amount of land under cultivation, owing to the deaths of so many labourers. This compelled the landowners drastically to increase wages, which in turn brought a weakening of the formerly rigid stratification of society as the working people began for the first time to travel about in search of employment or higher pay. In the arts – particularly painting and sculpture – there was a greater pre-occupation with death than before; in matters spiritual, the obvious inefficacy of prayer and the powerlessness of the Church against the plague shook the faith of many Christians. After 1350 Europe would never be quite the same again.

When the Roman Emperor-elect, Lewis IV of Bavaria, marched down into Italy in 1327 for his imperial coronation, it was with an attitude very different to that adopted by his predecessor, Henry of Luxemburg.[1] This time there was no idealism, no pretence at impartiality, no nod in the direction of Avignon. Lewis arrived at the invitation of the Ghibellines of Italy, bringing with him the most formidable of all the anti-papalists of his time, Marsilius of Padua. Only two years previously this ex-Rector of the Sorbonne had published his *Defensor Pacis*, in which he argued that the whole edifice of papal domination and canon law was contrary to the basic principles of Christianity. Such company was unlikely to increase Lewis's popularity at Avignon, and long before he reached Rome he had incurred a double sentence of excommunication and deposition from Pope John XXII; but by this time the papal prestige in Italy had sunk even lower than the imperial, and the decree went largely unheeded. When Lewis was crowned by Sciarra Colonna, representing the people of Rome, at St Peter's in January 1328 and three months later formally pronounced the Pope heretic and deposed, it almost looked as though he might re-establish imperial control; but when he advanced south into Neapolitan territory King Robert of Naples, grandson of Charles of Anjou, proved a far more serious adversary. Robert was his military match, and on returning to Rome Lewis found that the pendulum had swung. He realised, too, that he could never hope to establish a stable order in Italy until he was certain of Germany, where the situation was fast deteriorating. The year 1330 saw him back beyond the Alps. He too had learned his lesson: Italy had outgrown imperialism, even if she was not yet ready for a unity of her own making.

Between the south and the north the difference was still immense, so deep that the effects of it can still be felt today. The Kingdom of Naples, under Robert and his flighty successor Joanna I, could boast an enlightened and cultivated court and two of the best universities in Italy: Frederick II's foundation in Naples itself and the world-famous school of medicine, already more than five centuries old, at Salerno. Outside these centres, however, the land was dominated, just as in Norman days, by an irresponsible and obstreperous baronage. Sicily, under the house of Aragon, was less encumbered by feudalism and economically more coherent, but was otherwise permeated by much the same atmosphere of stagnation and inertia.

In the north, on the other hand, there is no escaping the sense of overpowering vitality. Gradually, as the fourteenth century progresses

---

[1] See Chapter XI, p. 197.

and the smaller city-states are drawn into the orbit of the larger, the great spheres of influence begin to appear: Venice, richer and more magnificent than ever, slowly outdistancing Genoa – by now her only serious maritime rival – and for the first time annexing important parts of the Italian mainland – Padua and Vicenza, Treviso and Verona – while still extending her influence beyond the Adriatic as one of the great powers of Europe; Milan, under the superb house of Visconti, flooding like a great tide over Lombardy and Piedmont and finally to engulf even Bologna, the centre of papal power in north Italy; and the Florence of Giotto, Orcagna and Andrea Pisano, her staunch republicanism foiling every attempt by a would-be despot, her great merchant bankers developing the art of international finance to undreamed-of levels of efficiency and sophistication. One of the advantages of Roman over canon law was that it made usury respectable; the way was now open for full economic growth and for the long-term credits which made possible the wealth and splendour that still dazzle down the centuries.

Across the centre of the peninsula and well beyond the effective control of their absentee landlord in Avignon, the Papal States succumbed in their turn to the prevailing fashion for despotism. The Este of Ferrara, the Pepoli of Bologna, the Malatesta of Rimini and their like might call themselves papal vicars and punctiliously acknowledge the suzerainty of St Peter, but within their respective cities their power remained absolute. Only in Rome itself, despite the attempts of the Colonna and their rivals the Orsini, was popular republican feeling strong enough to hold its own, but Rome was by now perhaps the saddest place in Italy. Deserted by the Popes, its principal *raison d'être*, its population reduced by malaria, famine and factional strife to a pitiable 20,000, the capital of Western Christendom had sunk to a level of degradation such as it had never before known. More than any other city, it now needed a leader who would focus its aspirations and restore its self-respect. At the moment of its darkest despair, it found one.

Cola di Rienzo, son of a Roman washerwoman, was a visionary, a fanatic, a superb showman and a demagogue of genius. In 1344, when he was thirty-one, he launched his campaign against the aristocracy of Rome, inflaming the popular imagination with his evocations of the city's past greatness and his prophecies of its glorious rebirth. Such was his success that three years later, on the Capitol, he was invested with the title of Tribune and limitless dictatorial powers; then, summoning a 'national' parliament, he solemnly conferred Roman citizenship on all the cities of Italy and announced plans for the election of an Italian Emperor. But appeals for Italian unity, whether pronounced by a German prince or a Roman demagogue, were doomed to failure. By the end of 1347 not only the other cities but the Roman mob itself had turned against Cola and forced him into exile. Seven years later he managed to return, but the old magic was gone; the mob, fickle as always, rose against him almost at once. In vain he showed himself on the balcony of the Capitol, clad in shining armour and bearing aloft the banner of Rome; they only jeered the louder. Disguising himself as a beggar, he tried to flee, but the gold bracelets glinting under his rags betrayed him. Minutes later his body was hanging by the feet in a public square – a fate eerily similar to that which befell, in the mid-twentieth century, his closest and most successful imitator.

And yet, in his comet career, Cola had somehow managed to clear the minds of his fellow citizens of much of the cumbersome detritus of the Middle Ages and to give them a new awareness of their classical past. What he had accomplished in the political sphere was paralleled in the world of letters by his friend and supporter Francesco Petrarch. It was in 1341, only twenty years after Dante's death, that Petrarch was crowned with the poet's laurels on the Capitol, but in those twenty years lay all the difference between late medieval scholasticism and the humanism of the Renaissance. Petrarch had none of Dante's gigantic vision, but his more slender genius led the way forward to a fresh, uncluttered outlook, based to some extent on the troubadour poets of Sicily and Provence but drawing its chief inspiration from the Latin authors of antiquity.

This new conception of the classical past as a signpost to the future led to a similar revival of interest in the literature of ancient Greece, long forgotten in the west and even in the Byzantine Empire largely neglected. This was principally the achievement of Giovanni Boccaccio, Petrarch's most gifted disciple, who kept for three years in his house an aged Greek of disgusting personal habits, preparing one of the first – and worst – translations of Homer into Latin. But it is not for his classical scholarship that Boccaccio is now remembered. His *Decameron* is a comparatively youthful work, but with it he did for Italian prose what Dante and Petrarch had done for poetry, simplifying it, refining it and forging it into a new literary instrument. The style which he developed, racy and astringent, gave the *Decameron* a

European reputation, starting a revived narrative tradition that can be traced through Chaucer and Shakespeare to La Fontaine and beyond.

To the Popes at Avignon, the impact of Cola di Rienzo and the success of the *Decameron* must have sounded a new note of danger. If the fullness of papal power were not soon reasserted in Italy, it would be lost forever. Cola's return to Rome had coincided with the appointment of Cardinal Gil Albornoz as legate to Italy, with the express task of bringing the States of the Church back into the papal fold. This terrifyingly able Spaniard succeeded to the point where, in 1367, Pope Urban V ventured to re-establish himself at the Lateran. He received a vociferous welcome from the people of Rome, and soon afterwards became the first and last Pope to receive visits from both Eastern and Western Emperors. But he was an old man; he soon grew homesick and, in 1370, despite warnings from St Bridget of Sweden that a return to Provence would be fatal, the attractions of Avignon became too strong for him. St Bridget was right. Within a few weeks he was dead.

Urban had shown with painful clarity why the Papacy had been so long absent from its rightful home. All the Avignon Popes and most of their curias had been Frenchmen – notoriously unwilling travellers at the best of times – to whom the ruins of Rome, insalubrious and smelly, must have constituted little enough temptation. It would take a serious crisis in Italy if, after seventy years, the papal conscience was to be reawakened. That crisis was not long in coming. In the States of the Church Albornoz had been succeeded by a horde of grasping French legates who made no secret of being out for what they could get and soon drove the unhappy cities to a state of open rebellion. In doing so they did not hesitate to make use of the so-called Free Companies – bands of foreign mercenaries who, when not otherwise employed, roamed the countryside supporting themselves on protection money, highway robbery and blackmail. In 1375 one of the worst of these, the English Company of Sir John Hawkwood, was despatched by the legate in Bologna to lay waste the Florentine harvests. To the Italian cities it seemed that papal iniquity could be carried no further. A wave of rabid anticlericalism swept through Tuscany, Umbria and the Papal States, and by the end of the year no less than eighty towns had expelled their papal garrisons.

Away in Avignon, Gregory XI acted quickly and firmly. Florence, the ringleader of the rising, was placed under an interdict; all the Christian princes of Europe were commanded to seize Florentine goods wherever they might be found and to sell all local Florentine merchants into slavery. These were fearsome measures, but they had no effect. Gregory saw that his only hope lay in an immediate return to Rome. Spurred on by the entreaties of St Catherine of Siena – carrying on where St Bridget had left off – he embarked with his reluctant curia at the end of 1376 and on 17 January 1377 made his formal entry into the city. It was a sad homecoming; in Florence his troops were taking hideous vengeance, while even in Rome his position was by no means secure. He was in fact seriously contemplating a return to Avignon when, fortunately for Rome, he died in the following year. The Romans had not always treated their Popes with particular affection or respect, but they were determined not to let them go again. '*Romano lo volemo, o almeno italiano!*'[1] they shouted throughout the ensuing conclave, and they got what they wanted – up to a point. The new Pope, Urban VI, showed every sign of being mentally unhinged and indeed tortured at least four of his cardinals to death, but he was at least an Italian.

The period of the Avignon Popes marks the close of the Middle Ages. When Clement V left Italy the old order was dying, but little had yet appeared to take its place. Though the imperial throne was temporarily vacant, men still remembered the magnificent Frederick, and wept for Manfred and Conradin. Papal pride had been brought low. Scholastic philosophy had reached, with St Thomas Aquinas, at once its highest pinnacle and its logical conclusion. It remained only for Dante to sum up, in the *Divine Comedy*, the achievements and the failures, the wisdom and the blindness, the ideals, the hopes and the fears of medieval Italy.

Gregory XI returned to a land which, though in some respects unchanged, in others could never be the same again. Unity was as remote a possibility as ever: Guelf and Ghibelline, their original differences long forgotten, still hammered away at each other and the blood continued to flow as it always had, copious and unavailing. But seventy years without a Pope or an effective Emperor had removed the old polarities, and in 1347–48 the Black Death seemed to draw yet another curtain across the past and to expose the present yet more mercilessly to the winds of change. The secular, enquiring spirit which now spread over the land was not in itself new. Its roots went back to Roger of Sicily and his Greek and Arab sages, to Frederick and his falcons, to Manfred and his troubadours, to Arnold of Brescia and the scholastics, to the doctors and lawyers of Salerno and Bologna. But the

---

[1] 'We want a Roman, or at least an Italian!'

fourteenth century had given it a new momentum – in the political sphere with Cola di Rienzo and the despots of the north, in the cultural with Petrarch and the humanists, in the theological with Marsilius of Padua – and at the same time the papal barriers that had so long blocked its progress suddenly disappeared. The Renaissance was under way.

CHAPTER XII

The Fall of Constantinople

When, with the fall of Konya to the Karaman Turks in 1308, the moribund empire of the Seljuks finally crumbled, many small Turkoman states – some of them hardly larger than the tribes they represented – rose from its ruins. Among them was that of a young warrior named Othman (or Osman) who after a whirlwind campaign had declared his independence as ruler of the extreme western end of Anatolia. This territory he governed wisely and well until his death in 1326, in which year his son and successor Orhan – who assumed the title of Sultan – conquered the city of Bursa and made it his capital.[1] Three years later he captured the great Byzantine city of Nicaea (Iznik). Then in 1354 Orhan's son Süleyman crossed the Dardanelles to capture the fortress of Gallipoli, which he converted into a permanent stronghold.

Here was the first Turkish base on European soil, and an invaluable bridgehead; almost at once, the Ottomans began their relentless progress. As early as 1359 an advance guard had reached the walls of Constantinople. Fortunately it was not large enough to constitute any immediate threat to the city, but the rest of Thrace, less well protected and exhausted by civil war, proved an easy victim. In 1362, Adrianople surrendered and became under the name of Edirne, Orhan's European capital. Its position on the great road leading from Belgrade to Constantinople provided a perfect base from which to drive deeper into the Balkans; it also effectively isolated Constantinople from its European possessions. In every city and village that was captured, a large part of the native population was transported to slavery in Asia Minor, its place being taken by Turkish colonists.

That same year, 1362, saw the death of Orhan. He was succeeded as sultan – Süleyman having died of a fall from his horse two years before – by his second son, Murad, who soon proved himself a more energetic and determined leader than either his father or his elder brother, campaigning not only in Thrace but also in Bulgaria, capturing Philippopolis (Plovdiv) in 1363 and putting considerable pressure on

---

[1] Othman did not live to see it, but Orhan had his father's body brought there for burial in the citadel. The town thus became something of a shrine, and the burial place of all the early Ottoman Sultans.

the Bulgar Tsar John Alexander to collaborate with him against Byzantium. After a decisive battle on the Maritsa river in 1371, Bulgaria became a Turkish vassal and was soon wholly absorbed. Murad's other signal achievement was to reduce the emirs of western Anatolia to a state of total subjection; henceforth, as the Ottoman Sultans advanced into Europe, their rear would be secure.

Murad was assassinated during the historic battle of Kosovo, 'the field of blackbirds', on 15 June 1389. On that day, under the inspired leadership of his son Bayezit – who was proclaimed Sultan on the field – the Serbian army was utterly destroyed, the Serbian nation effectively annihilated for four hundred years. Bayezit – known to his subjects as *Yilderim*, the Thunderbolt – was a man of superhuman energy, given to outbreaks of almost insane violence and utterly merciless to all who stood in his way. During his thirteen-year reign, the pace of conquest quickened still further. In the spring of 1394 an immense Turkish host marched against Constantinople itself, and by the beginning of autumn the siege had begun in earnest. The Sultan ordered a complete blockade, and for some time essential supplies in the city ran desperately short. The blockade was to continue in one form or another for eight years; fortunately for the citizens, however, as the ever-unpredictable Bayezit lost interest and involved himself in other operations that offered more immediate rewards, the pressure was soon relaxed.

Nevertheless, although Constantinople was spared for a little longer, other cities were less lucky. Thessalonica fell in 1394; in 1396, at Nicopolis (Nikopol) on the Danube, the Sultan smashed an army estimated at 100,000 – the largest ever launched against the infidel – raised by King Sigismund of Hungary. Thus it was that by the end of the fourteenth century the Ottoman conquest of eastern Europe and Asia Minor had acquired a momentum that could no longer be checked. Of the Sultan's Christian enemies, Serbia and Bulgaria were no more. Byzantium remained, but it was a Byzantium so reduced, so impoverished, so humiliated and demoralised as to be scarcely identifiable as the glorious Empire of the Romans that it had once been. And yet, doomed as it was, it was never to give up the struggle. Almost unbelievably, it was to endure another sixty years – and, at the last, to go down fighting.

For the Most Serene Republic of Venice, the last quarter of the fourteenth century had been traumatic indeed. The old rivalry with Genoa had come to a head. Beginning with a struggle over the island of Tenedos – which lay at the gateway to the Dardanelles, controlling the entrance to the straits – it had continued a good deal nearer home, with the siege and ultimate capture in August 1379 of Chioggia, a fortified city within the Venetian lagoon commanding a direct deep-water channel to Venice itself. Never in all its long history had the Republic been so seriously threatened; indeed, had the Genoese admiral Pietro Doria followed up his victory with an immediate assault on the city, it is hard to see how he could have failed. Fortunately for Venice, he decided instead to blockade it and starve it into submission, and the Venetian commander Vettor Pisani saw his chance. Chioggia, almost landlocked, depended on only three narrow channels; on midwinter night, 21 December, three large, stone-filled hulks were towed out in the darkness, and one sunk in each of them. The blockaders were blockaded. On 24 June 1380 the 4,000 beleaguered Genoese, half-dead with hunger, made their unconditional surrender.

It was not quite the end of the war; not until the following year did the two exhausted republics accept the offer of Count Amadeus of Savoy to mediate, and the consequent Treaty of Turin provided for the continuation of trade in the Mediterranean and the Levant by both Venice and Genoa side by side. But as time went on it gradually became clear that Venice's victory had been greater than she knew. Not for the first time, she was to astonish her friends and enemies alike by the speed of her economic and material recovery. Genoa, on the other hand, went into a decline. Her governmental system began to crumble; torn asunder by factional strife, she was to depose ten doges in five years and soon fell under a French domination which was to last a century and a half. Only in 1528, under Andrea Doria, was she finally to regain her independence; but by then the world had changed. Never again would she constitute a threat to Venice.

The Serenissima, by contrast, had emerged from six years of the most desperate war in her history with her political structure unshaken. No other state in Italy could boast such stability, or anything approaching it. Beyond her borders, all Italy had succumbed to the age of despotism; only she remained a strong, superbly ordered republic, possessed of a constitution that had effortlessly weathered every political storm, foreign and domestic, to which it had been exposed. The majority of her people, admittedly, had been shorn of effective power for the past hundred years,[1] but the civil service was open to all, the commerce and

---

[1] In fact, since the *serrata* (looking) *del Maggior Consiglio* in 1298, when the Greater Council was closed to all but those families whose names were inscribed in the Golden Book of the Republic.

the craftsmanship for which the city was famous provided a source of pride and satisfaction as well as rich material rewards, and few citizens ever seriously doubted that the administration – quite apart from being outstandingly efficient – had their own best interests at heart.

With the Genoese war now safely behind her, Venice set about rebuilding and extending her commercial empire. By the first years of the fifteenth century, thanks to a combination of political opportunism, diplomatic finesse, business acumen and an occasional touch of blackmail, she had acquired considerable territories on the Italian mainland, including the cities of Padua, Vicenza and Verona and continuing westward as far as the shores of Lake Garda – to say nothing of Scutari and Durazzo in southern Dalmatia; Nauplia, Argos and her old bases of Modone and Corone in the Morea; and most of the islands of the Cyclades and the Dodecanese. At last she could treat as an equal with nations like England, France and Austria – in her own right, as one of the great powers of Europe.

The Venetians had never considered themselves Italians. Cut off as they were from the *terra firma* by their lagoon, from earliest times their gaze had been fixed on the east, the source of almost all their commerce and their wealth. Thus their situation was as different from that of the cities of mainland Italy as it was possible for it to be. These cities too were independent republics, but they lacked Venice's extraordinary political constitution, with its intricate system of checks and balances that made it impossible for any one individual or family to acquire a stranglehold on the state. It was therefore inevitable that sooner or later, at some moment of foreign threat or domestic crisis, each would feel the need of a leader, and more than likely that, when the threat or the crisis was past, that leader would prove a good deal harder to get rid of than he had been to summon. Then, almost before the people knew it, he would have founded a dynasty.

This pattern – which, with minor variations, we find repeated time and again among the major cities of north and central Italy – was not without its advantages. The despot might well prove a tyrant, but he would depend for his position and his prestige on cutting a dash; this meant surrounding himself with a dazzling court, showing himself a munificent patron of the arts – and, incidentally, providing a perfect setting in which the Renaissance could flourish. One of the earliest, Can Grande della Scala of Verona, gave generous support to Dante and Giotto; other names that spring almost unbidden to the mind are those of the Visconti and the Sforza of Milan, the Gonzaga of Mantua, the Este of Ferrara, the Malatesta of Rimini, the Montefeltro of Urbino and above all the Medici of Florence.

What lent additional splendour to these Renaissance courts was the fact that, although the various rulers were almost constantly at war, they seldom if ever fought in person. Such fighting as needed to be done was the work of the *condottieri*, mercenary generals who sold their swords to the highest bidder. They were not invariably satisfactory; devoid of any emotional loyalty to their cause, they were often dilatory and occasionally duplicitous. But they spared their employers the discomforts of campaigning, allowing them still more time to pursue the arts of peace, and at their best they could be quite extraordinarily effective.

To the south of these Renaissance courts was the Papacy, now – with the return of the Popes from Avignon – on the threshold of a dramatic transformation. Cardinal Albornoz, the papal legate to Italy, had reorganised and consolidated the Papal States; with Venice, Milan, Florence and Naples, Rome was once again one of the five major powers in Italy. It was unfortunate, however, that at this moment the Church was once again rent by a particularly violent schism. Urban VI had so antagonised the cardinals of both the French and the Italian factions[1] that they had declared his election null and void and had elected a rival Pope, Clement VII, in his place. Urban, firmly entrenched in Rome, had refused to yield, and so the dispute had dragged on, with new Popes being elected on both sides as necessary. Finally, in March 1409, a General Council of the Church met in Pisa, repudiated both the rival Popes and elected a single successor. Its choice fell on the Cardinal Archbishop of Milan who, having started his life as an orphaned beggar boy in Crete, was to end it as Pope Alexander V.

But the Council had made one disastrous mistake. By calling the two rival Popes to appear before it – and declaring them contumacious when they refused – it implied its superiority over the Papacy, a principle which neither of the rival pontiffs could have been expected to endorse. Before long it became clear that its only real effect had been to saddle Christendom with three Popes instead of two. But it was unrepentant, and when Pope Alexander died suddenly in May 1410 it lost no time in electing his successor.

Baldassare Cossa, who now joined the papal throng under the name

---

[1] See Chapter XI, p. 215.

of John XXIII,[1] was widely believed at the time to have poisoned his predecessor. Whether he actually did so is open to doubt. He had, however, unquestionably begun life as a pirate; and a pirate, essentially, he remained. Morally and spiritually, he reduced the Papacy to a level of depravity unknown since the days of the 'pornocracy' in the tenth century. A contemporary chronicler records in shocked amazement the rumour current in Bologna – where Cossa had been papal governor – that during the first year of his pontificate he had violated no fewer than 200 matrons, widows and virgins, to say nothing of a prodigious number of nuns. His score over the three following years is regrettably not recorded; he seems, however, to have maintained a respectable average, for on 29 May 1415 he was arraigned before another General Council, this time at Constance. As Gibbon delightedly noted, 'the most scandalous charges were suppressed: the vicar of Christ was only accused of piracy, murder, rape, sodomy, and incest; and after subscribing his own condemnation, he expiated in prison the imprudence of trusting his person to a free city beyond the Alps.'

Next, in early July, Pope Gregory XII – Urban's third successor – was prevailed upon to abdicate with honour, with the promise that he would rank second in the hierarchy, immediately after the future Pope – a privilege that was the more readily accorded in view of the fact that, since he was by now approaching ninety and looked a good deal older, it was not thought likely that he would enjoy it for long. Indeed, two years later he was dead. By then, the anti-Pope Benedict XIII had been deposed in his turn, and with the election of Otto Colonna as Pope Martin V in 1417, the schism was effectively at an end.

It was Martin who, more than anyone else, was responsible for the Renaissance Papacy. Entering Rome in 1420 and continuing where Albornoz had left off, he took in hand the chaotic papal finances; in a largely ruined city with a population reduced to some 25,000, he initiated a programme of restoration and reconstruction of churches and public buildings; he strengthened papal power by dissolving the Council of Constance; and he succeeded – at least to some degree – in bringing under his control the Church in France, which had become quite impossibly arrogant and overbearing during the years of the Avignon Popes. Himself a member of one of the oldest and most

---

[1] The circumstances of his election and subsequent deposition have denied him a place on the canonical list of Popes. It was none the less somewhat surprising that Cardinal Angelo Roncalli should have adopted the same name on his election to the Papacy in 1958.

distinguished Roman families, he took the first significant steps in transforming the College of Cardinals and the curia from the genuinely international bodies that they had been heretofore into institutions that were predominantly Italian. (This aroused much criticism at the time, but it enabled him to create the first really efficient curia.) Finally, he re-established order in the Papal States.

The Papal States should never have existed. They were founded on the so-called Donation of Constantine,[1] a story deliberately fabricated by the curia in the early eighth century according to which Constantine the Great, on moving his capital to Constantinople in 330, had conferred upon Pope Sylvester I dominion over Rome and 'all the provinces, places and *civitates* of Italy and the Western regions'. No one thought to doubt its veracity until 1440, when the Renaissance humanist Lorenzo Valla proved the document on which it was based to be a forgery; by that time the six states had long been a *fait accompli*. Papal control over them varied considerably; Ferrara and Bologna, for example, were allowed almost complete self-government, while Pesaro and Forlì were kept on a much tighter leash, with the Popes frequently imposing their own vicars. All six, however, were obliged in one way or another to provide an annual subsidy to the papal coffers; together, they were often the Papacy's chief source of income.

Pope Martin's death in 1431 left his work still unfinished. His two separate responsibilities – on the one hand, that of re-establishing papal supremacy over the conciliar movement (an inevitable consequence of the recent schism) and, on the other, that of defending papal lands against his neighbours and several rapacious *condottieri* – had left him little time for anything else. His successor, Eugenius IV, was forced out of Rome three years later by a republican revolution and spent the next nine years in exile in Florence. There, however, he scored what appeared at the time to be a major diplomatic victory. Early in 1438 the Byzantine Emperor John VIII Palaeologus had arrived in Italy with a huge following – it included *inter alia* the Orthodox Patriarch of Constantinople, eighteen metropolitans and twelve bishops, including the brilliant young Bessarion, Metropolitan of Nicaea, and Isidore, Bishop of Kiev and all Russia – with the object of reaching some sort of accommodation with the Church of Rome. Neither John nor any of his

---

[1] See Chapter VI.

subjects had the slightest wish to reconcile their differences on theological grounds, but his empire seemed doomed and he knew that while it remained in Roman eyes heretical there was no hope of persuading the west to send a military expedition against the ever more threatening Turk. The conference began its deliberations at Ferrara, but subsequently moved to Florence – where, on 5 July 1439, an official Decree of Union was signed by all but one of the senior Greek churchmen. The Latin text of the decree began with the words *Laetentur Coeli* – 'let the heavens rejoice'. But the heavens, as it soon became clear, had precious little reason to do so.

The Emperor John had a sad homecoming. Back in Constantinople, he found the Council of Florence universally condemned. The Patriarchs of Jerusalem, Antioch and Alexandria had already disowned the delegates who had signed on their behalf. These and the other signatories were condemned as traitors to the faith, castigated throughout the capital and in several cases physically attacked – to the point where in 1441 a large number of them issued a public manifesto, regretting that they had ever put their names to the decree and formally retracting their support for it. Suddenly, the Emperor's own position on the throne looked distinctly uncertain. True, there were other distinguished pro-unionists who might have given him their support, but Bessarion of Nicaea, who had converted to Catholicism in 1439 and had almost immediately been made a cardinal, had left Constantinople in disgust within a few months of his return and taken the first available ship back to Italy, never again to set foot on Byzantine soil. His friend Isidore of Kiev, who had also been admitted to the cardinalate, was less lucky; on his return to Moscow he was deposed and arrested, though later he too managed to escape to Italy.[1]

For Pope Eugenius, on the other hand, there was no uncertainty. Church union now existed, at least on paper; and it was now his duty to raise a Crusade against the enemies of Byzantium. Were he not to do so, he would not only be going back on his word to the Emperor; he would be proclaiming to all that the Council of Florence had been a failure, the *Laetentur Coeli* worthless. In eastern Europe if not in the west, he found willing recruits, and an army some 25,000 strong, composed largely of Serbs and Hungarians, set off in the late summer

---

[1] In Rome Bessarion was to found an academy for the translation and publication of ancient Greek authors. By the time of his death in 1472 he had amassed an important library of Greek manuscripts, all of which he left to Venice, where they became the nucleus of the Biblioteca Marciana.

of 1443 under the Hungarian King Ladislas, the Serb George Brankovich and the brilliant John Hunyadi, Voyevod of Transylvania. It began promisingly enough: the cities of Nish and Sofia had both fallen by Christmas. The Ottoman Sultan Murad II, simultaneously threatened with serious risings by the Karaman Turks in Anatolia, by George Kastriotes – the famous Skanderbeg – in Albania and by the Emperor's brother Constantine Palaeologus, Despot of the Morea,[1] saw that he must come to terms and invited the three leaders to his court at Adrianople. The result was a ten-year truce, granted by the Sultan in return for a number of not very generous concessions in the Balkan peninsula.

When the news reached Rome, Eugenius and his curia were horrified. The Crusade had been intended to drive the Turks out of Europe; by the terms of this truce, they seemed almost as firmly entrenched as ever. The Pope's right-hand man, Cardinal Giuliano Cesarini, left at once for Ladislas's court at Szegedin, where he formally absolved the King from his oath to the Sultan and virtually ordered the Crusade on its way again. Ladislas should have refused. Absolution or no absolution, he was breaking his solemn word to the Sultan. Besides, his forces were by now dangerously diminished. Many of the erstwhile Crusaders had already left for home, and Brankovich – who had had his Serbian territories restored to him – was delighted with the truce and deter- mined to observe it. But the young King decided to do as he was bidden.

In September he was back with what was left of the army, and accompanied now by the cardinal himself. Somehow he managed to make his way across Bulgaria to the Black Sea near Varna, where he expected to find his fleet awaiting him. The allied ships, however – mostly Venetian – were otherwise engaged. Murad, on hearing of Ladislas's betrayal, had rushed back from Anatolia with an army of 80,000 men, and the ships were at that moment striving to prevent him from crossing the Bosphorus. They failed. Forcing his way across the strait, the furious Sultan hurried up the Black Sea coast and on 10 November 1444, just outside Varna, with the broken treaty pinned to his standard, tore into the Crusading army. The Christians fought with desperate courage; outnumbered, however, by more than three to one, they had no chance. Ladislas fell; so, shortly afterwards, did Cesarini.

---

[1] The Morea – better known to us as the Peloponnese – had seen its Frankish occupiers gradually wither away, and had been an autonomous despotate within the Byzantine Empire since the middle of the preceding century. It was usually entrusted to a senior member of the Emperor's family.

The army was annihilated; of its leaders, only John Hunyadi managed to escape, with a handful of his men. The last Crusade ever to be launched against the Turks in Europe had ended in catastrophe.

Resistance was not yet quite over. The following summer the Despot Constantine embarked on a raiding expedition through central Greece as far as the Pindus Mountains and into Albania. He was welcomed everywhere he went. Meanwhile his own governor of Achaia, with a small company of cavalry and foot-soldiers, crossed to the north shore of the Gulf of Corinth and drove the Turks out of western Phocis (the region around Delphi). This last insult was too much for Murad. Only a few months before, he had abdicated his throne in favour of his son; now he furiously resumed his old authority to take vengeance on these upstart Greeks. In November 1446 he swept down into the Morea at the head of an army of some 50,000. Phocis was once again overrun; Constantine hurried back to the Hexamilion, a great defensive fortification running six miles across the Isthmus of Corinth, roughly along the route of the present canal, determined to hold it at all costs. But Murad had brought with him something the Greeks had never seen before: heavy artillery. For five days his huge cannon pounded away at the wall, and on 10 December he gave the order for the final assault. Most of the defenders were taken prisoner or massacred; Constantine himself barely managed to make his way back to his capital at Mistra.

In one respect he was lucky: his capital was spared. It had been saved by one thing only: an unusually early and severe winter. Had the Sultan launched his campaign in May or June rather than in November, his army would have had no difficulty in reaching the furthest corners of the Peloponnese; Mistra would have been reduced to ashes, the Despot would have been killed – and Byzantium would have been deprived of its last Emperor.

On 31 October 1448 John VIII died in Constantinople, to be succeeded by his brother Constantine. Of all the Byzantine Emperors John is in appearance the best known, thanks to his portrait in the famous fresco by Benozzo Gozzoli that adorns the chapel of the Palazzo Medici–Riccardi in Florence. He had hardly deserved his posthumous celebrity; but he had done his best, and had worked diligently for what he believed to be right. Besides, the situation was already past all hope; anything he attempted would have been doomed to failure. And perhaps it was just as well. Byzantium, devoured from within, threatened from without, scarcely capable any longer of independent

action, reduced now to an almost invisible dot on the map of Europe, needed – more, perhaps, than any once-great nation has ever needed – the *coup de grâce*. It had been a long time coming. Now, finally, it was at hand.

Four months after John's death, on 13 February 1451 in Adrianople after an apoplectic seizure, Sultan Murad followed him to the grave. He was succeeded by his third son, Mehmet – the two older brothers having died some years before, at least one of them in suspicious circumstances – who was now eighteen. Mehmet was a serious, scholarly boy; by the time of his accession he is said to have been fluent not only in his native Turkish but in Arabic, Greek, Latin, Persian and Hebrew. On hearing the news he hastened to the capital, where he confirmed his father's ministers in their places or appointed them elsewhere. In the course of these ceremonies Murad's chief widow arrived to congratulate him on his succession. Mehmet received her warmly and engaged her for some time in conversation; she returned to the harem to find that her infant son had been murdered in his bath. The young Sultan, it seemed, was not one to take chances.

Within months of his succession Mehmet had concluded treaties with Hunyadi, Brankovich and the Doge of Venice, Francesco Foscari; messages of goodwill had been sent to the Prince of Wallachia, to the Knights of St John in Rhodes and to the Genoese lords of Lesbos and Chios. To the ambassadors despatched by Constantine XI in Constantinople the Sultan is said to have replied almost too fulsomely, swearing by Allah and the Prophet to live at peace with the Emperor and his people, and to maintain with him those same bonds of friendship that his father had maintained with John VIII. Perhaps it was this last promise that put the Emperor on his guard; he seems to have been one of the first European rulers to sense that the young Sultan was not all that he seemed. On the contrary, he was very dangerous indeed.

Mehmet may well have had similar feelings about Constantine, who in his days as Despot of the Morea had constituted a considerable thorn in the flesh of his father, Murad. Constantine Dragases – although a Palaeologus through and through, he preferred to use this Greek form of his Serbian mother's name – was now in his middle forties, twice widowed and – since neither of his marriages had proved fruitful – actively seeking a third wife. When he had heard of the death of Murad in 1451 he had had the brilliant idea of marrying one of the Sultan's widows: Maria, the Christian daughter of old George Brankovich.

After fifteen years in the harem she had remained childless, and it was generally believed that the marriage had never been consummated. She was, however, the stepmother of the new young Sultan; what better way could there be of keeping the boy under proper control?

There is little point in speculating on how history might have been changed had Constantine Dragases indeed married Maria Brankovich. Not, probably, very much. It is perhaps just conceivable that she could have succeeded in persuading her stepson to renounce his designs on Constantinople; in such an event the Byzantine Empire might possibly have struggled on for another generation or two. But it could never have recovered its strength. Powerless and penniless, a Christian island alone in a Muslim ocean, its days would still have been numbered, its eventual destruction inevitable. In fact, although her parents gave their delighted blessing to the plan, it foundered on Maria herself. She had sworn an oath, she explained, that if ever she escaped from the infidel she would devote the rest of her life to celibacy, chastity and charitable works. Subsequent events were all too soon to justify her resolution.

Mehmet, meanwhile, was losing no time. At that point on the Bosphorus where the straits were at their narrowest, immediately opposite the castle which his great-grandfather Bayezit I had erected on the Asiatic shore, he decided to build another; the two fortresses together would give him undisputed control of the channel. (It was true that the land on which this new castle was to stand was theoretically Byzantine but, as Mehmet pointed out, he could not help that.) In the early spring of 1452 all the churches and monasteries in the immediate neighbourhood were demolished to provide additional building materials, and on 15 April the construction work began. Nineteen and a half weeks later, on 31 August, the great castle of Rumeli Hisar was complete, looking essentially the same as it does today. The Sultan then mounted three huge cannon on the tower nearest the shore and issued a proclamation that every passing ship, whatever its nationality or provenance, must stop for examination. In late November a Venetian vessel, laden with food and provisions for Constantinople, ignored this instruction. It was blasted out of the water. The crew were executed; the captain, a certain Antonio Rizzo, was impaled on a stake and exposed as a warning to any other commander who might think of following his example.

Early the following year the Turkish fleet began to assemble off the Gallipoli peninsula. It seems to have comprised not less than ten

biremes and six triremes,[1] fifteen oared galleys, some seventy-five fast longboats, twenty heavy sailing-barges for transport and a number of light sloops and cutters. Even the Sultan's closest advisers were said to have been astonished by the scale of this vast armada, but their reactions can have been as nothing compared with those of the Byzantines, who saw it a week or two later making its way slowly across the Marmara to drop anchor beneath the walls of their city.

The Ottoman army, meanwhile, was gathering in Thrace. The Greek estimate of 300–400,000 is plainly ridiculous; Turkish sources – presumably fairly reliable – suggest some 80,000 regular troops and up to 20,000 irregulars, or *bashi-bazouks*. Included in the former category were about 12,000 janissaries. These elite troops of the Sultan had been recruited as children from Christian families throughout the empire, forcibly converted to Islam and subjected to a rigorous military and religious training; some had been additionally trained as sappers and engineers. Legally they were slaves, in that they enjoyed no personal rights outside their regimental life. But they received regular salaries and were anything but servile; as recently as 1451 they had staged a near-mutiny for higher pay, and janissary revolts were to be a regular feature of Ottoman history until well into the nineteenth century.

Mehmet was proud of his army and prouder still of his navy, but he took the greatest pride of all in his weaponry. Cannon, in a very primitive form, had already been in use for well over a hundred years; Edward III had employed one at the siege of Calais in 1347, and they had been known in north Italy for a good quarter of a century before that, but in those early days they were powerless against solid masonry. By 1446, as we have seen, they had grown effective enough to demolish the Hexamilion at Corinth; even so, it was not until 1452 that a German engineer named Urban presented himself before the Sultan and offered to build him cannon that would blast the walls of Babylon itself. The first of these had accounted for the Venetian ship off Rumeli Hisar; Mehmet then ordered another, double the size. This was completed in January 1453. It is said to have been nearly twenty-seven feet long, with a barrel two and a half feet in diameter. The bronze was eight inches thick. When it was tested, a ball weighing some 1,340 pounds hurtled through the air for well over a mile before burying itself six feet deep in the ground. Two hundred engineers were sent out to

---

[1] Unlike the ancient vessels of the same name, Turkish biremes and triremes possessed a single bank of oars only. In the triremes there were three rowers to each oar, in the biremes they sat in pairs.

prepare for the journey of this fearsome construction to Constantinople, smoothing the road and reinforcing the bridges, and at the beginning of March it set off, drawn by thirty pairs of oxen, with another 200 men to hold it steady.

The Sultan himself left Adrianople on 23 March. Medieval armies – particularly if they were carrying siege equipment – moved slowly, but on 5 April he pitched his tent before the walls of Constantinople, where the bulk of his huge host had arrived three days before. Determined to lose no time, he at once sent under a flag of truce the message to the Emperor that was required by Islamic law, undertaking that all subjects of the Empire would be spared, with their families and property, if they made immediate and voluntary surrender. If they refused, no mercy would be shown.

As expected, his message remained unanswered. Early in the morning of 6 April his cannon opened fire.

The people of Constantinople too had been at work: repairing and strengthening the defences, clearing out the moats, laying in stores of food, arrows, tools, heavy rocks and anything else that they might need. Meanwhile their Emperor had sent further appeals to the west, but the response had as usual been lukewarm. In February the Venetian Senate had finally agreed to the despatch of two transports, each carrying 400 men, with fifteen galleys as soon as they could be prepared, but this fleet did not leave the lagoon until 20 April. Fortunately for the honour of the Serenissima, the Venetian colony in the city produced a nobler response, undertaking that none of its vessels would return home; in all, the Venetians were able to provide nine merchant-men, including three from their colony of Crete.[1]

The defenders also included a Genoese contingent. Many of them came, as might have been expected, from the Genoese colony at Galata, the largely foreign quarter of Constantinople lying to the northeast of the Golden Horn; in addition, there was an honourable group from Genoa itself, some 700 young men who had been appalled by the pusillanimity of their government – it had promised Constantine just one ship – and had determined to fight for Christendom. Their leader, Giovanni Giustiniani Longo, was a member of one of the Republic's leading families and a renowned expert in siege warfare. Allies like

---

[1] It must sadly be recorded that, in defiance of their promise, on the night of 26 February seven Venetian ships, carrying some 700 Italians, slipped out of the Golden Horn and headed for home.

these were more than welcome, but though they may have afforded the Emperor some encouragement, they cannot have given him any real hope. His ships in the Golden Horn numbered just twenty-six, a pitiable number in comparison to the Ottoman fleet. Towards the end of March he had ordered his secretary George Sphrantzes – who has left us a full account of the siege – to make a census of all the able-bodied men in the city, including priests and monks, who could be called upon to man the walls. The population of the city had been dramatically reduced by ten separate visitations of the Black Death in the previous century; nonetheless, the final figure was far worse than he could have imagined: 4,983 Greeks and rather less than 2,000 foreigners. To defend fourteen miles of walls against Mehmet's army of 100,000, he could muster less than 7,000 men.

The land walls in which Byzantium put its trust during that fateful spring of 1453 ran from the shores of the Marmara to the upper reaches of the Golden Horn, forming the western boundary of the city. They were already more than a thousand years old. Known as the Theodosian Walls after the Emperor Theodosius II in whose reign they were built, they were in fact completed in 413 when he was still a child. In terms of medieval siege warfare they were impregnable. Any attacking army had first to negotiate a deep ditch some sixty feet across, much of which could be flooded to a depth of about thirty feet in an emergency. Beyond this was a low crenellated breastwork with a terrace behind it about thirty feet wide; then the outer wall, seven feet thick and nearly thirty feet high, with ninety-six towers at regular intervals along it. Within this wall ran another broad terrace, and then the principal element of the defence, the great inner wall, about sixteen feet thick at the base and rising to a height of forty feet above the city. It too had ninety-six towers, alternating in position with those of the outer bastion. The result was almost certainly the most formidable municipal fortification constructed in the middle ages.

But the middle ages were past. Over the next eight weeks the Sultan subjected those walls to a bombardment unprecedented in the history of siege warfare. Behind makeshift wooden stockades, the defenders worked ceaselessly to repair the damage, but it was clear that they could not continue to do so indefinitely. Only one of their defences seemed immune from any onslaught that the enemy could launch against it: the great chain which stretched across the entrance to the Golden Horn from a tower just below the Acropolis, on what is now Seraglio Point, to another on the sea walls of Galata. A few days after the siege began the Turkish admiral had led a number of his heaviest ships to ram it, but it had held firm.

It was one of the Sultan's characteristics that he would suddenly focus all his attention on a single objective, which he would pursue obsessively until it was gained; by the middle of April his mind was fixed on control of the Golden Horn. The method by which he proposed to achieve it seems barely credible to us today: he set his engineers to work on a road running behind Galata, from a point on the Bosphorus shore over the hill near what is now Taksim Square and down to the Golden Horn at Kasımpaşa. Iron wheels had been cast, and metal tracks; his carpenters, meanwhile, had been busy fashioning wooden cradles large enough to accommodate the keels of medium-size vessels. On Sunday morning, 22 April, the Genoese colony in Galata watched dumbfounded as some seventy Turkish ships were slowly hauled, by innumerable teams of oxen, over a 200-foot hill and then lowered gently down again into the Horn.

By the beginning of May, the Emperor knew that he could not hold out much longer. One hope only remained: a relief expedition from Venice. Was there a fleet on its way, or not? If so, how big was it, and what was its cargo? Most important of all, how soon would it arrive? On the answers to these questions the whole fate of Constantinople now depended. And so it was that just before midnight on 3 May a Venetian brigantine, flying a Turkish standard and carrying a crew of twelve volunteers all disguised as Turks, slipped out under the boom. On the night of the 23rd it returned, pursued by an Ottoman squadron. Fortunately, Venetian seamanship was still a good deal better than Turkish, and soon after nightfall it succeeded in entering the Horn. The captain immediately sought an audience with the Emperor. For three weeks, he reported, he had cruised through the Aegean; nowhere had he seen a trace of the promised expedition, or indeed of any Venetian shipping. When he realised that it was useless to continue the search, he had called a meeting of the sailors and asked them what they should do. One had advocated sailing home to Venice, arguing that Constantinople was probably already in Turkish hands, but he had been shouted down. To all the rest, their duty was clear; they must report back to the Emperor, as they had promised to do. And so they had returned, knowing full well that they would probably never leave the city alive. Constantine thanked each one personally, his voice choked with tears.

*

On 26 May the Sultan held a council of war. The siege, he told those around him, had continued long enough. The time had come for the final assault. The following day would be given over to preparations, the day after that to rest and prayer. The attack would begin in the early hours of Tuesday, 29 May. No attempt was made to conceal the plan from the defenders within the city. Some of the Christians in the Turkish camp even shot arrows over the walls with messages informing them of Mehmet's intentions, but such measures were hardly necessary; the frenzied activity day and night in the Turkish camp told its own story.

On the last Monday of the Empire's history, the people of Constantinople – including their Emperor – left their houses and gathered for one last collective intercession. As the bells pealed out from the churches, all the most sacred icons and the most precious relics were carried out to join the long, spontaneous procession of Greeks and Italians, Orthodox and Catholic alike, that wound its way through the streets and along the whole length of the walls. By the time it was finished, dusk was falling. From all over the city, as if by instinct, the people were making their way to the Church of the Holy Wisdom. For the past five months the building had been generally avoided by the Greeks, defiled as they believed it to be by the Latin usages that no pious Byzantine could possibly accept. Now, for the first and last time, liturgical differences were forgotten. St Sophia was, as no other church could ever be, the spiritual centre of Byzantium. In this moment of supreme crisis there could be nowhere else to go.

The service was in progress when the Emperor arrived to take communion with his subjects. Much later, when all but the few permanent candles had been put out and the great church was in darkness, he slipped back in and spent some time alone in prayer. Then he returned to the walls. He had no sleep that night, for Mehmet did not wait for dawn to launch his assault. At half past one in the morning he gave the signal. Suddenly, the silence of the night was shattered, the blasts of trumpets and the hammering of drums combining with the bloodcurdling Turkish war cries to produce a clamour fit to waken the dead. At the same time the bells of all the churches in Constantinople began to peal, a sign to the whole city that the final battle had begun.

The attacks came in wave after wave: first the irregular *bashi-bazouks* – untrained and with little staying power, but readily expendable and ideal for demoralising the defenders and making them easier victims for the more sophisticated fighters that would follow them; then the regiments of Anatolian Turks, fully trained and superbly disciplined, pious Muslims to a man and determined to win eternal rewards in paradise by being the first to enter the greatest city in Christendom; finally the janissaries, advancing across the plain at the double, their ranks unbroken and dead straight despite all the missiles that the defenders could hurl against them. Soon after dawn, a bolt struck Giovanni Giustiniani Longo and smashed through his chest. Confusion spread through the ranks of the Genoese, many of whom fled, but by now it hardly mattered. Within an hour the Turks had made a breach in the wall and were streaming into the city. The Emperor, seeing that all was lost, plunged into the fray where the fighting was thickest. He was never seen again.

By now it was morning, with the waning moon high in the sky. The hours that followed were horrible indeed. By noon the streets of Constantinople were running red with blood. Houses were ransacked, women and children raped and impaled, churches razed, icons wrenched from their golden frames, books ripped from their silver bindings. In the Church of the Holy Wisdom, matins were already in progress when the berserk conquerors were heard approaching. The poorer and more unattractive of the congregation were massacred on the spot, the remainder lashed together and led off to the Turkish camps for their captors to use as they liked. The officiating priests continued with the Mass for as long as possible before being slaughtered where they stood, at the high altar; there are among the Orthodox faithful those who still believe that at the last moment one or two of them gathered up the most precious of the sacred vessels and mysteriously disappeared with them into the southern wall of the sanctuary. There they will remain until the day Constantinople becomes once again a Christian city, when they will resume the liturgy at the point at which it was interrupted.

The Sultan had promised his men the three days of looting to which by Islamic tradition they were entitled, but the orgy of violence had been on such a scale that there were no protests when he brought it to a close on the same day as it had begun. He himself waited until the worst excesses were over before entering the city. Then, in the late afternoon, he rode slowly down the principal thoroughfare, the Mese, to St Sophia. Dismounting outside the central doors, he stooped and picked up a handful of earth which, in a gesture of humility, he sprinkled over his turban; only then did he enter the building. At his command the senior imam mounted the pulpit and proclaimed the name of Allah, the All-Merciful and Compassionate: there was no God but God, and Mohammed was his Prophet. That was the moment. Cross gave way to Crescent; St Sophia became a mosque; the Byzantine Empire was supplanted by the Ottoman; Constantinople became Istanbul. At twenty-one, Mehmet II had achieved his highest ambition.

The news of the fall of Constantinople, and with it the Byzantine Empire, was received with horror throughout Christendom. As the refugees spread westward they carried the epic story with them, and the story doubtless lost nothing in the telling. But western Europe, for all its deep and genuine dismay, was not profoundly changed. The two states most immediately affected, Venice and Genoa, lost no time in making the best terms they could with the Sultan.

The Venetian relief fleet – which had in fact been largely equipped by Pope Nicholas V – was anchored off Chios, waiting for a favourable wind to continue its journey to Constantinople, when some of the Genoese ships that had escaped from Galata drew alongside with the news. Its captain, Giacomo Loredan, promptly withdrew to Euboea, there to await further orders. Meanwhile, a special envoy, Bartolomeo Marcello, was sent at once to congratulate Mehmet on his victory, to emphasise the Republic's firm intent to observe the peace treaty concluded with his father and confirmed by himself, and to request the restitution of all Venetian ships remaining in Constantinople, pointing out that these were not warships but merchantmen. If the Sultan agreed to renew the treaty, Marcello was to ask that Venice should be allowed to maintain her trading colony in the city, with the same rights and privileges that she had enjoyed under Byzantine rule. Mehmet proved a hard bargainer. After the best part of a year's negotiation the ships and prisoners were released and the Venetian colony allowed to return; no longer, however, would it enjoy those territorial and commercial concessions on which its former power and prosperity had depended. The Latin presence in the east was already on the decline.

The Genoese had even more at stake than the Venetians, and had continued to play their double game. In Galata, their *podestà* had opened the gates the moment the Turks appeared, and had done everything he could to prevent his countrymen's unseemly exodus. After a time he was given assurances that the Genoese of Galata would remain in possession of their property and might practise their religion unhindered as long as they rang no bells and built no new churches, but they must surrender their arms and destroy their fortifications and citadel. Theoretically the Genoese trading colonies along the northern shore of the Black Sea – including the prosperous port of Caffa in the Crimea – would be allowed to continue, but since the death of Antonio Rizzo few sailors ventured through the straits and few merchants were prepared to pay the immense tolls demanded. With the exception of the island of Chios – which was to remain Genoese until 1566 – by the end of the century Genoa's commercial empire was gone.

In Rome, Pope Nicholas showed none of the cynicism and self-interest of the merchant republics. He did his utmost to galvanise the west for a Crusade, a cause which was enthusiastically supported by the two Greek cardinals, Bessarion and Isidore, as also by the papal legate in Germany, Aeneas Sylvius Piccolomini, the future Pope Pius II. But it was no use. Two or three hundred years before, Christian zeal had been enough to launch military expeditions for the rescue of holy places of pilgrimage; with the advent of Renaissance humanism, however, the old religious fire had been extinguished. Europe had dithered, and Byzantium had died. With the Ottoman army stronger than it had ever been, the old Empire was beyond all hope of resurrection.

The decade following the fall of Constantinople saw a number of mopping-up operations, notably in Greece, where the Latin Duchy of Athens ended in 1456 with the Turkish capture of the city. The last duke, Franco Acciajuoli, was murdered four years later when the Despotate of the Morea, in which he had taken refuge, came to a similar end. The Venetian colony of Negroponte – better known to us as the island of Euboea – fell in 1470. The still remaining Christian outposts included Crete, Cyprus, one or two strongholds in the Morea and a few of the Ionian Islands – notably Corfu, Cephalonia and Zante – together with a narrow strip of the Dalmatian coast. All of these remained Venetian. But in the Balkan hinterland, part of Bosnia had fallen as early as 1438 and the rest, together with Herzegovina in the south, was to crumble between 1463 and 1480.

There was, however, one other stronghold: the island of Rhodes, where since 1306 the Knights of St John had been simultaneously running their hospital and waging their own war against the infidel. For the west, they were now the first line of defence against the march of Islam: no longer a medieval anachronism but conceivably the very saviours of Christendom. For Sultan Mehmet, on the other hand, they were a permanent irritation, and in the spring of 1480 he moved against them. His army was probably about 70,000 strong, carried to the island by a fleet of some fifty ships. Also on board was a number of those formidable cannon which had served him so well at Constantinople. Against this huge host the Knights opposed about 600 members of their order, together with perhaps 1,500 paid foreign troops and local militia. They could also count on the active co-operation of the Rhodiots themselves, Christians to a man. They were commanded by their Grand Master, the fifty-seven-year-old Pierre d'Aubusson. Several years before, knowing that attack was inevitable, he had summoned the greatest military architects of the day to make the city of Rhodes as nearly impregnable as any city could be. Now that the Turks were at last on their way, he was ready for them.

The siege began on 23 May. Already by the middle of June parts of the city wall, pounded by nearly 1,000 cannonballs a day, were beginning to crumble, but somehow the Knights held firm. On 27 July came the final assault. As usual, the *bashi-bazouks*, untrained and expendable, led the way, followed by the janissaries. Bursting through what was left of the wall by the so-called Italian Tower, they managed to hoist the standard of the Prophet within the city; but then the Knights staged a massive counter-attack. The Grand Master was badly wounded a moment later, but suddenly panic spread through the *bashi-bazouk* line; they turned and fled. Why they did so remains a mystery. It has even been suggested that they were terrified by the sight of the Christian banners, emblazoned with pictures of the Virgin and saints, twisting and turning in the wind; they were after all Muslims, most of whom would never before have seen two-dimensional representations of the human face or figure. Whatever the reason, it is a rare thing indeed in the history of warfare for a besieging army to take flight after the walls are breached; for the Turkish army, triumph was from one moment to the next transformed into disaster. Probably some 4,000 lost their lives, including 300 janissaries who had invaded the Jewish quarter and had been cut off there.

The Knights had won a battle, but they had not yet won the war. Furious at his defeat, Sultan Mehmet immediately began preparing a fresh army, which he resolved to lead in person against them the following year. Had he done so, they would have stood no chance; the defences could never have been repaired in time. But in the spring of 1481, as he was riding south through Asia Minor on his way to take up his command, the Sultan was stricken by a sudden dysenteric fever. A day or two later he was dead. The Knights of St John were to hold their lovely island for another forty years, but now it was an island in more than just the geographical sense. The eastern Mediterranean had become, to all intents and purposes, a Muslim sea.

CHAPTER XIII

The Catholic Kings and the Italian Adventure

In the western Mediterranean on the other hand, Christianity was once again in the ascendant. The Spanish Reconquista was making slow progress, but the salient date for Spain – perhaps one of the most significant dates in all Spanish history – was 17 October 1469, which saw the marriage of Ferdinand II of Aragon to his cousin Isabella of Castile. Neither then possessed a crown, nor, technically, did the union at once give rise to a united Spain; the two kingdoms were not yet one. The monarchs – *los Reyes Catolicos*, 'the Catholic Kings', to give them the title conferred on them by the Spanish (Borgia) Pope Alexander VI – though soon to be sovereign in their own homelands, were but consorts in each other's. Of the two, Castile was very much the senior partner. In the marriage capitulations, Ferdinand bound himself to observe the laws and usages of Castile, to reside there (never leaving it without the consent of his wife) and to acknowledge her always as sovereign of Castile, he bearing the title of king by courtesy only. Nonetheless, when he succeeded to the Aragonese throne in 1479 his authority extended also over Catalonia, Valencia and the Balearic Islands, and included of course the great city of Barcelona, which had developed – since the fall of Constantinople had caused Genoa and Venice to draw in their horns – a commercial importance in all respects equal to theirs, with trading posts and consulates extending as far as Alexandria and even beyond.

Thus, from the beginning of their joint reign, Ferdinand and Isabella ruled over a far larger area of the Iberian peninsula than had been united for many centuries. They took immense pains, moreover, to display the closeness of their relationship: almost all official documents were issued in their joint names, and their propaganda endlessly – and exaggeratedly – stressed the love they bore each other. It seems legitimate, therefore, to see their marriage as the foundation-stone of modern Spain, and the vast conquests that they were to add to the kingdom during their lifetime served still further to emphasise its integrity.

The first of these conquests was that of the Muslim Kingdom of Granada, which despite its small size provided an example of civilised luxury which had no equal in Spain, and very few elsewhere. Despite the Arabic roots of its culture, relatively few of its people were in fact Arab; there had been little Arab immigration in recent centuries. In the towns the bulk of the population was composed of Berbers from North Africa; in the country the majority were native Spaniards, whose families had long since converted to Islam. As the Reconquista took its course, the kingdom had steadily diminished in size; Cordoba had been lost in 1236, Seville in 1248. By the end of the fifteenth century it could boast only two important cities: the city of Granada itself, with its population of about 60,000, and the port of Malaga, through which passed all the gold, the troops and the munitions collected from Africa and the Near East to carry on the holy war against Christian Spain.

On 2 January 1492, after ten years of resistance, the last Moorish ruler, Abu Abdullah Mohammed XI – known to Europeans as Boabdil – surrendered his kingdom and retired to Fez (though his wife Fatima and their children took Christian baptism and settled in Madrid). His surrender marked the beginning of the most crucial four months of Spanish history, seeing as they did both the intensification of that relentless course of religious persecution which was to have so disastrous an effect on the strength and vitality of Spain, and the launching of the most celebrated voyage of exploration ever known.

Few rulers in European history have shown themselves narrower or more bigoted than Isabella. Already in 1478 she and her husband had requested a papal bull introducing the Inquisition into Castile. It was at this time principally (and rather surprisingly) directed against the converted Jews – whose popular name, *marranos* (pigs), shows all too clearly how little their conversions had done to better their lot. Three years later all *marranos* charged with heresy were summoned to recant or face death at the stake. The first *auto-da-fé* was held in 1481, with six victims. By the time of Isabella's death in 1504 there had been more than 2,000.

Less than three months after the capitulation of Granada, the Queen felt strong enough to push her policy further. Encouraged by her Inquisitor-General Torquemada – who was himself originally Jewish – on 30 March she decreed that all Jews remaining unconverted by the end of June would be expelled from Spain, all their property confiscated. More than 100,000 were driven out, resulting in a vast Sephardic diaspora in northern Europe and the Near East. Several countries – notably the Netherlands – gave them a warm welcome; the

Ottoman Sultan Bayezit II went further, sending a whole fleet of ships to their rescue.[1]

Now it was the turn of the Muslims. By the terms of their capitulation they had been guaranteed their personal and religious liberty; Isabella had made no attempt to expel them, if only because she had no wish to see the country depopulated, its commerce and agriculture going to ruin. Instead, she had agreed to what was effectively a state within a state: an Islamic community whose faith, laws and customs were to remain inviolate. Many Muslims had nevertheless sought voluntary exile across the straits in Africa, particularly in Oran and Algiers, but to thousands of others the Queen's concessions must have seemed too good to be true – as indeed they soon proved to be. Isabella moved more carefully this time, only very gradually tightening the screw, but with every month that passed the Muslims found themselves treated more like pariahs, the practice of their religion more difficult and the pressure on them to accept Christian baptism more insistent. These attempts at forced conversion resulted in serious insurrections, and in 1502 a royal decree spelled out the choice once again: conversion, expulsion or execution. Unlike the Jews, the vast majority of the Muslims chose the first. By 1503, at least in theory, there were none left in Castile, but since few people believed in the genuineness of their conversion, the Moriscos (as the converts were called) supplied welcome new fodder for the Inquisition.

The war with Granada had been expensive; with its end spare funds again became available, and it was these that made possible the long-planned expedition by the Genoese Christopher Columbus, which was to end in the discovery of the Americas. Although Columbus had to defend his propositions to two separate commissions of enquiry, the first composed largely of churchmen and theologians, the second of philosophers, astronomers and cosmographers, the reasons for the Catholic Kings' eventual authorisation to him to proceed were not far to seek: the mopping-up of the eastern Mediterranean by the Turks had effectively closed the traditional Mediterranean trade route to the east. Fortunately it was now agreed that the world was round, and that the Indies could consequently be reached by sailing in either direction. The most important question now to be settled was which of the two routes

---

[1]Columbus, who was just setting out on his historic voyage from Genoa, was obliged to alter course because the sea ahead of him was so crowded with Turkish ships bringing Jewish refugees to safety.

was the shorter. The Portuguese, having learnt their seamanship from the Genoese and now inspired by their brilliant Prince Henry the Navigator, were already putting their money on the eastward route and feeling their way down the African coast.

There was nothing new about the idea of circumnavigating Africa. If we are to believe Herodotus, the Phoenicians had in effect achieved it around 600 BC,[1] and Genoa had made another attempt in 1291, sending the brothers Ugolino and Guido Vivaldi with two galleys to find their way to India by the ocean route. (Venice had never bothered; her compact with Mameluke Egypt and virtual control of the shipping lane through the Red Sea made it unnecessary.) The Vivaldis had been unlucky – they had foundered off the Canaries – and the fourteenth century had come and gone with no further attempts. In the later fifteenth, however – by which time there had been significant progress in the arts of shipbuilding, seamanship and navigation – it was a different story. The Cape of Storms (renamed by John II of Portugal the Cape of Good Hope) was rounded by the Portuguese Bartholomew Diaz in 1488; after that it was only a matter of time before the route to India was assured.

The age-old rivalry between Spain and Portugal naturally inclined the Spaniards to favour the westward alternative, and when Columbus set about persuading Ferdinand and Isabella of its virtues he was to a very large extent preaching to the converted. But the main purpose of his journey was, as always with the Spanish explorers, twofold: gold and the Gospel. From the Indies (parts of which were believed to have been evangelised by St Thomas) it was thought to be possible not only to open up a profitable trade in the fabled luxuries of the East but, with the help of the Great Khan – a wholly mythical figure who was believed to be friendly to Christians if not a Christian himself – to spread Christianity throughout the unknown subcontinent. Here was a proposal that went straight to the Queen's heart. True, her own kingdom had been theoretically cleared of the taint of Islam, but in the eastern and central Mediterranean the Ottoman advance showed no sign of slowing down. It had now reached as far as Italy, where bands of mounted Turkish irregulars had overrun the Friuli, laying waste the countryside, approaching so near to Venice that from the top of the campanile of St Mark the flames of the burning villages could be plainly seen. In 1480 the Sultan had launched a fleet of 100 sail against the port

---

[1] See Chapter I, p. 5.

of Otranto in Calabria and invested it without difficulty. Naples was now threatened, and even Rome itself. Clearly Christendom must take decisive action, but how? Pope Pius II had tried on two separate occasions to launch another Crusade, but had met with little response. In any case, the Ottoman army consisted of highly-trained professionals. In a direct confrontation it would be effectively invincible.

Here, perhaps, lay the answer to the problem: to approach the Turkish horde from the east, attacking it from the rear, where it would be weak and probably undefended. Isabella hesitated no longer. She was, she believed, financing not just the opening-up of a new and important trade route; she was taking the first exploratory but essential step towards what might be the last Crusade against the infidel. Ferdinand too was enthusiastic; Columbus later claimed to have brought a smile to the monarch's lips when he suggested that the profits from the great enterprise would pay for the conquest of Jerusalem. That smile may of course have been cynical, but Ferdinand could hardly have forgotten the old prophecy of the 'promised prince' who would raise his banner over the Holy City and rule the world. He and Isabella gave their formal approval on 17 April 1492, putting at Columbus's disposal the three tiny caravels – the largest of them little more than 100 feet long – that were to change that world beyond all recognition.

The story of Christopher Columbus and his epic voyage is not ours. It is important to us, however, in the effect it had on the fortunes of the Mediterranean. Just five years before the *Niña,* the *Pinta* and the *Santa Maria* set sail, Diaz had rounded the Cape; just six years afterwards, on 20 May 1498, his compatriot Vasco da Gama dropped anchor at Calicut (Kozhikode) on the Malabar coast of India. Da Gama's visit was not particularly successful; nobody wanted the distinctly shoddy merchandise he had brought with him, and he seems to have quite unnecessarily antagonised his hosts by his arrogance and quickness to take offence. His return journey, too, was plagued by bad luck. He missed the monsoon, thirty of his sailors died of scurvy, one of his ships had to be scuppered, and we do not even know the date he returned to Lisbon. But return he did, to uproarious acclaim. Not only had he found a continuous sea route to India; he had proved that Portuguese ships were capable – just – of getting there and back.

Another century and more was to pass before the Cape route was in regular use; throughout the sixteenth century there would be plenty of traffic passing through the Mediterranean. But henceforth the writing was on the wall. Even when the Turks did not make trouble – and they usually did – all cargoes bound for the further east had to be unloaded in Alexandria or some Levantine port. Thence they would be either transported overland to the pirate-infested Red Sea or consigned to some shambling camel caravan which might take two or three years to reach its destination. Now, merchants could look forward to a time when they could sail from London or Lisbon and arrive in India or Cathay in the same vessel. Meanwhile, thanks to Columbus and those who followed him, the New World was proving infinitely more profitable than the old, possessed as it was of a fabulous wealth, the lion's share of which went to Spain – and legally too. Within only seven months of Columbus's first landfall, Pope Alexander had issued the first of his five bulls settling the competing claims of Spain and Portugal over the newly discovered territories;[1] within twenty-five years, the galleons were regularly returning to their homeland loaded to the gunwales with loot. No wonder that the successors of Ferdinand and Isabella had their eyes fixed so firmly on the west. Jerusalem could wait.

It was not immediately apparent that this sudden opening-up of the oceans on both sides had dealt trade in the Mediterranean what would prove to be a paralysing blow. Gradually, however, men realised that – at least from the commercial point of view – the Middle Sea had become a backwater. To the east of the Adriatic it was now passable only with great difficulty and much good luck. To the west, it was still indispensable to Italy; but France was nowadays finding her northern ports on the English Channel a good deal more useful than Marseille or Toulon, while Spain, now entering her years of greatness, had other and better fish to fry. Not for another three hundred years, until the building of the Suez Canal, would the Mediterranean regain its old importance as a world thoroughfare.

It remained, as always, a battleground. In Italy, too, the year 1492 had been a milestone; it had seen the deaths of both Lorenzo de Medici (Lorenzo the Magnificent), ruler of Florence, and, just three months later, of Pope Innocent VIII. Lorenzo, now remembered principally for his patronage of the arts, had also been largely responsible for preserving the always tenuous balance of the Italian states; by main-

---

[1] The Pope ruled that the Catholic Kings were to be awarded all the land and islands, already discovered or thereafter to be discovered, that lay to the west of a line drawn from pole to pole, which itself ran 100 leagues to the west of the Azores and the Cape Verde Islands. Lands to the east of that line were allotted to Portugal (a concession which was later to allow the Portuguese to claim Brazil). This decision was ratified in 1494 by the Treaty of Tordesillas between the two countries.

taining the alliance of Florence, Milan and Naples he had provided a
focus for the smaller powers such as Mantua, Ferrara and some of the
Papal States, and had also kept in check the dangerous ambitions of
Venice. With his death and the succession of his feckless son Piero, that
moderating influence was gone. Pope Innocent, for all his corruption
and nepotism, had also been a force for peace; Rodrigo Borgia, the
Spaniard who succeeded him as Pope Alexander VI, was quite simply
out for what he could get. Italy lay once again open to attack, and that
attack was not long in coming.

The *casus belli* was Naples. Though it still claimed Sicily as part of
its kingdom, it had in fact been separated from the island proper ever
since the Sicilian Vespers, when the house of Anjou had been driven out
by that of Aragon and had retreated to the mainland. In 1435 the
Angevin line had died out with Queen Joanna II, and the mainland
throne of Naples, which she had left to an Angevin relative, had been
seized by the island ruler Alfonso of Aragon. Thus the two kingdoms
were now effectively reunited; each, however, had retained its separate
identity, and on Alfonso's death in 1458 they were separated again, the
mainland being devolved on his illegitimate son Ferdinand.[1] Ferdinand
inherited what continued to be, in every important respect, a medieval
monarchy. Feudal principles still prevailed; municipal liberties on the
northern model were still unheard of. The King – greedy, ruthless but
extremely capable – was feared and detested by his subjects, as was his
son Alfonso, who succeeded him in January 1494. But the bastard
grandson of a usurper, it was generally agreed, had but a tenuous claim
to the throne. Alfonso's position was open to challenge, and that
challenge came on 1 September 1494, when the twenty-two-year-old
King Charles VIII of France – described by the historian H. A. L. Fisher
as 'a young and licentious hunchback of doubtful sanity' – led an army
of some 30,000 into Italy to claim for himself, as a descendant of
Charles of Anjou, the Neapolitan throne. At once the two-hundred-
year-old rivalry between the houses of Anjou and Aragon flared up
again.

Charles's appearance was hardly what might have been expected in
a dashing young military adventurer. 'His Majesty,' reported the
Venetian ambassador[2] in that same year, 'is small, ill-formed and ugly
of countenance, with pale, short-sighted eyes, nose far too large and

---

[1] Not to be confused with Ferdinand of Spain, husband of Isabella.
[2] Venice had maintained a continuous embassy to the court of France since 1478 – the first
permanent diplomatic representation outside Italy.

abnormally thick lips which are always apart. He makes spasmodic movements with his hands that are most unpleasant to look upon, and his speech is extremely slow.' For him, too, 1492 had been significant, being the year in which he had been freed from the stern control of the former regent, his elder sister Anne de Beaujeu. She, certainly, would never have countenanced an adventure of the kind on which her brother had now embarked, from which his ministers had also done their best to dissuade him but in which he believed himself to be abundantly justified. He had no wish, he protested, to conquer the territory of others, only to claim such lands as belonged to him by right – which, for him, unquestionably included the Kingdom of Naples. And there was a further consideration: with this kingdom there had for the past three centuries been associated the style of King of Jerusalem,[1] a title which would give him the prestige necessary, once his Italian dominions were safely confirmed, to launch and lead the long-overdue Crusade of which he dreamed.

The expedition began promisingly enough. Charles, with his cousin the Duke of Orleans and his army – its cavalry drawn from the high nobility and gentry of France – his Swiss halberdiers and German pikemen, his Gascon archers and his quick-firing light artillery, crossed the Alps without incident over the Mont Genèvre pass, his heavy cannon having been shipped separately to Genoa. Milan, under its brilliant and all-powerful ruler Ludovico Sforza, received him with enthusiasm; so too did Lucca and Pisa; in Florence, welcomed as a liberator by the Dominican preacher Girolamo Savonarola, the King took the opportunity to expel Piero de' Medici – who displayed none of the statesmanship of his father Lorenzo. On 31 December Rome opened her gates, while a terrified Pope Alexander briefly took refuge in the Castel Sant' Angelo before sullenly coming to terms. Finally, on 22 February 1495, Charles entered Naples, while its people – who had never looked on the rival house of Aragon as anything other than foreign oppressors – welcomed him with enthusiasm. His Aragonese rivals fled to Sicily, and on 12 May Charles was for the second time crowned a king.

He did not remain long in his new kingdom; already his success was beginning to turn sour. The Neapolitans, delighted as they had been to get rid of the Aragonese, soon discovered that one foreign occupier was very much like another. Unrest also grew among the populations of

---

[1] See Chapter X, p. 189.

many smaller towns, who found themselves having to support, for no good reason that they could understand, discontented and frequently licentious French garrisons. Beyond the Kingdom of Naples, too, men were beginning to feel alarm. Even those states, Italian and foreign, who had previously looked benignly upon Charles's advance were asking themselves just how much further the young conqueror might be intending to go. Ferdinand and Isabella decided to send a fleet to Sicily; the Holy Roman Emperor-elect Maximilian,[1] terrified that Charles's successes might lead him in his turn to claim the imperial crown, also made his preparations; Pope Alexander, never happy about Charles, was becoming increasingly nervous; and even Ludovico Sforza of Milan, by now as alarmed as anyone, was further disconcerted by the continued presence at nearby Asti of the Duke of Orleans – whose claims to Milan through his grandmother, the Duchess Valentina Visconti, he knew to be no less strong than those of Charles to Naples. The result was the formation of what was known as the Holy League, ostensibly pacific but in fact with a single objective: to send the new King packing.

When news of the League was brought to Charles at Naples, he flew into a fury, but he did not underestimate the danger with which he was now faced. Only a week after his coronation, he left his new kingdom for ever and headed north. Following the west coast of the peninsula up to La Spezia, he then branched right along the mountain road that would bring him across the northern range of the Apennines and down again into Lombardy. Even in midsummer, the task of dragging heavy artillery over a high mountain pass must have been a nightmare. The ascent was bad enough, but the journey down was infinitely worse; it sometimes needed as many as 100 already exhausted men, lashed together in pairs, to restrain a single heavy cannon from careering over a precipice – and, if they did not act quickly, carrying them with it. At last, on 5 July, Charles was able to look down on the little town of Fornovo – and, deployed just behind it, on some 30,000 soldiers of the League under the command of the Marquis of Mantua, Francesco Gonzaga.

Gonzaga's army had every advantage. It outnumbered the French by three – possibly four – to one; it was fully rested and provisioned; and

---

[1] Maximilian was never to receive his imperial coronation by the Pope. In 1508, however, he was to issue the Proclamation of Trent, which allowed him to assume the title of Emperor without it, and which was reluctantly accepted by Pope Julius II.

it had had plenty of time to choose its position and prepare for the coming encounter. The French, by contrast, were exhausted, hungry and disinclined to fight. But fight they did, the King himself as bravely as any; the battle that followed was the bloodiest that Italy had seen for two hundred years. It did not, however, last long; according to the French ambassador to Venice, Philippe de Commines, who was present, everything was over in a quarter of an hour. Somehow Gonzaga managed to present it as a victory – even, on his return to Mantua, building a *chiesetta di vittoria* (a 'little church of victory') with a specially commissioned altarpiece by Mantegna; not everyone, however, would have agreed with him. The French admittedly forfeited their baggage train, but their losses were negligible compared with those of the Italians, who had utterly failed to stop them – as was seen when Charles and his men continued their march that same night and reached Asti unmolested only a few days later.

There was bad news awaiting them. A French naval expedition against Genoa had failed, resulting in the capture of most of the fleet. Louis of Orleans was being besieged in Novara by a Milanese army and unlikely to hold out much longer. Alfonso's son Ferrantino had landed in Calabria where, supported by Spanish troops from Sicily, he was rapidly advancing on Naples. On 7 July 1495 he reoccupied the city. Suddenly, all the French successes of the past year had evaporated. In October Charles managed to come to an agreement with Sforza which ended the effectiveness of the League; a week or two later he led his army back across the Alps, leaving Orleans behind to maintain a French presence as best he could.

Paradoxically, Charles's Italian adventure was to have its most lasting effect in northern Europe. When his army was paid off at Lyons in November 1495, it dispersed across the continent with reports of a warm, sunlit land inhabited by a people whose life of cultivated refinement went far beyond anything known in the greyer, chillier climes of the north, but who were too disunited to defend themselves against a determined invader. As the message spread, and as the painters, sculptors, plasterworkers and woodcarvers whom Charles had brought back with him from Italy began to transform his old castle at Amboise into a Renaissance palace, so Italy became ever more desirable in the eyes of her northern neighbours, presenting them with an invitation and a challenge which they were not slow to take up in the years to come.

The disbanded mercenaries carried something else too – deadlier far than any dream of conquest. Columbus's three ships, returning to Spain from the Caribbean in 1493, had brought with them the first cases of syphilis known to the Old World; through the agency of the Spanish mercenaries sent by Ferdinand and Isabella to support King Alfonso the disease had rapidly spread to Naples, where it was rife by the time Charles arrived. After three months of *dolce far niente*, his men must in turn have been thoroughly infected, and all available evidence suggests that it was they who were responsible for introducing the disease north of the Alps. By 1497 cases were being reported as far away as Aberdeen. In that year Vasco da Gama reached India, where the disease is recorded in 1498; seven years later it was in Canton.

But however swift the spread of the *morbo gallico* – the French disease, as it was called – death came to Charles VIII more quickly still. At Amboise on the eve of Palm Sunday 1498, while on his way to watch the *jeu de paume* being played in the castle ditch, he struck his head on a low lintel. He walked on and saw the game, but on his way back to his apartments, just as he was passing the place where the accident had occurred, he collapsed. Although it was the most sordid and tumbledown corner of the castle – 'a place,' sniffs Commines, 'where every man pissed that would' – his attendants for some reason thought it better not to move him. There he lay on a rough pallet for nine hours; and there, shortly before midnight, he died. He was twenty-eight years old.

Since Charles's only son had died in infancy, the throne now passed to his cousin the Duke of Orleans, thenceforth to be known as Louis XII. To the rulers of Italy, who had had plenty of experience of Louis in recent years, his succession could mean one thing only: a new invasion of the peninsula, this time to vindicate not only the Angevin claim to Naples but the Orleanist one to Milan. They were not in the least surprised to hear that the new King had expressly assumed the title of Duke of Milan at his coronation. The superiority of French arms had been proved at Fornovo, and the army that Louis was preparing bid fair to be considerably larger, better equipped and more efficiently organised than that of his predecessor. Pope Alexander might have objected, but Louis had managed to buy him without difficulty by offering to the Pope's son Cesare – who, bored with being a cardinal, had decided to abandon the Church in favour of a life of military adventure – the rich Duchy of Valentinois and the hand in marriage of Charlotte d'Albret, sister of the King of Navarre.

It was in mid-August 1499 that this second invasion took place. On

2 September Duke Ludovico Sforza fled with his treasure to the Tyrol, and on 6 October King Louis made his solemn entry into Milan. He still did not have things entirely his own way – exactly four months later, after the King's return to France, Sforza was back in the city – but ultimately the French army was too strong, and in April the Duke was taken prisoner, never to regain his liberty. Louis, however, was still not satisfied. Naples beckoned. His cousin Charles had won the city but then lost it again; he himself would be more careful. In November 1500 he concluded with Ferdinand of Aragon the secret Treaty of Granada, in which the two rulers would conquer Naples jointly. In return for his alliance – or at least his non-intervention – Ferdinand would receive a fair half of the kingdom, including the provinces of Apulia and Calabria. To Louis would go Naples itself, Gaeta and the Abruzzi. The Pope duly gave his approval, and in May 1501 the French army, supplemented by 4,000 Swiss mercenaries, was on the march.

The first news of the coalition to reach King Federico of Naples – brother and successor of Ferrantino, who had died soon after his return to his city – came from Rome, in the shape of a papal bull deposing him and dividing his kingdom according to the terms agreed at Granada. He retired to the island of Ischia, where after a time he accepted Louis's offer of asylum in France. Two days after his departure French garrisons occupied the castles of Naples, while other contingents headed north into the Abruzzi. Simultaneously, the celebrated Spanish captain Gonzalo de Cordoba occupied his master's share of the kingdom.

But alas, the Treaty of Granada had left too many questions unanswered. Nothing had been said about the province of the Capitanata, which lies between the Abruzzi and Apulia, nor about the Basilicata, on the instep of Italy between Apulia and Calabria. One might have thought it possible to settle such bones of contention by amicable means, but no: by July France and Spain were at war. The fighting continued on and off for two years, victory finally going to the Spaniards, who in 1503 smashed the French army at Cerignola. On 16 May Gonzalo entered Naples. In the last days of December he fell on the French yet again, by the Garigliano river. This time the battle was decisive, spelling the end of the French presence in Naples. Gaeta, the last French garrison in the kingdom, surrendered to Spanish troops on 1 January 1504. Thenceforth in the mainland kingdom, as well as in Sicily and Spain, the house of Aragon reigned unchallenged.

*

At this point in the story the spotlight shifts, briefly, to Cyprus. Some two and a half centuries before, the island had been bestowed by Richard Coeur-de-Lion on the hopeless Guy of Lusignan; and although it had from time to time fallen under foreign influences – notably that of Genoa in the fourteenth century and that of Cairo (to which it was still a tributary) in 1426 – the house of Lusignan had continued to reign. In 1460, however, James of Lusignan, bastard son of the former king John II, had seized the throne from his sister Queen Charlotte and her husband Louis of Savoy, forcing them to take refuge in the castle of Kyrenia for three years until they could escape to Rome. Once king, James needed allies, and, turning to Venice, he had formally requested the hand in marriage of Caterina, the beautiful young daughter of Marco Cornaro (or Corner, as the Venetians had it), whose family had long been associated with the island. Marco himself had lived there for many years and had become an intimate friend of James, for whom he had accomplished several delicate diplomatic missions, while Caterina's uncle Andrea was shortly to become Auditor of the Kingdom. On her mother's side her lineage was still more distinguished: there she could boast as a great-grandfather no less a personage than John Comnenus, Emperor of Trebizond.[1]

The prospect of a Venetian Queen of Cyprus was more than the government of the Serenissima could resist; lest James should change his mind, it arranged for an immediate marriage by proxy. On 10 July 1468, with all the considerable pomp and magnificence of which the Republic was capable, the fourteen-year-old Caterina was escorted by forty noble matrons from Palazzo Corner at S. Polo to the Doge's Palace. There Doge Cristoforo Moro handed a ring to the Cypriot ambassador, who placed it on the bride's finger in the name of his sovereign. She was then given the title of Daughter of St Mark – an unprecedented honour which caused the Bishop of Turin acidly to observe that he never knew that St Mark had been married and that, even if he had, his wife must surely be a little old to have a child of fourteen. Four years later, on 10 November 1472, Caterina sailed away, with an escort of four galleys, to her new realm.

The following year, however, King James died suddenly at the age of thirty-three, leaving his wife heavily pregnant. The inevitable suspicions of poison were probably unfounded, but Venice, fearing a

---

[1] See Chapter VIII p. 141.

coup to topple Caterina and reinstate Charlotte, was taking no chances. The Captain-General Pietro Mocenigo was sent at once to Cyprus with a fleet, ostensibly to protect the young Queen but in fact to watch over Venetian interests, with orders to remove all persons of uncertain loyalty from positions of power and influence. The fact that Cyprus was an independent sovereign state troubled the Republic not at all; Mocenigo was instructed to act through the Queen as far as possible, but was specifically empowered to use force if necessary.

Unfortunately, the measures he took served only to increase the resentment already felt by the Cypriot nobility at the continued interference by Venice in their affairs. A conspiracy soon took shape under the leadership of the Archbishop of Nicosia, and three hours before dawn on 13 November 1473 a small group – including the Archbishop himself – forced its way into the palace at Famagusta and cut down the Queen's chamberlain and her doctor before her eyes. Next it hunted out her uncle Andrea Corner and her cousin Marco Bembo. Both suffered a similar fate, their naked bodies being thrown into the dry moat beneath her window, where they remained until they had been half eaten by the dogs of the town. Finally Caterina was forced to give her consent to the betrothal of a natural daughter of her late husband to Alfonso, the bastard son of the King of Naples, and to recognise the latter as heir to the throne of Cyprus – despite the fact that James had specifically bequeathed his kingdom to her and that she had by this time given birth to a son of her own.

Mocenigo soon managed to lay hands on most of those responsible. One or two, including the Archbishop, had fled; of the others the ringleaders were hanged, the remainder imprisoned. The new arrangements for the succession were countermanded and the Venetian Senate sent out two trusted patricians who, under the title of Councillors, took over the effective government of the island in Caterina's name. The unhappy Queen remained on the throne, but now shorn of all her powers. Her baby son, James III, died in 1474, almost exactly a year after his birth; thenceforth she had to contend with the intrigues of her sister-in-law Charlotte on the one hand and young Alfonso of Naples on the other, while at home the great nobles of the island, seeing her less as their queen than as a Venetian puppet, hatched plot after plot against her. Her survival, as she well knew, was due only to Venetian protection, but even that was becoming intolerable; every important post at court or in the administration was in Venetian hands. At one period she and her father had to complain that her protectors had become more like jailers; she was forbidden to leave the palace, her servants were withdrawn and she was even compelled to take her meals alone, at a little wooden table. Daughter of St Mark or not, it was now plain to her that she was nothing but an inconvenience both to her subjects and to the Republic, which would not hesitate to get rid of her when the moment came.

The Venetian government bided its time. Since 1426 Cyprus had been held in vassalage to the Sultan of Egypt, to whom it was bound to pay an annual tribute of 8,000 ducats; its direct annexation might well cause diplomatic complications which Venice could ill afford. But then in 1487 the Sultan sent warning to Caterina that the Ottoman Sultan Bayezit was planning a massive expedition against him, and was likely to make an attempt at Cyprus en route. This development, offering as it did the prospect of Venice and Egypt allied against a common enemy, may well have encouraged the Senate to take the plunge; what certainly did so was the discovery, in the summer of 1488, of a further plot, this time with the object of securing the marriage of Caterina to Alfonso of Naples. Here was a possibility which could clearly not be contemplated. In October 1488 the decision was taken: Cyprus was to be formally incorporated into the Venetian Empire and its queen brought back – in state if possible, by force if necessary – to the land of her birth.

Anticipating some reluctance on Caterina's part – for marriage to Alfonso might well have seemed to her a welcome alternative to her present situation – the Venetian Council of Ten had secretly briefed her brother Giorgio to persuade her that a voluntary abdication would be for the good of all concerned. Cyprus, still dangerously exposed, could then be properly protected from Turkish cupidity, while she herself would acquire glory and honour for bestowing such a gift upon her motherland. In return for this she would be received in state, endowed with a rich fief and a generous annual income, and enabled to live in peace and luxury as the queen that she would always be. Her family, too, would gain immeasurably in power and prestige, whereas if she were to refuse they would be ruined.

Caterina protested bitterly, but she yielded at last. Early in 1489, at Famagusta, she formally charged the Captain-General to fly the standard of St Mark from every corner of the island; and in the first week of June she arrived in Venice. The Doge sailed out in his state barge to the Lido to greet her, accompanied by a train of noble ladies. Unfortunately a sudden storm arose; the barge was forced to ride it out for several hours, and when Caterina was able to embark its passengers were no longer at their best. But they nevertheless managed a stately progress up the Grand Canal while the trumpets sounded, the church bells rang, and the people of Venice – who probably cared little for Caterina but who dearly loved a parade – raised all the cheers that were expected of them.

Later the Queen went through a solemn ceremony of abdication in St Mark's, where she formally ceded her kingdom to Venice. In October she took possession of the little hill town of Asolo, where for the next twenty years she was to remain at the centre of a cultivated if vapid court, enjoying a life of music, dancing and the polite conversation of learned men – a life which, after her earlier tribulations, she richly deserved. Only in 1509, threatened by the advancing army of the Emperor Maximilian, was she obliged to return to her native city. There in July 1510, at the age of fifty-six, she died.

In February 1508 the Emperor Maximilian entered the territory of Venice at the head of a sizable army, ostensibly on his way to Rome for his imperial coronation. He had given the Republic advance notice of his intention the year before, requesting safe conduct and provisions for his army along the way, but Venetian agents in and around his court had left their masters in no doubt that his primary objective was to expel the French from Genoa and Milan and themselves from Verona and Vicenza, reasserting the old imperial claim to all four cities. The Doge had therefore politely replied that His Imperial Majesty would be welcomed with all the honour and consideration due to him if he came 'without warlike tumult and the clangour of arms'; if, on the other hand, he was to be accompanied by a military force, the Republic's treaty obligations and its policy of neutrality unfortunately made it impossible to grant his request.

Furious at this response, Maximilian had marched regardless on Vicenza – and found the opposition a good deal stiffer than he had expected. With French help, the Venetians not only turned him back but occupied three important imperial cities at the head of the Adriatic: Gorizia, Trieste and Fiume (now the Croatian port of Rijeka). By April, with his army's six-month contract expired and no money with which to extend it, the Emperor was obliged to agree to a three-year truce, allowing Venice to keep the territory she had gained. For him it was a salutary lesson; for Pope Julius II, on the other hand, who detested Venice and was hell-bent on her destruction, it was a piece of intolerable arrogance, and when within a few weeks the Republic refused to surrender some Bolognese refugees and appointed its own bishop rather than the papal nominee to the vacant see of Vicenza, he decided to act. A stream of emissaries was despatched from Rome: to the Emperor, to France and Spain, to Milan, Hungary and the Netherlands. All bore the same message: a call for a joint expedition by Western Christendom against the Republic and the subsequent dismemberment of her Empire. Maximilian would regain all the lands beyond the Mincio river that had ever been imperial or subject to the house of Habsburg, including the cities of Verona, Vicenza, Padua and Treviso and the regions of Istria and Friuli. To France would go Bergamo and Brescia, Crema and Cremona and all the lands, towns and castles east of the river Adda and as far south as its confluence with the Po. In the south, Trani, Brindisi and Otranto would revert to the house of Aragon; Hungary could have back Dalmatia; Cyprus would go to Savoy. Ferrara and Mantua would have their former lands restored to them. There would, in short, be something for everyone – except for Venice, which would be stripped bare.

The Pope himself intended to take back Cervia, Rimini and Faenza, but his long-term aim went far beyond any question of territorial boundaries. Italy as he saw it was now divided into three. In the north was French Milan, in the south Spanish Naples. Between the two, there was room for one – and only one – powerful and prosperous state; and that state, Julius was determined, must be the Papacy. Venice might survive as a city; as an empire she must be destroyed.

The princes of Europe had no interest in this theory. They were, however, well aware that Venice had a perfect legal right to the territories they planned to seize, a right enshrined in treaties freely entered into by both France and Spain and, more recently still, by Maximilian himself. However much they might try to present their action as a blow struck on behalf of righteousness by which a rapacious aggressor was to be brought to justice, they were all fully conscious of the fact that their own conduct was more reprehensible than Venice's had ever been. But the temptation was too great, the promised rewards too high. They accepted. So it was that on 10 December 1508, at Cambrai in the Netherlands, there was signed what appeared to be the death-warrant of the Venetian Empire. Venice was now confronted with an array of European powers more formidable than any Italian state had ever faced in history. Allies she had none. On 27 April 1509 the Pope announced a sentence of solemn excommunication and interdict over all Venetian territory.

Worse was to come. On 9 May, just outside the village of Agnadello, the Venetian army suffered a catastrophic defeat at the hands of King Louis. The whole mainland was as good as lost. What was left of it lay defenceless. Most of the objectives agreed upon by the League of Cambrai had been achieved at a single stroke. Had it not been for those treacherously shallow waters by which she was surrounded, Venice would have stood little chance of survival. A century earlier, she could have done without the *terra firma*, but times had changed. Her Levantine trade had never recovered from the fall of Constantinople in 1453. No longer was she mistress of the eastern Mediterranean; her colonial empire had now been reduced to a few tenuous and uncertain toeholds in an Ottoman world. No longer, if the Turks closed their harbours to her, could she trust to the more distant eastern markets for her salvation; the Portuguese had seen to that. No longer, in short, could she live by the sea alone. Nowadays Venetians tended to look west rather than east, to the fertile plains of Lombardy and the Veneto, to the thriving industries of Padua and Vicenza, Verona and Brescia, and to the network of roads and waterways that linked them to the rich merchant cities of Europe. It was on the mainland, now, that they had invested their wealth and reposed their hopes, and already Maximilian's specially empowered representatives were receiving the submission of one city after another – Verona, Vicenza and Padua, Rovereto, Riva and Cittadella – until the Venetians had fallen back on Mestre. All Lombardy and the Veneto were lost.

Or so, at least, it seemed; but already by July things were looking up. Many of the cities and towns that had surrendered had been perfectly content to live under Venetian rule, and were beginning to resent the heavier and far less sympathetic hand of their new masters. Less than two months after Agnadello came the first reports of spontaneous uprisings in favour of Venice. After just forty-two days as an imperial city, Padua returned beneath the sheltering wing of the lion of St Mark; many smaller towns in the region followed its example. Meanwhile, a *condottiere* named Lucio Malvezzo, temporarily in Venetian pay, had seized Legnago, a key town on the Adige, from which he was threatening Verona and Vicenza. Perhaps the situation was not quite so desperate after all.

Until now the Emperor Maximilian, after lending it his name, had not lifted a finger on behalf of the League. He had as yet sent no army, and indeed had not explicitly declared war until 29 May, three weeks after Agnadello. The news of the reconquest of Padua, however, stirred him into action. By August a heterogeneous and unwieldy army had started on its way to the city, to be joined at various stages of its journey by a force of several thousand French, a body of Spaniards and smaller contingents from Mantua, Ferrara and the Pope. Maximilian himself, meanwhile, decided to set up temporary headquarters at Asolo, in the palace of the Queen of Cyprus – who, with her numerous entourage, had wisely fled to Venice at the first news of his approach.

It was a good month before the imperial army was collected and ready, during which time the Paduans had plenty of time to strengthen their fortifications and to lay in plentiful stocks of food, water and ammunition. When on 15 September the siege at last began in earnest, they were well able to defend themselves. For a fortnight the German and French heavy artillery pounded away at the northern walls, reducing them to rubble, and yet somehow every assault was beaten back. At last the Emperor gave up the attempt. Making hurried arrangements to leave part of his army in Italy under the Duke of Anhalt for the garrisoning of other, less spirited cities and to provide an emergency force should the need arise, he led his shambling army back across the Alps whence it had come.

The Venetians were jubilant. To have recaptured Padua had been in itself a victory, but to have held it successfully against an army of some 40,000 – that was a triumph. And there was more to come. In November Anhalt surrendered Vicenza without any serious struggle, and in the weeks following more and more other towns voluntarily declared themselves for Venice. When Pope Julius heard of the reconquest of Padua he flew into a towering rage, and when after the failure of Maximilian's siege he learned that Verona too was likely to defect and that the Marquis of Mantua had been taken prisoner by the Venetians he is said to have hurled his cap to the ground and blasphemed St Peter. But he remained implacable, and the Venetians began to realise that despite their recent successes the situation had not fundamentally changed. The League was still in force; the imperial army remained intact. The French in Milan were also sharpening their swords. Meanwhile, Venice continued to stand alone, her army defeated, her treasury empty, most of her income from the mainland cut off, and without a single ally. When she sought help from England the new king, Henry VIII, expressed sympathy but offered no material support. Finally, in despair, she swallowed her pride and even appealed to the Sultan, but received no reply.

By the end of the year she was at the end of her tether, and was obliged to accept Pope Julius's conditions for peace. They were predictably savage. The Republic might no longer appoint its own bishops and clergy. It must compensate the Pope for all his expenses in recovering his territories and for all the revenues he had lost. The Adriatic would in future be open to all, free of the customs dues which Venice had always levied on foreign shipping. Finally, in the event of war against the Turks the Republic would provide not less than fifteen galleys at its own expense. On 24 February 1510, in the course of a long and deliberately humiliating ceremony outside the central doors of St Peter's, five Venetian envoys were made to kneel for a full hour while the agreement was read out in full, and were then handed twelve symbolic scourging rods from the twelve cardinals present. (The scourging itself was mercifully omitted.) Only when they had kissed the Pope's feet and received absolution were the great doors opened; the assembled company then proceeded in state to the high altar for prayers before going to Mass in the Sistine Chapel – all except the Pope, who, as one of the Venetians explained in his report, 'never attended these long services'.

The news of Pope Julius's reconciliation with Venice had not been well received by his fellow members of the League. The French in particular had done all they could to dissuade him from taking such a step, and at the ceremony of absolution their ambassador, together with his imperial and Spanish colleagues – all of whom were in Rome at the time – was conspicuous by his absence. Had he known just what that ceremony portended, his disapproval would have given way to horrified alarm. The Pope's scores with Venice had been settled; now it was the turn of France.

By all objective standards, the papal *volte-face* was contemptible. Having encouraged the French to take up arms against Venice, Julius now refused to allow them the rewards which he himself had promised, turning against them with all the violence and venom that he had previously displayed towards the Venetians. Conversely, just as he had previously been the chief architect of Venice's impoverishment and humiliation, so now he suddenly became her saviour. Not only did he step forth as the powerful champion she had so desperately sought; he took the principal initiative. The Republic could now withdraw from the centre of the stage. Henceforth the war would primarily be between the Pope and King Louis – together with Louis's chief Italian ally, the Duke of Ferrara. The Duke's salt-works at Comaccio were in direct competition with the papal ones at Cervia; moreover, as the husband of Lucrezia Borgia he was the son-in-law of Pope Alexander VI – a fact which, in Julius's eyes, was more than enough to condemn him.

As always, the Pope fought against his new enemies with all the means at his disposal: the military, the diplomatic and the spiritual. His first military action against the French – an attempt in July 1510 to drive them out of Genoa – ended in failure, but diplomatically he struck a more telling blow when, a few weeks later, he recognised Ferdinand of Aragon as King of Naples, passing over the old Angevin claims of King Louis. Shortly after that, in a bull couched in language that St Peter Martyr said made his hair stand on end, he anathematised and excommunicated the Duke of Ferrara. By this time he was approaching seventy. In October, lying with a high fever in Bologna, he narrowly escaped capture by the French, who took the city a few months later.[1] Another bout of sickness followed in the summer of 1511, during which his life was despaired of. But the energy with which he continued to pursue his vindictive policies was undiminished, and in the autumn he had recovered sufficiently to proclaim a new Holy League, this time against France.

King Louis, however, now played an important new card: his nephew Gaston de Foix, Duke of Nemours, who at the age of twenty-two had already proved himself one of the outstanding military commanders of his day. In February 1512 Nemours launched a whirlwind campaign against the papal and Spanish forces, ending on Easter Sunday at Ravenna with the bloodiest battle since Charles VIII's invasion nearly twenty years before. When it was over nearly 10,000 Spanish and Italians lay dead on the field. It had, however, been a Pyrrhic victory. The French infantry alone had lost over 4,000 men; most of the commanders had also perished, including Nemours himself. Had he lived, he would probably have rallied the remains of his army and marched on Rome and Naples, forcing the Pope to come to terms and restoring King Louis to the Neapolitan throne; and the subsequent history of Italy would have been different indeed.

By this time the three principal protagonists in the war of the League of Cambrai had gone through two permutations in the pattern of their alliances. First France and the Papacy had been allied against Venice, then Venice and the Papacy had ranged themselves against the French.

---

[1] The Bolognesi celebrated their liberation by toppling Michelangelo's magnificent bronze statue of the Pope and selling it for scrap to the Duke of Ferrara – who, in his turn, recast it into a huge cannon which he affectionately christened Julius.

It remained only for Venice and France to combine against the Papacy – which, in March 1513 at the Treaty of Blois, they did. Venice, having reasserted her position on the mainland, was determined that Pope and Emperor should not elbow her aside, and as the French no longer constituted any danger to her they were her obvious allies. But in fact the situation changed even before the treaty was signed: on 21 February 1513 the seventy-year-old Julius II died in Rome. In one of the most shameless acts of official vandalism in all Christian history, he had virtually completed his demolition of St Peter's. The new building designed by Bramante had scarcely begun to rise, and only one tiny chapel remained in which the assembled cardinals could elect his successor. Their deliberations were too slow for the guardians of the conclave, who in an effort to speed things up successively reduced the catering, first to a single dish per meal and later to a purely vegetarian diet. Even so, it was a full week before their choice was announced: Cardinal Giovanni de' Medici, who took the name of Leo X.

'God has given us the Papacy; now let us enjoy it.' Whether or not the new Pope actually uttered the superbly cynical words ascribed to him, few Italians of the time would have shown surprise. Leo was thirty-seven. He was immensely rich, immensely powerful – his family had been re-established in Florence in 1512, after an eighteen-year exile – and showed a far greater penchant for magnificence than his father, Lorenzo, had ever done. He was also, unlike Julius, a man of peace – within the curia he was known as 'His Cautiousness' – and his election was genuinely popular. On the other hand, he was enough of a realist to believe that King Louis would soon be once again on the warpath, and he was determined to protect papal interests wherever necessary.

But Louis's adventures in Italy were over. The Emperor Maximilian, having joined the Holy League, now decreed that all imperial subjects fighting with the French army should return at once to their homes on pain of death, while the French themselves were hurriedly recalled to their native soil to deal with the English – also League members – who had invaded France and had already captured Tournai. There were simply no soldiers left to carry on the Italian struggle; besides, the King no longer had the heart to continue. Worn out at fifty-two and already showing signs of premature senility, he had married during the previous autumn Princess Mary of England, sister of Henry VIII. She was fifteen years old, radiantly beautiful and possessed of all her brother's inexhaustible energy. Louis had done his best with her, but the effort had proved too great; he lasted just three months, dying in

Paris on 1 January 1515. In France, he had somehow acquired the title of 'Father of his Country'; in Italy he had achieved precisely nothing.

Just a year later, on 23 January 1516, King Ferdinand of Aragon followed him to the grave. Of all the monarchs involved in this twisted and tormented tale, only he had emerged consistently the winner. He had concluded with Louis the secret treaty of Granada to decide the fate of Naples; by its terms he had gained more than half its territory, together with the valuable provinces of Apulia and Calabria. Soon afterwards the entire kingdom was his; it was to remain under Spanish control for the next two centuries. After the death of his wife, Isabella, in 1504 he also ruled over both Castile (as regent for his mad daughter Joanna) and Aragon, together with Navarre, Roussillon and the former Kingdom of Granada, to say nothing of vast and unmeasured territories in the New World. He left behind him a Spain which, though still not completely unified, was infinitely richer, stronger and more powerful than ever before, and on the threshold of her golden age.

CHAPTER XIV

The King, the Emperor and the Sultan

The deaths of Louis XII and Ferdinand of Aragon within little more than a year of each other brought two young men, still relatively unknown, to the forefront of European affairs. They could hardly have been more unlike. King Francis I of France was twenty years old at the time of his accession and in the first flush of his youth and virility; he would have been a far better husband for young Mary Tudor than his poor cousin Louis, just as she would have been a far better wife for him than was Louis's prim and pious daughter Claude. He was already an accomplished ladies' man: not particularly handsome perhaps, but elegant and dashing, with a quick mind, a boundless intellectual curiosity and an unfailing memory which astonished all who knew him. He loved spectacle and ceremonial, pomp and parade; and his people, bored by a long succession of dreary, colourless sovereigns, took him to their hearts.

Charles of Habsburg, born in 1500 to the Emperor Maximilian's son Philip the Handsome and Ferdinand and Isabella's daughter Joanna the Mad, had inherited neither of his parents' primary attributes. His appearance was ungainly, with the characteristically huge Habsburg chin and protruding lower lip; he suffered also from a bad stammer, showering his interlocutors with spittle. He had no imagination, no ideas of his own; few rulers have ever been so utterly devoid of charm. What saved him was his innate goodness of heart and, as he grew older, a tough sagacity and shrewdness. He was also, in his quiet way, quite extraordinarily tenacious, wearing away those who opposed him by sheer determination and endurance. Though by far the most powerful man in the civilised world, he never enjoyed his empire in the way that Francis I enjoyed his kingdom – or, presumably, Leo X his Papacy – and when he finally abandoned his throne for a monastery, few of his subjects can have been greatly surprised.

His inheritance was vast, but it was not all undisputed, nor did it all fall to him at the same time. First came the Low Countries, formerly Burgundian, which his grandfather Maximilian had acquired through marriage to Mary of Burgundy. After the death of his father in 1506 Charles had been brought up by his aunt Margaret of Savoy, regent of the Netherlands; from the age of fifteen he had ruled them himself. Already by that time his mother, Joanna, now hopelessly insane, was being held under the restraint that she was to endure for more than half a century; technically, however, she remained Queen of Castile, while Ferdinand ruled as regent in her name. On Ferdinand's death, despite her condition, he left her his own crowns of Aragon and the two Sicilies, awarding the regency to Charles. The government of Castile, on the other hand, he entrusted to the octogenarian Cardinal Archbishop of Toledo, Francisco Ximenes – though one of the Archbishop's first acts was to proclaim Charles king, conjointly with his mother.

The young King who, at the age of seventeen, landed on the coast of Asturias and saw his Spanish kingdom for the first time was still a Netherlander through and through, utterly ignorant of the habits, the customs, even the language of his new subjects. He did not make a good start. The Spaniards saw him as the foreigner he was, and deeply resented the hordes of Flemish officials who now flooded the country. Rebellion was never far below the surface. Ximenes, who had done everything possible to smooth Charles's path, was elbowed aside by the Flemings and not even allowed a meeting with his new master; he was simply ordered back to his diocese. Two months later he was dead, and Charles was in full authority throughout the country. He did his best, as always; but he was quite unable to control his ambitious and endlessly grasping countrymen, while the Spanish *cortes* left him in no doubt that he was there on sufferance, and would be tolerated only so long as he did its bidding.

Francis I, at the outset of his reign, had a very much easier hand to play than Charles: his early successes in Italy stand out in sharp contrast to Charles's first tentative and ill-starred steps in Spain. Francis had revealed his Italian intentions clearly enough when, at his coronation, he had formally assumed the title of Duke of Milan; by July 1515 he had assembled an army of over 100,000 to make good his claim; and on 13 September he and the Venetians together inflicted a crushing defeat on a papal–imperial army – composed largely of Swiss mercenaries – at Marignano (now Melegnano), a few miles south of Milan. Francis himself fought in the thick of the battle, and was knighted on the field by the almost legendary Bayard, the original *chevalier sans peur et sans reproche*.[1] He took formal possession of Milan three weeks later. Then, in December, he met Pope Leo at

---

[1] 'Knight without fear and without stain'.

Bologna where, reluctantly, the Pope surrendered Parma and Piacenza; in the summer of 1516 he made a separate peace with Charles at Noyon, by which Spain recognised his right to Milan in return for French recognition of the Spanish claim to Naples.

His relations with two of the three main protagonists were now satisfactorily settled. There remained the Emperor Maximilian. Now politically isolated, he too was obliged to come to terms with France – and also with Venice, in whose favour he abandoned (in return, it must be said, for a substantial down payment by the Republic) his claims to all those lands that he had been promised at Cambrai, including his cherished Verona. Thus, eight years after the formation of the League, Venice had recovered nearly all her former possessions and resumed her position as the leading secular Italian state. These agreements, if they did not bring permanent peace to Italy, at least afforded a welcome breathing space: the year 1517 was the quietest that most Italians could remember. This is not to say that it was devoid of interest; no year that began with the capture of Cairo by the Turks and ended with Martin Luther's nailing of his Ninety-Five Theses to the church door at Wittenberg can be written off as easily as that. But the impact of these events, momentous as they were, was not immediate, and the people of Lombardy and the Veneto were able, then and in the twelve months following, to rebuild their shattered homes, resow their devastated fields, and sleep at night untroubled by terrors of marauding armies, of rape and pillage and blood.

Then, on 12 January 1519, the Emperor Maximilian died in his castle at Wels in Upper Austria. The succession of his grandson Charles was by no means a foregone conclusion. The Empire remained elective. There were many who preferred Charles's younger brother, the Archduke Ferdinand. A still more formidable rival was Francis I – who, in the early stages of his candidature, had the enthusiastic support of the Pope. (Henry VIII of England also at one moment threw his cap into the ring, but no one took him very seriously.) Fortunately for Charles, the German electors hated the idea of a French Emperor; the Fuggers – that hugely rich banking family of Augsburg – lined as many pockets as was necessary; and at the last moment Pope Leo abandoned his opposition. On 28 June Charles was elected, and on 23 October of the following year he was crowned – not in Rome but in the old Carolingian capital of Aachen – as the Emperor Charles V. In addition to the Netherlands and Spain, Naples and Sicily and the New World, there now devolved on him all the old Empire, comprising most of modern Austria, Germany and Switzerland. Milan, Bohemia and western Hungary were to follow a little later. For a man of modest talents and mediocre abilities, here was an inheritance indeed.

Charles's imperial coronation had repercussions both in Spain and in Europe as a whole. In Spain it vastly increased his popularity. The ruling class of Castile had, as we have seen, at first shown little enthusiasm for the foreign Habsburgs; but when their king was suddenly transmogrified, becoming overnight emperor of half the continent, he acquired a new respect among his subjects, who thenceforth identified themselves with both his dynasty and his destiny. No longer were they relegated to the remote southwestern tip of Europe. Their soldiers fought in Germany and the Netherlands, their writers and philosophers imbued themselves with the new humanism of Erasmus and his followers. At the same time, however, they were acutely conscious of being the one firm rock of Catholic orthodoxy which could support the Church against the heresies that were springing up in the north.

The coronation also completed the polarisation of continental Europe. The King of France was trapped in a vice, virtually encircled by the Empire; conversely, the Emperor found himself sovereign of a divided dominion, its two parts cut off from each other by a hostile state, and linked only by a neutral sea. From this moment onwards the two men were engaged in a deadly struggle for dominance in Europe and mastery of the western Mediterranean.

After the death of Sultan Mehmet II in 1481 Europe had breathed again. Mehmet had been a man of wide culture and scholarship. He had ordered Archbishop Gennadius, whom he had nominated as Orthodox Patriarch of Constantinople, to write for him a treatise on the Christian religion; he had a considerable knowledge of Greek, inviting Greek scholars regularly to his court; and he had summoned Gentile Bellini from Venice to paint his portrait.[1] But he was not known as *Fatih* – 'the Conqueror' – for nothing. His first and greatest triumph, the capture of Constantinople in 1453, had been only the beginning of a long succession of territorial acquisitions in the eastern Mediterranean, and, as we have seen, he was preparing yet another major offensive – against the Knights of St John in Rhodes – when his life was suddenly cut short. His successor, Bayezit II – who, though the

---

[1] Now to be seen in the National Gallery, London.

elder, gained the throne only after a monumental struggle with his brother Cem[1] – was very unlike his father. He consolidated Mehmet's conquests in the Balkans and appropriated the Venetian castles in the Morea, but with his much narrower mind he had no real interest in Europe – removing, for example, the Italian frescos that Mehmet had commissioned for the imperial palace and favouring instead the mosques, hospitals and schools that were so important an element of his fervent Islamic faith. His description by the Venetian ambassador – *'molto melancolico, superstizioso e ostinato'*[2] – sums him up as well as any.

In 1512 Bayezit's son Selim rebelled against his father and forced him to abdicate in his favour. (He may have poisoned him as well, since the old man died suspiciously soon afterwards.) Selim I, as he now became, was always known as *Yavuz*, 'the Grim'. His first act as Sultan was to eliminate, as potential rivals to the throne, his two brothers and five orphan nephews – the youngest of whom was five years old – by having them strangled with a bowstring; he is said to have listened with satisfaction to their screams from an adjoining room. He then turned his attention to the east, directing his formidable energies against Ismail I, the founder of the Safavid dynasty in Iran, massacring some 40,000 and incorporating various Kurdish and Turkoman principalities in eastern Anatolia into his empire. His next objective was Syria, still in the hands of the Mamelukes. Aleppo, Damascus, Beirut and Jerusalem fell in quick succession, and on 24 August 1516, at the battle of Marj Dabik, he effectively destroyed the Mameluke dynasty; its penultimate sultan, al-Ghawri, died on the field. In Egypt al-Ghawri's nephew Tuman Bey proclaimed himself Sultan and refused to submit, whereupon Selim marched his army across the Sinai desert and after one more particularly bloody encounter – at Raydaniye, near the Pyramids, in January 1517 – captured him and had him hanged at the gates of Cairo. Six months later the Sherif of Mecca made voluntary submission in his turn, sending Selim the standard and cloak of the Prophet and the keys of the Holy Cities. At last, with Egypt, Syria and the Hejaz all acknowledging him as their sovereign, the Sultan returned in triumph to the Bosphorus. His empire was not only increased; it was

---

[1] After his defeat Cem (pronounced 'Jem') fled first to Egypt and later to Rhodes, where Bayezit paid the Knights 45,000 gold pieces annually to keep him out of the way. He was in fact an invaluable hostage in the hands of Christendom. He died in Naples in 1495 – quite possibly poisoned by Pope Alexander VI, with the connivance of his brother the Sultan.
[2] 'Extremely melancholic, superstitious and obstinate'.

transformed. Possession of Mecca and Medina made it an Islamic Caliphate; henceforth the Ottoman Sultans were to consider themselves protectors of the Muslim world.

Dying in September 1520, Selim was succeeded by the only male member of his family whom he had left alive on his own accession: his son Süleyman, then aged twenty-six. Of the four larger-than-life monarchs who bestrode Europe during the first half of the sixteenth century – the other three being the Emperor Charles V, Henry VIII of England and Francis I of France – Süleyman was arguably the greatest. He was, in his own oriental way, a son of the Renaissance: a man of learning and wide culture, himself a sensitive poet, under whom the imperial pottery workshops of Iznik (Nicaea) were at their most inspired and the imperial architects – above all, the great Sinan – adorned the cities of the empire with mosques and religious founda- tions, caravanserais and schools, many of which still stand today. Like his forebears, however, Süleyman was also a conqueror, whose overriding ambition was to achieve in the west victories comparable to those of his father in the east. Thus he was to swell his already vast empire with conquests in Hungary, the Balkans and central Europe – to say nothing of North Africa, where Tripoli was to fall to him in 1551.

But that was for later. Like all the early Ottoman Sultans Süleyman was a fervently pious Muslim, and it was not long after coming to the throne that he turned his attention to the Christian enemy he most hated: the Knights of St John, whose island fortress of Rhodes lay at his very doorstep, ten miles off the Anatolian coast. The Knights were comparatively few, with neither an army nor a navy any match for his own, but, as his great-grandfather Mehmet had discovered to his cost forty years before, they were determined fighters. In those forty years they had worked unceasingly on their defences, building huge angled towers that would permit covering fire along exposed sections of the walls, and strengthening the ramparts against the heavy cannon that had smashed those of Constantinople in 1453 and by which they them- selves had been so nearly defeated in 1480. They would be hard indeed to dislodge.

Their Grand Master, Philippe Villiers de l'Isle Adam, a deeply religious French nobleman of fifty-seven who had spent most of his life in Rhodes, had received, within a week or two of taking office in 1521, a letter from the Sultan. In it Süleyman boasted of the conquests he had already made, including those of Belgrade and 'many other fine and well-fortified cities, of which I killed most of the inhabitants and reduced the rest to slavery'. Its implications were all too clear, but de l'Isle Adam was not intimidated; in his reply he proudly reported his own recent victory over Cortoğlu, a well-known Turkish pirate who had tried unsuccessfully to capture him on his most recent return to Rhodes.

Then, in the early summer of 1522, there came another letter:

To the Knights of Rhodes:

The monstrous injuries that you have inflicted upon my most long-suffering people have aroused my pity and my wrath. I command you therefore instantly to surrender the island and fortress of Rhodes, and I give you my gracious permission to depart in safety with your most valued possessions. If you are wise, you will prefer friendship and peace to the cruelties of war.

Any Knights who wished might remain, without paying homage or tribute, provided only that they acknowledged the sovereignty of the Sultan. To this second letter the Grand Master returned no answer.

The island of Rhodes forms a rough ellipse, running from northeast to southwest; the city itself occupies the northeastern extremity. On 26 June 1522 the first ships of the 700-strong[1] Ottoman fleet appeared on the northern horizon. More and more were to join this vanguard over the next two days, including the flagship carrying Süleyman himself and his brother-in-law Mustafa Pasha, who had marched down with the army through Asia Minor. Such was its size – not far short of 200,000 – that it took over a month to disembark and assemble: an overwhelming force, it might be thought, when measured against some 700 Knights, even after their numbers had been swelled by contingents from the various commanderies of the Order throughout Europe, by 500 Cretan archers, by some 1,500 other mercenaries and of course by the Christian people of Rhodes. On the other hand, the city's defences were immensely strong, perhaps even impregnable; and the Knights had spent the previous year laying in sufficient supplies of food, water and munitions to hold out for months.

In this type of warfare, moreover, life was always a good deal harder for the besiegers than for the besieged, since they had little protection either from the sweltering summer sun or from the cold and rain of winter. For the defenders, forced as they were into a passive role, the principal strain tended to be psychological; fortunately, however, there

---

[1] As always, numbers given by contemporary chroniclers at this period must be taken with a pinch of salt.

was endless work to be done. They had to keep a constant vigil over every foot of the wall, repairing damage as soon as it was inflicted and watching for any sign among the enemy below that might suggest the activity of sappers – for mining had become something of a speciality with the Ottoman armies, who well understood that many an impressive fortification was a good deal less vulnerable from the front than from beneath.

By the end of the month the heavy bombardment had begun in earnest, the cannon being even more powerful than those used against Constantinople, capable of hurling cannonballs almost three feet in diameter a mile or more. The Turkish army was now drawn up in a huge crescent to the south of the city; that of the Knights was divided into the eight tongues, each of which was responsible for the defence of its own section of the wall. The tongue of Aragon soon came under particular pressure, when the Turks began to throw up a huge earthwork opposite, from which they hoped to fire down into the city. Meanwhile, their sappers too were busy. By mid-September the Knights' worst fears were realised: there were some fifty tunnels running in various directions under the wall. Fortunately they had been able to secure the services of the greatest military engineer of his day, an Italian named Gabriele Tadini. He constructed his own warren of tunnels, from which he could listen – with the aid of tightly-stretched drums of parchment which could pick up every blow of a Turkish spade – and frequently deactivate the enemy fuses. He could not hope, however, to succeed every time, and early in September a mine exploded under the English section, creating a gap in the wall over thirty feet across. The Turks poured in, and there followed two hours of bitter hand-to-hand fighting before the Knights somehow prevailed and the exhausted survivors retired again to their camp.

Some time towards the end of October, a Portuguese in the service of Andrea d'Amaral, the Chancellor of the Order – second in importance only to the Grand Master – was caught firing a message into the enemy lines to the effect that the position of the defenders was now desperate and that they could not hope to hold out much longer. Put to the rack, he made an extraordinary confession: that he was acting on the orders of d'Amaral himself. Such an allegation is hard to believe. The Chancellor seems to have been generally disliked for his arrogance; having expected the Grand Mastership for himself, he also cherished a deep resentment of de l'Isle Adam personally. But would he really have betrayed the Order, to which he had devoted his life? We shall never know. Put on trial, he refused to plead one way or the other, saying nothing even when brought to his place of execution and refusing even the comforts of religion.

The gist of the message, however, was all too true. By December the Knights were at the end of their tether. Well over half their fighting force was now either dead or hopelessly disabled. Although the Sultan was offering honourable terms, for a long time the Grand Master kept his resolve. Rather than surrender to the infidel, he argued, every last Knight should perish in the ruins of the citadel. It was the native Rhodiots who finally persuaded him that if he continued to resist the result would be a massacre, of Knights and people alike. And so at last de l'Isle Adam sent a message to the Sultan, inviting him personally into the city to discuss terms – and Süleyman accepted. It is said that as he approached the gates he dismissed his bodyguard with the words, 'My safety is guaranteed by the word of a Grand Master of the Hospitallers, which is more sure than all the armies of the world.'

The negotiations were protracted, but on the day after Christmas 1522 the Grand Master made his formal submission. Süleyman is said to have treated him with the respect he deserved, congratulating him and his Knights on their tenacity and courage. A week later, on the evening of 1 January 1523, the survivors of one of the great sieges of history sailed for Crete. It is reported that the Sultan, as he watched them depart, turned to his Grand Vizir, Ibrahim Pasha. 'It saddens me,' he said, 'to force that brave old man to leave his home.'

Meanwhile, in Italy, the old struggle between France and Spain continued. It might be more correct to say 'between France and the Empire', but Charles's real interest in the peninsula was based on his Spanish heritage. Sicily, Naples and Sardinia he had all inherited from his grandfather Ferdinand, and he was determined to pass these on intact to his successors. He had no wish to acquire any further territory in Italy, and was only too pleased that the native rulers should remain in charge of their states, provided that they recognised the Spanish position and showed it due respect.

French influence, however, could not be tolerated. King Francis, for as long as he remained in Italy, constituted a challenge to the imperial hold on Naples and seriously endangered communications between the Empire and Spain. The Papacy, desperate to prevent either party becoming too strong, swung backwards and forwards between the two. Thus in 1521 a secret treaty was signed between Charles and Pope Leo,

20. Ravenna, St Vitale: the Emperor Justinian. Mosaic, 6th century

FOLLOWING PAGE
21. Ravenna, Mausoleum of Galla Placidia: the Good Shepherd. Mosaic, mid-5th century
22. Ravenna, St Apollinare Nuovo: the Three Magi (in Gothic dress). Mosaic, 6th century

+ SCS BALTHASSAR + SCS MELCHIOR + SCS GASPAR .

23. St Michael the Archangel: gold and enamel, precious and semi-precious stones. Byzantine, 12th century

26. The Emperor Alexius I Comnenus. Byzantine, vellum, c. 1100

24. King Roger II crowned by Christ: Palermo, Church of the Martorana. Mosaic, 12th century

25. The Emperor Frederick Barbarossa and his sons. German, vellum, 12th century

27. and 28. The Palatine Chapel, Palermo. The dome (*above*) and the nave and aisle (*below*). Mosaics, 12th century

29. Konya: Mevlana Tekke.
Seljuk, 13th century

30. Konya: Ince Minare madrasa.
Seljuk, 1260-65

31. Granada: fountain at the
Alhambra. 8th century

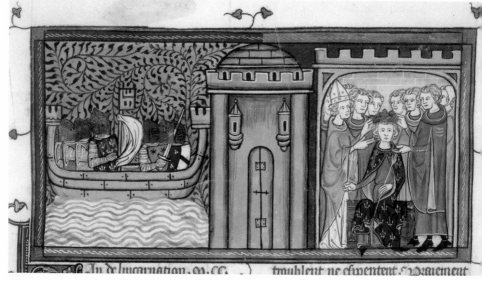

In de Imcarnation. m. CC.   ) tmublent ne efwentent.S2wzauement

32. Charles I of Anjou sailing to Rome (*left*) and his Investiture with the Kingdom of Sicily by the Pope, 1265

33. The siege of Damietta, 1249

34. The Emperor Frederick II. Illustration from his book, *De arte venandi cum avibus*

35. Siege of Acre

36. Crusader assault on Jerusalem, 1099

37. Saladin's army

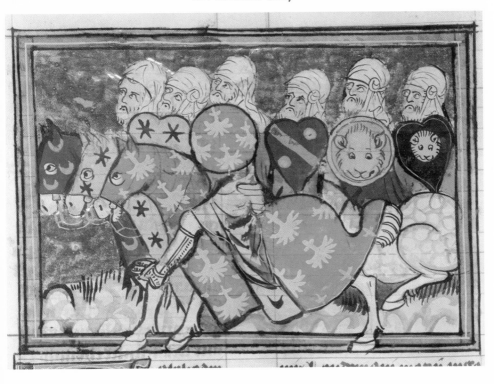

38. Cefalù Cathedral, Sicily: Christ Pantocrator. Mosaic, 12th century

as a result of which a combined papal and imperial force expelled the French once again from Lombardy, restoring the house of Sforza in the person of Ludovico's limp-wristed son Francesco Maria. Only three years later, however, in 1524, the new Pope Clement VII[1] joined with Venice and Florence in an equally secret alliance with France against the Empire, and Francis, with an army of some 20,000, marched back over the Mont-Cenis pass into Italy.

In late October Francis recaptured Milan, then turned south to Pavia, where he remained through the winter, trying unsuccessfully to divert the river Ticino as a means of taking the city; he was still there four months later when there arrived an imperial army, led not by a Spaniard or an Austrian but by one of his own countrymen: Charles, second Duke of Bourbon, one of the most exalted members of the French nobility and the hereditary Constable of the Kingdom. Charles should have been fighting beside his king, to whom he was distantly related, but Francis's mother, Louise of Savoy, had contested his inheritance and in a fit of pique he had sold his sword to the Emperor. He was now the imperial Commander-in-Chief in Italy. His army met that of Francis just outside Pavia, and on Tuesday, 21 February 1525, battle was joined.

The Battle of Pavia proved to be one of the most decisive engagements of European history. It was also, perhaps, the first to prove conclusively the superiority of firearms over pikes. The Swiss mercenaries – fighting this time on the French side – struggled valiantly, but their weapons, fearsome as they were, were no match for Spanish bullets. When the fighting was over the French army had been virtually annihilated; some 14,000 soldiers – French and Swiss, German and Spanish – lay dead on the field. Francis himself had shown, as always, exemplary courage; after his horse had been killed under him he continued to fight on foot until at last, overcome by exhaustion, he was obliged to give himself up. 'All is lost,' he wrote to his mother, 'save honour – and my skin.'

He was sent, a prisoner, to Madrid, and Charles V was once again master of Italy. The decisiveness of his victory sent a tremor through the whole peninsula, which depended – or so it believed – on the balance of power; but the Emperor had other preoccupations. Eight years before, in 1517, Martin Luther had nailed his Ninety-Five Theses

---

[1] Pope Leo X had died at the end of 1521. His successor, Adrian VI – a Dutchman from Utrecht and the last non-Italian Pope until John Paul II – lasted less than two years before being himself succeeded by Leo's cousin, Giulio de' Medici, as Clement VII.

to the church door at Wittenberg; three years after that, he had publicly burned the papal bull excommunicating him; and in 1521, at the Diet of Worms, he had effectively raised the standard of revolt against Pope and Emperor alike. The only hope of satisfying him, in Charles's view, lay in calling a General Council of the Church to discuss reform; but what was the use of a General Council if all the delegates from France and her allies were absent?

Then there was Süleyman to be considered. News of the fall of Rhodes had been received with horror throughout the west. Where, men asked themselves, would the Sultan strike next? Certainly he would continue his advance against the forces of Christendom. How could he be halted except by a concerted Crusade, led by the Emperor and backed by all the Christian powers? But how, in the circumstances prevailing, could Francis of France ever be persuaded to lend his support to such an effort? How was such a Crusade to be launched while Europe was so bitterly and brutally divided against itself?

It was perhaps considerations such as these that persuaded Charles to trust his royal captive, and to release him, after a year of not uncomfortable confinement, according to the terms of an agreement which Francis had absolutely no intention of observing – even though he left his two sons as hostages for his good behaviour. In what was known as the Treaty of Madrid, which he signed on 14 January 1526, the King readily renounced all his claims to the long-disputed Duchy of Burgundy, to Naples and to Milan. (He also, incidentally, restored all the disputed lands to the Duke of Bourbon, 'on condition that we never see him again'.) When Francis returned to Paris, however, and the terms of the agreement were made public, there was a general outcry. The Estates of Burgundy protested vociferously that the King had no right to alienate a province of the kingdom without the consent of its people. Pope Clement, too, was aghast; without a French presence anywhere in Italy, how could he hope to defend himself against Charles? Hastily he recruited Milan, Venice and Florence to form an anti-imperialist league for the defence of a free and independent Italy – and invited France to join. Though the ink was scarcely dry on the Treaty of Madrid, and though he and the Pope held widely differing views on Milan – the Pope favouring the Sforzas, while Francis wanted the city for himself – on 22 May 1526 the King, with his usual flourish, signed his name.

The League of Cognac, as it was called, introduced an exciting new concept into Italian affairs. For perhaps the first time, here was an agreement dedicated to the proposition that Milan, and so by extension all the other Italian states, should be free of foreign domination. Liberty was the watchword. Clearly there could be not yet be liberty for Italy, since Italy was still no more than a geographical expression; at the same time, it was clear to all the Italian signatories of the League that the only hope of resistance to the power of Charles V or Francis I lay in a settlement of their internal differences, a pooling of their resources and the presentation of a firmly united front to any would-be invader. The Risorgimento was still more than three centuries away, but here, perhaps, were the first glimmerings of the national sentiment that gave it birth.

It need hardly be said that Charles V did not view the League of Cognac in quite this light. To him it was a direct and deliberate challenge, and over the next few months relations between himself and the Pope steadily deteriorated. Finally, in September, two letters from the Emperor were despatched to Rome. They could hardly have been more outspoken if they had been written by Luther himself. The first, addressed personally to the Pope, accused him of failing in his duties towards Christendom, and Italy, and even the Holy See. The second, to the cardinals of the Sacred College, went further still. If, it suggested, the Pope refused to summon a General Council for the reform of the Church, it was the responsibility of the College to do so without his consent. Here was a clear threat to papal authority. To Pope Clement, indeed, it was tantamount to a declaration of war.

In and around Milan the fighting had hardly ever stopped; there must have been many Milanese who, on waking in the morning, found it difficult to remember whether they owed their allegiance to the Sforzas, the Emperor or the King of France. An imperial army had marched into the city in November 1525, and had spent the winter besieging the unfortunate Francesco Maria Sforza in the citadel. The League had sent an army under the Duke of Urbino to his relief, but largely owing to the Duke's lack of resolution it had failed, and Sforza had finally capitulated on 25 July 1526. The news of his surrender had plunged the Pope into black despair. His treasury was empty, he was deeply unpopular in Rome, and his theoretical ally Francis was not lifting a finger to help him. Meanwhile, the Reformation was daily gaining ground and the Ottoman threat still loomed. And now, as autumn approached, there were rumours that the Emperor was preparing a huge fleet, which would land some 10,000 troops in the Kingdom of Naples – effectively on his own doorstep. More serious still, Clement was aware that there were imperial agents in the city, doing everything they could to stir up trouble against him with the enthusiastic help of a member of his own Sacred College, Cardinal Pompeio Colonna.

For well over two centuries Rome had suffered from the rivalry of two of its oldest families, the Colonna and the Orsini. Away in the Campagna the two were for ever at war, often bringing out considerable armies on each side. Both were enormously rich, and both ruled over their immense domains as if they were themselves sovereign states, each with its own cultivated court. Their wealth in turn allowed them to contract advantageous marriages; people still talked of the wedding festivities of Clarice Orsini with Clement's uncle, Lorenzo de' Medici, the most sumptuous of the fifteenth century. Even before these, however, the Orsini enjoyed what might be called a special relationship with the Papacy, by reason of the fact that all the principal roads leading north out of Rome passed through their territory. Successive Popes, therefore, had long taken care not to offend them.

This alone was more than enough to antagonise their rivals, whose outstanding representative in the 1520s was Pompeio Colonna. The Cardinal had begun life as a soldier and should probably have remained one. He had entered the Church only because of family pressures; never could he have been described as a man of God. Julius II, indeed, had refused to promote him, and Pompeio in revenge had taken advantage of the Pope's serious illness in 1511 to stir up an insurrection among the populace, but his attempt had failed: Julius had recovered and stripped him of all his dignities. Surprisingly, it was the Medici Pope Leo X who had eventually admitted him to the Sacred College. His admission, however, only encouraged him to set his eye on the Papacy for himself, and any gratitude he might have felt towards Pope Leo was certainly not extended to Leo's cousin and second successor. For Clement he cherished a bitter hatred, powerfully fuelled by jealousy, and a consequent determination to eliminate him – either by deposition or, if necessary, by death.

In August 1526 Pompeio's kinsman Vespasiano Colonna came to Rome to negotiate a truce between his own family on the one hand and the Pope and the Orsini on the other. Pope Clement, much relieved, disbanded his troops – whereupon the army of the Colonna instantly attacked the city of Anagni, effectively blocking communications between Rome and Naples. The Pope had still not recovered from his surprise or had a chance to remobilise when, at dawn on 20 September, that same army smashed through the Gate of St John Lateran and poured into Rome.

At about five o'clock that same afternoon, after hours of heavy fighting, Clement fled along the covered passage that led from the Vatican to the Castel Sant' Angelo. Meanwhile the looting and plundering had begun. As one of the secretaries of the curia reported:

> The papal palace was almost completely stripped, even to the bedroom and wardrobe of the Pope. The great and private sacristy of St Peter's, that of the palace, the apartments of prelates and members of the household, even the horse-stalls were emptied, their doors and windows shattered; chalices, crosses, pastoral staffs, ornaments of great value, all that fell into their hands was carried off as plunder by this rabble.

The mob even broke into the Sistine Chapel, where the Raphael tapestries were torn from the walls. Golden and jewelled chalices, patens and all manner of ecclesiastical treasures were seized, to a value estimated at 300,000 ducats.

With proper preparations made, a Pope could hold out in the Castel Sant' Angelo for months; on this occasion, however, thanks to the incompetence of the castellan, Giulio de' Medici, the fortress was completely unprovisioned. Clement had no choice but to make what terms he could. The ensuing negotiations were hard, but their results were less than satisfactory to Pompeio Colonna, who now realised that his attempted coup had been a failure. Not only had Pope Clement remained on his throne, but public opinion had swung dramatically against his own family. Rome had been plundered and the Colonna had – rightly – been blamed. In November Pompeio was deprived – for the second time – of all his dignities and benefices, and the leading members of his family suffered similar fates. The family of Colonna lost all its property in the Papal States except for three small fortresses.

Clement had indeed survived, but only just.

> The Pope sees nothing ahead but ruin: not just his own, for which he cares little, but that of the Apostolic See, of Rome, of his own country and of the whole of Italy. Moreover, he sees no way of preventing it. He has expended all his own money, all that of his friends, all that of his servants. Our reputation, too, is gone.

So wrote another official of the curia, Gian Matteo Giberti, towards the end of November 1526. The Pope had good reason to be depressed.

Strategically he was vulnerable on every side, and the Emperor was exploiting his vulnerability to the full. And now there came the news of the defection of Ferrara, whose Duke, Alfonso d'Este, had joined the imperialist forces. 'The Pope,' wrote the Milanese envoy Landriano, 'seems struck dead. All the attempts of the ambassadors of France, England and Venice to restore him have been in vain . . . He looks like a sick man whom the doctors have given up.' And still his tribulations were not over. On 12 December a Spanish envoy delivered a personal letter from the Emperor repeating his demand for a General Council of the Church, in defiance of Pope Clement's wishes to the contrary. Early in the following year, there came the news that an imperial army under the Duke of Bourbon was advancing upon the Papal States.

Despite his treachery to his king, Bourbon was a charismatic figure, admired by all his men for his courage. He never shirked an engagement, and could always be found where the fighting was thickest, easily distinguishable by the silver and white surcoat that he always wore and by his black, white and yellow standard on which was emblazoned the word '*Espérance*'. Now, as he advanced southwards from Milan at the head of an army of some 20,000 German and Spanish troops, the citizens of all the towns along his route – Piacenza and Parma, Reggio, Modena and Bologna – worked frantically on their cities' defences. They could have saved themselves the trouble. The Duke had no intention of wasting time on them. He led his army directly to Rome, drawing it up on the Janiculum hill, immediately north of the city wall; and at four o'clock in the morning of 6 May 1527 the attack began.

In the absence of heavy artillery, Bourbon had decided that the walls would have to be scaled – a technique far more difficult and dangerous than that of simply pounding them until they crumbled. He himself was one of the first of the casualties. He had just led a troop of German landsknechts[1] to the foot of the wall, and was actually positioning a scaling-ladder when he was shot through the chest by an enemy arquebus. The fall of this unmistakable white-clad figure was seen by besiegers and besieged alike, and for an hour or so the fate of the siege hung in the balance; then the thought of revenge

---

[1] To describe them – as the *Oxford English Dictionary* does – as 'German mercenary footsoldiers of the fifteenth and sixteenth centuries' is not to say the half of it. Their preposterous clothes, slashed and swashbuckling, are reflected in the court cards of a European pack, and inspired Michelangelo when he came to design the uniforms of the Swiss Pontifical Guard. There is still a French card game called *lansquenet*. See Patrick Leigh Fermor, *A Time of Gifts*, pp. 84–86.

spurred the Germans and Spaniards on to ever greater efforts, and between six and seven in the morning the imperial army burst into the city. From that moment on there was little resistance. The Romans rushed from the wall to barricade their own homes, and many of the papal troops joined the enemy to save their own skin. Only the Swiss Guard and some of the papal militia fought heroically on until they were annihilated.[1]

As the invaders approached the Vatican the Pope was hustled out of St Peter's and led for the second time along the covered way to the Castel Sant' Angelo, already thronged with panic-stricken families seeking refuge. Such were the crowds that it was only with the greatest difficulty that the drawbridge could be raised. Outside in the Borgo and Trastevere, despite specific orders by their commanders, the soldiers embarked on an orgy of killing, cutting down every man, woman or child they encountered. Almost all the inmates of the Hospital of Santo Spirito were massacred; of the orphans of the Pietà, not one was left alive.

The imperial army crossed the Tiber just before midnight, the German landsknechts settling in the Campo dei Fiori, the Spaniards in Piazza Navona. The sack that followed has been described as 'one of the most horrible in recorded history'.[2] The bloodbath that had begun across the Tiber continued unabated: to venture out into the street was to invite almost certain death, and to remain indoors was very little safer; scarcely a single church, palace or house of any size escaped pillage and devastation. Monasteries were plundered and convents violated, the more attractive nuns being sold in the streets for a *giulio* each. Nor was any respect shown, even by the Spaniards, to the highest dignitaries of the papal curia. At least two cardinals were dragged through the streets and tortured; one of them, who was well over eighty, subsequently died of his injuries.

It was four days and four nights before Rome had any respite. Only with the arrival on 10 May of Pompeio Colonna and his two brothers, with 8,000 of their men, was a semblance of order restored. By this time virtually every street in Rome had been gutted and was strewn with corpses. One captured Spanish sapper later reported that on the north bank of the Tiber alone he and his colleagues had buried nearly 10,000, and had thrown another 2,000 into the river. Six months later,

---

[1] Near the church of Santo Spirito, an inscription still commemorates the papal goldsmith, Bernardino Passeri, who fell at that spot in the defence of Rome.
[2] J. Hook, *The Sack of Rome.*

thanks to widespread starvation and a long epidemic of plague, the population of Rome was less than half what it had been before the siege; much of the city had been left a smouldering shell, littered with bodies lying unburied during the hottest season of the year. Culturally, too, the loss was incalculable. Paintings, sculptures, whole libraries – including that of the Vatican itself – were ravaged and destroyed, the pontifical archives ransacked. The school of Raphael was broken up; the painter Parmigianino was imprisoned, saving his life only by making drawings of his jailers before escaping to Bologna.

The imperial army, meanwhile, had suffered almost as much as the Romans. It too was virtually without food; its soldiers – unpaid for months – were totally demoralised, interested only in loot and pillage. Discipline had broken down: the landsknechts and the Spaniards were at each other's throats. The only hope seemed to lie in the army of the League, under the mildly ridiculous Duke of Urbino. Given the present state of the imperialists he might well have broken into the city, rescued the Pope and saved the day; pusillanimous as ever, he did nothing. Eventually Clement was forced once again to capitulate. The official price he paid was the cities of Ostia, Civitavecchia, Piacenza and Modena, together with 400,000 ducats; the actual price was higher still, since the Venetians – in spite of their alliance – seized Ravenna and Cervia while the Duke of Ferrara made a grab for Modena. The Papal States, in which an efficient government had been developing for the first time in history, had crumbled away.

Even then, the fighting – now largely polarised between France and the Empire – continued. Peace, when it came, was the result of negotiations begun during the winter of 1528–29 between Charles's aunt Margaret of Savoy and her sister-in-law Louise, mother of King Francis. The two met at Cambrai on 5 July 1529, and the resulting treaty was signed in the first week of August. The Ladies' Peace, as it came to be called, confirmed Spanish rule in Italy. Francis renounced all his claims there, receiving in return a promise from Charles not to press the imperial claims to Burgundy; but France's allies in the League of Cognac were left entirely out of the reckoning and were thus subsequently forced to accept the terms that Charles was to impose at the end of the year – terms which included, for Venice, the surrender of all her possessions in south Italy to the Spanish Kingdom of Naples. Francesco Maria Sforza was restored to Milan (though Charles reserved the right to garrison its citadel); the Medici, who had been expelled from Florence in 1527, were also restored (though it took a ten-month siege to effect the restoration); and the island of Malta was given in 1530 to the Knights of St John.

It was a sad and – to those who felt that the King of France had betrayed them – a shameful settlement. But at least it restored peace to Italy and put an end to a long and unedifying chapter in her history, a chapter which had begun with Charles VIII's invasion of 1494 and had brought the Italians nothing but devastation and destruction. To seal it all, Charles V crossed the Alps for the first time for his imperial coronation. This was not an indispensable ceremony; his grandfather Maximilian had done without it altogether, and Charles himself, since his coronation at Aachen, had been nearly ten years on the throne without this final confirmation of his authority. The fact remained, nonetheless, that until the Pope had laid the crown on his head his title of Holy Roman Emperor was technically unjustified; to one possessing so strong a sense of divine mission, both the title and the sacrament were important.

Imperial coronations were traditionally performed in Rome. On landing at Genoa in mid-August 1529, however, Charles received reports of Süleyman's steady advance on Vienna and at once decided that a journey so far down the peninsula at such a time would be folly; it would take too long, besides leaving him dangerously cut off in the event of a crisis. Messengers sped to Pope Clement, and it was agreed that in the circumstances the ceremony might be held in Bologna, a considerably more accessible city which still remained firmly under papal control. Even then the uncertainty was not over: while on his way to Bologna in September Charles received an urgent appeal from his brother Ferdinand in Vienna, and almost cancelled his coronation plans there and then. Only after long consideration did he decide not to do so. By the time he reached Vienna either the city would have fallen or the Sultan would have retired for the winter; in either case, the small force that he had with him in Italy would have been insufficient to tip the scales.

And so, on 5 November 1529, Charles V made his formal entry into Bologna where, in front of the Basilica of S. Petronio, Pope Clement waited to receive him. After a brief ceremony of welcome, the two retired to the Palazzo del Podestà across the square, where neighbouring apartments had been prepared for them. There was much to be done, many outstanding problems to be discussed and resolved, before the coronation could take place. It was, after all, only two years since papal Rome had been sacked by imperial troops, with Clement himself a virtual prisoner of Charles in the Castel Sant' Angelo; somehow, friendly relations had to be re-established. Next there were the individual peace treaties to be drawn up with all the Italian ex-enemies of the Empire, chief among which – apart from the Pope himself – were Venice, Florence and Milan. Only then, when peace had been finally consolidated throughout the peninsula, would Charles feel justified in kneeling before Clement to receive the imperial crown. Coronation Day was fixed for 24 February 1530, and invitations were despatched to all the rulers of Christendom. Charles and Clement had given themselves a little under four months to settle the future of Italy.

Surprisingly, it proved enough. Well before the day appointed, Charles had laid the foundations of a pan-Italian league – a league which testified to the spread of imperial power across the length and breadth of Italy unparalleled for centuries past. And so the peace was signed; Clement's League of Cognac and Charles's sack of Rome were alike forgotten, or at least dismissed from minds; and on 24 February 1530, in S. Petronio, Charles was first anointed and then received from the papal hands the sword, orb, sceptre and finally the crown of the Holy Roman Empire. Something of a cloud was cast over the proceedings when a makeshift wooden bridge linking the church with the palace collapsed just as the Emperor's suite was passing across it, but when it was established that the many casualties included no one of serious importance spirits quickly revived, and celebrations continued long into the night.

It was the last time in history that a Pope was to crown an Emperor; on that day the 700-year-old tradition, which had begun in 800 AD when Pope Leo III had laid the imperial crown on the head of Charlemagne, was brought to an end. The Empire was by no means finished, but never again would it be received, even symbolically, from the hands of the Vicar of Christ on Earth.

CHAPTER XV

Barbary and the Barbarossas

Since the beginning of time men have preyed upon their fellows; and since the building of the first navigable ships, piracy had existed in the Mediterranean. Since the Dark Ages it had been practised by Christians and Muslims alike, with or without the excuse of war and often with the clearest of consciences. To the Turks, the activities of the Knights of St John during their years in Rhodes would have merited no other name; while Ferdinand and Isabella, after their defeat of the Kingdom of Granada, would hardly have seen the constant harassment of Spanish shipping by Muslim raiders from North Africa as an honourable continuation of the war on the part of the vanquished. Yet such, in the eyes of those raiders, it was, and as the sixteenth century got under way, so this harassment took on a new dimension: the Barbary – or Berber – Coast became synonymous with piracy.

After the first appearance of the Arabs nearly nine hundred years before, the North African coast – with the exception of Melilla, which had been occupied by the Spaniards in 1497 and remains to this day Spanish territory[1] – had been controlled by the Umayyad, Abassid and Fatimid Caliphates, the Almoravids and the Almohads, and various other smaller dynasties such as the Beni Hafs in Tunis, the Beni Ziyan in the central Maghreb and the Beni Merin in Morocco. Their rule, for the most part, was not unenlightened. They allowed freedom of worship to such modest Christian communities as existed within their borders; in the thirteenth century there was even a Bishop of Fez, where Leo Africanus – whose writings remained, for some four centuries, one of Europe's principal sources of information about Islam – had served as a registrar in the 'strangers' hospital'. He testified in about 1526 to the 'civilitie, humanitie and upright dealing of the Barbarians . . . a civill people [who] prescribe lawes and constitutions unto themselves' and were learned in the arts and sciences. It seems, moreover, that they normally enjoyed fairly close commercial relations with Sicily and the Italian mercantile republics, and were well known even to the English

---

[1] The other principal Spanish enclave on the African coast, Ceuta, was to be appropriated only in 1580.

merchants of the fifteenth century, for whom Algiers was a good deal more easily accessible than Constantinople or even Venice. But although their rulers could prohibit piracy, they could never prevent private freebooters from setting sail, and the Christian victims – especially the Sardinians, Maltese, Genoese and Greeks – gave as good as they got. Until the end of the fourteenth century, indeed, they gave rather better; they, rather than the Muslims, were the chief terrorists of the Mediterranean. Only with the coming of the large commercial fleets did their occupation lose something of its savour; thenceforth it is the Moorish corsairs who assume centre stage.

The fifteenth century, as we have seen, witnessed two cataclysmic events, one at each end of the Middle Sea: in the east, the fall of Constantinople in 1453 – with the consequent closure of the Black Sea to Christian navigation – and in the west the gradual expulsion of the Moors from Spain in the years following 1492. Both led to a proliferation of rootless vagabonds – in the east Christians, in the west Muslims – all of them ruined, disaffected and longing for revenge; and many of them adopted the buccaneering life. The Christians would normally establish their bases in the central Mediterranean: in Sicily, or Malta, or among the countless islands off the Dalmatian coast. The Muslims, on the other hand, could only join their co-religionists in North Africa. Between Tangier and Tunis there were some 1,200 miles and, in what was for the most part a fertile and well-watered coastal strip, innumerable tideless natural harbours ideal for their purposes. And so the legend of the Barbary Coast was born.

Of all the pirates of that coast, the two greatest were brothers: Aruj and Khizr – better known as Kheir-ed-Din – Barbarossa. Born on the island of Mytilene (the modern Lesbos), they were the sons of a retired Greek-born janissary, then working as a potter, and his wife who was formerly the widow of a Greek priest. (Since all janissaries had originally been Christians before their forcible conversion, the Barbarossa brothers possessed not a drop of Turkish, Arab or Berber blood – a fact to which their famous red beards were further testimony.) In his early youth Aruj – the elder of the two – had taken part in an unsuccessful expedition against the Knights of St John, during which he had been captured and forced to serve in their galleys. Ransomed – we have no idea by whom – he was soon afterwards entrusted with a privateer by merchants of Constantinople, and served under the Mameluke ruler of Egypt.

Some time during the very first years of the century, he and his brother appeared in Tunis with two galleots – basically open boats with about seventeen oars a side, each oar manned by two or perhaps three rowers; and in 1504, in the channel that runs between the island of Elba and the Italian mainland, Aruj won his first major prizes: two papal galleys, loaded to the gunwales with precious goods from Genoa. They were bound for Civitavecchia, but they never reached it; boarded and captured, they were brought proudly back to Tunis.

In the following years several Spanish vessels were also attacked, with similar results; and at last, in 1509, Cardinal Ximenes despatched the celebrated Don Pedro Navarro, with no less than ninety ships and an army of 11,000, ostensibly to spread Christianity along the North African coast but in fact to bring the miscreants to book. When Oran was captured at the cost of only thirty Spanish lives, 4,000 of its inhabitants were massacred in cold blood and 5,000 carried off to Spain, together with plunder valued at 500,000 gold ducats; in the year following, Bougie and Tripoli went the same way. But Aruj, who had by now taken over the island of Djerba as his base of operations, was growing steadily stronger, and in 1512 he responded to an appeal by the exiled ruler of Bougie – forced out by Don Pedro – to restore him in return for the free use of the port. After a week of heavy bombardment, the Spanish garrison was about to surrender when a lucky shot took off Aruj's left arm; the siege was raised and the fleet returned to Tunis, though not without capturing a Genoese galleot on the way.

The Genoese were shortly to have their revenge; their admiral Andrea Doria sped with twelve galleys to Tunis, sacked the fortress and captured half the pirate fleet. But Aruj, his wound healed, returned to the attack and in 1516 received another appeal – this time from Prince Selim of Algiers. The city had not been conquered by Don Pedro, but two years before, in an attempt to prevent the constant Algerian attacks on Spanish shipping, the Spaniards had fortified an offshore island in the bay known as the Penon, from which they virtually controlled the harbour, threatening all traffic in both directions. Aruj did not hesitate. Bad luck had prevented him from regaining Bougie, but Algiers was a far bigger prize and would, incidentally, make a superb capital for the great Barbary kingdom that had long been his dream.

By now Aruj was powerful enough to mobilise a fleet of sixteen galleots – under the command of his brother Khizr – and an army of some 6,000 men. With this he marched along the coast to Algiers, pausing only at Cherchel, some miles to the west, where another sea adventurer, a Turk named Kara Hassan, had carved out a little sultanate for himself and amassed a small army of Moors and Turks, together with a number of ships. These Barbarossa needed, but rather than negotiate an alliance with Kara Hassan he found it simpler, with a blow of his scimitar, to strike off his head. Arrived in Algiers, he at once began a heavy bombardment on the island fortress; three weeks later, however, he had made little appreciable impact and so, being clearly in danger of losing face with the Prince, changed his plan. A few days later Selim was murdered in his bath, and Aruj had himself formally proclaimed Sultan.

The people of Algiers saw all too clearly the mistake they had made in inviting Barbarossa to help them, and it was not long before they opened secret talks with the Spanish garrison on the Penon to bring about his downfall. But Aruj, with his network of spies throughout the city, soon got wind of what was happening. One Friday, when all the leading citizens were gathered in the great mosque, the doors were slammed shut and the worshippers found themselves surrounded by armed men. One after another they were bound with their own turbans, and were then led to the main door to witness the beheading of the chief conspirators.

News of the *coup* soon reached Spain, where Ximenes was seriously alarmed. In May 1517 he sent out his second expedition against Aruj: 10,000 men under the leadership of the country's leading admiral, Diego de Vera. Once again, Barbarossa acted quickly. Falling on the Spaniards while they were still unloading and before they had time to reform, he killed some 3,000 of them. The remainder hastily re-embarked and fled for their lives. Even then, luck was against them. Towards nightfall a sudden storm sprang up and drove many of the ships ashore, where Barbarossa's men were waiting. It was a dismally depleted fleet that struggled back to its homeland. A month later the ruler of Tenes, a city some ninety miles west of Algiers, was foolhardy enough to march against the corsair; his army in its turn was smashed to bits, and, although he himself managed to escape to the hills, a few days later his city fell to Aruj, who once more proclaimed himself Sultan. The city of Tlemcen, 200 miles further to the west and some way inland, quickly followed; when Aruj entered it in September, the head of its former ruler was borne before him on a lance. With the exception of Oran, Bougie, the Penon and a few other fortresses along the coast, Aruj Barbarossa was now master of virtually all the territory that forms the modern republic of Algeria. It had taken him just thirteen years.

But Oran was to prove his Achilles's heel. Soon after the arrival in Spain of Charles I – later the Emperor Charles V – in September 1517, the city's governor, the Marquis of Comares, had returned to Spain to pay him homage and to discuss the general situation in North Africa, which was now becoming desperate. The Barbarossas were growing more powerful with every month that passed; the few remaining Spanish possessions on the coast were increasingly threatened. Now, surely, was the moment to strike again, before it was too late; this time, however, the enemy's strength and military skill must not be underestimated, as they had so tragically been on previous occasions. The young King was quick to agree. He immediately gave orders for an expedition to be prepared through the coming winter. It was to sail in the early spring, when it had orders to track down Barbarossa and destroy him.

This time it was a veritable armada that reached Oran in the first months of 1518, and an army of trained veterans that at once set out for Tlemcen. Mistrusting the defences of the city, Aruj sent an urgent appeal for additional men and equipment from the Sultan of Fez, but the Sultan prevaricated; meanwhile, the Spanish army was approaching and there was no time to be lost. Tlemcen would have to be sacrificed; Aruj had no choice but to retreat to Algiers. But – probably owing to his fruitless waiting for the aid from Fez that never came – he had left it too late. Comares learned of his departure and set off in pursuit. Aruj had excellent horses, but they were no match for the Spanish thoroughbreds, and through forced marches the Spaniards steadily gained on him. It is said that Aruj scattered gold and jewels behind him to delay his pursuers, but Comares forbade his men to dismount and finally caught up with him as he and his army were fording a mountain river. Aruj and his vanguard had already crossed it, but he turned back to join the remainder who had not yet done so, thus presenting a united front to the Spanish force. It was on that riverbank that he made his last stand, and there, still laying about him with his one arm, that he was struck down in his forty-fourth year.

His end was worthy of all that had gone before. He had been fearless, sometimes reckless, perhaps the very first and greatest of those swash-buckling corsairs who were to blaze their trail through succeeding centuries. Of all his contemporaries, it was said that only Hernán Cortés was his equal for bravery. It might be added that in his own astonishing achievement – starting as he did a discredited foreigner without allies and, in the teeth of local hostility and everything that Spain could hurl against him, creating through sheer force of character in a few short years a strong and durable North African state – only he was the equal of the greatest of the conquistadors.

For the Marquis of Comares, the death of the first Barbarossa and the destruction of his army opened the way to Algiers. Had he marched on the city, it would surely have fallen, and with Algiers in Spanish hands, the rest of North Africa would soon have been his. But he did nothing of the kind. Instead, he returned directly to Oran – and the opportunity was lost to Spain for three hundred years. Meanwhile, Khizr – or, as we must now call him, Kheir-ed-Din – Barbarossa took on the mantle of his brother.

It was a hard act to follow, but Kheir-ed-Din had never lacked confidence. He may not have had quite the panache of Aruj, but he possessed all his brother's ambition, all his courage, and – arguably – rather more statesmanship and political wisdom. It is unlikely, for example, that Aruj would ever have considered sending ambassadors to Constantinople to make a formal presentation of the new Province of Algiers to the Sultan. For Selim I, who had conquered Egypt only the year before, here was an invaluable westward extension to his African empire. He instantly appointed Kheir-ed-Din his *beylerbey*, or governor-general, and provided him with a guard of honour of 2,000 janissaries. With their help all the Spanish conquests except Oran and the nigh-impregnable Penon outside the harbour of Algiers were regained.

Next, alliances were sealed with all the principal Arab and Berber tribes of the interior. In a remarkably short time the second Barbarossa, considerably more powerful than the first had ever been, dominated the central and western Mediterranean. Around him he gathered a splendid company of corsair captains. They included Dragut, another converted Christian, who became known as 'the Drawn Sword of Islam'; Sinan, 'the Jew of Smyrna', who was suspected of the black arts because he could take a declination reading with a crossbow; the redoubtable Aydin Reis, known by the Spaniards as *Cachadiablo*; and perhaps half a dozen others, all of them superb seamen. Between May and October of every year no foreign vessel was safe from their attacks; nor did they hesitate to pass through the straits to the open Atlantic, where they would lie in wait for the Spanish galleons returning from the Caribbean to Cadiz. But it was not only treasure that they were looking for; every bit as profitable were Christian prisoners, who could either be enslaved and set to work in the galleys or, occasionally, ransomed for gold.

One incident in particular illustrates the effect of the Barbary pirates in the Middle Sea. In 1529 Aydin Reis set out with fourteen small galleots on a raiding expedition to Mallorca, where he heard of a large party of Moriscos – 'converted' Muslims – who wished to escape from their Spanish masters and were ready to pay good money for a passage to North Africa. Landing secretly by night, he embarked 200 families and, with a considerable amount of treasure, set sail for home. It happened that at just that moment there arrived a fleet of eight large Spanish galleons under a certain General Portundo. It was returning from Genoa, whence Portundo had escorted Charles V to be crowned Emperor by the Pope at Bologna, and carried numerous grandees who had attended the ceremony. Aydin quickly landed his passengers then swung out to sea, attacked and boarded the flagship. In the hand-to-hand fighting that followed, Portundo was killed. By the time the battle was over, one of the galleons had escaped to Ibiza; the other seven had all been captured. The Muslim galley slaves were released from their chains, to be replaced at the oars by their erstwhile masters; the damaged ships were repaired; the Moriscos were re-embarked; and the seven great prizes – with their distinguished passengers, for whom good fat ransoms could be expected – were towed back in triumph.

At last Barbarossa felt himself ready to tackle the Penon. Situated as it was at the very entrance to Algiers harbour, it had long been a menace to his shipping, but it was only now that he had sufficient heavy artillery to make the necessary impact. On 6 May 1560 the attack began. The fortress was bombarded day and night for fifteen days before he ordered the final assault, by which time the men of the Spanish garrison had no fight left in them. The building was then dismantled and Christian slaves were employed for the next two years, to construct, using the stones, the huge mole which joins the island to the mainland and still protects the harbour on its western side.

Why, in the first half of the sixteenth century, did the Muslim world enjoy such a degree of naval supremacy in the Mediterranean? First of all, because it had few Christian competitors. Venice and Genoa controlled the Adriatic, together with the Ionian Sea immediately to the south, but the Knights of St John – the finest fighting seamen of their day – had been expelled from Rhodes in 1522 and found their new home in Malta only seven years later; it would be some time before they could hope to regain their former influence and strength. Spain, as we have seen, did her best to play an active part, but her principal energies were directed towards the New World. Besides, Christianity remained hopelessly divided. If Spain and France, Pope and Empire, the Eastern and the Western Churches, the Kingdoms of Naples and Sicily and the princes of north Italy could have made common cause, the outlook for the subjects of the Sultan might have been grim indeed, but Europeans always seemed far more interested in killing one another than in making a united stand against the Turk. Islam, by contrast, remained virtually united.

One Christian admiral only seemed able to hold his own. In 1532 the Genoese Andrea Doria won several victories over Ottoman fleets in Greek waters. Paradoxically, however, it was these successes that brought Barbarossa what was almost certainly the most glorious moment of his career. To Sultan Süleyman it was all too clear that the Turkish navy was vastly inferior to that of the corsair and must be drastically reorganised if it was to hold its own in the Mediterranean. Moreover, there was only one man who could do it. Thus it was that in the spring of 1533 a delegation from the Sublime Porte arrived in Algiers, commanding Kheir-ed-Din to come at his earliest convenience to Constantinople.

The corsair accepted with alacrity. As a loyal subject of the Sultan – which he undoubtedly was – he must have fully appreciated the honour that was being done him, but he also had reasons of his own. For some time he had had his eye on Tunis, his immediate neighbour to the east. It had once been his and his brother's headquarters, but in recent years neither he nor Aruj had paid it any particular attention. In 1526, however, a new ruler of the Beni Hafs dynasty had come to the throne, after the murder of (it is said) twenty-two of his brothers.[1] He had quickly proved a disaster, and by 1532 Barbarossa was receiving regular appeals from his friends in Tunis to assume power there himself. Before he could take such a step, however, he needed the Sultan's blessing; if he could also persuade Süleyman to provide him with arms and men, so much the better.

He set sail the following August, laden with appropriate presents for the Sultan which included – if we are to believe Sandoval, Bishop of Pamplona – some 200 young Christian women for his harem, each of them carrying in her hand a gift of gold or silver; and he was received

---

[1] Where polygamy is the rule, so large a family is less surprising than it would be otherwise.

in similar style. A few days later, with the title of Pasha, he was appointed member of the Divan and Captain General of the Fleet. He was to remain in Constantinople nearly a year, during which time he virtually created the Ottoman navy. The French Secretary in the city, Jean Chesneau, reported in 1543:

> The supremacy of Turkey at sea dates from Kheir-ed-Din's first winter in the dockyards of this city . . . Over at Pera [the northeastern side of the Golden Horn] there is a shipyard on the shore where they both build and maintain galleys and other ships. Normally there are two hundred skilled master-craftsmen working here . . . In charge of all this there is a Captain-General, whom the Turks call the Beylerbey of the Sea, who also has charge of the navy when it goes out . . . Before he took charge the Turks, apart from a few corsairs, knew nothing of the seaman's art. When they needed crews for a fleet, they went into the mountains of Greece and Anatolia and brought in the shepherds . . . and put them to row in the galleys and to serve aboard the other ships. This was quite useless, for they knew neither how to row or to be sailors, or even how to stand upright at sea. For this reason the Turks never made any showing. But all at once Barbarossa changed the entire system . . . Inspiring his men with his own marvellous energy, he laid out sixty-one galleys during the winter, and was able to take to the sea with a fleet of eighty-four vessels in the spring.

In July 1534 Kheir-ed-Din Barbarossa led his new fleet out of the Golden Horn, through the Sea of Marmara and down the Hellespont into the Mediterranean. Rounding the toe of Italy, he seized and sacked Reggio, then passed through the Straits of Messina and headed up the coast towards Naples. Oddly enough, there was no reaction from the Spanish viceroy; did he, one wonders, receive a secret message from the corsair promising that if he met with no opposition the city would be left untouched? At any rate, Naples was spared, and the fleet sailed on to Sperlonga[1] which proved rather less fortunate, the cream of its womanhood being seized and loaded on to the ships.

Barbarossa, however, had set his sights on one woman in particular – a woman whom he saw as a very special gift to the Sultan: Giulia Gonzaga, the exquisite young widow of Vespasiano Colonna. Generally accounted the most beautiful woman of her day, painted by

---

[1] Where the Emperor Tiberius had had a villa and had converted a neighbouring cave (which can still be seen) into a banqueting hall. One night, according to Suetonius, while he was feasting with his companions, part of the roof suddenly caved in. Many of his guests and serving-men were killed, but the Emperor escaped.

Sebastiano del Piombo and Titian, her praises sung by Ariosto and Tasso, she kept an elegant and cultivated little court in her palace at Fondi. This town lies some twelve miles inland from Terracina, and Kheir-ed-Din with his small raiding party had hoped to take it, and Giulia, by surprise. Fortunately she received warning a few minutes before their arrival and, still in her nightdress, made her escape with a single retainer – whom she later condemned to death on the grounds that he had taken advantage of her distress and been over-bold. (In the circumstances, one suspects, he probably had.) Fondi, as might have been expected, paid the usual price.

Laden with the captive women – most of them destined for the Turkish slave markets – and with loot from the pillaged towns, a few vessels now returned to Constantinople. They also carried the greater part of the janissaries made available by Sultan Selim – probably ordered home by Süleyman, who had gone to war with Persia and needed all the manpower he could lay his hands on. The bulk of the fleet, however, headed southwest, towards Tunis. For Barbarossa his Italian expedition had been merely a preliminary, a harmless little exercise designed to impress the Sultan with his new fleet in general and his new admiral in particular. Now it was time for the serious business: the toppling of Moulay Hassan and the annexation of his Tunisian kingdom. He arrived outside the harbour on 16 August and immediately began the bombardment, only to find that Moulay Hassan had already taken flight. Two days later, with 1,000 local irregulars, the fugitive ruler made a half-hearted effort to return, but when the corsairs opened fire a second time he once again hastily withdrew. All that winter Barbarossa kept his men busy, strengthening the harbour defences and building an imposing new fortress, big enough to accommodate a garrison of 500 men.

He need not have bothered, for this time he had overreached himself. Perhaps, when planning the Tunis operation, he had underestimated the probable reaction of Charles V, and the Emperor's power to retaliate; in any case, he had made a serious mistake. A glance at the map will show that Charles could not conceivably accept his annexation of a country less than 100 miles away from the two prosperous ports of western Sicily – Trapani and Marsala – and only very little more from Palermo itself. The idle and pleasure-loving Moulay Hassan had constituted no danger, but now that Barbarossa was in Tunis the Emperor's own hold on Sicily was seriously threatened. As soon as he heard the news, he began to plan an immense expedition to recover the city. The invasion fleet would number ships from Spain, Naples, Sicily, Sardinia, Malta – where the Knights of St John had recently established themselves following their eviction from Rhodes – and Genoa; Andrea Doria would once again be in command. The Emperor himself with the Spanish contingent – estimated at some 400 ships – sailed from Barcelona at the end of May 1535 to the agreed rendezvous at Cagliari in Sardinia, where they arrived on 10 June and picked up another 200. Then on the 13th they turned to the south, and on the following day hove to in the roadstead outside the port of Tunis.

Against such an armada, Kheir-ed-Din Barbarossa knew that there was little hope of retaining his hold on the city. Having no intention, however, of losing more ships than necessary, he had taken the precaution of sending fifteen of his best vessels along the coast to Bône, about half-way to Algiers, where they could be kept safely in reserve. He and his men fought valiantly, as they always did, but on 14 July – exactly a month after Charles's arrival – the fortress of La Goletta that defended the inner harbour was stormed by the Knights of St John, and a week later the 12,000 Christian captives who were being held in the city somehow smashed their way to freedom and flung themselves on their erstwhile captors. Tunis was effectively lost – and now it was Barbarossa's turn to flee. In company with his two fellow captains, Aydin Reis and Sinan, and as many other of his men who were able to follow him, he slipped out of the city and made for Bône.

At this point Charles should have ordered his army to leave at once in pursuit and force Kheir-ed-Din into a pitched battle. Had he done so, he might have destroyed the corsair forever, and the Emperor's 600 ships should have had no difficulty in preventing him from escaping by sea. But the soldiers – and probably the sailors too – were far too busy raping and plundering, as the rules of war allowed them to do for three days and nights. Having agreed to pay the Emperor an annual tribute, Moulay Hassan was then formally reinstated in the empty shell of his city, and the Spaniards, having repaired and refortified La Goletta, declared it Spanish territory and equipped it with a permanent garrison. The expedition, the victorious Christians all agreed, had been a huge success. Tunis was once again in friendly hands, Sicily was secure, thousands of their co-religionists had been freed from captivity, and – best of all, perhaps – the previously invincible Barbarossa had been conclusively defeated. They could all return to their various homelands, well satisfied with what they had achieved.

Or so they thought. The Emperor actually sent Andrea Doria on an expedition westward along the coast to find the fugitive corsair and bring him to book. He did not know his man. It was typical of Kheir-ed-Din Barbarossa that, instead of slinking back to Algiers as they had assumed he would, he put in at Bône only to collect more ships and supplies before immediately heading north to the Balearic Islands. As his squadron approached, the islanders understandably assumed it to be part of the imperial fleet returning to Barcelona, an impression confirmed when it was seen to be flying the imperial colours; there was no resistance, therefore, when it glided soundlessly into the harbour of Mahon in the southeast corner of Minorca. A Portuguese merchant-man which was lying there at anchor fired a friendly salute; then, suddenly, the squadron opened fire. The Portuguese, taken by surprise, defended themselves as well as they could; but their ship was easily captured. It was only a matter of hours before the whole port, and indeed the whole city, was sacked and destroyed.

In the late autumn of 1535 Barbarossa made his second journey to Constantinople. He was never to return to North Africa. His final years were to be spent less as a corsair than as Admiral of the Ottoman fleet, confounding the Sultan's enemies, notably the Spaniards, Venetians and Genoese. Until this time Venice had been allowed to pursue her mercantile activities largely unopposed. Süleyman's brilliant Grand Vizir, Ibrahim Pasha, is believed to have been born a Venetian citizen on the Dalmatian coast; certainly, after his forcible conversion to Islam, he always kept a soft spot for Venice in his heart and did his best to respect her Mediterranean possessions. In the spring of 1536, however, Ibrahim was murdered at the instigation of Süleyman's wife Roxelana, who wanted his post for her son-in-law Rüstem Pasha.[1] Henceforth the Serenissima would be as open to attack as were Spain and Genoa.

That same year an imperial fleet under Andrea Doria captured ten Turkish merchantmen off Messina, following up this coup with an intrepid raid on a section of the Ottoman fleet off Paxos, in the Ionian Sea. The Sultan, determined that these two insults should be properly avenged, conceived a daring plan. In the spring of 1537 he personally would lead an army of 20,000 men through Thrace and down the Balkan peninsula as far as Valona, in what is now Albania; meanwhile,

---

[1] Both are commemorated in modern Istanbul: Ibrahim Pasha by his palace on the north side of the Hippodrome, now the Museum of Turkish and Islamic Art; Rüstem Pasha by one of the loveliest small mosques in the city, built by the great architect Sinan in 1561, its walls covered with superb Iznik tiles.

Barbarossa would sail with a fleet of 100 ships to the same port. There he would embark the army and carry it across to Brindisi, whose governor had been suborned and had promised to open the city gates. Unfortunately for Süleyman, this plan misfired when the governor's treachery was discovered just in time. With both his army and navy already in the Adriatic, the Sultan had to decide quickly on an alternative. While he was deliberating, Barbarossa staged a series of lightning raids along the coast of Apulia, returning with the usual shiploads of treasure and slaves to learn that his master had decided to besiege the island of Corfu.

The largest of the Ionian Islands, Corfu had technically been a Venetian colony since the Fourth Crusade.[1] In the distribution of the former Byzantine territories of 1204, old Doge Dandolo had laid claim to a huge share, for which the Republic had no real appetite nor any means of properly digesting it. She had therefore had no choice but to leave the Ionian Islands to the Greek and Italian adventurers who occupied them. Since then Corfu had fallen into several successive hands. At first occupied by the Venetian family of Venier, it had at various times been held by the Despotate of Epirus, Manfred of Sicily and the house of Anjou, returning to Venice in 1386. Unlike all its neighbouring islands except Paxos, however, it had never been taken by the Ottomans (and, incidentally, never would be). In recent years it had been protected by its Venetian status, but Ibrahim Pasha was now dead and to Süleyman with his huge army it must have seemed easy prey. He landed his entire army and all his ordnance – some thirty cannon, including a gigantic fifty-pounder, the largest in the world at that time – surrounded the chief citadel of the town and began to pound it into submission.

Fortunately, Corfu's defences were strong. The town, half-way up the eastern coast of the island, lay behind and below the high citadel crowning the rocky peninsula that juts out towards the shores of Albania, commanding the approaches from both land and sea. Within this citadel was a garrison of some 2,000 Italians and roughly the same number of Corfiots, together with the crews of such Venetian vessels as happened to be in port at the time. Food and ammunition were in plentiful supply; morale was excellent. It needed to be, for the defenders now found to their dismay that they were faced not just with an attack from the sea but with a combined naval and military operation,

---

[1] See Chapter VII, p. 139.

carefully planned and on a considerable scale. The devastation suffered by the local peasants, as well as by the ordinary citizens, was appalling, but the citadel, despite constant battering from Turkish cannon on land and sea and several attempts to take it by storm, somehow stood firm. Then, mercifully, came the rain. Corfu has always been famous for the ferocity of its storms, and those which burst upon it in the early days of September 1537 seem to have been exceptional even by local standards. The cannon became immovable in the mud; dysentery and malaria spread through the Turkish camp. After barely three weeks' siege, the Ottoman army re-embarked on the 15th, leaving a triumphant if still somewhat incredulous garrison to celebrate its victory.

But the war was not over. Barbarossa's fleet was still active, and the other Mediterranean harbours and islands that remained in Venetian hands were not as defensible as Corfu. Many of them, though theoretically under the protection of the Republic, were in fact ruled by private families who had no means of staving off any sustained attack. But Barbarossa was remorseless. One by one they fell: Nauplia and Malvasia (now Monemvasia) on the east coast of the Peloponnese, then the islands – Skyros, Aegina, Patmos, Ios, Paros, Astipalaia – all of them considerably nearer to the Turkish mainland than to Venice, whose fleet was now blocked by the throng of Ottoman ships in the Adriatic narrows.

The Most Serene Republic had been brought to her knees, and it was Kheir-ed-Din Barbarossa who was responsible for her humiliation. No wonder that when he returned to Constantinople it was to a hero's welcome such as had never been known. But he gave as good as he received: 400,000 gold pieces, 1,000 young women and 1,500 youths. There was also a personal present for the Sultan: 400 more youths, dressed in scarlet and carrying vessels of gold and silver, bales of precious silks and embroidered purses almost bursting with gold coins.

For the Venetians, by the time the triumphant Barbarossa sailed into the Golden Horn the victory of Corfu had already gone sour; every week was now bringing them reports of new defeats, new losses. In 1538 he was again on the warpath, terrorising first Skyros and Skiathos in the Sporades and then Andros in the Cyclades, and many smaller islands nearby. From the larger and more important islands he exacted an annual tribute; the smaller were obliged to provide manpower for the galleys, since the vast fleet that he was building needed literally thousands of oarsmen, of whom there was a chronic shortage. He then turned south to Crete, still Venice's chief colony in the eastern Mediterranean. The fortifications of the capital, Candia, proved impregnable, but over eighty villages along the coast and several of the outlying islands were not so lucky.

Meanwhile, the European powers seemed incapable of forming alliances that were not poisoned by mutual suspicion and petty bickering almost before they began. In the summer of 1538 one such attempt, embarked upon by the Emperor, the Pope and Venice with all the fervour of a Crusade and a degree of optimism such that the participants actually made advance plans for the division of the Ottoman Empire between them, ended not as they had imagined, with the capture of Constantinople, but with a resounding victory for Barbarossa. It was while he was ranging along the south coast of Crete that he received reports of a huge combined fleet heading south down the Adriatic towards the Ionian Islands. The Venetian contingent alone consisted of eighty-one ships – some under sail but the majority oared galleys – under one of the Republic's leading admirals, Vincenzo Cappello; the papal contribution, of another thirty-six galleys, was commanded by another Venetian, Marco Grimani, and these were joined when they reached Corfu by another thirty from Spain. Yet even this was only the vanguard: expected shortly were the forty-nine vessels sent by the Emperor, which had been delayed pending the arrival of his secret weapon: a further squadron of fifty so-called galleons – literally, 'large galleys' – square-sailed and heavily armed, which had proved their worth in the Atlantic and the New World but which had never yet been seen in the Mediterranean. Predictably, Charles had entrusted the command of the whole enterprise to his trusted admiral Andrea Doria.

To set against this, Barbarossa could muster about 150 ships of his own, under Dragut, Sinan and several other former corsairs of long experience and tested courage. Here too was a formidable force; if numbers were all, however, it would have been no match for its opponents. But the Turkish fleet was united; the Christian was anything but. No Venetian, for a start, would willingly submit to being commanded by a Genoese; nor was there any love lost between Italians and Spaniards. There were differences, too, in long-term objectives. Cappello was interested above all in protecting the Ionian Islands, commanding as they did the gateway to the Adriatic. Grimani's chief concern was Italy's western seaboard, the ports of Civitavecchia and Ostia and indeed Rome itself, only a few miles from Ostia up the Tiber. The Spaniards cared for neither of these things: Spain was too far away.

They doubtless hoped to teach the Turks a lesson, but when that was done they wanted above all to get home with any prizes that might be obtainable. Discord, in short, could be virtually guaranteed, and tempers were not improved by the continued delay of Doria and his fleet, thanks to which the enforced inactivity at Corfu was prolonged from days into weeks.

At last Marco Grimani could stand it no longer. Leading the papal squadron out of Corfu, he sailed south to Preveza at the entrance to the Bay of Arta. This huge inlet of the Ionian Sea is in fact more of a gulf than a bay. Covering some 250 square miles, it is entered by a narrow, winding channel in places only a quarter of a mile wide. It thus provides an extraordinary natural harbour, and Grimani's purpose may well have been to satisfy himself that the Turkish fleet was not lying in wait there. It proved not to be; on the other hand, the fortress of Preveza was fully garrisoned and disposed to fight, and its cannon inflicted considerable damage on the raiders before they escaped to safety.

Had Grimani delayed his little expedition by another few days, he would have found his worst fears confirmed. Barely had his squadron disappeared over the northern horizon than Barbarossa's fleet sailed up from the south and turned straight into the bay. Here, off Actium, at the very spot where Octavian had met Mark Antony 1,570 years before, he prepared for battle.

It was not until 22 September that Andrea Doria finally arrived at Corfu with his galleons. By this time reports of Barbarossa's movements had reached the island, and on the 25th the entire fleet hove to off Preveza. But what was it to do next? To sail up the narrow channel in line under the guns first of the fortress and then of the Turkish fleet would have been suicidal; in the circumstances it would have been better to attack the fortress, capture it, and turn its guns against the enemy. Doria, however, refused to consider such a course. Any serious losses on land might disastrously weaken his fleet if a sea battle were to follow; he knew, too, that this was the season of the equinoctial gales, when the Mediterranean was at its most treacherous. In the event of a sudden storm – and September storms could blow up in half an hour from a clear blue sky – he might be obliged to withdraw the fleet to some lee shore, leaving any land forces unsupported. The situation looked suspiciously like a stalemate.

It was doubtless for this reason that, on the night of the 26th, Doria gave the order to weigh anchor and head south into Turkish waters.

Barbarossa, fully conscious of his enemy's strength but with no idea of his destination, would have no option but to pursue him, and the two fleets could meet in the open sea. To this degree Doria was right; as his ships sailed down the west coast of the island of Leucas, the Turks did indeed emerge from the Bay of Arta and follow them. His problem was that his fleet, consisting as it did partly of oared galleys and partly of sailing galleons, was impossible to keep together. When the wind was fresh, the galleons swept ahead; when it suddenly changed or dropped, the galleys either overtook them or threw away their advantage and – to the immense relief of the oarsmen – waited for them to catch up. Thus it was that by the time his flagship was rounding the southwestern cape of Leucas some of the heaviest galleons were lying almost becalmed only a few miles from their point of departure.

And then the wind did indeed change. On the morning of the 28th it was blowing from due south, and the fleet was strung out all along the west coast of the island. This, surely, would have been the moment for Doria to return, with all sails set, to the north, regroup his ships and meet the Turks head on. Inexplicably, he remained where he was. Meanwhile, the Ottoman fleet – almost entirely oared – rounded the northern tip of Leucas, Barbarossa in the centre, with Dragut commanding the right wing and Salah Reis the left. There, dead ahead of them, was the largest, strongest, heaviest and therefore – in the conditions prevailing – the slowest of all the allied vessels. She was known as the Galleon of Venice. Commanded by one of the Republic's most promising young captains, Alessandro Condulmer, she carried a huge weight of cannon – as much as the average coastal fortress – and was well able to defend herself; but, sheltered as she now was by the mountains of Leucas, she was immobile. Her commander despatched a fast pinnace to his admiral with an urgent appeal for help.

Barbarossa attacked, but Condulmer gave as good as he got – indeed rather better, waiting until the attacking Turkish ships came within point-blank range and then blasting them one after another out of the water. He knew, however, that he could not hold out indefinitely against such an enemy; everything depended on the swift arrival of Doria's galleys. But they did not come. With the wind behind them – which it was – they could have made the journey in three hours at the most; we know too that both Vincenzo Cappello and Marco Grimani pressed their admiral hard to sail with his whole fleet to the rescue. Dusk was falling when he eventually agreed; even then he insisted on taking the fleet in a wide arc to the west.

So Condulmer was obliged to fight on unaided – demonstrating, incidentally, that a sturdy galleon with a highly-trained, well-disciplined crew, even when becalmed, was a more effective fighting weapon than any number of oared galleys. Consequently he, his ship and most of his men survived. But he could not affect the outcome of the battle. By the time Barbarossa turned his ships back to Preveza at sunset he had captured at least two galleys, one Venetian and one from the papal squadron, and five Spanish sail. Doria, with the wind behind him, could still have pursued his adversary at first light the next morning. His forces were far stronger, his firepower infinitely superior. With no difficulty at all he could have turned the tables and inflicted heavy damage on the Turkish fleet. Instead, he ignored it utterly and headed back to Corfu.

Why did Genoa's foremost naval commander act as he did? In the words of a French naval historian – who was also an admiral – 'For less than this the English shot Admiral Byng in 1756.'[1] Was it simply Doria's hatred of Venice? Since he was neither a coward nor a fool, treachery or deliberate malice are the only possible explanations. Whichever is the true one, by his refusal to engage with a vastly inferior enemy he threw away an excellent chance of a decisive victory. Thanks exclusively to him, that victory belonged to Barbarossa. The immediate loser, beyond a shadow of doubt, was Venice.

It was by now clear that Venice must negotiate a peace with the Sultan on whatever terms she could. Of all her recent losses, those which crippled her most were Nauplia and Malvasia, her last trading posts in the Peloponnese, for the return of which she was prepared to pay a ransom of 300,000 ducats. This was by any standards a huge sum, and it was thought that Süleyman would be only too happy to accept it. He proved, however, to be nothing of the kind, and in October 1540 Venice was obliged to agree to a treaty on terms far harsher than she had ever contemplated. The sum she had offered as a ransom was exacted as general reparations, but there was to be no question of the return of Nauplia or Malvasia, or indeed any other of the territories lost in the past three years. In future, too, Venetian ships would not be allowed to enter or leave Turkish ports without permission. It was a blow from which the Republic was never entirely to recover, but it was symptomatic of a situation that was giving

---

[1] Jurien de la Gravière, *Doria et Barberousse*, Paris 1886. Quoted in Bradford, *The Sultan's Admiral*. (Byng's execution in fact took place in 1757.)

increasing concern to the entire Christian Mediterranean. Everywhere it was becoming brutally clear that the days of expansion were gone, that those of retrenchment had set in. The patterns of trade were changing fast; even though the adverse economic effects had not yet proved as bad as the pessimists feared, there were no long-term grounds for optimism. The Turk was at the gates, his advance relentless, his appetite apparently insatiable; and the Christian West had failed to offer him any concerted resistance.

Barbarossa was now about fifty-five. He still had before him some seven years of service to his Sultan, years in which he was to distinguish himself as brilliantly as ever he had, but henceforth he was to fight at the side of a somewhat surprising new ally: Francis I of France. Already two years before, in 1536, we find a Turkish squadron wintering in the harbour of Marseille; in the years following, relations between the two powers – to the disgust of the rest of Christian Europe and indeed of a large number of Frenchmen – seem to have grown steadily more cordial. For Francis, here was an invaluable ally prepared to fight his battles with the Emperor; for Süleyman the Magnificent, an unrivalled chance of splitting the forces of Christendom more drastically then ever.

It was not until 1543 that these improbable allies moved against their common enemy, but when they did so they moved in strength. In the early summer of that year, no less than 100 Turkish galleys attacked Charles where he was at his most vulnerable, in south Italy. Sweeping up from the south, they sacked Reggio – where, according to one account, Barbarossa captured and subsequently married the governor's daughter – and then, passing through the Straits of Messina, pressed remorselessly up the Calabrian coast, raiding and plundering as they went. On arrival at Gaeta they stormed and seized the fortress and wrought havoc within the city. A few days later they appeared off the mouth of the Tiber and fell upon Civitavecchia, before heading northwest to a prearranged rendezvous with the French at Marseille.

But now the trouble began. There was no sign of the stores and provisions which Barbarossa had ordered and upon which he had relied, and which Francis had promised would be awaiting him. The King's representative and commander of his galleys, the young Duke of Enghien, grovelled in apology – eyebrows were raised, then and later, at the seemingly exaggerated deference shown to the former pirate by all the leading Frenchmen with whom he came in contact – but

Barbarossa made no secret of his dissatisfaction, nor of his contempt for such unpardonable inefficiency; so angry, indeed, was he that he almost refused Enghien's proposal that the joint fleet should sail east along the coast to Nice. This city, which since the late fourteenth century had enjoyed peace and prosperity under the Dukes of Savoy, had become a bone of contention between Francis and Charles almost as soon as their long rivalry began; now it faced the most merciless bombardment of its history.

If the siege of Nice in August 1543 is remembered at all in the city today, it is because of the courage of its local heroine. Early in the morning of the 15th, Barbarossa and Enghien had opened a breach in the walls near one of the principal towers, and the garrison was on the point of taking flight when a local woman named Caterina Segurana, with a few brave men whom she had summoned to support her, blocked its passage and forced it to stand firm. The town was temporarily saved, but Caterina had only delayed the inevitable. Just a week later, on the 22nd, the governor formally surrendered. In doing so, he was entitled – and doubtless expected – to be offered honourable terms, but within two days Nice was sacked and put to the torch. Inevitably, the Turks were blamed; in fact it was almost certainly the French soldiers who were responsible. Such, certainly, was the opinion of the Maréchal de Vieilleville, dictating his memoirs shortly before his death in 1571:

> The city of Nice was plundered and burnt, for which neither Barbarossa nor the Saracens can be blamed, for when it occurred they were already far away . . . Responsibility for the outrage was thrown at poor Barbarossa to protect the honour and reputation of France, and indeed of Christianity itself.

Although the Ottoman fleet returned to Toulon for the winter, the siege and capture of Nice was the first and last joint operation of the Franco–Turkish alliance. In 1544 Francis made a pact with his old enemy Charles V and Kheir-ed-Din Barbarossa returned to a hero's welcome in Constantinople – ravaging en route Elba, Procida, Ischia and Lipari with its fellow Aeolian islands, all of which were imperial territory. Two years later he was dead, at the age of sixty-three. The only son that we know of, Hassan, in due course became ruler of Algeria, the kingdom that his father and uncle had created, but the old man's true successor was his long-time lieutenant Dragut – known as 'the living chart of the Mediterranean' – who continued his work. It was Dragut who in 1551 wrenched Tripoli after sixteen years from the hands of the Knights of St John,[1] and who nine years later utterly routed a Spanish fleet sent to dislodge him. He was subsequently rewarded with the Sultanate of Tripoli, but he never hung up his sword; in 1565, aged eighty, he was killed in action during the siege of Malta.

But the siege of Malta is another story.

---

[1] Tripoli had fallen in 1510 to Spain, which in 1535 had offered it to the Knights to garrison.

CHAPTER XVI

Malta and Cyprus

Malta's history really begins with the Phoenicians, who set up a trading post there around 800 BC. Perhaps surprisingly, in view of the number of Greek inscriptions, there seems to have been no Greek colony on the island. Its strategic importance became clear during the Punic Wars, and it was fought over by Rome and Carthage – changing hands several times – before it finally fell to Rome in 218 BC. For the next millennium and a half, its history was predictable enough: Roman, Byzantine, Arab, Norman. The first of the Norman rulers of Sicily, Count Roger I, conquered it in 1090. Tradition has it that he cut off part of his own scarlet standard and gave it to the Maltese as their flag. Finding this rather too small, they added a piece of white cloth to it; red and white – with the subsequent addition of the Cross of the Knights of St John – remain the colours of the Maltese flag to this day.

With the collapse of Norman Sicily at the end of the twelfth century, Malta was granted as a fief to the country's Grand Admiral, but it soon fell, with Sicily, to Charles of Anjou and then, after the War of the Sicilian Vespers, to the house of Aragon. Somewhere around 1250 King James I of Aragon expelled all the Muslims – who until then seem to have formed the considerable majority of the population – and the island remained at least technically under Spanish rule until Charles V presented it to the Knights in 1530. Just thirty-five years later it was to find itself at the centre of the Mediterranean stage.

On the international political scene during the nineteen years separating the death of Kheir-ed-Din Barbarossa in 1546 and the siege of Malta in 1565, there was a major change of cast. Henry VIII of England and Francis I of France died within two months of each other in 1547, and in 1556 the Emperor Charles V abdicated and retired to the monastery of Yuste in Extremadura, from which two years later he followed them to the grave. Spain he left to his son Philip II, the Empire to his brother Ferdinand; but Ferdinand himself died in 1564, to be succeeded by his son as Maximilian II. Only one of the old principals remained in the centre of the stage. Sultan Süleyman the Magnificent was now in his seventieth year, but his physical and mental powers were undiminished. So too was his ambition.

Süleyman had had plenty of time to regret his merciful treatment of the Knights of St John after the fall of Rhodes. His safe-conduct had been granted them in return for a promise never again to take up arms against him; never had a promise been so flagrantly or repeatedly broken. Clearly, the time had now come to expel them from Malta, just as he had expelled them from Rhodes. Now they were settled in their new home, they were threatening to become as persistant a nuisance as ever they had been. And the Sultan had another reason too. Malta occupied a key position in the central Mediterranean, forming a natural stepping-stone between Turkish-held Tripoli and Sicily, which belonged to Philip of Spain. Once it had fallen into Süleyman's hands, it would provide the perfect springboard for a conquest of Sicily, after which landings in south Italy would have followed as the night the day.

Charles V had been fully aware of this when in 1530 he made the island available to the Order. What better means could he hope for, at no cost to himself, of protecting the southern approaches to his empire? The Knights, it is true, had not been initially enthusiastic: they had considered the possibility of a move to Malta six years earlier, and had sent out eight commissioners to investigate its possibilities. 'The island,' the commissioners had reported,

> is merely a rock of soft sandstone called tufa, about six or seven leagues long and three or four broad;[1] the surface of the rock is barely covered by more than three or four feet of earth. This also is stony, and most unsuited for growing corn or other cereals. It does however produce quantities of figs, melons and other fruits. The principal trade of the island consists of honey, cotton and cumin seed. These the inhabitants exchange for grain. Except for a few springs in the centre of the island there is no running water, nor even wells, so the inhabitants catch the rainwater in cisterns. Wood is so scarce as to be sold by the pound and the inhabitants have to use either sun-dried cow-dung or thistles for cooking their food.

Malta was not, admittedly, a place designed to withstand a siege. It boasted, on the other hand, three immense advantages: a limitless supply of mellow, honey-coloured building stone; a fine tradition of quarrymen, builders, stonemasons and carvers; and perhaps the most astonishing natural anchorage in the world. To this day the first sight of Grand Harbour from the heights of Valletta cannot fail to catch the

---

[1] It is actually sandstone, and roughly eighteen miles by nine.

breath. It was unquestionably this that finally decided the Knights – after eight years' homelessness – to accept the Emperor's offer of a lease. The rent was reasonable enough: a single falcon, payable annually on All Souls' Day.

The Knights never forgot that they were first and foremost Hospitallers; for well over five centuries the care of the sick had been their *raison d'être*. No sooner had they settled in Birgu (now known as Vittoriosa), the northern of the two long headlands on the far side of Grand Harbour, than they set about building a hospital.[1] Its predecessor in Rhodes had been famous throughout Christendom and visited by the sick of every nation in the western world, and they were determined that a similar institution in Malta should be equally celebrated – as indeed it soon became. Their second priority was defence: the fortification of their superb harbour and their navy. Shipbuilding was no easy task on a treeless island; thanks, however, to massive imports of timber from Sicily, over the next thirty years they gradually built up a considerable fleet, until by 1560 their sea power was probably as great as it had been in the old Rhodian days. It was just as well; when they received the first reports of Süleyman's coming expedition, their navy at least was ready.

Certainly, they had no illusions about the danger they faced. Without vast reinforcements they knew that they would be hopelessly out-numbered, both in men and in ships, and they could expect little sustenance from their scanty, stony soil. They also knew, however, that that soil would show itself still more inhospitable to a besieging army. Whereas Rhodes had been only ten miles from the Turkish coast, Malta was nearly a thousand. Minor reinforcements might be brought in from North Africa; nonetheless, it was clear that the force which the Sultan was to hurl against them had from the first to be largely self-supporting. Small wonder that his invasion fleet, carrying as it did not only the entire army of some 40,000 men with their horses, cannon, ammunition and military supplies but food and water too and even fuel for cooking, was said to be one of the largest ever to embark on the high seas. It consisted of well over 200 ships, including 130 oared galleys, thirty galleasses[2] and eleven tub-shaped merchantmen which relied, like the galleons, entirely on sail. The remainder was made up of

---

[1] This first hospital still stands in Triq Santa Scholastica. It is now a convent of Benedictine nuns.

[2] A galleass might be described as a cross between a galley and a galleon. It was basically a cargo ship, largely dependent upon sail but also fitted with oars and a fair weight of guns.

assorted smaller ships, mostly barques and frigates. Swelling the numbers still further – though emphatically not part of the official expedition – were the privateers, circling like vultures around them.

In 1557, at the age of sixty-three – he was almost exactly the same age as Süleyman – Jean Parisot de la Valette had been elected forty-eighth Grand Master of the Order of St John. A Gascon, he is said by the Abbé de Brantôme to have been outstandingly handsome and to have spoken several languages fluently, including Italian, Spanish, Greek, Turkish and Arabic. He was also a hard, implacable defender of the Christian faith. As a young Knight of twenty-eight he had fought at the siege of Rhodes; later he had been captured and had suffered for a year as a Turkish galley slave. He was utterly single-minded in the service of the Order – a man, it was said, 'equally capable of converting a Protestant or governing a kingdom'. Faith, strength, leadership and steel discipline, all were his. He was to need them all in the ordeal that lay ahead.

The Knights, it need hardly be said, had their spies in Constantinople. They knew as soon as anyone when the Sultan had begun his preparations, and from the moment of his election La Valette had every able-bodied man in Malta working flat out to be ready for the battle to come. He had appealed for reinforcements of men and materials from the commanderies of the Order that were scattered throughout Christian Europe; even so, at the start of the siege he could count on only some 540 Knights with their servants-at-arms, together with about 1,000 Spanish infantrymen and arquebusiers and perhaps 4,000 local Maltese militia. He had also ordered emergency supplies of grain from Sicily and additional armaments and munitions from France and Spain. All his water cisterns were full, and he had no compunction in arranging for the waters of the Marsa – a low-lying region beyond Grand Harbour which he knew must be the principal source of water for any besieging army – to be contaminated with dead animals when the time came.

The great fleet appeared off the horizon on 18 May 1565. The Sultan had regretfully decided that he was too old to lead it in person, as he had led the last attack on Rhodes. Instead he divided the command in two, the naval force to be the responsibility of his young son-in-law Piale Pasha (who had recaptured Djerba from the Spaniards some years before), the land army that of his brother-in-law, the veteran general Mustafa Pasha. It was to prove a disastrous decision; the two men hated each other, Mustafa being deeply jealous of the younger man's success and his popularity with the Sultan.

Grand Harbour was obviously far too stoutly defended to be a possible site for disembarkation, and Piale eventually selected the harbour of Marsascirocco (now Marsaxlokk) at the southeastern tip, some five miles away across country from Birgu. The Knights made no attempt to stop him. They could have had little impact on so huge a force in the open sea or even at a beachhead; their one hope lay in their fortifications, from which they had no intention of emerging more than was absolutely necessary. The Turks, once ashore, then advanced towards the city and pitched their camp on the land sloping down to the Marsa, from which they had a commanding view of the whole anchorage. There, stretching out before them, was the long central sweep of water, with the three narrower creeks leading off to the right and, to the left, the long crest of Mount Sciberras – where Valletta stands today – with, at its furthest point guarding the entrance, the towering walls of Fort St Elmo.

Had Piale Pasha elected – as he certainly should have done – to keep his fleet in the south (where it would have been perfectly safe during the summer months), Fort St Elmo would not have loomed large in Turkish calculations. Instead, he decided to bring his ships up the northeast coast and into the harbour of Marsamuscetto (Marsamxett), which runs along the northern side of Mount Sciberras. This certainly provided more shelter; unfortunately it brought him once again into violent disagreement with Mustafa Pasha. It also involved sailing directly beneath the guns of the great fortress, the destruction of which thenceforth became a top priority.

A cursory examination of Fort St Elmo suggested that, as a star-shaped fort of a fairly traditional kind, it might not be a particularly tough nut to crack. The principal difficulty was the dragging of heavy guns for nearly two miles along the ridge of Mount Sciberras, where they would be within range of the guns from the headlands of Birgu and Senglea on the opposite shore. Trench-digging here was impossible; within a few inches the sappers' spades hit solid rock. If the troops manhandling the huge cannon up the slopes and along the crest were to be protected, it could only be by bringing up vast quantities of soil from the Marsa with which to construct earthworks. All this consumed the energies of most of the Sultan's army, providing a welcome breathing space for la Valette and his men as they worked around the clock to strengthen still further the defences of Fort St Angelo, their principal redoubt at the extremity of Birgu.

On 23 May the attack on St Elmo began in earnest. Night and day the bombardment continued. A few days later there arrived the most celebrated Ottoman commander on land or sea, Dragut himself, seemingly unaffected by his eighty years. He took personal command of the siege, setting up new batteries to the north and south of the fort, which was now suffering a remorseless bombardment from three sides at once. By the end of the month its walls were showing signs of imminent collapse. Every night under cover of darkness small boats from Fort St Angelo slipped across the harbour mouth to bring the garrison fresh troops and provisions, returning with the wounded for the hospital in Birgu; it was only thanks to them that the fort held out as long as it did. One night, however, a returning boat brought something more: a deputation from the besieged to tell the Grand Master that they could no longer continue. La Valette looked at them coldly and replied that in that case he would replace them with others who could, and that these would be led by himself. Ashamed, they returned to their posts. St Elmo might be doomed, but there would be no surrender.

Somehow, the fort survived for a total of thirty-one days. When at last on 23 June the Turks smashed their way in, only about sixty of the original 150-odd defenders remained alive. Of these, all but nine were instantly decapitated, their bodies nailed – in mockery of the crucifixion – to wooden crosses and floated across the harbour mouth to the waters below Fort St Angelo. When La Valette saw them he ordered the immediate execution of all Turkish prisoners. Their heads were then rammed into the breeches of the two cannon on the upper bastion and fired back into the ruins of St Elmo. There was no mistaking that message. From that time forward no quarter would be asked or given.

The Turks had now achieved their first objective. They had done so, however, at a cost of nearly a month of their time and some 8,000 of their finest troops – almost a quarter of their entire army. They had also lost Dragut, killed by a cannonball in the last stages of the siege of St Elmo. He lived just long enough to hear of the fall of the fortress – at which, we are told, 'he manifested his joy by several signs and, raising his eyes to heaven as if in thankfulness for its mercies, immediately expired'. Mustafa Pasha is said to have stood among the ruins, gazing through the summer heat across the harbour. 'If so small a son has cost us so dear,' he murmured, 'what price must we pay for the father?'

The father was, of course, Fort St Angelo itself. Behind it was the headland of Birgu, the Knights' fortified city. Beyond the narrow inlet to the southwest lay the neighbouring headland of Senglea. It was on the defence of these two parallel peninsulas, by now completely surrounded by the Ottoman army, that the Order of St John depended for its survival. They were connected by a flimsy bridge across the creek (now known as Dockyard Creek) and by a chain stretched on pontoons across its mouth. At the landward end, a palisade of stakes had been driven into the muddy bottom. No longer, however, after the fall of St Elmo, could the entrance to Grand Harbour itself be blocked; the Turkish ships could sail down its entire length, with only the guns of St Angelo to hinder them.

But there were consolations too. In order to move into their new positions south of Senglea and Birgu, the Turks would be obliged to drag all their heavy cannon, ammunition and supplies back along Mount Sciberras and then around the harbour, over a good four miles of roads that were little more than cart tracks and in the fierce heat of a Maltese summer. Moreover, on the very day that St Elmo fell, ships from Sicily carrying a relief force of perhaps 1,000 all told, including forty-two Knights, had managed to land and, a week later, to make their way by night to what is now Kalkara, beyond another creek to the northeast of Birgu. Not only the arrival of the force itself, but its almost miraculous success in avoiding the Turkish army, had an immense effect on the Knights' morale.

But the struggle continued. In mid-July a concerted attack on Senglea was made from the sea. It was foiled by the courage of the native Maltese, superb swimmers who tipped the Turks from their boats and fought them hand to hand in the water. A hidden gun emplacement completed the rout. On 7 August an Italian gunner with the Spanish army, Francesco Balbi di Correggio, who was later to write a fascinating eye-witness account of the siege, noted:

August 7: A general assault – 8,000 on St Michael's, 4,000 on the port of Castile . . . But when they left their trenches we were already at our posts, the hoops alight, the pitch boiling . . . When they scaled the works they were received like men who were expected . . . The assault lasted nine hours, from daybreak till after noon, during which the Turks were relieved by fresh troops more than a dozen times, while we refreshed ourselves with drinks of well watered wine and some mouthfuls of bread . . . Victory was given to us again . . . though not one of us could stand on his feet for wounds or fatigue.

But by this time it was becoming clear that the Turkish army too was weakening. The heat was merciless. Food was short and water shorter still, since the dead animals with which the Knights had deliberately fouled the wells of Marsa had now been supplemented by large numbers of Turkish corpses. By the end of August dysentery had spread through the Ottoman camp, its victims being carried in the blazing sun to the improvised sick tents where they died in their hundreds. The Turks knew, too, that it would soon be the time of the equinoctial gales, which would be quickly followed by the first winter storms. Mustafa Pasha was prepared to spend the winter on the island if necessary, in the hopes of starving out the besieged; Piale, on the other hand, would not hear of it. The navy, he argued, was more important than the army, and he could not risk wintering his ships without a proper anchorage and full maintenance facilities. He would be getting the fleet under way by the middle of September at the latest; if the army wanted to stay it was up to them, but they would be on their own.

Had Süleyman's forces remained, it is doubtful whether the Knights could possibly have held out. But then, on 7 September, came deliverance: the *Gran Soccorso*, as it was called, the Great Relief, sent by the Spanish viceroy in Sicily. Its 9,000 men were fewer than La Valette had expected, but they were enough. Mustafa hesitated no longer. Suddenly the guns were quiet; the clamour ceased; instead of smoke, there was only dust from the feet of what was left – little more than a quarter – of the once-proud army as it shambled back to the impatient ships. But the Christians too had sustained terrible losses. Two hundred and fifty Knights were dead, the survivors nearly all wounded or maimed. Only 600 men were now capable of bearing arms. And of the city of Birgu scarcely one stone was left on another; vulnerable to fire on every side, strategically it had proved a disaster. And so, when old La Valette limped forward to lay the first stone of his new capital, he did so not on the ruins of the old one but away on the heights of Mount Sciberras opposite, dominating Grand Harbour. As he richly deserved, the city was named after him: Valletta.[1] Three years later, on 21 August 1568, he died. Sir Oliver Starkey, his secretary – and, incidentally, the only Englishman to have fought at his side throughout the siege – wrote a Latin epitaph, which can still be read in St John's Cathedral. Translated, it reads:

> Here lies La Valette, worthy of eternal honour. He who was once the scourge of Africa and Asia, and the shield of Europe when he drove off the heathen by the might of his holy sword, is the first to be buried in this beloved city, whose founder he was.

---

[1] The additional 'l' in the place name cannot be satisfactorily explained.

One of the first major buildings to rise up in the new city was of course the hospital. Like its predecessor on Birgu, it still stands, but it is conceived on an infinitely more ambitious scale: its Great Ward, 155 metres long, is the longest hall (with unsupported roof) in Europe. By 1700, when it could accommodate nearly 1,000 patients, its walls were hung in winter with woollen tapestries, in summer with canvases by Mattia Preti.[1] It is full of light, space and fresh air, those virtues in which the Knights – virtually alone among the medical men of the sixteenth century – put their trust. Moreover, unlike other hospitals of the time, whose patients were normally fed from wooden platters crawling with bacteria of all kinds, the Order provided plates and cups of silver, thus drastically – if unconsciously – reducing the risks of infection. Each item was carefully numbered and stamped on the side with the emblem of the Holy Ghost. Finally, the Knights knew the value of good nursing; every one of them, whatever his seniority, would do his tour of duty in the ward, the Grand Master himself taking his turn on Fridays. For 'our lords the sick', only the best was good enough.

'With me alone do my armies triumph!' Süleyman's words when the news of the disaster was brought to him were all too true. Had he assumed sole command as he had in 1522, there would have been none of the destructive rivalry between Piale and Mustafa; his supreme authority, together with his inspired generalship, might have saved the day. His first reaction had been to swear personally to lead a new expedition to Malta the following spring, but he changed his mind, deciding instead to launch yet another campaign against Hungary and Austria. It was while he was encamped outside the Hungarian fortress of Szigetvar that he died of a sudden stroke – or possibly a heart attack – on 5 September 1566. The tenth of the Ottoman Sultans, he was also the greatest. He had not only greatly expanded his empire; he had set it on a firm institutional and legal basis and, largely through his own personal prestige, had raised it to the status of a world power. Had his successors possessed a fraction of his ability, the history of the Mediterranean might have been different indeed.

In the Christian west, still elated by the heroic resistance of the Knights in Malta, the news of the Sultan's death was greeted with jubilation. But the question remained: had the Turkish advance been

---

[1] Preti (1613–99) was a painter of the Neapolitan school who spent the last thirty-eight years of his life in Malta.

stopped for good, or was this only a temporary halt on its onward path? Süleyman's successor was his eldest son by his favourite wife, generally known to Europeans as Roxelana, the daughter of a Ukrainian priest. Selim II 'the Sot' – a nickname he richly deserved – could hardly have been more of a contrast to his formidable father. Short, fat and incorrigibly dissolute, he cared nothing for affairs of state, preferring to leave the administration of the empire to his Grand Vizir – who was soon to become his son-in-law – Sokollu Mehmet Pasha. Sokollu was by origin a Bosnian Serb who, as the last of Süleyman's Vizirs – he had actually closed the old Sultan's eyes in death – was fully qualified to carry on his former master's policies into the new reign. He had long cherished an ambition to build a canal across the isthmus of Suez, linking the Mediterranean with the Red Sea. This too, had he succeeded some three centuries before Ferdinand de Lesseps, would have changed the course of history; but now, for the first and last time in his life, Selim the Sot overruled him.

For Selim had his eye on Cyprus. It was always said – and may well have been true – that his determination to seize the island was due to his penchant for its unusually potent wines. In fact, its strategic importance was every bit as obvious as the fertility of its soil; the wonder is that Süleyman had not acted years before to rid himself of an unwanted Christian presence less than fifty miles from his own southern shores. Cyprus was a colony of the Venetian Republic, and it was to Venice that, in February 1568, there came a number of disquieting reports. Turkish agents were said to be active on the island stirring up disaffection among the local population, many of whom had no particular love for their Venetian overlords. Turkish ships were taking soundings in Cypriot harbours. Most worrying of all, the Sultan had recently concluded an eight-year truce with the new Emperor Maximilian II, and was consequently free to devote all his attention to a new enterprise. It was true that he had on his accession also signed a peace treaty with Venice, but he was still very much an unknown quantity, and was moreover rumoured to be growing more and more mentally and emotionally unstable.

All these rumours, and many others of the same kind, continued to spread throughout 1569, and towards the end of January 1570 news reached Venice which left no doubt of the Sultan's intentions. The Venetian *bailo* in Istanbul had been summoned by Sokollu, who had informed him in so many words that the Sultan considered Cyprus to be historically part of the Ottoman Empire. A day or two later there followed mass arrests of Venetian merchants and seizures of Venetian ships in the harbour, and on 28 March an ambassador specially sent from the Ottoman court delivered an ultimatum to the Doge: either Venice must surrender Cyprus of her own free will or the island would be taken from her by force. The Venetian reply was short and to the point. Venice was astonished that the Sultan should already wish to break the treaty he had so recently concluded; she was, however, the mistress of Cyprus and would, by the grace of Jesus Christ, have the courage to defend it.

Already the Republic had despatched appeals for help to all Christian states, but the response had been less than enthusiastic. The Emperor Maximilian had pointed out that his formal truce still had eight years to run. From France Catherine de' Medici, now effectively regent, was quarrelling with Spain over Flanders and had pleaded her old alliance with the Sultan. The King of Portugal had claimed that he was fully engaged in the east, and that anyway his country was being ravaged by plague. The Knights of St John – who were, incidentally, the biggest landowners in Cyprus – had been more obliging and had offered five ships; alas, four of them had been captured by the Turks soon after leaving Malta. No appeal had been addressed to Queen Elizabeth of England, who was under sentence of excommunication.

That left Pope Pius V and Philip II of Spain. The Pope had agreed to equip a dozen vessels if Venice would provide the hulls. Philip for his part had offered a fleet of fifty ships under the command of Gian Andrea Doria, great-nephew and heir of that Andrea whose hatred of Venice had twice led him to betray the Republic's trust, at Corfu and Preveza, some thirty years before. Even this was a niggardly enough contribution; Venice herself had mustered 144 ships, including 126 war galleys. But Philip had always mistrusted the Venetians, whom he suspected (not without some cause) of always being ready to make terms with the Sultan if the opportunity offered; and as events were to show, he had given Doria – whose feelings against the Republic were no whit less hostile than those of his great-uncle – secret instructions to keep out of trouble, to let the Venetians do the fighting, and to bring the Spanish fleet safely home again as soon as possible.

From the start, the expedition was ill-fated. The Venetian Captain-General, Girolamo Zane, who had understood that the Spanish and papal squadrons were to join him at Zara (Zadar) on the Dalmatian coast, waited there in vain for two months during which his fleet was ravaged by some unidentified epidemic, causing not only many deaths but a general demoralisation which led to hundreds of desertions. On 12 June 1570 he sailed to Corfu, where he picked up Sebastiano Venier, the erstwhile Proveditor-General of the island who had recently been appointed to the same position in Cyprus. Here he heard that the papal squadron under Marcantonio Colonna was awaiting the Spaniards at Otranto – but of Philip's promised fleet there was still no sign. Not until July was it learned that Gian Andrea Doria had simply remained in Sicily, on the pretext that he had received no instructions to go further. After urgent protestations from the Pope, Philip finally sent his admiral sailing orders, which arrived on 8 August; even then it was another four days before the Spanish fleet left Messina, and a further eight before it reached Otranto – a journey which, in the perfect weather then prevailing, should have taken no more than two.

Having at last joined his papal allies, Doria made no effort to call on Colonna or even to communicate with him; and, when Colonna decided to ignore this studied piece of discourtesy and to take the initiative himself, he was rewarded with a long speech implicitly recommending that the whole expedition should be called off. The season was late; the Spanish ships were not in fighting condition; and as Doria was at pains to point out, though his instructions were to sail under the papal flag, he was also under the orders of his sovereign to keep his fleet intact. Colonna somehow forbore to remind him who was to blame for the first two misfortunes, merely reiterating that both King and Pope expected their fleets to sail with the Venetians to Cyprus, so sail they must. Finally, with ill grace, Doria agreed.

Girolamo Zane had by now moved on to Crete, where the papal and Spanish fleets joined him on 1 September – almost exactly five months since his departure from Venice. A council was called, at which Doria at once began raising new difficulties. This time it was the Venetian galleys that were unfit for war; moreover, once the allied fleet left Crete there would be no harbours in which to take refuge. Now, too, the admiral revealed a fact that he had not, apparently, thought it necessary to mention before: he was instructed to return to the west by the end of the month at the latest.

Colonna remained firm. The season, though advanced, was not yet prohibitively so; there were still two clear months before the onset of winter. Cyprus was rich in admirable harbours. The Venetian ships had admittedly been undermanned after the epidemic and the desertions, but their long wait had given them plenty of time to find replacements and their crews were once again up to strength. Altogether the combined fleet now comprised 205 sail; the Turkish was thought to number 150 at the most. Why, therefore, should they fear an armed encounter? To retire now, before even sighting the enemy, would be nothing short of ignominious. Doria still prevaricated, and Zane sent a furious letter back to Venice accusing him of disrupting the whole enterprise. Then, on 16 September, after further delaying tactics, there came a report that the Turks had landed in Cyprus. It was now or never. On the night of the 17th the fleet sailed for the beleaguered island.

Almost immediately there came worse news still: Nicosia had fallen. Another council was called. Now, for the first time, the Marquis of Santa Cruz, who as commander of the Neapolitan contingent was technically a subordinate of Doria's but who had hitherto taken a considerably more robust line than his chief, also advised turning back. The capture of Nicosia, he pointed out, would mean a vast increase in the number of fighting men available for the Turkish fleet, and a corresponding upsurge in enemy morale – all this at the worst possible time, when the allied crews were becoming more and more dispirited. Colonna agreed with him; so, reluctantly, did Zane. The only voice raised in favour of a continued advance was that of Sebastiano Venier, who argued that however strong the Turks might be, they would almost certainly be a good deal stronger next year, when the allies were most unlikely to have a fleet of over 200 sail to throw against them.

They were brave words; but they failed to convince, and the mighty fleet, flying the banners of Christendom, turned about without once having come within sight of its enemy. In an almost pathetic attempt to salvage the last shreds of his reputation, poor Zane proposed that the allies should at least try to inflict some damage on enemy territory during their return journey; once again, his hopes were sabotaged by Doria's impatience to get home. By the time his ships reached Corfu on 17 November a new epidemic had broken out and he himself was, mentally and physically, a broken man. Lacking even the heart to return home, he wrote to the Senate in Venice asking to be relieved of his post. His request was granted, and on 13 December Sebastiano Venier was appointed Captain-General in his stead. Later Zane was to be summoned to Venice to answer several grave charges relating to his conduct during the expedition. After a long enquiry he was acquitted – but too late. In September 1572 he had died in prison.

The fate of Gian Andrea Doria was somewhat different. Philip II had been left in no doubt of the bitter feelings his admiral had aroused; Pope Pius, on receiving Colonna's report, had sent him a formal letter of complaint. But Philip chose to ignore it. Doria had obeyed his instructions to the letter, and was rewarded by immediate promotion to the rank of general, with seniority over all the commanders of the fleets of Spain, Naples and Sicily – in which capacity he was to do still further damage to the allied cause before his disastrous career was over.

In 1570 Venice had held Cyprus for eighty-one years. In 1489 Queen Caterina had been replaced by a Venetian governor – known as the Lieutenant – based in Nicosia. The military headquarters, on the other hand, was at Famagusta, where both the standing garrison and the Cyprus-based fleet were under the command of a Venetian captain. Famagusta, unlike Nicosia, was superbly fortified. Historically it was the island's principal harbour, although by 1570 Salines (the modern Larnaca) had overtaken it in terms of commercial traffic. The total population was about 160,000, still living under an anachronistically feudal system which the Republic had made little or no effort to change. At the top was the nobility, partly Venetian but for the most part still of old French crusader stock like the former royal house of Lusignan; at the bottom was the peasantry, many of them still effectively serfs. Between the two was the merchant class and urban bourgeoisie, a Levantine melting pot of Greeks, Venetians, Armenians, Syrians, Copts and Jews.

Cyprus, in short, cannot have been an easy place to govern, though it must be admitted that the Venetians – whose own domestic administration was the wonder and envy of the civilised world – might have governed it a good deal better than they did. By the time the Turks landed in the summer of 1570 the Republic had acquired a grim record of local maladministration and corruption, and had made itself thoroughly unpopular with its Cypriot subjects. Thus, even if the allied expedition for the relief of Cyprus had arrived on time and fought valiantly, it could scarcely have saved the island. A major victory at sea might perhaps have proved temporarily effective, delaying the inevitable for a year or two, but since the Turkish invasion fleet that dropped anchor on 3 July at Larnaca numbered not less than 350 sail – more than double Colonna's estimate – such a victory would have been, to say the least, unlikely. The truth is that, from the moment that Sultan Selim decided to incorporate the island into his empire, Cyprus was doomed.

It was doomed for the same fundamental reason that Malta, five years before, had been saved: the inescapable fact that the strength of any army in the field varies inversely with the length of its lines of communication and supply. Since Cyprus had neither the means, the ability, nor – probably – the will to defend itself, it could be defended only by Venice, from which all military supplies, arms and ammunition and the bulk of the fighting men and horses would have to come. But Venice lay over 1,500 miles away across the Mediterranean, much of which was now controlled by the Turks. They, on the other hand, had only fifty miles to sail from ports on the southern coast of Anatolia, where they could count on an almost limitless supply of manpower and materials.

Their success seemed the more assured in that the Cypriot defences, apart from those of Famagusta, were hopelessly inadequate. Nicosia, it is true, boasted a nine-mile circuit of medieval walls, but they enclosed an area considerably larger than the town and needed a huge force to defend them. They were moreover far too thin – the siege techniques of the sixteenth century were vastly different from those of the fourteenth – and despite the feverish last-minute efforts of Venetian engineers to strengthen them they stood a poor chance of survival against the massive artillery that had long been a speciality of the Turks. Kyrenia had once been a splendid fortress, but had long since fallen into ruin and was unlikely to withstand any serious attack. The defences of all other Cypriot towns were either negligible or nonexistent. Manpower and weaponry were both in short supply. Fra Angelo Calepio, who was present throughout, tells us that there were 1,040 arquebuses in the magazines, but that no instructions had been given as to their use, with the result that many soldiers found it impossible to fire them without setting light to their beards.

For this and many other shortcomings the principal blame must attach to the Lieutenant, Niccolò Dandolo. Uncertain, timid, forever vacillating between bouts of almost hysterical activity and periods of apathetic inertia, he was totally unsuited to the supreme command. Through the agonising months that were to follow he was to prove a constant liability, his lack of judgement and immoderate caution giving rise to suspicions – as it happened, unfounded – that he was in enemy pay. Fortunately, there was a better man at Famagusta: its captain, Marcantonio Bragadin.

The Turkish fleet had appeared off the coast on 1 July. Once again it was under the command of Piale Pasha. The army, on the other hand, had a new chief: Lala Mustafa Pasha, who thanks to Dandolo's timidity was able to land his entire force at Larnaca without opposition. By the 24th he and his men were encamped outside the walls of Nicosia. Now once again a chance was lost: the Italian commander of infantry begged for permission to mount an immediate attack while the enemy were still tired by their march of thirty miles through the heat of a Cyprus summer, their artillery and heavy cavalry still unprepared. But Dandolo declined to take the risk, and the Turks dug themselves in undisturbed.

And so the siege began. Dandolo, fearing a shortage of gunpowder, had rationed its use to the point where even those of his soldiers who had firearms and knew how to use them were forbidden to shoot at any group of Turks numbering fewer than ten. Yet somehow the city held out for forty-five days, all through a sweltering August; it was only on 9 September, after fourteen major assaults had been fought back and after Lala Mustafa's men had given a noisy and jubilant welcome to a further 20,000 troops freshly arrived from the mainland, that it finally yielded. Dandolo, who had taken refuge in the Lieutenant's palace some hours before, while his men were still fighting on the ramparts, now appeared at the doorway in his crimson velvet robes, hoping to receive the favoured treatment due to his rank. Scarcely had he reached the foot of the steps when a Turkish officer struck his head from his shoulders.

The usual atrocities followed, the usual massacres, quarterings and impalements, the usual desecrations of churches and violations of the youth of both sexes. Nicosia was a rich city, generously endowed with treasures ecclesiastical and secular, western and Byzantine; it was a full week before all the gold and silver, the precious stones and enamelled reliquaries, the jewelled vestments, the velvets and brocades had been loaded on to carts and trundled away – the richest spoils to fall into Turkish hands since the capture of Constantinople itself, well over a century before. Lala Mustafa, however, had no intention of losing momentum. Already on 11 September, just two days after the fall of Nicosia, he had sent a messenger to the commanders at Famagusta calling on them to surrender and bearing, as an additional inducement, the head of Niccolò Dandolo in a basin. The implication was plain. It would be their turn next.

Nicosia had given the Turks a good deal more trouble than they had expected, but the challenge of Famagusta was more formidable still.

With all its recent new fortifications it was now, to all appearances, as nearly impregnable as any town could be. Behind those tremendous walls the defenders were admittedly few – some 8,000 as compared with a Turkish force which, with new contingents arriving regularly from the mainland, probably now fell not far short of 200,000. On the other hand, they had in Marcantonio Bragadin and the Perugian captain Astorre Baglioni two superb leaders, for whom their admiration was steadily to grow during the trials that lay ahead.

The siege began on 17 September and continued all through the winter, the defenders – very unlike those of Nicosia – making frequent sorties outside the walls and occasionally even carrying the battle right into the Turkish camp. Towards the end of April Lala Mustafa ordered his corps of Armenian sappers to dig a huge network of trenches to the south. As they numbered some 40,000 and were further supplemented by forced labour from the local peasantry, work progressed rapidly; by the middle of May the whole region was honeycombed for a distance of three miles from the walls, the trenches numerous enough to accommodate the whole besieging army and so deep that the cavalry could ride along them with only the tips of their lances visible to the watchers on the ramparts. The Turks also constructed a total of ten siege towers, progressively closer to the town, from which they could fire downward on to the defenders. It was from there, on 15 May, that the final bombardment began.

The Venetians fought back with courage and determination, but slowly, as the weeks dragged on, they began to lose heart. Hopes of a great Venetian–Spanish relief expedition had faded. Powder was running short, food was even shorter. By July all the horses, donkeys and cats in the town had been eaten; nothing was left but bread and beans. Of the defenders, only 500 were now capable of bearing arms, and they were dropping through lack of sleep; yet still they fought on. Not until the last day of that nightmare month did Bragadin and Baglioni face the fact that they could hold out no longer. Only by a voluntary surrender might they still, by the accepted rules of warfare, avoid the massacres and the looting that were otherwise inevitable. Dawn broke on 1 August to reveal a white flag fluttering on the ramparts of Famagusta.

The peace terms were surprisingly generous. All Italians were to be allowed to embark, with colours flying, for Crete, together with any Greeks, Albanians or Turks who wished to accompany them. Greeks who chose to stay behind would be guaranteed their personal liberty and property, and would be given two years in which to decide whether they would remain permanently or not; those who then elected to leave would be given safe conduct to the country of their choice. The document setting out these terms was signed personally by Lala Mustafa and sealed with the Sultan's seal; it was then returned to Bragadin and Baglioni, with a covering letter complimenting them on their courage and their magnificent defence of the city.

On 5 August Bragadin sent word to Lala Mustafa proposing to call and formally present him with the keys of Famagusta; back came the reply that the general would be delighted to receive him. He set off that evening wearing his purple robe of office, accompanied by Baglioni with a number of senior officers and escorted by a mixed company of Italian, Greek and Albanian soldiers. Lala Mustafa received them with every courtesy; then, without warning, his face clouded and his manner changed. In a mounting fury, he began to hurl baseless accusations at the Christians standing before him. They had murdered Turkish prisoners; they had concealed munitions instead of handing them over according to the terms of the surrender. Suddenly he whipped out a knife and cut off Bragadin's right ear, ordering an attendant to cut off the other and his nose. Then, turning to his guards, he ordered the immediate execution of the whole delegation. Baglioni was beheaded; so, too, was the commander of the artillery, Luigi Martinengo. One or two managed to escape but most were massacred, together with a number of other Christians who happened to be within reach. Finally the heads of all those who had been murdered were piled in front of Lala Mustafa's pavilion. They are said to have numbered 350.

The worst fate of all was reserved for Marcantonio Bragadin. He was held in prison for nearly a fortnight, by which time his untreated wounds were festering and he was seriously ill. Only then, however, did his real torment begin. First he was dragged round the walls of Famagusta, with sacks of earth and stones on his back; next, tied to a chair, he was hoisted to the yardarm of the Turkish flagship and exposed to the taunts of the sailors. Finally he was taken to the place of execution in the main square, tied naked to a column and, literally, flayed alive. Even this torture he is said to have borne in silence for half an hour until, as the executioner reached his waist, he finally expired. After the grim task was completed his head was cut off, his body quartered, and his skin, stuffed with straw and cotton and mounted on a cow, paraded through the streets.

When, on 22 September, Lala Mustafa sailed for home, he took with him as trophies the heads of the principal victims and the skin of Marcantonio Bragadin, which he proudly presented to the Sultan. The fate of the heads is unknown, but nine years later one of the survivors of the siege, a certain Girolamo Polidoro, managed to steal the skin from the Arsenal of Constantinople and returned it to Bragadin's sons, who deposited it in the church of S. Gregorio in Venice. From here it was transferred in 1596 to SS. Giovanni e Paolo where, in the south aisle near the west door, it was placed in a niche just behind the urn which forms part of the hero's memorial.

On 24 November 1961, with the consent of Bragadin's direct descendant, the niche was opened. It was found to contain a leaden casket, in which were several pieces of tanned human skin.

CHAPTER XVII

Lepanto and the Spanish Conspiracy

The failure of the Cyprus expedition had been, both for Venice and for the Papacy, a humiliating blow; but already negotiations were under way for a firmer and more effective alliance. The prime mover of this new initiative was the Pope. Pius V had thought long and hard about the Turkish threat, and had realised that the principal obstacle to any close understanding between Venice and Spain was that Venice saw the problem in terms of her colonies in the Levant, while Spain was a good deal more anxious about the danger presented by the Sultan's Moorish vassals to her own possessions in North Africa. He had therefore concluded that the primary aim of Christendom should be to re-establish control of the central Mediterranean, cutting off the Sultan's African territories from those in Europe and Asia and thus effectively splitting his empire into two. In July 1570 he accordingly called a conference to draft the charter of a new Christian League, and over the following months, by patient argument and with active Venetian help, he gradually won King Philip round.

The resulting treaty was formally proclaimed on 25 May 1571 in St Peter's. It was to be perpetual, offensive as well as defensive, and directed not only against the Ottoman Turks but also against their Moorish vassals and co-religionists along the North African coast. The signatories – Spain, Venice and the Papacy (the way was left open for the Emperor and the Kings of France and Poland to join if they wished) – were together to furnish 200 galleys, 100 transports, 50,000 foot soldiers and 4,500 cavalry, with the requisite artillery and ammunition. These forces were to foregather every year, in the month of April at the latest, for a summer campaign wherever they thought fit. Every autumn there would be consultations in Rome to determine the next year's activity. If either Spain or Venice were attacked, the other would go to her assistance; both undertook to defend papal territory with everything they had. All fighting would be under the banner of the League; important decisions would be taken by a majority vote of the three generals commanding: Sebastiano Venier for Venice, Marcantonio Colonna for the Papacy, and for Spain the Captain-General of the combined fleet, the King's half-brother Don John of Austria.

Don John was the bastard son of Charles V by a German lady called Barbara Blomberg. Twenty-six years old, outstandingly good-looking and a natural leader of men, he had already gained a degree of fame – or notoriety – in the previous year by putting down a serious Morisco rising in Spain.[1] The Venetians expressed themselves delighted at the appointment – as well they might have been, since the King's first choice, about which he had luckily had second thoughts, had been Gian Andrea Doria. They would have felt rather less pleasure had they known that Philip, who suspected that the young prince's courage was apt to override his judgement, had ordered him on no account to give battle without Doria's express consent.

Although it was clearly too late to observe the timetable stipulated in the treaty, the allies had agreed that the summer of 1571 should not be wasted, and that the forces for the first year's campaign should muster as soon as possible at Messina, from which they would sail in search of the Ottoman navy. By August all had arrived, and Don John drew up his sailing orders. He himself, with Venier and Colonna, would take the centre, with sixty-four galleys. The right wing, with fifty-four, would be under Doria; the left, with fifty-three, under the Venetian Augustino Barbarigo. In addition there was to be a small vanguard of eight galleys and a rearguard of six, to be respectively commanded by Don Juan de Cardona and the Marquis of Santa Cruz. To each group were allotted six galleasses. The galleons and heavy transports, which – not being oared like the galleys – were considerably less manoeuvrable, were to form a separate convoy.[2]

Emboldened by the fall of Famagusta and by the departure of virtually the whole Venetian fleet for Messina, the Turks had by now entered the Adriatic in strength; their landings in Corfu and along the Dalmatian coast had aroused increasing fears in Venice of a sudden invasion which would find the city almost without defence. At the approach of the combined fleet, however, they had rapidly withdrawn to their bases in Greece; they had no wish to be blockaded within the narrow sea with the enemy all around them. Thus it was from Lepanto

---

[1] See p. 241.

[2] To remind the reader:

Galley: single deck, 120–180 feet long, 200-foot beam. Normally moved under sail, but always propelled by oars when in battle. Five guns mounted in bow, several smaller ones amidships. A metal beak of 10–20 feet was used for ramming.

Galleon: far heavier than galley, two decks, both thickly mounted with guns. No oars. Tall, unwieldy: a floating fortress.

Galleass: half-way between the two. High poop and forecastle (providing cover for oarsmen), 50–70 guns, lateen rigged.

(the modern Naupactos on the Gulf of Patras) that they sailed out, on 6 October, to meet the advancing Christians.

The Christians were in a fighting mood. Two days before, at Cephalonia, they had heard of the fall of Famagusta and, in particular, of the death of Marcantonio Bragadin; rage and vengeance were in their hearts. On the same day, however, there occurred an incident which almost proved disastrous. A Spanish officer and a few of the men on Sebastiano Venier's galley insulted some Venetians, and in the ensuing fight several of them were killed. Venier, without consultation and on his own initiative, had all those implicated hanged at the masthead. When this was reported to Don John he flew into a rage and ordered the captain's arrest – a command which, had it been obeyed, might well have torn the whole fleet apart. Fortunately, wiser counsels – probably those of Colonna – prevailed and he was persuaded to countermand his order, but he never forgave Venier. Henceforth all his communications with the Venetian contingent were addressed to the second-in-command.

The two fleets met at dawn on 7 October, a mile or two east of Cape Scropha at the entrance to the Gulf of Patras. The galleons had not yet arrived, but Don John was determined to engage the enemy at once. Only slightly revising his order of battle – Barbarigo and Doria received ten more galleys each – he drew his ships into formation and sailed to the attack. The Turks were ready for him, with a fleet that almost precisely matched his own, describing a huge crescent that extended from one shore of the gulf to the other. The admiral, Ali Pasha, commanded the central squadron, with eighty-seven galleys; on his right was Mehmet Saulak, governor of Alexandria, with fifty-four; on his left, opposite Doria, was Uluch Ali with sixty-one.

The battle began at about half past ten in the morning at the north end of the lines, where Don John's left wing under Barbarigo engaged Ali's right under Saulak. The fighting was fierce, Barbarigo's own flagship being at one moment set upon by five Turkish vessels which simultaneously loosed a hail of arrows, one of them wounding the Venetian admiral mortally in the eye. His nephew Marco Contarini took over the command, but within five minutes he too was dead. Yet the engagement ended in a total victory for the Christians, who eventually succeeded in driving the entire Turkish right wing into the shore. The Turks abandoned their ships and tried to escape into the surrounding hills, but the Venetians pursued them and cut them down as they ran. Saulak was taken prisoner, but he was already seriously wounded and did not long survive.

The focus now shifted to the centre where, at eleven o'clock or thereabouts, Don John's galleys, advancing in line abreast at a steady, even stroke, closed on those of Ali Pasha, the two flagships deliberately making straight for each other. They met, and entangled; to each side of them along the line the other galleys did the same, simultaneously closing in towards the middle until the sea was scarcely visible and men were leaping and scrambling from ship to ship, fighting hand to hand with swords, cutlasses and scimitars. Twice Ali's force of 400 picked janissaries boarded Don John's flagship, the *Real*; three times the Spaniards returned the attack, the last time under heavy covering fire from Colonna, who had just incapacitated the galley of Pertau Pasha, Ali's second-in-command. It was on this third occasion that Ali was struck on the forehead by a cannonball. Scarcely had he fallen before his head was sliced off by a soldier from Malaga, who stuck it on a pike and waved it aloft to give courage to his comrades. With their admiral killed and their flagship captured, the Turks rapidly lost heart. Many of their ships were destroyed in the mêlée; those that managed to extricate themselves turned and fled.

To the south, meanwhile, things were going less well. From the very beginning of the advance, at about ten o'clock that morning, Gian Andrea Doria had been uneasy about his position. The Turkish left wing under Uluch Ali which confronted him was longer and stronger – ninety-three vessels to his sixty-four – and, extending as it did further southward, threatened to outflank him. It was to avoid this danger that he had altered his course towards the southeast, a decision which left an ever-widening gap between Don John and himself. He should have known better. Uluch Ali saw the gap and instantly changed his plans, altering his own direction towards the northwest with the object of cutting straight through the Christian line and falling upon it from the rear. This new course led him against the southern end of Don John's squadron, which consisted of a few ships contributed by the Knights of Malta. The Knights fought bravely, but they had no chance against the overwhelming odds and were massacred to a man. Their flagship was taken in tow, and Uluch Ali raised their captured standard on his own.

By now Don Juan de Cardona, whose eight galleys had been held in reserve, was hurrying to the relief of the Knights. As he approached, sixteen Turkish galleys fell on him. There followed the fiercest and bloodiest encounter of the whole day. When it was over, 450 of the 500 fighting men of Cardona's galleys had been killed or wounded, and Cardona himself was on the point of death. Several ships, when boarded later, were found to be manned entirely by corpses. Others, meanwhile, were hurrying to the rescue: the second reserve force under Santa Cruz and – as soon as he could leave his own area of the battle – Don John himself. Uluch Ali stayed no longer, ordering thirteen of his galleys to quicken their stroke and heading with them northwest at full speed towards Leucas and Preveza. The remainder broke away in the other direction and returned to Lepanto.

Despite the confusion and the appalling losses sustained as a result of the cowardice and sheer bad seamanship of Gian Andrea Doria – and there were plenty of his colleagues after the battle to accuse him of both – the Battle of Lepanto had been an overwhelming victory for Christendom. According to the most reliable estimates, the Christians lost only twelve galleys sunk and one captured; Turkish losses were 113 and 117 respectively. Casualties were heavy on both sides, as was inevitable when much of the fighting was hand-to-hand, but whereas the Christian losses are unlikely to have exceeded 15,000, the Turks are believed to have lost double that number, excluding the 8,000 who were taken prisoner.[1] In addition there was enormous plunder; Ali Pasha's flagship alone was found to contain 150,000 sequins. Finally comes the most gratifying figure of all: that of the 15,000 Christian galley slaves set at liberty. For all this the lion's share of the credit must go to Don John himself, whose handling of his unwieldy and heterogeneous fleet was masterly and whose brilliant use of his firepower was to have a lasting effect on the development of naval warfare. In future, sea battles would be decided by guns rather than by swordsmanship. This in turn would mean bigger, heavier ships, which could be propelled only by sail. Lepanto was the last great naval engagement to be fought with oared galleys, ramming each other head on. The age of the broadside had begun.

It was 18 October before the galley *Angelo* reached Venice with the news. The city was still mourning the loss of Cyprus, raging against the bestial treatment of Bragadin and fearful as to what further reverses the

---

[1] Among the Christian wounded was Miguel de Cervantes, aboard the *Marquesa*. He was struck twice in the chest, a third shot permanently maiming his left hand – 'to the greater glory,' as he put it, 'of the right.' He was to describe Lepanto as 'the greatest occasion that past or present ages have witnessed or that the future can hope to witness', and to remain prouder of his part in it than of anything else in his life.

future might have in store. Within an hour of the *Angelo*'s appearance, trailing the Turkish banners in the water behind her stern, her deck piled high with trophies, the whole mood had changed. Venice had had her revenge; nor had she had to wait long for it. Suddenly jubilation was in the air, as everyone hastened to the Piazza to learn the details of the battle and to celebrate. The gates of the debtors' prison were opened in an act of spontaneous amnesty, while the Turkish merchants, with a contrary motion, barricaded themselves for safety inside the Fondaco dei Turchi until the excitement was over. In St Mark's, a *Te Deum* was followed by a High Mass of thanksgiving; that night there was scarcely a building in the city that was not illuminated inside and out by candles and torches. In more permanent celebration of the event, the great entrance portal of the Arsenal was enlarged and adorned by the addition of a winged lion of St Mark (with appropriate inscription) and two winged victories. A year or two later the pediment was to be surmounted by a statue of St Justina, on whose feast day the great battle had been won, and from 1572 to the fall of the Republic in 1797 that day, 7 October, was annually celebrated with a procession by the Doge and Signoria to the church of that same fortunate patron, outside which the captured Turkish standards were displayed.

And so Lepanto is remembered as one of the decisive battles of the world, the greatest naval engagement between Actium – fought only some sixty miles away – and Trafalgar. In England and America, admittedly, its continued fame rests largely on G. K. Chesterton's thunderous – if gloriously inaccurate – poem, but in the Catholic countries of the Mediterranean it has broken the barriers of history and passed, like Roncesvalles, into legend. Does it, however, altogether deserve its reputation? Technically and tactically, yes; after 1571 sea battles were never the same again. Politically, no. Lepanto did not, as its victors hoped, mark the end of the pendulum's swing, the point where Christian fortunes suddenly turned, gathering force until the Turks were swept back into the Asian heartland whence they had come. Venice did not regain Cyprus; only two years later she was to conclude a separate peace with the Sultan relinquishing all her claims to the island. Nor did Lepanto mean the end of her losses; in the following century, Crete was to go the same way. As for Spain, she did not appreciably increase her control of the central Mediterranean; only seventeen years afterwards, the historic defeat of her Great Armada by the British was to deal her sea power a blow from which it would not quickly recover. Nor was she able to break the links between

Constantinople and the Moorish princes of North Africa; within three years the Turks were to drive the Spaniards from Tunis, make vassals of the local rulers and reduce the area – as they had already reduced most of Algeria to the west and Tripolitania to the east – to the status of an Ottoman province.

But for all those Christians who rejoiced in those exultant October days, the real importance of Lepanto was neither tactical nor political; it was moral. The heavy black cloud which had overshadowed them for two centuries and which since 1453 had grown steadily more threatening, to the point where they felt that their days were numbered – that cloud had suddenly lifted. From one moment to the next, hope had been reborn. It was, perhaps, the Venetian historian Paolo Paruta who best summed up the popular feeling, in the course of his funeral oration in St Mark's on those who had been killed in the battle:

> They have taught us by their example that the Turks are not insuperable, as we had previously believed them to be . . . Thus it can be said that as the beginning of this war was for us a time of sunset, leaving us in perpetual night, now the courage of these men, like a true, life-giving sun, has bestowed upon us the most beautiful and most joyful day that this city, in all her history, has ever seen.

To every patriotic Venetian, it seemed essential that the glorious victory must be followed up at once. The Turk must be given no rest, no time to catch his breath; he must be pursued and brought to battle again, before he had a chance to repair his shattered forces and while the allies still maintained their forward impetus. This was the message that the government of the Republic now propounded to its Spanish and papal allies, but its arguments fell on deaf ears. Don John himself, one suspects, secretly agreed and would have been only too happy to press on through the winter, but his orders from Philip were clear. By the terms of the League, the allied forces would meet again in the spring; until then, he must bid them farewell. He and his fleet returned to Messina.

By the spring of 1572 it was plain to the Venetians that their instincts had been right. Spain was, as usual, prevaricating and procrastinating, raising one objection after another. Pope Pius did his utmost to spur them to action, but he was already a sick man and on 1 May he died. With his death the spirit went out of the League. At last, despairing of Spanish help, Venice decided to launch an expedition of her own, which Marcantonio Colonna willingly joined with his squadron of papal galleys. Only then were the Spaniards goaded into action. They had no wish to be left out if there was indeed another victory to be won. Philip's objections fell away and in June Don John was finally given permission to join his allies.

The fleet assembled at Corfu and sailed south in search of the enemy. The allies had learned with some dismay that in the eight months since Lepanto Sultan Selim had managed to build a new fleet of 150 galleys and eight galleasses – these latter being an innovation for the Turks, who had obviously been impressed by the brilliant use Don John had made of them at Lepanto. Rumour had it, however, that the shipwrights, aware of the fate that awaited them if they failed to meet the Sultan's deadlines, had been obliged to use green timber; that the guns had been so hurriedly cast that many of them were useless; and that the crews, press-ganged into service after the appalling losses at Lepanto, were scarcely trained. It was unlikely, in short, that they would give the allies much trouble. The principal problem would be to bring them to battle.

And so indeed it was. The two fleets met off Modone – for 250 years one of Venice's principal trading posts in the Peloponnese, until it had fallen to the Sultan in 1500 – and immediately the Turks ran for harbour. The allies followed them, took up their positions in the roadstead off Navarino (the modern Pylos) and settled down to wait. Modone, they knew, could not maintain a fleet of such a size for long. The mountainous hinterland was barren and without roads; all supplies must come in by sea. It was only a question of time before the enemy would be forced to emerge, and a second Lepanto would follow.

But once again Venice saw her hopes dashed, and once again the Spaniards were the cause. On 7 October – the first anniversary of the great battle – Don John suddenly announced that he could no longer remain in Greek waters and was returning to the west. The Venetian Captain-General Giacomo Foscarini, dumbfounded, asked why and, when the prince unconvincingly replied that his provisions were running low, at once offered to supply him from his own stock and order more from Venice as necessary. But Don John, clearly acting on new orders from Spain, could not be shaken. Colonna unaccountably took his side. Foscarini had to face the fact that his fleet was not strong enough to challenge the Turks alone. Fuming at the thought of the opportunity lost, he had no choice but to give the order to return.

All that winter the Venetian ambassador in Madrid worked on King Philip. The Turks, he argued, were bent on world domination; they had been constantly extending their territories for some five hundred years and were continuing to do so; the longer they were allowed to advance, the stronger and more irresistible they would become. It was surely the King's duty to Christendom – and to himself, if he wished to keep his throne – to take up arms against them, and not to rest until the work that had been so gloriously begun at Lepanto was thoroughly finished. But Philip refused to listen. He hated and mistrusted Venice; as far as the Turks were concerned he had done his duty the previous year, and with considerable success; after such a victory it would be some time before they raised their heads again. Meanwhile, he was fully occupied with William the Silent's revolt in the Low Countries. He did not go whining to Venice to help him with his problems; he saw no reason why he should assist her any further with hers.

Moreover, in those same winter months, Charles IX of France was also busy, intriguing against Philip on three separate fronts. In the Low Countries he was giving all possible support to the rebellion; in the Mediterranean he was manoeuvring to gain control of Algiers, where his machinations may well have been responsible for Don John's recall from Navarino; in Venice and Constantinople his ambassadors were working hard to bring about a peace between the Sultan and the Republic. By early spring they had succeeded. Venice had not wished for anything of the kind; since Lepanto she had done everything in her power to hold the League together and to persuade her fellow members to join her in an out-and-out offensive, stopping – with God's help – only at Constantinople itself. But she had failed. Philip was frankly not interested, the new Pope Gregory XIII scarcely more so. Deserted by her allies, knowing full well that to continue the war alone would be to invite new Turkish invasions of the Adriatic and, in all probability, the seizure of Crete – her last stronghold in the Levant – she had no choice but to accept the terms which were offered her. On 3 March 1573 the treaty was signed. Venice undertook, *inter alia*, to pay the Sultan 300,000 ducats over three years, and to renounce all her claims to Cyprus.

In the dominions of the Most Catholic King, there were cries of horror and disgust. In Messina, a furious Don John tore the League banner from his masthead and ran up that of Spain. How right Philip had been, said his subjects, not to trust those Venetians; they were bound to betray him sooner or later. It was, they protested, as if the Battle of Lepanto had never been won.

It was indeed. In spite of all the jubilation, the cheering and the shouting and the building up of the great Lepanto legend that still persists today, the truth is that one of the most celebrated naval battles ever fought proved to be of no long-term strategic importance whatever. And those who lamented loudest had only themselves to blame.

After the Battle of Lepanto a curious calm descended upon the Mediterranean. It was as if the whole vast basin had somehow exhausted itself. Until the last quarter of the sixteenth century – though the countries of northern Europe might latterly have disputed the fact – the Middle Sea had been, in a very real sense, the centre of the western world. It was the centre no longer.

For Spain, Christopher Columbus and his successors had opened new and exciting horizons. With her possession of Naples and Sicily in the south and Milan in the north[1] no longer disputed, with the island of Sardinia also hers and the city of Genoa now effectively a Spanish port, the rest of Italy and the Mediterranean had ceased to interest her. True, in 1601 she and a group of Italian states – but not Venice – despatched a powerful force of seventy galleys and 10,000 men to surprise and capture Algiers (since it was commanded by Gian Andrea Doria its failure was assured), but her real attention was now fixed on the west and the north, where her constant problems in the Low Countries and her rivalry with England were taking up almost all her time.

As for France, she was no longer the kingdom that she had been under Francis I. Foreign adventure in the south was now for her a thing of the past; instead, she was being almost literally torn apart by the Wars of Religion, which were to continue for more than thirty years and bring the country to the brink of disintegration. Even Italy was quiet – at least by Italian standards. Apart from Naples and the Papacy there was only one major power in the peninsula, and the Republic of Venice was always too keen on commerce to make war unless it absolutely had to. Between the various north Italian city-states internecine fighting went on as it always had, but most of it was of little if any lasting significance to the Mediterranean world.

Then there was the Ottoman Empire, and even the Turkish jugger-naut now seemed to be running out of steam. The great days of

[1] On the unexpected death of Francesco II Sforza in 1535 the Milanese state had returned to the control of Charles V, who in 1540 had invested his son – later Philip II – with the duchy. Milan was to remain under Spanish rule until 1706.

Süleyman the Magnificent were long since over, and his successor Selim the Sot died in 1574 – appropriately enough, after consuming a whole bottle of strong Cyprus wine at a single draught and then slipping on the wet floor of the baths. It is true that in that very same year the old corsair admiral Kilij Ali recaptured Tunis from the Spanish – the city and its hinterland became an Ottoman province – but this was the sum total of the Turkish gains in the Mediterranean. Selim's son Murad III – he had come to the throne only after ordering the strangulation of his five brothers – was more interested in what lay beyond his eastern borders, and preferred to concentrate his attention on Georgia and the Caucasus. His successors seem to have felt much the same way, and so it was that for very nearly a century the Turks were to do little to alter the map of the Middle Sea.

The only attempt to do so after the capture of Tunis came from an unexpected quarter. In 1578 Philip II's nephew, the headstrong young King Sebastian of Portugal, responded – for reasons that are still not entirely clear – to an appeal for help from the Sherif of Fez, who had recently been expelled from his city by a rival claimant. Sebastian had appealed in his turn to his uncle, who had somewhat grudgingly agreed to support him; he had thus been able to cross the straits of Gibraltar with an army of Spanish and Portuguese numbering some 15,000. On 3 August he reached the town of Alcacerquivir, to find on the following day a vastly greater Moroccan army drawn up against him. He had no choice but to fight, and in the ensuing battle he and both the rival sherifs were killed, as were over 8,000 of his men. Of the remainder nearly all were captured; barely 100 managed to make their escape.

The only real victor of the Battle of the Three Kings, as it was called, was Philip of Spain. Single-handedly, Sebastian had reduced Portugal to such a state of weakness and demoralisation that two years later Philip was able quite simply to swallow it up – doubling at a stroke his colonial empire and gaining valuable Atlantic harbours and shipping besides. Not until 1640 was Portugal to recover her independence.

Philip was to live another twenty years, dying at seventy-one in 1598. No king had ever taken his duties more seriously; none had ever worked harder. Trusting no one, he had spent the last forty years in Madrid or at his palace of the Escorial attending personally to every detail of government and administration, never giving himself time to look up from his desk and take a longer, broader view of the world around him. Morbidly pious, he was determined to perform what he believed to be the divinely appointed task of preserving the true

Catholic religion, in the cause of which he could be ruthless, tyrannical and cruel; but he was a lover of books and pictures and – when he was allowed to be – an affectionate husband and father. He was four times married – his wives were respectively Portuguese, English, French and Austrian – and four times widowed; they had given him, however, only two sons. The first was a lunatic, who died under mildly suspicious circumstances in prison at the age of twenty-three; the second – by his last wife – was to survive him as Philip III. His principal achievement from our point of view was to have built up his country as a serious military and naval power; by the 1570s his navy was at least four times stronger than it had been in his father's time. But he was a sad, lonely man, and his subjects were not sorry to see him go.

The unwonted inactivity of the great Mediterranean powers left the field free for the pirates, who as the new century opened became ever more of a menace. They consisted by no means only of Muslims from Barbary; included among them were plenty of European seamen like the infamous Captain John Ward, who in 1605 or thereabouts arrived in Tunis. There he came to an agreement with the Bey, by which he undertook to attack all Christians except Englishmen and to share the profits. Such was his success – particularly against the Venetians and the Knights of St John – that he was soon able to build himself in Tunis a palace 'beautified with rich marble and alabaster', second only in magnificence to that of the ruler himself. In 1609 he even acquired a noble second-in-command: Sir Francis Verney of Claydon in Buckinghamshire, who had left his distinguished family in disgust the previous year and was soon, in the words of an English historian, 'making havoc of his own countrymen . . . the merchants of Poole or Plymouth'.[1] Algiers, not to be outdone, then secured the services of a certain Simon Danzer or Dansker – of whose nationality we cannot be sure – who enjoyed a similar success. From these men the Barbary corsairs, who had hitherto used only galleys, learned the art of sail, greatly increasing their effectiveness. A dashing raid in 1609 by the Spanish admiral Don Luís Fajardo on the pirate fleet of Ward, Verney and their colleagues as they lay in Tunis harbour dealt them a serious blow, but the admiral was prevented from following up his advantage; at the critical moment he received orders from Madrid to participate in the wholesale expulsion of the Moriscos from Spain.

---

[1] Gardiner, *History of England*, vol. 3.

This – one of the major disasters of all Spanish history – was the brainchild theoretically of King Philip III but in fact of his favourite adviser, the Duke of Lerma. Philip had succeeded his father in 1598 at the age of twenty. Brought up entirely by monks and priests, he knew nothing of the world and was possessed of no great intelligence; he was therefore an easy prey to the Duke, who quickly became his *éminence grise*. This short-sighted bigot was a nobleman from the former Kingdom of Valencia (it had been incorporated into Castile in 1479) which was at that time very largely peopled by Moriscos: Spaniards whose families had been Muslim for centuries, many of whom – even though theoretically converted to Christianity – had retained their Moorish sympathies. The Moriscos were prosperous and hardworking, and by their own efforts had made the plain of Valencia one of the most fertile areas of the entire country; but their very prosperity had aroused the jealousy of their neighbours, and for half a century or more they had been the object of a campaign of vilification – led, it need hardly be said, by the Inquisition, which maintained (possibly with some reason) that they were still infidels at heart. In 1566 Philip II had issued an edict forbidding the Moriscos of Granada their language, costumes and culture; three years later, plagued and persecuted beyond endurance, they had rebelled and given the King many an anxious hour before their rebellion had been ruthlessly put down by Don John of Austria, but this had only increased their unpopularity. Lerma detested them, and had little difficulty in persuading the foolish young King that it was his duty to rid Spain of them once and for all.

To depopulate what had once been an entire kingdom was a major undertaking, and many of those, ecclesiastical and secular alike, who had been happy to oppress the Moriscos shrank from the idea of wholesale deportation. But Lerma was determined to carry his policy through to the end. On 22 September 1609 the dreadful edict was published; with the exception of six of 'the oldest and most Christian' Moriscos of each large village – who were to remain in order to teach others their system of cultivation – every one of them, male and female alike, was to be deported to Barbary, taking with them no money and only such personal property as they could carry. Ever since the spring, great fleets of galleys had been assembling in the Mediterranean ports; now at last the people knew why.

Over the next six months some 150,000 Valencian Moriscos were driven from the land that they and their ancestors had made fertile, herded down to the waiting ships, carried across the Mediterranean and dumped unceremoniously on the North African shore. And what had begun in Valencia was continued throughout Spain. In Castile and Aragon, in Andalusia and Extremadura, suspected Moriscos – it was often impossible to distinguish the new Christians from the old – were rounded up, dispossessed and expelled. Numbers are impossible to assess, but the total cannot have been much less than half a million and may have been substantially more. Nor, from these regions, were the victims primarily agriculturalists; they included large numbers of artists and craftsmen who had made immense contributions to the Spanish economy. Philip III and his evil counsellor cannot be accused of genocide, only because they did not deliberately decree the mass murder of those whom they expelled; but as an example of what might now be known as ethnic cleansing, it would be over three centuries before Europe was to witness its equal.

It would have been better for Spain if the Duke of Lerma had never been born; there was however another duke, Lerma's near-contemporary, to whom his country owes an enormous debt. He was Don Pedro Tellez Giron, third Duke of Osuna, who almost single-handedly transformed the Spanish navy. In 1603 as a young man Osuna had visited England, where he had captivated King James I by the elegance of his Latin conversation, and had settled down to a serious study of the English navy. Returning to Spain in 1607, he was made a member of the Privy Council, which found itself a year or two later discussing the appointment of a new viceroy in Sicily. Osuna spoke up. In the past thirty years, he pointed out, the Barbary corsairs had raided the island more than eighty times, on each occasion with complete impunity. Such a situation could not be allowed to continue. The King had only two courses before him: either he bought the pirates off with protection money or he made Sicily the base for a new, reformed navy that could sweep them from the seas. Philip, impressed, duly awarded him the viceroyship, and Osuna set to work.

Arriving on the island in 1611, he found a total of thirty-four galleys – twelve from Naples, ten from Genoa, seven Sicilian and five Maltese – all under the uninspired command of the Marquis of Santa Cruz, son of the luckless commander of the Great Armada. His first action was to commission six more to sail under his own personal flag, vessels which he could use as he liked, independently of the Admiral; he then turned his attention to his crews, increasing their pay, improving their diet and living conditions, giving them new drill and new discipline so that they

334

soon stood out in impressive contrast to their fellows. A lightning raid on Tunis was a complete success, with ten corsair ships burned at their moorings and several more captured. This was only the beginning; the next few years saw a succession of similar victories, and the resulting exhileration spread to the whole fleet. But Osuna was not yet satisfied. That fleet was still exclusively composed of oared galleys; and the future, as he well knew, lay with sail. He now laid down two galleons of his own, and eventually persuaded his government to send him twenty more under Prince Philibert of Savoy – a fleet which would, under a competent commander, have been enough to clear the whole sea of corsairs. Alas, Philibert proved to be a commander in the Doria mould, incapable of decisive action and tending always to return to harbour a few days after he had left, without having fired a shot. Even with his huge fleet he failed utterly to block the harbour of Navarino, in which a number of corsair ships had taken refuge; all were allowed to escape.

As always, Osuna knew exactly what he needed. In the Low Countries he had seen the little Dutch sailing ships lying just outside the Spanish ports and effectively sealing them off; but the government in Madrid refused all his requests. At least, however, he had his own two galleons, one of twenty guns and the other of forty-six; these he sent south to Egyptian waters, where they almost immediately captured a squadron of ten Turkish transports bound for Constantinople. It was a remarkable achievement, which should have been applauded in Madrid, but the Spanish government remained as unsympathetic as ever, merely pointing out that Osuna had infringed a century-old regulation forbidding the fitting out of sailing ships – as opposed to galleys – for privateering. In vain he pointed out that naval warfare was no longer what it had been a hundred years before; they continued to ignore him.

Until 1615. Then, suddenly, the whole situation changed: Osuna was appointed viceroy in Naples. Here he had far more independence – and far more money to spend – than he had had in Sicily, and he immediately ordered five new galleons – the Five Wounds, he called them – together with five other, lighter vessels and a pinnace. All but the last were heavily armed, more heavily indeed than any that the English navy could boast, but were otherwise organised entirely on English lines. He also put an end to the principle of dual captaincy – for long the bane of the Spanish armed forces – whereby all the soldiers in a given expedition were responsible to one commander and all the sailors to another. Henceforth a single officer would have command of the whole ship. In July 1616 his junior admiral Francisco de Ribera, with a squadron of six galleons, fought a a tremendous battle with a Turkish fleet of forty-five galleys. It lasted three full days, but when dawn broke on the fourth, there was no longer any sign of the enemy; the Turks had admitted defeat and, with what was left of their shattered ships, had retired to safer waters.

Here, by any standards, was a memorable victory, but it carried a lesson. It had been won by a fleet constructed and commanded not on Spanish but on English lines. That fleet had proved its superiority over the Turks. Could it not now be employed against Spain's most formidable enemy on the Italian peninsula, the Republic of Venice?

The fact that the Duke of Osuna reasoned thus should come as no surprise. He may well have been the architect of Spain's remodelled navy, but he was also a patriot, dedicated to the destruction of her enemies, and it was in large measure thanks to him that, as the seventeenth century got under way, the Spanish shadow began once again to loom ever more dangerously over the central Mediterranean. For a century or more, Spanish ambitions had been held in check by France, but the assassination of Henry IV in 1610, which left the throne to his nine-year-old son Louis XIII and the regency to his determinedly pro-Spanish widow Marie de' Medici, had ensured that the Most Catholic King would encounter no further opposition from that quarter. Spain was still supreme in Milan and Naples; in Florence Marie's cousin, the Grand Duke Cosimo II, was largely under Spanish control; so too, thanks to the influence of the Jesuits and the Spanish cardinals, was the Pope in Rome. Only two Italian states were determined to resist the growing threat. One was the Duchy of Savoy, where Duke Charles Emmanuel II had amassed an army of over 20,000 and was perfectly ready to take on any force that the Spanish governor of Milan might send against him. The other was Venice.

While Milan made trouble for Savoy (and vice versa), Venice was facing even greater difficulties with the other, eastern arm of the Spanish pincers: the Habsburg Archduke Ferdinand of Austria. The underlying cause was the piratical Uskoks, a heterogeneous but exceedingly troublesome community largely – but by no means entirely – composed of Christian fugitives from the Turkish advance, who had settled at Segna (now Senj) and elsewhere along the Dalmatian coast and had given themselves over to the traditional occupation of so many of its inhabitants. The problem was hardly new; piracy based on the innumerable islands and hidden creeks along the eastern shores of the Adriatic had constituted a threat to Venetian commerce for almost as long as the Republic itself had existed. With the Uskoks, however, there was an additional complication: their activities called down the wrath of the Turks, who after every Uskok attack on their own shipping would make a formal complaint to Venice, pointing out that as the power who claimed dominion over the Adriatic it was her duty to keep it efficiently policed. Since Dalmatia was now the territory of the Empire and the offenders technically imperial subjects, Venice in her turn would make ever more pressing representations to Ferdinand for effective measures to be taken against them; but despite repeated promises the Archduke did nothing, and the Uskoks remained a perennial anxiety.

Their culminating atrocity had occurred in 1613, with the beheading of a Venetian admiral, Cristoforo Venier. Still Ferdinand refused to lift a finger; indeed, as Venetian–imperial relations deteriorated he began to view the Uskoks with a steadily more sympathetic eye and, while feigning a few gentle remonstrations, gave them secret encouragement in every way he could. Finally Venice – not for the first time – took the law into her own hands and launched a punitive expedition. Ferdinand protested in his turn; and the resulting war, while it remained on a fairly desultory level, grumbled on until the autumn of 1617 when Venice, Savoy and the Empire patched up an uneasy peace, after which the fate of the Uskoks could be settled once and for all. Their harbours and fortresses were destroyed, their ships were burned, and all those who escaped a more disagreeable fate were transported with their families to the Croatian interior where, gradually over the years, they intermarried with the local populations and lost their separate identity.

This small victory did much to improve the security of the Adriatic, and indeed of all the central Mediterranean, but it did little to change the basic political situation. The overriding threat to the peace of the region remained Spain, and Spain was not looking only to armed force or to artful diplomacy to advance her interests. The late sixteenth and early seventeenth centuries were above all the age of intrigue. The idea itself, of course, was nothing new; in the Florence of the Medici, the Milan of the Visconti, the Rome of the Borgias, there had been instances aplenty of plots and poisonings, of spies and counterspies, of the stiletto beneath the cloak. But now, in France and England as well as in Italy, conspiracy became almost a way of life. Within the memory

337

of men still in their middle age, there had been the assassinations of Admiral Coligny and of Henry IV himself, the countless machinations that marked the sad, violent life of Mary Queen of Scots – and then, on 5 November 1605, the Gunpowder Plot.

There was no government in Europe more involved in the dark world of intrigue than that of the Most Serene Republic. Every embassy, every foreign household even, was thoroughly penetrated by Venetian agents, reporting directly back to the dreaded Council of Ten details of comings and goings, of letters steamed open and conversations overheard. A special watch was kept on the leading courtesans, several of whom were paid by the state to pass on any pillow talk that might prove of interest, for purposes of blackmail or otherwise. Normally, however, the Ten preferred to perform its more distasteful duties in secret; it was therefore with some astonishment that early risers, passing across the Piazzetta on 18 May 1618, saw the bodies of two men, each dangling by a single leg – a sure sign that their crime was treason – from a hastily erected gallows between the two columns at the southern end. More astonishing still was the fact that, even after the two bodies had been joined by a third bearing unmistakable signs of torture, no proclamation was made to identify the unfortunates or to explain the reason for their fate. Inevitably, rumours spread, most of them focusing on the likelihood of a major conspiracy against the Republic, of which there could be only one instigator. Hostile demonstrations were staged outside the Spanish Embassy, obliging the ambassador, the Marquis of Bedmar, to ask the authorities for special police protection. Meanwhile, he reported back to Madrid:

> The name of the Most Catholic King, and that of the Spanish nation, is in Venice the most odious that can be pronounced. Among the people the very word 'Spanish' is an insult . . . They seem to thirst for our blood. It is all the fault of their rulers, who have always taught them to hate us.

This was not strictly true. For years the Spanish Embassy had been the busiest centre of intrigue in the city, its anterooms and corridors teeming with sinister, slouch-hatted figures whispering together in groups while they awaited audiences with the ambassador. And when, the following October, the Ten finally disclosed in a full report to the Senate the details of what had taken place, the Marquis was revealed – as everyone had known he would be – as one of the leading figures in what came to be known as the Spanish Conspiracy.

It is entirely appropriate that this conspiracy should have indirectly furnished Thomas Otway with the material for his best and most celebrated play, *Venice Preserved*. The true story has all the elements of seventeenth-century melodrama. Here is the villain Don Pedro, Duke of Osuna and Spanish Viceroy of Naples, determined to destroy the power of Venice in the Mediterranean. Here is the Marquis of Bedmar, Spanish ambassador, cultivated and charming but in reality 'one of the most potent and dangerous spirits Spain ever produced', filled with an implacable hostility towards Venice and fully approving of Osuna's objective. Here are the two chief instruments of the conspirators: Jacques Pierre, Norman adventurer and corsair, now a Spanish secret agent with the Venetian fleet, practically illiterate but one of the most brilliant seamen of his day, and his inseparable antithesis Nicolas Regnault, educated and plausible with his mellifluous Italian and his exquisite handwriting. And here, finally, is the hero: the young Frenchman Balthasar Juven, who has come to Venice to enter the service of the Republic.

The conspiracy itself, too, was ambitious enough to satisfy the most demanding dramatist. It was also, like all its kind, complicated and convoluted in the extreme. A full account of it would be insufferably tedious, and has no place in this book.[1] For some weeks before the appointed day, Spanish soldiers in civilian clothes would be infiltrated in twos and threes into Venice, where they would be secretly armed by Bedmar. Then, when all was in readiness, Osuna's galleons, flying his own personal standard, would advance up the Adriatic and land an expeditionary force on the Lido, together with a fleet of flat-bottomed barges in which that force would be rowed across the lagoon to the city. The Piazza, Doge's Palace, Rialto and Arsenal would be seized, their armouries ransacked to provide additional arms for the conspirators and for any Venetians who might be prepared to lend them support. The leading Venetian notables would be killed or held to ransom. Venice itself would pass into the possession of Osuna; the loot and ransom money would go to the other conspirators to share among themselves.

Whether so wild an enterprise could ever have succeeded seems improbable; its originators, however, had no chance to put it to the test. The discovery of the plot was due to Juven, who was approached by a compatriot named Gabriel Moncassin, informed of all that was afoot

---

[1] Readers hungry for the full details – if such there be – are advised to turn to Vol. II of Horatio Brown's *Studies in the History of Venice*, pp. 245–95, where the whole story is set out in remorseless detail.

and invited to participate. What Moncassin did not know was that Juven was a Huguenot. Detesting Spain and the religion it stood for, he immediately informed the Venetian authorities, and the Council of Ten swung into action. Jacques Pierre was arrested and summarily dispatched; his body was sewn into a sack and dropped overboard. Regnault and two other conspirators, the brothers Desbouleaux, were seized, tortured and then, after they confessed, hung upside-down in the Piazzetta. As many as 300 minor participants were discreetly liquidated. Only Osuna and Bedmar were too powerful to be touched. They continued their intrigues from behind the walls of their respective palaces, but their grand opportunity had been missed. Venice was preserved.

CHAPTER XVIII

Crete and the Peloponnese

For a quarter of a century after the events described in the last chapter, the Mediterranean continued curiously calm. Occasionally a minor squall might ruffle its surface, but there were no storms, no epic upheavals on the scale of Malta, Cyprus or Lepanto. Simply in the light of the previous history of the Middle Sea, this is remarkable enough; it is more surprising still when we consider that the very year of the Spanish Conspiracy, 1618, also saw the beginning of the Thirty Years' War, which was to tear much of northern and eastern Europe to shreds.

From the Venetian point of view, however, the peace came just in time. In October of the same year there occurred an incident which, though Venice bore no part of the responsibility for it, was ultimately to result in the loss of her most valuable remaining colony: the island of Crete. Sooner or later, as she must have known, war was inevitable; Crete was too tempting a prize, the Turks too covetous an adversary, for her possession to go much longer uncontested. It remains ironic that the initial Turkish attack should have been the result of a piece of deliberate provocation on the part of a minor power which, after the Republic itself, stood to lose more than any other from the surrender of the last important Christian outpost in the eastern Mediterranean.

Although the Knights of St John possessed a priory[1] in Venice – inherited from the Templars after their dissolution in 1312 – they and the Venetians had for centuries cordially disliked each other. It could hardly have been otherwise. Since their order was immensely rich in property held all over Christian Europe, the Knights despised trade and commerce. As men of God, bound by the monkish vows of poverty, chastity and obedience, they disapproved of the Venetians' worldliness and love of pleasure. Finally, as men of the sword and children of the Crusades, their avowed object – apart from the cure of the sick – was to fight the infidel wherever they found him, and they deplored Venice's reiterated desire for peace with the Sultan, an

---

[1] It is still there, next to the Scuola di S. Giorgio degli Schiavoni.

attitude which they considered a shameless betrayal of the Christian cause.

By the 1640s the Knights were but a frail and feeble reflection of what they had been in those heroic days, only eighty years before, when they had successfully defended their island against the greatest fleet that Süleyman the Magnificent could hurl against them. They continued to run their famous hospital, where they still maintained standards of hygiene and of nursing far in advance of any to be found elsewhere, but their Crusading spirit was beginning to evaporate, and their naval operations tended all too often to savour less of holy war than of common piracy. Nor did they invariably confine their depredations to Muslim shipping; unprovoked attacks, launched on the flimsiest of pretexts, against Venetian and other Christian merchantmen were becoming increasingly frequent.

To the Venetians, in short, the Knights of Malta had become a nuisance only slightly less tiresome than the Uskoks in former days. Worst of all, they had adopted the old Uskok habit of harassing Turkish vessels in the Adriatic, a practice for which the Sultan invariably held Venice responsible – with much consequent damage to the friendly relations which the Venetians strove at all costs to maintain with the Sublime Porte. More than once, indeed, the Doge had been obliged to send for the local prior of the Order to make a vehement protest – never more forcefully than in September 1644, when he went so far as to threaten the sequestration of all the Knights' property in the territory of the Republic if they did not improve their behaviour. The Knights, as usual, took no notice.

Cruising in the Aegean at the beginning of October, a squadron of six ships of the Order fell upon and captured a rich Turkish galleon carrying several distinguished pilgrims bound for Mecca, among them the city's principal civil judge, the Chief Black Eunuch at the Sultan's court, some thirty ladies of the harem and about fifty Greek slaves. The squadron then sailed on with its prize to Crete, where, landing at some unguarded beach on the southern coast, the ships took on water and disembarked the slaves, together with a number of horses. Soon the local Venetian governor arrived and, not wishing to be implicated even after the event in what was, after all, an act of shameless piracy, ordered them away. Having made several attempts to put in at various ports of the island and meeting on each occasion with the same point-blank refusal, the Knights finally abandoned the Turkish vessel (which was no longer seaworthy) with its passengers and returned to Malta.

Occupying the Ottoman throne at this time was the half-mad Sultan Ibrahim.[1] When the news was brought to him he exploded with rage and ordered the immediate massacre of all Christians in his empire. This order, fortunately, he was later persuaded to countermand, but Venetian agents in Constantinople were by now sending reports of an immense war fleet being prepared on the Bosphorus, and it soon became clear that punitive action on an alarming scale was being contemplated. At first it was automatically assumed that this fleet was to be directed against Malta, an assumption that was confirmed by an official proclamation in March 1645, but despatches from the Venetian *bailo* in Constantinople warned that this was a deliberate feint. The Sultan, he reported, was convinced that the Venetians had been behind the whole incident; why else would the raiders have made straight for Crete? His true enemy was not the Knights, but Venice herself; his immediate objective was not Malta, but Crete.

It was not long before the *bailo* was proved right. On 30 April a Turkish fleet of 400 sail, carrying an estimated 50,000 fighting men, passed through the Dardanelles. At first it headed towards Malta as announced, sailing straight past Crete and putting in at Navarino, in the southwest corner of the Peloponnese, for reinforcements and supplies. Only on its departure from there on 21 June was it seen to have changed course. Four days later the invading army landed a little to the west of Canea (the modern Khania) and advanced on the town. The first round of the battle had begun.

Crete – or, as the Venetians called it after its capital city, Candia (now Heraklion) – had been Venice's first properly constituted overseas colony, dating from 1211 and the sharing out of the Byzantine Empire after the Fourth Crusade. Its government was based on that of the mother city, but it had never worked as easily or as well. The most fertile parts of the island had been largely swallowed up in vast feudal estates owned by prominent Venetian families, whose immense wealth and overbearing ways had done little to endear them to the local Greek population; these families in turn grumbled over their lack of any real political power, all the principal officials being sent out from Venice, where every major decision was taken. Defence was in normal times entrusted to feudal levies, raised and maintained at the expense of the

---

[1] Until his accession in 1640, Ibrahim had spent his entire life a virtual prisoner in the Seraglio. After a brief reign marked only by cruelty, frivolity and vice, he was destined to be executed in 1648 by his own exasperated subjects.

landowners, and to local militias of townsfolk and peasants; but both sides tended to shrug off their obligations, and discipline varied between the poor and the nonexistent. Corruption was endemic, and the colony was a constant drain on Venetian resources.

The moment it was apprised of the imminent danger, the government of the Republic ordered a new and vigorous defensive programme for the island, sending out to its Proveditor-General, Andrea Corner, a special remittance of 100,000 ducats, an army of 2,500 men including military architects and engineers, and a fleet of thirty galleys with two galleasses to supplement those already on the island. A further fleet, Corner was informed, was in preparation and would sail as soon as possible. All this was better than nothing, but his resources were still hopelessly inadequate for the magnitude of his task, and the time allowed to him far too short. Already as he hurried to the beachhead on that fateful midsummer day, he must have known that the colony's chances of survival were slim.

Much depended on the speed of the promised Venetian fleet; if it could arrive within a week or two, Canea might yet be saved. But it did not arrive. Corner would have been horrified to learn that it had orders to wait at Zante (Zakynthos) until it was joined by a further combined fleet of twenty-five sail, comprising ships from Tuscany, Naples, the Knights and the Pope; time was what counted now, not numerical strength. Meanwhile, the Turks were entrenching themselves more deeply with every day that passed. The island fortress of St Theodore fell to them, though only after its commander, Biagio Zulian, seeing that further resistance was hopeless, waited until it was overrun and then set light to the powder magazine, blowing up himself, his men, the attacking Turks and the building itself in a single epic explosion which must have been clearly audible in Candia. Canea was weakening fast, its ammunition and supplies running out, its defences steadily undermined by Turkish sappers. On 22 August it surrendered. The Turks, doubtless hoping by a well-timed show of magnanimity to encourage further surrenders as they advanced, promised to respect the lives, honour and property of the local population, allowing the garrison to leave the town with its colours flying and to embark unmolested for Soudha, beyond the Akrotiri[1] to the east.

Now more than ever, fortune seemed to favour the invaders. At

---

[1] The name (the Greek word for cape) is given to the land jutting out to the northeast of Canea and protecting the anchorage of Soudha Bay just beyond.

Soudha the Venetian admiral, Antonio Cappello, suddenly lost his head and abandoned the town; only its superb natural position and recently renewed fortifications saved it from capture. Then the combined fleet, at last arriving (in mid-September) in Cretan waters, made two attempts to recover Canea by surprise attack, but was each time driven back by equinoctial gales. Finally in October its non-Venetian element, under the command of the papal admiral Nicolò Ludovisi, Prince of Piombino – who from the start had shown extreme distaste for the whole expedition – announced its intention of returning home. Not for the first time, Venice's allies had done her nothing but harm. She would have been better off alone.

Her government, meanwhile, was on full war footing. Having no reason to believe that Sultan Ibrahim intended to confine himself to a single theatre of operations, it sent an additional garrison to Corfu and even began strengthening the defences of the Venetian lagoon. But top priority was naturally given to Crete. Galleys and transports were now sailing for the island almost daily, laden with munitions and supplies of every kind. One need, however, remained unfulfilled: that of a supreme commander, a man whose seniority and reputation would set him above the petty jealousies and rivalries which – particularly when Cretan Venetians were involved – were an ever-present danger. The appointment was long debated in the Senate, and in the ensuing vote the name that emerged with an overwhelming majority was that of the Doge himself, Francesco Erizzo.

One voice only was raised against the proposal. Giovanni Pesaro – later to assume the ducal throne himself – very reasonably argued that the cost of sending out the head of state, with his Signoria and an adequate staff and secretariat, was quite unjustifiable at a moment when the Republic needed every penny to pursue the war, and that such a step might well encourage the Sultan similarly to take the field in person, thus greatly intensifying the Turkish war effort. One other consideration was also perhaps worth bearing in mind: Erizzo was now just two months short of his eightieth birthday. But no one listened; all attention was fixed on the old Doge who, in a speech which brought tears to the eyes of all who heard it, declared himself ready to assume the formidable task that had been laid upon him. Fortunately for Venice, he never did so. The preparations alone proved too much for him, and just three weeks later, on 3 January 1646, he died. He was buried in the church of S. Martino, but his heart, in recognition of his unhesitating acceptance of his last commission, was interred beneath the pavement of St Mark's itself. There being no one else available in Venice of sufficient stature, the whole idea of a generalissimo was shelved, and is heard of no more.

Everything seemed to depend on containing the Turks in Canea, the only Cretan port that they as yet held. If they could be blockaded there while Venice built up her military strength in the other fortresses along the coast, it might not be impossible eventually to dislodge them. The young Tommaso Morosini, sent with twenty-three sail in an attempt to close off the Dardanelles and thus to pen up the Turkish reinforcement fleet in the Marmara, managed at least to delay it considerably; this delay so enraged the Sultan that he ordered his admiral to be beheaded forthwith. But the luckless admiral's successor, doubtless impelled as much by the fear of a similar fate as by a favourable wind behind him, finally smashed his way through the Venetian line and swept down through the Aegean to Candia, where the Captain-General, the seventy-five-year-old Giovanni Cappello, was too slow and indecisive to stop him entering the harbour. The Venetian ships fell back on Rettimo (Rethymnon), but they were not to remain there for long. After a prolonged struggle, the town was forced to surrender on 13 November.

The fall of Rettimo had one beneficial effect, in that it brought about the dismissal of the useless Cappello and his replacement by Gian Battista Grimani, a popular commander forty years younger whose arrival instilled new life into the fleet. Early in 1647 Tommaso Morosini, suddenly finding himself surrounded by no fewer than forty-five Turkish ships, was given an opportunity to take his revenge for his failure the previous year. In the unequal battle that followed he and his crew fought heroically, holding their fire until the enemy was almost upon them and then blasting out at point-blank range. Before long the Venetians were grappled by three of the Turkish vessels simultaneously and the fighting was hand-to-hand, Morosini himself continuing in the thick of it until a Turkish arquebusier managed to steal up behind him and blow his head off. At just about the same time the Turkish admiral also fell mortally wounded, but still the battle continued. Suddenly the exhausted Venetians saw three more ships approaching in close order, the banner of St Mark fluttering at their mastheads; Grimani, hearing the firing, had come to investigate. They too now plunged into the mélée, forcing the Turks to disengage. Four Ottoman vessels had gone to the bottom, the rest fled. Battered but still afloat, Morosini's ship was towed back to Candia, whence the remains of its courageous young captain were returned to Venice for a hero's burial.

But his heroism, inspiring as it had been, had in no way improved Venice's basic position in Crete. Of the four principal strongholds ranged along the northern coast of the island – the fifth, Sitia, was so far away to the east that it could for the moment be ignored – two were already in enemy hands; of the other two, Soudha had been blockaded from the sea for well over a year and was desperately short of food, and both it and Candia itself had now been struck by plague, which not only destroyed morale but made adequate garrisoning impossible. The Turks, however, outside the walls, remained free of the disease, and it was in the summer of 1647 that they first laid serious siege to Candia – on which, as the capital, the whole future of the colony depended.

The siege of Candia was to last for twenty-two years, during which Venice, virtually single-handed, defended the little town – its civilian population numbering only some 10–12,000 – against the combined military and naval force of the Ottoman Empire. In former times so long a resistance would have been inconceivable, if only because the interdependence of Turks and Venetians in commercial matters demanded that all hostilities between them should be short and sharp. But now that most of the carrying trade was in English or Dutch hands, such considerations no longer applied; the Sultan could afford to take his time. That Venice was able to hold out for so long was due less to the determination of the defenders within the walls – though that was considerable – than to her fleet which, by maintaining a continuous patrol of the eastern Mediterranean, not only frustrated every Turkish effort to blockade Candia from the sea; it actually increased its control over the Aegean to the point where, for the last ten years of the siege, the Turks were doing everything they could to avoid direct naval confrontation.

This is not to say that such confrontation never occurred; the story of the war is a national epic in every sense of the word, a story of innumerable battles, large and small, deliberate and unsought, their locations ranging from the mouth of the Dardanelles, where the Venetian fleet gathered every spring in the hope of blockading the enemy within the narrows, right through the Aegean archipelago to the roadstead of Candia itself. It is rich, too, in tales of heroism: of Giacomo Riva in 1649, pursuing a Turkish fleet into a small harbour on the Ionian coast and smashing it to pieces; of Lazzaro Mocenigo in 1651 off Paros, sailing in defiance of his admiral's orders to attack a whole enemy squadron and, though severely wounded by several arrows and a musket-shot through the arm, putting it to flight; of Lorenzo Marcello leading his ships right into the Dardanelles in 1656, but not surviving to witness one of the most complete and overwhelming victories of the entire war; and in 1657, of Lazzaro Mocenigo again, now Captain-General, his squadron of twelve vessels driving thirty-three of the enemy still further up the narrow straits and pressing on through the Marmara towards the walls of Constantinople itself.

And yet, however glorious the achievements, however superb the seamanship and the courage, one somehow feels that there was always lacking an overall plan: that a more organised defence of the immediate approaches to the beleaguered town might have been more successful in cutting off the assailants from their reinforcements and supplies. Despite all Venetian efforts, these continued to get through, and even in their most triumphant moments the defenders must have known in their hearts that the fall of Candia could be only a question of time.

One thing alone could have saved it: the unstinting and enthusiastic support of the European powers. It is arguable that the whole history of Ottoman expansion in Europe can be attributed to the perennial inability of the Christian princes to unite in defence of their continent and their faith. They had not done so, in all the fullness of their heart and soul, since the Third Crusade nearly five hundred years before; and they did not do so now. Again and again Venice appealed to them, emphasising always that it was not the future of an obscure Venetian colony but the security of Christendom itself that hung in the balance: that if Crete were lost, so too was half the Mediterranean. Again and again they refused to listen, just as they always had. From Germany the Emperor pointed out that he had recently signed a twenty-year truce with the Porte; from Spain, to the astonishment of all, His Most Catholic Majesty was actually sending an ambassador to infidel Constantinople; France, true to her double game, passed occasional small and secret subsidies to Venice with one hand but continued to extend the other in friendship to the Sultan. England – whence little was expected, since she was not yet a power in the Middle Sea – was prodigal with promises, but with little else. Successive Popes, seeing Venice's plight as a useful means of gaining some advantage for themselves, offered assistance only in return for concessions: Innocent X for the control of Venetian bishoprics, his successor Alexander VII for the readmission of the Jesuits, banned from the territory of the Republic since Paul V had laid it under an interdict in 1606.

Admittedly, as the years went by and the continuing resistance of Candia became the talk of Europe, foreign aid in the form of men, money and ships was a little more forthcoming, but such aid was invariably too little and too late. A typical example was the force of 4,000, under Prince Almerigo d'Este, sent out from France in 1660. It arrived not in the spring, when it might have been useful, but at the end of August; its first sortie against the enemy, over terrain which it had not troubled to reconnoitre, ended in panic and flight; a week or two later, laid low by dysentery, it had to be sent *en masse* to other more restful islands to recover its strength, after which the survivors – whose number did not, regrettably, include the Prince – returned to their homes having achieved precisely nothing.

So many, and so memorable, were the exploits of the Venetian commanders at sea that one all too easily forgets the still more heroic defence of Candia by the garrison itself, doomed to face twenty-two years of attrition – of all forms of warfare the most hopelessly discouraging – and to suffer constant disappointment when promised reinforcements from Venice's so-called allies proved time and time again to be worthless. Such forces as did appear always seemed intent either on saving their skins or – almost as bad – gaining personal glory for themselves, thus risking not only their own lives but also many others that, with the chronic shortage of manpower, could ill be afforded.

This latter phenomenon became more and more frequent in the last stages of the siege. By now the name of Candia was famous across Europe, and among the French in particular the young scions of noble families flocked to the island, determined to make proof of their valour on so glorious a field of battle. The most remarkable influx came in 1668, when Louis XIV was at last persuaded to take a personal interest in the siege. Even now he did not enter the war, or even break off diplomatic relations with the Sultan; French merchants in the Levant had taken full advantage of the sudden departure of their Venetian rivals, and were doing far too well for the King to dream of any open rupture. He did, however, compromise his principles to the point of allowing Venice to raise troops from within his dominions, under the overall command of the Lieutenant-General of his Armies, the Marquis of Saint-André Montbrun; the result was a 500-strong volunteer force, the list of which sounds less like a serious professional army than the roll-call at the Field of the Cloth of Gold. Foremost under Montbrun was the Duc de la Feuillade who, though by no means a rich man, had insisted on personally bearing the lion's share of the cost; then there were two more dukes, of Château-Thierry and of Caderousse, the Marquis of Aubusson, the Counts of Villemor and Tavanes, the Prince of Neuchâtel (who was barely seventeen) and a quantity of other young noblemen bearing names which numbered them among the proudest families in France.

On their arrival in Crete at the beginning of December the young French nobles were entrusted by the new Captain-General, Francesco Morosini, with the defence of one of the outer ramparts on the landward side of the town. They refused. They had not, they pointed out, made the long and uncomfortable journey to Crete only to be told to crawl through the mud to some advanced outpost – there to wait, patiently and in silence, until the Turks should decide to launch their next attack. Instead, they demanded a general sortie which would 'oblige the enemy to raise the siege'. Morosini very sensibly forbade any such thing. He had already made dozens of sorties, none of which had produced lasting results. His remaining men – there were by now fewer than 5,000 – were barely enough to defend the breaches in the walls that the Turkish sappers were regularly opening up. But his arguments went unheard. As one of France's own historians was to put it:

> Monsieur de la Feuillade sought only vigorous action and glory for himself; he would have concerned himself little over the loss of seven or eight hundred of the Republic's men so long as he could enjoy, on his return to France, the honour of having made a valiant sortie on Crete. Once out of the place, its subsequent loss through want of men to defend it would have occasioned him little distress.[1]

When he saw that the Captain-General would not be moved, La Feuillade, complaining loudly of Venetian timidity, announced his intention of making an unsupported attack on his own; this he did on 16 December, symbolically armed with a whip, at the head of a force whose numbers, we are told, had already been reduced from the original 500 to 280. The Turks resisted fiercely, but the Frenchmen, for all their foolhardiness, showed an almost superhuman courage, driving them back a full 200 yards and accounting for some 800 of them before, with the arrival of a fresh battalion of janissaries, they were finally forced to retire. The Counts of Villemor and Tavanes and some forty others were killed and over sixty badly injured, including the Marquis of Aubusson. La Feuillade himself,

---

[1] Philibert de Jarry, *Histoire du siège de Candie*.

streaming with blood from three separate wounds, was the last to return to safety.

It was magnificent, but it was no help to Crete or to Venice. When the moment of glory was past, the surviving young heroes could not get off the island quickly enough. They were gone within a week, though many of them – even those who had somehow escaped unscathed – never saw France again. They had taken the plague bacillus with them.

Soon after the survivors landed at Toulon another force, far larger, more professional and better equipped, set sail from France for Candia. At last Louis XIV had been persuaded by the Venetian ambassador – Giovanni Morosini, a kinsman of the Captain-General – to take his Most Christian responsibilities seriously, and in the spring of 1669 his first important contribution was ready: 6,000 men, 300 horses and fifteen cannon, all carried in a fleet of twenty-seven transports, with fifteen warships as an escort. But even now Louis tried to conceal his breach of faith from his Turkish friends; the fleet did not sail under the banner of the fleur-de-lys, but under that of the crossed keys of the Papacy.

The bulk of the army, some 4,000 strong, commanded jointly by the Ducs de Beaufort and de Noailles, arrived at Candia on 19 June. They were appalled at what they saw. One of the officers wrote:

> The state of the town was terrible to behold: the streets were covered with bullets and cannonballs, and with shrapnel from mines and grenades. There was not a church, not a building even, whose walls were not holed and almost reduced to rubble by the enemy cannon. The houses were no longer anything more than miserable hovels. Everywhere the stench was nauseating; at every turn one came upon the dead, the wounded or the maimed.

At once the story of La Feuillade began to repeat itself. So eager were the new arrivals for the fray that, refusing even to wait for the remainder of the army, they launched their own attack at dawn on 25 June. It began badly: the first body of troops on whom they opened fire proved to be a recently arrived detachment of Germans, marching up to give them support. Once order had been re-established they charged the Turkish emplacements, at first with considerable success. Then, suddenly, a stray Turkish shot ignited the powder barrels in one of the hastily abandoned batteries. The skill of the Turkish sappers was renowned; their mining operations had been a feature of the siege, and much of the damage to the defences of the town had been the result of subterranean explosions. The word now suddenly spread through the ranks of the French that the whole terrain on which they stood was mined, that the battery was a concealed blast-hole and that the detonation they had just heard was the first of a chain of similar explosions that would blow them all to smithereens. With the rumour went panic. They fled in terror, tripping over each other as they ran. Seeing this sudden and to them utterly unaccountable flight, the Turks regrouped and counter-attacked. Five hundred Frenchmen lost their lives; within minutes their heads, impaled on pikes, were being paraded in triumph before the Grand Vizir Ahmed. They included those of the Duc de Beaufort and of a Capuchin monk who had accompanied the army as its almoner.

Five hundred men out of 6,000 is not an intolerable loss; four days later the rest of King Louis's army arrived and Morosini started planning a fresh attack on Canea in the west. But the spirit of his new allies was already broken. On 24 July a French man-of-war of seventy guns approached too near a Turkish shore battery and was blown out of the water; a few days later Noailles coldly informed the Captain-General that he was re-embarking the army and returning home. Protestations, entreaties and threats, appeals from the surviving civilian population, even thunderings from pulpits were of no avail; on 21 August the French fleet weighed anchor. In the general despair that followed, the few auxiliaries from the Papacy, the Empire and even the Knights of Malta likewise set their sails for the west. Morosini and his garrison were left alone – and the Grand Vizir ordered a general attack.

Somehow it was repelled, but the Captain-General knew that he was beaten at last. His garrison was reduced to a mere 3,600 men. There would be no more reinforcements that year, the defences were in ruins and he knew that he could not hope to hold Candia for another winter. By surrendering now, on the other hand, rather than waiting for the inevitable taking of the town by storm, he might be able to secure favourable, even honourable, terms. Admittedly he had no powers to negotiate on behalf of the Republic, but he was aware that on at least three occasions in the past – the first as early as 1647, and then again in 1657 and 1662 – the question of a negotiated peace had been debated in the Senate and on every occasion had found a measure of support. In any case, he had little choice.

The treaty was agreed on 6 September 1669. The Grand Vizir, who had much personal admiration for Morosini, proved generous. The

Venetians would leave the town, freely and without molestation, within twelve days, though this term could be prolonged – as indeed it was – in the event of bad weather. All the artillery that had already been in place before the beginning of the siege must be left where it was; the remainder they could take with them. The Turks would be left as masters, but Venice could retain the Gramvousa Islands at Crete's northwestern extremity, their island fortress of Spinalonga and, in the extreme east, the town of Sitia which had never surrendered.

And so on 26 September, after 465 years of occupation and twenty-two of siege, the banner of St Mark was finally lowered from what was left of the citadel of Candia, and the last official representatives of the Republic returned to their mother city. With them went virtually all the civilian population of the town, none of whom had any desire to remain under their new masters. For Venice it was the end of an epoch. She had retained her three outposts, and there remained one or two pinpoints on the map of the Aegean where the winged lion still ruled, though his roar was gone and even his growl was barely audible; but Crete had been her last major possession outside the Adriatic, and with its loss not only her power but even her effective presence in the eastern Mediterranean was dead forever.

It had at least died magnificently. Never had Venetians fought longer or more heroically on land or sea; never had they faced more determined adversaries. The financial cost had been enormous, that in human lives greater still. Moreover, for nearly a quarter of a century, they had fought virtually alone. The assistance of their allies, on the comparatively rare occasions when it was given at all, had been grudging, half-hearted, inadequate or self-seeking; at times – as when it had caused long and inactive delays, or when it was suddenly withdrawn without warning – it had been positively detrimental to the common cause. Even in those last two or three years, when the former policy of attrition gave way to a frenzy of destruction and bloodletting, foreign interventions served only to demoralise and to discourage.

Yet it was neither demoralisation nor discouragement that drove Francesco Morosini to his surrender. It was the cold realisation that the loss of Candia was inevitable, and that the only choice was between departure on honourable terms now or wholesale massacre and pillage a very little later. Predictably, perhaps, he found himself in serious trouble when he returned to Venice. He was accused not only of having exceeded his legitimate powers by treating with the enemy as he had, but of cowardice, treason – even peculation and corruption.

Fortunately he had no lack of champions who were quick to defend him, and when the question was finally put to the Great Council its vote was overwhelmingly in his favour. He emerged from the affair without a stain on his reputation – determined, however, to be avenged.

And indeed it was not long before the pendulum began to swing. Only twelve years later, in 1681, the Hungarian Protestant subjects of the Emperor Leopold I rose in revolt against what they considered to be Habsburg Catholic oppression and, almost insanely, invited the Sultan to support them. Mehmet IV asked nothing better, and in the spring of 1683 set off for Edirne, where a substantial army awaited him. It included whole regiments of artillery and engineers, with a number of irregular units, composed principally of Tartars from the Crimea. When they reached Belgrade, the Sultan handed over the command to his Grand Vizir Karamustafa ('Black Mustafa'); and the last great Ottoman army to set forth against Christian Europe headed towards Vienna.

This was the second Turkish attempt on the imperial capital. Süleyman the Magnificent had set up his camp before the walls of Vienna in September 1529, but had been ultimately unsuccessful; after less than three weeks, the unexpectedly fierce resistance, the shortage of supplies and above all the approach of winter had forced him to retreat. Karamustafa had the advantage of an earlier arrival in the campaigning season: it was 13 July when he drew up his army outside the city. On the other hand, he had no heavy artillery – its transportation over such a distance would have been virtually impossible – and was obliged to rely largely on his sappers, mining beneath the fortifications in the hope of inducing a collapse from below. This had long been a Turkish speciality and proved, as always, highly effective; Vienna might well have fallen but for the arrival in the nick of time of a Polish army under King John Sobieski. Suddenly, the Turks found themselves caught in murderous crossfire between a desperate garrison and a brilliantly led relief force, and after a day-long battle fled in confusion. Süleyman had at least made a controlled withdrawal and had kept his army intact; Karamustafa suffered a debacle. In that one day, the reputation of the Ottoman Empire as an all-conquering power was gone forever. Never again would it constitute a serious threat to Christendom.

Vienna is well over 200 miles from the Mediterranean, and its unsuccessful siege would not have found a place in this book were it not for the fact that it encouraged the Emperor, the Pope and Sobieski to advance on the shattered Turks. Venice, still smarting from the loss of

Crete, now received increasingly urgent appeals to join a new offensive league by which, using her sea power combined with their own on land, the Sultan could be swept from Europe for good – an expulsion from which no nation would derive greater benefit than the Most Serene Republic itself.

Venice sent no immediate reply. She had taken well over a decade to recover from the effects of the Cretan war; was she really to stake everything yet again, on the fortunes of another confrontation? On the other hand, the situation had undoubtedly changed since the Turkish defeat at Vienna. The next phase of the war might be fought at least partially at sea; did not her own interests – let alone her good name – demand that she should now pursue a more active policy? The Turks were weak and demoralised: their Grand Vizir, the hated Karamustafa, had been executed on the Sultan's orders the moment he returned to Constantinople; their army was in shreds. Was this not the time to take the offensive, not only to avenge the loss of Crete but to recover it – and perhaps her other former colonies as well? After long debate, the imperial ambassador was informed on 19 January 1684 that Venice would join the league.

Her Captain-General at that time was once again Francesco Morosini. Despite his ultimate and inevitable surrender of Candia, he remained at sixty-four by far the ablest of Venice's captains; he assumed command of his fleet of sixty-eight fighting ships – together with a number of auxiliary vessels from the Pope, the Knights of Malta and the Grand Duke of Tuscany – with enthusiasm and determination. Once out of harbour he headed straight for his first objective, the island of Leucas, and captured it, after a sixteen-day siege, on 6 August. Few quick conquests could have had a more strategic value: from its situation between Corfu and Cephalonia, Leucas commanded the entrances to both the Adriatic and the Gulf of Corinth; it also provided a bridgehead from which, a few weeks later, a small land force crossed to the mainland and forced the surrender of the castle of Preveza. Meanwhile, further north along the coast, the Christian populations of Bosnia and Herzegovina rose in simultaneous revolt against their Turkish overlords and drove south into Albania and Epirus. Further north again, the armies of the Emperor and John Sobieski continued their advance through Hungary. By the time winter had set in, Venice and her allies had good reason to be proud of their success.

With the coming of spring in 1685 Morosini sailed against the old Venetian port of Corone – lost to the Turks in 1500 – landing some

9,500 men, including imperial, papal and Tuscan troops, as well as 3,000 Venetians and 120 Knights of St John. This time the Ottoman garrison put up a desperate defence; it was not until August that the white flag was raised on the citadel. Then, while the terms of surrender were being discussed, a Turkish cannon opened fire, killing several of the Venetians. Negotiations were immediately broken off; the allied troops burst into the town in fury and gave it over to massacre. A whole series of other fortresses followed; within another two or three months much of the southern Peloponnese was under allied control and a Swedish general, Count Otto William von Königsmark, had arrived – hired by the Republic at a salary of 18,000 ducats – to take overall command of the land forces.

Early in 1686, Morosini and Königsmark met on Leucas for a council of war. There were four main objectives from which to choose: Chios, Euboea, Crete or the rest of the Peloponnese. Largely, it seems, on the insistence of Königsmark, the last of these targets was selected. In the next two summers' campaigning the league forces accepted the submissions of Modone and Navarino, Argos and Nauplia, Lepanto, Patras and Corinth. Morosini, meanwhile, had sailed his fleet around to Attica and had begun to lay siege to Athens. And now there occurred the second of the two great tragedies of history the blame for which, alas, must be laid at Venice's door. The miserable story of the Fourth Crusade has already been told in Chapter VII; we must now sadly record that on Monday, 26 September 1687, at about seven o'clock in the evening, a mortar placed by Morosini on the Mouseion hill opposite the Acropolis was fired by a German lieutenant at the Parthenon – which, by a further curse of fate, the Turks were using as a powder magazine. He scored a direct hit. The consequent explosion almost completely demolished the *cella* and its frieze, together with eight columns on the north side and six on the south with their entablatures.

Nor was this the end of the destruction. After the capture of the city, Morosini – doubtless remembering the carrying off of the four bronze horses from the Hippodrome of Constantinople in 1205 – tried to remove the horses and chariot of Athena that formed part of the west pediment of the temple. In the process the whole group fell to the ground and was smashed to pieces. The determined conqueror had to content himself with lesser souvenirs: the two flanking lions of the four now standing at the entrance to the Venetian Arsenal.

It is unlikely that many tears were shed in Venice over the fate of the

Parthenon. The Venetians were too busy celebrating. Their last major victory at Lepanto had been well over a hundred years before; more important still, the conquests which Morosini was now making – unparalleled since the fifteenth century – seemed to point towards a final lifting of that black Ottoman cloud that had overshadowed them for so long, and perhaps even a return to those far-off days of commercial imperialism. No wonder they rejoiced, and no wonder that, when their Doge Marcantonio Giustinian died in March 1688, Francesco Morosini was elected, unanimously and at the first ballot, as his successor.

Morosini had, however, no intention of giving up his command. On 8 July 1688 he led a fleet of some 200 sail out of the Gulf of Athens and headed for his next objective, the island of Euboea (or Negroponte, as the Venetians called it). Like Crete, Euboea had first come into Venetian hands as a result of the partition of the Byzantine Empire after the Fourth Crusade, and although Venice had forfeited it to the Turks over two centuries before – in 1470 – its loss had never ceased to rankle. It was known to be heavily fortified, and the Turkish garrison of 6,000, even if it were to receive no reinforcements, was expected to put up a spirited resistance. But the league forces numbered twice that many, and neither Morosini nor Königsmark had any serious doubts that the island would soon be theirs. They had reckoned, unfortunately, without acts of God. Suddenly their luck changed, and no sooner had the siege begun than an appalling epidemic – probably dysentery or malaria – struck their camp. Within a few weeks the army had lost a third of its men, including Königsmark himself. In mid-August the arrival of a 4,000-strong relief force from Venice encouraged Morosini to continue, but almost immediately he found a mutiny on his hands. The imperial troops from Brunswick–Hanover flatly refused to fight any longer. With disaffection spreading almost as fast as disease, he had no choice but to order a general re-embarkation.

Yet even now he could not reconcile himself to the humiliation of a direct return to Venice. One more victory, however modest, would be enough to redeem his honour and enable his subjects to greet him as a hero after all. The fortress of Malvasia (Monemvasia) in the south-eastern corner of the Peloponnese, one of the few mainland strongholds left to the Turks, would serve the purpose admirably. There was, however, a problem. The castle, set high on its virtually impregnable rock, could be approached only by a narrow path, most of it less than a yard across – useless for a besieging army.

Bombardment was the only hope, and Morosini ordered the construction of two gun emplacements; but even before they were completed he himself was struck down by illness. Leaving the command to his Proveditor-General, Girolamo Corner, he sailed home in January 1690, sick and disconsolate, to a stirring welcome which he was quite unable to enjoy.

Corner proved a worthy successor, and a luckier one. He took Malvasia, where the standard of St Mark was hoisted on the battlements for the first time in 150 years; then, hearing that an Ottoman fleet was heading through the archipelago, sailed north again to meet it and scattered it off Mytilene (Lesbos), inflicting considerable damage in the process. Returning once more to the Adriatic, he launched a surprise attack on Valona, captured it and dismantled its defences. He was still there when the fever struck him; a day or two later he was dead. His successor showed himself a broken reed.

With the prospect of the Turkish war, which had begun so magnificently, grinding to an ignominious halt, the Venetians looked once again to their Doge for active leadership. Morosini, now seventy-four, had never properly recovered his health; nevertheless, when he was invited to resume his command he did not hesitate. He sailed from Venice, amid scenes of great pomp, on 25 May 1693 – but his last campaign proved another sad anticlimax. The Turks had taken advantage of the winter and spring to strengthen the defences of both Euboea and of Canea in Crete. Contrary winds persuaded Morosini against another attempt on the Dardanelles. He reinforced the garrison in Corinth and one or two other strong-points in the Peloponnese, and chased a few Algerian pirates; finally – in order not to return completely empty-handed – he occupied Salamis, Hydra and Spetsai before putting in to Nauplia for the winter. By then it was clear that his exertions had taken their toll. Throughout December he was in constant agony from gallstones, and on 6 January 1694 he died. Never again until the fall of the Venetian Republic was a Doge of Venice to go to war.

In the history of Venice's tragic attempt to regain control of the Mediterranean, only one short chapter remains. The island of Chios had been one of the four possible objectives considered by Francesco Morosini and Count von Königsmark in 1686. It boasted a predominantly Christian population, both Catholic and Orthodox, each with its own bishop; the Turkish garrison was thought to number some 2,000 at the most. Antonio Zen, the Venetian Captain-General who on

7 September 1694 landed 9,000 men on the island, expected no difficulties.

Nor, at the outset, did he encounter any. The bombardment began at once; the harbour, together with three Turkish ships that chanced to be lying at anchor, was captured without a fight and the garrison surrendered on the 15th in return for a guarantee of safe conduct to the mainland. Venetian spirits were high, and they rose higher still when reports reached Chios of a Turkish fleet of some fifty sail, rapidly approaching. For years now the Turks had done their utmost to avoid naval engagements, and Zen's captains had little admiration for their seamanship or indeed their courage. Unfortunately, just as the Captain-General was about to emerge from the narrow straits that separate Chios from the mainland and to make for the open sea, the wind dropped. In the flat calm that followed, no confrontation was possible, and when on the 20th a very faint breeze sprang up it threatened the Turks – who, seeing their danger, quickly made for home and reached the harbour of Smyrna before the Venetians could catch up with them. Zen, still ready to fight, anchored in the roadstead outside the harbour, but no sooner had he done so than he was visited on board his flagship by the local consuls representing the three European powers outside the league – England, France and the Netherlands – who implored him not to risk Christian lives and property in the city by any unprovoked attack – backing up their entreaties, it is reported, with a considerable sum of money. Knowing that he was also running short of supplies, Zen agreed and returned to Chios.

But the great sea battle that most of the Venetian captains so eagerly awaited was not much longer to be delayed. The Sultan, furious at the loss of one of his most valuable offshore islands, had given orders for its immediate recovery, and early in February 1695 a new Ottoman fleet was signalled, consisting of twenty of his heaviest capital ships – *sultanas*, as they were called – supported by twenty-four galleys. Antonio Zen at once sailed out to meet it with a roughly comparable fleet – it included a sizable squadron made available by the Knights of Malta – and on the morning of the 9th battle was finally joined at the northern end of the straits. The fighting was long and violent, marked by several deeds of outstanding courage on the part of the Venetians – and probably on that of the Turks too, though these are not recorded in the Venetian reports; but when the two fleets separated at nightfall, despite heavy casualties on both sides – for the Venetians, 465 dead and 603 wounded – the result was inconclusive.

This proved, however, to be only the first phase. The fleets anchored off Chios, just out of range of each other's guns, and waited ten full days, watching. Then, on 19 February, with a strong north wind behind them, the Turks once again bore down upon their adversaries. As they fought, the wind rose to gale force; the sea grew increasingly rough until close manoeuvring became impossible. The Venetians fought desperately to get to windward, but gradually they were forced down the narrow channel to the harbour. In such weather entry into port was impossible; the vessels could only lie to in the roadstead, where they were raked again and again by the pursuing Turks. It was a disaster. The Venetian losses were immense, the Turkish comparatively slight. The Captain-General called a council of war, but the outcome seems to have been a foregone conclusion. There were no longer enough men available for the adequate manning of the fortress; the defences were in lamentable condition; the treasury was empty and supplies were running low. Long before any help could be expected, the Turks were bound to attack again, and when they did, the consequences would be catastrophic.

So it was that the island of Chios was won and, within less than six months, was lost again. On the night of 20 February all the war materiel that could be carried away was loaded on to the ships, the remaining defences dismantled or destroyed. Then, on the morning of the 21st, the fleet sailed out of the harbour. With it, to escape the vengeance of the Turks, went most of the leading Catholic families of the island, who were granted new estates in the Peloponnese to compensate them for what they had left behind. Even on her departure, Venice's ill fortune went with her. Scarcely was the last ship round the mole when one of Zen's most important remaining vessels, the *Abbondanza Richezza*, laden with arms and ammunition, struck a hidden rock. All endeavours to free her failed and she had to be abandoned with most of her cargo still intact on board.

To the people of Venice, who had so recently been celebrating the recovery of Chios, the news of its loss was a matter less for sorrow than for anger. The Senate demanded an immediate inquiry, pending which the miserable Zen, together with several other senior officers, was brought back to Venice in chains. He died in prison in July 1697 while the inquiry was still in progress. Its findings were never made known.

The Turks were not beaten; but they were undeniably battered, and seemed likely to welcome the opportunity for a negotiated peace. The

Emperor Leopold for his part was anxious that they should, for he knew that a fresh crisis was approaching – not on his eastern border this time but in the west, where the half-mad and childless King Charles II of Spain obviously had not long to live. There were two principal contenders for his throne – Leopold himself and Louis XIV of France, both grandsons of Philip III and sons-in-law of Philip IV – and Leopold understandably wished to have his hands free to deal with the struggle ahead. England and Holland, horrified at the prospect of seeing France and Spain united under Louis, offered their mediation with the Sultan; Poland and Venice, on the assumption that they would retain the territories they had conquered, were only too pleased to lay down their arms after fifteen years of war. The arrangements were quickly made, and on 13 November 1698 the various powers concerned met at Karlowitz in Hungary (now the Serbian town of Sremski Karlovci).

The negotiations did not run as smoothly as had been expected, the representatives of the Sultan pointing out that their master, not having surrendered, saw no reason why he should be required to abandon all the territories now in Christian hands. In particular he had in mind certain of his Mediterranean possessions. Venice could have the Peloponnese; he would make no difficulty about that. She could also retain Leucas on one side and Aegina on the other, and a number of fortresses on the Dalmatian coast. He himself, however, was determined to keep Athens, Attica and all Greek territory north of the Gulf of Corinth. The Venetian representative objected violently, but received little support. The Emperor, once he had been assured of Hungary and Transylvania, was anxious to get home as quickly as possible; he let it be known to the Venetians that, if they insisted on making difficulties, he would have no hesitation in concluding a separate peace. For a time the Republic continued to argue, and when the treaty was signed on 26 January 1699 she was not among the signatories. But at last wisdom triumphed over pride, and on 7 February the Doge finally appended his seal.

It was as well that he did so, for the Treaty of Karlowitz is the one diplomatic instrument above all others that marks the decline of Ottoman power; and Venice, which had directly confronted that power for longer than any other Christian state, had more right than any to be a party to it. On the other hand, her forced renunciation of an important part of her conquests was not just a blow to her self-respect; it made it considerably more difficult for her adequately to defend that part which remained. There was now nothing to prevent the Turks from invading the Peloponnese from Attica, or indeed from anywhere along the north shore of the Gulf of Corinth – a point which they were, all too soon, to prove.

CHAPTER XIX

The Wars of Succession

On Friday, 1 November 1700, King Charles II of Spain died in his palace in Madrid. Weak in body as in mind, he had come to the throne at the age of four on the death of his father, Philip IV, and one glance at the luckless child had been enough to convince the court of his total inadequacy for the tasks that lay ahead of him. Charles looked like a caricature of a Habsburg, his chin and jaw projecting so far that the lower teeth could make no contact with the upper ones. He was always ill, to the point where many suspected witchcraft. Few of his subjects believed for an instant that he would grow up to assume power over his immense dominions. But grow up he did, and after a ten-year regency under his mother, Mariana – daughter of the Emperor Ferdinand III – he took over, at least in theory, the reins of government. Thus, from the day of his accession in 1665 and for the next thirty-five years Spain was effectively a great monarchy without a monarch. Never was there a suggestion that Charles might have a personal policy of his own. He was hardly ever at his desk except when there were papers – almost always unread – for him to sign, and the day in May 1694 when he was obliged to miss his lunch caused such astonishment that it was recorded in a contemporary journal. Government of the country was left to a succession of Prime Ministers of varying ability, and to the grandees of Spain.

And, above all, to the Church and its principal instrument, the Inquisition. As the King himself told the British ambassador, he never meddled in religious affairs. Jews and Protestants were the Inquisition's most usual victims, but in fact no foreigner was safe. When the ambassador's chaplain died in 1691 he had to be buried in secret; even then, his body was subsequently dug up and mutilated. And there is no doubt that the expulsion of the Moriscos[1] in 1610 – achieved by the Inquisition acting with the dreadful Duke of Lerma – had dealt Spain a blow from which it took centuries to recover. On the Moriscos had depended much of the agricultural production of the country: cereals,

---

[1] Those former Muslims whose families had converted to Christianity – at least in theory – as a result of the persecutions by Queen Isabella. See Chapter XIII.

sugar, rice, cotton, even paper. What little industry Spain could boast had also been in their hands. Thus by 1700 Seville and Toledo, Segovia and Burgos were pale shadows of what they had been a hundred years before. For the peasantry and the working-class populations of the towns, conditions grew bleaker with every year that passed. In 1699 came famine: a crowd of 20,000 assembled before the royal palace, and a full-scale revolution was narrowly averted.

It came as no surprise that Charles II, despite two marriages, had failed to produce any offspring, and as the century drew to its close the question of who should succeed him grew steadily in importance. The problem was that the Spanish crown was coveted – and indeed claimed – by the two mightiest dynasties of Europe. Of the two daughters of King Philip III the elder, Anne, had been married to Louis XIII of France; the younger, Maria, to the Emperor Ferdinand III of Austria. Anne had in due course given birth to the future Louis XIV, Maria to the Emperor Leopold I. Louis might have been thought to have a secondary claim through his wife, Maria Teresa, who was Charles II's elder sister; unfortunately for him, however, his bride had been obliged on her marriage formally to renounce all her hereditary rights in the Spanish dominions.

Charles's younger sister Margaret, on the other hand, had made no such renunciation when she had married the Emperor Leopold I; her small grandson Joseph Ferdinand – son of her daughter Maria Antonia and Max Emanuel, Elector of Bavaria – was consequently the Habsburg claimant. Already the scene seemed to be set for a struggle. When in 1698 Charles made a will confirming Joseph Ferdinand as his heir and successor, the matter might have been thought to be settled, but in February 1699 the young prince unexpectedly died. His sudden death was attributed, rather unconvincingly, to smallpox; there were many, among them the boy's own father, who suspected poison and did not hesitate to say so. Once again, intricate diplomatic negotiations began – not only among the three powers most directly concerned, but also with the participation of England and Holland.[1] These two maritime countries both carried on immensely profitable trade with Spain; there were several British and Dutch merchants permanently

---

[1] In the early part of the sixteenth century the Netherlands had, as we have seen, become a province of the Spanish Habsburgs. Then, during the Reformation, the northern provinces had been converted to Calvinism and Prince William of Orange (William the Silent) had led them in a revolt against Spain. In 1579 they shook off Spanish rule and became the United Provinces of the Netherlands – though Spain did not recognise their independence till 1648. The southern provinces remained Spanish.

resident in Cadiz and other Spanish ports. Through much of the seventeenth century the two had been at loggerheads; now, however, they shared a common concern: to keep out the French. If Spain were to pass from the hands of the weakest monarch in Europe into those of the strongest, what chance was there that trade would be allowed to continue?

Backwards and forwards shuttled the ambassadors between the European capitals, until in June 1699 what was known as the Second Treaty of Partition (never mind the First) was signed by William III of England and Louis XIV of France; it was hoped that the States-General of Holland and the Emperor Leopold would give their assent later. By its terms the formerly Spanish kingdoms of Naples and Sicily were allotted to France, together with the Spanish lands along the coast of Tuscany and – in exchange for Milan – the Duchy of Lorraine. Spain and the rest of Charles II's inheritance would fall to the Emperor's younger son, the Archduke Charles. In March 1700 the States-General signed up; only Leopold held out. He saw no reason why France should help herself to any imperial territories, and he was particularly incensed at the idea that he should surrender Milan. So far as he was concerned, his son should assume the entire Spanish inheritance – and he was prepared to fight for it.

Leopold's reactions were moderate, however, in comparison to those of the Spanish court when, in June, the terms of the treaty were communicated to Madrid. It was reported that, on receipt of the news, the King 'flew into an extraordinary passion, and the Queen in her rage smashed to pieces everything in her room'. Clearly, Spain's greatest hope of support lay with Austria, a natural ally against the partitioning powers. Letters flew between King and Emperor, and the prospect of war began to loom larger still. But Charles had one more surprise up his sleeve. By the autumn of 1700 it was plain that he had not long to live, and on 3 October he put his tremulous signature to a new will, by the terms of which he left all his dominions without exception to Louis XIV's seventeen-year-old grandson, Philip, Duke of Anjou. A month later he was dead.

What caused this sudden change of heart in favour of France? Above all, the Church. The Inquisition, and indeed the whole hierarchy and clergy of Spain, had long favoured a French solution, and Pope Innocent XII – who was actually to die five weeks before the King – had himself written to him recommending the Duke of Anjou. With the consciousness of approaching death and the voice of his father confessor whispering into his ear, Charles no longer had the strength to argue.

'Never,' wrote King William III of England on 16 November 1700, 'did I much rely on engagements with France; but I must confess I did not think they would have broken, in the face of the whole world, a solemn treaty before it was well accomplished.' He cannot in truth have been all that surprised; Louis – or at least his grandson – had been offered on a plate far more than he could ever have hoped for, and the King's character was certainly not such as to pass it all up for the sake of a treaty upon which the ink was scarcely dry. Well aware that Leopold would not accept this new dispensation without protest, he lost no time in packing the young claimant off to Madrid to assume his throne without delay, in company with a bevy of French officials to take over all the key posts of government and, as his special guide and mentor, the redoubtable Princesse des Ursins.[1] In fact, Philip V was to be readily accepted in his new kingdom, only Catalonia proving hostile, but this was by no means enough to ensure an uncontested succession. What Louis could not have known was how long and how desperate the ensuing war would be, or what a price he would have to pay for his grandson's throne.

The Treaty of Partition was now hardly worth the paper it was written on; clearly it would have to be replaced. And so, on 7 September 1701 at the Hague, representatives of England, Holland and the Empire signed what was to become known as the Grand Alliance. In certain areas its terms were left deliberately vague, but its principal objectives for the coming war – the imminence of which could no longer be in doubt – were plain enough. The imperial aims were frankly political: Leopold was out to recover for the Empire all the Spanish possessions in Italy. Those of England and Holland, on the other hand, were almost exclusively commercial: they wished only to secure the future of their navigation and trade.

But seven months before, in February of that same year, Philip of Anjou had entered Madrid as Philip V of Spain, and French troops had occupied the Spanish Netherlands.[2] The war had already begun.

*

---

[1] Born Marie-Anne de la Trémouille in 1642, she married in 1675 as her second husband Flavio degli Orsini, Duke of Bracciano; their palace in Rome became the centre of French influence in Italy. Widowed again in 1698, she returned to France, gallicised her name and became Mistress of the Robes to the Queen. From the day of her arrival in Spain she virtually ran the country.

[2] I.e. the southern provinces, which had remained Spanish after the secession of the northern.

The War of the Spanish Succession is, for most of us, associated with the great Duke of Marlborough; and it was in northern Europe, not in the south, that he created his magnificent legend. Those blood-soaked battlefields of Blenheim and Ramillies, of Oudenarde and Malplaquet, are hundreds of miles from the Mediterranean and no business of ours. But the Middle Sea too played its part; indeed, the war began with a brief land campaign on Italian soil, during which the French were able to secure various formerly Spanish possessions in Lombardy and the Po valley; and at the very outbreak of hostilities in 1701, a considerable allied army had assembled in the south Tyrol under the command of Prince Eugene of Savoy[1] with the object of expelling them. Meanwhile the French commander, the splendidly named Marshal Nicholas Catinat de la Fauconnerie, who had no intention of being expelled and assumed that the Prince would follow the valley of the Adige, drew up his army on the shores of Lake Garda and awaited the attack. But Eugene was too clever for him. Sending a small detachment along the right bank of the Adige as a feint, he brought the bulk of his army – 16,000 foot and some 6,000 horse – by narrow and obscure mountain paths over Monte Baldo, finally approaching the French unexpectedly, on their right flank.

Catinat lost his head. Taken completely off guard and uncertain of Eugene's intentions, he spread out his army in small detachments over some sixty miles. It was a fatal mistake, of which the Prince took full advantage. Attacking one detachment after another, he scored a succession of small but decisive victories – culminating in a midwinter raid on Cremona to capture another marshal, the Duc de Villeroi[2] – and threw the French into total confusion. The following year they recovered: Catinat had been succeeded by the Duc de Vendôme – an infinitely better general – whose army had received massive reinforcements sent by Philip of Spain from Naples. Eugene, his lines of communication with Vienna suddenly cut off, was thrown for the first

---

[1] Prince Eugene (1663–1736) was the imperial field marshal who was known as the greatest soldier of his time. He had fought his first battle – during the Turkish siege of Vienna in 1683 – at the age of twenty. He was the teacher of Frederick the Great, and the only strategist whose campaigns Napoleon considered worthy of careful study.

[2] How Villeroi had become a marshal no one ever knew: he lost virtually every battle he ever fought. After his capture and for the rest of the war, French soldiers on the march would sing:

> Parsembleu! la nouvelle est bonne
> Et notre bonheur sans égal:
> Nous avons conservé Cremone
> Et perdu notre général.

time on to the defensive. By then, however, the epicentre of the war had shifted. Italy was largely forgotten.

But not the Mediterranean. Already at the time of the Partition Treaty, the future of the Middle Sea had been much in King William's mind. It was not only the continuation of trade with Spain that preoccupied him; it was also the realisation that, if Spain were to pass into Bourbon hands, England might be excluded from the entire Mediterranean basin unless she could find herself a secure stronghold within it. He had long had his eye on Minorca, and he was also planning with his admiral, Sir George Rooke, to occupy Cadiz before the French could do so.[1] William's death in March 1702 put paid to this latter idea; Rooke had never had much enthusiasm for it, and his attack on the port the following autumn proved a fiasco. Two years later, however, he redeemed it in full – when, with an Anglo-Dutch fleet, he captured Gibraltar.

The Rock had been in Spanish hands since 1462, and in 1501 had been formally annexed to Spain by Queen Isabella; but its defences were poor and its tiny garrison showed little appetite for resistance. It surrendered to Rooke on 4 August, having held out for just three days, at a cost to the attackers of sixty killed and some 200 wounded. The admiral had a real chance to show his mettle only three weeks afterwards when, on 23 August, off the Spanish coast near Malaga, he ran into a French fleet of about fifty sail under the Count of Toulouse. What followed was later described by Rooke as 'the sharpest day's service I ever saw'. Losses were high on both sides. There was no doubt, however, that the British had the best of it; when day broke on 27 August there was not a Frenchman in sight. The French fleet had withdrawn to Toulon, and for the rest of the war made no effort to dispute the allied control of the Mediterranean.

The capture of Gibraltar had not immediately made it a British colony. Technically, Rooke had taken it on behalf of the imperialist claimant, the Archduke Charles, and almost exactly a year after its fall, on 2 August 1705, the Archduke had disembarked from a British naval vessel and had been formally recognised there as King Charles III of Spain. Meanwhile the Rock was garrisoned by two British and two Dutch regiments, and although its governor, Major-General Sir John Shrimpton, was an Englishman, he and his staff continued to

---

[1] Cadiz is technically an Atlantic port rather than a Mediterranean one, but close enough to the straits to provide a base from which to control them.

acknowledge Charles's sovereignty. On the King's birthday in 1705 three rounds from thirty-five guns were fired in salute; on that of Queen Anne five months later, there was only one round from twenty-one guns. But these were early days, when Charles still seemed to have a fair chance of winning the Spanish throne. Later, as those chances diminished, the future of Gibraltar took on a different complexion. Surely there could be no question of its passing to the hated Philip V – and through him, for all anybody knew, to his still more hated grandfather, Louis XIV? How much safer if it were kept, permanently, in British hands . . .

The next major Italian campaign opened only in 1706. Prince Eugene had recognised that further progress was impossible without substantial reinforcements, and had returned to Vienna to find them. Taking advantage of his absence, Vendôme had launched a surprise attack on the imperial army at its camp near Brescia and had driven it back into the Tyrol. He had, however, reckoned without Eugene who, with 24,000 troops from Germany – raised thanks to an English subsidy of £250,000 – entered Italy early in July down the valley of the Adige and marched south to the Po. Crossing it, he then headed west along the right bank, driving the enemy before him. At Villa Stellona, just south of Pavia, he joined another army under the Duke of Savoy, and together they advanced on Turin, where – though easily out-numbered – they inflicted a resounding defeat on the French forces. It was the end. In March 1707, by the Convention of Milan, Louis XIV abandoned northern Italy.

In Spain, on the other hand, he continued to fight; indeed, he had no choice. In the spring of 1706 a squadron commanded by Admiral Sir Clowdisley Shovell had carried a force under the Earl of Peterborough through the Straits of Gibraltar to the east coast, where Barcelona had willingly accepted the imperial claimant as King Charles III. Meanwhile an English–Dutch–Portuguese army under the Earl of Galway[1] had invaded Extremadura from Portugal and had continued eastward to Madrid. It entered the city on 26 June, only to evacuate it again after a few weeks in recognition of one indisputable fact: that outside

---

[1] Formerly the Marquis de Ruvigny and member of an old Huguenot family, Galway had commanded a French regiment before settling in England after the revocation of the Edict of Nantes in 1685 and becoming a British subject. Five years later he had entered the English service as a major-general of horse. In 1692 he had been appointed commander-in-chief in Ireland, and had soon afterwards been awarded a peerage.

Catalonia and Valencia Spain was overwhelmingly in support of King Philip. Disappointment over Madrid was, however, easily outweighed by allied successes in northern Europe, to the point where, in August, King Louis made it known that he was ready to come to terms: he would leave Spain to Charles in return for the recognition of Philip's right to Milan, Naples and Sicily.

At that time, it need hardly be said, neither England nor the Empire were prepared to listen; twelve months later, they may well have wished that they had. The year 1707 saw no great victories in the north and, in the south, two disasters. The first was when on 25 April Galway's motley force of some 15,000 men was heavily defeated at Almansa, some sixty miles southwest of Valencia, by a greatly superior army of French and Spaniards under King Louis's leading general the Duke of Berwick, the natural son of King James II of England by the Duke of Marlborough's sister Arabella.[1] At a single blow Valencia, Murcia and Aragon were lost to the allies. Worse still, perhaps, they were therefore unable to supplement the forces of Prince Eugene when, in July, he attacked Toulon. Eugene was almost as great a general as was his chief, the Duke of Marlborough; it is sad indeed that his last venture in the Mediterranean should, through no fault of his own, have cast something of a shadow over his reputation. If his attempt on Toulon proved a failure, this was due entirely to his two principal allies, the Emperor Leopold and the Duke of Savoy. Leopold had at the critical moment seen fit to detach some 13,000 men to attack Naples; Savoy for his part had shown himself to be weak and indecisive – so much so that by the time Eugene eventually landed on Provençal soil on 26 July the battle was already as good as lost. Ten thousand men were needlessly sacrificed. It was perhaps some consolation to know that, rather than allowing Toulon to fall into allied hands, the French had deliberately scuttled their squadron of some fifty sail in its harbour; the fact remained that their principal southern port, which should have been Eugene's for the taking, had been forfeited through sheer inefficiency and muddle, and the English fleet was still deprived of the one thing it needed more than any other: a good, safe harbour in the Mediterranean where it would be protected from winter storms, where its provisions and supplies could be safely stored and where its ships could be properly refitted.

---

[1] This is probably the only battle in history in which the British forces were commanded by a Frenchman, the French by a Briton.

As things turned out, it did not have to wait much longer. Minorca, the furthest of the Balearic Islands to the northeast and consequently the nearest to France, had long been an object of interest to the British navy; and in the summer of 1708 Major-General James Stanhope – who had been sent to Spain as Minister, but who had some months before succeeded Galway as Commander-in-Chief – received orders from Marlborough to take the island's capital, Port Mahon. Supported by a fleet of thirty-four ships under Admiral Sir John Leake – who had hastened to Minorca from Sardinia, where he had been bombarding Cagliari[1] – he landed in Minorca on 14 September with about 1,200 British, 800 Spanish and 600 Portuguese troops. It was another fortnight before he was ready to attack. A road had to be constructed to carry the guns and provisions the mile from his landing-place to his first objective, Fort St Philip; even then, the fort's commanding position overlooking the harbour made it almost impregnable. Stanhope dealt with the problem by offering generous terms for its surrender and threatening to slaughter the entire garrison if these were not accepted. The French and Spanish commanders might even then have continued to resist, had it not been for the large number of women and children who had taken refuge there. They therefore decided to surrender – a decision they were later to regret. Both were subsequently imprisoned, and the Spanish commander killed himself.

Other forts quickly followed St Philip's example, the speed of Stanhope's progress being due largely to the goodwill of the local population, who had had quite enough of both French and Spaniards: the magistrates of Mahon willingly handed over the keys to the city as soon as the invaders approached. By the end of the month the entire island was effectively in British hands. It was to remain so, with a short intermission between 1756 and 1763, for very nearly a century. To Stanhope it mattered little that the island, like Gibraltar, had technically surrendered to King Charles III of Spain, who was indeed formally proclaimed as its king on 8 November. 'England,' he wrote, 'ought never to part with this island, which will give the law to the Mediterranean both in time of war and of peace.' To emphasise the fact, he left a garrison consisting entirely of British troops, all the Spanish and Portuguese being returned to Spain to assist King Charles. By June 1709 he had spent £11,000 on the island's defences.

---

[1] Cagliari itself was forced to surrender, but the British never conquered Sardinia as a whole. It was to become a major bargaining counter in the years following the Treaty of Utrecht.

To Galway on the Spanish mainland, meanwhile, matters were looking increasingly grave. He tended to blame his reverses principally on his Portuguese troops – at Almansa they had been a distinct liability – and early in 1708 marched them back to their homeland. They were replaced by Germans made available by the recent armistice in Italy, under their commander Count von Starhemberg, but even then it proved impossible to stop the imperialists taking Tortosa, so cutting communications between Barcelona and Valencia. Not until 1710 was any progress made, when the allies marched for the second time on Madrid. The city fell on 23 September, but once again Charles failed to hold it: by the end of the year he had to retreat to Catalonia. Even there, his hold was tenuous enough: in January 1711 the French captured Gerona.

Then, just three months later on 17 April, the Emperor Joseph I died in Vienna at the age of thirty-three – this time it was unquestionably smallpox – and the entire European political scene was transformed overnight. Joseph had succeeded his father, Leopold, in 1705, had done much to reform the Empire's chaotic finances and had warmly espoused the claims of his younger brother Charles to Spain. But Charles was now not just a Spanish claimant; he was the obvious successor to his brother on the imperial throne. The Grand Alliance had been formed only in order to prevent a single family, the Bourbons, from becoming too powerful; if Charles were to succeed to the Empire – as indeed he did, being elected in the following year – the Habsburgs threatened to be more powerful still, with all their dominions once more united as in the days of his great-great-great-great-uncle Charles V. Inevitably, many months were to pass before the European powers were able to come to terms with the new situation; it was not until New Year's Day 1712 that negotiations began between the allies and France in the Dutch city of Utrecht.

Before we leave for Utrecht, however, we must return briefly to Minorca and to Gibraltar, whose status remained ambiguous. In England the Whigs, who had dominated the first half of Queen Anne's reign,[1] had been replaced by a Tory government, and the new ministry had decided that the Emperor Charles VI was now a far more serious danger than the Bourbons had ever been and no longer merited British support. Besides, the Bourbons too were now ready for peace. The war

---

[1] Queen Anne had succeeded to the English throne on the death of William III in 1702.

in the north was threatening France with disaster – Marlborough was still carrying all before him – and King Louis was increasingly anxious to come to terms. Concessions would therefore have to be made, preferably – Louis being Louis – with other people's property; and what concessions could be more acceptable to the British than the acknowledgement of their claim to Gibraltar? On 31 May the King informed Queen Anne: '*On a parole du Roi d'Espagne de laisser aux Anglais Gibraltar pour la sûreté réelle de leur commerce en Espagne et dans la Méditerranée.*'[1]

In fact, he had nothing of the kind, but Philip was in no position to complain. Hitherto he had been a good deal more fortunate than his grandfather: the war in Spain against Charles and his allies had been moderately successful. But for how long would his luck hold? The succession of Charles to the Empire meant that the latter would hence-forth have all its resources at his disposal. There were also rumours that Prince Eugene might be sent to take over the command in Spain, and Philip was all too well aware that he had no generals with half the Prince's experience or brilliance to set against him. Finally, if France and Britain made a separate peace, he would be deprived of all French military support. He saw that he had no choice, and so he reluctantly informed King Louis that he was ready to offer the British both their recent conquests.

Peace negotiations were quietly and discreetly set in train: Britain recognised Philip V as King of Spain, while Spain and France were obliged to accept that Minorca and Gibraltar would remain in British hands. At first Louis kept quiet about Minorca. The Rock was of little strategic value to him; the island, on the other hand, was only a day's sail from France and, as he had recently seen, could be used as a springboard for an attack on Toulon and his Mediterranean coast, so he had no intention of handing it over unless he had to. What he did not know was the admonition that had been given to the British negotiators before they left for Utrecht: that they were to insist that 'Gibraltar and Port Mahon, with the island of Minorca, be for the future annexed to the Crown of these realms' – and not to take no for an answer.

There was still a little trouble with the Dutch. They had played their part in the taking of the Rock in 1704, and they had provided an

---

[1] 'We have the promise of the King of Spain to leave Gibraltar to the English as a true safeguard for their commerce in Spain and in the Mediterranean.'

important part of its garrison ever since. They had understandably expected to be rewarded; now, equally understandably, they felt betrayed. At first they refused to withdraw their troops from Gibraltar, even threatening to continue the war alone. But no one took them too seriously. The truth was that they desperately needed British support to protect them in the Netherlands – and both they and the British knew it.

What is generally known as the Treaty of Utrecht was in fact a whole series of treaties in which, after a European upheaval that had lasted for eleven years, France and Spain attempted once again to regulate their relations with their neighbours. Most of the subjects upon which agreements were reached do not concern us here. Where the future of the Mediterranean was concerned, however, both countries made major concessions. France and Spain both formally recognised Duke Victor Amadeus II of Savoy – who happened to be King Philip's father-in-law – as King of Sicily, his northern dominion extending to include the formerly French city of Nice. Spain in addition accepted the transfer to the Empire of the formerly Spanish areas of Italy and the Netherlands, and effectively handed over Minorca and Gibraltar to Britain. She did not, however, do so unconditionally. Although the treaty conferred on the British Crown perpetual property rights over part of the present territory of Gibraltar (Britain has shamelessly extended it since), provided that the Catholic religion should continue to be freely exercised and that Jews and Moors should be prohibited from settling there, the ultimate sovereignty over the Rock she explicitly reserved to herself.[1] What is rather less well known is that she also put her name to the so-called *asiento* agreement, by which she gave the British the exclusive right to supply her overseas colonies with African slaves, at the rate of 4,800 slaves a year for thirty years.

The Emperor Charles fought on until 1714, and the final peace had to be signed without him. It was essentially on his behalf that the great struggle had continued for the past twelve years, and by distancing himself from the peacemakers he did his Empire a lasting disservice. His

---

[1] It is this subtle distinction that forms the basis of the Spanish claim to the Rock: that it has been part of the sovereign territory of Spain since the days of Ferdinand and Isabella, and that this status was not affected by the Treaty of Utrecht. The Spanish position is often accused of being hypocritical because of a supposed parallel between Gibraltar and the Spanish cities of Ceuta and Melilla on the North African coast. Spaniards reply that these two cities are not colonies but have always been Spanish territories, just as much as the Balearics or the Canaries; they have never formed part of the Moroccan state.

interests were not altogether ignored during the long negotiations at Utrecht, but since they were fundamentally opposed to those of France, Bourbon Spain and the United Provinces – as the Dutch now called themselves – while Britain remained largely indifferent, it was inevitable that they should have been to some degree neglected. Nevertheless, when the negotiators returned to their homes, Charles found himself master not only of the body of his Empire but also of the Catholic Netherlands, Milan, Naples and Sardinia. He was hardly in a position to complain, but with a modicum of diplomatic finesse he could probably have done better still.

And the Spanish throne? This was of course the most important question of all, the original *casus belli*, the reason for the deaths of hundreds of thousands of men across the continent. It was at last resolved – as it by now virtually had to be – in favour of Philip. His kingdom had been drastically amputated – though he would certainly not miss the Low Countries, which had long been a millstone round the Spanish neck. Anyway, there were compensations. He kept Spanish America and all the wealth that it brought him, and he was, thenceforth and for the next thirty years, to rule uncontested as King Philip V of Spain.[1]

Where he must stand condemned is in his treatment of the Catalans. Despite the fact that they had been staunch champions of Charles of Habsburg, in Article XIII of the Anglo-Spanish Treaty Philip formally accorded to them, by reason of his respect for the Queen of Great Britain, a complete amnesty and all the privileges at that time enjoyed by the Castilians, 'of all the peoples of Spain, that which the King cherished most'. It was plain from the start, however, that he had no intention of forgiving them for what he considered their disloyalty, and early in 1713 he had demanded their unconditional submission. They not surprisingly had refused, and had set up a provisional government of their own; whereupon in July 1714 Philip had sent a detachment of troops to invest Barcelona. The city fought back, and indeed held out for nearly two months; even after the besiegers had been joined by a French army under the Duke of Berwick and a French fleet, it refused to surrender. On the night of 11 September there was a general assault. The Catalans doggedly defended every street, often every house, until they could fight no more. The survivors were sold into slavery, and the

---

[1] There was a brief interregnum in 1724, when in a fit of religious mania Philip abdicated in favour of his eldest son Luís; but he resumed the throne when Luís died of smallpox seven months later.

standards of Catalonia were, by the King's orders, burned in the public market by the common hangman.

Whether Philip V ever felt remorse for his treatment of the Catalans is doubtful. He soon, however, had cause to regret his surrender of Spanish Italy. Soon after the death in 1714 of his first wife, Maria Louisa of Savoy, he married the twenty-two-year-old Elizabeth Farnese, niece and stepdaughter of the Duke of Parma. The new Queen – undistinguished by beauty, education or experience – began as she meant to continue. Before she even reached Madrid she picked a quarrel with the Princesse des Ursins – who had travelled half-way across the country to meet her – on the stairs of a wayside inn and bundled her unceremoniously, alone and shivering, over the snowy Pyrenees and back to France. On arrival in the capital she immediately summoned her uncle's agent, a highly intelligent if unscrupulous churchman named Giulio Alberoni, the son of a gardener in Piacenza. From that day all French influence vanished from the Spanish court; it became Italian through and through, and Alberoni – whom just three years later she persuaded Pope Clement XI to appoint a cardinal – quietly set to work on the general reconstruction of Spain, with particular reference to the creation of a fleet.

Since Queen Maria Louisa had left three sons, Elizabeth could have little hope of the Spanish throne. Her long-term objective was therefore to ensure her succession after her uncle's death to Parma and Piacenza, and also perhaps to Tuscany by virtue of her descent from the Medici. Nor was she alone in desiring it. The Emperor Charles was still unhappy with the recent dispensations. He was particularly riled by the grant of Sicily to the house of Savoy, and was known to be in contact with Victor Amadeus with a view to exchanging it for the island of Sardinia. Elizabeth and Alberoni were equally determined that he should do nothing of the kind: Sicily, once it had become part of the Empire, would constitute a permanent threat to Spain's Mediterranean coast. They first moved, however, against imperial Sardinia. In August 1717 an expedition sailed from Barcelona to Cagliari, and by the end of November the island was theirs. Only then, emboldened by this easy success, did they decide to move directly on Sicily. On 1 July 1718 Spanish troops were landed near Palermo, where they received a warm welcome – giving strength to the Spanish argument that both islands, having been in the possession of Aragon since the thirteenth century and thus for more than a hundred years before that kingdom's union with Castile, were far more Spanish than much of Spain.

And so at that time they were; but the argument was unlikely to appeal to Charles VI, and Charles had just concluded what was rather misleadingly described as the Quadruple Alliance with Britain and France.[1] The Empire had no navy, but Britain did; and so it was that a British fleet under Admiral Sir George Byng hastened to Sicily, where it totally destroyed the Spanish fleet off Cape Passero, at the island's southeast corner. Unfortunately Britain was not at that time at war with Spain; she was acting only on behalf of her ally the Emperor. Byng's action thus created a tidal wave of violence, the effects of which were felt throughout Europe, as far away as the Sweden of Charles XII and the Russia of Peter the Great. Victor Amadeus, too, was loud in his protests, but he had to submit to the inevitable. The Kingdom of Sicily was taken from him and given to Charles; that of Sardinia was granted to him in its stead. Where Britain was concerned, Alberoni's rage was such that he launched a second Armada, a threat which in London was taken very seriously indeed. On 17 December 1718 Parliament declared war; less than a month later France followed suit.

The Armada, when it sailed in the summer of 1719, proved no more successful than its famous predecessor: it ran into storms in the Bay of Biscay and was wrecked off Finisterre, never even reaching English waters. A separate expedition headed for Scotland and actually landed a Spanish force in the Western Highlands – of which, however, the clans soon made short shrift. More serious for Spain, and a good deal more surprising, was the arrival of a French army under the Duke of Berwick. Philip V had difficulty in believing that his own country would take up arms against him, or that Berwick would march against his old friend, but he was soon disillusioned. There was nothing much he could do about it, since his army was away in Sicily. He had to watch, powerless, while Catalonia was invaded and Vigo occupied.

Alberoni, the ultimate author of all these misfortunes, could no longer hold out. In December 1719, the victim of a conspiracy led by his old patron the Duke of Parma, he was dismissed and banished from Spain. In foreign affairs he had been an adventurer and an intriguer, impatient and over-ambitious; domestically, on the other hand, he had

---

[1] Holland was technically a party to it, but in name only; the anti-war policy of the Dutch merchant class was too powerful.

shown himself a fine administrator, and although primarily a patriotic Italian he had worked hard and on the whole effectively for the benefit of his adopted country. After his departure there seemed no reason to continue hostilities, and Philip hoped for favourable terms. He was disappointed. Britain, France and the Empire refused absolutely to listen to him until Spain too had joined the Quadruple Alliance – which on 17 February 1720, with extreme reluctance, she did.

When all those international agreements collectively known as the Treaty of Utrecht were signed during the first four months of 1713, Venice had been in possession of the Peloponnese for just over a quarter of a century. Her new experiment in empire had not been a success. The years of Turkish occupation that had preceded her reconquest had reduced a once prosperous land to a place of poverty and desolation; all too soon she had realised that the task of administration would be expensive and largely thankless. The downtrodden local populations, their patriotism nurtured and sanctified as always by the Orthodox clergy, dreamed of a nationhood of their own and saw little advantage in having their infidel overlords replaced by Christian schismatics who showed no greater sympathy with their aspirations. Defence was another problem. In former days, when the Venetian presence had been confined to a few important commercial colonies and garrison towns, it had been manageable enough; but how could nearly 1,000 miles of serrated coastline be made safe from invaders? Even such new defences as were deemed indispensable, like the lowering fortress of Acrocorinth – still today one of the most impressive examples of Venetian military architecture in existence – served only to antagonise still further the local inhabitants, with whose taxes it was paid for and with whose conscript labour it was built. No wonder that when in 1715 Turkish troops appeared once again on the soil of the Peloponnese, they were welcomed as liberators.

Damad Ali, Grand Vizir to the Sultan Ahmet III, had planned a combined operation, in which a land force would march down through Thessaly while a fleet sailed simultanously southwest through the Aegean; in the course of the summer both prongs of the attack scored success after success. By the time the fleet reached its destination it had already forced the surrender of Tinos and of Aegina, while the army captured Corinth after a five-day siege. Nauplia followed, then Modone and Corone, Monemvasia (Malvasia) and the island of Cythera. Meanwhile, the Turks in Crete, encouraged by reports of their compatriots' success, had attacked and seized the last remaining Venetian outposts. By the end of 1715, with Crete and the Peloponnese both lost and all the great victories of Francesco Morosini set at naught, the Turks were once again at the gates of the Adriatic. For Venice only a single bulwark remained: Corfu.

The army that, early in 1716, the Grand Vizir flung against the citadel of Corfu consisted of 30,000 infantry and some 3,000 horse. For the Venetians, estimates differ. They were certainly outnumbered; but in siege warfare comparative strengths are less important than the sophistication of offensive and defensive techniques, and here Venice could count on the knowledge and skill of one of the leading soldiers of his day. Marshal Matthias Johann von der Schulenburg had fought under Marlborough at Oudenarde and Malplaquet, then after the peace had sought service with Venice. He had spent much of the winter improving the fortifications of Corfu, and though he could not prevent the Turkish army from disembarking, he was able to confront it with a defensive system far superior to anything it had previously encountered.

All through the heat of the summer the siege continued. Early in August, however, there arrived reports that gave new encouragement to the defenders and struck gloom into Turkish hearts. Venice had concluded an alliance with the Empire, which had entered the war. The almost legendary Prince Eugene was once again on the march. He had routed a Turkish army, appropriately enough at Karlowitz – the very town in which, eighteen years before, the Turks had signed that treaty which they had now so shamefully broken – and shortly afterwards had won a still more crushing victory at Peterwardein, where he had killed 20,000 of the enemy and seized 200 of their guns at the expense of fewer than 3,000 of his own men.

This unexpected necessity of fighting simultaneously on two fronts probably convinced the Turkish commander that if he could not take Corfu quickly he would be unlikely to take it at all. On the night of 18 August he ordered a general assault, to the usual accompaniment of an ear-splitting din of drums, trumpets, rifle and cannon fire and hideous shrieks and war-cries – psychological warfare of a primitive but by no means ineffectual kind. Schulenburg was instantly at his post, summoning every able-bodied Corfiot – women and children, the old and infirm, priests and monks alike – to the defences. After several hours the fighting was still desperate, and he decided to stake all on a sudden sortie. Shortly before dawn, at the head of 800 picked men, he slipped out of a small postern and fell on the Turkish flank from the rear. His success was immediate – and decisive. The Turks were taken by surprise and fled, leaving their rifles and ammunition behind them. Their bewildered colleagues along other sections of the wall saw that the assault had failed and also retired, though in better order. The next night, as if to consolidate the Venetian triumph, a storm broke – a storm of such violence that within hours the Turkish camp was a quagmire, the trenches turned to canals, the tents torn to ribbons or, with their guy-ropes snapped, lifted bodily into the air and carried off by the gale. Out in the roadstead many of the Turkish ships, similarly driven from their moorings, crashed into each other, splintering like matchwood.

When dawn broke and the full extent of the damage was revealed, few of the erstwhile besiegers wished to remain another moment on an island where the very gods seemed to be against them; indeed, within a matter of days the Turkish commander received orders to return at once. Corfu was saved; Schulenburg was awarded a jewelled sword, a life pension of 5,000 ducats, and the honour of a statue erected in his lifetime in the old fortress.[1] The Turks withdrew, never again to seek to enlarge their empire at the expense of Christian Europe.

The effect on Venetian morale was enormous. Early the following spring a new fleet of twenty-seven sail set out from Zante for the Dardanelles under the command of a brilliant young admiral, Ludovico Flangini. On 21 June 1717 it met the Turks head-on, and after a battle that lasted several days won a splendid victory, marred only by the death of Flangini who, mortally wounded by an arrow, insisted on being carried up to his quarterdeck to watch, through glazing eyes, the last stages of the conflict. A month later, off Cape Matapan, the Ottoman fleet was again beaten and put to flight. By then Prince Eugene had reoccupied the all-important river fortress of Belgrade, and the Turks were retreating on all fronts.

Had the war continued another season and the Venetians managed to sustain their momentum, the Peloponnese might have been theirs once more – though whether this would have been in their long-term interests is open to doubt. But the Turks decided to sue for peace, and it was now that Venice was to discover how ill-advised she had been to conclude her Austrian alliance. The Empire, faced with new threats

---

[1] It was transferred during the British occupation of the island to its present position on the Esplanade.

from Spain, was anxious to reach a quick settlement and paid little heed to Venetian territorial claims, on the entirely spurious grounds that the victory of Corfu and the subsequent upsurge of Venice's fortunes were the direct results of Prince Eugene's victory at Peterwardein. Thus, when the parties met in May 1718 at Passarowitz – together with representatives of England and Holland as mediators – the Venetian envoy, Carlo Ruzzini, found that he could make little impression on his colleagues. For six hours he pleaded, calling for the restitution to Venice of Soudha and Spinalonga, of Tinos, Cythera and the Peloponnese – or, in default of this last, an extension of Venetian territory in Albania as far south as Scutari and Dulcigno, a pirate stronghold that she was eager to eliminate. But his appeal coincided with the news that 18,000 Spanish troops had landed in Sardinia, and he was overruled.

The treaty was signed on 21 July 1718. Two months later to the day, in another of those terrifying Mediterranean summer storms, a bolt of lightning struck the powder magazine in the old fortress of Corfu. The explosion ignited three smaller ammunition stores, and the citadel was virtually destroyed. The governor's palace was reduced to rubble, killing the Captain-General and several of his staff. Nature, in a split second, had achieved more than the combined Turkish forces had in several months; the futility of the recent war was more than ever underlined.

At Passarowitz the frontiers of the Venetian Empire were drawn for the last time. There would be no more gains, or losses, or exchanges. In the Mediterranean, apart from the historic city and the towns and islands of the lagoon, the empire embraced Istria, Dalmatia and its dependent islands; then northern Albania, including Cattaro (Kotor), Butrinto, Parga, Preveza and Vonitsa; then the Ionian islands of Corfu, Paxos and Antipaxos, Leucas, Cephalonia, Ithaca and Zante; finally, to the south of the Peloponnese, the island of Cythera. That was all. The age of imperial greatness was past. Still, there were compensations. Morosini's conquests had given Venice nothing but trouble; she was better off without them. Passarowitz, inglorious as it may have appeared, settled her differences with the Turks and proclaimed eternal friendship with Habsburg Austria, the only other power which might have posed a serious political threat. The result was peace – peace which was to last the best part of a century, until the coming of Napoleon brought the Republic itself to an end.

*

When George I – having arrived somewhat reluctantly from Hanover – succeeded Queen Anne on the British throne in 1714, he expressed himself perfectly ready to return Gibraltar to Spain. So, somewhat more surprisingly, did Stanhope, the hero of Minorca, who now effectively held the rank of Foreign Secretary and who more than once gave it as his opinion that the Rock was more a liability than an advantage. When he suggested as much in Parliament, however, he was met by such a barrage of protest that he hastily withdrew, fearing a formal resolution which might make it even harder to dispose of. Then, in March 1721, a treaty of mutual defence was signed at Madrid between Spain and France in which the eleven-year-old Louis XV promised his enthusiastic support for the restoration of Gibraltar. Stanhope had died six weeks before, but his policy was pursued by his successors. King George actually wrote to Philip promising to restore it, in return for certain concessions, as soon as the consent of Parliament could be obtained – which was not, as it turned out, very soon; in June he even put his name to the treaty. Once again, in the great international game of musical chairs, the music had stopped: Britain, France, Spain and Prussia[1] were now aligned against the Emperor and the Tsar.

It soon started again. Queen Elizabeth Farnese was always an impossible bedfellow, and she had been far from pleased when young Louis XV had summarily dismissed the young Spanish Infanta whom he had been due to marry. In April 1725 representatives of Austria and Spain signed a treaty at Vienna. Now it was the Emperor who promised to use all his good offices to induce the British to surrender both Gibraltar and Minorca to Spain. But the British had hardened their hearts: Foreign Secretary Lord Townshend showed a very different attitude from that of his predecessor Stanhope. 'The Imperialists,' he wrote in June 1725,

> are thoroughly sensible of the great fondness the Parliament and even the whole nation have for Gibraltar; they likewise know that by our laws and Constitution the Crown cannot yield to any foreign power whatsoever any part of his dominions without the consent of Parliament, and that Gibraltar, being yielded to Great Britain by the Treaty of Utrecht, is as much annexed to the Crown as Ireland, or any part of England.

---

[1] Prussia had become a nation in 1701, when Frederick, son of the Elector of Brandenburg, had crowned himself king at Königsberg.

39. Sultan Mehmet II. Watercolour, Turkish, 15th century

40. Dante, *The Divine Comedy: Inferno*. Illustration to Canto xxxiii

41. Jacques de Molay, Grand Master of the Templars, burnt at the stake in 1314

42. The conquest of Constantinople, 1453. (To the left, Turkish ships being lowered into the Golden Horn.)

43. Rumeli Hisar: castle built by Mehmet II on the Bosphorus, 1452

44. Ferdinand of Aragon   45. Isabella of Castile

46. Francis I, King of France

47. The Emperor Charles V

48. 'The Captain General Francesco Morosini Pursues the Turkish Fleet, April 1659'

49. The siege of Rhodes, 1480: Turkish forces prepare for battle

50. The battle of Lepanto, 7 October 1571. Venetian, contemporary painting

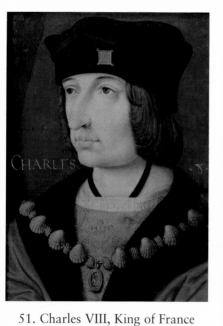

51. Charles VIII, King of France

52. Süleyman the Magnificent

53. Philip II, King of Spain

54. Francesco Morosini,
Doge of Venice

55. The execution of Admiral Byng, 14 March 1757

56. The battle of the Nile: destruction of *L'Orient*, 1 August 1798

57. Eruption of Vesuvius, 9 August 1779

58. Maria Carolina, Queen of Naples

59. The arrival of Napoleon on Elba, 4 May 1814

60. The battle of the Pyramids, 21 July 1798

Nor did he stop there. He devoted the next year to the formation of a great league of northern powers – it included Sweden, Denmark, and many of the small German principalities – and by 1727 Europe was an armed camp. Already in February of that year Spain declared war on England and laid siege – unsuccessfully – to Gibraltar, while Britain concentrated with rather better results on blocking the annual Spanish treasure fleet from the Americas. Neither party, however, showed much enthusiasm for the war, and hostilities were suspended early in 1728. The ensuing peace, a lady wrote to Lord Carlisle, was rather like the peace of God: it was long in coming and passed all understanding.

Now, yet again, Queen Elizabeth changed sides. On 9 November 1729 at Seville, the representatives of England, France and Spain signed a treaty in which Spain was induced to grant, perhaps for the first time, an ungrudging recognition of the full consequences of the Treaty of Utrecht, including the British occupation of Gibraltar. In return, England and France promised to facilitate the introduction of Spanish garrisons into Tuscany and Parma – which, two years later, they did. Elizabeth's uncle Antonio Farnese died suddenly in 1731, and her greatest ambition was realised in March 1732 when her son Don Carlos – with a mother like his, he was despite his name far more an Italian than a Spaniard – was formally installed as Duke of Parma and Grand Prince of Tuscany. That same year, infuriated by the increase of Mediterranean piracy, she sent a large expeditionary force to North Africa. Oran was taken, but soon afterwards the Spanish advance was checked and the commander killed in battle.

The Queen, however, was not discouraged; indeed, the success of her son in Italy had whetted her appetite for more. Skilful diplomacy with Louis XV now ensured France's agreement that Don Carlos should also claim Naples and Sicily, at the Emperor's expense. In the spring of 1734 he accordingly marched south through the Papal States and on 10 May made a triumphal entry into Naples; by the end of the autumn, despite some resistance from the citadels of Messina, Trapani and Syracuse, Sicily too had welcomed her new invaders. (Just four years later Austria was to be forced to make formal cession of the Two Sicilies, and Don Carlos could succeed to the Neapolitan throne as King Charles III.)

Elizabeth now turned her full attention back to Great Britain, the one enemy she detested more than any other. Of all the issues between the two countries, Gibraltar and Minorca inevitably remained by far the most important. They were not, however, the only bone of contention: there were other quarrels, on both sides of the Atlantic. In Spain,

English merchants and seamen were constantly harried by the Inquisition, and even by the ubiquitous press-gangs. English ships provisioning Gibraltar were also subjected to a good deal of interference. In the Americas, there were disputes over boundaries and frontiers, over rights to cut timber and several other issues besides, but the most important was the lucrative smuggling trade that was being shamelessly carried on by the British between Jamaica – in their hands since 1655 – and the Spanish colonies in the Caribbean.

Spain protected her interests as best she could with a fleet of coast guards, some of whom, it appeared, were less humane than others. In 1738 an English mariner named Robert Jenkins appeared before Parliament brandishing aloft his amputated ear, which he claimed had been cut from his head by one of these *guarda-costas*. It was, perhaps, only a minor atrocity, but the Whig opposition howled for blood and the whole country echoed with cries for revenge. The resultant War of Jenkins' Ear was declared in 1739.[1] Once again Gibraltar and Minorca were under threat; they were, however, well protected by the navy's Mediterranean fleet under its Commander-in-Chief, the happily-named Admiral Nicholas Haddock, who successfully blockaded both Cadiz and Barcelona and went on to capture two Spanish treasure ships, each reputed to be worth a million dollars. A war fought on so footling an issue should not have lasted long, but on 20 October 1740 the Emperor Charles VI died in Vienna at the age of fifty-five – and all Europe was once again plunged into confusion.

It must be accounted a misfortune for readers – and indeed for writers – of European history in the eighteenth century that the great struggle for the throne of Spain should have been followed after only twenty-seven years by another, this time for the throne of Austria. The War of the Austrian Succession had, however, less bearing on the Mediterranean, and will therefore take up a good deal less of our time.

The Austrian Empire, being not so much the successor to as the continuation of the Holy Roman, remained theoretically elective; during the three centuries of Habsburg rule, however, the duties of the electors had become more ceremonial than anything else and the throne

---

[1] London in particular was delighted with the declaration. Frederick Prince of Wales, roistering with his friends in the Rose Tavern, drank lustily to the confusion of the Papists, and the church bells rang from all the steeples. This was the occasion on which the Prime Minister, Sir Robert Walpole, was guilty of the lamentable pun by which he is chiefly remembered: 'They now ring the bells; soon they will be wringing their hands.'

was by now to all intents and purposes hereditary. Unfortunately, like their Spanish cousins, at this point in their history the Austrian Habsburgs suffered from an acute shortage of male heirs – to the point where, as early as 1703, Leopold I had specifically decreed that, in default of males, females should be allowed to succeed, the daughters of his elder son, Joseph, naturally enough taking precedence over those of his younger son, Charles. But, as we have seen, everything was changed by Joseph's sudden death in 1711 and Charles's succession the following year. By a secret family arrangement, known for some reason as the Pragmatic Sanction, Charles – now Charles VI – gave his own daughters priority over those of his brother, insisting at the same time that in future the Habsburg possessions in northern and central Europe should be indivisible.

When his one son predeceased him, Charles was the only male Habsburg alive; he was therefore determined to be succeeded on the Austrian throne by his daughter Maria Theresa. This, according to the Pragmatic Sanction, should have posed no problems, and indeed for the first few months after her father's death in 1740 all promised well. Charles had taken care to obtain solemn guarantees from all the principal European powers that they would respect his daughter's succession: the Papacy and the Republic of Venice, England and Holland all willingly recognised the twenty-three-year-old Queen,[1] France though noncommittal was friendly and reassuring, and the new King of Prussia, Frederick II – later to be known as 'the Great' – not only gave his recognition but even offered military assistance should she ever need it. He spoke, as it happened, with a forked tongue, but Maria Theresa was not to know it until, on 16 December 1740, a Prussian army of 30,000 invaded the imperial province of Silesia. The War of the Austrian Succession had begun.

It was to continue until 1748. Like its predecessor it was fought mainly in northern and central Europe – the Mediterranean was never at any stage a primary theatre. Indeed, to one of the two principal protagonists, Frederick of Prussia, it hardly figured at all. To two other rulers on the European stage, on the other hand, it mattered a great deal. Those rulers were Philip V of Spain and the King of Sardinia, Charles Emmanuel III. As we know, in 1718 Charles Emmanuel's father, Victor Amadeus II of Savoy, had been obliged to surrender Sicily

---

[1] She became Empress only in 1745. On the death of her father Charles VI the Empire had passed to her distant cousin from the Bavarian side of the family, who became Charles VII; only on his death was her husband Francis of Lorraine elected to the imperial throne.

to the Austrian Habsburgs, receiving in exchange the comparatively unimportant island of Sardinia; from 1720 – when he formally took possession of his new realm – until 1861, when his distant cousin Victor Emmanuel II became the first king of a united Italy, he and his successors were also known as Kings of Sardinia, although they continued to reign from their ancestral capital of Turin.

Charles Emmanuel was formidably intelligent, and ruled his subjects both wisely and well. As a European statesman, on the other hand, he would stop at nothing to extend his frontiers and increase his country's power: Sardinia – or Savoy – was not to be known as 'the Prussia of Italy' for nothing. Cardinal Fleury, the octogenarian Chief Minister of Louis XV, prophesied that one day a King of Sardinia would throw the Bourbons out of the whole peninsula, while that most shrewd of observers President Charles de Brosses[1] went still further. 'Of all the states of Italy,' he noted, 'the Italians fear only the King of Sardinia; he, they claim, is at their throats, and sooner or later he will throttle them.'

The body of Charles VI was scarcely cold before Elizabeth Farnese forced her ever-compliant husband to lay claim to all the Habsburg hereditary possessions. Their grounds were shaky, and she knew it. What she was really after, as always, was the Italian provinces, and she now had a new and valuable ally on the spot: her son Don Carlos, now King Charles III of Naples. Within weeks a Spanish army had crossed the Pyrenees and was advancing through the Languedoc and Provence; meanwhile, the Spanish Duke of Montemar sailed a further division to Orbetello (near the modern Porto Ercole), where it was joined by Neapolitan troops.

Almost simultaneously with the Spanish claim, Charles Emmanuel let it be known that the province of Milan was rightfully his – was not his great-great-grandmother the daughter of Philip II of Spain? – but as soon as he saw that Spain was also on the warpath with the same objective in view, he thought again and decided to throw in his lot with Maria Theresa. Henceforth Austria and Sardinia were pitted against the two Bourbon kingdoms of France and Spain. They had other allies too: in August 1742 a British naval squadron commanded by the sixty-six-year-old admiral Thomas Mathews appeared off Naples and threatened to bombard the city unless King Charles withdrew at once from the Bourbon coalition. The threat was gratifyingly effective;

---

[1] The Presidency of Charles de Brosses (1709–77) was only that of the *parlement* of Dijon; but he has somehow always managed to keep his title. President or not, he is a consistently interesting and amusing writer, whose views are always worthy of respect.

Mathews then turned against a squadron of French and Spanish ships, driving it back into Toulon and thus cutting off all naval communications between Italy and Spain. But the allies did not have it all their own way: that same month a Spanish army under Charles III's brother Don Philip invaded Savoy. Despite desperate resistance by the terrorised population, it was to remain there for the next six years.

The war might have gone on a good deal longer than it did but for the death, on 9 July 1746, of Philip V of Spain. Philip himself had been anything but bellicose, spending much of his time either at his devotions or listening to the music he loved. From the moment of their marriage, however, he had been utterly dominated by his wife, whose Italian ambitions had done much to exacerbate the current hostilities, and in his last years his increasingly frequent bouts of insanity had strengthened her hold on him still further. The new king, Ferdinand VI – the sole survivor of Philip's four children by his first wife, Maria Louisa of Savoy – had inherited all his father's indolence and readiness to be guided by his consort; on the other hand, his Portuguese queen, Maria Barbara of Braganza, possessed none of her predecessor's fire. For the moment, the war continued, but close ties had existed between Britain and Portugal since the days of John of Gaunt in the fourteenth century, and negotiations quietly began between the courts of Lisbon and London to bring about a peaceful settlement. One of Ferdinand's first actions on ascending the throne was to dismiss his Foreign Minister, the openly pro-French Marquis of Villarias, and to replace him with an Anglophile descendant of Gaunt's, Don José de Carvajal y Lancaster.

At last, thanks largely to the Queen and Carvajal, the Treaty of Aix-la-Chapelle was signed in 1748 and the war came to an end. The only true victor was Frederick of Prussia, who had started it in the first place. Charles Emmanuel kept Savoy and Nice, together with a strip of Lombardy which brought his eastern frontier to the river Ticino. Don Philip secured Parma and Piacenza. The Pragmatic Sanction was given renewed guarantees, and Maria Theresa's husband was duly recognised as the Emperor Francis I. True, Anglo-Spanish relations were now friendlier than they had been for half a century and more; to many people, nevertheless, the War of the Austrian Succession must have seemed to have been hardly worth the fighting.

As we know, the British had had their eye on the island of Minorca since the beginning of the century. They had successfully insisted upon it at Utrecht and had confidently believed that it would be a permanent addition to their empire. In fact, this first period of British rule was to last less than fifty years; on the outbreak of the Seven Years' War in 1756, one of the first actions of Louis XV was to despatch an expedition under the famously libertine Duc de Richelieu to capture the island. With his garrison of barely 3,000 men, the eighty-four-year-old Irish Lieutenant-Governor, William Blakeney, put up a splendid resistance, but he knew that without substantial reinforcements he could not hold out for long. Fortunately, such reinforcements were available: a squadron of ten ships of the line was lying at Gibraltar under the command of Admiral Sir John Byng, who had clear instructions that in the event of any attack on Minorca 'he was to use all possible means in his power for its relief'.

Although the Governor of Gibraltar had at the last moment refused to part with the battalion of infantry which he had been ordered to send – a decision which was subsequently to lead to his court-martial and disgrace – Byng sailed on 8 May and reached Port Mahon eleven days later. On the afternoon of the following day, 20 May, he bore down on the French fleet. In point of numbers the two were equal, but the French vessels were considerably larger, carrying heavier armament and more men. Such a superiority should not by itself have proved decisive, but Byng, almost at the start of the engagement, made a disastrous tactical error, leaving his line dangerously exposed to the enemy guns. The French took full advantage and left the British fleet effectively disabled. They made no attempt to follow up their victory; nevertheless, after holding a council of war, Byng decided to head back to Gibraltar, abandoning Minorca to its fate.

Still Blakeney refused to surrender, though his garrison in Fort St Philip was now under constant fire. By this time the besiegers too were beginning to suffer, both from dysentery – always a danger in siege conditions – and from the unremitting heat. They were well aware that another British fleet, greatly superior to Byng's, was on its way to the island under the command of Admiral Sir Edward Hawke, and Richelieu was anxious to conclude matters before its arrival. He accordingly ordered a night attack, and at a council of war held by Blakeney the morning after, 29 June, all its members but three agreed that – given reasonable terms – the only sensible course was surrender. Approaching Mahon a few days later, Hawke passed a French convoy carrying the surviving members of the garrison back to Gibraltar; only then did he realise that he was too late.

When the news reached London, there was a surge of enthusiasm for Blakeney – who, it was revealed, had never once removed his clothes during the seventy days of the siege. King George II appropriately made him a Knight of the Bath, honorary colonel of the Enniskillen Regiment and finally Lord Blakeney of Mount Blakeney in the peerage of Ireland. Admiral Byng was less lucky. On 27 January 1757 a court-martial at Portsmouth found him guilty of dereliction of duty and sentenced him to death. The court added a strong recommendation to mercy, on the grounds that it did not believe that the admiral's action was prompted by cowardice or disaffection, but the King refused to commute the sentence. On 14 March 1757 Byng was shot on the quarterdeck of HMS *Monarque* in Portsmouth harbour.

After Sicily, Sardinia and Cyprus, the island of Corsica is the fourth largest in the Mediterranean. Its early history was very much what might have been expected: after a fairly active prehistory, successive occupations by Greeks, Carthaginians, Etruscans, Romans, Vandals, Goths, Lombards and Arabs. In the eighth century, rather more surprisingly, it passed into the hands of the Papacy, who in 1077 entrusted it to the Bishop of Pisa. Under the Pisans, Corsica knew efficient and enlightened government for the first time. The island's economy developed, the arts began to flourish: those two magnificent flowers of early Romanesque, the cathedral of Nebbio and the church of La Canonica, date from the beginning of the twelfth century. Inevitably, however, such a pearl in Pisa's crown aroused the cupidity of her implacable rival, Genoa, and during the bitter struggles between the two sea republics throughout the later Middle Ages – in which they were sometimes joined by the Kingdom of Aragon – anarchy returned. Eventually, in the middle of the fifteenth century, Genoa established firm control over the island, which it was to maintain, with a few wobbles, for some three hundred years.

There then appeared on the Corsican scene the heroic figure of Pasquale Paoli. His father, Giaquinto, had led an uprising against Genoa in 1735, but after four years' fighting had been ultimately unsuccessful; he and Pasquale had been lucky to escape a worse fate than exile to Naples. There Pasquale had studied at the military academy, preparing himself to carry on the struggle for independence, and in 1755 he was ready. He returned to Corsica, overcame the Genoese – who, however, refused to renounce their claim – declared an independent state and was elected to power under a constitution as liberal and democratic as any in Europe. Over the next nine years he pacified the hitherto turbulent island. He encouraged industries, built a fleet and instituted a system of national education, complete with university. Throughout this period he kept up a defensive and initially inconclusive war against Genoa, but Genoa sought the assistance of France and, in 1768, sold to the French her rights. France strengthened the Corsican garrisons to six full regiments, and in 1769, after twelve months of guerrilla warfare, Paoli was obliged to flee to England.

On 15 August of that same year, a baby boy was born in a house on the Rue Saint-Charles in Ajaccio. His name – in the Italian which was then Corsica's national language – was Napoleone Buonaparte.

Almost exactly ten years before Napoleon's birth, in August 1759, the Spanish King Ferdinand VI died at the age of forty-six. His mental powers had never been strong, and the death of his beloved wife in the previous year had had a disastrous effect upon him. He had become more and more reclusive, refused to speak and eventually lapsed into complete insanity. Strangely enough, he had been a remarkably good king. With the help of Queen Barbara he had restored the national finances, built up a formidable fleet, enthusiastically encouraged the arts and sciences and clamped down on the Inquisition, putting an end to the public *autos-da-fé* that so shocked eighteenth-century Europe. Many a monarch has done worse.

His kingdom now passed to his half-brother Charles III of Naples, the Queen Dowager Elizabeth Farnese becoming regent pending Charles's arrival in Spain. The new king's eldest son being an imbecile, as part of this royal reshuffle Charles designated his second son – also called Charles – to be Prince of Asturias and heir to the Spanish throne, abdicating the crown of Naples and the Two Sicilies in favour of his third son Ferdinand, then a child of eight. These dispensations completed, he and his wife, Amalia of Saxony, set sail for Barcelona with their family. On 9 December they reached Madrid, where the King was reunited with his mother for the first time since his departure twenty-eight years before. The two embraced affectionately, but Charles soon made it clear that he was his own man and had no intention of allowing Elizabeth any influence in state affairs. She soon retired to her palace at San Ildefonso, and never – even after the death of Queen Amalia only three months later – returned to Madrid.

Although Charles may not have been exceptionally intelligent, he was industrious, conscientious, deeply pious and utterly honest, and could call on over a quarter of a century's experience as a ruler. At the same time he was a Bourbon through and through, and he had neither forgiven nor forgotten the British threat to bombard Naples seventeen years before. Now, with the Seven Years' War half-way through its course, he hated to see British arms almost everywhere triumphant over French. As a Spaniard, he was well aware of his country's continuing grievances against England over smuggling, contraband and the searching by the British of Spanish ships, to say nothing of various other disputes ranging from claims to the coast of Honduras to fishing rights off Newfoundland. When, therefore, the French Foreign Minister, the Duc de Choiseul, suggested to him that an English victory might prove calamitous to the Spanish dominions in the Americas, he found a ready listener.

The result was the signature, in August 1761, of two treaties together known as the Family Compact, whereby France agreed to make any conclusion of peace conditional on the settlement of Spanish grievances, while Spain undertook in return to enter the war at once if these terms were rejected. At this point – and before there was any question of peace between Britain and France – the British government demanded an explanation of Spain's obvious military preparations. Spain refused to reply, expelled the British ambassador Lord Bristol and imposed an embargo on all British shipping in Spanish ports. The Seven Years' War had now entered a new, Mediterranean phase. This proved, however, to be of remarkably short duration, and to have repercussions as far afield as the Caribbean and the Pacific. In August 1762 one British fleet captured Havana, and little more than a month later another one accepted the surrender of Manila. No wonder that by the year's end France and Spain were ready for peace.

The treaty that ended the Seven Years' War was signed in Paris on 20 February 1763. It contained only one clause of direct relevance to the Mediterranean: the restitution of Minorca to Britain. The Americas, on the other hand, were largely transformed. Britain acquired Canada, Nova Scotia, Cape Breton and a number of islands in the Caribbean from France, which also surrendered Senegal; in return France regained Martinique and Guadeloupe, and was guaranteed fishing rights off Newfoundland.[1] Her former settlements in India were also restored to her, with the proviso that they might not be fortified. Spain for her part

---

[1] Some of the islands in the Caribbean were to be again redistributed by the terms of the Peace of Versailles in 1783.

recovered Havana from Britain, but had to cede Florida in exchange; she also recovered Manila and the Philippines. Her most important new acquisition, however, was the formerly French territory of Louisiana. This was presumably some compensation for the loss of Florida, but to Charles III it must have been all too clear that he had made his first major mistake as King of Spain: to have listened to Choiseul. His predecessor's policy of strict neutrality had been the right one. The Seven Years' War would have been more wisely followed from the sidelines.

CHAPTER XX

The Siege of Gibraltar

On 4 July 1776, as all the world knows, the British colonies of North America declared their independence. The conflict that had begun as a dispute over British colonial affairs had developed in just two years into a crisis after which the world would never be the same. In March 1778 France joined the fray on America's side, Louis XVI – who had succeeded his grandfather four years before – doing everything he could to persuade Charles III of Spain to follow his example. Charles was initially doubtful. His last-minute participation in the Seven Years' War had proved catastrophic; more recently, an expedition against the Algerian pirates in 1774 had been less of a disaster than a disgrace. He desperately needed a few military successes. Moreover, he himself possessed vast colonies in the New World – did he really want to encourage revolution among them? Finally, he was angry with Louis. By the terms of the Family Compact the French King should have consulted him before entering into his American alliance; now he was calling on Spain to join him in the name of that very same pact. Charles therefore offered his services as mediator between the two sides. Britain, he proposed, should suspend hostilities for a year; during that time the American colonies were to be treated as independent and there would be a peace conference in Madrid, in which the American representatives would be on an equal footing with those of Britain. The price of this mediation would, it need hardly be said, be Gibraltar.

The British government, not altogether surprisingly, turned him down flat. His proposal, it declared, 'seemed to proceed on every principle which had been disclaimed, and to contain every term which had been rejected'. Faced with this, in June 1779 Charles too declared war. For the future of Britain's American colonies he cared not a jot, but Gibraltar and Minorca were prizes worth the winning. The question was, how could they best be won? He considered no less than sixty-nine separate suggestions. One of the first – and perhaps one of the best – was an invasion of England. He and the French together could easily have mustered both a fleet large enough to overwhelm the Royal Navy in the Channel and an army capable of dealing with the relatively few British forces who were not fighting in America. But the idea did not ultimately appeal: Charles preferred something more direct. He decided to put Gibraltar under siege.

That siege began on 11 July 1779, when the newly-arrived Spanish commander, Martín Alvarez de Sotomayor, fired a single shot from Fort St Barbara across the border. The British general Sir William Green replied – it was the first time that his guns had been fired in anger for over half a century – and kept up the barrage for some twenty-four hours. Over the next two months the besiegers dug themselves in, built gun emplacements and provided themselves with shelter for the coming winter, while their forces steadily gathered in strength: by the end of October they numbered well over 14,000. The British garrison, by contrast, amounted to some 4,000 officers and men, plus 1,300 Hanoverians; the Governor, General George Augustus Eliott, also had to reckon with some 1,500 soldiers' wives and children and a local population of another 2,000. Food, he saw, would be a serious problem. Since the Spanish blockade was not yet total, he encouraged all who felt like it to leave the Rock as soon as possible. A number of Jews and Genoese agreed to do so, and made their way in small boats to Portugal or the Barbary Coast; the remainder were obliged to stay until the arrival of a convoy from Britain – if one got through.

From the start, Green set a stern example to his men. To save food – and to augment its supply – he had one of his own horses shot. To calculate minimum food needs, he lived for a week on four ounces of rice a day. And he stood no nonsense: one of his officers, Captain John Spilsbury, wrote in his diary:

> October 3. It seems one 58th was overheard saying that if the Spaniards came, damn him that he would not join them: the Governor said he must be mad and ordered his head to be shaved, to be blistered, bled and sent to the Provost on bread and water, wear a tight waistcoat and be prayed for in church.

It was not until 16 January 1780 that the good news finally came. A fleet of twenty-one ships[1] under Admiral Sir George Rodney had attacked a squadron of ten Spanish vessels off Cape St Vincent, destroying two, taking four and putting the rest to flight. In a separate engagement he had also captured fifteen merchantmen. The blockade was broken; provisions and supplies were landed, together with 1,000

---

[1] One of the ships, the *Prince George*, numbered among its midshipmen Price William Henry, second son of George III and the future King William IV.

Highlanders; the wives and children of most of the rank and file were carried away to safety. There was only one cause for distress: the relief had brought no wine or rum. As the Governor pointed out, 'The want of strong liquor will perhaps be more severely felt by the Soldier than the curtailing of a small part of his provisions, and possibly might affect his health, from the alteration of a habit he is accustomed to.'

Meanwhile, the siege was by no means over. By early spring a savage epidemic of smallpox broke out on the Rock and was soon taking a heavy toll. The Spanish blockade was tightened again, and as the year dragged on provisions once more grew desperately short. The Spaniards meanwhile were quiescent, and the defenders had to contend with another serious threat to their morale: boredom.

The new year of 1781 began badly. On 11 January two Moorish galleys were seen approaching under a flag of truce. They carried the British consul in Tangier and his wife, together with about 130 British subjects, all expelled from Morocco after its Sultan had leased Tangier and Tetouan to Spain. This meant that no more supplies could be expected from Barbary, and that Eliott had another 130 mouths to feed. Yet somehow he managed to struggle on until at last, at daybreak on 12 April, Admiral George Darby brought his fleet into the Bay of Algeciras. At first it was obscured by a mist, but, wrote another eye-witness, Captain John Drinkwater:

> As the sun became more powerful the fog gradually rose, like the curtain of a vast theatre, discovering to the anxious garrison one of the most beautiful and pleasing scenes it is possible to conceive. The convoy, consisting of near a hundred vessels, were in a compact body, led by several men-of-war; their sails just enough filled for steerage, whilst the majority of the line-of-battle ships lay-to under the Barbara shore, having orders not to enter the bay lest the enemy should molest them with their fire-ships. The ecstasies of the inhabitants at this grand and exhilarating sight are not to be described. Their expressions of joy far exceeded their former exultations.

It was a quarter to eleven when the first vessel dropped anchor, and at that very moment the Spanish emplacements opened fire. Instantly, rejoicing changed to astonishment, astonishment to panic. The threat of bombardment had existed since the beginning of the siege, but for eighteen months there had been nothing but an occasional desultory shot, and the people had largely forgotten the danger. Now, suddenly, the horror was upon them – a hail of shells and cannonballs, spreading devastation and havoc through the little town. In the early afternoon it slackened, then stopped altogether – even with the future of Gibraltar at stake, the Spaniards were not going to forgo their siesta – but it started again at five o'clock that evening and continued throughout the night.

The next morning revealed a town in ruins – and also, through the crumbling walls of the houses, the storerooms of the traders, many of them bursting with secret provisions of every kind which they had deliberately withheld in order to dole them out item by item for exorbitant prices. Inevitably there was wholesale looting, particularly from the wine merchants. On Sunday morning, 15 April, Captain Spilsbury noted with distaste that 'such a scene of drunkenness, debauchery and destruction was hardly ever seen before.' In an attempt to restore order, a group of officers armed with axes made a round of the provision stores, staving in barrels until the streets ran with wine and brandy.

Through it all, the unloading went on at the rate of ten ships a day. Admiral Darby had orders to sail with the first favourable wind, and the victuallers had no wish to be left behind. It was soon discovered, however, that the government in England had forgotten to send one all-important commodity: gunpowder. Eliott had no alternative but to beg as much as possible from Admiral Darby, who was happy to oblige with 2,280 barrels. 'It is,' he wrote, 'the noble defence you are preparing to make which has induced me to stretch this supply to the utmost . . . Happy am I in doing everything in my power for the Service of the Garrison on which are fixed the Eyes of the whole World.'

On 20 April the Admiral was ready to sail. Whereas on the outward journey the vessels had been loaded to the gunwales with stores, the freight they carried on their return was largely human: most of the officers' wives and children, and virtually all the remaining Jews and Genoese, many of whom had paid dearly for their places on board. They probably amounted to half the total population of the Rock.

May 7th 1781.

My Lord,
   I must not conceal from you the scandalous irregularity of the British Regiments composing this Garrison ever since the Enemy opened his Batteries; except Rapes and Murders, there is no one crime but what they have been repeatedly guilty of and that in the most daring manner. . . Things are so bad that not a sentinel at his post but will connive at and assist in robbing even The King's Stores under his charge . . .

This letter, written by Eliott to Lord Amherst, Commander-in-Chief of the British armed forces, makes it all too clear that the town of Gibraltar, already largely destroyed, was now being systematically sacked by its supposed defenders. The Governor took firm measures against them: the artificers Samuel Whitaker and Simon Pratts were hanged on 30 May, and William Rolls of the 58th Regiment was given a thousand lashes, administered in public on the South Parade. Even without legal retribution, however, the looters were still risking their lives: the bombardment continued without remission. The several diaries and logbooks take a gruesome delight in describing the casualties: 'Two men killed one of which was in the office easing Nature when a Ball took off his head and left His Body, the only remains to finish Nature's cause.' Nor was all the damage done by the shore batteries; there were now quantities of small Spanish gunboats lying off the Rock and keeping up a constant barrage at anything that moved. They were particularly dangerous at night; Mrs Catherine Upton, wife of one of the ensigns, described how 'a woman, whose tent was a little below mine, was cut in two as she was drawing on her stockings.' 'These infernal spit-fires,' she added, 'can attack any quarter of the Garrison as they please.' On 23 May, her diary continued,

> at about one o'clock in the morning, our old disturbers the gun-boats began to fire upon us. I wrapped a blanket about myself and the children, and ran to the side of a rock . . . Mrs Tourale, a handsome and agreeable lady, was blown almost to atoms! Nothing was found of her but one arm. Her brother who sat by her, and his clerk, both shared the same fate.

The good news was that the besiegers had abandoned the blockade. It had not anyway been singularly successful, and now that it had failed to prevent the delivery of enough stores and provisions for the next two years there seemed little point in going on. Communications with the outside world were restored, and food and drink were once again plentiful, but the siege went on regardless.

The summer heat, too – the worst that Captain Spilsbury had experienced in his twelve years in Gibraltar – began to take its toll on both sides. By the end of July the Spaniards were firing only three shots a day, so regularly that the garrison began to refer to them as the Father, Son and Holy Ghost. (A major explosion in their powder magazine on 9 June may have been partly responsible.) Among the besieged, tempers grew short. On 22 July a major and the adjutant of the 72nd fought a duel with three pistols each; fortunately they missed with all six. A few days later the garrison watched tight-lipped while a Franco-Spanish invasion fleet sailed eastward through the straits bound for Minorca. There was no doubt that the island's Lieutenant-Governor, General James Murray, would need all the help he could get.

With the approach of autumn the atmosphere on the Rock, both physical and social, improved. In October, however, the defenders saw to their anxiety that the Spaniards were building two new parallel batteries along the isthmus, uncomfortably close to the boundary and protected by huge banks of sand which were virtually impenetrable by the British guns. It was plain that an all-out assault was intended.

And so, on 27 November at a quarter to three in the morning, over 2,000 men and 100 sailors – about a third of the whole garrison – led by a detachment of Hanoverian grenadiers, filed in silence out of the fortress, through the devastated town and out on to the isthmus. The Governor – he was to turn sixty-five on Christmas Day – was among them. His absence from the garrison was distinctly improper, but he had been unable to resist. There was some counter-fire, but surprisingly little; after a few token shots the Spaniards, taken entirely by surprise, fled before the invaders. One by one the Spanish emplacements were destroyed, their powder magazines ignited. By five o'clock all was over and the force returned, with eighteen prisoners, to the Rock. The operation had been a complete success. Equally important, perhaps, was the effect on the garrison's morale. The looting stopped as if by magic. The total casualties were five killed, twenty-five wounded; one of the Highlanders, it was reported, had lost his kilt.

While Gibraltar was holding its own, Minorca was fighting for its life. In early August 8,000 Spanish troops had landed on the island. They were commanded by the sexagenarian Duc de Crillon, who had joined the Spanish army when Spain entered the Seven Years' War. Against such a force Governor Murray's 2,700 men, many of whom were sick, could only retreat to Fort St Philip, where Crillon sent the Governor a message, asking him frankly how much he would charge for an immediate surrender. Murray rejected the offer with indignation, and the siege began.

Despite the arrival in September of 4,000 French troops to swell the Spanish ranks, Crillon at first made little progress. At the end of the year, however, scurvy appeared in the fortress, and within weeks created havoc among the British ranks. There was nowhere where fruit or vegetables could be grown, nor were there any friendly ports nearby from which they could possibly be infiltrated through the Spanish blockade. The only hope was a relief expedition from England, but none came. Within a month many of the men had to be carried to their posts; at a roll-call on 1 February 1782 only 760 of the 2,700 were able to answer, and three days later 100 of those were in the infirmary. On 5 February, after a heroic resistance of five and a half months, Murray surrendered. Minorca was Spanish again.[1]

The news did not reach Gibraltar until 1 March, when a Spanish officer appeared under a flag of truce with a detailed report. It was received philosophically, having long been expected, and seems to have had little long-term effect on morale. Winter had been grim enough – the Rock too had seen a serious outbreak of scurvy, and by 20 December over 600 men had been hospitalised – but early in February three vessels had arrived from Portugal loaded with oranges and lemons, and the beneficial effect had been immediate. The weather too was improving fast, and early in March HMS *Vernon* sailed in with two frigates and four transports carrying welcome reinforcements, including ten gunboats and a whole new regiment. Thanks to these, the garrison was able to face the coming year with confidence and hope.

What its members did not realise was that while they had been defending their Rock the outside world had changed. The American War of Independence was over; Europe, as well as America, wanted peace. Only Spain held out. Charles III had entered the war for one reason only: to recover Minorca and Gibraltar. Minorca was now his, but Gibraltar, for all its obvious proximity to his kingdom, seemed as far away as ever. In France, Louis XVI and his government cared little for Gibraltar; on the other hand, by the secret Convention of Aranjuez which they had been incautious enough to sign in 1779, they were bound to continue fighting until Spain had recovered it. With the greatest reluctance, therefore, they prepared to show her how the job should be done.

On 1 April 1782 a mysterious figure named Chicardo arrived in a small boat from Portugal with a report that the Spaniards had commandeered twelve ships at Cadiz, and that they were lining them with cork, oakum and old rope cables for use against Gibraltar. Ten

---

[1] Away in St Petersburg, Catherine the Great – advised by her counsellor-lover Prince Potemkin – is said to have suggested to George III that he might cede Minorca to Russia on condition that a Russian fleet went at once to its assistance: one of the many instances in history of Russia's longing for a presence in the Mediterranean.

THE SIEGE OF GIBRALTAR

days later came further confirmation: these ships were to be used as floating batteries under the direction of a celebrated French military engineer. They appeared in the harbour of Algeciras on 9 May: large Indiamen in such an advanced state of dilapidation that, as one observer reported, 'most people think they are more fit for fire-wood than attacking a fortress.' By this time the harbour and roadstead were filling fast, as more Spanish ships arrived almost daily. Spring turned to a sweltering summer, and the defenders had little to do but watch, and try to interpret, the frantic activity that continued in the Spanish lines. On 17 June they were horrified to witness the arrival of a fleet of sixty transports, escorted by three French frigates; here was the first detachment of Louis's army, estimated to be not less than 5,000 strong. Then, just five days later and quite without warning, the bombardment stopped. After well over a year of unremitting thunder, the sudden silence was distinctly unnerving. Only later was its significance understood: it signalled the succession of the Duc de Crillon, fresh from his triumph at Minorca, to the command of the combined armies of France and Spain.

On 14 July a Spanish deserter – presumably fleeing from justice – slipped through the lines and presented himself to the sentries. He too had much of interest to report. The floating batteries – there were now ten of them – were being roofed and would be ready by the end of August. The army before Gibraltar now consisted of thirty-seven battalions of Spanish and eight of French infantry, two battalions of Spanish and four companies of French artillery, and several companies of dragoons and cavalry: a total of some 28,000 men. The good news was that there was much discontent, and almost daily desertions. Ten days later, on the 25th, two ships arrived from Leghorn bringing a certain Signor Leonetti, a nephew of Pasquale Paoli, who had with him two Corsican officers, a chaplain and sixty-eight volunteers. They also brought the welcome news of Admiral Rodney's victory over the French in the West Indies at the Battle of the Saints. That same afternoon the Governor ordered a *feu de joie* to be fired by the heavy ordnance at one o'clock, and by the riflemen of the various regiments at six: 'Three cheers when the firing is finished, to begin on the right, and pass along in the same manner as the firing did.' The French and Spaniards, watching from below and confident that the Rock would soon be theirs, must have been confirmed in their long-held opinion that all the English were mad.

*

Great preparations are making in Spain to attack the Garrison; when at Algeciras we saw them hard at work at what you call Cork-ships; the sides of these ships are covered with large square green timber and junk, the whole to be about seven or eight feet thick; only one side is to be covered in this manner, the other to remain as before; the deck is to be made shot and shell proof, at least so they endeavoured to make us believe. These ships are ready to be ranged along the Front of the Garrison in order to make breaches in the Wall, when the Troops are to be landed in Boats building at Carthagena for that purpose. While at Seville we saw them shipping off brass guns.

So wrote a Mr Anderson from Tavira (on the south coast of Portugal, just across the border from Spain) on 1 June 1782. The monstrous constructions he describes were the brainchild of a French engineer, the Chevalier Jean-Claude-Eléonor Le Michaud d'Arçon. D'Arçon had apparently persuaded Charles III and the entire Spanish government that, being *incombustibles et insubmersibles*, they would render the garrison powerless and ensure its speedy surrender. One man only, as we now know, remained utterly unconvinced; he was, unfortunately, the designated Commander of the Franco-Spanish army, the recent hero of Minorca, the Duc de Crillon. He tells in his memoirs of two stormy interviews at Madrid in May, first with d'Arçon himself and then with the Spanish Minister of State, the Conde de Floridablanca. In the second he made his position clear and tendered his immediate resignation, but Floridablanca refused to hear of it, and finally persuaded him to continue only on the understanding that he would officially declare his disagreement and disapproval, and that if the plan failed this declaration should be made public.

In fact, Crillon went further still. Then and there he wrote a memorandum, which he deposited with a friend with instructions that it should be opened and published the moment the news reached the capital that the attack had begun:

> In leaving for Gibraltar I declare that I accept the command only in obedience to the King's orders . . . I have done my utmost to explain to His Majesty my opposition to the plan . . . and I declare that, just as – if the place is taken thanks to the success of the floating batteries, which I greatly doubt – all the glory and the credit will go to M. d'Arçon the French engineer, so – if the batteries fail – shall I incur no reproach, having taken no part in it . . .

The Duke left no less than twenty copies of the letter to be distributed in France and Spain. In the words of a recent historian of the siege,[1] 'never before or after did a general advancing to the attack cover his own retreat with such care, or reveal his own dishonesty and hypocrisy in accepting a command in which he had no faith.'

When Crillon arrived at San Roque – the small Spanish town across the frontier – and set up his headquarters just outside it, the force under his command had swelled to over 32,000 which, even allowing for deserters and sick, was at that time possibly the largest ever deployed against a single fortress. Its weakness was in its command structure. Crillon and d'Arçon made no secret of their mutual loathing, being united only in their cordial dislike of the much younger and insufferably bumptious admiral Don Buenventura de Moreno, who had commanded the Spanish navy at Port Mahon and was now boasting that once his fleet had taken up its positions Gibraltar would fall to him within twenty-four hours. At one point d'Arçon is said to have cried out in despair: '*Crise, contradiction, fâcherie et jalousie!*'[2] It seems to have been a pretty fair description.

Meanwhile, the defenders – some 7,000 of them, with another 400 in hospital – were waiting: waiting for the grand attack, which would plainly not be long in coming, and waiting too for the promised relief fleet, the arrival of which was beginning to seem a good deal less certain. In London, the government continued to prevaricate. Lord North's administration, after twelve disastrous years, had fallen in March; the new ministry of Lord Shelburne was paralysed by indecision. To the King's repeated urgings for immediate action, Shelburne could only reply – by this time it was the beginning of August –

> As to the relief of Gibraltar . . . this depends so much upon local as well as naval knowledge of the Bay and other circumstances, that I dare not offer to decide and I am apprehensive the Cabinet not being naval men will find a good deal of difficulty in doing so. It appears to me that a great deal should depend upon the experience and convictions of the officer who commands.

This continued dithering was the more surprising in that the siege of Gibraltar had caught the popular imagination of western Europe. The entire Bay of Algeciras formed a vast theatre from which the spectacle could be watched from a safe distance, and spectators were by now arriving from all over France and Spain to witness the coming drama. They included two French Princes of the Blood, the Comte d'Artois and

---

[1] Jack Russell, *Gibraltar Besieged*, from which much of the present account has been taken.
[2] 'Crisis, contradiction, quarrel, jealousy!'

the Comte de Bourbon, who had recently arrived at San Roque, and it was perhaps in their honour that the date for the grand attack had been set for St Louis's Day, 25 August. Somehow the information had filtered through to the Rock, and as dawn broke the garrison was standing to; but nothing happened. The floating batteries, it seemed, were not yet ready.

And so, on Sunday, 8 September, the garrison launched its own assault. Over the past few weeks the Spaniards had built a vast wall right across the isthmus, composed of some million and a half sandbags and sand-filled casks, and was now engaged in bringing up guns and mortars to fill the new emplacements. This work, however, was also unfinished, and the Lieutenant-Governor, General Robert Boyd, had conceived the idea of launching upon it a sustained barrage of red-hot shot and incendiary bombs. Technically, this was a difficult operation, seldom attempted in land warfare although it was quite popular at sea; the cannonballs took about three hours on a huge grill to heat to the required temperature, after which the process of loading them presented major problems. On the other hand, they were formidable in their effect, setting fire to wood the moment they touched it and inflicting hideous wounds on any man unfortunate enough to be in their path. Beginning soon after midnight, this barrage continued for nine relentless hours, with some 5,500 rounds fired at the rate of ten a minute; the flames ran along the Spanish lines like fuses along a trail of powder. The Spaniards, taken by surprise and at first unaware of the heat of the cannonballs, were slow to act, but once started they fought like tigers, tearing down the burning wood with their bare hands as the missiles continued to rain down around them. General Boyd, watching from the Grand Battery, could not withhold his admiration: 'braver men,' he wrote, 'were never seen.'

But personal courage could not conceal the disaster – or the humiliation. In order to save what face he could, Crillon ordered an immediate reply in kind: a sustained bombardment from five new batteries, to begin at daybreak the following morning. Almost as many shots were fired on the 9th as on the 8th – the official count registered 5,403 – but the balls were cold, and the Rock of Gibraltar was a very different proposition from the low, sandy isthmus. The bombardment continued throughout the following day, both from the shore batteries and from Admiral Moreno's ships, but little serious harm was done.

Then, at eight on the morning of the 12th, the lookouts reported the sails of a large fleet approaching from the west, and hearts rose: had relief from England come in the nick of time? It had not. The sails were those of an immense French and Spanish armament, including forty-seven ships of the line alone, flying the flags of no less than ten admirals. With its arrival, the defenders of the Rock found ranged against them an army of nearly 40,000, with some 200 pieces of heavy artillery. Their own relief fleet would now be useless even if it were to arrive; hopelessly outnumbered, it would have no hope of entering the harbour. Many of the defenders must by now have been feeling something very like despair.

They might have been rather more cheerful had they had any idea of the bickering and growing confusion in the enemy camp. Crillon was urging an immediate attack; his honour was at stake, autumn was approaching, the delays and postponements had gone on long enough. D'Arçon was protesting that his *flottantes* were not yet ready; no markers had been placed to guide them to their positions, no soundings had been taken of possible shoals or sandbanks, no anchors had been sunk to allow the vessels to be warped back if necessary. Caught between the two of them, Moreno felt frustrated and ignored, and sulked. It was, however, Crillon who prevailed. Shortly before seven on the morning of 13 September, the first three of the ten *flottantes* moved off to their allotted stations along the western shore. Moreno flew his flag on the twenty-four-gun *Pastora*. A furious d'Arçon, knowing that they were all headed straight for a sandbank, had been obliged to board the next largest, the twenty-three-gun *Talla Piedra*, commanded by Don Juan Mendoza, Prince of Nassau. The seven other captains, whether their vessels were ready or not, followed soon afterwards. Three hours later all ten were drawn up, broadside on, some 800 yards offshore, covering the thousand yards between the Old Mole in the north and the South Bastion. The battle began.

Late that night, Samuel Ancell, quartermaster of the 58th, wrote to his brother:

> Tired and fatigued I sit down to let you know that the battle is our own, and that we have set the enemy's ships on fire. When they came on at nine o'clock this morning, they proceeded successively to their different stations, and as they moored began to fire with the utmost vivacity; at the same time we began a discharge of cold shot upon them, but to our great astonishment we found they rebounded from their sides and roofs, even a thirteen inch shell would not penetrate one! however we were not much disheartened, although we had several killed, but with all possible speed we kindled fires in our furnaces, and put in our pills of thirty-two pound

weight to *roast*. If you could have peeped over the rock, and viewed our several employs, you could not have forbore smiling; some stationed to work the guns like Ethiopians black by rubbing their faces with their hands dirtied with powder – the sons of Vulcan were blowing and sweating, while others were allotted to carry the blazing balls, on an iron instrument made for that purpose, but as these did not afford a sufficient supply for the batteries, wheel-barrows were procured fill'd with sand, and half a dozen shot thrown into each. The fire was returned on our part without intermission, and equally maintained by the foe, but the continual discharge of red hot balls, kept up by us, was such as rendered all the precautions taken by the enemy in the construction of the *flotantees* [sic] of no effect, for the balls lodging in their sides, in length of time spread the fire throughout – This we found to be the case repeatedly during the day, though the foe frequently kept it under, but a continuance of the same inconvenience, rendered it impossible at last to work their guns. Just at the close of day-light, we observed one of the largest to be on fire in several places, and soon after another in the same condition. This gave the troops additional courage, and the fire was redoubled upon the remaining eight.

One o'clock in the morning. [14 September]

The floating batteries have ceased firing, and one of them has just broke out in flames, the hands on board them are throwing rockets as signals for assistance . . . A report is now received that an officer and eleven men were drove on shore, upon a piece of timber, being part of a floating castle that was sunk by a shell from the garrison, as she was steering to co-operate with the *flotantees*.

What had happened? First of all, as we have seen, there had been no firm leadership, only a trio of squabbling prima donnas. Second – and this was to some extent a consequence of the first – the *flottantes* had been abandoned by the combined fleet. They had never been intended to operate alone; the original plan had called for thirty gunboats and thirty mortar-boats to take up positions between them and on their flanks, from which to maintain a steady barrage against the shore batteries. Had they done so, they might well have affected the whole course of the battle. But of these boats there had been no sign. For reasons of his own the admiral, Don Luís de Cordoba, had refused to move. Third, the Chevalier d'Arçon had overestimated the strength of his creations. *Insubmersibles* they may have been; *incombustibles* they were not. The very thickness of their defences meant that a red-hot cannonball could penetrate deep into the cladding, there to smoulder undetected and eventually ignite the timber around it.

What was now to be done? For the Spanish the day had been a disaster, and that evening at Crillon's headquarters there was consternation. The first concern was for the *flottantes*, which still had some 5,000 men aboard. In two of them – including the *Talla Piedra*, the worst hit – there were quite serious fires, but their powder had been damped and they were unlikely to explode. On the other hand, their masts and rigging had been shot away and they were immobile. If somehow they could be towed to safety they might still be saved, but how could this be done? And did Crillon want it done anyway? He had always hated the things, and while they remained unburned and unsunk d'Arçon could claim a certain measure of success. There was also the possibility that the British would take them as prizes. Far better that they should be destroyed – but first they would have to be evacuated. At about ten thirty that night the general set off with the Prince of Nassau (who had abandoned the *Talla Piedra* immediately after the outbreak of fire) to ask de Cordoba to send his frigates to take off the crews. But the old admiral refused outright: he could not expose his ships to enemy fire for such a purpose. Only his small boats would be available.

The first of these reached the ten huge hulks around midnight, carrying orders to each of the ten captains to fire his vessel before abandoning it. There followed scenes of nightmare confusion. The exhausted men, who had kept their heads and fought bravely under heavy bombardment for over twelve hours, now panicked in their anxiety to escape. Some of the boats were so overloaded that they sank; others were destroyed by the shore batteries even before they could take on their complement. It soon became clear that those remaining possessed nowhere near the capacity required and would need to make two or more journeys to the shore, but by now the captains had obeyed their orders and all ten vessels were in flames. In each there were men who had failed to get away and had no choice but to leap over the side; it was better to drown than to burn.

At daybreak on Saturday 14 September, Mr Ancell continued his letter:

> Our bay appears a scene of horror and conflagration, the foe are bewailing their perilous situation, whilst our gun-boats are busily employed in saving the unhappy victims from surrounding flames and threatening death, although the enemy from their land batteries

inhumanly discharged their ordnance upon our tars to prevent their affording them relief. But never was bravery more conspicuous, for notwithstanding the eminent dangers which were to be apprehended from so daring an enterprize, yet our boats rowed along side of the floating batteries (though the flames rushed out of their port holes) and dragged the sufferers from their desperate state – the contempt paid by the *British* tars to the enemy's fire, of round and grape shot, and shells, will ever do honor to *Old England*.

Seven o'Clock

The enemy's ships are blowing up one after another half full of men, and our boats having staid as long as possible, they are now returning with a body of prisoners.

Ten o'Clock

The floating batteries have not all exploded – One of them has almost burnt to the water's edge, the crew having thrown the powder overboard. The enemy's land batteries maintain their cannonade upon the garrison, while on the opposite shore confusion and consternation visibly appears. The Nobles and Grandees who had assembled to view the capture of the place are withdrawing from the *Spanish* camp to carry the direful news to *Philip's* court . . .

It must be a galling vexation to our foes, to behold their Royal Standard displayed on our *South Parade* – where it is tyed to a gun and reversed.

The grand attack had failed – but the Rock was not yet out of danger. The combined fleet still lay out in the bay, and the armies of France and Spain were still encamped on the isthmus, where the bombardment had resumed as if nothing had happened. But there was now a degree of coming and going between the two sides under flags of truce, and on 6 October prisoners were exchanged. It was from one of these that the defenders learned that the relief fleet, under Admiral Lord Howe, was on its way at last.

Howe had a hard time bringing his ships into Gibraltar. The equinoctial gales were doing their worst and the fleet was blown right out into the Mediterranean, the enemy in hot pursuit; but somehow battle was avoided, and eventually every British vessel came safely into port. From that moment the French and Spanish forces began gradually to disappear. Sporadic firing continued, but no one's heart seemed really to be in it. Gibraltar, everyone knew, would not be taken by storm; if ever it were to be surrendered to Spain, it would be by peaceful agreement and not by force.

Preliminary negotiations began on 20 October. They were long and complicated, and continued until just before Christmas. In the early stages Britain showed herself perfectly prepared to give up Gibraltar – for the right price: she would naturally expect the return of Minorca and the two Floridas,[1] and several of the Caribbean islands as well. At the opening of Parliament on 5 December, however, Charles James Fox turned to the subject in the course of his reply to the King's Speech. 'Gibraltar,' he declared, 'has been of infinite use to this country by the diversion of so considerable a part of the force of our enemies which, employed elsewhere, might have greatly annoyed us.' The Parliamentary Report of his speech continues:

> The fortress of Gibraltar was to be ranked among the most important possessions of this country; it was that which gave us respect in the eyes of nations . . . Give up to Spain the fortress of Gibraltar, and the Mediterranean becomes to them a pool in which they can navigate at pleasure, and act without control or check. Deprive yourselves of this station, and the states of Europe that border on the Mediterranean will no longer look to you for the maintenance of the free navigation of that sea; and having it no longer in your power to be useful, you cannot expect alliances.

He was enthusiastically applauded, and it was largely thanks to his words that the government decided to hold on to the Rock at all costs. Instead, the Spaniards were offered Minorca and East and West Florida – which, with some reluctance, they accepted. King George III was unhappier still. At the conclusion of the talks on 19 December, he wrote to his Principal Secretary of State, Lord Grantham: 'I should have liked Minorca, and the two Floridas and Guadeloupe better than this proud fortress, in my opinion source of another War, or at least of a constant lurking enmity.' They were wise words; a few fertile islands would have been of infinitely more use to his kingdom than a barren rock. But it was not only Parliament that remained adamant; there can be little doubt that the British people felt the same way. They had just lost their American colonies; they had no intention of giving up their only foothold in Europe, the symbol not only of their naval supremacy in the Mediterranean but also – in the past four years – of endurance, fortitude and courage.

---

[1] East and West Florida extended well beyond the borders of the present state, comprising also parts of Alabama, Mississippi and Louisiana.

CHAPTER XXI

The Young Napoleon

Napoleon Bonaparte[1] was a Corsican, and thus a man of the Mediterranean. When he was born in 1769, Corsica had been French for only a few months; in its language – apart from a characteristic local accent – and culture it remained wholly Italian. His father, Carlo Maria, had been one of Pasquale Paoli's most trusted lieutenants, and the boy grew up a fervent Corsican patriot, detesting the French as oppressors of his island. The family was, by Corsican standards, well-to-do and highly educated: Carlo Maria had strong literary inclinations, though these had not stopped him taking to the hills with Paoli for the long guerrilla war against the French. It was only after their final victory that he accepted the inevitable. The Bonapartes were not noble – Corsican nobility was a contradiction in terms – but they were landowners with a few small and scattered agricultural estates, and somehow Carlo Maria managed to scrape together the four heraldic quarterings which enabled his son to qualify, at the age of nine, for a free primary education in a so-called military college – it was in fact run by a monastic order – at Brienne.

Despised by his fellows for what they considered his humble birth, Corsican origins and still heavily accented French, Napoleon not surprisingly became surly and withdrawn, given to occasional outbursts of violent temper. But he was a good scholar and a hard worker, and his brilliance in mathematics earned him in October 1784 a place at the national *Ecole Militaire* in Paris.[2] Even here he made no secret of his Corsican patriotism, lashing out with his fists or any weapon that came to hand against all who mocked him; but he worked harder than ever, and in September 1785, when still only sixteen, he passed out as an officer. He was sent first to the artillery training school at Valence, and then in 1788 to Auxonne in Burgundy; it was in Auxonne that he heard the news that was to transform his life. On 14 July 1789 the Bastille had fallen:

---

[1] He would sign his name Napoleone Buonaparte until 1796, when he translated it into French. It seems simpler however to stick to the French form for him and his family throughout this book.

[2] 'Commanding character, imperious and opinionated,' noted the examiner.

France was in revolution. A month later his regiment mutinied.

As an instinctive hater of the *ancien régime*, Napoleon flung himself with enthusiasm into the revolutionary cause. He considered going straight to Paris, but in view of the general chaos in the capital he decided instead to return temporarily to his home, where he was confident of his ability to shape events. His father had died, aged only thirty-eight, in 1784; back in Corsica, despite the presence of his elder brother Joseph, Napoleon now effectively made himself head of his family, advancing its interests in true Corsican style in any way he could. Before long his influence extended well beyond family limits. It was he who drafted, and was the first to sign, a letter to the National Assembly in Paris demanding that action be taken against the royalists who were still in charge of the island – a letter which seems to have been largely responsible for the Assembly's decision shortly afterwards to declare Corsica an integral part of the French state. He remained there throughout 1790, during which time republican-dominated munici-palities were elected in Ajaccio and the other principal towns, and when the Ajaccio Jacobin Club[1] was established in January 1791 he became a founder member. In October, after a flagrantly dishonest election, he acquired command of the local volunteer militia. Sadly, however, he and his family fell out with the returned Paoli who, while still striving for Corsican independence, was now *de facto* ruler of the island under the French and had no patience with the revolutionary adventurers which he now conceived the Bonapartes to be.

He was certainly right where Napoleon was concerned. Matters came to a head when the bumptious young officer proposed that his battalion of militia should replace the French garrison in the Ajaccio citadel. Paoli, outraged, refused to consider the idea, whereupon Napoleon launched an attack on the fortress on his own initiative. The fighting went on for three days, during which several men were killed; then French reinforcements arrived and the besiegers were forced to retire. A report was sent to the Ministry of War in Paris, where Napoleon had already been recorded as having seriously overstayed his leave. If he wished to continue his military career, he would have to return and explain himself. By the end of May 1792 he was back in Paris.

---

[1] The original Jacobin Club had been founded to protect the gains of the revolution against possible aristocratic reaction, but it soon became identified with extreme egalitarianism and violence, leading to the Revolutionary Government from mid-1793 to the fall of Robespierre in July 1794. By July 1790 there were 152 affiliate Jacobin Clubs all over France.

His reception at the Ministry was warmer than he might have expected. The authorities were inclined to accept the various specious documents which he had brought from Corsica to explain his long absence. They had little choice: France was now at war and needed every man she could get. Since the outbreak of the revolution vast numbers of royalist officers had left the army in disgust, and its present depleted strength – particularly in the cavalry and the artillery – was causing grave concern. Of the fifty-six officers of Napoleon's own class, only six now remained. He too had been given up for lost, and now that the prodigal son had returned the authorities had no intention of losing him again. The incident of the Ajaccio citadel was conveniently forgotten. He was restored to duty, and promoted to captain.

He made one more visit to Corsica – how he was permitted to take such a vast amount of leave has never been properly explained, especially since he had shown himself apt to exceed his allowance by several months – this time ostensibly to escort his sister Marianna back from the royal convent school at Saint-Cyr, which circumstances had forced to close down. They sailed from Marseille on 10 October. There was, predictably, no welcome from Paoli; ignoring him completely, Napoleon at once reinstated himself as lieutenant-colonel in the volunteers – a rank which he had had to renounce on his return to the army in Paris. He then flung himself into a campaign to get his brother Joseph elected as a Corsican representative to the National Convention.

But Corsica, he realised, was rapidly becoming a backwater. The revolution was no longer purely French: it was beginning to involve all Europe. In April 1792, despite the ruinous state of her finances, the depletion of her armed forces and the chaos still prevailing throughout the country, France had declared war on Austria. Two months later she had done the same to Prussia and to Sardinia. One reason for these displays of naked aggression was, paradoxically enough, economic: in their present state, the only way the French armies could support themselves was by commandeering food and all their other needs from countries they invaded. Inevitably, however, revolutionary idealism played its part: the theory that under the shock of war all the peoples of Europe would rise up against their sovereigns, and the spirit of the revolution would spread across the world. This, fortunately, failed to happen, but the initial success of the French armies certainly surpassed anything that could have been expected. An Austrian and Prussian invading army was turned back at Valmy in September; in October a French army swept through the Rhineland, and a month later another defeated the Austrians at Jemappes, occupied Brussels and part of the Netherlands, while a fourth annexed Savoy. In February 1793 the Convention declared war on England, and a month later on Spain. Meanwhile, on 21 January, King Louis XVI had been beheaded on the guillotine in the Place de la Concorde, before a cheering crowd.

In all this stirring international drama, Napoleon Bonaparte's first role was one of almost laughable insignificance. Pasquale Paoli had received instructions from Paris to support an invasion of Sardinia. He was loath to do anything of the kind. Sardinia was Corsica's neighbour and natural ally; her Piedmontese king had always been the friend of the Corsicans and of their cause, and had in the past often been generous with supplies and munitions. Still, orders were orders, and he gave his reluctant approval to an expedition by the Ajaccio battalion of the militia to seize and fortify the small island of La Maddelena, opposite Corsica off the north Sardinian coast; at the same time, however, he murmured to the expedition's leader, his nephew Colonel Colonna-Cesari, that it would be an excellent thing if the whole enterprise went up in smoke.

The Colonel took the hint. The battalion, hopelessly ill-equipped, sailed on 20 February, and by the 24th was strategically placed to take the island. Captain Bonaparte, it need hardly be said, was of the company. From the start he distinguished himself by his sheer professionalism – a quality in lamentably short supply among his fellows – and was confident that within a matter of hours La Maddelena would be theirs; but Cesari identified a few grumbling sailors as an incipient mutiny and ordered the expedition's immediate return to Corsica. Napoleon objected fiercely, but was overruled. As a final humiliation, he was obliged to spike two of his guns and consign them to the sea. He addressed a letter of furious protest to Paoli, sending copies to the War Minister in Paris as well as to the two Corsican representatives. Almost simultaneously Paoli was the subject of another attack, this time by Napoleon's brother Lucien Bonaparte, in a speech to the Jacobin Club at Toulon. Paoli, declared Lucien, was a traitor to France whose only object was to deliver Corsica to the British. His words made a deep impression on the Convention in Paris, who ordered the General's immediate arrest and sent three commissioners to investigate the charges.

The commissioners found the island openly hostile. Paoli somehow *was* Corsica, and his people were prepared to fight for him – against the Bonapartes, against the Convention, against anyone. To make matters worse, Lucien had stupidly sent his brother a letter, in which he had written: 'Paoli and Pozzo[1] are to be arrested; our fortune is made.' This letter was intercepted by Paoli's police before the commissioners arrived, as a result of which the Bonapartes were condemned to 'perpetual execration and infamy' – tantamount, in the Corsican code of honour, to a death sentence. To remain on the island was to risk assassination. Besides, Paoli had now begun an armed insurrection against the French, and the island was on the verge of civil war. For a moment Napoleon considered a republican counter-rising of his own, with the object of taking over Ajaccio and turning the tables on his enemies, but it was too late. Clearly, there was no longer a future for him in Corsica. By the middle of June he and his whole family were on their way to France.

On his arrival Napoleon rejoined the army and, finding himself in Nice at the beginning of September, made contact with his old friend and fellow Corsican Jean-Christophe Saliceti. Saliceti was one of the two 'representatives of the people' with the revolution's Army of Italy; it was at that time besieging Toulon, which had been occupied a week or two before by royalist, British and Spanish forces. It chanced that some days previously the French artillery commander had been badly wounded; a replacement was urgently needed, and Saliceti saw that Captain Bonaparte was just the man. Napoleon asked nothing better. From one moment to the next, his Corsican patriotism was forgotten. Henceforth he was a Frenchman – a Frenchman, indeed, such as there had never been before.

The state of the army which he found drawn up before Toulon was enough to make any trained officer weep. Most of the old royalists had emigrated, to be replaced by republican volunteers with virtually no experience; the artillery consisted of a few broken-down old cannon and mortars, all of which were dangerously short of ammunition. On the credit side there was only Napoleon himself, one of the few officers in the whole Army of Italy who was a professional through and through. True, he was only a captain, but he had the powerful support of Saliceti, and his genius did the rest. One of his first actions was to send for more heavy guns from Nice and Marseille (which also

---

[1] Pozzo di Borgo, colleague of Paoli and mortal enemy of the Bonapartes.

provided 5,000 sandbags); others he requisitioned from the forts at Martigues, Antibes and Monaco. Wood was ordered from Le Ciotat for the construction of proper platforms; at Ollioules he created a veritable arsenal and repair centre with eighty blacksmiths, wheelwrights and carpenters. From the outset, however, he found himself at loggerheads with his commander, the politically irreproachable but militarily idiotic General Carteaux, whose only idea was to pour as much shot as possible into the town. Napoleon, on the other hand, seeing at once that the key to its continued resistance was the British fleet under Admiral Lord Hood which lay just off the coast, pressed insistently for the capture of the little peninsula of Le Caire, from which red-hot cannonballs could be fired into Hood's ships. Finally, with the help of Saliceti, he obliged a grudging Carteaux to give his permission.

The first attempt on Le Caire failed, as Carteaux – furious at having been overruled – had released only 400 men for the task. Thanks largely to the influence of the newly promoted Major Bonaparte, the hopeless old general was dismissed in October; his successor, General Jacques-François Dugommier, who had joined the army at thirteen and was another thoroughgoing professional, immediately recognised his subordinate's genius and backed him to the hilt. The result was a full-scale assault on Fort Mulgrave, recently constructed by the British on the highest point of Le Caire. It took place on 17 December, in pouring rain, but was ultimately successful; in the early hours of the following morning the British garrison evacuated the fort, while Hood's ships hastily weighed anchor and made for the open sea. On the following day, 19 December 1793, Toulon was French again.

There was no doubt in anyone's mind to whom the credit belonged. Napoleon Bonaparte – who had had his horse shot under him and had been wounded by a bayonet in the thigh – had been proved right. Dugommier had already sent urgent – and prophetic – advice to the War Minister in Paris: '*Récompensez, avancez ce jeune homme; car, si l'on était ingrat envers lui, il s'avancerait de lui-même.*'[1] Three days after the recovery of Toulon he was appointed brigadier. He was just twenty-four years old.

The long-delayed Corsican expedition took place in March 1795. It proved a fiasco: the British fleet was standing off the island in force, and

---

[1] 'Reward this young man, and promote him; for if his services are not recognised, he will promote himself.'

took so severe a toll of the French transports that they were unable to land. Once again, for a moment, Bonaparte's luck seemed to have deserted him. He returned to Paris, officially on sick leave, and awaited his next opportunity. It came on 5 October – 13 *vendémiaire*, in the new republican calendar – when he was ordered by Paul Barras, the Commander-in-Chief of the Army of the Interior, to put down a threatened royalist rising. With the memory of Corsican insurrections behind him, he did not hesitate. There would be no negotiation; he preferred to put his faith in heavy artillery. Fierce fighting broke out at the Tuileries, with heavy casualties on both sides, but the final issue was never in doubt. When the Directory was established just a week or two later, Barras was nominated the first of its five members and Bonaparte appointed second-in-command of the Army of the Interior. In March 1796, when the Directory resolved to launch a new campaign against Austria through Italy, the slim, solemn young Corsican, bilingual in Italian, seemed the obvious choice to lead it.

Shortly before his departure, in a civil ceremony held on 8 March 1796, Napoleon Bonaparte married one of the many 'widows of the guillotine': Josephine de Beauharnais, a cast-off mistress of his friend Barras. (Both lied about their ages, the twenty-six-year-old groom actually producing the birth certificate of his elder brother, Joseph.) Two days later he bid his bride farewell and headed south to Nice, there to take up his new command. This was to be the beginning of his first prolonged campaign, which was also to prove one of his greatest. Its intention was to mop up northern Italy, then to advance through the Tyrol into Austria and finally to meet up with the Army of the Rhine, carrying the war into Bavaria. It started with an advance into Piedmont. Nobody – except possibly Bonaparte himself – could have foreseen the measure and speed of his success: almost every day brought news of another victory. Towards the end of April Piedmont was annexed to France, King Charles Emmanuel IV abdicating and retiring to Sardinia, which remained under his authority. On 8 May the French crossed the Po, and two days later forced the narrow bridge over the Adda at Lodi. On the 15th Bonaparte made his formal entry into Milan.

His army was of course living off the conquered land, requisitioning food and accommodation as necessary, but for the members of the Directory this was not enough. Their instructions were to levy huge contributions both from the Italian states and from the Church, not just to support the troops but to send back to Paris, and Napoleon obeyed them to the letter. The neutral Duke of Parma, to take but one example, was obliged to hand over two million French *livres* and twenty of his best pictures, to be chosen personally by the Commander-in-Chief; few of the major towns escaped having to give up their Raphaels, their Titians and their Leonardos. Many of these found their way to the Louvre or to other French museums, where they still hang today.

With the occupation of Milan all Lombardy was now in French hands, save only Mantua. But the Austrians fought back, with such determination that by 13 November we find Bonaparte confessing to the Directory, in a mixture of exhaustion and despair, his fears that all Italy might soon be lost. Only in early 1797 did his spirits begin to recover. On 14 January he engaged the Austrians at Rivoli, a village some fourteen miles north of Verona between the Adige river and Lake Garda. He lost 2,200 men in the action, but his army inflicted 3,300 casualties on the enemy and took 7,000 prisoners. The following day his general Joubert, pursuing the fleeing Austrians, captured another 6,000; meanwhile, Joubert's colleague André Masséna, having marched southward all night, surrounded and captured a second Austrian column now isolated outside Mantua. From that day Mantua was cut off, without hope of relief. On 2 February its starving garrison surrendered. Another 16,000 men and 1,500 guns were taken.

At last the way was clear for the invasion of Austria. True, it lay across the neutral territory of Venice, but that could not be helped. Such considerations were certainly not heeded by the Austrians, who were regularly crossing Venetian lands without let or hindrance. But if Venice did not protest – and her imperial sympathies were well known – Napoleon certainly did, taking every opportunity to browbeat and even threaten the local Venetian authorities. What they did not know was that his anger on these occasions was nothing but a simulated display, and that most of his threats were empty. His real purpose in his dealings with Venice at this time was not to enlist her aid or even to persuade her to take a more firmly neutral line; rather it was to frighten her, to put her in the wrong, to make her feel guilty and inadequate, to erode her pride, confidence and self-respect to the point where her moral resistance would be reduced to the same level as her physical.

Towards the end of March 1797 Napoleon led his army north over the Brixen Pass and into the Tyrol. There he took the road to Vienna, leaving behind him only a few light garrisons in Bergamo and Brescia, with a rather more considerable force in Verona. He seems, however, to have had a secret purpose in mind: to stir up, throughout the Veneto, a revolutionary mood and to promote, wherever possible, open risings against Venice. The danger was, of course, that such risings might back-fire against the French themselves – which indeed they did. On Easter Monday, 17 April, despite the strength of the garrison, the people of Verona came out in open insurrection and, in what came to be known as the *pâques véronaises* – the Veronese Easter – massacred a consider-able number of Frenchmen, both soldiers and civilians. Similar though less serious outbreaks took place in Bergamo and Brescia, though these were principally directed against Venice. If, as is generally believed, all this was the work of French *agents provocateurs*, Napoleon would certainly have deemed the losses well worth while; they would have provided him with a further excuse for attacking the Venetian Republic, which he was by now determined to eradicate once and for all.

When the news of these risings, and of many others which followed them, reached Venice, it caused something akin to panic. All the *terra firma* west of the Mincio river was effectively lost. The new frontier must be defended at any price; armed militias raised among the local peasantry were the only hope. The local French commander, General Balland, was informed of Venice's intentions, it being emphasised to him that the measures proposed were to be purely defensive, directed not against the French but against rebellious citizens of the Republic. What nobody seems to have foreseen was that these peasants – there were probably at least 10,000 of them – finding themselves for the first time with weapons in their hands, might not be over-conscientious in the manner of using them. They had no quarrel with the Italian rebels; they did, on the other hand, have plenty of outstanding scores to settle with the French, whose foraging parties regularly made free with their crops, their livestock and, as often as not, their wives and daughters into the bargain. It was not long before the serious sniping began. Balland's reprisals were swift and savage, but they had no effect. By early April every pretence of civility between French and Italians was gone.

Napoleon, on the road to Vienna, had been kept fully informed of the worsening situation. Already on 10 April he had dictated an ultimatum to the Doge, to be delivered in person by his aide-de-camp General Andoche Junot. Junot arrived in Venice on the evening of Good Friday, the 14th, and demanded an audience with the Doge early the following morning. The reply was polite but firm. Holy Saturday was a day traditionally set aside for religious observances, and neither then nor on Easter Sunday itself could any government business be transacted. The Doge and his full

Collegio[1] would however be happy to receive the General early on Monday morning. But Junot was not interested in religious observances and said so. His orders were to see the Doge within twenty-four hours, and he intended to obey them. If he were not accorded an audience within that time, he would leave and Venice would have to take the consequences. They would not, he suggested, be pleasant.

Thus, when the Collegio reluctantly received him early on the Saturday morning, its dignity was already bruised. Ignoring the seat to which he was shown, on the Doge's right hand, the General remained standing; then, without preliminary, he pulled Bonaparte's letter from his pocket and began to read:

Judenberg, 20 Germinal, year V

All the mainland of the Most Serene Republic is in arms. On every side, the rallying-cry of the peasants whom you have armed is 'Death to the French!' They have already claimed as their victims several hundred soldiers of the Army of Italy. In vain do you try to shuffle off responsibility for the militias that you have brought into being. Do you think that just because I am in the heart of Germany I am powerless to ensure respect for the foremost people of the universe? Do you expect the legions of Italy to tolerate the massacres that you have stirred up? The blood of my brothers-in-arms shall be avenged, and there is not one French battalion that, if charged with such a duty, would not feel the doubling of its courage, the trebling of its powers.

The Venetian Senate has answered the generosity we have always shown with the blackest perfidy . . . Is it to be war, or peace? If you do not take immediate measures to disperse these militias, if you do not arrest and deliver up to me those responsible for the recent murders, war is declared.

The Turk is not at your gates. No enemy threatens you. You have deliberately fabricated pretexts in order to pretend to justify a rally of the people against my army. It shall be dissolved within twenty-four hours.

We are no longer in the reign of Charles VIII. If, against the clearly stated wishes of the French government, you impel me to wage war, do not think that the French soldiers will follow the example of your own militias, ravaging the countryside of the innocent and unfortunate inhabitants of the terra firma. I shall protect those people, and the day will come when they shall bless the crimes that obliged the army of France to deliver them from your tyranny.

BONAPARTE

---

[1] Roughly comparable to a modern Cabinet, it was composed of thirteen members including the Doge himself. It functioned as the executive arm of the government. The chairman – a post which rotated weekly – was thus effectively Prime Minister of the Republic.

In the shocked silence that followed, Junot flung the letter on the table in front of him, turned on his heel and strode from the room.

Napoleon, meanwhile, continued his march. His manner with his men was, as always, cheerful and confident; in his heart, however, there must have been a growing anxiety – on two counts. The first was strategic. His army was now poorly supplied, dangerously strung out in narrow mountain valleys where there was little hope of forage – let alone pillage – with a hostile population around it and a formidable Austrian army awaiting it in front. The second, to him, was more serious still. His army formed only one prong of the French attack. There was also the Army of the Rhine, commanded by his brilliant young contemporary and chief rival Lazare Hoche, which was now advancing eastwards through Germany at terrifying speed and threatening to reach Vienna before him. This was a possibility that he refused to contemplate. He, and no one else, must be the conqueror of the Habsburg Empire; his whole future career depended on it. He could not allow Hoche to steal his triumph.

He was wrestling with these two problems when suddenly – and to him almost miraculously – the imperial government panicked and sued for an armistice. It must have been difficult to conceal his delight: his signature on such a document would stop Hoche in his tracks. Thus it came about that on 18 April 1797, at the castle of Eckenwald just outside Leoben, a provisional peace was signed between Napoleon Bonaparte, acting in the name of the French Directory – although in fact he had never bothered to consult it – and the Austrian Empire. By its terms (details of which remained secret until they were confirmed six months later at Campo Formio) Austria was to renounce all claims to Belgium and to Lombardy, in return for which she would receive Istria, Dalmatia and all the Venetian terra firma bounded by the Oglio, the Po and the Adriatic. Venice was to be compensated – most inadequately – by the formerly papal territories of Romagna, Ferrara and Bologna.

Bonaparte, it need hardly be said, had no conceivable right to dispose in such a way of the territory of a neutral state. He would probably have argued that Venice was a neutral state no longer; still, there was no escaping the fact that the laws of international diplomacy did not look kindly on arbitrary settlements of this kind. However hollow Venice's professed neutrality might be, she would still have to be shaken out of it, and if, during the process, she could be made to appear in an unfavourable or even aggressive light, so much the better. Now, thanks to the complete demoralisation of her government, she offered Bonaparte a perfect opportunity.

We can have nothing but sympathy for Francesco Donà and Lunardo Giustinian, the two Venetian envoys sent off to Bonaparte with the reply to his letter and instructions to placate him as best they could. Even the physical aspect of their task was disagreeable enough. Napoleon was famous for the speed at which he travelled, and for two middle-aged Venetians those gruelling days and nights spent trying to catch up with him, the endless jolting over some of the worst mountain roads in Europe only occasionally interrupted by a few hours' rest snatched at some verminous and foul-smelling inn, must have been a nightmare. Nor can their spirits have been improved by the prospect of the stormy scenes that they knew lay ahead of them when they finally ran their quarry to earth. And even that was not all: in every town and village at which they stopped, the same rumours besieged their ears. France had made peace with Austria, and on the altar of that peace Venice was to be sacrificed.

The pursuit lasted over a week; it was not until 21 April, at Graz, that the two exhausted deputies finally drew up before the French camp. Bonaparte received them courteously enough, and listened in silence to their protestations of friendship. Then, suddenly, his mood changed. Striding back and forth across the room, he launched into a searing diatribe against Venice, her government and her people, accusing them of perfidy, hypocrisy, incompetence, injustice, 'medieval barbarities' and – most serious of all in his eyes – hostility to himself and to France. He demanded the immediate release of all political prisoners – threatening, if this were not done, to break open the prisons himself. What, he continued, of all the Frenchmen whom the Venetians had murdered? His soldiers were determined to have their revenge, and he would not deny it to them. Any government unable to restrain its own subjects was an imbecile government and had no right to survive. He ended with those terrible words that were soon to echo in the heart of every Venetian: *'Io sarò un Attila per lo stato veneto'* – 'I shall be an Attila to the state of Venice.'

When the two envoys returned to Venice with their report, Doge Lodovico Manin and his colleagues saw that the Republic was doomed. War was imminent; further negotiation was impossible; the *terra firma* was as good as lost. The only hope of saving the city itself from destruction lay in capitulation to the conqueror's demands, and these demands were terrible indeed: nothing less than the abdication of the entire government and the abandonment of a constitution that had lasted more than a thousand years – the suicide, in fact, of the state.

On Friday, 12 May 1797, the Great Council of Venice met for the last time. Many of its members having already fled the city, it fell short – by sixty-three – of its constitutional quorum of 600, but the time for such niceties was past. The Doge was just completing his opening speech when the sound of firing was heard outside the palace. At once, all was in confusion. To those present, such sounds could mean one thing only: the popular uprising that they had so long dreaded had begun. Their only hope of survival was to escape from the palace while there was still time. Within minutes, the true source of the firing had been established: some of the Dalmatian troops, who were being removed from Venice on Bonaparte's orders, had symbolically discharged their muskets into the air as a parting salute to the city. But the panic had begun; reassurances were useless. Leaving their all-too-distinctive robes of office behind them, the remaining legislators of the Venetian Republic slipped discreetly out of the palace by the side entrances. The Serenissima was no more.

Lodovico Manin himself made no attempt to flee. In the sudden stillness that followed the break-up of the meeting, he slowly gathered up his papers and withdrew to his private apartments. There he removed his *corno* – that curiously shaped cap which was the principal symbol of his office – and handed it to his valet. 'Take this,' he said, 'I shall not be needing it again.'

From the inauguration of the first Doge in 726 to the resignation of the last in 1797, the Venetian Republic had lasted 1,071 years – only half a century less than the Empire of Byzantium. For much of that time Venice had been the acknowledged mistress of the Mediterranean – politically, constitutionally, commercially, artistically and architecturally a wonder of the world. How pleasant it would be to record a less ignominious end, with her people showing, as their Republic began to totter, some spark of that endurance and courage that they had shown often enough in defending their colonies against the Turks – or that their own grandchildren were to show against the Austrians half a century later. One would not have asked for – and certainly not have expected – a heroic resistance such as had been seen on the walls of Constantinople in 1453: merely a flash of the old Venetian spirit, which would have allowed the Serenissima to pass into history with some semblance of honour. But even that was lacking. The last tragedy of Venice was not her death; it was the manner in which she died.

Thus it was that when the Treaty of Campo Formio was signed on 17 October, Austria received even more than she had expected at Leoben: not just the Venetian *terra firma*, but the city itself. Napoleon Bonaparte, however, was well pleased. He had always believed – probably rightly – that he could master Italy so long as it remained divided. Already in December 1796 he had formed his Cispadane Republic[1] out of the merger of the duchies of Reggio and Modena and the papal states of Bologna and Ferrara. The following June he had established his Ligurian Republic with its capital in Genoa, and in July his Cisalpine Republic based on Milan. As for Venice, he himself had never set foot there and had no desire to; he saw it – quite erroneously – in his mind's eye as a brutally repressive police state, its dungeons bursting with political prisoners. Meanwhile, there was peace all over continental Europe. Only England remained an enemy. It was England, now, that must be invaded and destroyed. The Directory agreed, appointing Bonaparte Commander-in-Chief of the Army of England, but after the best part of a year's consideration he reluctantly decided against the project. The expense would be too great, the necessary manpower unavailable; above all, the French navy was in a deplorable state, no match for the British and with no commander who could hold a candle to Hood, Rodney or St Vincent – still less to Nelson.

The alternative was Egypt. As early as July 1797 the Foreign Minister, Charles-Maurice de Talleyrand-Périgord,[2] had proposed an Egyptian expedition, and seven months later had produced a long memorandum on the subject. Inevitably this contained a section deploring the cruelty of the local beys and pressing the necessity of delivering the Egyptian people from the oppression that it had so long endured; more worthy of attention was the suggestion that with an army of 20–25,000, which would land at Alexandria and occupy Cairo, a further expedition could be launched against India – possibly through a hastily dug Suez Canal. On 2 March 1798 the Directory gave its formal approval. Not only would the proposal keep the army employed and their terrifying young general at a safe distance from Paris; it also offered an opportunity to take over the British role in

---

[1] The sole distinction of this otherwise footling state was to have chosen for its standard the red, white and green tricolour. It is curious indeed that one of the earliest manifestations of French conquest should have given rise to the Italian national flag.

[2] Talleyrand had dissociated himself from the revolution after the execution of the royal family in 1793 and gone into voluntary exile in America. He had returned in 1795 after the fall of the Jacobins and became Foreign Minister in 1797.

India, while providing France with an important new colony in the eastern Mediterranean. Finally, if a little more problematically, it would achieve a major diversion of English sea power to the east, which might make the delayed invasion possible after all.

Napoleon, it need hardly be said, accepted the command with enthusiasm. Since his childhood he had been fascinated by the Orient, and he was determined that the expedition should have objectives other than the purely political and military. To this end he recruited no less than 167 *savants* to accompany it, including scientists, mathematicians, astronomers, engineers, architects, painters and draughtsmen. Egypt had preserved her ancient mysteries for too long; she was a fruit more than ready for the plucking. The country had been effectively under the Mamelukes since 1250. In 1517 it had been conquered by the Turks and absorbed into the Ottoman Empire, part of which, technically, it still remained; by the middle of the seventeenth century, however, the Mameluke beys were once again in control. A French invasion would doubtless evoke an indignant protest from the Sultan in Constantinople, but his empire, though not yet known as 'the sick man of Europe', was a decadent and demoralised shadow of its former self and unlikely to represent much of a threat. Unfortunately there were other risks a good deal more serious. The 300 French transport ships were poorly armed, their crews practically untrained. True, they had a naval escort of twenty-seven ships of the line[1] and frigates, but Nelson was already known to be cruising in the Mediterranean. Were he to intercept them, their chances of escape – and those of the 31,000 men aboard them – would be negligible.

The fleet sailed in four separate divisions, the largest from Toulon, the other three from Marseille, Genoa and Civitavecchia just north of Rome. Napoleon himself left Toulon in his flagship *L'Orient* on 19 May 1798. His first objective was Malta. The island had been in the possession of the Order of the Knights of St John since 1530. The Knights had conscientiously maintained their hospital and had heroically withstood the dreadful Turkish siege of 1565, but as fighters for Christendom they had grown soft. When Bonaparte reached the island on 9 June and sent messengers ashore to the Grand Master, a

---

[1] Ships of the line were the largest category of naval vessels, being those fit to stand in the line of battle. They were three-masters, and were subdivided into six rates, only the first three of which, by the end of the eighteenth century, were considered solid enough for warfare. A first-rate ship of the line carried a hundred or more guns, a second-rate eighty-four to ninety-eight and a third-rate seventy to eighty, all with armaments on two or more decks. Frigates, corvettes and brigs were normally two-masted, with diminishing numbers of guns.

German named Ferdinand Hompesch, to demand the admission of all his ships into the harbour to take on water, he received a reply stating that, according to the regulations of the Order, states that were at war with other Christian countries might send in only four vessels at a time. A message was returned swiftly from *L'Orient*: 'General Bonaparte is resolved to obtain by force that which ought to have been accorded to him by virtue of the principles of hospitality, the fundamental rule of your order.'

At dawn on 10 June the assault on the island began. The 550 Knights – nearly half of them were French, and many more too old to fight – resisted for only two days. On the morning of the 12th they requested a truce; that same night a delegation came on board the flagship. The Order would give up its sovereignty over Malta and Gozo, so long as the French government used its good offices to find Grand Master Hompesch some small principality to which he could retire, together with a pension of 300,000 francs to enable him to live in a style that befitted his rank. Napoleon accepted, and immediately set to work on a programme of reform. In less than a week he managed to convert the island into something tolerably like a French *département*. The people were ordered to wear the red, white and blue cockade; slavery – such as it was – was abolished; 600 Turks and 1,400 Moors were to be repatriated; the number of monasteries was reduced and the power of the clergy drastically restricted. All gold and silver was to be removed from the churches, and all the treasure from the palace of the Knights – which included the famous silver service regularly used by the Order to feed the sick in the hospital – melted down into 3,500 pounds of bullion for Napoleon's war chest. Three thousand French soldiers under General Claude Vaubois were left behind to provide a garrison, and within a week of its arrival the fleet was ready to continue its journey. On the 19th, Napoleon himself set sail.

France, however, was not to keep the unhappy island for long. In 1800, enraged by the behaviour of Vaubois, who had even tried to impose French as the official language and who now proposed to auction the entire contents of the Carmelite church in Mdina, the Maltese – led by their clergy – rose in revolt, hurling the French commander of militia out of a window. Vaubois quickly ordered all his men to Valletta, where he locked the city gates. Thenceforth the French found themselves under siege. Meanwhile, the Maltese appealed to the British navy for help, and several ships arrived to blockade any French vessels that might attempt to relieve their garrison. These were followed shortly afterwards by 1,500 British troops. Vaubois held out heroically, until – thanks to the blockade – he had only three days' rations left. He was then allowed an honourable surrender and safe repatriation for the garrison, taking with him – to the further fury of the Maltese, who were not consulted – much of the treasure that his men had looted during their stay.

With the departure of both the Knights and the French, the Maltese found themselves under the authority of a British Civil Commissioner until such time as their long-term future could be settled. In 1802 the Treaty of Amiens – which declared peace between Britain and France, although Napoleon intended to observe it only for as long as it suited him[1] – provided for the return of the island to the Order of St John; the Maltese, however, who had no more love for the Knights than they had for the French, let it be known that their own strong preference was for the security afforded by the British Crown – which, by the Peace of Paris in 1814, they were finally to obtain.

On the night of 1 July 1798, nearly two weeks after its departure from Malta, the French fleet dropped anchor off Marabout, some seven miles west of Alexandria. The landing of so many men, and so much equipment, in the small boats which were all that was available was a long and complicated task. It began only in the late afternoon, when a storm was already brewing. The vice-admiral, François-Paul Brueys d'Aigaïlliers, had advised delaying the operation until the following morning, but Napoleon had refused to listen. He himself did not reach the shore until shortly before midnight. Fortunately for him, there was no resistance until the army reached Alexandria, and even there the crumbling walls and the tiny garrison could do little to delay the inevitable. The whole city proved to be in a state of advanced decay, its population reduced from the 300,000 that it had boasted in Roman times to a sad and apathetic 6,000. Apart from 'Pompey's Pillar' (which had nothing to do with Pompey) and 'Cleopatra's Needle' (which had no association with Cleopatra),[2] there was nothing to evoke its days of glory.

---

[1] It actually lasted less than fourteen months, owing to Napoleon's indignation that the British had not left Malta immediately, and British concern at his having annexed Piedmont, Elba, Parma and Piacenza in 1802.

[2] The pillar in fact dates from the time of Diocletian at the end of the third century. The obelisk, dating from the reign of Thutmose III – nearly 1,500 years before Cleopatra's day – was given to the British government by Mohammed Ali in 1819, although it did not reach London's Embankment until 1878.

To the French army, therefore, the capture of Alexandria came as an anticlimax. The July heat was demoralising enough, but men who had expected a rich and magnificent city – with commensurate opportunities for pillage – and who had found only a heap of pestiferous hovels felt not only disappointed but betrayed. Napoleon saw that they must be given no time to brood, but must march at once on Cairo. Advancing along the western side of the Nile delta, they captured Rosetta without a struggle and on 21 July met the main body of the Mameluke army at Embabeh, just below Gezira Island. Napoleon's exhortation to his troops, 'Think, my soldiers, from the tops of these pyramids forty centuries look down upon you!' has gone down in history, but was hardly necessary: the Battle of the Pyramids was a walkover. Mameluke swords, however valiantly wielded, were no match for French musketry. The following day he entered Cairo – to his men a slight improvement on Alexandria, but scarcely a *vaut-le-voyage*.

Nelson, meanwhile, had been pursuing the French ships across the Mediterranean. Misled by information from a Genoese vessel that Bonaparte had left Malta on 16 June – three days earlier than he actually did – he had hastened to Alexandria; then, finding to his astonishment no trace of the French fleet, he had sailed again on 29 June to search for it along the coast of Syria. As a result of this confusion, it was only around 2.30 p.m. on 1 August that he returned to Egypt, to find thirteen French men-of-war – he himself had fourteen – and four frigates anchored in a two-mile line in Aboukir Bay, one of the mouths of the Nile. But they were still nine miles away; it would take another two hours to reach them, and a lot longer still to draw up his own ships in a regular line of battle. Night encounters in those days were hazardous things; there was a danger of running aground in unknown waters, and a worse one of firing into one's fellows by mistake. Most admirals, in such circumstances, would have elected to wait until morning; Nelson, however, seeing that the French were unprepared and that there was a favourable northwest wind running, decided on an immediate attack. He began by sending four ships inshore along one side of the French line, while he himself in his flagship, the *Vanguard*, led a parallel attack down the offshore side. Each enemy vessel was thus subjected to a simultaneous cannonade from both sides. That was at about six o'clock; the ensuing battle lasted through the night. By dawn all the French ships but four had been destroyed or captured, including their flagship, *L'Orient*, on which

Admiral Brueys had been killed by a cannon shot. The vessel still lies beneath the waters of Aboukir Bay, together with all the treasure looted from the palaces and churches of Malta.

The Battle of the Nile, as it was called, was one of the greatest victories of Nelson's career.[1] At a stroke he had not only destroyed the French fleet; he had severed Napoleon's line of communication with France, leaving him marooned and frustrating all his plans of conquest in the Middle East. His victory also had a serious effect on French morale – though not, apparently, on Bonaparte's. Almost before the ships' guns had cooled, Napoleon was at work transforming Egypt into a strategic base. What the British were attempting to achieve little by little in India, he set himself to complete in a few months. He devised new and more efficient systems of administration and taxation; he established land registries; he gave orders for hospitals, improved sanitation and even street lighting. The scientists and engineers whom he had brought with him were put to work on such problems as the purification of the Nile water and the local manufacture of gunpowder.

Where he failed, unsurprisingly, was in his attempts to win the trust and support of the Egyptians. He did his best, taking every opportunity to stress his admiration for Islam; he even issued a 'Proclamation to the People of Egypt', in which he seemed to go still further:

> I, more than any Mameluke, worship God, glory be to Him, and respect His Prophet and the Great Koran . . .
> O you sheikhs, judges, imams, tell your nation that the French are also sincere Muslims . . .

The fact remained, however, that his men were living off the country and behaving as if they owned it. Small-scale revolts were constantly breaking out, with attacks on isolated French garrisons or individual Frenchmen in the street. A more serious uprising in October was put down with brutal efficiency; over 3,000 Egyptians were killed and the entire al-Azhar quarter sacked, including its mosque. From that day forward Napoleon decreed that any Egyptian found carrying a firearm was to be beheaded and his body thrown into the Nile. It was no wonder that the longer the occupation continued, the more detested it became.

Beyond the Egyptian frontiers, too, enemies were gathering. On

---

[1] In his despatches Nelson had reported that the engagement had taken place not far from the (Rosetta) mouth of the Nile, hence the slightly misleading name. It would have been more accurate to call it the Battle of Aboukir.

2 September 1798 the Ottoman Sultan Selim III declared war on France, and the Turkish governor of Syria, Djezzar ('the Butcher') Pasha, began to raise an army. This could easily march south, then turn across the Sinai peninsula and invade Egypt from the east; worse still, it could be carried by English ships straight to the Nile delta. Rather than risk such an eventuality, Napoleon decided to act first: to destroy Djezzar's army even before it was fully formed. In early February 1799 he marched his men across the deserts of Sinai and up into Palestine. On 7 March Jedda fell; 2,000 Turks and Palestinians were put to the sword, another 2,000 taken down to the sea and shot. In an effort to improve his image after these atrocities, the Commander-in-Chief visited a plague hospital and, we are told, was ill-advised enough personally to carry a plague victim out to his grave. He was not infected; otherwise, this exercise in public relations does not seem to have been outstandingly successful.

Acre was his next objective; but Acre was well defended and well garrisoned, the Turkish commander having enlisted additional support from the British navy under the swashbuckling Commodore Sir Sidney Smith, famous for having escaped from the Temple prison in Paris during the revolution. Smith had brought with him his friend Colonel Phélippeaux, a military engineer who had been at the *Ecole Militaire* with Bonaparte and who was able to contribute invaluable expertise to the defence of the town. For two months the French army besieged the city; fortunately, however, Smith had succeeded in capturing the eight gunboats carrying their siege artillery, stores and ammunition. Napoleon had only his field guns, and it was not until 25 April that he was able to bring up six heavy cannon from Jaffa. On 10 May he launched his final assault. Like its predecessors, it was thrown back with heavy losses, and he had no course but retreat. By this time plague had taken hold in the army; he himself advocated killing all the patients with overdoses of opium, but his chief medical officer refused outright. The hundreds of stretchers carrying the sick and wounded considerably slowed the return journey; it was a miserable body of men that finally limped back into Cairo.

As always, Bonaparte did his best to dress up defeat as victory. Turkish prisoners were paraded, captured Turkish flags proudly displayed. What was left of the army, cleaned up as far as possible, staged a triumphal march through the city and, on 25 July, made short work of a Turkish force which, with British assistance, had been landed at Aboukir. But no one, least of all the Egyptians, was fooled. The

Middle Eastern expedition had been a failure, and had done little for Napoleon's reputation. He was alarmed, too, by reports reaching Cairo that Europe was once again at war, that the Italian Cisalpine Republic which he had established two years before was now under Austrian occupation, that the Russian army was on the march and that the domestic situation in France itself was once again critical. For the first time in his career – but not the last – he left his army to get home as best it could and, at five o'clock in the morning of 22 August 1799, slipped stealthily from his camp and sailed for France. Not even his successor in command, General Jean-Baptiste Kléber, knew of his departure until he was safely away.

In Paris, the *coup d'état* of 30 *prairial* (18 June) 1799 had expelled the moderates from the Directory and brought in men who were generally considered to be Jacobin extremists, but confusion continued to reign and one of the new Directors, Emmanuel Sieyès, declared that only a military dictatorship could now prevent a return of the monarchy. '*Je cherche un sabre*,' he said – 'I am looking for a sabre.' That sabre was soon to hand, and from the moment Napoleon arrived in Paris on 14 October – having almost miraculously escaped the British fleet – he and Sieyès started planning a *coup* of their own. It took place on 18–19 *brumaire* (November 9–10), abolished the Directory and established a new government, the Consulate. There were technically three consuls, but effectively only one: the First Consul, Napoleon Bonaparte, was henceforth master of France.

He spent the winter reorganising his army, and – Russia having by now withdrawn from the anti-French coalition – preparing for a campaign against his principal remaining enemy, Austria. At that moment the Austrians were besieging Genoa, capital of one of his more ephemeral creations, the Ligurian Republic. A lesser general would have marched south from Paris and down the valley of the Rhône; Napoleon turned east at the Alps and took his men over the Great St Bernard Pass before the snow had melted, appearing in Italy behind the Austrian army and taking it entirely by surprise. The Austrian general Michael von Melas had no course but to leave Genoa and regroup, concentrating all his forces on Alessandria. Napoleon followed them, and on the evening of 13 June 1800 reached the village – it was in fact little more than a farm – of Marengo, some two and a half miles southeast of the town.

The encounter that followed might have spelled the end of

Napoleon's career. Melas did not wait to be attacked; the following morning, with a force of some 31,000, he lashed out at the 23,000 French, pounding them remorselessly with his eighty guns for over five hours. In the early afternoon their line began to give way; they were forced to retreat nearly four miles to the village of San Giuliano. The Austrians' victory seemed certain; strangely enough, however – perhaps because the seventy-one-year-old Melas now retired to Alessandria, leaving the command to some relatively incapable subordinate – their pursuit was slow and half-hearted, giving Napoleon time to regroup and to welcome substantial reinforcements under General Louis Desaix which just then providentially arrived from the southeast. As evening drew on he launched a counter-attack. Desaix was killed almost immediately, but his 6,000 men, fresh and rested, gave new spirit to their fellows, and by nightfall the Austrians were in full retreat. When the battle ended they had lost 9,500 men, the French less than 6,000.[1]

Melas now had no choice but to come to terms, withdrawing all his troops east of the river Mincio and north of the Po, giving the French complete control of the Po valley as far as the Adige. Napoleon, his reputation unstained despite the narrowness of his victory, returned to Paris, where he took over both the military and the civil authority. In 1801 Austria was forced to sign the Treaty of Lunéville, whereby France regained the old frontiers that Julius Caesar had given to Gaul: the Rhine, the Alps and the Pyrenees.

Napoleon's star was now high in the sky – and was still rising.

---

[1] The news of Napoleon's victory at Marengo reached Rome some hours after the reports of his defeat. The sudden change from celebration to lamentation lends additional drama to Act II of Puccini's *Tosca*.

CHAPTER XXII

Neapolitan Interlude

The news of Nelson's victory on the Nile was received with jubilation in England – but still more so, perhaps, in Naples. Its king, Ferdinand IV,[1] had come to the throne in 1759 at the age of eight. He and his queen, Maria Carolina – daughter of the Empress Maria Theresa of Austria and elder sister of the unfortunate Marie Antoinette – were an ill-assorted couple. Ferdinand – 'the scoundrel king', as he was universally known, '*il rè lazzarone*' – was a childish boor who loved only hunting and horseplay, possessed not a shred of natural dignity and boasted of never having read a book. The Queen was comparatively intellectual, acutely conscious of her rank yet surprisingly tolerant of her insufferable husband,[2] to whom she was to bear eighteen children; though herself only sixteen years old at the time of her marriage, it was not long before she was effectively running the kingdom, her foreign policy being dictated by her understandable detestation of the French Revolution and all it stood for.

Ever since 1797, to Maria Carolina, to her subjects and even to King Ferdinand, French intentions in south Italy had been only too clear. In Rome on 22 December of that year, the local Jacobins staged an armed demonstration against the Pope, in the course of which a twenty-seven-year-old French officer named Léonard Duphot was shot by a papal corporal. The French ambassador, Napoleon's elder brother Joseph, refused to listen to the Vatican's explanations and reported to the Directory that one of his country's most brilliant young generals had been murdered by the priests. As a result General Louis Berthier was ordered to march on Rome. He met with no opposition and on 10 February 1798 occupied the city. Five days later the new republic was proclaimed in the Forum. Pope Pius VI, aged eighty, was abominably treated – his rings were torn forcibly from his fingers – and was carried

---

[1] Of Sicily he was Ferdinand III, of the Two Sicilies he was Ferdinand I. The historian – and his readers – must tread warily indeed.

[2] '*Er ist ein recht guter Narr,*' ('He's a right good fool') she remarked to her brother, the Emperor Joseph, when he came to Naples. Joseph left a hilarious account of his visit. (See H. Acton, *The Bourbons of Naples*, pp. 135–49.)

off to France, where he was to die miserably at Valence in August 1799.[1]

What was Naples to do? The French were now on its very doorstep; what was to prevent them from crossing the frontier, and who could stop them if they did? With Napoleon's seizure of Malta in June 1798 the threat loomed still larger. No wonder that the Neapolitans rejoiced at the news of the Battle of the Nile, or that when Nelson himself arrived on his flagship *Vanguard* towards the end of September he was accorded a hero's welcome – with, on the 29th, a magnificent fortieth-birthday banquet for 1,800 guests, given at Palazzo Sessa by the British Minister, Sir William Hamilton, and his wife, Emma. But the party, as far as Nelson was concerned, was not a success. On the following morning he wrote to Lord St Vincent:

> I trust, my Lord, in a week we shall all be at sea. I am very unwell, and the miserable conduct of this Court is not likely to cool my irritable temper. It is a country of fiddlers and poets, whores and scoundrels. I am, etc.

Indeed, the next three months were a nightmare. The Austrian field marshal Baron Karl Mack von Leiberich arrived in early October to assume command of the Neapolitan army of 50,000 men, who duly marched north, a quivering King among them. Needless to say, they proved quite incapable of stopping the French advance, and by early December more and more of them, officers and men alike, had shed their uniforms and returned to their homes. The Queen – her sister's dreadful fate always in her mind – wrote several times to Lady Hamilton deploring their cowardice, but when her husband deserted in his turn there were no more letters on the subject. On 18 December there arrived a despatch from an utterly demoralised Mack, confessing that his army – which had not yet fought a single battle – was now in full retreat and imploring Their Majesties to leave while there was still time. 'I do not know,' wrote Nelson to the Minister at Constantinople, 'that the whole Royal Family, with 3,000 Neapolitan émigrés, will not be under the protection of the King's flag this night.'

And indeed it was, though thanks to atrocious weather and the usual Neapolitan confusion, the *Vanguard* did not leave Naples until the evening of the 23rd. On Christmas Eve Nelson recorded that 'it

---

[1] His body was later exhumed and returned to Rome, where Canova designed him a splendid tomb.

blew harder than I have ever experienced since I have been at sea'. On board, there was general panic. Of the distinguished passengers, only Emma Hamilton kept her head; Sir William was found in his cabin with a loaded pistol in each hand – since, he explained to his wife, he was determined not to perish with 'the guggle-guggle-guggle of salt water in his throat'. Little Prince Albert, aged six, died of exhaustion in Emma's arms; but at two in the morning on the 26th the vessel finally dropped anchor in the harbour of Palermo, and a few hours later His Sicilian Majesty made a formal entry into his kingdom's second capital.

The King and Queen settled as best they could into what passed for the royal palace. Nelson, meanwhile, moved in with the Hamiltons. He was desperately tired, and not yet completely recovered from a head wound sustained at Aboukir Bay; he was quarrelling with the Admiralty, and his relationship with his wife was also giving him cause for serious concern. He desperately needed emotional support, and Emma Hamilton gave it him. Her long experience as a courtesan did the rest. It was in Sicily that their celebrated affair began.

When the French troops under General Jean-Etienne Championnet arrived in Naples in mid-January, they found the populace a good deal more spirited than the army. The mob – the so-called *lazzaroni* – was prepared to attack the invaders tooth and nail, and for three days there was bitter house-to-house fighting. In the end the *lazzaroni* had of course to give in, but not before they had stormed and gutted the royal palace. They had done so with a clear – or almost clear – conscience. Had not their king abandoned them? And besides, would he not have preferred his treasures to go to his own subjects rather than to his French enemies? When at last peace was restored, a French officer remarked that if Bonaparte had been there in person he would probably have left not one stone of the city standing on another; it was fortunate that Championnet was a moderate and humane man. Quietly and diplomatically he established what was known as the Parthenopean Republic[1] on the French Revolutionary model. It was officially proclaimed on 23 January 1799 and acquired a number of loyal Italian adherents – though it was perfectly obvious to all that it had been the result of conquest, and that the French army of occupation was its only support.

*

[1] Parthenope was an early Greek settlement on the site of Naples in the sixth century BC.

To Queen Maria Carolina, life in Sicily was 'worse than death'. She and her husband, she believed, had been dishonoured and disgraced. The winter of 1798–99 was perishingly cold, with snow on the ground – a rare phenomenon in Palermo – and the royal apartments possessed neither fireplaces nor even carpets. The news of the sack of the royal palace in Naples had caused her deep distress. Worst of all, perhaps, her husband had turned against her, blaming her for forcing him into that shameful campaign and for saddling him with the hopeless General Mack. But her spirit was undaunted; she dreamed only of counter-revolution and enthusiastically welcomed a proposal for just such an operation, despite the fact that it came from a most improbable quarter.

Cardinal Fabrizio Ruffo was already over sixty. He had been papal treasurer to Pope Pius VI, but in Rome all his suggested reforms had been rejected as too radical. He had consequently retired to Naples, from where he had duly followed the court to Palermo. He now proposed a landing in his native Calabria, first to defend it from any further French advance – as well as from Italian republicanism – and ultimately to recover Naples for its king. This would, he emphasised, be nothing less than a Crusade, and he had no doubt whatever that all his fellow Calabrians would rally to the Cross.

Ruffo landed as planned on 7 February, with eight companions. Eighty armed *lazzaroni* joined him almost at once, and by the end of the month the strength of the 'Christian Army of the Holy Faith' had risen to 17,000. He was a born leader, and quickly won their love and trust; in 1799, wrote his secretary–biographer Sacchinelli, 'there was not a miserable peasant in all Calabria but had a crucifix on one side of his bed, a gun on the other.' On 1 March the Cardinal was able to establish his headquarters in the important city of Monteleone. Catanzaro followed, and then Cotrone. Admittedly, he had his problems. His ramshackle army was totally without discipline, his 'Crusaders' comporting themselves no better than their medieval predecessors; Cotrone, for example, was delivered over to a sack from which it never recovered. Such atrocities could not but damage his reputation, though he personally was mild and merciful, always preferring peaceful conversion to violence. But his momentum was unstoppable, and his successes encouraged other, similar movements throughout south Italy. He himself, having recovered the whole of Calabria, marched eastwards into Apulia, where he had similar success. By the beginning of June he was at the gates of Naples – which, thanks to a blockade of the bay by a British fleet under Rear Admiral Sir Thomas Troubridge, was by now on the brink of starvation.

On 11 June, hearing of the Cardinal's approach, the people of Naples broke out in open rebellion. There was fighting throughout the city. Desperate for food, mercilessly bombarded by the French from the Sant' Elmo, Nuovo and Ovo castles, the *lazzaroni* fell on every Jacobin that they could lay their hands on, French or Italian, with unbridled barbarity. There are accounts of unspeakable atrocities: of dismemberment and cannibalism, of severed heads paraded on pikes or kicked around like footballs, of women suspected of Jacobinism being subjected to ghastly humiliations. The horrified Cardinal did what he could, but many of his own men had plunged joyfully into the bloodbath; in any case, against mob hysteria he was powerless. The orgy of destruction continued for a week. Negotiations were seriously impeded by the inability of the commanders of the three castles to communicate with one another, and it was only on the 19th that the French formally capitulated, St Elmo alone still holding out. Even then there were problems: the King and Queen – and of course the Hamiltons – insisted that no mercy be shown to any of the Jacobin survivors, while Ruffo and his friends saw all too clearly the danger of bringing home a royal couple who thought only of revenge.

Nelson, understandably but most unfortunately, took the monarchist side. Politically he was extraordinarily naive, his knowledge of the situation in Naples being limited to the highly tendentious opinions that he had picked up from the King and Queen and the Hamiltons. He spoke not a word of any language but his own. As a down-to-earth, right-wing English Protestant he mistrusted the Cardinal, and on his arrival in Naples had no hesitation in overruling him, insisting – as his friends also insisted – on unconditional surrender. Some 1,500 rebels, whom Ruffo had saved from the mob and to whom he had given refuge in the municipal granaries, marched out according to the terms of the capitulation, expecting safe conduct to their homes. They were seized by the new royalist government, and many of them were executed. Was Nelson guilty of betraying them? Probably not. All that we know of his character suggests that he would never knowingly have done such a thing, but the Hamiltons' influence was paramount and he always accepted their point of view.

He has also been condemned, with a good deal more justification, for his treatment of Commodore Francesco Caracciolo, the former senior officer of the Neapolitan navy who had transferred his allegiance to the republicans. After ten days on the run in disguise, Caracciolo had been found hiding in a well and was brought before Nelson on the *Foudroyant*. At ten in the morning of 30 June he was court-martialled, at noon he was found guilty of high treason and condemned to death, and at five in the afternoon he was hanged from the yardarm. There his body remained until sunset – it was virtually midsummer – when the rope was cut and it fell into the sea. He had been allowed no witnesses for his defence, no priest to hear his last confession. His request to be shot rather than hanged was refused outright. Traitor he may have been, but he had deserved better than that. Why had Nelson allowed it? Simply because of his infatuation with Emma. With a ship and the ocean beneath him he was invincible, infallible; on land he was literally out of his element, and when in the arms of his mistress little better than a child.

Leaving Maria Carolina in Palermo, the King returned to Naples in the first week of July, but he did not stay there long. Never, during his forty years on the throne, had he believed that he had enemies in the city; now he knew that he did, and the knowledge had shaken him to the core. Henceforth he preferred the safety of Palermo, where he could still fool himself that he was popular. On 8 August he sailed back into its harbour with Nelson on the *Foudroyant*. The Queen came on board, and the two together then made their formal disembarkation to a salute of twenty-one guns before driving in state to a *Te Deum* in the cathedral.

For Ferdinand and Maria Carolina, for the Hamiltons and for Nelson, life now continued much as it had before – except that there was no longer any cogent reason to stay in Palermo. The Queen yearned for Naples; the King, on the other hand, had worked himself up about it until dislike had turned to detestation. Never, he said, would he willingly go back. The Hamiltons, while from the political point of view advocating return, were in fact perfectly content where they were. Sir William, being accredited personally to Ferdinand, was required to remain with him, and Naples may well have held poignant memories since his second collection of Greek vases had been lost in a shipwreck in August 1798.

The saddest fate was Nelson's. He was to remain ashore in Palermo until June 1800, ten months in which his infatuation with Emma Hamilton not only sapped his morale but even seems to have affected his conscience and his sense of duty. For the first half of that period he was acting Commander-in-Chief, Mediterranean, but he left virtually all the work to his subordinates. He was not there to intercept Napoleon Bonaparte when he slipped out of Egypt; had he made the effort and succeeded, history might have taken a very different turn. His colleagues grew increasingly concerned for him and disturbing reports even reached London, where the Admiralty began to lose patience and the First Lord, Lord Spencer, very nearly relieved him of his command. In January 1800 his superior, Lord Keith, returned to duty and ordered Nelson to join him in an inspection of the blockade of Malta, but the admiral returned almost at once to Palermo, where Emma – now shamelessly pregnant – received him publicly with open arms.

He and the Hamiltons were back in Malta in April 1800, though their voyage savoured more of a pleasure cruise than a serious naval visit. At that moment Sir William received his letters of recall, so finally in July all three of them sailed for England – since Keith had refused Nelson a battleship, he commandeered ships from the blockade of Malta without permission – taking with them on the first leg of the journey Queen Maria Carolina, who was on her way to visit her family in Vienna. They landed her at Livorno, where they ran into General Sir John Moore, on his way to Egypt. 'It is really melancholy,' he noted, 'to see a brave and good man, who has deserved well of his country, cutting so pitiful a figure.'

The Hamiltons finally settled in London, where Nelson's daughter Horatia was born the following January. On the very same day he was named second-in-command of the Baltic fleet, an appointment which very probably saved his reputation and his career.

CHAPTER XXIII

Egypt After Napoleon

When Napoleon slipped so ignobly out of Egypt in August 1799, he left his deputy Kléber in an impossible position – and perfectly furious. The army's morale, after the long and abortive Syrian expedition, was lower than ever. Many of its soldiers were sick, food was scarce, drinkable water scarcer still. Kléber managed, however, to negotiate an armistice with Sir Sidney Smith, by the terms of which his army would be returned to France at the expense of the Sultan and his allies. It must have seemed almost too good to be true, and so indeed it proved to be, since both parties were blatantly disobeying orders. As Kléber well knew, the First Consul had given clear instructions that the army was to remain in Egypt until the signature of a general treaty of peace, while Smith, desperate to get the French out of the country, had similarly ignored an equally explicit order from London that no terms were to be made which did not involve the surrender of French troops as prisoners of war. Not surprisingly, the Commander-in-Chief, Mediterranean, Lord Keith, flatly refused to approve the document.

Meanwhile, the Turkish janissaries were once again on the march. Kléber had no choice but to put his men once again on a war footing – and conclusively proved that there was life in them yet. On 20 March 1800 he defeated the Turks at Heliopolis, and a month later accepted the surrender of the Cairo garrison. By this time the British government had decided after all to ratify Smith's armistice, but these last successes had put a very different complexion on such matters. However ailing and homesick the French army might be, it was now back in control. To most of its senior officers evacuation was no longer an issue. One of the few who still had his doubts was Kléber himself, but on 14 June – the very day of Marengo – he was assassinated in Cairo by a Muslim fanatic, to be succeeded by the pompous and pot-bellied General Jacques – or, as he now preferred to be called, Abdullah – Menou. Menou had recently converted to Islam – largely, it was thought, the better to enjoy the companionship of an Egyptian wife, daughter of a bathhouse keeper in Rosetta, of which town he had formerly been governor. Though reasonably brave and not unintelligent, he was sadly

438

deficient in judgement and, in short, a bit of a joke – by no means the man to shoulder the responsibilities that lay ahead.

With Austria finally off his back, Napoleon's thoughts had returned to the Nile. 'The great affair now,' he wrote to his brother Lucien in December 1800, 'is Egypt . . . to inspire the troops there with a sense of their important mission.' Egypt was the bridgehead, the springboard, the gateway to the east. The old dream was revived: of a glorious expedition from Suez which would sweep through the Red Sea and, perhaps in a single campaign, drive the British from India forever. He, Napoleon, would then be master of his own mighty oriental realm, a latter-day Alexander the Great.

Meanwhile, in England, the same dream assumed the form of a nightmare, and there were those who took the danger very seriously indeed. Among them was the head of the War Department, Henry Dundas, a dour Scottish lawyer of whom his chief, William Pitt, had declared that 'his comprehensive knowledge of the history of India . . . though it might have been equalled in the House, had never been excelled.' It was plain to Dundas that the only solution lay in a pre-emptive strike, and equally clear that this strike should be carried out by the British force of some 22,000 men under his kinsman and fellow Scotsman General Sir Ralph Abercromby, then stationed at Gibraltar. Its purpose would be not to occupy Egypt, but quite simply to get the French out. Dundas had a hard time persuading some of his colleagues – King George III himself, remembering all too well the American war of a quarter of a century before, gloomily predicted that any army sent to Egypt would perish of starvation or disease or both – but at last, with Pitt's strong support, the decision was taken.

Abercromby was now sixty-six. He was a man of the highest integrity, who had already refused a peerage and a grant of land in the West Indies. He had resigned a command in Ireland on a matter of principle, and had avoided service in America because of his sympathy for the rebels. He had, however, fought in the Low Countries and the Caribbean, where in 1796 he had commanded the largest expeditionary force ever sent abroad, and despite fearsome epidemics of malaria and yellow fever had recovered several important islands, including Trinidad, from the French. His most recent operation, an attempt in October 1800 to destroy the Spanish fleet and arsenal at Cadiz, had been a fiasco: the British troops had failed even to make a landing. The principal fault, however, had been that of his superior, Lord Keith, and a sudden tempest of almost tropical violence had done the rest. Abercromby had reached Gibraltar with his pride seriously hurt but his record untarnished.

Though he was naturally determined that the coming Egyptian campaign would restore his reputation, he had no delusions as to its difficulty. He possessed no wagons or beasts of burden, few cavalry and still fewer teams of artillery. Nor did he have a single map of the region; the French, thanks to their professional surveyors, by now had whole sheaves of them. Water, too, would be a problem; the British would almost certainly have to depend on the navy for their supplies. Theoretically he should have invaluable support from the Turkish army, but Major-General John Moore, whom he sent on a fact-finding mission to the Turkish headquarters at Jaffa, returned to report that the Turks were poorly provisioned, utterly undisciplined and commanded by an elderly one-eyed Grand Vizir who was devoid alike of qualities of leadership and of military knowledge. The British would be better off on their own.

The combined naval and military force assembled during the winter of 1800–01 at Marmaris, on the coast of Asia Minor. At dawn on 22 February Admiral Lord Keith gave the order to weigh anchor, and for the next ten hours the fleet – numbering no less than 175 vessels – sailed one by one out of the bay. 'Never was the honour of the British army more at stake,' wrote Abercromby's son Robert from the deck of HMS *Kent*, 'but an equal number of Britons never assembled who were more determined to uphold their own and their country's valour.'

On 2 March 1801 the fleet hove to in Aboukir Bay, but by now the weather was steadily deteriorating, and it was another week before the sea was calm enough for a general disembarkation. Thanks to assiduous practice in Marmaris this was finally effected on the 8th, with some 13,000 infantry, 1,000 cavalry and 600 artillery all being landed in a single day. The French were waiting for them, but Menou, who had persisted in believing that the Aboukir landing would be merely a diversion, had kept the main bulk of his army in reserve in Alexandria and sent off a subordinate, General Louis Friant, with just 2,000 men to oppose the invaders. Friant, with three iron cannon and a dozen field-guns, was confident in his ability to deal with a ragged line of boats and small parties of men struggling ashore as best they could; but the intensive training to which the British troops had been subjected at Marmaris had not been for nothing. Ignoring the French fire, Moore led them fearlessly in parade order up the beach, where they quickly formed a line, fixed their bayonets and charged. The French, hopelessly outnumbered, turned and ran.

Nonetheless, the British losses that morning were heavy. The army lost 625 men, the navy nearly 100. Enemy casualties were somewhat fewer, but there was no doubt as to the result of the battle. It had been the most spectacular success against the French that anyone could remember, and the British soldiers' coolness and courage under fire had been beyond praise. They had won – and won heroically – their first foothold in Egypt. Morale soared. They looked forward to the future, as well they might. Abercromby, however, advanced down the peninsula to Alexandria only with the greatest caution. March on the city he must, but the terrain was unfamiliar and the French were unlikely to make the same mistake again. His column was attacked on 13 March and again on the 18th, but these engagements proved to be only minor skirmishes. Just three days after the second of them came the moment of truth.

The Battle of Alexandria began at dawn on Saturday, 21 March, and lasted for the next four hours. Both sides fought with courage, their generals – except Menou – setting a superb example to the men under them. Of the French, General François Lanusse, killed in battle at the age of twenty-nine, was perhaps the bravest – but also one of the most clear-sighted. To Menou, who rode up and spoke to him as he lay dying, he remarked simply that he was *foutu* – like Menou's entire Egyptian colony.[1] Of the British, Moore was once again the hero of the hour. Early in the fighting he had been seriously wounded in the knee and soon afterwards had had his horse shot under him, but he had fought on in a manner described by an eye-witness as 'almost beyond belief'. As for Abercromby himself, in the early stages of the battle he had been hit by a musket-ball that had lodged in his hip; the doctors were astonished at the way he had continued to move about the battlefield. Only after the fighting ceased did he allow himself to be laid on a stretcher. A junior officer picked up a soldier's blanket and put it as a pillow under his head.

'What's that?' he muttered.

'Only a soldier's blanket,' the officer replied.

'Only a soldier's blanket?' he echoed. 'A soldier's blanket is a thing of great consequence. Return it to him at once.' A week later he died.

---

[1] P. Mackesy, *British Victory in Egypt, 1801*, from which much of the material in this chapter has been taken.

His successor, Major-General John Hely-Hutchinson, was as much disliked in the army as Abercromby had been loved – to the point where a number of senior officers actively plotted his downfall. They would probably have succeeded but for determined opposition on the part of the still convalescent Moore. Hely-Hutchinson's colleague Sir Henry Bunbury, who knew him well, wrote:

> He was forty-four years of age, but looked much older, with harsh features jaundiced by disease, extreme shortsightedness, a stooping body and a slouching gait, and an utter neglect of his dress . . . He shunned general society, was indolent, with an ungracious manner and a violent temper.

From the start, the major-general found himself in a difficult position. The British had won another victory, so much was certain; they had inflicted some 3,000 casualties on the French, at a cost of 1,400 of their own. But Alexandria remained in enemy hands, held not by a small and demoralised garrison but by the bulk of the French army of Egypt, still probably more numerous than his own, under a Commander-in-Chief who had no intention of leaving. Nor could that army be starved out: the road to the west was wide open. Little effective help could be expected from the Turks. There was always the possibility that the French would themselves take the initiative, but Menou seemed bent on playing a waiting game.

Something clearly had to be done to break the stalemate, and Hely-Hutchinson at last decided to send a small force of two and a half battalions, plus 4,000 recently arrived Turks, to attack Rosetta on the westernmost branch of the Nile delta. The expedition was a success, the garrison at Fort Julien[1] laying down its arms on 19 April after a three-day resistance. The way was now clear for shipping on the Nile, and possibly even for a major river operation. On the other hand, such an operation would seriously deplete the garrison which would have to be left outside Alexandria, and it was to protect this – and also to cut Menou's line of communication – that Hely-Hutchinson now decided to flood the dried-up Lake Mareotis immediately to the south of the city. The canal dyke was cut in two places, and the waters of Lake Aboukir plunged down in ten-foot cataracts, carrying away 300 feet of the banks. Leaving his deputy, General Eyre Coote, to hold the front at

---

[1] It was in one of the towers of this fort that the French had discovered in 1799 the famous Rosetta Stone – now one of the most popular exhibits of the British Museum – which provided the key to the deciphering of ancient Egyptian hieroglyphics.

Alexandria, Hely-Hutchinson set off on 21 April for Rosetta, and on 5 May headed up the riverbank towards Cairo.

The march took seven weeks – weeks during which the exhausted men, many of them sick with dysentery, were obliged to contend with 110-degree temperatures by day and monstrous spiders and scorpions by night. There were several skirmishes with the French along the way – but also, surprisingly, an unexpected meeting with the Turkish army, which to everyone's surprise had somehow marched under its one-eyed Grand Vizir from Jaffa, defeating a French force en route. 'It was the worst army that ever existed,' wrote Hely-Hutchinson, 'but bad as they are they will fight to a certain degree in their own way.' On 7 June there was a violent sandstorm, but when it cleared there, on the horizon, were the Pyramids. By the 21st the last units had arrived, and the British and Turks together had Cairo effectively surrounded. Unfortunately Hely-Hutchinson now had only some 4,000 soldiers fit for duty. The Cairo garrison, he had learned from French prisoners, amounted to about 5,000, although their morale was said to be low.

In the event, it proved even lower than he had been led to believe. On 22 June, the day the batteries were to be drawn into position, the gates of the city opened. The siege of Cairo was over before it had begun.

General Augustin-Daniel Belliard, commanding the Cairo garrison, had had little choice. There were less than two months' rations in the city, and foraging was no longer possible. Ammunition too was desperately short, down to 150 rounds per gun. His men had no stomach for the fight; all they wanted was to get home. He also had to remember the local population, who had no love for his army and who would not hesitate to rise up against it when they saw the chance. There might perhaps have been a hope of retiring into Upper Egypt and continuing the resistance there, but another British force, from India, was rumoured to be on its way to Quseir on the western shore of the Red Sea, from which it would advance on Cairo from the south.

Most worrying of all was the realisation that his Commander-in-Chief had gone off his head. Just a week before, a courier from Alexandria had delivered a letter from Menou, describing how he had reported to Bonaparte that the British had suffered appalling losses on their way from Rosetta. Belliard himself, according to the same report, had destroyed the Turkish army and was now advancing down the Nile towards Alexandria. Meanwhile, reinforcements from France were on their way. Cairo must be held until they arrived.[1]

To the luckless general it was now clear that he could no longer hope for any reasonable orders from his chief; henceforth, he was on his own. Having no authority to make terms, he summoned a council of war; it was only after assuring himself of the support of his senior officers that he sent one of them under a flag of truce to report his readiness to negotiate. An armistice was agreed at once, the capitulation signed on 28 June. The French, with their arms, baggage and artillery, would march under British escort to Rosetta, where they would be shipped back to France within fifty days.

During the ensuing period of well-deserved rest and recreation for the British – and, for the French, of preparation for their coming departure – Hely-Hutchinson arranged for officers and men alike to visit the Pyramids. Several of them, according to contemporary accounts, cut their names into the stone; Sergeant Daniel Nicol wrote in his journal: 'I wrought very hard and got D. NICOL, 92 REGT carved, and broke my knife while finishing the job; this is in the south-east corner, and is likely to stand some time.'[2] Few, mercifully, seem to have shared the enthusiasm of a certain Colonel Cameron of the 79th, who in his eagerness to carry home a souvenir ordered one of his men to attack the royal sarcophagus with a sledgehammer.

For the citizens of Cairo, 9 July 1801 was the worst day that any of them could remember: it was the day when the French evacuated the city and when it was engulfed by swarms of Turkish soldiers, who had made no secret of the fact that the unrivalled prospects of murder, rape and pillage which it offered were the sole reason for their having crossed the deserts from Syria. The Grand Vizir's army had always been cheerfully anarchic; now, as the orgies and the bloodbaths began, the last faint suggestions of discipline vanished. There was nothing the British could do as they formally took over the garrison; the Turks were their allies, and had given plenty of warning of their intentions. As for the French – who had withdrawn to Giza – they can have felt nothing but relief to be out of the city at last.

British, French and Turks together set off down the Nile on 14 July.

---

[1] On 17 June Menou had indulged his imagination still further, assuring the Minister of the Interior that Belliard had won a major victory over the British just outside Cairo and that Hely-Hutchinson had been killed.
[2] Before condemning Nicol and his fellows as vandals, we should remember that ten years later Lord Byron was to do precisely the same at the Temple of Poseidon at Sunion.

The British were astonished to find that the French numbered not the 5,000 that they had estimated, but nearly three times that number. They were accompanied by some 300 small river boats carrying the sick and wounded with the baggage, vast quantities of loot and the corpse of Kléber, to be reburied under an appropriate memorial in France.[1] Three weeks later, on 5 August at Rosetta, their embarkation was complete; on the 9th the last ship sailed for Toulon. Now finally the British could turn their full attention on Alexandria, and so – they very much hoped – draw a line under the whole Egyptian adventure.

Throughout the journey to the coast, the army was commanded by Moore. Hely-Hutchinson, having fallen sick, spent most of July recovering at Giza. Only on the 29th did he arrive by river at Rosetta, where he immediately boarded the flagship *Foudroyant* and remained there for another fortnight. It was essential that he should properly regain his strength before marching on Alexandria, and in any case no major operations could begin until Moore had finished supervising the French embarkation. By then, however, the Major-General had his plans ready: he would attack the city simultaneously from east and west. It lay at the centre of a narrow isthmus separating the Mediterranean to the north from the recently flooded Lake Mareotis to the south. From Rosetta, some forty miles east of Alexandria, he would advance with his heavy artillery. Coote, meanwhile, would be shipped with three brigades across the lake and take up a position on the isthmus some eight or ten miles beyond the city to the west. In a classic pincer movement, the two would then come together.

The attack began in the evening of the 16th, when under cover of darkness some 300 gunboats, carrying 4,000 men, sailed westward over Lake Mareotis. Then, at dawn on the 17th, two divisions under Moore and General Sir John Cradock advanced along the isthmus and attacked the advanced French positions. The expedition was successful, but Moore, to whom it had given an opportunity to see the eastern fortifications for the first time, found them formidable indeed and seriously doubted whether, with his existing resources, they could be overcome. Fortunately the defences to the west of the city were known to be a good deal weaker; on Coote, it seemed, the success of the operation might well depend.

*

---

[1] The body was first taken to Kléber's native city of Strasbourg, where it was kept for twenty years in the cathedral. It was then brought to Paris and buried beneath the monument in the *Place* that bears his name.

Coote was certainly showing himself dependable. By the evening of the 21st, after superhuman exertions by his men in pitiless heat, he had taken the Marabout Fort, on a small island commanding the further end of the long and shallow lagoon, known as the Old Harbour, to the west of the city. At dawn on the 22nd he began his advance along the isthmus, flanked by the navy in the Mediterranean on his left and the gunboats in the lake on his right. Nothing, it seemed, could stop him; the French forward positions dissolved at his approach. By ten o'clock that morning they had lost about 200 killed, wounded and prisoners; British losses were three killed and forty wounded. That afternoon Hely-Hutchinson himself sailed across the lake to confer with Coote and look at the western fortifications for himself. There was no doubt that those he saw before him were far weaker than those on the other side of the city. There and then he decided that the main force of the assault must be from the west.

More – and heavier – guns were hastily embarked on the lake and carried across to Coote's camp. The moment they were in position the artillery bombardment began, and with it the steady advance on the city. Rather than heading immediately for Alexandria, however, Coote's plan was to occupy a vantage point on the high ground just above Pompey's Pillar to the southeast of the city, from which he could fire down on its defences. This, however, proved unnecessary: at about half past four on the afternoon of the 26th a French officer arrived at one of his advance posts with a request for an armistice. Coote immediately suspended the firing while the letter was taken to the Commander-in-Chief; and when a little after midnight he heard that Hely-Hutchinson had agreed he stood down his men. The fighting was over.

True, there were moments in the next few days when it looked as if it might be resumed. General Menou, having obtained his armistice, did his best to wriggle out of his obligations. First he asked for a brief extension of the armistice period; then he suggested a convention rather than a capitulation; then he proposed a return of all the men-of-war and most of the artillery to France; then the retention of all Egyptian public property in French hands. Finally he even tried to have the armistice prolonged until 17 September, on the understanding that the French might then resume hostilities if their expected reinforcements had arrived. But Hely-Hutchinson was having none of it. He simply sent Menou his terms: repatriation for his army with personal arms and ten pieces of artillery, all shipping and public property to remain in

61. *Greece Expiring on the Ruins of Missolonghi*. Painting by Delacroix, 1826

62. Theodore Kolokotronis

63. Byron, in Albanian costume

64. *The Massacre of Chios*. Painting by Delacroix, 1824

65. Isabella II, Queen of Spain

66. Alfonso XII, King of Spain

67. General Baldomero Espartero

68. *Daniele Manin and Nicolò Tommaseo freed from prison.*
Painting by Napoleone Nani

69. Garibaldi lands at Marsala

70. Victor Emmanuel II

71. The inauguration of the Suez Canal at El-Guisr

72. Map of the Suez Canal, 1869, with portraits of Ferdinand de Lesseps and the Khedive Ismail and views of the Canal

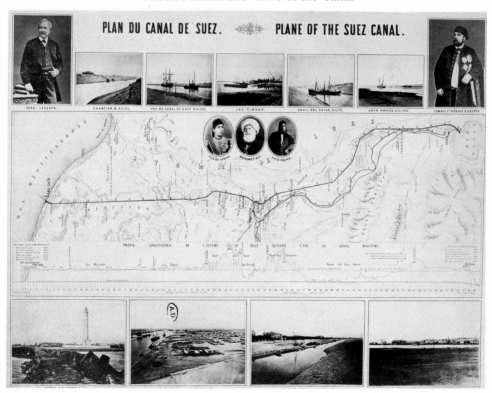

73. Turkish soldiers riding through Constantinople, 1911

74. Troops landing on a beach at Gallipoli, 15 October 1915

75. Eleftherios Venizelos

76. Sultan Abdul-Hamid II

77. Allenby in Jerusalem. (He had entered
the city on foot before remounting.)

78. Mustafa Kemal (later Kemal Atatürk)

79. Faisal at Versailles. (Colonel T. E. Lawrence—to the right.)

80. Clemenceau, Wilson and Lloyd George, after signing the Treaty of Versailles

Egypt. If these terms were not immediately accepted, Alexandria would be blown to bits.

Menou gave in. There was no fight left in him, still less in his exhausted and demoralised men. A capitulation was signed, on what were still remarkably generous terms. At 11 a.m. on 2 September the British took over Alexandria, while the band of the 54th assembled around Pompey's Pillar and played the national anthem. It was just at this triumphant moment that the force despatched from India arrived at Rosetta after its long march from the Red Sea. Hely-Hutchinson's men – who were half-starved and had lived in their clothes through appalling heat for the past six months – were incredulous when they saw it: it included whole regiments of cooks, with exotic foods, wines and spirits; its tented camp looked more like the Field of the Cloth of Gold. The sepoys, for their part, were shocked by the shabbiness of the British troops. No wonder that Hely-Hutchinson thought it wiser to keep the two forces well apart.

So the bulk of the British army sailed away – from the point of view of every single fighting man, not a moment too soon. In its determination to prevent any attempt by the French to return, however, the government in London ordered a surprisingly large garrison – 6,000 strong – to remain at Alexandria at least until the peace, under the command of a reluctant and angry General Moore, who despite his grave wound still thirsted for action. A further 7,000 got no further than Malta, where a strong base was deemed essential, but Malta – where many of the men had left their wives – was a paradise after Egypt, and there were few complaints.

The cost of the Egyptian expedition had been considerable, and not only in financial terms. It left behind 633 British killed or missing; about another 1,000 had died of wounds or disease. The wounded who lived to be repatriated numbered over 3,000, including 160 blinded by ophthalmia. Politically and strategically, on the other hand, the operation had been a triumphant success. In six months British forces had achieved their objective: to show Napoleon that Egypt would never be his. In doing so they had captured both Cairo and Alexandria, and throughout had shown quite astonishing steadiness and discipline, impressing their own officers almost as much as they impressed the French. They had also proved wrong the pessimists at home. A heartwarming story is told of how one day King George III had ridden out to the home of old Dundas in Wimbledon, where he had raised a glass of madeira to the only begetter of the expedition. 'When a person has been perfectly in the wrong,' he declared, 'the most just and honourable thing for him to do is to acknowledge it publicly.'

The British had been victorious; the French had been defeated. '*Quand les armées croient possible de sortir d'une position critique avec une convention sans se déshonorer, tout est perdu*,'[1] wrote Napoleon. He spoke no more than the truth. But what, it may be asked, of the Egyptians themselves, who had probably suffered more from the three years of fighting than anyone else? Once the foreigners had gone, they were left in much the same situation as before: in theory under the hopeless misrule of the Ottoman Empire, in fact under the tyranny of the Mameluke beys. But this situation did not last long. On 22 October 1801 all the principal beys were invited to a banquet on board the flagship of the Capitan Pasha, admiral of the Ottoman fleet, which was lying at anchor off Alexandria. Most of them were mowed down by a Turkish gunboat before they had even reached the vessel; the remainder were imprisoned as soon as they arrived on board. Although a few survived – some had been in Constantinople, others had remained in Cairo – and struggled on for two or three more years, their power was broken. Nor could they continue to recruit their soldiers from the slave markets of the east, since in 1802 the Sublime Porte prohibited the exportation of young boys to Egypt. Unfortunately, however, the moribund Ottoman Empire was incapable of instituting an effective government in their place. Thus it was that, virtually overnight, Egypt ceased to be a bone of contention and became a vacuum. Writing in 1803, Lieutenant-Colonel Robert Wilson – who had kept a meticulous journal throughout the expedition and subsequently published a detailed history of it – expressed his astonishment that 'no adventurer endowed with fortitude, talents and ambition had proposed to command a body of auxiliaries to act against the Mamelukes', while in the following year a nameless American gentleman wrote from Cairo to Admiral Sir Alexander Ball, Governor of Malta, that 'Egypt has no master . . . she must have a new master, and the first comer will be welcome.'

That first comer was to be not an Englishman nor a Frenchman, but a member of a race that has not until now merited a mention in this book. He was, it is generally believed, an Albanian. His name was Mohammed Ali.

*

---

[1] 'When armies believe it possible to escape from a critical position with a convention that does them no dishonour, all is lost.'

Mohammed Ali was born in 1769 at Kavalla in eastern Macedonia. After his father's death he was brought up by the governor of the town. At eighteen he married one of the governor's relations, who was to bear him five children. (An assortment of other ladies was responsible for the other ninety.) The lucrative tobacco trade seems to have engaged him for some years; he then joined the Ottoman army – in which, having attained a relatively senior rank, he in due course found himself under the command of the Grand Vizir, fighting the French. For as long as the Europeans remained on Egyptian soil he fought bravely enough, but after their departure his Albanian regiment, commanded by a certain Tahir Pasha and just about the only disciplined unit in the Turkish army, broke out in open mutiny.

There is no reason to believe that Mohammed Ali had personally engineered the mutiny – such risings of unpaid soldiery were frequent enough in Ottoman history – but after the murder of Tahir he quickly assumed control, and by dint of various intrigues was appointed in 1805 the Sultan's viceroy in Egypt. For the next forty-four years he ruled the land as a virtual dictator, eliminating the last vestiges of Mameluke rule, expropriating the property of the old landowning classes and ruthlessly crushing successive insurrections. By 1815 nearly all agricultural land along the banks of the Nile and in the delta had been nationalised, profits from agriculture going directly into his own coffers. He vastly improved the all-important irrigation system and introduced various new crops – notably cotton – which promised high returns. He also built up a fleet and a considerable army, conscripted from the peasantry but commanded by Turks and other foreigners. These he used at first on the Sultan's behalf, suppressing revolts in Arabia and in Greece; later, in his own interests, he invaded the Sudan with similar success.

He was to live until 1849; but for the moment a far greater man once again claims our attention.

CHAPTER XXIV

The Settlement of Europe

Napoleon Bonaparte had failed in Egypt; in Europe, on the other hand, he was going from strength to strength. In December 1804, in the presence of Pope Pius VII, he had laid the imperial crown on his own head in Paris; five months later, in May 1805, he had staged a second self-coronation, this time – his pettifogging little Italian republics now forgotten – as King of Italy in Milan cathedral. His decision to use for the ceremony the ancient iron crown of Lombardy, for centuries the property of the Holy Roman Empire, gave mortal offence to the Austrian Emperor Francis, who thereupon joined the alliance formed by Britain and Russia a week or two before.

Having thus consolidated his past conquests, Napoleon now embarked on a new campaign against Austria, and there was much rejoicing in the *Grande Armée* when, on 20 October 1805, an Austrian army of 33,000 capitulated at Ulm. It was ironic that, on the very day following, Nelson smashed a combined Franco-Spanish fleet at Trafalgar, he himself being mortally wounded at the moment of victory; but even such a disaster as this would not have remained long on the Emperor's mind since only six weeks later, on 2 December, his army of 68,000 triumphed over a combined force of 90,000 Austrians and Russians at Austerlitz in Moravia. On the day after Christmas, by the terms of a treaty signed at Pressburg (now Bratislava), Austria was obliged to return to France, *inter alia*, all the Venetian territories she had acquired in 1797 at Campo Formio – to constitute, with the coasts of Istria and Dalmatia, part of the new Napoleonic Kingdom of Italy.

The Emperor had refused to admit into the Treaty of Pressburg any stipulations on behalf of the Neapolitan Bourbons; indeed, on the day the treaty was signed he had declared his intention to 'hurl from the throne that criminal woman who has so shamelessly violated everything that is sacred among men'. This verdict on Maria Carolina may seem a little harsh; it must, however, be admitted that his conclusion of a treaty of neutrality with Naples earlier in the year had not prevented her from appealing to her allies for assistance, and towards the end of November 1805 no fewer than 13,000 Russians, accompanied by 7,000 British troops from Malta, had disembarked in the Bay of Naples. They were joined by a few thousand Neapolitans, and by mid-December the combined army had advanced to the papal frontier. But then there arrived the news of Austerlitz, and the whole expedition came to an abrupt and premature end. It had been a bad idea from the beginning, since in sending it the Queen had played straight into the Emperor's hands. In his subsequent proclamation to his army he was able to say: 'Shall we trust again a court without loyalty, without honour, without sense? No, no! The dynasty of Naples has ceased to reign: its existence is incompatible with the peace of Europe and the honour of my crown.'

The dynasty had not of course ceased to reign, nor would it finally do so for another half-century; but it could not stand up to the French army of 40,000 men who now marched through the Papal States[1] into south Italy under Marshal Masséna, with Joseph Bonaparte as the Emperor's personal representative. On 11 February 1806 the royal family fled, for the second time, to face the winter miseries of Palermo; and on the 14th, in drenching rain, a French division under General Partouneaux entered Naples. There was no resistance; whereas seven years previously the *lazzaroni* had fought like tigers and caused appalling carnage, this time they were listless and apathetic, making no protest when Joseph Bonaparte staged his own procession on the following day and took up his residence in the royal palace. Later that year, by imperial decree, Joseph was proclaimed king.

'Naples captured, everything will fall,' Napoleon had written to Joseph soon after the second flight of the royal family. Not for the first time, however, he had underestimated his enemy. Calabria proved a very much harder nut to crack. On 1 July 1806 a British force from Palermo under General Sir John Stuart, consisting of 4,800 infantry and sixteen guns, disembarked on the west coast of Calabria; three days later it attacked a French force near the village of Maida, and after a savage bayonet assault routed it. The victory was welcomed with enthusiasm, not only locally but also in England, where the battlefield is still remembered in the name of Maida Vale.[2] Unfortunately the fall – after a heroic resistance – of the city of Gaeta, together with Masséna's decision to concentrate far greater forces against him,

---

[1] When Pius VII registered a somewhat nervous protest, he was put firmly in his place by a personal message from the Emperor: 'Your Holiness will show the same respect for me in the temporal sphere as I bear towards him in the spiritual . . . Your Holiness is the Sovereign of Rome, but I am its Emperor.'

[2] Until a few years ago there stood at the southern end of Maida Vale a pub named The Hero of Maida, with a portrait of General Stuart on its sign.

obliged Stuart to re-embark his troops in September. This meant that guerrilla warfare now took over, with the usual atrocities perpetrated on both sides. The Calabrians had no deep love for the Spanish Bourbons, but they vastly preferred them to the French invaders; besides, had not the Pope refused to recognise Joseph Bonaparte as their king? They were of peasant stock, and when the fighting began they pulled no punches.

As for Sicily, an island ruled solely by King Ferdinand and Queen Maria Carolina would probably have presented Masséna with few problems. Nelson was dead, and the royal family had had a far cooler reception on their arrival than on their previous visit. The Sicilians by now knew their sovereigns all too well, and were fully conscious of the fact that the King saw their island as nothing more than a hunting reserve and an occasional funkhole. In the Palatine Chapel in Palermo[1] he had even destroyed a number of the superb twelfth-century mosaics simply to give himself more convenient access to the building. Moreover, all the principal administrative posts were taken over by Neapolitans, and many Sicilians – including in particular the younger sons of the nobility – found themselves unemployed. In such circumstances, a French invasion might have met with little enough resistance.

But the true situation was very different. First of all, Ferdinand had invited the British to take over the defence of the island – which was just as well, as they would have done so anyway – and the Straits of Messina were now constantly patrolled by British gunboats. Secondly, the British had taken over a good deal more than Sicily's defence; in all but name, they were now masters of the island itself, with more than 17,000 soldiers and some thirty consuls or vice-consuls stationed there. Sicily also enjoyed a direct subsidy from Britain, to say nothing of a number of sizable loans and a good deal of private investment; the impact on the formerly sluggish Sicilian economy can well be imagined.[2]

British influence grew still greater after 1811, when the Commander-in-Chief in the Mediterranean, Lord William Cavendish-Bentinck, was additionally appointed envoy to the court of the Two Sicilies. Though Bentinck was still only thirty-seven, he had already served as Governor of Madras and had subsequently fought in the Peninsular War. Able and energetic, he soon made himself effective governor of the island,

---

[1] See Chapter VI, p. 104.
[2] Such was the prevailing Anglophilia that the swells of Palermo affected to speak the Sicilian dialect with an English accent.

embarking on a number of sweeping constitutional changes. In that same year the King had arrested and deported five of his leading opponents in the Sicilian assembly; by threatening to withdraw his army and suspend the subsidy, Bentinck now forced Ferdinand to reinstate them and to replace his largely Neapolitan ministry with a more liberal one which actually included three of the deportees. In 1812 he introduced a liberal constitution on British lines, and soon afterwards he went still further: Queen Maria Carolina, who had rendered his task infinitely more difficult by thwarting him in every way she could, suddenly found herself exiled. No wonder she called him a wild animal – *una bestia feroce*.

Though not permitted to perform the ceremony, Pope Pius VII had been invited to attend Napoleon's coronation in Paris – an invitation which, much as he might have wished to, he could not have refused. In the years immediately following, however, relations between Pope and Emperor grew worse and worse. Napoleon seized the all-important ports of Civitavecchia and Ostia, and by the beginning of 1808 – by which time the Papal States were French in all but name – the imperial army entered Rome itself and occupied the Castel Sant' Angelo. Finally, on 17 May 1809, from the castle of Schönbrunn in Vienna, the Emperor issued a decree announcing his annexation of Rome. '*Consummatum est*,' the Pope is said to have murmured when he heard the news. On 10 June the papal standard which normally flew above the castle was replaced by the tricolour – and the despoilers of the Holy City were formally excommunicated.

The Pope was careful not to mention the Emperor by name; even so, it was a brave step for him to take, and retribution was not long in coming. On the night of 5 July he was arrested and carried off, by a strangely roundabout route that took him through Grenoble, Valence and Nice, to Savona. There he was to remain for three years, until – while suffering a fever so severe that he received the last unction – he was transported, more dead than alive, in a locked carriage to Fontainebleau. Unlike his predecessor, who had died in his French exile, he was to return to Rome in May 1814. He lived on until 1823, by which time Christendom had assumed a complexion very different from that which he had known in the early years of his pontificate.

In the autumn of 1807, when the Portuguese had refused to close their ports to British shipping, Napoleon had despatched General Junot

– whom we last met in Venice ten years before – with an army of 30,000 men across Spain and into Portugal. The Portuguese royal family instantly fled to Brazil, leaving the French in possession of the country. Much of the invading army then moved into northern Spain. Meanwhile, Napoleon had sent his brother-in-law, the brilliant cavalry general Joachim Murat,[1] to occupy Madrid and to bring the Spanish King Charles IV and his son Ferdinand to meet him at Bayonne. There, on 5 May 1808, they both abdicated their rights to the throne, Napoleon promising in exchange that Spain should remain Roman Catholic and independent, under a ruler whom he would shortly name. Soon afterwards, he did so: and the name was that of his brother Joseph. But Joseph's reign was doomed before it had even begun. On 2 May, the people of Madrid had risen against the invader.

Joseph Bonaparte had started well enough in Naples. On his brother's orders he had initiated a programme of dismantling the vast feudal estates in the kingdom; he had reformed the monastic orders and done his best to regularise the financial, educational and judicial systems. But he had never been happy there, and when Napoleon offered him the crown of Spain he was only too glad to accept. The Emperor replaced him in Naples with Joachim Murat. Murat indulged himself with an expensive, extravagant and slightly ridiculous court, but he continued the work that Joseph had begun, carrying out a number of important social reforms, breaking up the vast landed estates and replacing the old, somewhat slap-happy laws of Naples with the Code Napoléon. He was to remain in Naples until his departure in 1812 on the Russian campaign, during which he once more distinguished himself by his bravery at Borodino; but having been left by Napoleon in charge of the shattered *Grande Armée* during the retreat, he in his turn abandoned it in an effort to save his Neapolitan kingdom. When the news of the Emperor's escape from Elba reached Italy Murat, back in Naples, was one of the first to declare for him, immediately putting himself at the head of an Italian army; but on 3 May 1815, in defiance of the Emperor's instructions, he was foolish enough to challenge a large Austrian contingent and was soundly beaten at Tolentino. He sought refuge in Corsica, and in October made a last attempt to recover Naples, but by then the Neapolitans had enough. They took him prisoner and shot him.

*

---

[1] He was married to the Emperor's youngest sister, Caroline.

The Madrid rising was quickly and brutally suppressed, but other provincial insurrections sprang up all over Spain, whose people as always showed their superb capacity for guerrilla warfare. The French were driven back from Valencia, and General Pierre Dupont, who had advanced into Andalusia, was ultimately forced to surrender with his entire army at Bailén on 23 July. The rebels now advanced on Madrid and expelled Joseph a few weeks later. By this time the British had joined the fray, British forces under Arthur Wellesley – the future Duke of Wellington – having landed in Portugal on 1 August. It was largely thanks to them that the massive French counter-attack the following winter failed to crush the revolt altogether.

The Peninsular War was to continue until 1814, through Portugal and northwestern Spain – but although Spain is a Mediterranean country, the war was in no sense a Mediterranean war, nor was Napoleon Bonaparte directly involved in it. His history, after his departure from Egypt in 1799, has not indeed greatly concerned us; he had moved his theatre of operations back to northern and central Europe, where it was to remain for the next fifteen years. During most of those years his star continued to rise; but in 1812 came the disastrous Russian campaign, after which little went right for him. The allies were now drawing the net ever closer, and in October 1813 the Emperor's defeat at Leipzig sealed his fate. There was one more last, hopeless campaign, but on 30 March 1814 Marshal Marmont was obliged to surrender Paris to the allies. Less than a fortnight later Napoleon formally announced his abdication, and soon afterwards began his period of exile on the island of Elba.

Elba had had a chequered history. In antiquity it was known principally for its iron ore, which was mined first by the Etruscans and then by the Romans. During the early Middle Ages it was subject to Pisa, but in 1290 it passed to Genoa and in 1399 to the Dukes of Piombino, who ceded it in 1548 to Cosimo de' Medici of Florence. Since then it had been ruled by Spain, and later by Naples; only in 1802 was it ceded to France. On the arrival of Napoleon it became an independent principality, with himself as its ruler.[1] He landed on 4 May 1814, and the whole island was instantly galvanised. 'I have never seen a man,' wrote the British Commissioner, Sir Neil Campbell, 'in any situation in life with so much activity and restless perseverance.'

---

[1] After his departure it would be returned to Tuscany, with which it would pass in 1860 to a united Italy.

Napoleon took Elba seriously, seeing the island not as a prison but as a state to be governed. He set its population of some 112,000 to work building new roads and bridges, even establishing a miniature court – with the strict etiquette on which he always insisted – and hoisting over his palace at Portoferraio a new standard, emblazoned with his imperial bees. His mother and his sister Pauline arrived in July; soon, too, there arrived his Polish mistress, Maria Walewska, with their little son. So far as he was concerned there was only one absentee: his second wife, Marie Louise – the eldest daughter of the Austrian Emperor Francis I – whom he genuinely loved, desperately missed and for whom he had carefully prepared the country palace of San Martino; but her parents were determined to keep her in Vienna. He was never to see her again.

Meanwhile, he watched and waited. There were plenty of encouraging signs. Most of his army remained loyal; in Paris, the arch-reactionary Louis XVIII was making himself more and more unpopular; the Congress of Vienna had reached a deadlock. In Elba, on the other hand, his finances were dwindling, and his mother was constantly encouraging him to 'fulfil his destiny'. And so, in February 1815, Napoleon made up his mind. The day after Campbell had left on a visit to Italy he ordered his only ship, the brig *Inconstant*, to be made ready. On the 26th he sailed, landing on 1 March without opposition at Golfe-Juan, between Fréjus and Antibes. The most straightforward route to Paris would have been up the Rhône valley, but Provence was fanatically royalist and had greeted him with hostile demonstrations on his way south the previous year. Besides, it was obviously the route that would be taken by any royalist army sent to oppose him. He therefore chose instead the mountain road that leads through Digne, Sisteron and Grenoble, known ever since as the *Route Napoléon*. That road, which took the Emperor back to Paris – and, after the Hundred Days, to Waterloo – takes him also out of our story.

Only then could the Bourbons return to Naples; Queen Maria Carolina, however, was not among them. Effectively abandoned by her miserable husband – who at the time of her deportation by Bentinck had not lifted a finger to help her – she had returned to her native Austria; it was there, in the castle of Hötzendorf just outside Vienna, that her dead body was found on the morning of 8 September 1814. She had been a woman of spirit, even of courage; but she was consistently wrong-headed, and it was very largely to her that the Bourbon Kingdom of Naples owed its decline and its eventual collapse.

*

Little more than a week before Waterloo, on 9 June 1815, the Congress of Vienna held its last session. It had opened the previous September, five months after Napoleon's abdication, and had suffered an awkward moment when the news arrived of his escape from Elba; but it had continued to sit – casting all the time a wary eye to the west – and its final settlement was to prove the most comprehensive treaty that Europe had ever seen. Tsar Alexander I was there in person to defend the interests of Russia; the Austrian Emperor Francis II was represented by his First Minister, Prince von Metternich, the King of Prussia by Prince von Hardenberg, and King George III of England by Lord Castlereagh. The later admission of Bourbon France to the Congress brought to Vienna the most brilliant of them all, Prince Talleyrand.[1] Spain, Portugal and Sweden were also represented, and the numbers were supplemented by countless European noblemen and their ladies, all come to enjoy the most brilliant social season that the continent had to offer.

The majority of the decisions reached in Vienna affected the northern states of Europe and need not detain us. Where the Mediterranean was concerned, Venice – together with Lombardy and the Veneto – found herself once more in Austrian hands; Genoa was absorbed into Piedmont; Tuscany and Modena went to an Austrian archduke, while Parma was given to another Austrian, the Empress Marie Louise – she who had been ill-advised enough to marry Napoleon just five years before. The Papal States – which in 1798–99 had formed part of the Cisalpine and Roman Republics and in 1808–09 of the Kingdom of Italy – were generously restored to the Pope.

There remained a certain amount of tidying-up to be done, notably with the seven Ionian Islands off the west coast of Greece. The respective histories of these islands vary to some degree, but the basic pattern remains very much the same: first Byzantine, then Norman Sicilian (conquered by Robert Guiscard), then Venetian after the Fourth Crusade, then Turkish (except Corfu and Paxos, which

---

[1] Talleyrand, by now sixty, had had an astonishing career. Having first entered the Church, he had risen to the rank of bishop. Later he had represented his government in London, working hard in the cause of Anglo-French relations; but after the execution of the King and Queen he had sought refuge in America, where he had remained for two years. Returning to Paris, he was appointed Foreign Minister under the Directory, and soon became Napoleon's principal adviser on foreign policy; eventually, however, disgusted by the Emperor's insatiable ambition, he began secretly to plan for a Bourbon restoration. With the return of Louis XVIII in 1814, he had found himself once again Foreign Minister.

457

remained Venetian till 1797). After Napoleon's occupation of Venice in that year, one of his first actions was to send 2,000 men to the islands, possession of which he believed to be essential to his eastern – and, in particular, to his Egyptian – plans. By August they were all in French hands, and two months later the French rule was legalised at Campo Formio. As in Venice, the Golden Books of the local nobilities were systematically burned, the lions of St Mark chiselled off the gateways; but the French soon made themselves hated, first by their anticlericalism and then by their insistence on granting the Jews equal status with the Orthodox Christians. So it was that when Russia and Turkey joined the Second Coalition against Napoleon in 1798 and – taking advantage of the French defeat at the Battle of the Nile – despatched a joint fleet under Admiral Feodor Ushakov to recover the islands, the Orthodox Russians (if not the Turks) were greeted as liberators. Only on Corfu did the French have a big enough garrison to put up a fight, but after several months of siege that too was forced to surrender.

Under the terms of a Russo-Turkish convention of May 1800 the islands now became an independent federal republic, under the protection of the Tsar and paying annual tribute to the Sublime Porte; when war was resumed between Britain and France in 1803 it seemed at first as if their independence would be respected. But Napoleon still remained obsessed by Corfu, and by an annex to the Treaty of Tilsit – signed with the Tsar on a raft in the middle of the river Niemen in July 1807 – the islands were transferred from Russian to French protection. A year later came a further setback to British *amour-propre*, when the French captured Capri; the Commander-in-Chief, Mediterranean, Lord Collingwood, having heard from a number of Cefalonian and Zantiot merchants that the islanders were eager to regain their independence, decided to retaliate by taking as many of the Ionian Islands as he could. The considerable force that sailed from Sicily in 1809 easily recovered Cefalonia and Zante, Ithaca and Cythera, but Corfu was too strongly defended for direct assault. The only alternative was a blockade, which in fact proved little better than a farce: it was maintained by only two small frigates, and as soon as these were out of sight the French boats would run out across the straits to Albania and return with all the food they needed. Thus for the next six years the military representatives of the two powers – at daggers drawn in Europe – pursued similar peaceful policies on islands often within sight of each other.

Neither side found the islanders easy to govern. Blood feuds were part of the normal way of life, murder was an everyday occurrence, ignorance and superstition were everywhere. An English traveller reported that when the governor of Cephalonia attempted to introduce the potato to the island, 'some of the priests laboured to convince the peasants that this was the very apple with which the serpent seduced Adam and Eve in Paradise'. Gradually, however, they were won over, and by March 1811 a Major Richard Church had succeeded in raising on Zante what he called the 1st Regiment, Duke of York's Greek Light Infantry. A second regiment, raised on Cephalonia and officered almost entirely by Greeks, took part in the capture of Paxos in February 1814. Though both regiments were disbanded at the end of the Napoleonic Wars, many of their Greek officers and men were later to turn their experience to good use as leaders in the Greek War of Independence – notably the great Theodore Kolokotronis, nearly all of whose portraits and statues show him inseparable from his British helmet.

In November 1815 it was jointly agreed by the plenipotentiaries of Britain, Prussia, Russia and Austria that the Ionian Islands should henceforward be an independent state, under British protection and governed by a British High Commissioner. A month later there arrived to take up this post the then Governor of Malta, Sir Thomas Maitland. Sir Charles Napier, who served under him, describes him as 'a rough old despot . . . insufferably rude and abrupt', 'particularly dirty in his person' and 'constantly drunk and surrounded by sycophants'. Despite these failings, however, and a Scottish accent that rendered him almost incomprehensible to Corfiots and compatriots alike, 'King Tom' was to rule the islands for the next ten years with a firm but surprisingly enlightened hand.

Meanwhile, across the straits on the Albanian mainland, a far more portentous drama was beginning to unfold. It was unleashed because of the ambitions of the nominal Turkish governor in the city of Iannina, a certain Ali Pasha. When Byron visited him in 1809, he wrote:

> His Highness is sixty years old, very fat and not tall, but with a fine face, light blue eyes & a white beard, his manner is very kind & at the same time he possesses that dignity which I find universal among the Turks . . . He has the appearance of any thing but his real character, for he is a remorseless tyrant, guilty of the most horrible cruelties, very brave & so good a general, that they call him the Mahometan Buonaparte.

Ali had started life as a brigand, which is essentially what he remained. In his youth, he and his followers had instituted something like a reign of terror in Albania and Epirus. The Ottoman authorities had done their best to crush him, but time and again he had outwitted or outfought them, until at last in despair they had decided to bribe him with high imperial office. He had become governor of Iannina as early as 1787, and from this power base he and his family had extended their authority over virtually all Greece and Albania, apart from Attica and Athens itself. He had also transformed his capital. Iannina had always been beautiful, set in a spectacular setting of lake and mountains. He improved its roads, instituted two trade fairs a year, built caravanserais for the merchants and even dug a ship canal. His sumptuous palace contained the largest Gobelins tapestry ever made, which had previously hung at Versailles.

The changing fortunes of the Ionian Islands were always of interest to Ali, and sometimes of concern. During the years of Venetian rule, Venice had also controlled the four chief coastal towns on the mainland opposite: Butrint (now in Albania), directly across the strait from Corfu; Preveza and Vonitsa, flanking the entrance to the Gulf of Arta; and Parga, opposite Paxos. When in 1807 the islands became French, Ali had seized the first three before anyone could stop him, but the Russians, who maintained a strong garrison at Parga, had handed it over to France as agreed. The local population, who had no love for the French, at first had little option but to put up with them as best they could, but when the Napoleonic star began to sink they hoisted the Union Jack and appealed to the British to support them. Thus it was that on 22 March 1814 a small British military force took possession of the town. All now should have been well; unfortunately, when in the following year the Congress of Vienna made the Ionian Islands a British protectorate, the mainland towns were specifically excluded and passed instead to the Turks, with the proviso that any inhabitant of Parga who wished to cross to the islands should be allowed to do so.

Had the Congress left it at that, most of the Pargiots would probably have remained where they were, but it went further, stipulating that all emigrants should be compensated by the Ottoman government for the mainland property that they had abandoned. As a result, every single citizen chose to leave, and the Turks, faced with huge compensation payments, offered Parga to Ali. The amount of compensation was finally fixed at £150,000, which in due course Ali paid; and on Good Friday 1819 some 3,000 Pargiots, with their icons, their holy relics and in some cases even the bones of their ancestors, crossed the straits to Corfu, where the money was divided among them. They were, we are told, inconsolable, and their story was to become one of the great legends of Greek suffering under Turkish rule. The point is less often made that they left their homes voluntarily and were compensated for them, and that by remaining in Parga they would have fared no worse than the populations of the neighbouring towns, who were denied all chances of leaving.

Ali Pasha did not live long to enjoy his new acquisition. An attempt in February 1820 to assassinate one of his relations, a certain Ismail Pasha who had incurred his displeasure and fled to Constantinople, was traced back to him and gave Sultan Mahmoud II the opportunity he had long been seeking. He thereupon appointed Ismail governor of Iannina in Ali's place, gave him a small army and ordered him to do the rest. That same autumn, with Ismail's troops closing in, Ali set fire to the city and retreated to his citadel, which stood on a promontory projecting into the lake and was additionally protected by a broad moat. Here he seemed likely to hold out indefinitely, but in January 1821, with a stalemate still persisting, Mahmoud dismissed Ismail and replaced him with the infinitely more capable Khurshid Pasha, governor of the Morea. Khurshid, seeing that nothing could be expected of Ismail's motley army – which consisted of a number of separate forces each going its own way under the command of its own pasha – spent the next year putting it into shape; then, at the beginning of 1822, he smashed his way into the citadel. There were various stories about how Ali met his end; a few days later his severed head was exhibited on a pike in Iannina before being borne back in triumph to Constantinople.

CHAPTER XXV

Freedom for Greece

The beginning of the Greek struggle for independence from Turkish rule can be dated to September 1814, when three young Greeks in Odessa founded a secret society. To avoid suspicion, they called it by the deliberately noncommittal name of the *Philiki Eteria*, the Friendly Association. None of the three had so far acquired any distinction: Nikolaos Skouphas was a hatter, Emmanuel Xanthos was a bankrupt dealer in olive oil, Athanasios Tsakalov had no settled occupation. They got off to a slow start. Although they had all three been born in Greece, as expatriates they were unable to tap into the resources of the mainland, while even among the Greek diaspora around the Black Sea they were too insignificant to be taken seriously by the rich merchants whose support they needed.

Little by little, however, the Association's numbers increased. Its founders moved their base to Constantinople, where in those days there were almost as many Greeks as Turks, and whence they sent emissaries into Greece itself: one to Macedonia and Thessaly, one to the Peloponnese and the wealthy islands of Hydra and Spetsai, and two to the Mani (the central of the three promontories of the southern Peloponnese). The Mani had been the focus of an earlier, unsuccessful uprising instigated in 1770 by Catherine the Great through her lover, Count Gregory Orlov.[1] As a somewhat paradoxical result of this incident, the Ottoman authorities had removed it from the jurisdiction of the governor of the Peloponnese and subjected it directly to the Capitan Pasha, head of the Turkish armed forces and overlord of the Aegean, and he in his turn had devolved his power to the head of one of the local families, with the title of bey. The eighth of these beys,[2] appointed in 1815, was to be one of the heroes of the Greek Revolution – of whose family no fewer than forty-nine were to fall in battle during the coming struggle. His name was Petrobey Mavromichalis.

Petrobey was, like all his family, outstandingly handsome – only to

---

[1] Their joint membership of the Orthodox Church has always provided a close emotional link between Russia and Greece.
[2] For a fascinating summary of the lives of the previous seven, see Patrick Leigh Fermor, *Mani*, p. 49.

be expected, perhaps, his ancestor George having reputedly married a mermaid. This quality he combined with graciousness of manner, high intelligence and, as he was later to show, indomitable courage. Like any tribal leader, he was capable of cruelty when he believed it to be justified, but he was also generous and – in his own territory – a man of peace, settling blood feuds wherever he could and doing his utmost to create the solidarity which he knew would be necessary in the years ahead. When approached by the Association, he instantly gave it his support.

Before there could be any question of taking up arms, however, the movement had to find a leader. The most distinguished Greek living at that time – and the obvious first choice – was Iannis Kapodistrias, more usually known outside Greece as Capodistria. Born in Corfu, he came from an ancient family which had emigrated to the Ionian Islands from Italy in the fourteenth century. In his youth he had been active in local political life, so impressing the occupying Russians that he had been invited to join the administration in St Petersburg. In normal circumstances his status as a civil servant of the Russian Empire might not have prevented his accepting the presidency of the Association; unfortunately, however, in 1815 Tsar Alexander had appointed him joint Foreign Minister, so that when in 1820 Emmanuel Xanthos requested an audience and extended the invitation, he was turned down flat.

The Association's eye next fell on a dashing imperial aide-de-camp named Alexander Ipsilantis, who though still in his twenties had already lost his right arm in the service of the Tsar. Two of his brothers were already members, and he accepted without hesitation. There was still a long way to go: total membership numbered only 1,000 or so. But Ipsilantis was impatient, and on 8 October 1820 issued a proclamation calling upon all Greeks to prepare themselves for the struggle ahead. The revolution, he declared, must be unleashed in the Peloponnese before the end of the year. Characteristically, he had failed to consult his contacts on the spot, who were now obliged to inform him that the Peloponnese was not yet ready; he therefore decided to begin in the north rather than the south: in the Danubian principalities of Moldavia and Wallachia.

It was in many ways a surprising choice. Neither of these regions – both of them lying in present-day Romania – formed part of Greece. Nor, technically, were they part of the Ottoman Empire; their legal status was that of vassal states, into which the Sultan was forbidden by treaty to send troops without Russian consent. This meant that the

Tsar, in the interests of his Orthodox co-religionists, might be persuaded to prevent Turkish forces from opposing the insurgents. An additional advantage was that for the past century the two regions had been governed by Greeks from Constantinople, who could be expected to give whatever support they could. Encouraged by such considerations, on 6 March 1821 Ipsilantis, with two of his younger brothers and a few companions, crossed the border into Moldavia. That same evening they entered the capital, Iasi, where another proclamation was issued, promising 'with very little effort' to annihilate the Turks completely, 'while a mighty empire defends our rights'.

There was in fact every indication that the mighty empire would do no such thing, both Capodistria and the Tsar himself having made it clear to Ipsilantis that they disapproved of the whole project and would have nothing whatever to do with it, and from that moment on the campaign – if so it could be called – was an unmitigated disaster. In Galatz, a town some 100 miles south of Iasi, the rebels massacred the Turkish garrison and all the Turkish merchants, and when the news reached Iasi the Turkish guard there of some fifty men, who had already disarmed on the promise that their lives and property would be spared, was also put to the sword. Moreover, when Ipsilantis realised that the funds which he had confidently expected in Iasi were not forthcoming, he had resorted to extortion from rich bankers. Meanwhile, the unpaid troops that he had assembled were looting the local villages. Now seriously alarmed, Ipsilantis marched on Bucharest – only to find that a local adventurer, Theodore Vladimirescu, had got there before him and occupied the city, summoning the local Wallachians to rise up, not against the Turks, but against the Phanariot Greeks,[1] 'dragons that swallow us alive'.

But the two greatest blows were yet to fall. First, the Orthodox Patriarch of Constantinople, supported by twenty-two bishops, sentenced Ipsilantis and the other leading rebels to be 'excommunicated and cursed, and not forgiven, and anathematised after death, and to suffer for all eternity'. Then the rising was formally denounced by the Tsar himself. In a statement drafted by Capodistria, Ipsilantis was cashiered from the army on the grounds that he had abandoned 'all the precepts of religion and morality'. He and his colleagues would receive absolutely no support from Russia, to which he was forbidden ever to return.

---

[1] From the Phanar district of Constantinople, seat of the Greek Orthodox patriarchate.

Fortunately Vladimirescu was soon captured and taken to Ipsilantis's camp, where he was quickly despatched. Their numbers swelled by Vladimirescu's disaffected followers, the rebels then decided to tackle the Turks head-on, and on 19 June they encountered a considerable Ottoman force in the village of Dragasani. In the ensuing battle half of them were cut to pieces; the other half fled. Ipsilantis escaped into Austria, but was arrested as he crossed the border. He was imprisoned at Mohacs until 1827, and died the following year. In Greek popular legend he is usually seen as a hero and a martyr, and so in a way he was; but he possessed neither the intelligence nor the experience required to lead a successful rebellion, and it was due as much to his sheer incompetence as to anything else that the first campaign of the Greek War of Independence ended in fiasco.

In the Peloponnese the prospects for the coming revolt looked somewhat brighter, particularly after the departure in January 1821 of Khurshid Pasha, governor of the Morea, to deal with Ali Pasha of Iannina. Khurshid had been a considerable force in the region, and his replacement by a young and ineffectual deputy led to an immediate slackening of Turkish authority. Only days later there arrived from Zante the boisterous, black-moustachioed, fifty-year-old ex-brigand who was, more than anyone else, to personify the Greek War of Independence: Theodore Kolokotronis. With his commanding presence, his resounding laughter and his terrifying rages he was a born leader of men; within days of his arrival he had impressed his personality on all around him.

The fuse had already been laid, but it was Kolokotronis who lit the match, fixing the day of the rising as 25 March.[1] Even then, a few communities jumped the gun. In the little town of Areopolis a plaque in the square of St Michael's church reads: 'From this historic square was launched the great uprising under the leadership of Petrobey, 17 March 1821'. To Mavromichalis, therefore, belongs the honour of being first in the field. But Kolokotronis was not far behind, marshalling on the 20th some 2,000 armed men who marched through Kalamata amid cheering crowds. Three days later they accepted the

---

[1] In the early nineteenth century the Orthodox Church still used the Julian calendar (Old Style), which was twelve days behind the Gregorian (New Style). This latter had been instituted by Pope Gregory XIII in 1582 – though it was not generally adopted by the Protestant countries for a considerable time. (Britain went over to the New Style in September 1752.) Since 25 March is so important a date in Greece, it would be pedantic – as well as confusing – to call it 6 April; in this chapter, therefore, Old Style dates are used throughout.

surrender of the Turkish garrison, having promised them that their lives would be spared. (Alas, they were not; as a contemporary writer put it, 'the moon devoured them'.)[1] In little more than a week, the entire Peloponnese was in revolt.

Not everywhere, however, did the rebels have it all their own way. In Patras, the chief city and port, the rising in the last days of March met with serious opposition, the Turks barricading themselves in the citadel and firing their cannon down on the besiegers below. And within a few days there was further disappointment. Bishop Germanos – who not only held the see of Patras but was also the leading churchman and figurehead of the whole revolution – had appealed to all the Christian powers for support, and on 29 March received a reply from Sir Thomas Maitland in Corfu. Ionian subjects, wrote Maitland, were forbidden to involve themselves in the struggle on either side; were they to do so, they would instantly lose their government's protection.

Then on Palm Sunday, 3 March, a Turkish force of several hundred men reached Patras under the command of a certain Yussuf Pasha. Yussuf had recently left the siege of Iannina to take up a new appointment as governor of Euboea; calling en route at Missolonghi (now Mesolongion), he had heard of the disturbances and had hurried at once to the city's relief. He and his men entered Patras at dawn, surprising the Greek population in their beds. Most of them rose, panic-stricken, and fled for their lives, while Yussuf ordered the houses of all the leading citizens to be burned to the ground. With a strong *scirocco* blowing to fan the flames, some 700 buildings were destroyed. Meanwhile, the streets filled with rampaging Turks, all of them out for Greek blood. Of those Greeks who had stayed behind, forty were beheaded in the next few hours.

Patras was to remain a battleground until the end of the war, with Greeks and Turks alternately getting the upper hand but never so decisively as to bring the fighting to an end. Despite constant battering from the Greek guns, the Turks never lost control of the citadel, nor were they ever driven from the two other great castles, of Roumeli and the Morea, which face each other across the Gulf of Corinth at the point where the straits are at their narrowest. Without this invaluable bridgehead – for the Greeks were firmly ensconced at Corinth – the vast peninsula would have been impenetrable to them from the north, their

[1] Quoted by David Brewer, from whose superb history, *The Flame of Freedom*, I have drawn liberally in this chapter.

seat of government at Tripolis dangerously isolated; with it, they were able to make life for the rebels difficult indeed.

There was no doubt now that the Peloponnese was to be the heart-land of the struggle. It was there that Kolokotronis – now officially *archistrategos*, commander-in-chief – won his first pitched battle, at Valtetsi only five miles from the seat of the Turkish government at Tripolis. The Turks lost some 700 killed or wounded, the Greeks perhaps 150. It was there too that the Greeks captured from the Turks their first great stronghold: Monemvasia in the southeast corner, whose immense outcrop of rock many had thought impregnable. In Roumeli, on the other hand – which is to say, all Greece to the north of the Gulf of Corinth – the occasional outbreaks of fighting were largely directed towards stopping the Turks from advancing southward. There was, for example, a significant Greek victory at Vasilika, the road running through a long and narrow pass, very similar to – and not far from – the pass of Thermopylae, where King Leonidas of Sparta and his army had perished in their heroic stand against the Persians twenty-three centuries before.[1]

The sea also saw its share of battles. The opposing forces were hopelessly unequal. Greek ships were essentially merchantmen, though they normally carried a number of guns to defend themselves from the pirates who still infested the eastern Mediterranean. The Turks, on the other hand, had a navy. This, on the face of it, should have made the whole concept of naval warfare between the two unequal in the extreme, but the Greeks had one immense advantage: they were seamen to their fingertips, while the Turks – originating as they had in landlocked Central Asia – were anything but. This meant that while the fighting men on board a Turkish warship were almost certainly Turks, for seamanship and navigation they tended to rely on Greeks – which, after the outbreak of the revolution, they were unable to do. Moreover, the smaller size of the Greek vessels made them faster and more manoeuvrable, just as were the victorious English ships that, two and a half centuries before, had sailed out against the Spanish Armada.

It comes as no surprise, therefore, to read that of the three separate Turkish naval expeditions despatched from Constantinople in 1821 – with the dual purpose of reimposing Turkish control over the Greek islands in revolt and of bringing reinforcements and provisions to the Turkish garrisons around the Peloponnese – two were hopeless failures.

---

[1] See Chapter II, p. 18.

The first retired after its second largest vessel was destroyed by a Greek fireship, the flames of which reached its powder magazine and blew the whole thing to smithereens with the loss of over 500 lives. The second, which was intended to subdue the island of Samos just off the Anatolian coast, was driven back having achieved nothing. Only the third succeeded, having sailed around the Peloponnese and into the Ionian Sea, where the British authorities still allowed the Turks to use the island harbours. Here it took on provisions at Zante and continued with an attack, by a largely Egyptian flotilla, on the port of Galaxidi on the northern shore of the Gulf of Corinth. Thirty-four Greek ships with thirty sailors were captured, the town burned to the ground. The fleet then returned to the Bosphorus by the way it had come, anchoring in the Golden Horn with the prize ships behind it, the bodies of the dead captives swinging from their yardarms.

As relations between Greek and Turk deteriorated, it was only to be expected that civilians as well as fighting men should suffer. There was an ugly incident at Smyrna (Izmir) in June 1821 when, in the course of an attack on the large Greek community, hundreds of men and women were slaughtered and raped, but the most notorious atrocity was perpetrated in Constantinople, and by order of Sultan Mahmoud II himself. Shortly after dawn on Easter Sunday, 22 April 1821, Patriarch Grigorios V – who, it must be emphasised, had never voiced the slightest support for the Greek revolt – was formally stripped of his rank, and at noon on the same day was hanged from the central doors of the Patriarchate. According to Robert Walsh, chaplain to the British Embassy, 'his person, attenuated by abstinence and emaciated by age' – he seems to have been not far short of eighty – 'had not weight sufficient to cause immediate death. He continued for a long time in pain, which no friendly hand dared abridge, and the darkness of night came on before his last convulsions were over.' A few hours later the Sultan is said to have come in person to see the body, which was left swinging for three days.

Nor was the old Patriarch the only victim. All over the Ottoman Empire Christian churches were attacked and burned, and many of the clergy – including no less than seven bishops – were executed. And yet, though the whole western world was shocked by the outrage, only Orthodox Russia lifted its voice in protest – the Austrian and British Foreign Ministers, Metternich and Castlereagh, who could always be trusted to oppose any movement of national liberation, easily overcoming the initial hesitancy of Prussia and France. The Tsar was accordingly obliged to act alone, but he did not mince his words. In an ultimatum drafted by Capodistria, he declared that:

> the Ottoman government has placed itself in a state of open hostility against the Christian world. It has legitimised the defence of the Greeks, who will henceforth be fighting solely to save themselves from inevitable destruction. In view of the nature of that struggle, Russia will find herself strictly obliged to offer them help, because they are persecuted; protection, because they need it; and assistance, jointly with the whole of Christendom, because she cannot surrender her brothers in religion to the mercy of blind fanaticism.

This was presented to the Turkish government on 18 July. On the 25th, having received no reply, the Russian ambassador, Count Stroganoff, broke off diplomatic relations with the Porte and closed his embassy.

Meanwhile, in the Peloponnese, Kolokotronis and his army were preparing to capture their greatest prize to date: Tripolis. Though garrisoned by some 10,000 men – including a body of 1,500 formidable Albanian mercenaries – the town seemed at first a comparatively easy target. Standing in the middle of an open plain, it could rely on no natural defences, merely a stone wall some fourteen feet high. Nor could it be provisioned from the sea. It was also known to be dangerously overcrowded, its civilian population of about 15,000 having been swelled by considerable numbers of local Turks for whom life in the surrounding countryside was no longer safe. In the Greek summer heat, it would be unlikely long to survive a siege.

By mid-July the Greek forces were drawn up to the north and west. Kolokotronis was in command, and there was a reserve force in waiting under Mavromichalis. Just as they were about to attack, there arrived an unexpected visitor: Dimitrios Ipsilantis, brother of the ill-fated Alexander. This alone would not have seemed much of a recommendation, even though the news of Alexander's final débâcle had not yet reached the Peloponnese. Physically, too, Dimitrios was more than usually unimpressive: less than five feet tall, skeletally thin and with a curious impediment in his speech. And yet there was something about him that inspired confidence. From the moment of his first appearance no one was in any doubt of his integrity, and when within a few days he offered to assume the leadership of a new Peloponnesian government, together with the supreme command of the armed forces, a surprising number of leading revolutionaries gave him their support. Among them was Kolokotronis himself, conscious as he was that the new Greece rapidly taking shape was much in need of an acknowledged head, and probably seeing Ipsilantis as an eminently suitable candidate whom he would have little difficulty in bending to his will. After some discussion it was agreed that the provisional government, the so-called Peloponnesian Senate, established only a month before, should continue in being, with Ipsilantis as its president and Commander-in-Chief.

The siege began, and went much as the Greeks had expected. Before long Tripolis was desperately short of food and water, and disease rapidly followed. At the end of August came the news that a Turkish relief force, advancing from the north via Thermopylae, had been successfully cut off by the Greeks, and a few days later the embattled Turks in the city signified their readiness to negotiate. They held a single card in their hands: a party of thirty-eight Greek hostages, captured with their servants at the beginning of the siege. All were being held in a single tiny cell, the masters shackled by one chain round their necks, the servants by another, both chains so tightly drawn that if any one man chose to sit down or stand up, the rest had to do the same. Perhaps it was this flagrant inhumanity that enraged the besiegers. With the promise of plunder in the air their numbers were now rapidly increasing, and their mood grew steadily more ugly as they began to discuss the division of the spoils.

Shortly before the expected surrender, Kolokotronis persuaded Ipsilantis to leave the camp. The excuse given was that the Turkish fleet had appeared off the west coast and that it was his duty to prevent its disembarkation. (In fact, the single two-pounder gun that he took with him would have had little effect on the Ottoman navy – which, as we know, proceeded unopposed to Galaxidi.) The real reason seems to have been that, as Kolokotronis well knew, the capture of Tripolis would end in an orgy of bloodshed. It would be better if the high-minded Ipsilantis were not there to witness it, or to risk – as head of the government – being held responsible.

Of course he was perfectly right. The peace talks were still in progress when the Greeks burst into Tripolis on 5 October, to find the unburied bodies of those who had died of hunger or disease lying scattered over the streets; within hours they had been covered by hundreds more, victims this time of a lust for indiscriminate slaughter. Nor did this occur only within the town; some 2,000 refugees, mostly women and children, who had left of their own free will on guarantee of safe conduct, were also massacred. Ipsilantis, returning a few days after the nightmare had ended, was appalled. It has been suggested that he should have stayed, using his influence to curb the frenzy of his countrymen; but that influence, never great, was already beginning to decline, and there is little in any case that he could have done. War, as we know, all too easily dehumanises those who engage in it; history is full of such horrors, and the sack of Tripolis was neither the first nor the worst of them. It is sad, nonetheless, that the often heroic story of Greek independence should be tarnished with so indelible a stain.

The Greeks were fighting for liberty and nationhood, but they were not yet a nation. The Peloponnesian Senate was all very well, but its members had not been elected – many, indeed, were self-appointed – and its writ, such as it was, was by its very definition confined to southern Greece. North of the Gulf of Corinth there were similar organisations in both East and West Roumeli – the latter, based on Missolonghi, being firmly under the control of Alexander Mavrogordatos, a highly sophisticated westerniser who spoke seven languages and had recently arrived from Pisa, where he had been a close friend of the poet Shelley and had given Mary Shelley lessons in Greek. The moment he heard of the revolt he had hurried to Greece, landing at Missolonghi in the middle of August, and from that moment on his was the dominant influence in the revolution.

What was now urgently needed was a supreme body which would unite these three bodies, together with several other smaller groups which had formed in individual cities and towns. With that objective, representatives of all the organisations met during the last weeks of the year in Piada, an insignificant little village some five miles away from the great classical theatre of Epidaurus. The Assembly of Epidaurus, as it was called, was to draft Greece's first constitution. This first proclaimed the 'political existence and independence' of the Greek nation, adopting Greek Orthodoxy as the state religion; it went on to list the civil rights which would be guaranteed; finally, it laid down the essentials of the administrative machinery, with a five-man executive and a Senate. Mavrogordatos was elected president of the executive, effectively head of state; Ipsilantis, away besieging Corinth, was fobbed off with the presidency of the Senate, with Mavromichalis as his vice-president.

But it was one thing to proclaim independence and a constitution; it was quite another to bring these into active existence and to have them universally accepted. The delegates at Epidaurus had made one serious mistake: they had omitted to choose a capital. Perhaps, at so early a stage, such a decision might have seemed premature, but it meant in practice that when their deliberations were over they all returned to their individual seats of power, and that very little administrative work was done to make the national government a reality. Mavrogordatos himself, fully aware that the Turkish fleet was still lingering in the southern Adriatic, left immediately for Hydra and Spetsai – two of the three islands (the third was Psara in the Aegean) on which the revolutionary navy depended for its ships and crews, and whose support would be vitally necessary in the maritime struggle to come. He returned only in May 1822, when he went straight to Missolonghi to strengthen the town's defences.

Thus it was that the Greek constitution, in the minds of Greeks and of foreigners alike, still partook to some degree of a dream. We may regret, but not perhaps be entirely surprised by, the reply given by Sir Thomas Maitland in Corfu to the new Greek government when it requested the return of an impounded ship:

> His Excellency has just received letters from persons who give to themselves the name of the Government of Greece, by a messenger now in this port . . .
>
> His Excellency is absolutely ignorant of the existence of a 'provisionary government of Greece', and therefore cannot recognise such an agent . . . He will not enter into a correspondence with any nominal power which he does not know.

For the Greeks, the first year of their revolution had been a surprisingly successful one. The Greek uprising had by now caught the imagination of Europe. From England and France, from Germany and Spain, from Piedmont and Switzerland, even from Poland and Hungary, parties of young philhellenes – with recent memories of a good sound classical education to inspire them – were seizing any available ship that would take them to the scene of the struggle.

Alas, all too many of them were doomed. The year 1822 was a good deal less happy than its predecessor. Most of the foreign volunteers, speaking not a word of Greek and understandably alarmed by the obvious brigands by whom they found themselves surrounded, stuck together in battalions of their own; nearly all of these were mobilised in July, when Mavrogordatos ill-advisedly challenged the Turks to a pitched battle on the plain of Peta, just outside Arta. It was fought on the 16th, and the result was catastrophe. Among the dead were no less than sixty-seven of the philhellenes. Fewer than thirty survived – most of them seriously wounded – to make their way back to Missolonghi, where several more were to die, of their wounds or of disease, during the following winter. The dream was over.

Yet the disaster at Peta was as nothing compared with the tragedy which was simultaneously being enacted 150 miles to the east, on the island of Chios. Of all the isles of Greece, Chios had been, until the revolution, the richest and the happiest. Unlike many of its neighbours it was enviably fertile and, after many centuries of Italian occupation, quite exceptionally sophisticated, boasting a number of great merchant families – including the Mavrogordatos – whose names were well-known throughout the eastern Mediterranean. Thanks to its wealth and its influence – twenty-two of its villages, producers of the mastic gum so much in demand at Constantinople, were the property of the Sultan's sister – the Ottoman yoke was light. Left to themselves, the people of this blessed island would never have dreamed of rebelling; indeed, when in May 1821 a fleet from Hydra arrived with an invitation to join the revolution, they categorically refused. It was only in the following year – when another fleet, this time from the neighbouring island of Samos, unceremoniously landed 1,500 troops and a good deal of heavy artillery on their shores – that they found themselves swept up into a nightmare.

It was the Samians, not the Chiots, who were responsible for the attack on the Turkish-held citadel of Chora, the island's principal town. It was they who burned down the customs house and stripped the lead from the roofs of the mosques to melt down into bullets. But it was the Chiots who suffered. Eighty of their most prominent citizens were taken prisoner, three of them sent as hostages to Constantinople. On 11 April 1822 an Ottoman fleet arrived under the admiral Kara Ali. Some 15,000 Anatolian toughs were landed and deliberately left to their own devices. The Samians fled, and the massacre began. It was Tripolis all over again, but this time the Turks were the butchers, the Greeks the victims. Not a man, woman or child in Chora was left alive, and the rest of the island was scarcely safer. Two thousand terrified refugees huddled in the great monastery of Nea Monì, famous throughout the Byzantine world for its glorious mosaics; all were put to the sword. Another monastery, Agios Minas, gave shelter to another 3,000; on Easter Sunday, 14 April, it was burned to the ground with everyone within it. A month later forty-nine of the eighty hostages were publicly hanged, eight from the yardarms of the Turkish flagship, the remainder on the trees lining the road which is still known as the Street of the Martyrs.

The Greeks scored one victory. On the night of 18 June they sent fireships against the Turkish fleet lying outside Chora, targeting in particular the flagship of Kara Ali himself. The operation was wholly successful: within minutes of the strike, the flagship was in flames. Kara Ali tried to escape in a lifeboat, but was hit on the head by a falling spar and died the next day. Turkish casualties are said to have numbered over 2,000. But by now those Chiots left alive hardly cared. They had lost some 70,000 of their compatriots: 25,000 dead and another 45,000 – nearly half the original population – carried off into slavery.

The celebrated painting by Delacroix – bastard son of Talleyrand – of the *Massacres of Chios*[1] is only one indication of the wave of revulsion and horror which swept through western Europe as the news of the atrocity spread. The Turks were not quickly forgiven.

Elsewhere, there was better news for the Greeks. The most dramatic of their successes – though not, perhaps, the most strategically important – was their capture of the Acropolis of Athens. Apart from this majestic elevation, the city would have been unrecognisable to anyone who had known it in the days of Pericles, still less to anyone who knows it today. Its population was no more than 10,000, at least half of whom were Albanians; Greeks and Turks together made up the rest. Already in the summer of 1821 the Greeks had begun a blockade of the Turkish garrison on the Acropolis, but they made little headway until the end of the year, when they managed to seize the well just outside the walls to the south, which they promptly poisoned. This left the garrison entirely dependent on rainwater, and it chanced that that winter and the spring of 1822 were among the driest in living memory. Every attempt to take the great rock by storm failed, but it hardly mattered; thirst, and the disease which it brought in its train, proved far more effective. On 22 June what was left of the garrison – it numbered some 1,150 – surrendered.

It did so on honourable terms – safe conduct and passage home at Greek expense – but although the Greek captains swore an oath before the archbishop to respect them, the Greek population of Athens felt differently. The fate of Chios, only a few weeks before, was fresh in their minds; they remembered too the so-called 'Greek hunts' of the previous year, when the Turkish leader Omer Vrionis had led out mounted parties of some fifty to a hundred in search of Greek peasants

---

[1] It was bought by King Louis XVIII and is now in the Louvre.

and then, having given them a few minutes' start, pursued them at the gallop, firing at them as they ran and beheading them when they were caught. In consequence, they did not feel merciful. By the middle of July at least half the garrison had been massacred, and the remainder were lucky indeed to escape with their lives.

Just a fortnight after the surrender of the Acropolis garrison, a Turkish army left Lamia – opposite the northern end of the island of Euboea – and marched south, first to recover the citadel of Acrocorinth, high above Corinth town, captured by the Greeks some months before, and then to relieve its beleaguered comrades who were being besieged at Nauplia. It was a huge force; the death of Ali Pasha had released several thousand men from Iannina, who had swelled the ranks to what may have been well over 20,000 – many times the number of the Greeks against whom it was sent. Its leader was a certain Mahmoud who, being Pasha of Drama some miles east of Thessalonica, was commonly known as Dramali.

For the first few weeks Dramali carried all before him. After the surrender of Acrocorinth he headed south towards Nauplia, where an armistice had been declared to facilitate the negotiations for the coming surrender of the Turkish garrison. The first Greek national government had hastily moved from Corinth a week or two before and settled in Argos, just ten miles or so inland. It now fled a second time, in the Greek ships which were waiting at Nauplia to carry away the Turks, and its reputation never recovered. The Greek military captains, on the other hand, showed no lack of courage. They poured men into the citadel of Argos, and were joined there by Dimitrios Ipsilantis and soon afterwards by Kolokotronis himself, who had been appointed by the Peloponnesian Senate to the supreme command. Dramali, he knew, would now march on the former Turkish headquarters at Tripolis; his own plan, therefore, would be to block the way forward and then, by sending smaller bodies of troops into the narrow mountain passes between Argos and Corinth, to cut off the retreat.

After so promising a start, Dramali had lost his momentum. In the heat and desiccation of the Greek summer, he was having difficulty in feeding – and above all in watering – his men. Meanwhile, Ipsilantis was holding out in Argos, while in Nauplia the negotiations had broken down and the Turkish garrison in the citadel was once again under siege. There was nothing for it but to return to Corinth; unfortunately, as Dramali now realised, he had omitted to post guards on the passes and ravines through which he would have to march.

Kolokotronis's plan worked perfectly. As the Turkish advance guard entered the narrow valley of the Dervenakia on 6 August, the Greeks opened fire from the rocks above; the result was another massacre, and when two days later Dramali himself took a different route, it was the same story. Thanks to his bodyguard, he himself got through to safety, but he lost his sword and his turban – and his self-respect.

Still more satisfactory for the Greeks than the number of the enemy dead and wounded, estimated at about 2,000, was the plunder: virtually the whole of the Turkish baggage train, with 400 horses, 1,300 beasts of burden and several hundred camels. In December the Turkish garrison at Nauplia finally gave in, and the survivors of the expedition who had made it back to Corinth were almost cut off; their only chance was to head west to Patras, which was still in Turkish hands. The thousand-odd sick and wounded were sent by sea; the 3,500 who had escaped unharmed set off on foot. About half-way along the southern shore, however, where the road narrows to cross the river Krathis, the Greeks suddenly struck, cutting them off both in front and behind. For six weeks they held out, first eating their horses and finally, we are told, resorting to cannibalism. Only the following March did a Turkish flotilla from Patras succeed in rescuing the 2,000 survivors, many of them more dead than alive.

The abject failure of the largest Turkish force seen in Greece for well over a century to make any impact on the revolution put new heart into the Greeks, but although their military successes had been impressive, the movement itself was becoming dangerously fissile. The Assembly of Epidaurus had been intended to last for only a year; its successor, which met in April 1823 near Astros – on the eastern coast of the Peloponnese, some twenty miles south of Nauplia – with 260 delegates, was more than four times the size and infinitely more chaotic.

Already the insurgents were split down the middle: on the one hand, the politicians surrounding Mavrogordatos; on the other, the warriors led by Kolokotronis. And there were territorial divisions too: the inhabitants of the Peloponnese, of Roumeli and Epirus, and of the islands had little love for each other and resented it bitterly if their rivals received what they considered preferential treatment. Every time an important appointment was made to a senior post, it would be challenged; in the ensuing discussion pistols were fondled and tempers flared. On one occasion an infuriated Kolokotronis went so far as to threaten the whole new assembly, being pacified only when he was offered a place on the executive committee; even then, among his friends and enemies alike, jealousies and deep indignation continued to smoulder.

Such, briefly, was the situation when on 3 August 1823 George Gordon, Lord Byron, landed in Cephalonia. Byron was no stranger to Greece; he had been there fifteen years before, in 1809–10, when he had visited Ali Pasha in Iannina. On this occasion he was greeted by the British Resident, who promised him all possible assistance provided only that it did not compromise the British policy of strict neutrality between the two sides. His first problem was to discover exactly what was happening. The British could tell him virtually nothing, so he hired a small boat in which to slip through the Turkish blockade with a letter to Marcos Botsaris, who had been described to him as 'one of the bravest and most honest of the Greek captains'. Botsaris replied at once, inviting Byron to join him and adding that he was going into battle the next day.

Byron would certainly have accepted the invitation; it was a disappointment to him that the news of the captain's death came before he was able to start out. He therefore remained in Cephalonia, moving into a small villa in the village of Metaxata. There he spent the entire autumn, defending himself as best he could against a deluge of appeals for money and support. The young George Finlay – a passionate philhellene who was later to write a definitive history of the Greek Revolution – wrote:

> Kolokotrones invited him to a national assembly at Salamis. Mavrocordatos informed him that he would be of no use anywhere but at Hydra, for Mavrocordatos was then in that island. Constantine Metaxa, who was governor of Mesolonghi, wrote, saying that Greece would be ruined unless Lord Byron visited that fortress. Petrobey used plainer words. He informed Lord Byron that the true way to save Greece was to lend him, the bey, a thousand pounds . . .

The rebels, it was all too clear, did not speak with a single voice. Matters reached their peak in December, when Kolokotronis's son Panos burst into the Senate while it was in session at Argos, physically driving the senators from the building, following them home and wrecking their houses. All attempts to heal the rift failed, and by the beginning of 1824 Greece had effectively two rival governments, one based at Kranidi in Argos, the other – backed by the Kolokotronis clan – at Tripolis.

By this time, however, Byron had finally acted. The proximity of their fleet in the Ionian Sea strongly suggested that the Turks would return to the attack. On 13 November, therefore, Byron had undertaken to lend the Greek government – such as it was – £4,000, with the specific purpose of funding a squadron from Hydra and Spetsai to patrol the waters off the coast. That squadron reached Missolonghi in mid-December, carrying with it Mavrogordatos, who had been entrusted with the town's defence; and four days after Christmas Byron sailed from Cephalonia to join him, with his Newfoundland dog Lyon, his valet, William Fletcher, and his page, a good-looking fifteen-year-old from the Peloponnese called Loukas Chalandritsanos.

It was a dangerous journey, for the Turkish fleet was out in force: there was one particularly unpleasant moment when, in the early hours of 31 December, they encountered a huge Turkish vessel bearing down upon them. The captain turned their own ship round and they were able finally to outdistance it, but Byron soon afterwards put Chalandritsanos ashore with instructions to find his way to Missolonghi by land. As he wrote to Colonel Stanhope, the agent in Greece of the London Greek Committee:

> I am uneasy at being here: not so much on my own account as on that of a Greek boy with me, for you know what his fate would be; and I would sooner cut him in pieces, and myself too, than have him taken out by those barbarians.

At noon on 4 January 1824 they entered the port of Missolonghi. Byron remained on board until the following morning when, at eleven o'clock and in full military uniform designed by himself, he made his formal entry into the town. An eye-witness remembered:

> Crowds of soldiery, and citizens of every rank, sex, and age were assembled on the shore to testify to their delight. Hope and content were pictured in every countenance. His Lordship landed in a Speziot boat, dressed in a red uniform. He was in excellent health, and appeared moved by the scene.

It was, perhaps, the most glorious moment of Byron's visit to Greece – for the story of his last three months makes depressing reading. He achieved none of his declared objectives. The idea that he should personally lead an expedition against Naupactos (Lepanto) came to nothing; a plan for a meeting of the Greek leaders at Salona also failed to materialise. The vast quantities of money that he spent – as well as the £4,000 in November and the living costs for his considerable retinue, he advanced another £2,000 to a perfectly useless regiment of Souliot troops,[1] made a personal loan of £550 to Mavrogordatos and paid £800 to support a drunken though entertaining adventurer named William Parry – did nothing to advance the Greek cause. The house in which he lived, almost devoid of furniture, looked out on to the featureless lagoon, muddy and malarial. The winter rain poured down every day; he would return from his daily rides chilled to the bone. It was no wonder that his health began to suffer.

The first seizure occurred on 9 April. He was attended by a Dr Julius van Millingen, then serving as a surgeon with the Greeks,[2] who weakened him still further by daily or even twice-daily bloodletting; meanwhile, just about every drug known to Greek science was forced down his throat. His constitution, already wrecked by years of drinking and dissipation – he looked nearer fifty than his true age of thirty-six – could no longer stand the strain. He died at six o'clock on the evening of Easter Monday, 19 April. What precisely caused his death remains a mystery: malaria, typhoid, uraemia, syphilis and stroke have all been suggested. Byron had never expected to return from Greece and had no fear of death, but his hope had been to die in battle, fighting for the independence of a land he loved, not – as he himself put it a few days before his death – 'slowly expiring on a bed of torture'.

Still, he did not die in vain. He cast the international spotlight on the Greek struggle as no one else could have done. Thanks to him, all Europe embraced the cause; countless young men were to follow in his tracks in search of death or glory. Greece, we may be sure, would have won her freedom even if he had never existed, just as Serbia had already done, and as her two other neighbours Romania and Bulgaria were later to do; but she would have done so, as they did, without that element of romance which only Byron could instil. The first two decades of the nineteenth century, it must not be forgotten, saw the beginning of the Romantic movement. The Greek War of Independence was anything but romantic; heroism was there, to be sure, but so too

---

[1] Albanians from the wild Souli district southwest of Iannina, who lived on extortion and plunder. Byron had high hopes of them but they proved insufferable. 'I will have nothing more to do with the Souliotes,' he wrote, 'they may go to the Turks or – the devil . . . they may cut me into more pieces than they have dissensions among them, sooner than change my resolution.'

[1] Shortly afterwards Dr van Millingen was taken prisoner by the Turks, but was later released after urgent representations by Sir Stratford Canning, then British ambassador to the Sublime Porte. In 1827 he settled permanently in Constantinople, where he served as court physician to five successive Sultans.

were cruelty, brutality and barbarism on a scale scarcely seen for centuries. Yet somehow that war epitomised all that Romanticism stood for. The West consequently looks back on it with admiration, the Greeks remember it with pride – and among them the name of Byron is not forgotten.

Already by the beginning of 1824, Greece was effectively in a state of civil war. In certain areas in the east of the country and elsewhere in the Mediterranean the Turks remained a force to be reckoned with, but in the Peloponnese and southern Roumeli Greeks were fighting Greeks. By the time Byron died in April the government forces had regained Argos, together with Tripolis and Corinth, while the Kolokotronis clan and their followers still held Nauplia. By midsummer Nauplia too had been surrendered, and the Senate and administration moved in. This did not mark a permanent end to the hostilities, but it afforded a breathing space, during which the Greek government saw the arrival of £80,000, the first two instalments of a loan of nearly £500,000 subscribed in London. Much of this was, predictably enough, to go to waste or to find its way into the wrong pockets; nonetheless, it left the government immeasurably strengthened.

Infighting broke out for the second time towards the end of October, when the citizens of Arcadia (now Kiparissa, in the southwestern Peloponnese) rose up in protest against what they considered disproportionate levies by the government. A force of 500 was sent down to restore order, under the command of a captain named Makriyannis. They would have had little difficulty in suppressing the revolt had the rebels not been joined by Theodore and Panos Kolokotronis, who brought with him a substantial number of disaffected troops from the continuing siege of Patras. Makriyannis could only return to Nauplia, whereat the rebels, much encouraged, marched on Tripolis, which had been largely garrisoned by forces from Roumeli. Immediately the fighting took on a territorial aspect, and in one particularly violent encounter Panos Kolokotronis was killed.

Only at this point did the government realise that it had on its hands not a localised rising, but a second civil war which must be stamped out while there was still time. In the existing circumstances Peloponnesian troops would clearly be untrustworthy; the government accordingly approached the Roumeliots, offering them not only money from the loan but – most irresponsibly – the possibility of the wholesale plunder of the Peloponnese. By the end of the year the Roumeliot captains, each with his own small army behind him, were swarming across the Gulf of Corinth to take full advantage of their opportunity.

The rebels, though now hopelessly outnumbered, fought on until February 1825, when Kolokotronis surrendered, followed by twelve of his principal captains. All were imprisoned in the fortified monastery of the Prophet Elijah in the hills of Hydra. The government had won – but at a heavy price. The Roumeliots had pillaged and plundered wherever they had gone, looting indiscriminately from government supporters and neutrals as well as rebels, from rich and poor, landowner and peasant alike. Makriyannis, who seems to have had a higher sense of morality than most of his colleagues, was appalled – not only by the violence but also by the realisation that his country was more dangerously split than ever before: the people of the Peloponnese would not easily forgive their northern neighbours.

He was not to know how soon national unity was to be enforced, when the Ottoman Empire was to fling its forces once more into the fray.

Even in 1824, the Turks had not been completely idle. Although their impact had scarcely been felt in the Greek mainland, in July the little Aegean island of Psarà – the principal eastern base of the Greek navy – had been sacked by a Turkish fleet, which was soon afterwards threatening the two other key naval centres, the offshore islands of Hydra and Spetsai. But the most formidable Islamic enemy that Greece now had to face was not Turkish; it was Egyptian.

The impressive figure of Mohammed Ali has already made an appearance in these pages, when we saw him appointed imperial viceroy in Egypt in 1805, at the age of thirty-six. Nineteen years later, in what would then have been thought of as late middle age, he was at the height of his powers. He had already transformed the country; in particular, he had given it for the first time an efficient army and navy, trained on European lines by European officers. To the Sultan Mahmoud II it was now plain that these must be swiftly employed if Greece were to remain part of his empire. An incentive was easy enough to find: if Mohammed Ali would help him to recover the Peloponnese, his son Ibrahim could take over as its pasha.

The fleet which Mohammed Ali and Ibrahim now prepared consisted of no less than fifty-five ships of the line and well over 300 transport vessels, carrying some 14,000 infantry, 2,000 cavalry with their horses, and 150 cannon in the charge of 500 artillerymen. It sailed from

Alexandria on 19 July 1824 and met the Turkish fleet at Bodrum (the ancient Halicarnassus) on the western coast of Asia Minor; but the Greeks were waiting, with a fleet of about seventy ships from Hydra, Spetsai and Psarà. A battle followed almost immediately – off Cape Yeronda, a mile or so to the north of the Bodrum peninsula – which, though inconclusive, was enough to persuade Ibrahim that his expedition would have to be postponed until the following year. He withdrew his ships to Crete – which had already been for over a century and a half under Ottoman rule – while the Turks returned to Constantinople for the winter.

So, at least, they intended; but in December a French captain gave Ibrahim valuable advice. There were three fortresses in the Peloponnese still in Turkish hands: Patras, and the former Venetian colonies of Methoni and Koroni.[1] Ibrahim, the captain suggested, should concentrate on pouring as many troops as possible into one of these – Methoni, with its direct access to the shore, would be best – and should do so immediately, without waiting for the Turks or for the spring, so that his heavy ships could still take advantage of the winter winds. And so Ibrahim sailed on 23 February 1825, and the next day disembarked his infantry and cavalry at Methoni, where they dug themselves in. A few days later they entered Koroni. Meanwhile, the Egyptian army fanned out to the northeast, to subjugate the rest of the Peloponnese.

If it was to have any chance at all of checking Ibrahim's advance, the Greek government now needed every man it could lay its hands on. Kolokotronis was quickly released with his fellow captains from their prison on Hydra and once again given supreme command of the Greek forces, while another decree required each district in the country to provide one conscript for every hundred of its population. But it was too late; the Egyptians were spreading rapidly across the whole peninsula. Kolokotronis, believing that Tripolis was the key to the entire Peloponnese, decided to destroy the city before their arrival, but once again he was unlucky: Ibrahim's troops arrived before much damage was done and soon had the fires under control before first setting about the plunder and destruction and then relighting them. Once again the barbarity was appalling. Dr Samuel Gridley Howe,[2] an

---

[1] Modone and Corone must henceforth be known by their Greek names.
[2] He was, incidentally, the husband of Julia Ward Howe, author of *The Battle Hymn of the Republic*. ('Mine eyes have seen the glory . . .')

American surgeon who had arrived in Greece earlier in the year, wrote in his journal:

> I went on shore at sunrise and . . . went over the little ground, where still lay the dead, horseman and horse, which the enemy had not been able to carry off. They were all beheaded, and bodies savagely mangled by the Greeks, who committed on them every possible indignity. It was not enough to leave their bodies unburied, but they must show towards them a brutality the most savage.

Only two days later, on 28 June, he added:

> But what is poor Greece to do? Ibrahim Pasha, with his army, has traversed the whole Morea from Modon to Napoli [Nauplia]. He has passed unharmed through defiles where five hundred resolute men might keep at bay his whole army. He has burnt Argos, Tripolitza, and Kalamata, the three largest towns in the Morea. It is not so much the loss of these places, and the immense property which they have ruined in their route, but it shows lamentably the weakness of the country that cannot resist an army which is not the fifth part of what the enemy can bring.

Dr Howe spoke no more than the truth. He could not know that the most dramatic disaster of all was still to come.

In the whole story of the Greek War of Independence, the name of Missolonghi stands out above all others. This is not only because of its resistance to two concerted attacks, in 1822 and 1823, thanks to which it was the only town north of the Gulf of Corinth to have remained in Greek hands since the beginning of hostilities; nor is it altogether due to the death there of Lord Byron in 1824, though this did much to make it celebrated throughout Europe. Missolonghi became a symbol above all as a result of the unique experience which it suffered on the eve of Palm Sunday 1825, and which captured the horrified imagination of the world.

The Turkish army that marched south from Arta early that year under the command of Reshid Pasha drew up outside the town at the end of April. It numbered some 8,000 fighting soldiers, as opposed to the Missolonghi garrison of less than half that number. Unlike the unified Turkish force, however, this garrison was characteristically composed of about a dozen different groups, each under its own captain. Concerted action was hard to achieve until one natural leader emerged above the others, a Souliot captain named Notis Botsaris. Thanks in large measure to him, in that first phase of the siege the defenders successfully withstood everything that Reshid could hurl against them. They knew too that they could not be starved out, since they still had a supply line from Zakynthos and the other Ionian islands across their lagoon, whose waters were too shallow to allow the passage of the heavy Turkish ships. When the October rains began and the Turks withdrew from the walls for the winter, there was high optimism among the Greek leaders.

But they were reckoning without the Egyptians. Since Ibrahim's departure from Alexandria his father had built up a whole new fleet: some 135 vessels of all sizes, including a further squadron from Turkey and others from Algiers and Tunis. Ibrahim had returned to take command, and in the first days of 1826 this new armada, carrying 10,000 troops and a quantity of heavy artillery, cast anchor in the waters outside Missolonghi. After a few weeks of preparation, at dawn on 24 February the cannon opened fire, and it has been calculated that over the next three days more than 8,500 cannonballs and mortar shells were fired into the town. The destruction was appalling – but somehow the defences held.

Ibrahim – who had taken over the supreme command, making no secret of his contempt for his Turkish colleague – now turned his attention to the lagoon. Once he had gained control of those shallow waters the people of Missolonghi could be starved into submission, but the task was not an easy one. Reshid had tried it the year before, when he had launched thirty-six shallow-draft boats to attack the town by sea; but they had been turned back by heavy fire from the little island of Vasiladi. Ibrahim now tried something a good deal more powerful: a fleet of eighty-two even shallower vessels, together with five huge rafts carrying thirty-six-pounder cannon. Once again the gunners of Vasiladi put up a magnificent performance, but towards evening there was an explosion in their powder magazine and their resistance came to an end. After that the other lagoon islands quickly surrendered until only one remained: the island of Klisova, half a mile southeast of the town. Here, the attackers were obliged to disembark several yards from the shore and wade through the mud; they made easy targets, of which the island's defenders took full advantage. Both Reshid and Ibrahim himself were wounded and the attempt on the island failed, but it made little difference. The Turks had gained control of the lagoon. Missolonghi's lifeline was cut. Henceforth its surrender would be only a matter of time.

Unless, that is, its entire population broke out and made a bid for liberty across the plain to the northeast of the town; and this is precisely what the people of Missolonghi resolved to do. They numbered some 9,000 all told, men, women and children; it was decided that when night fell on 22 April, every able-bodied adult and adolescent would scramble over the walls, carrying the younger children who would be drugged with laudanum. They would cross the defensive ditch on makeshift bridges, and then take shelter and wait behind the outer rampart until they heard firing: this would come from a party of troops under one of the captains, George Karaiskakis, staging a diversionary attack to keep the besiegers busy. Then they would all move forward together. Those too old, too sick or too weak to leave would be gathered into a few neighbouring houses, with an explosive charge beneath them which they would ignite when the Turks approached.

It was a desperate plan, which could hardly have been expected to succeed even as well as it did. There was none of the long-awaited firing from Karaiskakis; after standing for an hour behind the rampart the refugees lost patience and burst out on to the plain. Then, suddenly, there were cries of 'Opiso! Opiso!' – 'Back! Back!' – and all was confusion. Some continued forward, others retreated. Such was the crowding and jostling on the bridges that many fell into the ditch; those who got back into the town were made short work of by the Turkish troops who, seeing the walls undefended, had lost no time in smashing their way in. Those still hurrying across the plain were attacked first by Turkish cavalry and, later, by Albanian soldiery; the men were killed, the women and children taken prisoner. Behind them, meanwhile, Missolonghi was a blazing inferno. Dr Howe could not contain his feelings. He wrote on 30 April:

> Missolonghi has fallen! Her brave warriors have thrown themselves in desperation upon the bayonets of their enemies; her women and children have perished in the flames of their own dwellings, kindled by their own hands; and their scorched and mangled carcasses lie a damning proof of the selfish indifference of the Christian world . . . For ten months have the eyes of Christian Europe been turned upon Missolonghi. They have seen her inhabitants struggling at enormous odds against the horrors of war and famine; her men worn out, bleeding and dying; her women gnawing the bones of dead horses and mules; her walls surrounded by Arabs, yelling for the blood of her warriors, and to glut their hellish lusts upon her women and children. All this they have seen, and not raised a finger for their defence . . .

As for the casualties, it is impossible to give an exact figure; by the end of that ghastly night, however, it seems likely that nearly half the population of Missolonghi – perhaps 4,000 – were dead and some 3,000, mostly women and children, captive. Less than a quarter – 2,000 at the most – had made their way to safety.

Even more than the tragedy of Chios, the fate of Missolonghi was mourned throughout Europe. Once again an outraged Delacroix seized his brush in protest: his tremendous painting, *La Grèce sur les ruines de Missolonghi*, did much to focus the prevailing indignation, and across Europe his contemporaries – painters and sculptors, writers and poets – enthusiastically followed his lead. The western powers could no longer sit on their hands in the name of neutrality; the time had come to gird on their swords and hasten to Greece's aid.

The disaster of Missolonghi left all Greece demoralised; and it was soon afterwards followed by another, greater still. In June 1826 Reshid Pasha launched, with an army of 7,000 men, a concerted attack on Athens. The city, because of its position, had never been the Greek capital; it was exceptional, however, for two reasons. The first was the obvious one: it had been the scene of the greatest achievements of classical antiquity and still, for all its long *dégringolade*, remained a symbol of the artistic, cultural and intellectual distinction of which the Greeks had once been capable and, it was hoped, might one day be capable again. The second, less romantic, had still greater relevance to the present situation. After the fall of Missolonghi it was the only city in Greek hands north of the Gulf of Corinth. Despite recent Turkish and Egyptian successes, it now seemed likely that the continuing struggle, together with the increasing sympathy for it among the powers of western Europe, would result in at least some degree of Greek autonomy. With Athens back in Muslim hands, that autonomy might well be limited to the Peloponnese; if, on the other hand, the Greeks were able to hold the city, the frontier would have to be a good deal further north.

By mid-August Reshid was in control of the whole city except the Acropolis, where a Greek garrison of 500 held out through the following winter – during which time the Greek government, such as it was, fell victim to yet another outbreak of factional strife. Once again, Kolokotronis seems to have been largely to blame, and by the summer of 1827 there were no less than seven separate conflicts in progress. Oddly enough, it was two Britons who managed to impose some degree of calm, though both failed ultimately to distinguish themselves. The first was General Sir Richard Church, who had raised the Anglo-Greek regiment on Zakynthos sixteen years before. In the interim he had served in the army of the King of Naples, but his heart had remained in Greece. He returned there in March 1827, having been offered the supreme command of the Greek land forces – only a foreigner, it seemed, could hope to establish order over so chaotic a country – but he had refused to take up his post until the two rival governments had settled their differences.

Church was followed a week later by a still more remarkable figure. Thomas, Lord Cochrane – later 10th Earl of Dundonald – had early in his career been court-martialled for insubordination, and in 1814 had been put on trial for fraud on the Stock Exchange. In the first instance he had been acquitted, in the second found guilty.[1] Nonetheless, he was generally accounted England's greatest admiral since Nelson. He had spent seven years in South America, where he had fought for the independence of Chile, Peru and Brazil, and as early as November 1825 he had been offered the command, such as it was, of the Greek navy. The delay had been occasioned by his insistence, as a condition of his employment, on the provision of six steamships and two frigates, to be designed by another British aristocrat, Frank Abney Hastings, who had served as a ship's boy at Trafalgar and had reached the rank of captain before being dismissed from the service.

Steamships were still in their infancy. Even they were still normally propelled by sail, using their primitive engines only in calm or in battle. Cochrane's order was to be paid for by a second loan, organised in London, of £566,000, but it was never fulfilled. One of the two frigates had to be sold to the American government to pay for the other, and only two of the six steamships ever reached Greece, neither of them – thanks to design failings, poor construction, corruption and the activities of Egyptian agents – to be trusted an inch. When he eventually arrived in Greece – on his yacht – in the spring of 1827, Cochrane took an even stronger line than Church. How, he demanded, could the Greek leaders make such fools of themselves, squabbling about where to hold their next assembly, when they should have been attacking the Turks and Egyptians, driving them out of the country before it was totally destroyed? His words had their effect: the two sides were forced into an agreement, according to which a new Assembly should meet at Trizini, the ancient Troezen. By the end of March both Church and

---

[1] The two judgements should almost certainly have been reversed.

Cochrane had withdrawn their objections and assumed their posts, and only a week or two later the Assembly resolved to offer the presidency of Greece to Capodistria, who had now left the Russian service and was living quietly in Geneva.

Meanwhile, in Athens, the Acropolis was still under siege. In an attempt to break the deadlock, it was decided early in 1827 to despatch a force of 2,300, under the English philhellene commander Thomas Gordon. Gordon was soon joined by Karaiskakis with several detachments of local troops, so that his numbers were probably not far short of 10,000 by the time Cochrane arrived at Piraeus in his flagship, the *Hellas*, shortly to be followed by Church in a commandeered schooner. Various plans of action were now put forward, but Cochrane had determined on a direct march on Athens and, as usual, rode roughshod over any opposition. 'Where I command,' he is quoted as saying, 'all other authority ceases.' Karaiskakis, realising that such an advance would involve a dangerous crossing of an open plain almost certainly surrounded by Turkish cavalry, did not immediately accept this view, but a day or two later he was shot by a Turkish musketeer and there were no more objections. So it was agreed that at midnight on 5 May 1827 a force of 2,500 should disembark from the near side of Phaleron Bay and march on Athens, while the remainder – almost three times as many – should remain at Piraeus to await further orders.

Karaiskakis had, of course, been perfectly right. But if the plan was foolhardy, its execution was little short of shameful. Gordon commented afterwards:

> As the Admiral had nothing to do with the motions of the troops when once ashore, and the General [Church], satisfied with having sketched a disposition, staid in his vessel till daylight, the captains, all on a footing of equality, acted independently, halting where they chose; so that the column was scattered over a space of four miles, the front within cannon-shot of Athens, the rear close to the sea, and the soldiers, unprovided with spades and pickaxes, dug the earth with their daggers, in order to cover themselves from the charge of horse.

Reshid attacked at dawn, with all too foreseeable results. The Greeks lost 1,500 men, more than on any single day since the beginning of the war. When, after a comfortable night's rest, Cochrane and Church disembarked from their respective ships, it was to find the survivors, exhausted and terrified, dragging themselves back to the shore and clambering into the small boats in which they hoped to escape to safety. Church, in an attempt to restore his reputation, held out heroically with a handful of men at Phaleron for three more weeks, but by the end of the month heat and thirst had compelled him to surrender. The garrison on the Acropolis gave in a few days later.

Who was to blame? In one way or another, just about everyone: Cochrane for his overweening arrogance and refusal to listen to other, wiser men; Church for not standing up to him; both of them for staying on board their ships when they should have been with their men; the Greek captains for demonstrating once again their hopeless lack of discipline and inability to agree on a supreme commander. Their failure proved a tragedy, and it served them right.

Meanwhile, the question of European intervention dragged on, as ambassadors shuttled between London, Paris and St Petersburg. British interests were in the capable hands of the Foreign Secretary, George Canning, who in April 1827 succeeded Lord Liverpool as Prime Minister; it was largely through his efforts that the Treaty of London was signed by Britain, France and Russia on 6 July. By its terms Greece would enjoy autonomy, theoretically as a dependency of Turkey (in that she would pay an annual tribute) but effectively independent, as the three powers would recognise by establishing commercial relations with her. She and Turkey must conclude an armistice within a month – Canning later shortened this to a fortnight – after which, if they had failed to do so, the powers would intervene. For the Greeks this was good news indeed. Turkey, they knew, would reject any idea of an armistice, so intervention was virtually certain.

Events were to prove them right. Some months before, the Sultan had appointed Mohammed Ali titular supreme commander of all land and sea forces in Greece, Turkish as well as Egyptian; Mohammed Ali had thereupon raised a new army of nearly 15,000, and a new fleet consisting of three Turkish ships of the line, sixty smaller vessels – five of them French-built – forty transports and six fireships. All told, they carried some 3,500 guns. This was the force which dropped anchor on 7 September in the Bay of Navarino, where Ibrahim was waiting.

The three allied navies hastened to Navarino; but their respective admirals had strict orders not to go directly into battle. They were first to do everything in their power to 'encourage' all Turkish and Egyptian warships to return peaceably to Constantinople or Alexandria, though Canning made it clear that, if they persisted in remaining in Greece, the orders of the British admiral, Sir Edward Codrington, 'were to be enforced, if necessary and when all other means are exhausted, by cannon shot'. Codrington – another veteran of Trafalgar, where he had commanded HMS *Orion* – had been appointed Commander-in-Chief, Mediterranean, the previous December. He was the first to reach Navarino, where he was joined by his French colleague, the Comte de Rigny, a few days later. The Russians having not yet arrived, on 25 September the two admirals, accompanied by a few of their senior officers and by Codrington's son Henry, a midshipman on his father's ship, had an interview with Ibrahim in his tent just outside the neighbouring town of Pylos.

The conversation, as recorded by Henry Codrington, was polite and cordial, accompanied by quantities of coffee and the smoking of enormous jewel-studded chibouks. It went very much as might have been imagined, with Codrington issuing his courteous warning and Ibrahim agreeing to take no action until he received new instructions from Alexandria and Constantinople. All the same it is a pity that no minutes were taken, for it soon became clear that the two sides had very different ideas of the conclusions. Ibrahim apparently believed that the Greeks as well as the Turks were bound by the temporary armistice; he also assumed that there would be no allied objection to his taking supplies and provisions to the Turkish garrison at Patras.

The Greeks for their part saw no reason to call a halt. They after all had accepted the terms of the Treaty of London; it was the Turks who had rejected them. Thus it was that in the last days of September, while Church was leading an expedition against Patras, Ibrahim sailed for the city with a fleet of no less than forty-eight ships – far more than could have been needed for a simple supply drop. But he never reached it: Codrington was there to block him, and ferocious equinoctial gales did the rest. Ibrahim then changed his tactics. The admirals might frustrate him by sea, but they were powerless to check him on land. Very well, he would continue with the devastation of the Peloponnese.

With the agreement of 25 September now little more than a dead letter, the three admirals – Codrington and de Rigny had now been joined by the Russian, the Dutch-born Rear-Admiral Count Heiden – decided on a show of strength. The ten French naval officers on board the Egyptian ships as advisers were summoned back at once, and in the late morning of 20 October Codrington – in his flagship, the *Asia* – led the three fleets, together numbering eleven ships of the line, eight large frigates and eight smaller vessels, through the narrow entrance to the Bay of Navarino.

Both sides were still under orders not to begin hostilities, but in so tense a situation it was impossible to tell whether any individual action was merely provocative or actually aggressive. Moreover, unlike the allied admirals, the Turkish and Egyptian commanders had agreed on no overall plan to guide them. Sooner or later, battle was inevitable. It began at about two o'clock in the afternoon, and continued until about six. Those four hours saw the last naval battle ever fought in which no steamship took part. More remarkable still was the fact that the ships were all lying at anchor, at close quarters in a small bay; they could manoeuvre only by swinging round on the anchor cables so that the guns along their broadsides could face their chosen target. Dr Howe unforgettably described the scene:

> The Turkish ships, more than triple the number of their opponents, opened all their broadsides, and seconded by the batteries onshore, poured such tremendous volleys of shot as, if well directed, must have annihilated the Europeans, but the latter sent back, if a smaller, yet a far more destructive fire, for every gun was pointed, every shot told . . . The allies, sending out their boats, cut the cables of the Turkish fire-vessels, and setting fire to them, let them drive down upon their own fleet. In a few minutes several ships-of-war, taking fire, added to the horror of a scene already terrible; the two long lines of ships, from which roared nearly two thousand cannon; the blazing fire-ships, driving to and fro among the huge Turkish vessels, whose falling masts and shattered hulls began to show how the battle went; the sea covered with spars and half-burnt masses of wood to which clung thousands of sailors escaped from their exploded vessels; the lines of batteries upon the shore, which blazed away all the time, and were covered by the whole Turkish army most anxiously watching a scene upon which their own fate depended . . . But a contest could not be long where one side had only a vast superiority of force, directed by blind fury alone, against cool courage, discipline, and naval skill.

Strangely enough, the allied losses at Navarino were comparatively light: not a single ship was sunk, the casualties amounting to 174 killed and 475 wounded. For the Ottoman fleet, however, it was a very different story. From the start it had been at a disadvantage. Its supreme commander Ibrahim Pasha missed the whole engagement, being still away in the Peloponnese; the Egyptian admiral, Moharrem Bey, had no stomach for the fight and had left with the French officers before it began. There remained only the Turk, Tahir Pasha, whose flagship was sunk at an early stage of the battle. Of the eighty-nine fighting ships under his command, only twenty-nine survived.

Codrington estimated that some 6,000 Turks and Egyptians were killed, and another 4,000 wounded.

The pendulum had swung dramatically. Little more than five months before, on 6 May, the Turkish recovery of Athens had seemed to sound a death-knell to Greek hopes; after Navarino, Greek independence was certain.

All was not quite over. Ibrahim's troops – some 24,000 of them – remained in the devastated Peloponnese; it was not until September 1828 that they were finally embarked on Egyptian ships and returned to Alexandria. Fighting continued, too, beyond the Gulf of Corinth: the further the Greeks could advance to the north, the more territory they could claim for their new state. Church in the west and Dimitrios Ipsilantis in the east pushed steadily forward, the former as far as Arta, the latter to Thermopylae, opposite the northern tip of Euboea – although he was unable to dislodge the Turks from Athens itself.

Meanwhile, Capodistria had finally arrived to take up his presidency. He immediately antagonised the revolutionary captains by making no effort to conceal his contempt for the way in which they had failed to unite, endlessly bickering and squabbling amongst themselves while the fate of their country hung in the balance. But he worked sixteen hours a day to rebuild the country, and his immense reputation abroad had a decisive effect on the deliberations of the London Conference, which now had the task of drawing the boundaries of the new Greek state. In September 1828 the ambassadors to Constantinople of the three allied powers met on the island of Poros to consider this specific question, and three months later they announced their recommendation: a line running from Arta in the west to Volos in the east, with the inclusion of the islands of Euboea, Samos and possibly Crete.[1] The only problem was Turkey, which refused outright to come to the negotiating table; this was finally resolved only by the Treaty of Adrianople, which ended a Russian–Turkish war in September 1829. By its terms the Turks finally agreed to abide by whatever future decisions on Greece might eventually be taken by the allies. Finally, on 3 February 1830 in London, Greece was declared an independent nation under the protection of Britain, France and Russia.

It was to be some years yet before peace returned. Capodistria was

---

[1] The territory north of the Arta–Volos line was to remain part of the Ottoman Empire until May 1913, after the First Balkan War.

assassinated on 9 October 1831, and the country was plunged back into confusion. But in July 1832 the Turks gave their final approval to the Arta–Volos line – though not to the inclusion of Samos and Crete – and Greece became a sovereign state. Even then, however, its sovereignty was not absolute. The western powers had determined that it should be a monarchy, and had selected as its king the seventeen-year-old Prince Otto of Wittelsbach, son of King Ludwig I of Bavaria. He arrived in Nauplia on the morning of 6 February 1833 and was given a tremendous welcome, cheered everywhere to the echo.

Greece's long-cherished dream had finally become a reality – but her troubles were by no means over.

CHAPTER XXVI

Mohammed Ali and North Africa

The Ottoman Sultan Mahmoud II deserved better than he got. He was, in many ways, an enlightened ruler and reformer, who did everything within his power to modernise his creaking empire. In 1826 he had got rid of the janissaries – for five hundred years the empire's crack military corps, but now becoming increasingly mutinous – by the simple expedient of massacring them wholesale. He established a new army, under his own direct control and trained by German instructors, with a military college modelled on Napoleon's Saint-Cyr; he slashed the power of the religious *ulema*, depriving them of their secular responsibilities; he centralised and to some extent streamlined his civil service; he virtually introduced modern principles of education; he inaugurated a postal service and the first Turkish-language newspaper in Istanbul; he established a school of medicine and introduced new laws on public health. Finally – and perhaps rather sadly – he abolished the old Turkish dress. Away went the long robes and turbans, the billowing pantaloons and soft slippers. In came the fez, the frock coat, the European trousers and the black leather boots.

It was sad indeed for him that he had to preside over the loss of his navy, of southern Greece and of several other previously Ottoman territories – and then was still obliged to cope with that perennial thorn in his flesh, Mohammed Ali in Cairo. As a reward for his intervention in the Peloponnese, Mohammed Ali had expected the pashalik of Syria; Mahmoud, however, had fobbed him off with Crete, which his viceroy considered shamefully inadequate. In the spring of 1832 Mohammed Ali therefore sent his son Ibrahim with an army to Syria, instructing him to occupy it by force. Ibrahim obeyed him to the letter. Gaza fell, and Jerusalem, and – after a short siege – Acre; Ibrahim then swept north to Damascus and Aleppo, whence he led his army through Anatolia until he was threatening Istanbul itself.

With his capital now in a state not far short of panic, the Sultan sent an urgent plea to London for aid. The British Foreign Secretary, Lord Palmerston, however, was not interested; Mahmoud had no choice but to call upon his old enemy Russia. Tsar Nicholas, ever ready to meddle in Turkish affairs, asked nothing better; early in 1833 he landed 18,000 troops at Scutari, directly across the Bosphorus from Istanbul. Against such a force Ibrahim knew that he had no chance; sensibly enough, he decided to negotiate. By this time Palmerston had woken up to the seriousness of the situation, as had the French government; together they prevailed upon the Porte to insist on the Russians' withdrawal, in return for certain major concessions. Mohammed Ali was confirmed in the pashaliks of Egypt and of Crete, and was now in addition presented with that of Syria, which included Damascus, Tripoli, Aleppo and Adana. Simultaneously but in a separate treaty, Mahmoud confirmed an offensive and defensive agreement with Russia, a secret clause of which gave Russian warships the right to pass freely through the straits from the Black Sea to the Mediterranean – a privilege denied to all other foreign powers without Turkish consent.[1]

The Sultan had successfully averted both the Russian and the Egyptian threats, but he had paid a heavy price. With the whole of the southeastern Mediterranean under his control, Mohammed Ali was now a serious rival, and although Syria had been specifically awarded to him for his lifetime only, Mahmoud was well aware that he had every intention of turning his possessions into what would effectively be an independent hereditary monarchy. Five years later he was proved right, when in 1838 Mohammed Ali refused to pay his annual tribute to the Porte. The Sultan seized his opportunity and the following year declared war, sending an army of 24,000 and a supporting fleet to Syria with explicit orders to drive out the Egyptians once and for all.

The result, from his point of view, was catastrophic. On 24 June Ibrahim's army, though heavily outnumbered, routed Mahmoud's forces at Nezib in northern Syria. Thanks to generous Egyptian bribes vast numbers of Turkish troops deserted, while the commander of the fleet – presumably for much the same reason – sailed it straight to Alexandria; and on 1 July 1839, the very day that Sultan Mahmoud died in Istanbul, handed it over to Mohammed Ali. The French, who believed their own best interests to lie with Egypt, declined to take any action, but the other powers were horrified. On 15 July 1840 a conference in London, presided over by Palmerston himself and including both Austria and Prussia, presented Mohammed Ali with an ultimatum. He must withdraw all his troops from northern Syria and

---

[1] This was the Treaty of Unkiar–Skelessi, little known because short-lived. In July 1841 the powers guaranteed Ottoman independence and declared the Dardanelles and the Bosphorus closed to all nations in time of peace.

Crete and return the Turkish fleet to Istanbul. If he did so, he would be recognised as hereditary Pasha of Egypt, and Pasha of southern Syria for his lifetime; if he refused, the British and Russian fleets would together put both Egypt and Syria under a blockade.

In the hopes of receiving substantial aid from France – which, it need hardly be said, was not ultimately forthcoming – Mohammed Ali refused, and the British at least were as good as their word. That autumn a British squadron under Captain Charles Napier bombarded the forts of both Beirut and Acre and destroyed them; it even landed an expeditionary force, also commanded by Napier, which with the help of the local Arabs – who had greatly suffered under Mohammed Ali's regime – easily defeated the Egyptian army of occupation at the battle of Boharsef (one of the Royal Navy's most unlikely victories). The French, furious at what they denounced as unprovoked aggression, threatened war but were not taken very seriously; as King Louis-Philippe himself was later to point out, there was all the difference in the world between threatening war and making it. Napier then sailed on to Alexandria, which would surely have suffered the same fate as the two Syrian ports if Mohammed Ali had not agreed to negotiate. He hastily returned the Turkish fleet to Istanbul and resumed his annual tribute to the Sultan, withdrawing altogether from Syria and Crete.

The old ruffian lived on until 1849, dying at the age of eighty. He continued to rule as hereditary Pasha of Egypt and Sudan, but always under Ottoman suzerainty. And he made no further attempts at territorial expansion. He was a man of high intelligence and, we are told, great personal charm. He was also energetic and efficient: his rule in Egypt certainly marked a dramatic improvement on what had gone before. But he was uneducated and possessed no real political vision or ideology. He governed by Ottoman principles and, though he went some way towards creating a new and more forward-looking society, much of his time was spent consolidating his own position and resisting repeated attempts by sultan after sultan to get rid of him. In this he was remarkably successful. The dynasty that he established was to last well over a hundred years, until the middle of the twentieth century, and if he missed his opportunity of laying the foundations of a modern Egyptian state, he at least cleared the way for his successors. If they too failed, the blame for their failure can hardly attributed to him.

*

One April day in 1827 Hussein, Dey[1] of Algiers, angrily struck the French consul three times with his fly-whisk. Outraged at such treatment of its official representative, the French government despatched a naval squadron to the city to demand an apology and reparations. When the Dey refused, the consul and all French residents were put on board the ships and Algiers blockaded. Then, in July 1830, a French expeditionary force landed at Sidi-Ferruch, some twenty miles to the west of Algiers, while the city itself was simultaneously subjected to a formidable naval bombardment. It fell a few weeks later. The Dey went into exile. The French occupation of Algeria had begun.

The occupiers did not, however, have it all their own way. As early as 1832 fighting broke out in the interior under a twenty-five-year-old resistance leader named Abd el-Kader and continued for the next fifteen years, but by the time Abd el-Kader surrendered in 1847 to Marshal Thomas-Robert Bugeaud, French colonists were pouring into Algeria. Already by 1841 there were over 37,000 of them, and well before the end of the century they accounted for a good 10 percent of the total population. It was, they found, an easy place in which to settle – indeed, many different peoples had already done so: Carthaginians, Romans, Byzantines, Arabs and Turks. Recently the power of the Barbary corsairs had grown to the point where they were virtually the masters of the land – though not its governors, if only because they made no attempt to govern. What is unquestionable is the fact that under the French army and Bugeaud's *bureaux arabes* Algeria was more efficiently and more fairly administered than it had been for many centuries.

Along the coast and in the northern mountains, the Algerian climate is typical of the Mediterranean, with warm, dry summers and mild, rainy winters. Before the arrival of the French the land had been by no means uncivilised – as early as 1834 a French general noted that illiteracy hardly existed, since every village boasted two schools – but although technically under Ottoman domination its successive governments had been chronically unstable: of the Dey's twenty-eight predecessors, over half had met a violent death. Property rights were vague, and to the French unimportant. Addressing the National

---

[1] The office of dey – the word actually comes from the Turkish, meaning maternal uncle – had been first instituted in 1671. In the early years the dey was elected by the corsair captains, taking over the duties of the pasha appointed by the Ottoman Sultan. It was he who nominated the beys as provincial chiefs.

Assembly in 1840, Bugeaud made his own opinion clear: 'Wherever there is fresh water and fertile land, there we have to put settlers [*colons*], without concerning ourselves as to whom these lands belong.' On the other hand, there were about a million hectares – some 4,000 square miles – which had been the property of the Ottoman government and which the French could be said to have inherited, together with other vast tracts which had been taken over, either because they were lying uncultivated or as the result of some malfeasance on the part of the former owners.

In the early days Bugeaud's regime was fairly dictatorial, with relatively little comprehension between rulers and ruled. Gradually, however, the French attitude became more enlightened. Soon after the establishment of the Second Empire in 1852 Napoleon III was to say that, while he hoped that an increased number of settlers would keep Algeria French, it should be remembered that France's first duty was to its three million Arabs. Algeria was 'not a French province but an Arab country, a European colony and a French camp'. Military rule, however, was to continue until after the fall of the Second Empire in 1870. Before that time the Governor-General of Algeria – a title first given to Bugeaud in 1845 – was almost invariably a high-ranking army officer. It was only in 1870 that the *colons* – otherwise known as the *pieds noirs* – by now over 200,000 strong, insisted on more control over their own affairs, similar to that enjoyed by their compatriots across the Mediterranean. Algeria was now formally annexed, constituting an integral part of France itself, and was governed through the French Ministry of the Interior in Paris.

Because of this, Algeria's position was essentially different from that of her neighbours to east and west, Tunisia and Morocco. Here too French influence was strong, but since there was relatively little immigration these two countries were deemed to be protectorates only and were dealt with by the Ministry of Foreign Affairs at the Quai d'Orsay. Tunisia too had been technically an Ottoman province, although in fact entirely autonomous. When in 1830 the French occupied Algiers, the reigning Bey of Tunis had cautiously accepted French assurances of non-intervention, but then in 1835 the Ottoman Empire seized the opportunity of a disputed succession in neighbouring Libya to depose the ruling dynasty there and re-establish direct Ottoman rule. Thereafter Tunisia found herself most delicately placed, sandwiched as she was between the two great powers of France and Turkey, both of which were casting covetous eyes upon her. It says much for the Bey and his successors that she performed a successful balancing act until 1881, when the French, on the flimsy enough pretext that a bunch of Tunisian tribesmen had settled in Algerian territory, invaded the country, transferred to France the Bey's authority in finance and foreign affairs and appointed a French Resident Minister.

The Sultanate of Morocco – the only North African country with coastal exposure to both the Mediterranean and the Atlantic – was in a different position again. Because of its lack of natural harbours, its rugged mountainous interior and the immense distance separating it from imperial centres in the east, it was still, in the middle of the nineteenth century, very largely isolated. It was this isolation – encouraged by successive rulers – which had enabled it firstly to preserve, to a far greater degree than was possible elsewhere, its ancient Islamic, Berber and African traditions, and secondly to resist exterior pressures, notably that of the Spanish Reconquista in the fifteenth and sixteenth centuries. Morocco thus remains the only Arab country never to have become part of the Ottoman Empire, which for so long controlled virtually all the rest of the Arab world.

The arrival of the French in neighbouring Algeria could not, however, be ignored. Relations deteriorated sharply in 1844, after the rebel Abd el-Kader took refuge in Morocco, and the Sultan despatched an army to the border. The French responded by bombarding Tangier in early August, and Mogador ten days later; on the 14th they virtually destroyed Sultan Moulay Abd el-Rahman's army at Isly, near Oujda. The Sultan was obliged, *inter alia*, to promise that he would intern or expel the rebel should he ever again enter Moroccan territory. He proved as good as his word: in 1847, when Abd el-Kader sought refuge for the second time, he was arrested by Moroccan troops and forced to surrender. It comes as a relief to report that the French were merciful towards him: he was to spend the rest of his life in honourable exile in Damascus.

On the Sultan's death in 1859, the spotlight briefly switches to Spain, with which a bitter dispute took place over the boundaries of the Spanish enclave at Ceuta.[1] This ended in a declaration of war by

---

[1] This free port on the coast of Morocco had first become independent in Byzantine days, but because of its importance as a trading post in ivory, gold and slaves, its ownership had always been bitterly contested. In 1415 Portugal gained control, but in 1580 it passed to Spain, to which it was legally assigned by the Treaty of Lisbon in 1688. With nearby Melilla, it has remained Spanish ever since. Never has it formed part of Moroccan territory.

Madrid and, in the following year, the Spanish capture of Tetouan, the Sultan being obliged to agree to a large indemnity and a considerable increase in the size of the Ceuta enclave. Meanwhile, the British and the Italians were also hoping somehow to win their slice of the Moroccan cake, but both were bought off by France: Britain agreed to give the French a free hand there in return for a French undertaking not to interfere with her own plans in Egypt, while Italy did much the same in relation to Libya. In 1880 the British, French, Spanish, Germans, Italians and Americans had concluded a convention at Madrid which – in theory at least – virtually guaranteed Moroccan independence, but this did not prevent France from concluding in 1904 – with full British connivance – a secret treaty with Spain agreeing on respective 'spheres of influence' within the country. This was the situation when at the end of March 1905 Kaiser Wilhelm II arrived at Tangier on the liner *Hamburg* – and, as so often, put the cat among the pigeons. In his reply to the speech of welcome he declared first for the complete sovereignty and independence of the Sultan, second for the integrity of his realm, and third for 'a Morocco open to the peaceful competition of all nations, without annexation or monopoly'.

It all sounded innocuous enough, but to the European powers it was clearly a deliberate attempt to put a spoke into the French – and to a lesser extent the Spanish – wheel. The previous year the Kaiser had proposed that Germany should lease Port Mahon in Minorca from Spain – an idea that had met a frigid reception from both France and Britain, the island being situated where it could command the approaches to Toulon and on a direct line between the two vital British bases of Malta and Gibraltar. The last thing either nation wanted was to have Wilhelm meddling once again in the affairs of the western Mediterranean. The whole issue was finally hammered out and – it seemed – satisfactorily resolved in 1906, when a conference of the signatories to the 1880 convention was called at Algeciras to discuss the whole Moroccan question. This reaffirmed the integrity of the country and the economic equality of the powers, but sanctioned French and Spanish policing of Moroccan ports and the collection of customs dues.

Even now the story was not quite over. In 1907 France – always eager to increase her influence in North Africa – occupied Casablanca; then Abd el-Hafid, the brother of the Sultan Abd el-Aziz, led a rebellion against him, claiming that he had betrayed Muslim traditions. Abd el-Aziz took refuge in Tangier, while in Fez Abd el-Hafid was proclaimed

Sultan. He was duly recognised in the following year by the European powers, but never managed to impose order throughout the country and eventually, with disorder steadily increasing, was obliged to ask the French to rescue him. The result was the Treaty of Fez of 1912, by the terms of which Morocco became a French protectorate. Tangier, long the seat of the European diplomatic missions, was put under separate administration.

Finally, a word about Libya. Anyone who has ever visited the country will have been struck by its extraordinary geography. To the west – with its capital at Tripoli – is Tripolitania where, in sites like Leptis Magna or Sabratha, we can still feel the impact of ancient Rome; to the east is Cyrenaica – based on Benghazi – which, at Apollonia, Cyrene and elsewhere, immediately takes us back to the world of classical Greece. Between the two, however, are some six or seven hundred miles of virtually nothing, except the nondescript little town of Sirte at what is roughly the half-way mark. The country has probably been kept together by two things only: the Sanussi order that preached a puritanical form of Islam – though even this was largely concentrated in Cyrenaica – and, later, Italian colonialism.[1] Like its neighbours, it had been more or less autonomous, although under nominal Turkish rule, until in 1835 the Ottoman Empire took advantage of one of the endless disputes over the succession to reimpose a direct government. For the next seventy-seven years the country was administered by civil servants from Istanbul, until in 1911 Italy took over, gave it its present name and governed it until after the Second World War.

---

[1] See Chapter XXXI.

CHAPTER XXVII

The *Quarantotto*

When, on Wednesday, 12 January 1848 – the thirty-eighth birthday of King Ferdinand II[1] – the people of Palermo rose up against their Bourbon masters, they could have had no idea of what they were starting. Risings in the kingdom were nothing new: there had been unsuccessful ones in Naples in 1820 and in Piedmont in 1821; in Sicily itself there had been another as recently as 1837, sparked off by an epidemic of cholera – the first appearance of the disease in western Europe. But the consequent angry manifestations had been relatively easily dealt with. What happened in 1848 – the *quarantotto*, as Italy remembers it – was something else. It was a revolution, and by the end of the year it had been followed by other revolutions: in Paris, Vienna, Naples, Rome, Venice, Florence, Lucca, Parma, Modena, Berlin, Milan, Parma, Cracow, Warsaw and Budapest.

Already, as the year opened, student riots had prompted the authorities to close the university; several eminent citizens known for their liberal views had been arrested, and an unsigned manifesto circulated calling upon the people to rise up on the King's birthday. A large proportion of the insurgents were mountain brigands – the forerunners of the *mafiosi* of today – or simple peasants, few of whom probably had much idea of what they were fighting for, apart from a generally better life; but they fought no less fiercely for that. Many of the smaller villages and towns were devastated, as was much of the countryside.

The Bourbons had some 7,000 troops in the Palermo garrison, but they proved almost useless. Communications were bad, the roads execrable, and they could not be everywhere at once. In despair they decided to bombard the city – a decision which they soon had cause to regret.[2] The infuriated mob fell on the royal palace, sacked it – sparing, thank heaven, the Palatine Chapel – and set fire to the state records and archives. The garrison retreated, and soon returned to Naples. In the

---

[1] Ferdinand I had died in 1825, and was succeeded by his son Francis I, who reigned for only five years. His son Ferdinand II was to reign from 1830 to 1859.
[2] It was this incident that gave Ferdinand the nickname King Bomba.

following days a committee of government was formed under the presidency of the seventy-year-old Sicilian patriot (and former Neapolitan Minister of Marine) Ruggero Settimo; meanwhile, the revolt spread to all the main cities – except Messina, which held back through jealousy of Palermo – and well over a hundred villages, where the support of the peasantry had by now been assured by lavish promises of land. It encountered no opposition worthy of the name.

By the end of the month the island was virtually free of royal troops, and on 5 February Settimo announced that 'the evils of war had ceased, and that thenceforth an era of happiness had begun for Sicily'. He failed to mention that the citadel of Messina was still in Neapolitan hands; nonetheless, it was clear to King Ferdinand that he had his back to the wall. Owing to almost continuous demonstrations in Naples on the Sicilian model, on 29 January he offered a liberal constitution to both parts of his kingdom, providing for a bicameral legislature and a modest degree of franchise. 'The game is up,' wrote the horrified Austrian ambassador, Prince Schwarzenberg, to his chief, Metternich, 'the King and his ministers have completely lost their heads.' Metternich simply scribbled in the margin, 'I defy the ministers to lose what they have never possessed.'

The news that reached him towards the end of February must have distressed him still more. In Paris, the 'Citizen King' Louis-Philippe had been toppled on 24 February and a republic proclaimed. Now the landslide began. Ferdinand, who had enjoyed a brief popularity after his grant of a constitution, was more than ever execrated; liberal constitutions were no longer enough. The Sicilians, meanwhile, had refused the offer. 'Sicily,' they coldly informed him, 'does not demand new institutions, but the restoration of rights which have been hers for centuries.' In Palermo he was declared deposed, the Bourbon flag being replaced by the revolutionary tricolour and that strange device of a sort of rimless wheel with three legs as its spokes.[1]

Sicily was now truly independent, for the first time since the fourteenth century. The difficulty was that it lacked any machinery for its effective administration. Armed bands sprang up throughout the island; kidnappings and protection rackets were rife. But all this was symptomatic of a greater malaise. Trade plummeted, unemployment soared, the legal system virtually collapsed. To most Sicilians, the year

---

[1] A very similar design is used in the arms of the Isle of Man. Here, however, the legs are armoured and spurred.

1848 was no longer the year of revolution; it was the year of destruction and chaos.

Towards the end of August, Ferdinand sent a combined military and naval force under Field Marshal Carlo Filangieri to restore order on the island. The rebels fought back, and the age-old hatred between Neapolitans and Sicilians gave rise to atrocities on both sides – to the point where the British and French admirals in Sicilian waters, shocked by the bloodshed and brutality, persuaded Ferdinand to grant a six-month armistice. Here, one might have thought, was an opportunity to end the stalemate, but every offer of settlement was refused out of hand. As a result, Filangieri captured Taormina on 2 April 1849 and Catania on the 7th; on 15 May he entered Palermo. By their inefficiency, their lack of unity and their refusal to compromise, the Sicilians had perfectly demonstrated how a revolution should not be run. Their neighbours the Greeks had shown similar defects, but they had the active support of the western powers. The Sicilians had not – and they paid the price.

The revolution in Venice, though it too was ultimately unsuccessful, was handled with far more assurance and skill. Already in June 1844 three young Venetian naval officers – the brothers Attilio and Emilio Bandiera and their friend Domenico Moro – had sailed from Corfu to Calabria, where they planned to join a minor insurrection that had broken out against Bourbon Naples. Their expedition was ridiculously quixotic: they had made virtually no preparations, had taken no precautions and were almost immediately arrested. A month later they were executed in the valley of Rovito, near Cosenza.[1] The news of their deaths had an immense impact on Italian public opinion. If three Venetians – to say nothing of several fellow martyrs from Perugia, Rimini and other cities – were prepared to die for Naples, then Italian unity must after all be something more than an empty dream. It seemed unthinkable that such heroes should have perished in vain. In Venice it was now generally agreed that the moment had come when the whole population of the city must speak out with a single voice – and the voice with which it spoke was that of Daniele Manin.

He was born in Venice on 13 May 1804. His Jewish father had converted to Christianity in his youth, and had adopted the name of his

---

[1] They were commemorated in Venice by the renaming of the former Campo S. Giovanni in Bragora, now known as Campo Bandiera e Moro in their honour.

godfather, Pietro Manin – brother of the last Doge, Ludovico. Determined to be a lawyer like his father, Daniele had published his first work, a legal treatise on wills, when he was twelve. By the time he was awarded his doctorate at Padua University at the age of twenty-one, he had a good working knowledge of Latin, Greek, Hebrew, French and German, as well as Italian and his native Venetian. Brought up by his father to share his own republican and liberal ideas, he had already been politically active for some sixteen years when in 1847, with nationalist feeling growing throughout Italy, he launched what he called his *lotta legale*, or legal struggle, against Austrian despotism. He was not at this stage demanding full Venetian independence, merely home rule under the Habsburg Empire. Only when this had been refused – as he knew full well that it would be – would he call his fellow citizens to arms.

The first moment of open defiance came on 30 December 1847, when the distinguished academic Niccolò Tommaseo gave a lecture. Its ostensible subject was 'The State of Italian Literature'; in fact, it proved to be a direct attack on the Austrian censorship. At the end he circulated a petition, which was signed by over 600 leading names in Venice and the Veneto. As a further indication of their anger, the Venetians followed the example set a few weeks before by the Milanese and gave up smoking.[1] They had always made a point of not applauding the concerts by the Austrian military band in the Piazza; henceforth, at the opening bars, they turned on their heels and left. A week later, Manin followed up with a sixteen-point charter, demanding, *inter alia*, vastly increased rights for all Italians under Austrian rule, a separate north Italian government answerable to the Emperor alone, and finally the complete abolition of censorship. This, for the imperial authorities, was the last straw. On 18 January 1848 Manin and Tommaseo were arrested and marched to the old prisons next to the Doge's Palace. Once the Venetians had discovered where they were, crowds collected daily to stand in respect, bareheaded and silent, on the Riva below.

In early March, to everyone's surprise, the two were acquitted, but the Austrian chief of police insisted that they should remain in prison. It was a disastrous mistake. The annual Carnival was cancelled, and Manin's fellow lawyers took over all his work without pay. The Venetians, however, aware that the Austrian army in Venetia-

---

[1] Austria drew substantial revenue from Lombardy by heavy taxes on cigars. The Austrian army's reply to this was to issue vast quantities of free cigars to both officers and men, with orders to puff the smoke in the Italians' faces.

Lombardy under the eighty-one-year-old Marshal Josef Radetzky[1] numbered no less than 75,000, still hesitated to take up arms. Then, on 17 March, the postal steamer from Trieste brought the news that Vienna itself was in revolt, that the rebels had triumphed and that, just four days before, the hated Prince Metternich had fled for his life. Overnight, the situation was transformed. As the word spread through the city, an immense crowd flocked to the governor's residence on the south side of the Piazza shouting '*Fuori Manin e Tommaseo!*'[2] The people, it was clear, would no longer be gainsaid.

The Austrian governor, Count Pàlffy, eventually appeared at the window and protested that even if he had wished to release the prisoners, he had no power to do so. The crowd, led by Manin's sixteen-year-old son Giorgio, then streamed across the Piazzetta to the prison and began hammering on the doors, which were finally opened. It was typical of Daniele Manin – always a lawyer – that he should have refused to leave the building until he had an official order to do so, an order which Pàlffy, at the urgings of his near-hysterical wife, hastily signed. Only then did he and Tommaseo emerge, to be carried shoulder-high to the governor's residence. The crowds made as if to break down the doors, but Manin restrained them. 'Do not forget,' he told them, 'that there can be no true liberty, and that liberty cannot last, where there is no order.' Only when they had calmed down did he allow them to bear him off to his home.

Metternich's resignation and flight on 13 March had inspired Italy to action, but had left Austria in chaos. The government was rudderless, the army bewildered and uncertain of its loyalties. Here, unmistakably, was the signal to insurgents and revolutionaries throughout Italy. In Milan, the great insurrection known to all Italians as the *cinque giornate* – the five days of 18–22 March – drove the Austrians from the city and instituted a republican government. On the last of those days, in Turin, a stirring front-page article appeared in the newspaper *Il Risorgimento,* written by its editor, Count Camillo Cavour. 'The supreme hour has sounded,' he wrote. 'One way alone is open for the nation, for the government, for the King. War!'

---

[1] Radetzky had taken part in the very first Austrian campaigns against Napoleon more than half a century before, and had been Chief of Staff at the battle of Leipzig in 1813. He had fought in seventeen campaigns, had been wounded seven times and had had nine horses shot under him.
[2] 'Release Manin and Tommaseo!'

Two days later, King Charles Albert of Savoy proclaimed from Piedmont his country's readiness to give full support to Venetia–Lombardy in the forthcoming struggle, together with his own intention personally to lead his army into battle. Unfortunately, although able immediately to mobilise some 70,000 men, Piedmont was hopelessly unprepared for war; in her entire army, we are told, there was not a single map of Lombardy. Unfortunately, too, the King was to prove uninspired as a general – certainly no match for old Radetzky, who had been commanding armies since before Charles Albert was born.

On the other hand, although the eventual outcome of the hostilities between Austria and Piedmont might have been a foregone conclusion from the military point of view, the King must have been greatly encouraged by the reaction of the other Italian states. Grand Duke Leopold II of Tuscany at once despatched an army composed of both regular troops and volunteers. Rather more surprisingly, there was a similar response from King Ferdinand of Naples, who sent a force of 16,000 under a huge Calabrian general called Guglielmo Pepe. Strategically these contributions probably made little difference; they showed, however, beyond all possible doubt, that the cause was a national, Italian one. As they took their places beside the Piedmontese, Charles Albert's fellow rulers saw themselves not as allies but as compatriots.

Daniele Manin alone made no pretence of fighting for Italy; his cause was Venice. A few months before, he might have welcomed the news that arrived on the evening of his release from prison, to the effect that the Emperor had agreed to the principle of constitutional government for Venetia–Lombardy; but such an offer was now too little and too late. He was resolved to settle for nothing less than the expulsion of all Austrians from Venetian territory. On the morning of March 22 – a date now commemorated in the name of Venice's principal shopping street – he and his men occupied the Arsenal without a struggle and commandeered all the arms and ammunition that were stored there. He then led a triumphal procession to the Piazza, where he formally proclaimed a republic, ending his speech with a ringing cry of '*Viva San Marco!*' It was the first time that the words had been heard in public for over half a century. Pàlffy, meanwhile, had signed a formal act of capitulation, leaving effective power in the hands of 'the provisional government which is to be formed' and undertaking that all Austrian troops would be evacuated – without their arms – to Trieste.

Venice was once more a republic; but it was plain, from its earliest days, that that republic was in mortal danger. The Austrians had retreated, but they were by no means beaten; the revolution, after all, had been confined only to the major towns. Radetzky was still in control of most of the countryside, and after the fall of Vicenza on 10 June the whole of the Venetian *terra firma* was back in Austrian hands. Venice could not hope to stand alone. And so, on 4 July, the newly-elected Venetian Assembly reluctantly voted for fusion with Piedmont, where Cavour was calling ever more insistently for the unification of Italy. It was a tragic day for Daniele Manin, who at once handed over to an interim ministry and retired from public life. (A few days later he was spotted in the uniform of a private in the Civic Guard, on sentry-go in the Piazzetta.) Meanwhile, 3,000 Piedmontese troops were billeted in the city; for many Venetians, it was almost as bad as having the Austrians back again.

> Each day the Pope shows himself more lacking in any practical sense. Born and brought up in a *liberal* family, he has been formed in a bad school; a good priest, he has never turned his mind towards matters of government. Warm of heart and weak of intellect, he has allowed himself to be taken and ensnared, since assuming the tiara, in a net from which he no longer knows how to disentangle himself, and if matters follow their natural course, he will be driven out of Rome.

These prophetic words were written by the Austrian State Chancellor Prince Metternich to his ambassador in Paris in October 1847. Their subject was Giovanni Maria Mastai-Ferretti, the former Bishop of Imola and Archbishop of Spoleto who, the previous year at the age of fifty-four, had been elected Pope Pius IX. By the liberals of Italy and indeed all western Europe, the news of his election had been greeted with excitement and delight. The new pontiff, it seemed, was one of themselves. In his first month of office he amnestied more than 1,000 political prisoners and exiles.[1] A few weeks later he was giving garden parties – for both sexes – at the Quirinal. Meanwhile, he actively encouraged plans for railways (anathema to his predecessor, Gregory XVI, who called them *chemins d'enfer*) and for gas lighting in the streets of Rome. He established a free – or very nearly free – press. He made a start on tariff reform, introduced laymen into the papal government and abolished the ridiculous law whereby Jews were

---

[1] 'God doesn't grant amnesties,' growled Metternich, 'God pardons.'

obliged to listen to a Christian sermon once a week. Mobbed wherever he went, he was the most popular man in Italy.

But his reputation carried its own dangers. Every political demonstration, from the mildest to the most revolutionary, now claimed his support; his name appeared on a thousand banners, frequently proclaiming causes which he violently opposed. With the outbreak of the revolutions of 1848, his position became more untenable still. '*Pio Nono! Pio Nono! Pio Nono!*' – the name became a battle-cry, endlessly chanted by one mob after another as it surged through the streets of city after city. When the Pope concluded one speech with the words 'God bless Italy', his words were immediately seen as an endorsement of the popular dream of a united Italy, freed forever from Austrian rule. (Pius, it need hardly be said, had no desire to see Italy united; apart from anything else, what then would become of the Papal States?) In short, the Pope now found himself on a runaway train; his only hope was to try to apply the brakes in whatever way he could.

Already by the end of January of that fateful year, the spate of new constitutions had begun. Ferdinand had given one to Naples on the 29th; in Florence, just a week later, the Grand Duke had offered another. On March 5, after the Paris revolution and the flight of Louis-Philippe, King Charles Albert of Savoy had granted one in Turin. Then on 13 March it had been the turn of Vienna, and Metternich himself had taken to his heels. This was the most important news of all; new hope surged in the breast of every Italian patriot – who, as always, looked to the Vatican for a lead. There was nothing for it: on the 15th, Pope Pius granted a constitution to Rome. It was not exaggeratedly liberal – his Chief Minister, Cardinal Antonelli,[1] had seen to that – nor, as things turned out, did it last very long; but it served its purpose. Pius, unwilling as he was to spearhead European revolution, could hardly be seen to be lagging behind.

On 24 March – the very day that Charles Albert declared war on Austria – General Giovanni Durando led the advance guard of a papal army out of Rome, to protect the northern frontier of the Papal States against any possible Austrian attack. This was conceived as a purely

---

[1] Antonelli was largely responsible for enabling the Papacy to cling to its temporal power for as long as it did. He was a brilliant politician with immense charm and – as his countless bastards attested – an extremely *mouvementé* sex life. 'When he stops in a salon near a pretty woman, when he stands close to speak to her, stroking her shoulders and looking deeply into her corsage, you recognise the man of the woods and you tremble as you think of post-chaises overturned at the roadside.' (Edmond About, *La question romaine*, quoted by Holt, *Risorgimento*, p. 139.)

defensive measure, but the warmongers refused to accept it as such. Austria, they claimed, had declared war on Christian Italy. This was therefore a holy war, a Crusade, with the divine purpose of driving the invader from the sacred Italian soil. Pope Pius was predictably furious. Never for a moment would he have condoned such a policy of aggression, least of all against a Catholic nation. It was clearly essential for him to make his position clear once and for all. The result was the so-called Allocution of 29 April 1848. Far from leading the campaign for a united Italy, he declared, he actively opposed it. God-fearing Italians should forget the whole idea of unification and once again pledge their loyalty to their individual princes.

The Allocution was welcomed by King Ferdinand, who saw it as a perfect excuse to recall the army he had sent north under General Pepe. (Pepe, to his eternal credit, was to disobey him and lead 2,000 of his men to the defence of Venice.) By true Italian patriots up and down the country, on the other hand, the news was received with horror; yet, as things turned out, the cause of unification was almost unaffected. The movement was now so widespread as to be unstoppable. The only real damage done was to the reputation of Pius himself. Until now he had been a hero; henceforth, he was a traitor. Moreover, the Allocution had shown, as perhaps nothing else could have shown, just how powerless the Pope was to influence events. All his fantastic popularity disappeared overnight; now it was his turn to look revolution in the face. For the next seven months he struggled to hold the situation, but when his Chief Minister, Count Pellegrino Rossi, was hacked to death as he was about to enter the Chancellery, he realised that Rome was no longer safe for him. On 24 November, disguised as a simple priest, he slipped secretly out of the Quirinal Palace by a side door and fled to Gaeta, where King Ferdinand gave him a warm welcome.

At first the Piedmontese army enjoyed a measure of success. All too soon, however, on 24 July, Charles Albert was routed at Custoza, a few miles southwest of Verona. He fell back on Milan, with Radetzky in hot pursuit; and on 4 August he was obliged to ask for an armistice, by the terms of which he and his army withdrew behind their own frontiers. Two days later the Milanese also surrendered, and the indomitable old marshal led his army back into the city.

The first phase of the war was over, and Austria was plainly the victor. It was not only that she was back in undisputed control of Venetia–Lombardy. Naples had made a separate peace; Rome had capitulated; France, in the person of her Foreign Secretary, the poet Alphonse de Lamartine, had published a republican *Manifesto* which had made encouraging noises but had offered no active or material help. Less than five months after the proclamation of the new Venetian Republic, the forces of the counter-revolution were triumphant across mainland Italy.

Venice was not sorry to say goodbye to the Piedmontese, but once again she stood alone. Her only hope was Manin, who now cast aside his private's uniform and on 13 August was invited by the Assembly to assume dictatorial powers. He declined, on the grounds that he knew nothing of military matters, but he was eventually persuaded to accept the leadership of a triumvirate. Such was his reputation that his two colleagues allowed themselves to fade into the background: Manin was in fact a dictator in all but name. It was under his sole guidance that the Venetian Republic was to fight on throughout the following winter, courageously but with increasing desperation.

For all the states of Italy, the *quarantotto* had been a momentous year. Strategically, the situation had changed remarkably little; in most places Austria remained master. Politically, on the other hand, there had been a dramatic shift in popular opinion. When the year began, most patriotic Italians were thinking in terms of getting rid of the Austrian forces of occupation; when it ended, the overriding objective – everywhere except in Venice – was a united Italy. Change was in the air. At last, it seemed, the Italians were on the verge of realising their long-cherished dream. The Risorgimento had begun.

CHAPTER XXVIII

Risorgimento

'Italy,' declared Metternich, 'is a geographical expression.' He spoke no more than the truth. Never in all its history had the Italian peninsula constituted a single nation; even in the days of imperial Rome it had been merely a part – and usually quite a small part – of the Roman state. Since the early Middle Ages, however – and perhaps even earlier – the concept of Italian nationhood had existed as a distant ideal: Dante and Petrarch had both dreamed of it, as later had Machiavelli. Geographically and linguistically, it obviously made sense; but the land was so deeply divided against itself, the medieval rifts and rivalries so bitter between city and city, Guelf and Ghibelline, Emperor and Pope, that the nineteenth century was already half-way through its course before unification was seen even as a possibility.

But then came the *quarantotto*, and all was changed. The distant dream had suddenly become an attainable objective. Count Camillo Cavour had no good reason to call his newspaper *Il Risorgimento* – there could be no question of resurgence towards an objective that had never existed before – but the word had a fine ring to it and was soon generally adopted. What was now needed was leadership.

As 1849 opened, there was only one serious contender on the national level. Venetia-Lombardy was still under Austrian rule. Rome was obviously excluded since, although Pope Pius had been for some weeks in voluntary exile, the problem of the Papacy – and therefore of the Papal States, which effectively divided the peninsula into two – remained unsolved. Naples under the sadly unreconstructed King Bomba was scarcely worth considering, and the other states of Italy were too small and weak to qualify. Piedmont was the obvious choice. Though still smarting from its defeat the previous year, it was energetic, ambitious and steadily increasing in size.[1] Its King, Charles Albert, had been on the throne since 1831 and was uncompromisingly anti-Austrian.

But Charles Albert, as a reigning monarch, could not give the movement – which was, after all, largely republican – the charismatic

---

[1] At this time it comprised not only the traditional territory of the ancient Dukes of Savoy, with its capital at Turin; there was also the island of Sardinia, the County of Nice and, since 1815, the city of Genoa.

personal leadership that it so obviously required. This, in the early years at least, was to be the task of Giuseppe Mazzini. Mazzini had been born in Genoa in 1805, but ten years later the dispensations of the Congress of Vienna had automatically made him a Piedmontese citizen; though he somewhat desultorily studied both medicine and law, from his university days onward he was obsessed by the idea of Italian regeneration – to the point where his subversive activities resulted in a brief sentence of internment, followed in February 1831 by exile in Marseille. Living principally there and in London, he was to remain essentially an exile for the rest of his life.

It was on his arrival in Marseille that Mazzini founded the movement that he called *la giovine Italia* – Young Italy. As its name implied, it was directed exclusively at the under-forties, in an attempt to develop their national consciousness; it would be a 'great Italian national association', which had as its avowed object the liberation of Italy, by revolution if necessary. It had an immediate success: within two years of its foundation it could boast some 60,000 members. It also ran a periodical – bearing the same name as the society – of which six copies were produced in the first two years: no mean achievement, considering that each number contained some 200 pages, many of them written by Mazzini himself.

By 1833 he was ready for action. Young Italy had attracted a remarkably large number of the young officers and men of the Piedmontese army; with his boyhood friend Jacopo Ruffini he now planned simultaneous risings in Genoa and Alessandria, which he believed would spread across the country, overthrowing the government and eventually toppling Charles Albert. Alas, before these risings were even begun the plot was discovered. The discovery was in fact the fault of neither of the two chief conspirators, but virtually all their associates were arrested, twelve of them being executed by a firing squad. Ruffini slashed his veins in prison.

Mazzini, over the border in France, was in no immediate danger, but Marseille was full of Piedmontese agents, and soon afterwards he left for the greater safety of Geneva. Three years later, however, after several more unsuccessful conspiracies, even Switzerland had become too hot for him. In January 1837 he arrived in London, where he was to spend the next eleven years and which was to become his second home. Here he flung himself once again into a whirlpool of feverish activity: breathing new life into Young Italy, working to improve the lot of Italian immigrants, establishing a free school for Italian children, founding another newspaper, writing dozens of letters every day to Italian patriots and exiles throughout the world – for by now there were revolutionary committees not only in Italy but in several other European countries as well as in the USA, Canada, Cuba and Latin America.

Such was his energy and his industry that this remarkable Italian soon became a well-known figure in London. Seven years after his arrival, however, he was to enjoy a sudden and unexpected celebrity which proved of immense benefit to his cause. Early in 1844 he began to suspect that his letters were being secretly opened before delivery – a fact which a few simple experiments were enough to confirm. He at once complained to a friendly Member of Parliament, who obligingly put a question in the House of Commons. The Home Secretary, Sir James Graham, at first denied the accusation, but when faced with the evidence was compelled to admit that his office had indeed been opening the letters, at the request of the Austrian ambassador. The resulting scandal – people began writing 'Not to be Grahamed' on their envelopes – not only threw Mazzini into the limelight; it also enabled him to write an 'open letter' to Graham which set out the Italian case in detail and – since it was widely reprinted – gave him just the publicity he needed. His friend Thomas Carlyle maintained that the opening of his letters was the best thing that had ever happened to him.

The hurried departure of the Pope took Rome by surprise. The Chief Minister of the papal government, Giuseppe Galletti – an old friend of Mazzini's who had returned to Rome under the amnesty and had courageously succeeded the murdered Rossi – first sent a delegation to Gaeta to persuade Pius to return; only when this was refused an audience did Galletti call for the formation of a Roman Constituent Assembly, of 200 elected members, which would meet in the city on 5 February 1849. Time was short but the need was urgent, and 142 members duly presented themselves in the palace of the Cancellaria on the appointed date. Just four days later, at two o'clock in the morning, the Assembly voted – by 120 votes to ten, with twelve abstentions – to put an end to the temporal power of the Pope and to establish a Roman republic. Mazzini was not present; by far the most dominant personality in the proceedings was a forty-one-year-old adventurer named Giuseppe Garibaldi.

Born in 1807 in Nice – which would be ceded to France only in 1860 – Garibaldi was, like Mazzini, a Piedmontese. He had started his professional life as a merchant seaman, and had become a member of Young Italy in 1833. Always a man of action, he was involved the following year in an unsuccessful mutiny – one of the many failed conspiracies of those early years – and a warrant was issued for his arrest. Just in time, he managed to escape to France; meanwhile, in Turin, he was sentenced *in absentia* to death for high treason. After a brief spell in the French merchant navy he joined the navy of the Bey of Tunis, who offered him the post of Commander-in-Chief. This he declined, and finally, in December 1835, he sailed as second mate in a French brig bound for South America. There he was to stay for the next twelve years, the first four of them fighting for a small state that was trying – unsuccessfully – to break away from Brazilian domination. In 1841 he and his Brazilian mistress, Anita Ribeiro da Silva, trekked to Montevideo, where he was soon put in charge of the Uruguayan navy, also taking command of a legion of Italian exiles – the first of the Redshirts, with whom his name was ever afterwards associated. After his victory at the minor but heroic battle of Sant' Antonio in 1846 his fame quickly spread to Europe. By now he had become a professional rebel, whose experience of guerrilla warfare was to stand him in good stead in the years to come.

The moment Garibaldi heard of the revolutions of 1848, he gathered sixty of his Redshirts and took the next ship back to Italy. His initial offers to fight for the Pope and then for Piedmont having both been rejected – Charles Albert, in particular, would not have forgotten that he was still under sentence of death – he headed for Milan, where Mazzini had already arrived, and immediately plunged into the fray. The armistice following Charles Albert's defeat at Custoza he simply ignored, continuing his private war against the Austrians until at the end of August, heavily outnumbered, he had no choice but to retreat to Switzerland. There he spent the next three months with Anita, but on hearing of the flight of the Pope hurried at once with his troop of volunteers to Rome. He was elected a member of the new Assembly, and it was he who formally proposed that Rome should thenceforth be an independent republic.

Mazzini was, surprisingly, not present during these stirring events. From Milan he had travelled on to Florence – from which Grand Duke Leopold had somewhat hurriedly decamped – with the vain hope of persuading the government to proclaim a republic and unite it with that of Rome; it was only at the beginning of March that he made his way – for the first time – to the new capital, where a seat in the Assembly was awaiting him. He was, predictably, given a hero's welcome, and was invited to sit at the President's right hand.

It was unfortunate that the King of Piedmont should have chosen this moment to denounce the armistice concluded less than seven months before and to resume his war with Austria. Why he did so remains a puzzle. It may be that he feared another insurrection and the loss of his throne; more probably he saw himself as the champion and liberator of Italy, and was determined not to allow the defeat of Custoza to spell the end of his military career. That defeat had shown him, however, that he was no general; for the next phase of the war, while retaining the nominal supremacy, he entrusted the effective command to a Pole, a veteran of the Napoleonic wars named Wojtiech Chrzanowski.

Chrzanowski doubtless did his best, but as a general he proved little better than his chief. Less than a fortnight after the war was resumed the Piedmontese found themselves up against Radetzky at Novara, some thirty miles west of Milan. As at Custoza, they were no match for the slightly outnumbered but infinitely more disciplined and professional Austrians. Charles Albert showed exemplary courage, moving fearlessly across the field as the bullets whistled around him. He survived unscathed, but his troops were routed and the battle lost. One city, Brescia, stood alone for a few more days, but it was soon subdued in its turn by the Austrian General Julius von Haynau, with all the savagery and brutality for which he was notorious.[1] Charles Albert, declaring that he could not face signing another armistice, abdicated in favour of his son Victor Emmanuel, Duke of Savoy. Permitted as a private citizen to pass through the Austrian lines, he retired to Oporto, where he died only four months later of what seemed suspiciously like a broken heart.

Giuseppe Mazzini had long believed that imperial Rome and papal Rome would be followed by a third Rome: a Rome of the people. Now that dream had come true. The Assembly had put the new republic in the hands of a triumvirate; of its three members, however, two were virtually ignored. Mazzini was now effectively dictator of Rome. He was by no means the first, nor would he be the last, but it can safely be

---

[1] Notorious even in England. On 4 September 1850, with two friends, Haynau visited Barclay's Brewery in London. He was soon recognised by his grotesquely long moustaches and attacked by the employees, who threw buckets of dirt all over him. He fled down Bankside and, pursued now by a large mob, took refuge at the George Inn, where he was finally rescued by the police.

said that no other was remotely like him. In his cramped little office in the Quirinal Palace he was accessible to all comers; he ate every day at the same cheap *trattoria*; his monthly salary of thirty-two lire he gave to charity. Now, too, the propagandist and demagogue became a quietly conscientious administrator. He abolished the death penalty, introduced universal male suffrage, declared total freedom of the press and restored order to the Papal States, which had been terrorised by republican extremists. He would doubtless have done a great deal more, but he knew that he was working against time: 'We must act,' he told the Assembly, 'like men who have the enemy at their gates, and at the same time like men who are working for eternity.' He spoke no more than the truth; in early April there came ominous news from Paris. A French expeditionary force was on the march.

On 18 February Pope Pius in Gaeta had addressed a formal appeal for help to France, Austria, Spain and Naples. By none of these four powers was he to go unheard; to Mazzini, however, the greatest danger was France – whose response would clearly depend on the complexion of its new republic and, in particular, on Prince Louis Napoleon, its recently elected president. Nearly twenty years before, the Prince had been implicated in an anti-papal plot and expelled from Rome; he still had no particular affection for the Papacy. Since Novara, on the other hand, he could see that Austria was more powerful in Italy than ever; how could he contemplate the possibility of the Austrians now coming south and restoring the Pope on their own terms? If he himself were to take no action, that – he had no doubt at all – was what they would do.

He gave his orders accordingly, and on 25 April 1849 General Nicholas Oudinot – son of one of Napoleon's marshals – landed with a force of about 9,000 at Civitavecchia and began the forty-mile march to Rome. From the start he was under a misapprehension. He had been led to believe that the republic had been imposed by a small group of revolutionaries on an unwilling people and would soon be overturned; he and his men would consequently be welcomed as liberators. His orders were to grant the triumvirate and the Assembly no formal recognition, but to occupy the city peacefully, if possible without firing a shot.

He was in for a surprise. The Romans, although they had little hope of defending their city against a trained and well-equipped army, were busy preparing themselves for the fight. Their own forces, such as they were, consisted of the regular papal troops of the line, the *carabinieri* – a special corps of the Italian army entrusted with police duties – the

1,000-strong Civic Guard, the volunteer regiments raised in the city amounting to some 1,400, and – by no means the least formidable – the populace itself, with every weapon it could lay its hands on. But their total numbers were still pathetically small, and great was their jubilation when, on the 27th, Garibaldi rode into the city at the head of 1,300 legionaries which he had gathered in the Romagna. Two days later there followed a regiment of Lombard *bersaglieri*, with their distinctive broad-brimmed hats and swaying plumes of black-green cock's feathers. The defenders were gathering in strength, but the odds were still heavily against them and they knew it.

That first battle for Rome was fought on 30 April. The day was saved by Oudinot's ignorance and incomprehension. He had brought no siege guns with him, and no scaling-ladders; it was only when his column, advancing towards the Vatican and the Janiculum hill, was greeted by bursts of cannon-fire that he began to realise the full danger of his situation. Soon afterwards Garibaldi's legion swept down upon him, swiftly followed by the *bersaglieri* lancers. For six hours he and his men fought back as well as they could, but as evening fell they could only admit defeat and take the long road back to Civitavecchia. They had lost 500 killed or wounded, with 365 taken prisoner, but perhaps the humiliation had been worst of all.

That night all Rome was illuminated in celebration, but no one pretended that the French were not going to return. The French had now learned that Rome was to be a tougher nut to crack than they had expected; nonetheless, they intended to crack it. Little over a month later – during which time Garibaldi, with his legionaries and the *bersaglieri*, marched south to meet an invading Neapolitan army and effortlessly expelled it from republican territory – Oudinot had received the reinforcements he had requested, and it was with 20,000 men behind him and vastly improved armament that, on 3 June, he marched on Rome for the second time.

Advancing as he was from the west, his primary objectives were the historic Villa Pamfili and Villa Corsini, high on the Janiculum hill. By the end of the day both were safely in his hands, his guns drawn up into position. Rome was effectively doomed. The defenders fought back superbly for nearly a month, but on the morning of 30 June Mazzini addressed the Assembly. There were, he told them, three possibilities: they could surrender; they could continue the fight and die in the streets; or they could retire to the hills and continue the struggle. Around midday Garibaldi appeared, covered in dust, his red shirt soaked in blood and sweat; his mind was made up. Surrender was obviously out of the question. Street fighting, he pointed out, was also impossible; when Trastevere[1] was abandoned – as it would have to be – French guns could simply destroy the city. The hills, then, it would have to be. '*Dovunque saremo*,' he told them, '*colà sarà Roma*.'[2]

Strangely enough, the majority of the deputies disagreed, choosing a fourth possibility: not to surrender, but to declare a ceasefire and remain in Rome. This was a course which Mazzini appeared not to have previously considered; eventually, however, he decided to adopt it himself. The French, who had been led to believe that he was a hated tyrant, were astonished to see a man who walked fearlessly through the streets hailed and greeted with respect wherever he went, to the point where they did not dare to arrest him. But Mazzini knew that even if he remained at liberty he would henceforth be powerless, and after a few days he slipped back to London. 'Italy is my country,' he used to say, 'but England is my home – if I have one.'

Garibaldi, meanwhile, appealed for volunteers. 'I offer,' he declared, 'neither pay, nor board, nor lodging; I offer only hunger, thirst, forced marches, battle and death. Let him who loves his country in his heart, and not with his lips only, follow me.' Four thousand men hastened to join him, though it was to be little more than a handful that a month later, having escaped the attentions of no less than three enemy armies, dragged itself to refuge in the little republic of San Marino.[3] There the troop disbanded, and Garibaldi, with Anita and a few faithful followers, set off for the only Italian republic which was still fighting for survival: Venice.

Alas, the vessel in which they sailed was intercepted by an Austrian warship. Garibaldi was forced to disembark on a remote stretch of the coast – now known as Porto Garibaldi – and before he could reach the Venetian lagoon his beloved Anita died in his arms. Temporarily, the spirit went out of him. Once again he left Italy, and a few weeks later arrived in New York, there to begin his second period of American exile.

Even if Garibaldi had managed to reach Venice, there was little that he could have done. All through the previous winter, despite an

---

[1] The area of Rome lying to the west of the Tiber.

[2] 'Wherever we are, there shall be Rome.'

[3] San Marino, with its area of 23.5 square miles, is still an independent republic. It is completely surrounded by Italy, with the Romagna on the west and the Marche on the east. It remains the last relic of the self-governing city-states of the middle ages and Renaissance.

intermittent Austrian blockade, Daniele Manin had concentrated on building up an effective army – a task which he entrusted to General Pepe, who cheerfully proclaimed his readiness to give his life for Italy and the Venetian Republic. As a Calabrian, Pepe proved able to recruit a large number of officers and men formerly in the Neapolitan army; the result, by the beginning of April 1849, was a reasonably disciplined fighting force some 20,000 strong, which gave the Assembly the confidence to publish a heroic decree: 'Venice will resist Austria at all costs. President Manin is invested, for that purpose, with unlimited powers.'

The blockade continued until May 1849, when the Austrian commander finally accepted that a lagoon ninety miles in circumference could never be completely cordoned off, while a city of some 200,000 inhabitants would take a long time to starve; there was nothing for it but a full military siege. The first target was the fort at Malghera (now Marghera), at the mainland end of the railway bridge. After three weeks' bombardment it finally gave in, but the bridge itself, with several other makeshift forts along its length, somehow held. Early in July the Austrians had the extraordinary idea of trying to drop bombs on Venice from a fleet of large balloons; the experiment proved a fiasco and gave the Venetians at least something to laugh about – but they had very little else. The siege had at last given rise to a serious shortage of food, and as the month wore on they found themselves on the brink of famine. Even fish – the Venetian staple – was in short supply, since the amount furnished by the lagoon was hopelessly inadequate for the city's population. Bread rationing was introduced, but the situation continued to deteriorate. On 28 July Manin formally asked the members of the Assembly whether it was possible for Venice to resist any longer; his hearers, however, were determined to fight to the end.

On the night of the 29th, the bombardment of Venice began in earnest. It was confined to the western half of the city, if only because the Austrian guns, even when raised to their highest elevation, could lob their cannonballs no further; the Piazza was fortunately just out of range. Fortunately, too, the vast majority of the projectiles were merely balls, and not shells that exploded on impact. The Austrians frequently made them red-hot before firing, but there were not enough furnaces to heat them all and the occasional small fire that resulted could normally be dealt with by the Venetian fire brigade – which now included Daniele Manin as one of its members.

Nevertheless, the sheer intensity of the bombardment over the next three and a half weeks could not fail to take its toll on Venetian morale, and by now the city had fallen victim to the greatest scourge of all: cholera. By the end of July the disease was raging in every quarter of the city. In the heat of August it grew worse still, especially in the hideously overcrowded easternmost region of Castello, to which most of the people from the exposed western areas had fled. The grave-diggers could not hope to keep pace – burial is anyway a difficult process in Venice – and the corpses awaiting their attention remained piled up in the *campo* of Venice's old cathedral, S. Pietro di Castello. The smell, we are told, was asphyxiating.

It was plain that the end was near. On 19 August two gondolas set off for Mestre flying white flags; three days later, agreement was reached. The Austrian terms were surprisingly generous. Their principal require-ment was that all officers and all Italian soldiers who were subjects of the Empire and had fought against it should leave Venice at once; forty leading Venetians were also to be expelled. On 27 August the Austrians reoccupied the city. That same afternoon the French ship *Pluton* sailed from the Giudecca. On board were, with thirty-seven others, Guglielmo Pepe, Niccolò Tommaseo and Daniele Manin.

Manin, with his wife and daughter, settled in Paris, where he wrote articles for the French papers and gave lessons in Italian. By now he had given up his republican ideals; his sights, like Mazzini's, were set on his country's unification. 'I am convinced,' he wrote, 'that our first task is to make Italy a reality . . . the republican party declares to the house of Savoy: "If you create Italy, we are with you; if not, not."' He died in Paris on 22 September 1857, aged fifty-three. Eleven years later his remains were brought back to Venice and placed in a specially designed tomb against the north wall of St Mark's. Outside his house in the former Campo S. Paternian – now Campo Manin – there crouches a huge bronze lion, angrily lashing his tail.

Had the *quarantotto* been in vain? By the autumn of 1849 it certainly seemed so. The Austrians were back in Venice and in Lombardy; Pius IX had returned to a French-occupied Rome; in Naples, King Bomba had torn up the constitution and once more wielded absolute power; Florence, Modena and Parma, all under Austrian protection, were in much the same state. In the whole peninsula, only Piedmont remained free – but Piedmont too had changed. The tall, handsome, idealistic Charles Albert was dead. His son and successor, Victor Emmanuel II, was short, squat and unusually ugly, principally interested – or so it seemed – in hunting and women. But he was a good deal more

intelligent than he looked; despite his genuine shyness and awkward-
ness in public, politically speaking he missed very few tricks. It is hard
to imagine the Risorgimento without him.

Yet even Victor Emmanuel might have foundered had it not been for
his Chief Minister, Camillo Cavour, who succeeded the strongly
anticlerical Massimo d'Azeglio at the end of 1852 and remained in
power, with very brief intermissions, for the next nine years – years
which were crucial for Italy. Cavour's appearance, like that of his
master, was deceptive. Short and pot-bellied, with a blotchy complexion, thinning hair and spectacles that looked more like goggles, he
was shabbily dressed and at first acquaintance distinctly unprepossessing. His mind, on the other hand, was like a rapier, and once
he began to talk few were impervious to his charm. Domestically, he
continued d'Azeglio's programme of ecclesiastical reform – often in the
teeth of opposition from a pious and conscientiously Catholic king –
while doing everything he could to strengthen the economy; his foreign
policy, meanwhile, was ever directed towards his dream of a united
Italy, with Piedmont at its head.

But what, it may be asked, did the cause of a united Italy have to do
with the Crimean War, in which Piedmont allied herself with the
western powers in January 1855? Cavour had several reasons. He
knew, first of all, that Britain and France were hoping to bring Austria
into the war; this in turn might lead to a long-term Franco-Austrian
alliance which would effectively destroy his chances of ending the
Austrian presence in the peninsula. If, on the other hand, Italy could
show the world her fighting spirit, those chances would be pro-
portionately increased; the greater her military glory, the more likely it
was that Britain and France would at last take her aspirations seriously.
The experiment was not entirely successful: the Piedmontese were to
fight in one battle only, and that a relatively insignificant one. Just
twenty-eight of them were killed, few indeed compared with the 2,000
lost to cholera by the end of the year. Infuriatingly, too, it was Austria's
threat to enter the war which persuaded the Russians to sue for peace.
But if Piedmont failed to impress on the field of battle, she at least
earned invitations for Victor Emmanuel to pay state visits to Queen
Victoria and Napoleon III[1] in December 1855 and gained a seat at the
Paris peace table two months later. It was, moreover, in the course of

---

[1] Prince Louis Napoleon had taken advantage of the fall of King Louis-Philippe in 1848, and
in December of that year had been elected President of the Second Republic of France. In 1852
he had been confirmed as the Emperor Napoleon III.

his conversations with the French at this time that Cavour began to entertain a new and exciting hope: that Napoleon III, after his distinctly unhelpful policies in the past, might now be prepared to assist in the long-awaited Austrian expulsion.

It is a curious fact that what seems finally to have decided the Emperor to take up arms on Italy's behalf was a plot by Italian patriots to assassinate him. The attempt took place on 14 January 1858, when he and the Empress were on their way to the Opéra for a performance of *William Tell* and bombs were thrown at their carriage. Neither was hurt, though there were a number of casualties among their escort and surrounding bystanders. The leader of the conspirators, Felice Orsini, was a well-known republican who had been implicated in a number of former plots. While in prison awaiting trial he wrote the Emperor a letter, which was later read aloud in open court and published in both the French and the Piedmontese press. It ended: 'Remember that, so long as Italy is not independent, the peace of Europe and Your Majesty is but an empty dream . . . Set my country free, and the blessings of twenty-five million people will follow you everywhere and forever.'

Although these noble words failed to save Orsini from the firing squad, they seem to have lingered in the mind of Napoleon III, who by midsummer 1858 had come round to the idea of a joint operation to drive the Austrians out of the Italian peninsula once and for all. His motives were not, however, entirely idealistic. True, he had a genuine love for Italy and would have been delighted to present himself to the world as her deliverer, but he was also aware that his prestige and popularity were fast declining. He desperately needed a war – and a victorious war at that – to regain them, and Austria was the only potential enemy available. The next step was clearly to discuss the possibilities with Cavour, and in July 1858 the two met secretly at the little health resort of Plombières-les-Bains in the Vosges. Agreement was quickly reached. Piedmont would engineer a quarrel with the Duke of Modena and send in troops, ostensibly at the request of the population. Austria would be bound to support the Duke and declare war; Piedmont would then appeal to France for aid. In return, she would cede to France the county of Savoy and the city of Nice. The latter, being the birthplace of Garibaldi, was a bitter pill for Cavour to swallow, but if it was the price of liberation, then swallowed it would have to be.

To set the seal on this agreement, the two men agreed on a dynastic marriage: Victor Emmanuel's eldest daughter, the Princess Clotilde, should be espoused to the Emperor's cousin, Prince Napoleon. When this engagement was announced there were many – especially in Piedmont – who threw up their hands in horror. The princess was a highly intelligent, pious and attractive girl of fifteen; her fiancé – universally known as Plon-Plon – a well-known and slightly ridiculous *roué* of thirty-seven. Victor Emmanuel, who had apparently not been consulted in advance, made no secret of his displeasure and left the final decision to Clotilde herself. It says much for her sense of duty that she agreed to go through with the marriage – which, to everyone's surprise, proved to be a not unhappy one.

The wedding ceremony took place at the end of January 1859, while France and Piedmont were actively – and openly – preparing for war. Soon afterwards Napoleon III began to have second thoughts about the whole affair – to the dismay of Cavour, who was well aware that his country could not possibly tackle Austria alone. Worse still, Britain, Prussia and Russia were now talking of a possible international congress, which would almost certainly involve the voluntary disarmament of Piedmont. Cavour, in short, was staring disaster in the face. He was saved in the nick of time by Austria herself, which sent an ultimatum to Turin on 23 April demanding that very disarmament within three days. Austria had now declared herself the aggressor; Napoleon could no longer hope to wriggle out of his commitments and did not attempt to do so. He ordered the immediate mobilisation of the French army. Of its 120,000 men, one section would enter Italy across the Alps while the rest went by sea to Genoa.

Cavour was well aware that all this would take time; meanwhile, the Austrians were already on the march. For at least a fortnight, the Piedmontese would have to face the Austrians alone. It was a daunting prospect; fortunately he was saved again – this time by torrential rains and dissension over strategy within the Austrian staff. The consequent delay gave time for the French to arrive, led by the Emperor himself who, landing at Genoa on 12 May, for the first time in his life took personal command of his army. It was on 4 June that the first decisive battle took place – at Magenta, a small village some fourteen miles west of Milan, where the French army, fighting alone under General Marie-Patrice de MacMahon – whom Napoleon subsequently promoted to marshal and made Duke of Magenta – defeated an Austrian army of 50,000. Casualties were high on both sides, and would have been higher if the Piedmontese, delayed by the indecision of their own commander, had not arrived some time after the battle was over. This misfortune did not, however, prevent Napoleon and Victor Emmanuel from making a joint triumphal entry into Milan four days later.

After Magenta the Franco-Piedmontese army was joined by Garibaldi, who had returned from America in 1854 full of all his old ardour and enthusiasm. He had now been invited by Victor Emmanuel to assemble a brigade of *cacciatori delle Alpi*,[1] and he had won a signal victory over the Austrians some ten days before at Varese. Army and *cacciatori* then advanced together and met the full Austrian army on 24 June at Solferino, just south of Lake Garda. The ensuing battle – in which well over 250,000 men were engaged – was fought on a grander scale than any since Leipzig in 1813. This time Napoleon III was not the only monarch to assume personal command: Victor Emmanuel did the same, as did the twenty-nine-year-old Emperor Franz Josef of Austria, who had succeeded his uncle Ferdinand in 1848. Only the French, however, were able to reveal a secret weapon: rifled artillery, which dramatically increased both the accuracy and the range of their guns.

The fighting, much of it hand-to-hand, began early in the morning and continued for most of the day. Only towards evening, after losing some 20,000 of his men in heavy rain, did Franz Josef order a withdrawal across the Mincio river. But it was a Pyrrhic victory; the French and Piedmontese lost almost as many men as the Austrians, and the outbreak of fever – probably typhus – that followed the battle accounted for thousands more on both sides. The scenes of carnage made a deep impression on a young Swiss named Henri Dunant, who chanced to be present and organised emergency aid services for the wounded. Five years later, as a direct result of his experience, he was to found the Red Cross.

Nor was Dunant the only one to be sickened by what he had seen at Solferino. Napoleon III had also been profoundly shocked, and his disgust for war and all the horrors it brought in its train was certainly one of the reasons why, little more than a fortnight after the battle, he made a separate peace with Austria. There were others too. Things had gone badly for the Austrians, but they remained secure in what was known as the Quadrilateral – the four great fortresses of Peschiera, Verona, Legnago and Mantua – from which the Emperor had no realistic hope of removing them. He was worried, too, about German reactions. The German Confederation was mobilising some 350,000

---

[1] 'Alpine hunters'.

men; were they to attack, the 50,000 French soldiers remaining in France would be slaughtered.

Finally, there was the situation in Italy itself. Recent events had persuaded several of the smaller states – notably Tuscany, Romagna and the duchies of Modena and Parma – to think about overthrowing their former rulers and seeking annexation to Piedmont. The result would be a formidable state, immediately over the French border, covering virtually all north and central Italy: a state which in time might well absorb some or all of the Papal States and even the Two Sicilies. Was it really for this that those who fell at Solferino had given their lives?

And so on 11 July 1859 the Emperors of France and of Austria met at Villafranca, near Verona, and the future of north and central Italy was decided in under an hour. Austria would keep two of the fortresses of the Quadrilateral, Mantua and Peschiera; the rest of Lombardy she would surrender to France, who would pass it on to Piedmont. The former rulers of Tuscany and Modena would be restored to their thrones,[1] and an Italian confederacy would be established under the honorary presidency of the Pope. Venice and Venetia would be a member of this confederacy, but would remain under Austrian sovereignty.

The fury of Cavour when he read the details of the Villafranca Agreement can well be imagined. Without Peschiera and Mantua, not even Lombardy would be entirely Italian; as for central Italy, that was lost even before it had been properly gained. He himself would have nothing to do with the agreement; after a long and acrimonious interview with Victor Emmanuel, he submitted his resignation. 'We shall return,' he wrote to a friend, 'to conspiracy.' Gradually, however, he recovered himself. There had at least been no mention in the agreement of the French annexation of Savoy and Nice, which he had reluctantly offered at Plombières; the present situation, if not all that he had hoped, was certainly a good deal better than it had been the year before.

Over the next few months that situation improved still further, as it gradually became clear that Tuscany and Modena refused to accept the fate prescribed for them; nothing, they made it clear, would induce them to take back their former rulers. In Florence, Bologna, Parma and

---

[1] There was no mention of Romagna, Parma or Piacenza, for which neither emperor was directly responsible.

Modena virtual dictators had sprung up, all of them determined on fusion with Piedmont. The only obstacle was presented by Piedmont itself. The terms agreed at Villafranca were now incorporated in a formal treaty signed at Zurich, and General Alfonso La Marmora, who had succeeded Cavour as Chief Minister, was unwilling to take any action in defiance of it. But the dictators were quite prepared to bide their time. Florence, meanwhile, kept her independence; Romagna (which included Bologna), Parma and Modena joined together into a new state which – since the Roman Via Aemilia ran through all three of them – they called Emilia.

Camillo Cavour, who had withdrawn after his resignation to his estate at Leri near Vercelli, followed these developments with satisfaction; the Villafranca Agreement had not turned out so badly after all. When, therefore, in January 1860 Victor Emmanuel – not without some personal reluctance[1] – recalled him to take over a new government, he was happy to return to Turin. Scarcely was he back in office before he found himself swept up in negotiations with Napoleon III, and it was not long before the two reached agreement: Piedmont would annex Tuscany and Emilia; in return, Savoy and Nice would be ceded to France. Plebiscites were held in all these states, and in every one the majority in favour of the arrangement was overwhelming. In Emilia, for example, the voting was 426,000 against 1,500; in Savoy, 130,500 to 235. There was a predictable explosion of wrath from Garibaldi, but against such majorities there was little that he could do. But in fact, of the powers principally concerned, only the annexed territories were entirely happy. Piedmont hated losing Savoy and Nice; France opposed the annexation of Tuscany, which the Emperor feared would give too much strength to Piedmont at the expense of the central Italian kingdom that he would greatly have preferred; Austria, quite apart from the loss of Lombardy, mourned the departure of the Grand Duke of Tuscany and the Duke of Modena, both of whom she had effectively controlled.

One of Garibaldi's closest political colleagues was a Sicilian lawyer named Francesco Crispi. In 1855, during a period of exile in London, this man had also been a friend of Mazzini's, and Mazzini had long dreamed of an invasion of Sicily. Four years later Crispi had visited

---

[1] He had never quite forgiven Cavour for his hard words after Villafranca, nor for having successfully opposed – after the death of Queen Maria Adelaide in 1855 at the age of only thirty-three – his marriage to his long-time mistress.

Sicily in disguise and under a false name, and returned to London convinced that it was once again ripe for revolution. A small armed expedition was all that was required, and the whole island would be up in arms. The only question was, who was to lead it? The name of Garibaldi immediately sprang to mind, but Garibaldi was hesitant. He was still seething over Villafranca, and he himself had a rather different dream: the capture of Nice and its return to Piedmont.

Thoughts of Nice, however, were soon to be indefinitely postponed. On 4 April 1860 there was a popular insurrection in Palermo. If all had proceeded according to plan it would have been accompanied by a simultaneous rising among the aristocracy, but something went badly wrong. The Neapolitan authorities had been secretly informed, and the insurgents found themselves surrounded almost before they had left their homes. All who were not killed instantly were executed later. The operation, like virtually every other inspired by Mazzini, had been a disastrous failure, but it provided a spark for many others throughout northern Sicily, and the authorities could not cope with them all. Nor could they suppress the rumour that ran like wildfire across the island, adding fuel to the revolutionary flames that Garibaldi was on his way.

At the time it was wishful thinking, but when Garibaldi heard the news he acted at once. Cavour refused his request for a brigade from the Piedmontese army, but within less than a month he had assembled a band of volunteers, who sailed from the little port of Quarto (now part of Genoa) on the night of 5 May 1860, landing unopposed at Marsala in western Sicily on the 11th. They represented a broad cross-section of Italian society, about half consisting of professional men such as lawyers, doctors and university lecturers, the other half drawn from the working classes. Some were still technically republicans, but their leader made it clear to them that they were fighting not just for Italy but also for King Victor Emmanuel – and this was no time to argue.

From Marsala, the Thousand – as they came to be called, though there were actually 1,089 of them – headed inland, where their numbers were soon doubled by Sicilian volunteers. At Calatafimi, some thirty miles to the northeast, they found Bourbon troops awaiting them. The battle was fought on 11 May and lasted several hours, most of the fighting being hand-to-hand, with bayonets rather than rifles. Garibaldi's men were massively outnumbered; on the other hand, he could count on a huge psychological advantage. To every Italian this army of Redshirts – with its whole string of victories in South America as well as in Italy – was by now of almost legendary fame, its members often credited by the simple with a magic invulnerability to bullets. The Neapolitan soldiers were frightened and had little stomach for the fight; the Thousand were fighting for an ideal in which they all passionately believed, under a leader whose swashbuckling charisma was a constant inspiration. If they could win this first battle, Garibaldi told them, there was a strong probability that the opposition would melt away; then, in just a week or two, they would be masters of Sicily.

And they won it. And Garibaldi was proved right. There was no more obstruction before Palermo; on the contrary, thousands of Sicilians rallied to his colours, and when he arrived on 26 May it was to find that the citizens had already risen against the Bourbon government. There was a little desultory fighting, but it was not long before the Neapolitan commander gave the order to evacuate Palermo. By the end of the month Garibaldi was master of the city. There followed a brief period of consolidation, during which substantial reinforcements arrived from north Italy; then in early July he continued his advance. His last Sicilian battle was fought at Milazzo, a fortified seaport some fifteen miles west of Messina. It was harder fought than the others, but it opened the way to Messina itself, which surrendered without a struggle, apart from a small but courageous Bourbon garrison which held out for a little longer in the citadel.

The Neapolitans had withdrawn their forces from every other town and city, so with this negligible exception Sicily was free. Cavour sought its immediate formal annexation to Victor Emmanuel's rapidly-growing kingdom – an idea hotly opposed by Garibaldi and Francesco Crispi, now his right-hand man. To all intents and purposes, they argued, Sicily was already part of the kingdom. The Sicilians certainly assumed as much, and the long legal formalities could surely wait until the rest of the fighting was over. They were worried, too – though they took care not to say so – that if the island were annexed Cavour might use his new authority to refuse to allow them to make it a springboard from which to advance on Naples, Rome and Venice.

These fears were by no means groundless. On 1 August Cavour wrote in desperation to his *chef de cabinet* and close friend Costantino Nigra:

> If Garibaldi can pass to the mainland and take possession of Naples as he has of Sicily and Palermo, he becomes the absolute master of the situation . . . King Victor Emmanuel loses almost all his prestige; to most Italians he is simply the friend of Garibaldi. He will probably keep his crown, but that crown will shine only with the reflected light that a heroic adventurer

chooses to throw on it . . . The King cannot take the crown of Italy from the hands of Garibaldi; it would lie too unsteadily on his head . . .

We must ensure that the government of Naples falls before Garibaldi sets foot on the mainland . . . The moment the King is gone, we must take the government into our own hands in the name of order and humanity, while snatching from Garibaldi's hands the supreme direction of the Italian movement.

This brave, you may say audacious, measure will provoke cries of horror from Europe, will cause serious diplomatic complications, may even involve us at a somewhat later stage into a war with Austria. But it saves our revolution, and it preserves for the Italian movement that quality which is at once its glory and its strength; the quality of nationhood, and of monarchy.

Cavour had already persuaded Victor Emmanuel to write officially to Garibaldi asking him not to invade the mainland. The King had done so, but had followed up his letter with another, private note to the effect that these official instructions could perhaps be ignored. It now appears that this second note may never have been delivered – when it was found the seal was still unbroken – but it hardly mattered: Garibaldi's mind was already made up. Cavour then sent *agents provocateurs* to stir up trouble in Naples in the hope of sparking off a liberal revolution. Naples, however – in striking contrast to Palermo – proved numb and apathetic. There was nothing to do but allow events to take their course.

On 18 and 19 August 1860, Garibaldi and his men crossed the Straits of Messina on the first step of their march on Naples. If Cavour had been alarmed, the twenty-four-year-old King Francis II,[1] who had succeeded his father Ferdinand the previous year, was panic-stricken. The British diplomat Odo Russell, at that time serving on a mission to Naples, had reported that when Garibaldi entered Palermo the King 'telegraphed five times in twenty-four hours for the Pope's blessing', and 'Cardinal Antonelli . . . sent the last three blessings without reference to His Holiness, saying that he was duly authorised to do so.' Francis knew that his army was incapable of further resistance to the seemingly invincible Redshirts, and that he himself was equally incapable of breathing further life into it; the only alternative was flight. On 6 September he took ship for Gaeta. Less than twenty-four hours later, Garibaldi entered Naples.

---

[1] He is described in the *Enciclopedia Italiana* as 'serious, taciturn, melancholic, timid, awkward, eternally doubtful of himself and everyone else'.

His journey through Calabria had been ridiculously easy. As against the 16,000 Neapolitan soldiers in the province, his vanguard consisted of only 3,500, but after a token resistance at Reggio there was no more opposition. For his men there were still 300 miles to cover in the broiling summer heat, but with Bourbon troops instantly surrendering their arms as they approached he had no fear for their safety. On the other hand, he was anxious to get to Naples as soon as possible – he did not trust Cavour an inch, and feared a preemptive strike. Fortunately for him, the late King Ferdinand had recently built a railway; Garibaldi now requisitioned all the rolling stock he could find and filled it with his army. He himself, with six companions, climbed into an open carriage and trundled into Naples on the afternoon of 7 September. That evening he addressed a cheering populace from the balcony of the royal palace, thanking the Neapolitans 'in the name of all Italy which, thanks to their cooperation, had at last become a nation'. It was a shameless lie – they had not lifted a finger – but, he doubtless felt, a little flattery at this stage would do no harm.

Naples was the largest city in Italy, and the third largest in Europe. For the next two months Garibaldi ruled it – with Sicily – as a dictator. Meanwhile, he was planning his next step, which was to be an immediate march on the Papal States and Rome. But this step was never taken. Cavour, who had been unable to prevent his invasion of the mainland, was now determined to stop him in his tracks – knowing full well that to allow him to continue might well mean war with France. The Redshirts would have found the well-trained French a very different proposition to anything they had encountered so far, and Italy might well have lost everything she had gained in the past two years. There were other considerations too: as he had feared, Garibaldi was now far more popular than Victor Emmanuel himself; the Piedmontese army was deeply jealous of his recent successes; and there was always the lurking danger that Mazzini – who arrived in Naples on the 17th September – and his followers might persuade Garibaldi to desert the King of Piedmont and espouse the republican cause.

Garibaldi was well aware of Cavour's hostility, just as he believed in the King's tacit support, and soon after his arrival in Naples he had even gone so far as publicly to demand the Chief Minister's resignation. In doing so he badly overplayed his hand. Victor Emmanuel, realising that he could no longer continue to play off the two men against each other, found it safer to accept the policy of his government. None of this, however, nor any number of letters (inspired by Cavour) from distinguished foreigners ranging from the Hungarian patriot Lajos Kossuth to the British social reformer Lord Shaftesbury, weakened Garibaldi's resolve to march on Rome. The only argument that could have had an effect was the one that eventually did so: *force majeure.*

Suddenly he found two formidable armies ranged against him: the Neapolitan and the Piedmontese. King Francis in Gaeta had managed to raise a new army, and not long after Garibaldi and his men left Naples on the first stage of their advance to the north they found a force of some 50,000 ranged along the bank of the Volturno river. It was here that they suffered their first defeat since their landing in Sicily; outside the little town of Caiazzo, in the leader's temporary absence, one of his generals tried and failed to cross the river and lost 250 men in the attempt. On the first day of October, however, Garibaldi had his revenge. The battle was fought just outside Capua, in and around the little village of S. Angelo in Formis.[1] It was an expensive victory – some 1,400 killed or wounded – but it saved Italy.

Meanwhile, the army of Piedmont was also on the march. Cavour, determined to recapture the initiative from Garibaldi, had launched an invasion of his own into the papal territories of Umbria and the Marches. Leaving Rome untouched, he had neatly avoided antagonising France and, quite possibly, Austria; he had also opened the way into the south, where – since Garibaldi was now dictator – he could claim that the Piedmontese army was urgently needed to save Naples from the forces of revolution. Most important of all, he had removed the geographical barrier which, so long as it lasted, would always divide Italy into two separate parts and make unification impossible. The campaign itself was unspectacular but effective. The Piedmontese army overcame a spirited resistance at Perugia, scored a small victory over a papal army near the little village of Castelfidardo near Loreto and a rather larger one when, after five days' fighting, they captured Ancona, taking 154 guns and 7,000 prisoners – including the commander of the papal forces, the French General Christophe de Lamoricière. That was the end of the papal army; henceforth there was no further trouble.

Victor Emmanuel himself, accompanied by his long-term mistress, Rosina Vercellana – dressed, we are told, to kill – now came to take titular command of his army. From that moment Garibaldi's star began

---

[1] It is something of a miracle that the church of S. Angelo was not destroyed. It is the grandest monument in all Campania, its interior walls covered in eleventh-century frescos in a quite astonishing state of preservation.

to set. The battle of the Volturno had already persuaded him that a march on Rome was no longer a possibility, and now, with the King himself on his way, he saw that his rule in the south must come to an end. This was confirmed in late October, when plebiscites were held in the Kingdom of Naples and in Sicily, in Umbria and in the Marches, on whether voters wished their land to form an integral part of Italy under Victor Emmanuel. The votes in favour were overwhelming: in Sicily – to take but one example – 432,053 voted in favour, 667 against.

Garibaldi gave in gracefully. He rode north with a large escort to meet the King, and on 7 November the two of them entered Naples side by side in the royal carriage. He asked one favour only: to be allowed to govern Naples and Sicily for a year as viceroy. But this was refused. He was after all a dangerous radical and anticlerical, who still dreamed of capturing Rome from the Pope and making it the capital of Italy. In an attempt to sugar the pill, Victor Emmanuel offered him the rank of full general together with a splendid estate, but Garibaldi would have none of it. He remained a revolutionary, and for as long as Austria still occupied the Veneto – and the Pope continued as temporal ruler in Rome – he was determined to preserve his freedom of action. On 9 November he sailed for his farm on the little island of Caprera off the Sardinian coast. He took with him only a little money – borrowed, since he had made none during his months of power – and a bag of seed for his garden.

On Passion Sunday, 17 March 1861, Victor Emmanuel II was proclaimed King of Italy. Old Massimo d'Azeglio, Cavour's pre-decessor as Chief Minister, is reported to have said when he heard the news: 'L'Italia è fatta; restano a fare gli italiani.'[1] But although the first half of the statement was true – an Italian nation had indeed come into existence, even if it was not yet complete – the second half was truer still. Francis II kept up his resistance; the country had been divided since the end of the Roman Empire, and few indeed of Italy's twenty-two million people thought of themselves as Italians. North and south had virtually nothing in common, with radically different standards of living (as indeed they still have today). New roads and railways had to be built as a matter of urgency. A national army and navy had somehow to be created, together with a single legal system, civil administration and common currency. In the meantime, there was no alternative to the adoption of Piedmontese institutions; but this forcible

---

[1] 'Italy is made; now we have to make the Italians.'

'Piedmontisation' was widely resented and did little to help the cause of unity. Even the King's decision to keep his designation 'the Second' caused offence. As King of Italy he was surely Victor Emmanuel I; was the Risorgimento really the rebirth of Italy, or was it simply the conquest of Italy by the house of Savoy?

Less than three months after the royal proclamation Cavour was dead. He had spent his last weeks in furious debate over the future of Rome – in which, it should be recorded, he had never once set foot. All the other major Italian cities, he argued, had been independent municipalities, each fighting its own corner; only Rome, as the seat of the Church, had remained above such rivalries. But though the Pope must be asked to surrender his temporal power, papal independence must at all costs be guaranteed – 'a free church in a free state'. He encountered a good deal of opposition – the most vitriolic from Garibaldi, who emerged from Caprera in April, strode into the Assembly in his red shirt and grey South American poncho, and let loose a stream of abuse at the man who, he thundered, had sold off half his country to the French and done his best to prevent the invasion of the Two Sicilies. But he succeeded only in confirming the general view that however brilliant a general he might be, he was certainly no statesman; Cavour easily won the vote of confidence that followed. It was his last political victory. He died suddenly on 6 June, of a massive stroke. He was just fifty years old.

If Camillo Cavour had lived just one more decade he would have seen the last two pieces of the Italian jigsaw fitted into place. Where Rome was concerned, the situation was not helped by Garibaldi, who in 1862 made a faintly ridiculous attempt to repeat his triumph of two years before. Adopting the slogan 'Rome or death!', he raised 3,000 volunteers at Palermo, with whom he took possession of a complaisant Catania; then in August, having commandeered a couple of local steamers, he crossed with his men to Calabria and began another march on Rome. This time, however, government troops were ready for him. He had got no further than the Aspromonte massif in the extreme south of Calabria – the toe of Italy – when they attacked. Fearing a civil war, Garibaldi ordered his men not to return the fire, but there were a few casualties nonetheless, he himself having his right ankle shattered. He was arrested and sent in a gunboat to Naples, where he was promptly freed; he remained a hero, and the government did not dare take action against him.

Meanwhile, quiet diplomacy was proving rather more successful. Pope Pius himself was refusing to yield an inch; so far as he was concerned, he held the Papal States for the Catholic world and was obliged by his coronation oath to pass them on to his successor. Napoleon III, by contrast, was becoming steadily more amenable to negotiation, and by what was known as the September Convention, signed on 15 September 1864, he agreed to withdraw his troops from Rome within two years. Italy in return pledged herself to guarantee papal territory against any attack, and agreed to transfer her capital within six months from Turin to Florence.

The Convention, which was to remain in force for six years, did not directly improve the prospects of incorporating Rome into the new Italian state; indeed, it seemed at least temporarily to guarantee the *status quo*. On the other hand, by putting an end to the fifteen years of French occupation it cleared the ground for the next steps, whatever these might be, and by freezing the situation in Rome it enabled the government to turn its mind to the other overriding necessity in those early years of Italian nationhood: the recovery of the Veneto. For some time past King Victor Emmanuel had been toying with the idea of an invasion of the Balkans – led, it need hardly be said, by Garibaldi – to stir up revolt among the Austrian subject peoples; with Austria fully engaged in restoring order, it would be a simple matter to occupy the Italian lands. Unfortunately Napoleon III – whose support would have been vital – had pooh-poohed the idea and the King had reluctantly put it to one side.

But now, by a stroke of quite unexpected good fortune, there appeared a *deus ex machina* who was effectively to drop both the coveted territories into Italy's lap. This was the Prussian Chancellor, Otto von Bismarck, who was now well on the way to realising his dream of uniting all the German states into a single empire. The one stumbling-block was Austria, whose influence in Germany he was determined to eliminate. He therefore approached General La Marmora – now once again Victor Emmanuel's Chief Minister – with a proposal for a military alliance: Austria would be attacked simultaneously on two fronts, by Prussia from the north and by Italy from the west. Italy's reward, in the event of victory, would be Venetia. La Marmora readily agreed, and Napoleon III signalled that he had no objection. The treaty was signed on 8 April 1866, and on 15 June the war began.

Six weeks later it was over. For the Prussians, a single battle was enough. It was fought at Sadowa, some sixty-five miles northeast of Prague, and it engaged the largest number of troops – some 330,000 – ever assembled on a European battlefield. (It was also the first in which railways and the telegraph were used on a considerable scale.) The Prussian victory was total. It bankrupted the military resources of the Austrian Emperor Franz Josef I and opened the way to Vienna. Bismarck had achieved exactly what he wanted, and was glad to accede to Austria's request for an armistice.

Italy, unfortunately, did less well. Her main army, under the King, La Marmora and General Enrico Cialdini, Duke of Gaeta, was defeated several times in and around Custoza – always unlucky for the house of Savoy – and at sea her navy was largely destroyed off Lissa (now the Croatian island of Vis). The only good news was provided by Garibaldi, who had delightedly obeyed a summons to lead a force of 35,000 into the Tyrol. While scoring no major victory, he certainly caused the Austrians a good deal of discomfiture. The Italian government, now settled in Florence, though mildly aggrieved that it had not been consulted over its terms, nevertheless welcomed the armistice – not least because it provided for the cession of the Veneto. Since Austria had not yet granted recognition to the new kingdom of Italy, the same procedure was followed as for Lombardy five years before: the province was ceded to Napoleon III, who instantly passed it on to Victor Emmanuel.

The cession was confirmed by a plebiscite, the result of which was a foregone conclusion. There was a measure of disappointment in that the area ceded did not include the South Tyrol – what the Italians called the Trentino – or Venezia Giulia, which included Trieste, Pola and Fiume (the modern Rijeka); for those Italy would have to wait until after the First World War. But Venice was an Italian city at last, and Italy could boast a new and invaluable port on the northern Adriatic.

Only Rome remained.

By the end of 1866 the last of the French army had left Rome. The motley array of mercenaries that Pope Pius had managed to recruit seemed to constitute little enough threat to anyone; by the beginning of 1867 the old conspirators were once again out in force. Mazzini, playing on Bismarck's fears of a Franco-Italian alliance, was demanding money and munitions with which to overthrow the government in Florence; Garibaldi, not for the first time, was preparing for a march on Rome and actually went so far as to issue a proclamation calling on all freedom-loving Romans to rise in rebellion. Since the September Convention still had four years to run, the government had little choice but to arrest him and send him back to Caprera, but he soon escaped – he was now in his sixtieth year – reassembled his volunteers and began his promised march.

He had reckoned without the French. Napoleon III, having realised that he had withdrawn his troops too soon, sent a fresh army equipped with the deadly new *chassepot* rifles, which landed at Civitavecchia in the last week of October. The volunteers, outnumbered and outclassed, stood no chance. A day or two later, at Mentana, they met their fate. Garibaldi himself managed to slip back across the frontier into Italy – and into the arms of the authorities. Back he was sent to Caprera, where he remained – this time heavily guarded – under house arrest. His men were less lucky. No less than 1,600 of them were taken prisoner.

Yet again, by his swift reaction, the Emperor Napoleon had saved the temporal power of the Papacy; none could have expected that less than three years later he would be instrumental in bringing about its downfall. The prime mover, once again, was Bismarck, who had cunningly drawn France into a war by his threat to place a prince of the ruling Prussian house of Hohenzollern on the throne of Spain. That war was declared – by France, not Prussia – on 15 July 1870. It was to prove a bitter struggle; Napoleon was going to need every soldier he had for the fighting that lay ahead. By the end of August there was not one French soldier left in Rome.

Pope Pius was fully aware of the danger. Only his little mercenary army remained to protect him. Just three days after the declaration of war, during the First Vatican Council[1] and at the height of the most violent thunderstorm that any Roman could remember, he sought to bolster his position by proclaiming the doctrine of Papal Infallibility. It was a step that arguably did his cause more harm than good,[2] but there was little point in arguing it: Napoleon's defeat at Sedan on 1 September spelled the end of the Second Empire and the destruction of Pius's last hopes. In the minds of the Italian government, the only question still to be decided was one of timing: should their army occupy Rome immediately – the September Convention was on the point of

---

[1] The Pope had summoned it in 1868 to discuss a wide range of subjects, both theological and administrative.
[2] Mazzini addressed the 700 bishops who attended: 'Science goes forward, regardless of your doctrines, caring nothing for your denunciations and your councils, tearing up, with every new discovery, another page of the book that you call infallible.'

expiry, and with the elimination of one of the signatories was anyway a dead letter – or should they wait for a popular rising or mutiny?

Meanwhile, Victor Emmanuel addressed a last appeal to the Pope, writing (as he put it) 'with the affection of a son, the faith of a Catholic, the loyalty of a king and the soul of an Italian'. The security of Italy and of the Holy See itself, he continued, depended on the presence of Italian troops in Rome. Would His Holiness not accept this unalterable fact and show his benevolent cooperation? Alas, His Holiness would do no such thing. He would yield, he declared, only to violence, and even then he would put up at least a formal resistance. He was as good as his word. When Italian troops entered Rome on the morning of 20 September 1870 by the Porta Pia, they found a papal detachment waiting for them. The fighting was soon over, but not before it had left nineteen papalists and forty-nine Italians dead in the street.

Over the next few hours Italian troops swarmed through Rome, leaving only the Vatican and the Castel Sant' Angelo, from which there now flew the white flag of surrender. There was no more resistance. Pope Pius withdrew inside the walls of the Vatican, where he remained for the last eight years of his life. The plebiscite that was held shortly afterwards registered 133,681 votes in favour of the incorporation of Rome into the Kingdom of Italy, and 1,507 against. Rome was now part of Italy not by right of conquest but by the will of its people. Only the Vatican city now remained an independent sovereign state.

It was not until 2 July 1871 that Victor Emmanuel made his official entry into his new capital. The streets were already being decorated for the occasion when he sent a telegram to the mayor, Prince Francesco Pallavicini, forbidding all signs of festivity. As a pious Catholic, he had been not only saddened but terrified when sentence of excommunication had been passed upon him. Ferdinand Gregorovius, the Prussian historian of medieval Rome, wrote in his diary that the procession was 'without pomp, vivacity, grandeur or majesty; and that was as it should have been, for this day signals the end of the millenary rule of the Popes over Rome'. In the afternoon the King was urged to cross the river to Trastevere, where some ceremony had been prepared by the largely working-class population. He flatly refused, adding in the Piedmontese dialect of which few of those about him would have understood a word, 'The Pope is only two steps away, and would feel hurt. I have done enough already to that poor old man.'

CHAPTER XXIX

The Queens and the Carlists

On 30 September 1868, Queen Isabel II of Spain boarded a train with her children at San Sebastian and trundled off into exile. Her departure marked the end, not only of a reign, but of perhaps the most turbulent period in the entire history of her country.

The story began with her father, Ferdinand VII, who, with her grandfather Charles IV, had in 1808 abdicated his right to the throne.[1] The fall of Napoleon clearly rendered these abdications null and void, and Ferdinand, having succeeded in 1814, had ruled Spain with singular ineptitude for fifteen years when, in 1829, he was widowed for the third time. None of his three wives had produced a child that survived infancy, and Ferdinand was desperate for a son. What with his crippling gout and his regular fits of apoplexy, his chances looked slim enough; but he refused to give up hope. His problem was to find a suitable wife. As it happened, his youngest brother, Francisco de Paula, was married to a daughter of King Francis I of Naples; she had been christened Maria Luisa Carlotta, but in Spain was known simply as Carlota. It was she who showed the King a miniature of her twenty-three-year-old sister, Maria Cristina, and Ferdinand looked no further. On 12 December 1829 he married the young princess at the church of Our Lady of Atocha in Madrid.

Maria Cristina was devastatingly attractive, shamelessly flirtatious, with a huge capacity for enjoyment; to the suffocating stuffiness of the Spanish court she came as an invigorating breath of fresh air. Immediately, she won all hearts. Or nearly all; for the marriage came as a severe blow to the heir apparent, the King's younger brother Don Carlos, and even more to his wife, Maria Francisca of Braganza. They were an ill-assorted couple. Don Carlos was almost a dwarf, though fully endowed with the hideous Bourbon chin and nose; he was morbidly pious, fanatically absolutist and weak as water. To the English diarist Henry Greville he was 'an imbecile . . . bigoted and perverse . . . a coward too, without a spark of energy or talent'. Maria Francisca by contrast was statuesque, intelligent, with a commanding

---

[1] See Chapter XXIV, p. 454.

presence and formidably ambitious. Heretofore she had been virtually certain of her husband's succession; now there was a chance that it might be taken from him. And worse was to come. When, three months after the wedding, it was announced that the new Queen was pregnant, Ferdinand promulgated the old Pragmatic Sanction, whereby the even older Salic Law – barring females from the succession – was set aside. In other words, the long-awaited child, whether boy or girl, would inherit the throne of Spain.

It was a girl, born on 10 October 1830 and christened Maria Isabel Luisa. The Carlists – as the adherents of Don Carlos now came to be called – could derive little immediate comfort from the fact, but as time went on, with the King's health steadily worsening, the prospect of a reigning queen began to cause serious concern. Then, in July 1832 on the way to his summer palace at La Granja, Ferdinand was seriously injured in a carriage accident, and two months later he still lay at the point of death. The Queen, who in those two months had seldom left his bedside, took advice from one of his chief ministers and was horrified when she was told that the whole country would immediately rally around Don Carlos. Maria Francisca, we may be sure, uttered her own dire warnings, and the King, by now barely conscious, was persuaded that the Pragmatic Sanction must be revoked if a bloodbath was to be avoided. A decree was hastily drafted, which he signed with a quavering hand. Shortly afterwards he was pronounced dead. Don Carlos, it seemed, was king.

But he was not. Suddenly, the undertakers who came to prepare the body for its lying in state detected signs of life, and slowly Ferdinand began to recover. Even so, the document which he had so recently signed, and on which the ink was scarcely dry, would probably have remained in force had it not been for his sister-in-law Carlota. The moment the astonishing news reached her in Cadiz, she ordered her carriage and set off at top speed, over 400 miles of execrable roads, for La Granja. The state of the King's health was of relatively little interest to her, but she detested Don Carlos and his wife and had no intention of letting them deprive her niece of her rightful crown. On her arrival she went straight to the Queen, berated her for her fecklessness and demanded to see the revocation decree. When it was shown to her she snatched it out of the official's hand and tore it to pieces.

Ferdinand lived for another year, during which he presided over an elaborate ceremony in the ancient church of Los Jeronimos in Madrid, designed to strengthen yet further the claim of his little daughter to the succession. One by one all the grandees of Spain – with one significant exception – filed past, kissing the hands of the King, the Queen and the two-year-old Infanta. Then, on 29 September 1833, Ferdinand suffered an apoplectic stroke. This time there was no resuscitation. The Infanta was proclaimed Isabel II, with her mother as regent. She was recognised by Britain, France and Portugal; Don Carlos, on the other hand, who had proclaimed himself King Charles V, was favoured by Russia, Austria, the Pope and – most surprisingly of all – Maria Cristina's brother, Ferdinand II of Naples. As for Spain itself, it was split across the middle. Madrid and the south were overwhelmingly in favour of Isabel; many of the cities and towns of the north, however, immediately rose in support of Don Carlos. The Carlist Wars – the last in European history in which two rival claimants fought for a crown – had begun. They were to continue, on and off, for the best part of half a century.

Or perhaps even longer: it could be argued that the Nationalists in the Spanish Civil War were Carlists at heart. For Carlism came to mean something a great deal more than loyalty to Don Carlos and the unwavering conviction that he was the legitimate ruler of Spain. It also represented all the old reactionary Spanish traditions: devout Catholicism, with unquestioning obedience to the Church and even nostalgia for the Inquisition ('that most august tribune, brought down by angels from heaven to earth'); political absolutism under an authoritarian and all-powerful king (never, in any circumstances, a queen); and that unbending austerity which was for so long a feature of the Spanish character. Set against all this was the great wave of liberalism which swept across Europe throughout the nineteenth century and was now improbably represented by little Isabel and her loyal subjects. The Spanish royal family had never, heaven knows, been known for their left-wing views; compared with the Carlists, however, they were rabid revolutionaries. Anyway, they desperately needed liberal support, so liberals they reluctantly became – proving it by reinstating the remarkably liberal constitution of 1812.[1]

Spain was now rent by civil war – and of all forms of warfare civil war is the most cruel. Fighting was fierce throughout the north, with hideous atrocities committed on men, women and children by both sides. Finally, in August 1839, the Carlists secretly negotiated a

---

[1] The constitution of 1812 – known as the Constitution of Cadiz – considerably restricted the powers of the monarchy, instituted a single-chamber parliament (with no special representation for the nobility or the Church) and introduced a modern system of administration based on provinces and municipalities.

surrender agreement. Don Carlos sadly crossed the border into France, where he, his second wife[1] and his three sons were to maintain a mildly ridiculous little court at Bourges. He lived another fifteen years, but never returned to Spain.

Towards the end of August 1840, the Regent Maria Cristina set off for Barcelona, ostensibly to take the waters at Caldas but in fact to meet the country's leading general, Baldomero Espartero, and to ask his advice. The constitution of 1812 had conferred a considerable degree of independence on the country's municipalities, many of which had taken what she considered unwarranted advantage of their new privileges during the recent war. The more conservative members of the government were now keen to cut them once again down to size by what was known as the Municipal Bill, and Maria Cristina whole-heartedly agreed with them; the liberals, on the other hand, were determined that they should do no such thing. It was obvious that serious trouble was brewing. Considering that Catalonia had never had much love for the royal family, Maria Cristina was surprised and gratified by the warmth of her reception; it proved, however, to be nothing like the rapturous welcome accorded to Espartero a day or two later, and when the general informed her of his strong opposition to the bill, such was her irritation that – just to spite him – she signed it on the spot.

That night Barcelona erupted in protest. The palace was surrounded by a furious mob, cheering the General and the constitution and threatening death to the Regent and her ministers. At 1 a.m. a terrified Maria Cristina begged Espartero to bid the crowds disperse, but he refused to do so until she had revoked her signature to the bill. She did so, then a few days later attempted to change her mind; once again, chaos resulted. She fled to Valencia, but the fuse had been lit: on 1 September Madrid rose in revolt and denounced the government, and other cities quickly followed its example. Only when she swallowed what was left of her pride and invited Espartero to form a government did a semblance of order return. It was then that Maria Cristina dropped her bombshell. She announced her abdication as Regent. Espartero begged her to reconsider, but she was adamant. Her last words to him are said to have been, 'I made you a Duke [of Morella],

---

[1] After the death of Maria Francisca in 1834 he had married his Portuguese sister-in-law, the Princess of Beira.

but I could not make you a gentleman.' She then said goodbye to the two little Infantas, now aged ten and eight respectively – the younger, Maria Luisa Fernanda, had been born in 1832 – and on 17 October, with her second, semi-secret family,[1] a vast amount of money and virtually all the jewels, silver and linen in the palace,[2] boarded a ship for France.

The loot that Maria Cristina had taken with her was probably enough to have kept her and her family in comfort for the rest of their lives; in fact, her abdication proved to be short-lived. She and her family received the warmest of welcomes in Paris, King Louis-Philippe travelling out as far as Fontainebleau to meet them, and were given a splendid apartment at the Palais-Royal. In December they paid a visit to Rome, where she signed a written act of repentance for the anticlerical laws to which she had given her approval, receiving a full absolution from Pope Gregory XVI before returning to Paris. But then, on 8 November 1843, at the age of thirteen, Queen Isabel II was declared to be legally of age. There was now no political obstacle to her mother's return to Spain; such problems as existed were chiefly financial. The liberals demanded that Maria Cristina should first pay compensation for all that she had taken away at the time of her departure. This resulted in endless legal wrangling, particularly after she had lodged an enormous counterclaim in respect of an unpaid pension, but by the time matters were finally settled she was substantially richer than ever. At last she was ready for her homecoming.

At every stage of her journey through Spain she received a tumultuous welcome. She showed, too, that after fifteen years – and despite a formidable increase in weight – she had lost none of her youthful exuberance and charm. On her return to Madrid the court recovered, almost overnight, all its old brilliance. Balls, banquets and dazzling receptions followed thick and fast, at all of which Maria Cristina completely overshadowed her somewhat surly daughter who, realising that she was outclassed, grew surlier still. Such moods, however, are not uncommon in teenage girls, and Isabel too was soon to change.

---

[1] Soon after – or perhaps before – Ferdinand's death she had taken a lover: a corporal in the Guards named Fernando Muñoz. The two were secretly married on 27 December 1833, after which she named him Groom of the Bedchamber. Although they were to have four children, the marriage was not publicly admitted until 1845, when Muñoz was created Duke of Riánsares.

[2] According to the French Prime Minister François Guizot, who knew her well, 'there were not six spoons left.'

*

On 3 April 1846 the Comte de Bresson, French ambassador to the Court of Spain, sent his Foreign Minister, François Guizot, a terse message. '*La Reine*,' he reported blandly, '*est nubile depuis deux heures*.'[1] Few ambassadors have ever been quicker off the mark, but Maria Cristina, it need hardly be said, had not waited for this happy moment. For months already, she had devoted most of her waking hours to the question of her daughter's marriage. No one, of course, thought of consulting Isabel herself. Away in Bourges, Don Carlos was intriguing hard on behalf of his son, the Count of Montemolin, even going so far as to abdicate in his favour. Such a marriage would obviously have eliminated the Carlist question once and for all; it would, however, have relegated Isabel to the status of Queen Consort – a position which her mother refused absolutely to contemplate. In Paris, Louis-Philippe favoured his own son, the Duc de Montpensier, while in London – where the thought of a royal union between France and Spain was anathema – Queen Victoria and Lord Palmerston were pressing for the Prince Consort's cousin, Prince Leopold of Coburg. This in turn was unacceptable to Louis-Philippe, who politely pointed out that there were already Coburg princes in Brussels, London and Lisbon and that four would be really too many. The King of Naples proposed his brother the Count of Trapani, but as he was studying in Rome with the Jesuits, who were at that time banned in Spain, his claim was not even seriously considered.

Eventually Maria Cristina was obliged to lower her sights and to look within her own family, it being finally agreed that the unfortunate Isabel should marry her own first cousin Francisco de Asís,[2] son of her now deceased aunt Carlota. It was not a pleasing prospect: her intended husband was short and unprepossessing, with a high-pitched voice and a manner which would nowadays be described as distinctly camp. He was generally believed to be homosexual and probably impotent as well. All this would have been bad enough, but it was made still more unbearable by the decision that the Queen's younger (and much prettier) sister, Luisa, should simultaneously marry the sophisticated, charming and pleasingly virile Duc de Montpensier.

The dual marriage took place on 10 October 1846, Isabel's sixteenth birthday. When Francisco de Asís – who looked, we are told, 'like a

---

[1] 'The Queen has been nubile for two hours.'
[2] *Asís* is Assisi in Spanish.

young girl dressed up as a general' – and Isabel were declared man and
wife, they both burst into tears. Years later a close friend asked the
Queen about her wedding night. 'What shall I say,' she answered, 'of a
man who was wearing more lace than I was?' In fact, there is good
reason to believe that even before the marriage she had taken the first
of her innumerable lovers. He was General Francisco Serrano, 'the
handsomest man in Spain', but when in the late summer of 1847 Her
Majesty showed signs of pregnancy and an official rapprochement with
her husband became essential, Serrano was packed off to Granada with
the rank of captain-general. Isabel did not – even privately – mourn his
departure, since she had by now taken up with a young singer from the
opera.

Already by the time of her marriage, the introduction of love into her
life had transformed her. The surliness was gone. She was never
beautiful, but she was now seen to have inherited much of her mother's
warmth. Despite her sexual voraciousness she was genuinely pious,
kind and considerate – and generous to a fault. In the first years of her
reign, therefore, she seems to have been loved by her subjects. But
gradually, as a constant succession of soldiers, sailors, singers, dancers,
composers and a dentist beat a path to her bedroom, the rumours
spread until the Queen's behaviour was the talk not only of Spain but
of all western Europe.

The family reputation was not improved by her mother. Since her
second marriage Maria Cristina's domestic life had been irreproachable, but her name had now become a byword for corruption. Though
the Spanish industrial revolution was still but a poor reflection of the
British, this was an age of commercial rights and concessions,
particularly in the roads and railways; she was always happy to use her
considerable influence in return for cuts and kickbacks, and was
famous for her insider dealings on the Bourse. Corruption, infectious as
it always is, had now spread through the government and
administration, until by the summer of 1854 Spain was ripe for revolt.
The serious disturbances began on the evening of 17 July, when the
mob launched a concerted attack on Maria Cristina's palace, looting
whatever they could carry away and wantonly destroying everything
else. Had the old queen not in the nick of time taken refuge with her
daughter, she would not have survived the night.

Desperate, Isabel took the only course open to her: she sent for
General Espartero. There had been no love lost between them since her
mother's abdication; she recognised, however, that, if she herself were

to remain queen, he represented the only hope of restoring order. The condition on which he now insisted – that she should reform her private life – roused her to a fury, but she was forced to accept it. On 28 July the General entered Madrid. Dead wood was swept away from government and court alike, and there seemed a good chance that Isabel could keep her throne. Maria Cristina, on the other hand, remained a liability. On 28 August, in the small hours of the morning, accompanied by Muñoz and their children, she left Madrid for her second – and this time permanent – exile.

Isabel had been badly frightened, but somehow she clung on. The undertaking that she had reluctantly given to Espartero was soon forgotten; before long she had taken up with Carlos Marfori, the middle-aged, paunchy son of an Italian pastry-cook, whom she appointed Chief of the Royal Household. By the beginning of the 1860s the writing was once more on the wall. Her final downfall came at the hands of one of her former supporters, a general named Juan Prim. Prim's first idea was to replace her with her sister Luisa and Luisa's husband the Duc de Montpensier, and Montpensier paid him several thousand pounds to help finance a rising in their favour; unfortunately for him, the general made the fatal mistake of informing Napoleon III, from whom he also hoped for financial support. Napoleon – who had by now supplanted Louis-Philippe on the French throne – had no intention of allowing his predecessor's son and daughter-in-law to occupy that of Spain, and the Duke's hopes were dashed.

Meanwhile, another challenge came from a different source, an admiral by the name of Juan Bautista Topete, commander of the squadron at Cadiz. With him was the Queen's old lover General Serrano; soon the two were joined by Prim. A new revolution broke out on 18 September 1864 and quickly spread across the country. Isabel was at San Sebastian, only a few miles from the French border. Her first instinct was to return at once to Madrid, but before she could do so there came the news that Serrano had marched on the capital, which had risen in revolt against her. She did not abdicate as her mother had done; she simply went quietly to the railway station with her husband, lover and children and, on 29 September 1868, took the next train for France. Still only thirty-eight, she had reigned for thirty-five years and was to live for another thirty-six. Apart from her nymphomania she was not a bad woman, but she had been a hopeless queen and her country was better without her.

*

Or promised to be – but much depended on her successor. Of her four daughters and one son all, we may be pretty sure, had different fathers, but she had remained married to Francisco so there were no doubts as to their legitimacy. Her son Alfonso, born in 1858, is thought to have been the result of his mother's brief affair with an American dentist's assistant named McKeon, but from his birth he had been recognised as heir to the throne and had been accorded the traditional title of Prince of Asturias. Inevitably, however, Isabel's abrupt departure had given new hope to the Carlists.

Since the end of the First Carlist War in 1839 they had maintained a fairly low profile. The Count of Montemolin, in whose favour Don Carlos ('Charles V') had abdicated in 1846, had shown himself almost as unimpressive as his father.[1] Several times in his life he dramatically summoned the Spanish people to rise against the usurpers in favour of their rightful king, but nobody paid much attention and he himself was never there when he was wanted. His brother Don Juan, who most unwillingly became the pretender after Montemolin's death in 1861 but preferred to live quietly in Brighton, was if anything even more feckless, and Carlist fortunes were at a low ebb until the appearance on the scene of Don Juan's eldest son, Don Carlos. Tall, outstandingly good-looking, a superb horseman with a passion for soldiering, he was convinced of the justice of the Carlist cause and determined to fight for it until he himself could mount the throne which was rightfully his. He was also extremely rich, thanks to the enormous dowry brought by his wife, Princess Margaret of Parma. Small wonder that at a meeting of the Great Carlist Council, held in London in the summer of 1868, the twenty-year-old Don Carlos was formally acclaimed and cheered to the echo. A few weeks later Don Juan signed a formal act of abdication in favour of his son.

Don Carlos would almost certainly have made a splendid king, and now it seemed that he might even have the edge over young Alfonso of Asturias, who had followed his mother into exile and was still only ten years old. Two years later Queen Isabel was finally persuaded to abdicate in Alfonso's favour; the difficulty now – for both claimants – was that an emergency junta formed after her departure from Spain had formally resolved that the Bourbons had forfeited all rights to the

---

[1] During his youth in London he had been engaged to Miss Adeline de Horsey, who subsequently became the second wife of the Earl of Cardigan, leader of the Charge of the Light Brigade at Balaclava.

throne. Nonetheless, Spain was still a monarchy. All it now needed was a king.

But how was it to find one? The crown was offered in vain to the King of Portugal, to Prince Leopold of Hohenzollern–Sigmaringen[1] and to the Duke of Genoa. Finally Victor Emmanuel's second son, Amadeo, Duke of Aosta, was persuaded to accept, and triumphantly entered his new capital on 31 December 1870. The fact, however, that that very day also saw the assassination of the kingmaker, General Prim, made it all too clear that although Amadeo was happy to accept Spain, Spain was from the very start less enthusiastic about him. Dissatisfaction continued to grow, until in April 1872 Don Carlos called for a general rising. On 2 May he entered Spain from France with a handful of men, but instead of finding – as he had hoped – the whole country up in arms he was met by only a couple of thousand untrained and ill-equipped guerrillas. They had got no further than the mountain village of Oroquieta, only a few miles inside the border, when they were attacked and routed by government troops. Seven hundred were taken prisoner. Don Carlos himself, uninjured, escaped back into France.

Amadeo struggled on for a few more months, but he was opposed by both republicans and Carlists – of whom there were many in the *cortes* – and at last, in February 1873, was obliged to abdicate in his turn. This caused still more chaos. Eventually Spain was proclaimed a republic – and the Carlists, outraged, seized their opportunity. They had always been strong in the northern territories – Catalonia, Navarre and the Basque country – and once again they called Spain to arms in defence of the monarchy. This time they were a good deal more successful than in the previous year. The fighting on both sides was barbarous and brutal, but by midsummer virtually the whole country north of the Ebro – apart from a few towns – was in Carlist hands. Had Don Carlos now marched directly on Madrid, he would almost certainly have won the day. Unaccountably, however, he preferred to lay siege to Bilbao, leaving the southward advance to his brother Don Alfonso Carlos and to Don Alfonso's formidable nineteen-year-old Portuguese wife, Maria de las Nieves, who wore a man's uniform and always fought at her husband's side. These two, at the head of an army of some 14,000, actually captured Cuenca, only some eighty miles east of the capital.

---

[1] Who first accepted it, then refused. Had he turned it down at once, the Franco-Prussian War – which was fought entirely because Napoleon III was not prepared to contemplate a dynastic alliance between Prussia and Spain – would never have taken place. See Chapter XXVIII, p. 537.

Appalling bloodshed followed, doing serious harm to the Carlists' reputation.

Now at last the tide began to turn. In May 1874 Serrano raised the siege of Bilbao. Henceforth the Carlists were on the defensive, and at the end of the year they suffered a truly disastrous blow: a young brigadier, Arsenio Martinez Campos, issued a *pronunciamiento* calling for the return of Alfonso. The response, outside the Carlist north, was immediate and overwhelming. Alfonso set off at once from England – where he had been studying at the Royal Military College, Sandhurst – boarded a Spanish man-of-war at Marseille, landed at Barcelona and on 10 January 1875 entered Madrid as King Alfonso XII to a rapturous welcome. He had been summoned back by his own subjects, and he had been recognised by the Pope; his enemy Don Carlos no longer had a leg to stand on.

Unfortunately Don Carlos did not immediately agree, and continued the fight all through the following year. Only after the fall of Estella on 19 February 1876 did he capitulate. On the 28th he crossed the French frontier. Although he threatened to return, the Second Carlist War was over. Under the benevolent reign of Alfonso XII, *El Pacificador*, Spain entered on a quarter of a century of stable government, the first she had known since the death of King Ferdinand forty-three years before.

With her son now firmly installed on the Spanish throne, Queen Isabel and her daughters returned to Spain. They were not, however, allowed to settle in Madrid; instead, they were given commodious apartments twenty-five miles away, in Philip II's immense palace of the Escorial. It proved a wise precaution. All her life Isabel had been a compulsive meddler, and her years in exile had not cured her. Scarcely had she settled in than she had entered into an interminable wrangle with the Treasury over her pension, and before long she began scheming on her own behalf with the Pope, thereby provoking an unedifying public quarrel with the Prime Minister, with both sides openly attacking each other in the press. Something, it was clear, had to be done. She could hardly be exiled once again, but it was decided to send her still further away from the capital, to the old Moorish Alcazar in Seville. 'So, within a few months,' wrote her daughter Eulalia, 'we went from the chilly monotony of a northern court to the oppression and ennui of an oriental harem.'

But it took more than a change of residence to stop Isabel's intrigues. She now devoted her energies to finding a suitable bride for her son.

Alfonso, however, forestalled her by himself announcing his engagement to his cousin Mercedes, the ravishing sixteen-year-old daughter of the Duc de Montpensier. His mother did everything she could to prevent him, but it was a genuine love match; realising that she was powerless, she returned in a huff to Paris, leaving her daughters behind her. The wedding took place on 23 January 1878, the couple's obvious happiness, together with the bride's beauty and charm, winning all hearts. Then five months later, when not yet eighteen, Mercedes died of gastric fever. Alfonso never recovered from the blow. He was remarried at the end of 1879 to another Maria Christina, daughter of Archduke Karl Ferdinand of Austria, but it was to remain a *mariage de convenance*. This time old Isabel approved, and returned to Spain for the ceremony.

The new Queen's grandmother-in-law and namesake had died, in her home at Sainte-Adresse near Le Havre, less than two months after Mercedes. Her second husband, Muñoz, had already been long in his grave, so her body was brought back to Spain and buried near that of her first, Ferdinand VII, at the Escorial. And then, on 25 November 1885 – just three days before his twenty-eighth birthday – King Alfonso died of tuberculosis. His little daughter, the five-year-old Infanta Mercedes, became Queen of Spain, but not for long: Queen Maria Christina, who had loved her husband dearly despite his countless infidelities and in his last days had never left his bedside, was three months pregnant, and in May 1886 she gave birth to a boy – born a reigning king, the first in five centuries. His father had wanted him to be named Fernando, but Maria Christina had determined otherwise. Five days later, with a miniature Order of the Golden Fleece around his neck, he was baptised Alfonso – inauspiciously enough, the thirteenth of that name.

Meanwhile, the baby's grandmother, old Isabel – now the last queen but two – lived on, still interfering whenever she had the chance, and even making a determined attempt to take over the regency from her daughter-in-law. When this failed she eventually yielded to pressure and returned to Paris and the life of endless party-going and entertaining that she had always loved. Her other proclivities also remained undiminished; she had by now found a new 'secretary-treasurer', a man of villainous aspect by the name of Haltman, who never left her side. She remained nevertheless every inch a queen, corresponding with both Queen Victoria and her fellow exile the Empress Eugénie, widow of Napoleon III. Indeed, it was probably her insistence on waiting in a draughty corridor for the Empress's arrival, and again to bid her farewell, that brought about her death. The resulting nasty cough turned to pneumonia, and on 9 April 1904 she died. She was seventy-three.

CHAPTER XXX

Egypt and the Canal

The first Suez Canal was dug by Pharaoh Necho in the seventh century BC. So, at least, we are informed by Herodotus, who adds that 120,000 Egyptians perished during the digging, and that the finished canal was four days' journey in length and wide enough for two armies abreast. But there was little or no trace of it two and a half millennia later, when Napoleon ordered the first detailed survey of the isthmus. His chief surveyor, Jean-Baptiste Le Père, concluded that the extremities of a canal would be at different levels – he actually estimated the southern end to be some ten metres higher – but the theory soon became academic: by the time he produced his final report the French were no longer in Egypt, and the British who had ejected them were determined to get out themselves as soon as possible. The project was once again forgotten, and remained so for another half-century.

Then, in 1854, the Ottoman Sultan's Khedive (or viceroy) – by now Mohammed Ali's fourth son, Saïd – granted to a young French visionary named Count Ferdinand de Lesseps, acting on behalf of his French-owned company, the right to construct a canal running almost exactly 100 miles across the isthmus, from the Mediterranean to the Red Sea. Work began in 1859 and took ten years instead of the six that de Lesseps had estimated; there were early labour troubles among the largely Egyptian workforce and in 1865 an outbreak of cholera which threatened to bring the whole enterprise to an end. But the difficulties were eventually overcome, Le Père's anxieties proved unfounded – the Canal has no locks – and at half past eight on the morning of 17 November 1869 the French imperial yacht, the *Aigle*, with the Empress Eugénie and de Lesseps himself on board, entered it at Port Said. This was followed by forty-five more vessels bearing the Khedive – by this time Saïd had been succeeded by his nephew Ismail – and his official guests, the foreign ambassadors and other high dignitaries. On the morning of the 20th the *Aigle* entered the Red Sea, and the ship's band struck up, somewhat inappropriately, with *'Partant pour la Syrie'*.

There is a popular misconception that Verdi's *Aida* was written to celebrate the opening of the Canal. In fact, the historic event seems to have left him cold – so cold, indeed, that he deliberately turned down a commission to produce an inaugural hymn for the occasion. It was not until the early months of 1870 that he was sent a scenario by the French Egyptologist Auguste Mariette, based on an invented story set in Egyptian antiquity. This had an immediate appeal for him. An opera was commissioned by the Khedive Ismail, and he set to work with a will. Although the première was scheduled for Ismail's new opera house in Cairo, it was decided that the sets and costumes should be prepared in Paris – an unfortunate decision, as it turned out, since the Franco-Prussian War and the consequent siege of the city held them up for weeks. They were freed at last, and the opera duly opened on Christmas Eve 1871. Verdi was, somewhat surprisingly, not present, though he did attend the Milan première early the following year.

For the lands and seaports of the eastern Mediterranean, the opening of the Suez Canal was a godsend – though it took them a little time to realise the fact. No longer were they stuck in a comparative backwater; now at last they could recover their old status as important stopping places on the trade routes of the world. Even the countries of the Far East profited, as their own commercial links with the west were strengthened. The world had become a smaller place.

From the day of the Canal's opening, however, the Suez Canal Company was in financial trouble. The shareholders, persuaded by de Lesseps that they had invested in a gold mine, wanted an immediate return on their money; but Europe was slow to take advantage of the new possibilities. In its first year of operation, fewer than two ships a day passed through the Canal. De Lesseps had expected an annual income of ten million francs; he received only four. There followed a fierce international argument over the finances, which a conference called by the Sublime Porte did little to settle. At last a furious de Lesseps threatened to close down the Canal altogether, whereupon the Khedive – backed up by the Porte – sent a military force to the Canal and two warships to Port Said, with instructions to seize the Canal if the Company persisted in its plans. France, which had previously backed de Lesseps, now withdrew its support and he had to admit defeat.

But the Franco-Prussian War had dealt the Second Empire its death blow, and French influence in Canal affairs was on the wane. That of Britain, on the other hand, was rapidly increasing. The government of Lord Palmerston and its successors had violently opposed the construction of the Canal, which they had seen as a French imperialist threat, but now that the French were effectively out of the way, opinion in London was changing fast. Suddenly, the distance to India had been halved; from Bombay to Calcutta, what was later to be known as the tourist industry took wing. Within twenty years the annual influx of marriageable young women arriving in India in search of husbands – generally known as the Fishing Fleet – became an institution.[1] From 1873 onwards the fortunes of the Canal itself began to improve, with more and more ships using it with every passing year. Two-thirds of those vessels were British, and the Khedive told the British Agent in Cairo not only that he would be glad to see the Canal the property of an English company, but that in the event of such a company being formed he would do everything in his power to facilitate its transfer into their hands.

Egypt, meanwhile, was plunging further and further into debt, and by November 1875 the Khedive found himself in urgent need of some four million pounds to meet his obligations. His only course was to sell or mortgage his own shares in the Suez Canal Company. Two separate groups of French bankers began contending with each other in Paris, but neither was as quick or decisive as Benjamin Disraeli, who had recently succeeded Gladstone as Prime Minister and who was being kept informed of exactly what was going on by his friend Lionel de Rothschild, with whom he regularly dined on Sunday evenings. Negotiations dragged on for a while, but on 24 November 1875 it was agreed that the British government would purchase from the Khedive of Egypt 177,642 shares in the Suez Canal Company for four million pounds sterling. 'You have it, Madam,' Disraeli wrote to the Queen. 'The French government has been out-generalled.' The Queen replied that this was indeed 'a great and important event'. 'The great sum,' she added characteristically, 'is the only disadvantage.'[2]

But the four million pounds still had to be raised. Once again Disraeli turned to de Rothschild, to whom he sent his Private Secretary, Montagu Lowry Corry. In later years Corry loved to tell the story of how he went to Rothschild's office and told him that the Prime Minister wanted four million pounds.

'When?' asked Rothschild.

'Tomorrow.'

---

[1] A less happy consequence was that Indian army officers were obliged to put away their native wives and bring their memsahibs out from Britain – often with disastrous results to British-Indian relations.

[2] A rather more surprising reaction was that of the Crown Prince of Prussia, later Kaiser Wilhelm II: 'How jolly!'

Rothschild picked up a muscatel grape, ate it, spat out the skin, and asked: 'What is your security?'

'The British government.'

'You shall have it.'

A few days later the shares were delivered to the British Consulate-General in Cairo. They were counted, and were found to number only 176,602 – 1,040 short of the number contracted for. The price was accordingly reduced to £3,976,582. Lionel de Rothschild was not, one suspects, unduly concerned.

Britain, it should be emphasised, had not bought the Canal; she had not even bought control. With her 40 percent holding, however, she had prevented that control from passing entirely into French hands, as it would assuredly have done had she not acted as she did. She now had the right to appoint three out of the twenty-four directors on the board of the Company – a figure which a few years later was to be increased to ten. Of all the shareholders, moreover, she was the strongest and the richest.

Was her purchase of the shares in some degree a prelude to the re-establishment of a British presence in Egypt? The Liberal Opposition certainly suspected – and suggested – as much. In fact, Disraeli seems to have had no particular interest in anything of the kind. At the same time, it was obviously of vital importance that the Canal should be adequately protected, and whereas in former days such protection might have been satisfactorily afforded by the Ottoman government, the Sultan's power had now been effectively assumed by the Khedive, who had shown again and again by his extravagance and irresponsibility that he could not be trusted – to the point where in 1876 the Egyptian budget was placed under the supervision of two controllers, one British and one French. The Dual Control, as it was called, checked the collapse to some extent, but all too soon it became clear that the Khedive would have to go. Britain and France made a joint appeal to the Sultan, and in June 1879 he was deposed. His son Tewfik, who succeeded him, was almost immediately faced with a major revolt by the Egyptian nationalists who in 1881 staged a *coup d'état*, establishing what was in effect a military dictatorship. This was followed nine months later by riots in Alexandria, during which more than fifty Europeans were killed.

By this time Britain had sent a naval squadron to Alexandria, in response to which the nationalist leader, Lieutenant-Colonel Ahmed

Orabi – known in the West as Arabi Pasha – had begun to construct new fortifications on the seaward side. The British admiral ordered him to stop, and when he refused to do so shelled the buildings to bits. A British force was then landed in the name of the Khedive and went on to occupy the city. But Arabi now replied with a new threat: to block the Sweet Water Canal, which linked the Nile with the isthmus of Suez, providing it with virtually its only supply of fresh water. With the situation fast deteriorating, a full-blown British expeditionary force under the famous General Sir Garnet Wolseley landed on 19 August 1882 at Port Said, further troops being already on their way from India to Suez. A month later, on 13 September, this force had little difficulty in inflicting a decisive defeat on Arabi at Tel el-Kebir on the edge of the delta, and occupying Cairo on the following day.

Where, it might be asked, was France during this crucial time? She too had sent a squadron to Alexandria, but this had almost immediately – and unaccountably – sailed on to Port Said, taking no part in the bombardment or the landings. Had it remained and followed the British example, Britain would certainly not have objected; indeed, she would probably have welcomed such participation. But by this time the French government seems to have lost interest. Thanks largely, we are told, to the violent opposition of the young Georges Clemenceau, it failed to vote the funds necessary for military intervention, thus sacrificing at a stroke France's traditional influence in Egypt and giving her British rival a free hand to do as she liked. At the end of 1882 the Dual Control was abolished.

When in the past British troops had occupied Egypt, they had thought only of getting out again as soon as possible; this time, however, they had a lifeline to defend. For many years Britain was to claim that her occupation of Egypt was nothing but a temporary measure. As for full annexation, successive governments would protest that nothing was further from their minds; Egypt was part of the Ottoman Empire, and they were more than happy that she should remain so. But the Canal had to be protected, and it was Britain's task to do it. If such protection involved the occupation of Egypt, then that was that.

Britain had now guaranteed for herself the effective control of the Canal in the event of war, but she recognised that such an *ad hoc* arrangement would not satisfy the other powers. So strategic a waterway could ultimately be protected only by a complete neutralisation. The diplomatic negotiations required before this could be achieved were delicate and complicated, but at last, on 29 October 1888, the representatives of nine nations at Constantinople signed the Suez Canal Convention, establishing 'a definite system designed to guarantee at all times and for all Powers the free use of the Suez Maritime Canal'. The Canal was, it stipulated, to be open to all vessels of whatever provenance, in time of war as in time of peace. Its entrances were not to be blockaded, nor were any permanent fortifications to be erected on or along its banks. No belligerent warships might disembark troops or munitions in its ports or anywhere along it. Under the terms of the original concession of 1854, however, the Convention would remain in force only until 1968, ninety-nine years after the Canal's opening. Its ownership would then revert to the Egyptian government.

This chapter requires, perhaps, a brief postscript. In November 1914 Britain declared war on the Ottoman Empire and proclaimed a protectorate over Egypt, with Khedive Abbas – his title of viceroy being no longer appropriate – being redesignated Sultan. Only four years later, however, Egypt was granted full independence (with a few reservations) and became, in its own right, a kingdom. The first ruler, King (formerly Sultan) Fuad I, was succeeded in 1936 by his son Farouk, who reigned until 1952, when a group of Egyptian army officers inspired by Colonel Gamal Abdel Nasser overturned the monarchy and declared Egypt a republic. In 1954 they concluded a treaty with Britain, whereby all British forces were to be withdrawn from the Canal Zone; two years later, on 26 July 1956 – twelve years before the automatic reversion – the Canal was seized and nationalised. At the end of October, all diplomatic representations having failed, the recently formed state of Israel, joined by Britain and France, invaded Egypt with the purpose of recovering the Canal by force. British troops were landed at Port Said under cover of a naval bombardment, while the Israelis invaded the Sinai peninsula. Soon, however, international disapproval for the operation – and particularly that of the United States – became so strong that in December the Anglo-French forces were obliged to withdraw, leaving Nasser – despite severe military losses – triumphant and the Canal firmly in Egyptian hands. British influence in Egypt was at an end. Port Said was reoccupied, and the statue of Ferdinand de Lesseps – without whose vision and determination the Canal would never have come into being – was torn from its pedestal. In the hearts of dictators, gratitude is a rare emotion indeed.

CHAPTER XXXI

The Balkan Wars

Greece, in her first years of independence, remained an unhappy land. Her new king in particular had been a disappointment. It was perhaps too much to hope that the seventeen-year-old Otto speaking not a word of Greek and not even a member of the Orthodox Church, would be able to endear himself to his swarthy, battle-scarred subjects. The King's father, Ludwig I of Bavaria, in the name of the London Conference powers – Britain, France and Russia – had therefore appointed a Regency Council of three, all Bavarian, only one of whom had ever set foot in Greece. None showed the least sensitivity to local custom or tradition, introducing their own legal and educational systems, gagging the press and imposing taxes that were both oppressive and unjust. They continued in this way for almost three years – years that were known as the *Bavarokratia*, the Bavarocracy – but even after Otto came of age in 1835 there was little real change. Bavarian influence was as strong as ever, and was increasingly resented. Was it for this, the Greeks asked themselves, that they had fought so long and so valiantly? Their new rulers were even worse than the Turks.

Matters came to a head in 1843, when a virtually bloodless military coup forced Otto to grant a constitution. On paper, this seemed liberal enough, providing *inter alia* for nearly universal male suffrage (though women had to wait for their vote until 1952). Meanwhile, the Bavarian ministers were dismissed and replaced by a new ministry composed exclusively of Greeks, together with a Greek National Assembly. In fact, traditional Greek society had – thanks to the long Turkish occupation – evolved in a totally different manner from the societies of western Europe, and the people were quite unprepared for a sophisticated modern democracy; it seemed, nonetheless, that Greece had taken a significant step forward, and there were grounds for hoping that there might be better times ahead.

Alas, such hopes were vain. All that had happened was that a Bavarian oligarchy had been set aside in favour of a Greek one, even more ham-fisted than its predecessor. It was certainly understandable that, on the outbreak of the Crimean War in March 1854, the Greeks

558

should have identified themselves emotionally with Russia – then the only other sovereign power with a national Orthodox Church – and violently opposed the Ottoman Empire, which had held them in thrall for nearly five hundred years. It was, on the other hand, sheer folly that led them to launch an utterly abortive invasion of Turkish-held Thessaly and Epirus, the only result of which was that British and French fleets occupied Piraeus, landing detachments of foreign troops which were to remain on Greek soil until 1857. So much, it seemed, for Greece's newly acquired and much vaunted sovereign status.

In the last years of his reign Otto showed genuine patriotism for his adopted country, and was much influenced by what was known as the Great Idea: in essence, the elimination of the Ottomans and their replacement by a reborn Byzantium, a Greek Christian empire with its capital once again in Constantinople. But he was never popular with his subjects. In 1862, on one of his progresses round the Peloponnese, an insurrection broke out in the old Venetian fortress of Vonitza. Before the royal yacht could return to Athens, the government had proclaimed its king deposed. Otto returned to Germany and settled in Bamberg, where five years later he died.

The Powers had accepted his expulsion without protest, and his former subjects set about looking for a successor. The search took them two years. Their first choice was Prince Alfred, second son of Queen Victoria; unfortunately, however, it had been laid down in the agreements of 1827 and 1830 that no member of the reigning families of the three powers should occupy the Greek throne; the proposal was accordingly turned down flat. Only then was an approach made to the seventeen-year-old son of Christian IX of Denmark, whose sister Alexandra had recently married the Prince of Wales. His name, William, smacked too much of the north and was more or less unwritable in the Greek alphabet, but he was only too happy to change it; it was thus as King George I of the Hellenes that he was to ascend the throne in 1863 and occupy it for the next half-century until 18 March 1913, when he was assassinated in Thessalonica while taking an afternoon stroll.

King George's reign got off to an auspicious start when Britain voluntarily – despite the powerful opposition of William Ewart Gladstone – ceded to Greece the Ionian Islands, which had been under its protection since 1815.[1] It continued with another success: the

---

[1] See Chapter XXIV.

introduction in 1864 of a new constitution, a huge improvement on that of 1844. George's later popularity was largely due to his having adopted principles precisely contrary to those of Otto; instead of trying to impose his own personality and leadership he made a point of remaining a figurehead, interfering with government as little as possible and allowing his ministers a free hand to do much as they liked.

With the Ionian Islands now safely incorporated within the kingdom, the next territorial problem was posed by Crete. This island had a far longer experience of foreign domination: after four centuries under Venice, it had – unlike Corfu and most of its fellows[1] – already suffered two more under Ottoman rule, which was as firmly established as ever. In Venetian days it had been in a state of almost constant insurrection, and the War of Independence had still further increased nationalist feeling among the Christian population, to the point where the Cretans had now set their sights not simply on the expulsion of the Turks but on union with the new Greek kingdom. Crete had sent delegates to the National Assembly of Argos in 1829, but in the following year, as we have seen, Sultan Mahmoud had bestowed the island on Mohammed Ali as a reward for his services in the recent hostilities. This union with Egypt – unnatural, to say the least – lasted for only ten years; in 1840, furious at his viceroy's insubordination, the Sultan took it back again.

To the Cretans it mattered little whether they were under the Egyptians or the Turks. Their call was for *enosis*, union with Greece. The insurrections continued, by far the bloodiest of them breaking out in 1866. It was in the course of this that Maneses, abbot of the monastery of Arkadion and one of the great heroes of Cretan history, blew up his powder magazine – though it may be wondered why monasteries *had* powder magazines – rather than surrender. The ensuing bloodbath, in which large numbers of women and children were killed in cold blood, caused an international scandal; the British government in particular came under severe censure when it was revealed that it had ordered the Royal Navy not to rescue Cretan civilians of whatever age or sex who were threatened with massacre, lest such operations be seen as departures from the strict neutrality which Britain was determined to preserve.

At last the Sultan, exasperated by the blatant support that was being given by the Greek government to the Cretan insurgents, presented it in

---

[1] Leucas (Lefkas) is the only one of the Ionian Islands that was for any length of time under Turkish rule.

1868 with an ultimatum: within five days Greece must undertake to cease the equipment of ships designed for acts of aggression against Turkey. There were other points too, but they were academic; Greece angrily refused. Diplomatic relations were broken off, and a certain Hobart Pasha, a retired Royal Naval captain who had taken service with the Sultan and was now commanding the Turkish fleet, threatened the country with a blockade. War seemed imminent, but a conference of European ambassadors managed to persuade the Greeks to accept the Turkish terms and relations were resumed the following year. In return the Sultan granted Crete a constitution, which provided for a degree of self-government and – temporarily at least – soothed Cretan feelings.

In the summer of 1876 the Balkan peninsula burst into flame.[1] The conflagration began when the Serbian Orthodox populations of Bosnia and Herzegovina rose up against their Ottoman masters. Serbia and the neighbouring principality of Montenegro – also Orthodox and Serbian-speaking – rallied to their aid, and it was then unthinkable that the only other Slav people in the Balkan peninsula, the Bulgars, should remain unmoved. Insurrection in the Vilayet of the Danube – as Bulgaria was officially styled – broke out in May 1876. It was in itself relatively insignificant, but it was suppressed with almost unbelievable brutality. In the village of Barak, which after a brief resistance had already surrendered, most of the male population was butchered; women and children were herded into the village church and school, both of which were then set on fire. Barak alone lost some 5,000 of its 7,000 inhabitants; it was estimated that the total number of Christians massacred in that one month fell not far short of 12,000.

The news was received with horror throughout the civilised world – particularly in Russia, where the Tsar instantly voiced his solidarity with his co-religionists. In London 'the Bulgarian atrocities' were the subject of a furious pamphlet by Mr Gladstone – at that time out of office – who also castigated the pro-Turkish policy of the Disraeli administration. The revulsion expressed on all sides had its impact even in Constantinople, where some 6,000 theological students staged a mass demonstration demanding the dismissal of the Grand Vizir and the Chief Mufti. Sultan Abdul-Aziz capitulated at once, but the demonstrators – and indeed the people as a whole – remained

---

[1] For this section and those immediately following, I must record my thanks to Mr Alan Palmer, on whose compulsively readable history, *The Decline and Fall of the Ottoman Empire*, I have shamelessly drawn.

unsatisfied. From that moment, according to the British ambassador, 'the word "constitution" was in every mouth'.

Meanwhile, the Turkish army had soundly defeated the Serbs, and would have marched on Belgrade had not the Powers – now joined by Germany and Austria – put their foot down just in time and insisted on an armistice. The Tsar and the Austrian Emperor together, supported by Germany, drew up what was known as the Berlin Memorandum, designed to put pressure on the Porte to institute radical reforms, and now requested British cooperation. Disraeli turned the request down flat. Britain, he pointed out, had not been consulted in advance, and refused to join the three powers 'in putting a knife to the throat of Turkey'. Further, to bolster Turkish morale, he ordered a squadron of the Mediterranean fleet to take up its station at the mouth of the Dardanelles. Determined to avert the war on which Russia had clearly set its heart, he then called for a six-power conference, to be held at Constantinople the following December.

The situation in the city was not improved by the fact that the mental health of the Sultan was already giving rise to serious concern. Abdul-Aziz had succeeded his half-brother Abdul-Mejid in 1861. Few Sultans in modern times had been more terrifying. Nearly seven feet in height – his eight-foot bed may still be seen in the Dolmabahçe Palace – with a thick black beard and a ferocious temper, he seemed to many of his courtiers a throwback to the worst days of the seventeenth and eighteenth centuries. In 1867, when he was thirty-seven, he had been invited by Napoleon III to France for the Great Universal Exhibition and had visited Vienna and London on the way. He had thus been the first Sultan in Ottoman history to set foot peaceably in Christian Europe, and the experience had gone badly to his head, instilling in him a determination to acquire a fleet of modern warships (despite an embarrassingly public attack of seasickness while reviewing the Home Fleet with Queen Victoria at Spithead) and a passion for railways, which he managed to bring to Constantinople only six years later. But with every year that passed his paroxysms of rage became more furious and ungovernable, and by 1876 his extravagance had brought the state to the brink of bankruptcy.

Thus it was that not long after the theologians had dispersed, in the early hours of 30 May of that terrible year, the Commander-in-Chief of the army, Hüseyin Avni, surrounded the Dolmabahçe with two battalions of infantry while a naval squadron drew up immediately opposite on the Bosphorus. On entering the palace he instantly found himself confronted by the Sultan, standing on the staircase in his nightshirt with drawn sword; when the act of deposition was presented, however, Abdul-Aziz offered no resistance and obediently boarded the state barge which was waiting to take him to the old palace of Topkapi. There he was lodged for the night – somewhat insensitively, it might be thought, in the room in which his predecessor Selim III had been murdered in 1808 – before being rowed back the following day a little further up the Bosphorus to the Çiragăn Palace (next to which there today rises one of modern Istanbul's most glamorous hotels). Just four days later he was found dead in his new apartment, having slashed his wrists with scissors. There were the usual rumours of something a good deal more sinister than suicide, but the testimony of eighteen doctors to the contrary seems finally to have been accepted.

All this should have been excitement enough; but the drama was only beginning. A week later, Abdul-Aziz's favourite young Circassian wife died in childbirth, a tragedy which so affected her brother – who was serving as an equerry in the Sultan's household – that on 14 June he burst into a meeting of the Council of Ministers, shooting dead both the Commander-in-Chief and the Foreign Minister. This latest development had a profound effect on the new Sultan, Murad V. Already, on hearing of his uncle's death, he had fainted dead away and vomited for thirty-six hours; the news of the two later assassinations sent him into a deep depression, which his chronic alcoholism did little to relieve. On the last day of August he went the same way as Abdul-Aziz. This time, however, there were no scissors; Murad was to remain a prisoner in the Çiragăn for the next twenty-eight years.

Of the new Sultan, Abdul-Hamid II, it can safely be said that he was an improvement on his two predecessors; he was not, however, a great improvement. Having lost his Circassian mother at the age of seven, he was virtually ignored by his father, Abdul-Mejid, and had retreated back into himself, totally without friends or even companionship. Cruel, scheming and vindictive as a man, weak and vacillating as a ruler, with a morbid fear of assassination which dominated his life and kept his public appearances to the minimum, he hated Abdul-Mejid's Dolmabahçe with its exposed position on the shore of the Bosphorus, creating for himself a whole new seraglio – a centre of government and power – behind the high and impenetrable walls of his park at Yildiz, high in the hills above. From here this hunched and stooping figure, hook-nosed, black-bearded and sallow-skinned, always apparently cowering from some imagined attacker, spun his webs of intrigue, secretly received his regiments of spies and informers and directed, after a fashion, his crumbling empire.

Abdul-Hamid was not, one would have thought, the type of ruler to present his people with a constitution; he was, however, astute enough to realise that if he did not go at least some way towards assuaging popular discontent he might well become the third Sultan to lose his throne within that fateful year. He was also anxious to reassure the European delegates to the coming conference: after all, if it could now be seen that Turkey had a complete plan of her own for constitutional reform, what part was there for the Powers to play? It was certainly no coincidence that the decree promulgating the new constitution was published on the very morning the conference opened. But the delegates, it need hardly be said, remained unconvinced. Even the leader of the British party, the Marquess of Salisbury, who as Secretary of State for India in Disraeli's administration might have been expected to share his chief's sympathies, made no attempt to conceal his disgust. Unlike most of his fellows he was granted an audience with Abdul-Hamid, but described him afterwards as 'a wretched, feeble creature, who told me he dared not grant what we demanded because he was in danger of his life'.[1]

Thus, thanks in part to the constitution – which, as soon became apparent, was not worth the paper it was printed on and was anyway soon suspended – and in part to the fact that the Sultan had no intention of granting autonomy to Bulgaria, Bosnia and Herzegovina simply because the Powers demanded it, the Constantinople conference was an utter failure. War was now inevitable.

The first nation to act was Russia, whose armies simultaneously crossed the European and the Asiatic frontiers of Turkey on 24 April 1877. A month later Romania declared her independence and joined the combatants, and before long the Turks were retreating on all fronts. At last, on 31 January 1878, the Sultan agreed to an armistice. It was virtually an act of surrender; even so, it did little to assuage the state of panic prevailing on the Bosphorus. There seemed a real possibility that, after more than four centuries, the Crescent might once again give way to the Cross.

---

[1] His opinion may perhaps have been affected by the Sultan's decision to confer upon Lady Salisbury – who had accompanied him – the Order of Chastity (Third Class).

But such a prospect held little appeal for Austria, which was now casting a covetous eye on Bosnia and Herzegovina, nor indeed for Britain, where Disraeli had always been a friend of Turkey and where the people, still remembering the Crimean War, lustily bellowed the contemporary music-hall song:

> We don't want to fight, but by jingo if we do,
> We've got the ships, we've got the men, we've got the money too;
> We've fought the Bear before, and while Britons shall be true,
> The Russians shall not have Constantinople!

To emphasise the point still further, in mid-February Britain ordered a squadron from her Mediterranean fleet to sail up through the narrows into the Sea of Marmara, returning fire if necessary, and to take up a station opposite the city. If, as seems likely, this was intended to have a calming effect, it was unsuccessful. The Sultan was more terrified than ever, while the Russians chose to regard it as a hostile act and themselves advanced to the Marmara, halting only at San Stefano (now Yeşilköy, site of the international airport). With Britain and Russia now drifting ever nearer to war, the Grand Duke Nicholas – commanding the Russian forces – agreed to advance no further, Admiral Sir Phipps Hornby consenting on his side to withdraw his ships to the Princes' Islands, about eight miles south of the Golden Horn.[1]

Where the Greeks were concerned, recent events suggested that the Great Idea was perhaps no longer the pipe dream that it once had been; the vision of the Greek flag flying over St Sophia was not one that any true Greek could resist. There was the additional hope that open hostilities might encourage the Greek populations within the Ottoman Empire to rise in revolt, and insurrections did indeed break out in Thessaly and Epirus, and once again – inevitably – in Crete. Thus it was that Greece entered the field. Alas, her timing could hardly have been worse: she declared war on 2 February 1878, having no knowledge of the armistice concluded just forty-eight hours before. The Greek army, which had actually crossed the Turkish border, was – not without some embarrassment – hastily recalled. Peace was soon restored in Epirus

---

[1] As it happened, Prince Louis of Battenberg was serving on the appropriately named HMS *Sultan*, while his brother Prince Alexander was a staff captain in the army of the Grand Duke. Alexander was given a warm welcome aboard the *Sultan* by its commanding officer, who chanced to be none other than Prince Alfred, Duke of Edinburgh, second son of Queen Victoria and husband of the Tsar's only surviving daughter.

and eventually in Thessaly also; in Crete, however, desultory fighting continued.

The armistice led directly to the Treaty of San Stefano, signed by the Russian and Turkish delegates on 3 March. It was an extraordinary agreement, satisfying as it did no one except Bulgaria, to which it would virtually have restored her once-great medieval empire, and putting an end to all Greek aspirations in Macedonia. Its other provisions do not concern us; suffice it to say that it could never possibly have worked. The Great Powers – now including also the Ottoman Empire – therefore met together just three months later at Berlin, where their deliberations initially proved a good deal more favourable to Greece; but the Ottoman government reneged on its promises, endlessly prevaricating and procrastinating, and it was three more years before the Greeks received even part of what they had been awarded. They eventually had to be content with Thessaly – admittedly a very valuable province, which had been Turkish for five centuries – and part of Epirus, including Arta.

Crete still remained in Turkish hands. In that same year of 1878, however, the Sultan granted it what was in effect a supplementary constitution. This established a General Assembly of forty-nine Christians and thirty-one Muslims, and decreed *inter alia* that Greek should be the language of both the Assembly and the law courts, and that half the annual revenues should go to the building of schools, hospitals, harbours and roads, on which virtually nothing had been spent since the days of the Venetians. This dispensation kept the island relatively quiet for a decade; it was not until 1889 that a new insurrection broke out, to be followed in 1896–97 by two more. These last were considerably more serious, the second of them resulting in a massacre of Christians in the streets of Canea and the burning of the Christian quarter of the town.

After these atrocities Greece could no longer remain inactive. Prince George, the King's second son, left Salamis with a flotilla of torpedo boats to prevent the landing of reinforcements by the Turks; on 15 February 1897, 1,500 armed Greek volunteers landed near Canea – with memories of Garibaldi's Redshirts in Sicily to spur them on – to take over the island in the name of the King. Perhaps, even at this point, firm and concerted action by the European powers might have prevented open hostilities, which neither the King nor the Sultan wanted, but such action was not forthcoming and on 17 April Turkey declared war.

The King himself had assured foreign visitors that in the event of war the Greek communities throughout the Sultan's empire would rise up against their oppressors, and that most other Christian minorities would follow the Greek lead. Alas, nothing of the kind occurred; the Thirty Days' War, as it came to be called, gave rise to an almost unbroken series of disasters for Greece. According to the *Cambridge Modern History*, 'the Greek navy, which was superior to that of the Turks . . . effected nothing except the futile bombardment of Preveza, the capture of a cargo of vegetables at Santi Quaranta, and that of a Turcophil British Member of Parliament.' On land, the Greek performance was very little better. It was lucky for Greece that the Powers intervened when they did and forced the belligerents to agree to an armistice. All Greek combatants were withdrawn from Crete, which was to be policed by an international force. Greece – already nearly bankrupt – had to pay a heavy indemnity to the Sultan; on the other hand, Abdul-Hamid was finally obliged to fulfil his twenty-year-old promise by the formal cession of Thessaly.

Only then did the Powers make a serious effort to solve the Cretan problem once and for all. The Sultan was persuaded to go one step further, giving the island autonomous status under Ottoman suzerainty. In November 1898 the last Turkish troops withdrew from Crete; and from the end of the year a High Commissioner in the person of Prince George, second son of the Greek King, governed from Canea, while British, French, Italian and Russian troops occupied the chief towns. Crete was given her own flag, coinage and postage stamps.

Abdul-Hamid's grip had once again been loosened. Even then, however, he could not bring himself finally to let go. It was to be another fifteen years before the Cretans received their reward.

The Congress of Berlin did, however, affect the fate of one other major Mediterranean island. Cyprus had been under Ottoman rule since the Turks captured it from the Venetians in 1570. At first, among the vast majority of the people, the change of government was welcomed. The Turks had permitted the re-establishment of the Greek Orthodox Church, the hierarchy of which soon assumed the role of ambassador for its flock, engaging itself regularly as spokesman and mediator with the Turkish administration. The feudal system had been abolished; the serfs had been freed; once again Cypriots could own land – even though by doing so they became taxpayers. They were less happy, however, to see some 3,000 Turkish soldiers given land and settling permanently on the island – a development that was to have dire consequences in our own day. Strangers as the two communities were through both their language and their religion, there was little or no intermarriage. From the start, therefore, the Cypriots were sharply divided; divided they still remain.

With the outbreak of the Greek War of Independence, the Turkish governor of the island had become seriously alarmed. Summoning the Archbishop, Kyprianos, and other leading churchmen – they included the Bishops of Paphos, Kitium and Kyrenia and the Abbot of Kykko monastery – to Nicosia, he had had them murdered in cold blood.[1] Other influential clerics were given asylum by the foreign consuls at Larnaca, but the power of the Cypriot hierarchy was, from one day to the next, dramatically eclipsed.

By the middle of the century conditions on the island had begun once again to improve. Sultan Abdul-Mejid undertook to accord equality of treatment to all his subjects regardless of race or creed, and abolished the iniquitous practice of tax-farming.[2] He also ordered that the governorship should in future be by appointment, rather than sold to the highest bidder as it had been in the past. Then in 1869 came the exciting news of the Suez Canal, from which Cyprus stood to gain immeasurably in commercial importance. One of the first statesmen to realise this was Benjamin Disraeli, who managed to conclude with Turkey what was known as the Cyprus Convention. By its terms, Britain undertook to join the Sultan in the defence of his Asiatic dominions against any further Russian attack. The better to enable her to do this, the Sultan assigned to her Cyprus as what was called 'a place of arms' in the Levant, on payment of an annual tribute.

Until that moment, the only historical link between Britain and Cyprus had been the island's conquest by Richard Coeur-de-Lion in 1191. Now – although technically it would remain part of the Ottoman Empire until its formal annexation by Britain in November 1914 – it was once again effectively in British hands. Since surplus revenues were still payable to Constantinople, the island was always a financial liability; nonetheless, both before and after the annexation and over the

---

[1] It will be remembered that the Orthodox Patriarch Grigorios had suffered a similar fate in Constantinople at much the same time (See Chapter XXV, p. 468), as had hundreds, if not thousands, of Greeks, secular and priestly, throughout the Ottoman Empire.
[2] By which individual entrepreneurs purchased from the government the right to levy taxes, and then bled the local populations.

next eighty years, Britain was to pour money into it, transforming its agriculture, initiating ambitious programmes of reforestation, constructing roads and public buildings. Cyprus, in short, had never had it so good – although among the Greek population thoughts of *enosis* were seldom far away.

One day in the late summer of 1901 Miss Helen Stone, an American Protestant missionary from Boston, was ambushed by Macedonian revolutionaries when travelling by cart near the town of Bansko. With her was her friend, known only as Madame Tsilka. The two were quickly surrounded and carried up into the mountains. It was only then that their captors discovered a complication: Madame Tsilka was pregnant. There was nothing they could do; they treated their captives with every consideration circumstances would allow until, one stormy December night in a village wine cellar, a healthy girl was born. Everyone was delighted; the health of mother and daughter was drunk all round; and when shortly afterwards the village was raided by Turkish troops and they all had to flee, Madame Tsilka rode by herself while one of the *comitadjis*, on another horse, carried her baby.

The ransom money, the equivalent of $66,000, was willingly supplied by the United States government (though the approval of President McKinley had to be assumed since he was at that moment on his deathbed, the victim of a terrorist's bullet a few days before). The head of Miss Stone's mission, a Dr House, himself carried the gold, packed in wooden chests, to Bansko, but he learned just in time that the Turks planned to seize it at the moment of collection. Having first courteously warned the kidnappers what he was doing, he therefore hid the money at a prearranged place and filled the chests with scrap iron. The Turks duly fell upon them and carried them all the way back to Serres before they discovered the deception. Meanwhile, the two ladies and the baby were released in the neighbouring town of Strumica. Everybody, it was felt, had behaved well; Miss Stone in particular was so delighted with her treatment that when she returned to Boston she became the foremost American champion of the Internal Macedonian Revolutionary Organisation, soon to become famous as the IMRO.

By this time Macedonia had been part of the Ottoman Empire for over five centuries. It had given its conquerors no particular trouble until 1870, when Russia, determined to extend her influence in the Balkans through the Orthodox religion, persuaded Turkey to allow the formation of an autocephalous Bulgarian Church. This had inevitably roused the wrath of both Greece and Serbia. The Greek Patriarch declared the new Church to be schismatic, and violently resisted the spread of Bulgarian influence – national and cultural as well as ecclesiastical – in Macedonia. The Serbs, despite being fellow Slavs, felt much the same resentment towards their Bulgar neighbours. Thus began the three-sided contest for the province, which became quadrilateral with the appearance of the Macedonian separatists, who had founded IMRO as a secret society in 1896, somewhat naively choosing for its standard a black flag bearing a crimson skull and crossbones.

The Helen Stone affair gave the organisation just the international publicity it needed. The eyes of the Powers turned towards Macedonia, and the Ottoman government settled back with a sigh to the usual lectures by western ambassadors on the importance of further reforms in the Balkan lands – lectures which were given additional force by a dramatic increase in the number of bomb outrages in Thessalonica and elsewhere.[1] All but one of the Powers, however, were fundamentally in favour of the continuation of Ottoman rule; only Britain wanted the complete withdrawal of Ottoman troops from the area.

What the Powers did not perhaps fully understand was that the Sultan had on his plate a number of more immediate concerns, the most important of which was another secret society, this time on his own doorstep: the Young Turks. This too seems to have originated in the last decade of the century – the very first cell is in fact said to have been formed by army medical students as early as 1889 – and though its members were by no means all military, nearly all were from the young officer class. They were not, in these early stages, dedicated to the overthrow of the Ottoman Empire; all they wanted was reform, and in particular westernisation. They remained, nonetheless, a potentially dangerous threat, and as time went on gave ever-increasing anxiety to Abdul-Hamid's secret police. Part of this anxiety was due to the fact that the Young Turks found a particularly fertile field for recruitment in the Balkan peninsula, especially Macedonia, adding yet another element to a region that was rapidly becoming a seething cauldron of unrest. There many of them established organisations of their own. One of these, founded in 1906, was the *Vatan*, or Fatherland Movement, the creation of a young staff captain of twenty-five born in Thessalonica, but whose political activities in Macedonia had already

---

[1] Europe had also been profoundly shocked by the recent appalling massacres of the Sultan's Armenian subjects. These had begun in 1894 and are believed to have accounted for at least 30,000 by the end of the following year.

resulted in his transfer to distant Damascus. His name was Mustafa Kemal; thirty years later he would be known to the world as Atatürk – Father of the Turks.

Internal organisations like *Vatan* were of necessity secret; outside the empire, by contrast, the Young Turks sought as much publicity for their movement as they could get. They called their first congress in Paris as early as 1902; a second was held in the same city in December 1907, and it was soon after this second assembly that the leaders assumed the name of the Committee of Union and Progress (the CUP), establishing a permanent secretariat and absorbing many of the smaller societies – *Vatan* included – before they could yield to centrifugal forces and start opposing one another.

It was in 1908 that matters came to a head, when on 3 July a certain Major Ahmed Niyazi, stationed deep in the Macedonian hinterland between Monastir and Lake Ochrid, brought out his men in armed rebellion. Many junior officers from other Macedonian stations joined him, the CUP gave its enthusiastic support and by the end of the summer most of what is now northern Greece was up in arms. Troops sent hurriedly across from Anatolia were almost immediately infected by the prevailing mood, and Abdul-Hamid saw that he would have to act quickly if he were to save his throne. On 24 July he announced that the suspended constitution of 1876 would be immediately restored. This announcement was followed by a general amnesty for political prisoners and exiles. Finally, on 1 August, a further imperial decree proclaimed the abolition of the secret police, freedom from arbitrary arrest, the right to foreign travel, equality of race and religion and a promise that all existing governments within the empire would be reorganised.

Preempted by the speed and scope of the Sultan's reaction, the CUP were thrown seriously off balance, but the rest of his subjects were jubilant. They had expected Abdul-Hamid to hold tightly to the absolutist principles he had cherished for the past thirty-two years; concessions, if any, would have to be wrung out of him one by one. Now, suddenly, and without a single shot being fired from anywhere closer than Macedonia, he was offering them on a platter far more than they had dared to hope. That Friday he drove through the streets of Constantinople amid cheering crowds to pray in St Sophia – a mosque since the Turkish conquest of 1453. It was the first time in a quarter of a century that he had summoned up sufficient courage to cross the Golden Horn.

*

Such dramatic developments as these could not but have their effect far beyond the boundaries of the Ottoman Empire. In Vienna the principal concern was with the territory of Bosnia–Herzegovina, which although technically Turkish had long been treated by the Austrians as one of their own colonies: what if it were required to send deputies to the new bicameral parliament that was shortly to open in the Çirağan Palace? The government of the Emperor Franz Josef lost no time; on 6 October 1908, only a few weeks after the Sultan's bombshell, Austria–Hungary annexed Bosnia–Herzegovina by decree. Just twenty-four hours earlier in Sofia, Prince Ferdinand of Saxe-Coburg – who had been made Prince of Bulgaria in 1887 – had shaken off Ottoman suzerainty and proclaimed himself Tsar of the Bulgarians (a title which he was forced to downgrade to king as the price of recognition by the Powers a few months later). Meanwhile, Crete made yet another attempt at her long-awaited *enosis* – though the arrival of a British naval squadron in Cretan waters served as a salutary reminder that Britain would countenance no transfer of sovereignty until such time as she was ready to do so.

In Constantinople it soon became clear that the peaceful revolution had gone too far, too fast. Fundamentalist Muslims, shocked by the unveiled women who suddenly appeared in the streets, began to campaign for the readoption of their traditional values. To this end a so-called Society of Islamic Unity was established, with the Sultan's fourth son as a founder member. Rumours that it received financial support from Yildiz abounded, but were never proved. Then, in April 1909, another of those demonstrations by theological students – backed, surprisingly enough, by numbers of troops from the local garrisons – went further still, demanding the resignation of the government and its replacement by a Muslim fundamentalist regime that would govern strictly according to Sharia law and would emphasise the authority of the Sultan in his religious role as Caliph. To these demands Abdul-Hamid – it was thought a little too eagerly – gave his consent.

It proved his undoing. In the new parliament there was an immediate uproar. A manifesto formally condemning the Sultan's actions was published. Once again he gave way – but it was too late. Constitutional government of the kind Turkey now hoped to enjoy could clearly not be entrusted to a ruler who instantly bowed his head to every passing breeze. On 27 April 1909 Abdul-Hamid was deposed in his turn. There could be no question of consigning him, like his two immediate predecessors, to the Çirağan Palace, which was now teeming with parliamentarians; it was decided instead to send him into exile. On hearing the news, the Sultan fainted dead away into the arms of his Chief Eunuch. That same night, with two princes, three wives, four concubines, five eunuchs and fourteen servants, he was packed into the train which was to deposit him nearly twenty-four hours later in the city where – ironically enough – all his troubles had begun: Thessalonica.

With the departure of Abdul-Hamid from the scene, the Ottoman Empire was never the same again. His half-brother and successor, Mehmet V, already sixty-four, had spent most of his life in semi-enforced seclusion, consoled by industrial quantities of alcohol and regiments of concubines. He was not unintelligent and was deeply read in Persian literature, but he was totally incapable of governing – a drawback which was in fact of little importance, since he was never asked to do so. Power was now – at least in theory – in the hands of the parliament, and reforms in any number of fields followed thick and fast. There remained areas – freedom of the press and of public gatherings, for example – in which repression continued; nonetheless, had the new government been granted a few years of peace and stability it might have achieved much.

Alas, it was not. The old empire was too divided – and, frankly, too big. There were too many national minorities who still felt themselves to be second-class citizens. Macedonia remained an open sore; in 1910 Albania rose in revolt; there were further serious troubles in Armenia; the Muslims from Syria and Lebanon founded a Young Arab movement on the model of the Young Turks, while their brethren in the Arabian peninsula and the Hejaz stirred up rebellions which were soon causing the government in Constantinople serious anxiety – to the point where they were obliged to send most of their garrisons in what is now Libya to the affected areas. This resulted in a serious weakening in the last section of the North African coast to remain under Turkish control, and the Italians saw their chance.

For the past thirty years – ever since France had occupied Tunisia in 1881 – the Italians had looked upon Libya with a covetous eye. The withdrawal of all but some 3,000 of the Ottoman army of occupation convinced them that the time had come for action; if they did not move fast, there could be little doubt that the French would invade from the west, extending their influence from Morocco to the Egyptian border. By the summer of 1911 it was clear that Italian forces were preparing for the attack. All that the Turkish government could do was to ensure that the local tribesmen were well provided with arms and ammunition.

When the moment came – on 27 September 1911 – the time-worn procedure was followed: the issue of an ultimatum making various accusations, usually exaggerated, accompanied by demands known in advance to be unacceptable; then, immediately this was rejected, the declaration of war. On the 28th, Italian troops were landed simultaneously at Tripoli, Benghazi, Derna and Tobruk. These landings were accompanied by the first air raids in history, with the pilots of early biplanes flying low over their targets and lobbing small bombs out by hand. Against such overpoweringly superior forces the Turks could do little. Inland, however, the situation was reversed. The invaders, who knew nothing of desert warfare, were no match for the tribesmen and failed utterly to penetrate far into the interior. But partial success was enough: on 5 November the Italian government announced its formal annexation of Tripolitania and Cyrenaica. Five months later, in April 1912, it went a good deal further: an Italian naval squadron bombarded the forts protecting the entrance to the Dardanelles. Failing to force an entrance, it then turned back to seize Rhodes and the rest of the Dodecanese, which for the previous four centuries had been part of the Ottoman Empire.

The Empire was now obviously rocking on its heels. If Italy, after little more than forty years as a single nation, could inflict such damage upon it, then surely the way was open for all its other enemies to move in on their own behalf. By the end of the summer Serbia, Greece, Bulgaria and Montenegro had managed to set aside their differences and form a Balkan League, with the objective of driving the Turks once and for all from the European continent. Hostilities began in early October and a week later, its forces outnumbered by more than two to one, the Ottoman government made a panicky peace with Italy, by the terms of which it recognised Italian suzerainty over Tripolitania and Cyrenaica in return for the return of the Dodecanese – a condition to which the Italians agreed, but which they were never to fulfil. By the end of November the Bulgarians had overrun Thrace; the Serbs had occupied Kosovo, Monastir, Skopje and Ochrid; and – most significant of all – the key Mediterranean port of Thessalonica was in the hands of the Greeks.[1]

---

[1] Poor Abdul-Hamid was hurried with his family on board the German steamship *Lorelei* and returned to Istanbul, to spend his six remaining years in the Beylerbey Palace on the Bosphorus.

In December came a pause; Bulgaria, Serbia and Montenegro agreed to an armistice – though Greece pointedly did not – and five days before Christmas a peace conference opened in London. But there was too much unfinished business, and at the beginning of February 1913 war broke out again. Another armistice followed in mid-April and a peace treaty was signed in London on 30 May. Turkey had lost Crete (formally annexed by Greece on 13 December), Macedonia, Thrace, Albania and most of her islands in the Aegean. All that was left of 'Turkey in Europe' was the city of Constantinople and its hinterland – little more than half the area that it occupies today; the present frontier, just beyond Edirne, is the result of what was known as the Second Balkan War, which lasted only a week or two. It was caused by the Bulgarians who, resentful at the Greek and Serbian gains in Macedonia, in the early hours of 29 June (of that same year, 1913) launched a surprise attack on their former allies, who were joined soon afterwards by Romania. The Turks decided to intervene, and a certain Major Enver – later Enver Pasha – who had been one of the moving spirits of the Young Turks, led his cavalry at breakneck speed across eastern Thrace to Edirne, capturing the city virtually without firing a shot. It was a brave adventure, and a successful one, but it could not conceal the fact that in little more than a year the Ottoman Empire had lost four-fifths of its European territory and more than two-thirds of its European population.

For these losses it was generally agreed that its army was to blame. It clearly needed extensive reorganisation and reconstruction. The men had gone unpaid for months; all of them were ragged, many of them were hungry, and morale had sunk almost to the point of mutiny. The fleet, too, was hopelessly out of date and in appalling condition. The first German officers who arrived to set the armed forces on their feet again are said to have been horrified to discover that the Turkish language had no word for 'maintenance'.

The Germans, it went without saying, were the people to do the job. For some years past, Kaiser Wilhelm II had been waging a goodwill offensive. Like several other powers, he had heard of the recent discovery of vast oil deposits in Mesopotamia, and was anxious to obtain the Sultan's agreement to the extension of the existing Berlin–Constantinople railway eastward to Baghdad. He had first called at Constantinople on his yacht, the *Hohenzollern*, as early as 1889, the year after his accession; on his second visit in 1898, he and Abdul-Hamid together crossed the Bosphorus and formally opened the magnificent new Asiatic terminus at Haydarpaşa. He had then sailed on to Palestine, where on 29 October 1898 he had made a state entry into Jerusalem – the first by a German Emperor since that of Frederick II in 1229 – on a coal-black charger, wearing white ceremonial uniform, his helmet surmounted by a golden eagle. The effect may have been faintly ridiculous – 'revolting,' wrote the Empress Maria Fyodorovna to her son Tsar Nicholas II – but it certainly ensured that Wilhelm would not be easily forgotten. And now, on 30 June 1913 – the very day of the Bulgarians' surprise attack – the Kaiser appointed General Otto Liman von Sanders to lead a German military mission to Constantinople.

How much that mission would have achieved we shall never know. A year later almost to the day, the Archduke Franz Ferdinand fell victim to an assassin's bullet in Sarajevo – and all Europe was at war.

CHAPTER XXXII

The Great War

The First World War, as everyone knows, was fought principally in the trenches of northern France and Belgium. It was not in any sense a Mediterranean war. On three occasions, however, it spilled out into the Middle Sea to concentrate on its eastern enemy, the Ottoman Empire. The first was the ill-starred campaign of the Dardanelles and Gallipoli; the second, the Allied landings at Salonica; the third took place in Palestine.

On 27 December 1914 Winston Churchill, then First Lord of the Admiralty, characteristically addressed to the Prime Minister, Herbert Henry Asquith, a long letter of advice. The war, he suggested, had reached an impasse. The two armies were so firmly dug in that an advance of a few hundred yards was likely to involve casualties of several thousand. What was needed was a breakout, to some completely new theatre of war. 'Are there not other alternatives,' he asked, 'than sending our armies to chew barbed wire in Flanders?' It seemed to him that there were two. One idea was the invasion and seizure of Schleswig–Holstein, enabling Denmark to join the Allies and opening up the Baltic to Allied shipping; the Russians could then land an army within ninety miles of Berlin. This would certainly be his own preference.

But he also put forward another idea, still more ambitious and imaginative: an invasion of the Gallipoli peninsula, control of which would allow the Royal Navy to force a passage through the Dardanelles and into the Sea of Marmara. Anchoring at the mouth of the Golden Horn, it could then threaten a bombardment of Constantinople – a terrible threat indeed in view of the narrow streets and tumbledown wooden houses of the old city. The destruction of the Galata Bridge would cut off Pera from Stamboul; the only two munitions factories in Turkey both stood on the water's edge, where they would be an easy target for the British guns. All this would oblige the Sultan's government to sue for peace, after which there would be no difficulty, Churchill believed, in persuading the still neutral Greece, Romania, Serbia and Bulgaria to throw in their lot with the Allies. It was a typically Churchillian plan which, had it succeeded, would have greatly shortened the war. But it did not succeed – and for the best part of a century military historians have been trying to analyse why a plan which at first appeared so promising led to the greatest disaster of the war.

The chief problem seems to have been the lack of a concerted overall plan. Churchill had originally envisaged a combined military and naval operation; by mid-January 1915, however, he was advocating an attack by the Navy only, despite the furious opposition of the First Sea Lord, his friend – but occasionally also his *bête noire* – Admiral Sir John Fisher. Only a month later, less than a week before the naval bombardment of the Dardanelles began, was it decided to send troops in support. This was largely due to the fact that Churchill, who was providing all the energy and drive behind the plan, was only a cabinet minister, responsible exclusively for the navy. He had no power over the army; the Secretary of State for War, Lord Kitchener – who did – was half-hearted, the Prime Minister still more so. Had Churchill possessed the authority that he was to enjoy twenty-five years later, the Gallipoli campaign might well have ended very differently.

Over the navy, however, he was supreme; thanks to him, the fleet assembled by the British and French was the greatest concentration of naval strength ever seen in the Mediterranean. Apart from cruisers, destroyers and lesser craft, the British had contributed fourteen battleships, including the recently completed *Queen Elizabeth*, whose fifteen-inch guns – possessed by no other vessel – made her probably the most powerful ship afloat. Most of the others had twelve-inch guns, but these alone easily outclassed anything the Turks could boast in the eleven fortresses – on both sides of the straits – which constituted their principal defence. To this already considerable force the French added four more battleships and their auxiliaries.

By 18 February 1915 the combined fleet was in position, and at 9.51 a.m. on the following morning the attack began. It continued throughout the day, the fleet gradually drawing nearer, bombarding the forts from ever closer range. Meanwhile, minesweepers were at work, clearing the approach to the straits. By nightfall there was as yet no conclusive result. The Allied commander, Vice-Admiral Sackville Carden, saw that nothing of importance could be achieved unless his ships could approach much closer still to their targets; unfortunately that night the weather broke, and rough seas made accurate bombardment impossible. Not until five days later did the storm blow itself out and allow the battle to continue. On the 25th Vice-Admiral John de Robeck advanced right up to the straits themselves and the defenders withdrew to the north. Over the next few days small parties of sailors and marines actually landed on both the European and Asiatic shores, destroying such Turkish equipment as they could find, but most of the territory seemed deserted. On 2 March Carden telegraphed to London that given fine weather he hoped to be at Constantinople in about a fortnight.

How wrong he was. The Dardanelles, he soon discovered, were one vast minefield; the minesweepers were prevented from doing their job by the enemy guns, and the Navy could not silence the guns until the mines had been swept. A fortnight later, instead of dropping anchor in Constantinople, Carden was on his way back to London with a nervous breakdown. He was succeeded in the command by de Robeck, who led an attack on the straits on 18 March; alas, it was a failure, owing largely to an undetected line of mines that sank one French and two British battleships. De Robeck was not to know – though he might have suspected – that the Turkish emplacements were now running seriously short of ammunition and had little immediate prospect of obtaining any more. He was aware only of his heavy losses and of the fact that Constantinople seemed as far away as ever. As for the Turks, their 60,000 men, skilfully deployed and commanded by General Liman von Sanders, had won their first victory for many years – and over the Royal Navy, which they, and much of the rest of the world, had long believed to be invincible. Constantinople had been saved from British clutches. Once again, they could walk with their heads held high.

It was by now clear to most of the British government that the navy could not achieve a breakthrough alone. 'Somebody,' wrote Admiral Fisher to David Lloyd George, 'will have to land at Gallipoli some time or other.' By mid-March Kitchener had reluctantly agreed to send out the 29th Division from England – totalling some 17,000 men – together with the Australian and New Zealand divisions (another 30,000) that were then awaiting orders in Egypt. In addition, there was one French division of 16,000 and the Royal Naval Division of 10,000. In overall command he appointed his old friend from Boer War days, General Sir Ian Hamilton. It was agreed that the armies would assemble on the island of Lemnos, where they would receive their stores and equipment and draw up their plans for the coming campaign.

At Lemnos, however, another disappointment was in store. The transports from England had been loaded with no thought for the army that was to receive them. Horses and guns arrived on one ship, saddles, harness and ammunition on another. Landing craft had apparently been forgotten altogether. A number of heavy lorries had been loaded, despite the fact that the Gallipoli peninsula had no roads. Nor, it seemed, did the army possess any accurate maps or charts of the area over which it would be fighting. Finally, landing and other facilities on Lemnos were found to be inadequate or nonexistent, with the result that everything had to be re-embarked and carried on to Alexandria, where the whole army could be regrouped and somehow made ready for battle. There was now no chance that the combined force would be ready until mid-April at the earliest. That would give Hamilton some three weeks to prepare and plan the most ambitious amphibious operation in the history of warfare.

The navy had been more fortunate with its supplies. A new fleet of destroyer-minesweepers had arrived, together with three dummy battleships, humble vessels which had been decked out with elaborate superstructures and wooden guns to serve as decoys and, with any luck, to persuade the German fleet to come out and fight.[1] The Royal Flying Corps was represented by Air Commodore Charles Samson. When his thirty aircraft were uncrated, twenty-five were found to be unserviceable; for the remainder, however, there was a number of bombs designed to be lobbed overboard by the observer. Where the aircraft really came into their own was in the field of reconnaissance. The aerial photography of the enemy emplacements, with their vast fields of barbed wire, filled Hamilton with gloom.

The long-delayed landings finally took place in the early hours of 25 April. The British disembarked at Cape Helles on the western tip of the peninsula, the Australians and New Zealanders in a small bay – henceforth to be known as Anzac Cove – some thirteen miles along the north coast. The French, meanwhile, were put ashore at Kum Kale on the southern coast. The defending Turks, though outnumbered and outgunned and subject to constant shelling from the ships, kept up a courageous resistance. The Allied troops fought equally bravely, but their task was made harder by the extraordinary preference of Hamilton and his two subordinate generals, Aylmer Hunter-Weston and Sir William Birdwood – commanding the British and the Anzacs respectively – to remain at sea throughout the vital first hours after the

---

[1] Alan Moorehead tells us that one of these was 'subsequently torpedoed by a U-boat off Malta, and must have occasioned some surprise to the Germans. As the ship settled, her wooden turrets and her twelve-inch guns floated away on the tide.'

landings. Thus, when the signalling arrangements began to fail and there was an almost immediate breakdown of Allied communications, each individual unit was left to look after itself, with no knowledge of what was happening on the next beach to its own. By the end of the first day, after heavy casualties on both sides, the invading forces were still largely confined to the shore.

Anyone who has ever visited the Gallipoli peninsula will have been struck by the intense hostility of the terrain. Of scenic beauty there is plenty, with the plain of Troy extending beyond the Dardanelles to the south and, rising from the sea in the west, the islands of Imbros and Samothrace. But the beaches themselves, set in what is essentially a succession of small coves, are small and narrow, and they are overhung by cliffs, rising almost perpendicular only yards from the shore, slashed by precipitous ravines and so densely covered with scrub and bracken as to be in many places utterly impassable. Thus the Turks on the heights above, hidden in the thick vegetation, had a perfect field of fire on the forces trapped on the beaches below.

How, one wonders, can those who planned the operation have believed that it had the faintest chance of success? Hamilton and a few of his senior officers had done a rough reconnaissance by sailing a little way up the coast in a destroyer, and there were a few aerial photographs. But no one had a proper map, and there were some areas – notably Anzac Cove – which had never been mapped at all. Nonetheless, when the Australians and New Zealanders splashed ashore in the early hours of that Sunday morning, they fought like tigers. Some of them managed to cut a path with their bayonets through the scrub, and by 8 a.m. it seemed that in several places the Turks were on the run. At that moment, however, there arrived on the scene one of the half-dozen most remarkable men of the twentieth century.

Mustafa Kemal – he made a brief appearance in the preceding chapter – was by now, at the age of thirty-four, a divisional commander. Called out with one small battalion to engage the invaders, he first single-handedly stopped a group of his retreating countrymen and by the sheer force of his personality persuaded them to turn and fight; then, realising that the battle was far more serious and on an infinitely larger scale than he had been led to understand, he summoned – on his own responsibility – a crack Turkish regiment and one of the Arab units as well. In doing this he was blatantly exceeding his authority, but it was not until the early afternoon that he even informed his headquarters of what he had done. By this time the progress of the battle had proved him right; he returned to his unit with effective authority over the whole of the Anzac front.

All day he kept up the pressure, and the Dominion troops who had managed to advance a short distance into the hinterland began to fall back towards the sea. By now Birdwood had discovered to his horror that he had landed his men on the wrong beach. He had expected to find a strip of coast at least a mile long; he found instead a cove little more than half that length, with only some thirty yards between the water and the cliff. Here everything had to be brought: guns, ammunition, stores of all kinds, pack animals – and, all too soon, an endless stream of stretchers bearing the dead or wounded. That night he sent a message to the Commander-in-Chief seeking permission to abandon his whole position and to re-embark his men.

But Hamilton refused. Any such re-embarkation, he pointed out, would take at least two days; meanwhile it had just been reported to him that an Australian submarine had passed through the narrows and entered the Sea of Marmara, where it had already torpedoed a Turkish gunboat. There was nothing the poor general could do but tell his men to dig themselves in.

Birdwood, busy with the Anzacs, would have been even more discouraged had he known how the European troops had fared. The French, to be sure, had done well: they had landed near the reputed tomb of Achilles, had seized and occupied the ruined fortress of Kum Kale and were now ready to join their British allies at Cape Helles. Here, however, the landings had been catastrophic. The Turks had held their fire until most of the transports had been drawn up to the beach and the men disembarked, and had then suddenly loosed a murderous hail of bullets. For the British troops there was no protection, and soon, as Air Commodore Samson reported after observing the scene from the air, 'the calm blue sea was absolutely red with blood for fifty yards from the shore, a horrible sight to see.' In the shallows, all the little ripples were dyed scarlet. Within three hours, nearly a thousand corpses were strewn across the beach. At the other four nearby landing places the situation had been rather better; it was known, too, that the Turks had also suffered appalling casualties. Nevertheless, Hamilton's continued optimism remained astonishing. 'Thanks to God who calmed the seas,' he wrote on April 26, 'and to the Royal Navy who rowed our fellows ashore as coolly as if at a regatta; thanks also to the dauntless spirit shown by all ranks of both Services, we have landed

29,000 upon six beaches in the face of desperate resistance.' But as other reports filtered back to London there could be no doubt in anyone's mind that the cost of the Gallipoli operation in human life alone had already been far greater than foreseen, and that its long-term prospects were in serious doubt.

After three days there was a lull, followed by what seemed a stalemate. The British and the Anzacs had somehow managed to advance a mile or two into the hills, and to dig themselves in; try as they might, the Turks could not dislodge them. For some time it looked as though the action in the trenches of the peninsula might become almost as static as in Flanders. Meanwhile, in London, all the stresses and strains within the government were mercilessly exposed. First, on 15 May, Admiral Fisher resigned – or, more accurately, walked out; for some hours he was missing, and was finally run to earth at the Charing Cross Hotel. Next, Prime Minister Asquith was obliged to form a coalition government, from which – in the most dramatic reverse of his political career to date – Winston Churchill was determinedly excluded.

For the men on the beaches of Gallipoli, and the others on the cliffs above, the summer was long indeed. As the weather grew steadily hotter, the flies became more and more insufferable: the food, the corpses in no man's land, the countless suppurating wounds, the proximity of the latrines, all these things attracted them in their millions and made life an even greater misery than it would otherwise have been. In the wake of the flies came the dysentery. By July a thousand totally incapacitated men were being shipped off every week to Lemnos or one of the other islands. But there was good news too: in June it was agreed in London to send out five more divisions, giving Hamilton a total of some 120,000 men. De Robeck also – now that Fisher was safely out of the way – received substantial reinforcements to his fleet. In these dramatically changed conditions a new landing was clearly indicated, and the choice fell on Suvla Bay, a few miles to the north of Anzac Cove. From here it was hoped to advance quickly the four miles to the narrows, cutting off the bulk of the Turkish army on the tip of the peninsula.

Suvla Bay seemed at first full of promise. Unlike the shallow crescents of most of the other bays, it formed a perfect horseshoe; its waters thus provided an ideal anchorage for the fleet. It had no tall cliffs to dominate it and was, perhaps for that reason, only lightly defended – as it turned out, by some 1,800 men distributed around the bay, without barbed wire or machine-guns. It was, moreover, just around the headland from Anzac Cove; once its possession was assured it could accommodate many of the unhappy Dominion troops and so relieve the nightmare overcrowding which they had endured for so long. The landings began under cover of darkness on 4 August and continued until the night of the 6th, the Turks apparently suspecting nothing. It was only after all were disembarked that things began to go seriously wrong. The newly arrived troops were inexperienced and undisciplined, their commanders old and for the most part incompetent, seemingly unable to cope with the hellish conditions prevailing. The chain of command soon broke down, Hamilton remaining hopelessly out of touch: orders were countermanded at the last moment; generals and brigadiers were encouraged to act at their own discretion; seldom was it clearly explained to the soldiers what was required of them.

There were a few temporary successes. The heroic attack by the Australians at Lone Pine cost them 4,000 men, but it won them no less than seven Victoria Crosses and resulted in the capture of the Turkish front line. The New Zealanders smashed through another part of the line and found themselves to the rear of the Turkish positions. But for every success there were several failures, and on the evening of 8 April the Allies had been forced back into their own trenches, having sustained horrific casualties and with none of their main objectives achieved. At the end of August Hamilton confessed his failure to Kitchener. He could do no more, he said, without heavy reinforcements; he mentioned the figure of 95,000 men, but the Field Marshal only shrugged. The War Cabinet, it appeared, had decided to concentrate once again on the Western Front. Was Gallipoli to be written off?

In the last week of September there came a further blow. Bulgaria mobilised; it was virtually certain that within a week at the most she would enter the war on the side of Germany and Austria and would march with them against Serbia. This threatened to change the whole situation in the Balkans; the Allies therefore decided to transfer two divisions, first a French and then a British, from Gallipoli to Salonica, whence they could march north to help the Serbs. It seemed then that Hamilton must be prepared to abandon Suvla altogether. And there was another possibility, even more depressing: on 11 October Kitchener cabled Hamilton: 'What is your estimate of the probable losses which would be entailed to your force if the evacuation of the Gallipoli Peninsula was decided upon? No decision has been arrived at yet . . . but I feel I ought to have your views.' Hamilton replied at once; 50 percent, he suggested, might be a realistic figure, adding, 'On the other hand, with all these raw troops at Suvla and all those Senegalese at Cape Helles, we might have a veritable catastrophe.' When this message was put before the Dardanelles Committee on 14 October, Hamilton's fate was sealed. Two days later he received his dismissal.

Lieutenant-General Sir Charles Monro, Hamilton's successor, had come straight from the Western Front, and from the day of his arrival made no secret of the fact that he considered the whole Gallipoli expedition misconceived. The war, he believed, would be won in France; any distraction or diversion from the main thrust was to be deplored. Since his orders were to advise on whether the peninsula should be evacuated or not, the nature of his advice seemed a foregone conclusion. Nor, on his arrival, did he see anything to make him change his mind. Although the weather was growing rapidly colder, no winter clothing had been received from London. Many units were now at half strength or less, the remaining soldiers reduced to skin and bone. The guns were rationed to two shells a day. Monro's first sight of Suvla Bay confirmed his worst fears. 'Like *Alice in Wonderland*,' he was heard to murmur, 'curiouser and curiouser.' The following day he sent Kitchener his recommendation.

But all was not yet lost. Commodore Roger Keyes, Admiral de Robeck's chief of staff, saw fit to disagree. His plan was quite simple: to gather the entire Mediterranean fleet, which had been lying all summer at various points in the Aegean, and – while keeping up a terrific bombardment of the Turkish shore batteries – to make a determined attempt on the straits. This would, he believed, take the Turks by surprise. Once in the Marmara, it would be a simple matter to block the isthmus of Bulair at the northern end of the peninsula, cutting off the twenty Turkish divisions stationed there. De Robeck was sceptical, but generously allowed Keyes to return to England to plead his case. He did – and made a considerable impact on all the principal admirals, on the First Lord of the Admiralty Arthur Balfour, and of course on Winston Churchill.

There remained Lord Kitchener, who had been appalled by the speed and tenor of Monro's reply. It was he who had personally chosen Hamilton for the Gallipoli command, and he had not enjoyed seeing his friend humiliated. He immediately fell in with Keyes's idea, asked him to try to get some sort of definite undertaking from the Admiralty, and then announced – to Birdwood rather than to Monro – his decision to leave personally for the Dardanelles the following day. The message ended: 'I absolutely refuse to sign order for evacuation, which I think would be the greatest disaster and would condemn a large percentage of our men to death or imprisonment. Monro will be appointed to command the Salonica force.' Then he set off, via Paris – where the French confirmed that they were firmly opposed to evacuation – to Marseille and thence in HMS *Dartmouth* to Gallipoli.

Had Keyes accompanied him – as Kitchener had asked him to, but the message was never delivered – he might have kept the Field Marshal steady, but the climate of opinion among the commanders on the spot had swung considerably since Keyes's departure and Kitchener immediately found himself surrounded by Monro, de Robeck and Birdwood, all three now firmly in favour of evacuation. No one spoke up for Keyes and his plan. After two days of discussions the Field Marshal went off on a tour of inspection of the three principal bridgeheads, and was duly depressed by what he saw, though somewhat less so than Monro. On 22 November he cabled to London a recommendation that Suvla and Anzac Bay should be evacuated at once, Cape Helles being held 'for the time being'. Two days later he sailed for England.

By this time no one remotely involved with the operation, from the highest to the most humble, felt anything but loathing for the Gallipoli peninsula; but they had not yet seen it at its worst. On 27 November it was hit by the fiercest blizzard for at least forty years. Twenty-four hours of deluge were followed by north winds of hurricane force, bringing with them heavy snowfalls and two nights of intense frost. Torrents came sweeping down from the hills, carrying the bodies of drowned Turks. At Anzac Cove, in particular, where many of the Australians and a small Indian contingent were probably seeing snow for the first time, there was virtually no protection from the piercing cold; winter clothing still had not been issued, and the soldiers could do nothing but huddle in their soaking wet blankets, which soon froze solid. For three days and three nights the torment continued. When it was over, 200 men had been drowned or died of cold, 5,000 were suffering from severe frostbite. Many of them had in the past opposed evacuation, determined to see the operation through to the end; now, however great the inherent dangers, they could not get away fast enough.

The evacuation was clearly going to be a long and difficult job.[1] In

---

[1] There is a superb account of the evacuation in Chapter XVII of Alan Moorehead's *Gallipoli*, to which for this all too brief account of the campaign I am hugely indebted.

the Suvla–Anzac bridgehead alone there were 83,000 men, to say nothing of the 5,000 horses and donkeys, 2,000 motor vehicles, nearly 2,000 guns and several tons of supplies. The only hope was to withdraw silently and secretly over perhaps two or three weeks. Even then there were formidable dangers: a sustained Turkish bombardment could easily make embarkations impossible; bad weather and a rough sea could ruin the best-laid plans – and the winter solstice was fast approaching. But there was no alternative; from the second week of December nightly flotillas of barges and small boats crept into the bays, leaving before dawn weighed down to the gunwales with men, animals and arms. The sick and wounded were embarked first; fifty-six temporary hospital ships had been prepared for them, and 12,000 hospital beds were waiting in Egypt. During the day, to allay Turkish suspicions, life continued precisely as usual: the endless mule teams continued to toil up from the beaches to the front, down from the front to the beaches. The only difference was that the crates and boxes that they carried were empty. As the evacuation progressed the deception became more difficult: the same men and animals were obliged to march round and round again like a stage army. No tents were struck; thousands of extra cooking fires were lit every night.

After a week the pace quickened; by 18 December half the force – some 40,000 – had been taken off. The enemy could no longer be fooled; it was agreed that the remainder of the army would leave over the next two nights. In some sectors of the front, the Allied and Turkish trenches were less than ten yards from each other (many of them can still be seen) and it must have seemed impossible to leave them without alerting the enemy; yet somehow it was done. Just before daybreak on the 21st the last boats pulled away from the beach. At Anzac Cove two men were wounded by stray shots just as they were boarding; at Suvla Bay every single man and animal was safely taken off. The last thing they did before they left was to light the fuses that had been carefully laid all over the beaches. Ten minutes later they heard with deep satisfaction the series of deafening explosions as the ammunition dumps went up.

What about the British? For their four divisions – some 35,000 men – in the Helles bridgehead, the situation looked grave indeed. The Turks had allowed the Anzacs to disappear from right under their noses; surely they would not make the same mistake again. Instead, no longer tied down at Anzac and Suvla, they would throw the whole weight of their army against them. There could no longer be any question of hanging on, and Monro, Birdwood and de Robeck – who had been briefly invalided home but who returned just before Christmas – were now all agreed. Evacuation, however problematic, must be attempted.

It began on Saturday, 1 January 1916. The French left first, and after a week the number of British troops remaining was down to 19,000. Up to this point there had been surprisingly little enemy opposition. Then, in the early afternoon of the 7th, the Turks launched their attack – in a bombardment that lasted for four and a half hours. After the guns had fallen silent there came the inevitable charge. The British in their trenches faced it with guns and rifles blazing, and were astonished to see the Turkish infantry – well-known for its discipline and courage – stopping dead in its tracks, flatly refusing to advance further. When night fell not a single Turkish soldier had penetrated the British line. For the next twenty-four hours there was no more trouble, and the evacuation continued.

Meanwhile, however, the weather was worsening. By the evening of 8 January the glass was falling fast, and soon the wind was gusting at 35 miles an hour. Two lighters broke adrift and smashed one of the makeshift piers; everything stopped while it was repaired – no easy job in the dark, with a stormy sea. The wind and the rain also slowed down the few remaining troops as they marched the three or four miles from their trenches to the beach, but at 3.45 a.m. the last man was on board, the last boat heading out to sea. Ten minutes later, as at Anzac and Suvla, the ammunition dumps exploded in a dramatic finale. The ill-starred adventure was over at last.

Nothing became it like its end. It is one of the many ironies of Gallipoli that, after the chaos and confusion that had blighted the whole operation from the beginning, the final evacuations were models of superb organisation and planning. There were scarcely any casualties; not a man was left behind. But there is, perhaps, a greater irony still: that the great expedition, failure as it may have been, was nevertheless a brilliant concept, which should – and could – have succeeded. Some years after the war, an official report on the campaign by the Turkish General Staff confessed that the naval battle of 19 March had left it virtually without ammunition; had de Robeck returned immediately to the attack he would very probably have been able to advance unhindered through the straits to Constantinople, in which case 'the eight divisions retained there would have been unable to defend it'. With Constantinople occupied, it is doubtful whether the

Russians would ever have signed a separate peace – and the Russian Revolution might never have occurred. Even after the landings victory might have been possible; the Turkish report also admitted that twice during the campaign – during the first Anzac landing in April and at Suvla Bay in August – the Allies would almost certainly have broken through had it not been for the astonishing personal magnetism of Mustafa Kemal.[1] Had they managed to do so, had the campaign succeeded – as it so very nearly did – the Great War would probably have ended three years earlier, and a million lives would have been saved.

The Greek attitude towards the landing of troops in Salonica was ambiguous and uncertain. The Prime Minister, Eleftherios Venizelos, secretly welcomed the plan, though for form's sake he registered a formal protest. King Constantine, on the other hand – who had succeeded his father George two years before and was married to the Kaiser's sister – was violently opposed, on the grounds that until the Bulgarian army actually crossed the frontier, the presence of foreign troops on Greek soil would be a violation of Greek neutrality. As for the Greeks themselves, they were overwhelmingly on the side of the King. They had no desire for an Allied presence, feeling that they were being forced against their will into the war. The result was what came to be known as the National Schism, and Venizelos was forced to resign.

It is always a mistake for constitutional monarchs to meddle in foreign policy; this time it was calamitous. The King now opened secret talks with the Germans, and on 23 May 1916, on his orders, the Greek army surrendered the frontier castle of Roupel, allowing German and Bulgarian troops to overrun eastern Macedonia. Kavalla too was ordered to surrender, its Greek garrison being carted off to Germany as prisoners of war. 'Where,' shouted Venizelos in parliament, 'where at least are your thirty pieces of silver?' It was not perhaps the most diplomatic preface to a last appeal to the King to join the Allies before it was too late. Predictably, Constantine turned a deaf ear.

For the expeditionary force, the situation was becoming more and more impossible. From the day of its arrival it had found itself extremely unwelcome, being obliged to camp several miles outside the

---

[1] The official British historian went further still: 'Seldom in history,' he wrote, 'can the exertions of a single divisional commander have exercised, on three separate occasions, so profound an influence not only on the course of a battle but, perhaps, on the fate of a campaign and even the destiny of a nation.'

city while the consuls of the enemy remained at liberty within. That winter the Serbs had been driven back to the Adriatic and Serbia had been occupied. What, the Allies asked themselves, were they meant to be doing? It was then that the French commander in Salonica, General Maurice Serrail, had taken the law into his own hands, putting all the enemy consuls and agents under arrest and imprisoning them in the castle while simultaneously taking possession of another fortress guarding the entrance to the bay. Now the gloves were off: the Allied powers officially demanded the demobilisation of the Greek army, the dissolution of parliament and the dismissal of the government. In September 1916 Venizelos slipped away to his native Crete, where he raised a revolt against the King. He then returned to Greece and established a provisional government in Thessalonica, which the Allies recognised a month later.

In December the British and French, their demands still unfulfilled, landed troops at Piraeus in an attempt to force the King to surrender his armaments and munitions. This, however, proved a mistake: the Greeks fought back and the royal palace was bombarded by the French fleet. Venizelos, understandably but quite unjustifiably, was blamed, and on 26 December was solemnly excommunicated by the Archbishop of Athens. The Allies then put southern Greece under a blockade and in June 1917 demanded the abdication of the King – the French reinforcing the demand by landing troops at Corinth. Constantine refused to abdicate, but left with his eldest son for Switzerland.

Now, overnight, the whole situation changed. Constantine was succeeded in Athens – now starving owing to the continuing blockade and virtually under French occupation – by his second son, Alexander. A few days later Venizelos returned from Salonica with his government, received a warm welcome and became the new King's Prime Minister – celebrating his reappointment with a nine-hour speech to parliament. Now it was the royalists who suffered; indeed they were purged – government, civil service, army, even the Church. Greek society was torn in two, and was to remain so for at least a generation. At last, and not a moment too soon, Greece entered the war on the Allied side. Her army, conscripted and largely untrained, fought magnificently in Macedonia. With the British they invaded and defeated Bulgaria; with the French and Serbs, they drove the Germans out of Serbia. As a final triumph, Greek troops entered Constantinople for the first time since 1453. For Eleftherios Venizelos, it was his finest hour.

*

The initial excitement and subsequent despair over Gallipoli completely overshadowed yet another theatre of war: that of the Middle East. This too formed part of the Ottoman Empire, and saw the Turkish army under constant pressure from the Allies, both in Mesopotamia and in Palestine.

The Palestinian campaign was, once again, an attempt to boost the morale of an increasingly war-weary Britain: to give its people something to think about other than the continuing holocaust in the trenches of Flanders, while at the same time landing a telling blow on the enemy at his weakest point. Its principal instigator, however, was not Winston Churchill – still out of the government thanks to the Gallipoli debacle – but the Prime Minister, Asquith's successor David Lloyd George. His objective could be summarised in just three words, 'Jerusalem before Christmas', and the man he chose to achieve it was General Sir Edmund Allenby. Allenby was not universally popular in the army, where his immense height, commanding presence, furious temper and frequently hectoring manner had earned him the nickname of the Bull;[1] in fact, his aggression concealed a genuine passion for nature and a deep love of music, literature and philosophy.[2] A soldier through and through, he had been desolated when ordered to leave the trenches for Palestine; he little knew that the unwelcome transfer was to make his name and fame, securing him a field marshal's baton, a viscountcy and the gift from a grateful nation of £50,000.

The Egyptian Expeditionary Force (as it was called) was manned largely by Australians. It existed primarily to protect the Suez Canal – but it was also expected to fight the Turks. The Canal was safe enough; against the Turks, however, though superior both in numbers and equipment to the ramshackle army facing it beyond the Sinai Peninsula, the EEF had achieved remarkably little. 'In Palestine and Mesopotamia,' Lloyd George had written, 'nothing and nobody could have saved the Turk from complete collapse in 1915 and 1916 except our General Staff.' The spring of 1917 showed no sign of improvement. There had been two half-hearted attempts to take Gaza; both had ended in defeat. Allenby's first task, therefore, when he arrived in Cairo on 28 June, was to breathe new life into this sadly demoralised army –

---

[1] 'One Colonel of the Royal Engineers was sick on the floor outside Allenby's office after an interview; another officer had to be actually carried out of Allenby's room, having collapsed on the floor before his desk.' (Brian Gardner, *Allenby*, p. 177).

[2] Not many British officers during the Boer War, one suspects, would have written from South Africa asking to be sent a copy of A. N. Majestrat's *L'Art du Croire, ou Préparation Philosophique à la Foi Chrétienne*.

and within a few weeks he had done so. His predecessor, General Archibald Murray, had preferred to maintain his headquarters at the Savoy Hotel in Cairo; Allenby moved it forward to a sweltering, fly-blown camp of tents and huts just behind the front line at Gaza and immediately embarked on a round of all the advanced units, establishing direct personal contact with his officers and men. It was the height of summer, the noonday temperature often hit 120 degrees, sandstorms were frequent and asphyxiating – but nothing seemed to stop the enormous general in full uniform, sitting bolt upright in an old Ford truck beside a diminutive Australian driver in vest and shorts, bouncing over the desert, investigating defence works and water supplies, barking out orders and quick to express his dissatisfaction in no uncertain terms. Wherever he went, morale soared.

Allenby's first task had been to gain a clear idea of the forces at his command; his next was to draw up a plan of campaign. This required substantial reinforcements: two further divisions to supplement the seven already in Palestine. To plead his case with the War Office he sent to London a young liaison officer, Lieutenant-Colonel A. P. Wavell (the future field marshal of the Second World War and subsequently Viceroy of India). It was largely thanks to Wavell's persuasive powers and already growing reputation that he got what he wanted, together with extra artillery and further units of the Royal Flying Corps; soon afterwards, it was Wavell who explained Allenby's plan to the Chief of the Imperial General Staff and the War Cabinet. Briefly, this consisted of a main thrust to the plentiful wells at Beersheba, some thirty miles inland from Gaza, to be protected by a feint attack on Gaza itself. As always, Allenby's preparations were thorough: 30,000 camels were assembled to carry water to the advance troops; new roads were built and new maps prepared, far more accurate – thanks to recent aerial reconnaissance – than their predecessors, which had been prepared by 'H. H. Kitchener, Lt.' in the 1870s. Meanwhile, he read everything on the area that he could get his hands on, from Herodotus and Strabo to histories of the Crusades and the latest papers of the Royal Geographical Society.

It was during this period of preparation, in the late summer of 1917, that Allenby met for the first time the one British officer whose fame in the area was to surpass even his own: the twenty-nine-year-old Captain T. E. Lawrence. Lawrence, second of the five illegitimate sons of an Anglo-Irish baronet, had had his first experience of the Arab world in 1908, when he had toured Syria and Lebanon recording their still little-known Crusader castles. Later, as an archaeologist, he had worked on the British Museum's excavations at Carchemish in Syria until the outbreak of war, when he had found himself in Cairo as a subaltern in the military intelligence department of the Egyptian Expeditionary Force. There he might well have remained, but for the Arab Revolt.

This had begun on 10 June 1916, when Sherif Hussein of Mecca and the Hejaz had led an uprising against the Turks. Three months later, however, the insurgents had run out of steam. They had failed, after repeated efforts, to dislodge the Turks from Medina and their morale was flagging. Lawrence had met the leaders, and had been particularly impressed by Hussein's second son Feisal, with whom he had evolved a plan to capture Aqaba, the principal Ottoman port at the northern end of the Red Sea. Two British naval expeditions there had failed; Lawrence believed, however, that Aqaba could be taken from the land. At the beginning of July, after nearly a month's march across some 800 miles of desert and with a scratch force of local Arabs largely recruited en route, he took the surrender of the Turkish garrison. His name was made.

One would like to have been present on the day Lawrence, distinctly undersized and – as always by now – in full Arab fig, strode into the office of the huge and immaculately uniformed Allenby. Many a commanding officer would have dismissed him with orders to come back when he had got out of his fancy dress; Allenby simply glared – but listened, while Lawrence explained how he would spread the revolt northwards via Aqaba against Damascus, making constant attacks on the single-track Hejaz railway which was virtually the only link between there and Medina. His manner – vanity combined with arrogance – may have been insufferable, but his arguments were persuasive. The General promoted him on the spot, making him – and Feisal's force – responsible directly to himself and promising him all the help he could give.

Certainly, this was the way for Allenby to achieve his primary purpose, the destruction of the Ottoman Empire; it was also, as he well knew, a guarantee of trouble in the future. In the spring of the previous year Britain had entered into an agreement with France and Russia, whereby French pretensions with regard to Syria might be reconciled with British pledges and promises to the Arabs. Russia had earmarked Constantinople, with a few miles of hinterland on both sides of the Bosphorus, together with a good deal of eastern Anatolia running to the Caucasus; France laid claim to most of Syria and the Lebanon, much of southern Anatolia and the Mosul district of Iraq; Britain's share consisted of the rest of modern Iraq – including both Baghdad and Basra – and a strip of Palestine which included the ports of Haifa and Acre. If Lawrence's plan for a northward thrust were successful, it was unlikely – to say the least – that the victorious Arab armies would countenance such an arrangement. But there would be time enough to deal with problems such as these.

The main advance against Gaza and Beersheba was launched towards the end of October 1917. Despite heavy fortification of the line by the German commander General Kress von Kressenstein, Beersheba fell on the last day of the month, Gaza a week later. Allenby, determined to maintain the momentum, spared neither himself nor his troops, to whom he allowed no rest; in some regiments the horses were watered only once in seventy-two hours as they pressed on relentlessly to the north, stretching the lines of communication and supply to the utmost limit. Jaffa fell on 16 November, and the exhausted, thirsty army assembled in the Judaean hills for the final attack on Jerusalem. Allenby's determination that there should be no fighting in the Holy City itself involved a long and complicated encircling manoeuvre. To make matters worse the weather had at last broken, the thermometer plunging; the horses were either sinking to the fetlocks in mud or slithering hopelessly over the slippery rocks. Yet the advance continued, and in the first week of December the Turkish governor informed Damascus of the evacuation of the city before personally smashing his telegraph equipment with a hammer. The city itself surrendered on 9 December, and two days later Allenby made his official entry into Jerusalem. With him was Colonel Wavell and Major Lawrence, in a borrowed army uniform. Nineteen years before, Kaiser Wilhelm had ridden in on his charger; Allenby, it was everywhere noted, entered on foot. After 730 years, Jerusalem had passed once again into Christian hands, but on his orders no official flag was flown. He merely issued a short proclamation. It ended as follows:

> Since your city is regarded with affection by the adherents of three of the great religions of mankind, and its soil has been consecrated by the prayers or pilgrimages of multitudes of devout people of these three religions for many centuries, therefore I make it known to you that every sacred building, monument, holy spot, shrine, traditional site, endowment, pious bequest or customary place of prayer of whatsoever form of the three religions will be maintained and protected according to the existing customs and beliefs of those to whose faiths they are sacred.

*

After the taking of Jerusalem, there was a pause of almost a year before the continuation of the campaign. Allenby knew that if he was to advance on Aleppo he would need a substantially larger force than he had commanded up to now, and he refused to move until that force had been provided. In fact, his army was completely reorganised; some units returned to Europe, others were brought in from India and elsewhere until he had at his disposal troops from a dozen or more countries and colonies, including Singapore and Hong Kong, South Africa, Egypt and the West Indies. There was even a detachment from Rarotonga in the South Pacific. The three battalions of Jews sent as a result of the Balfour Declaration[1] included David Ben-Gurion, later to be the first Prime Minister of the state of Israel.

Thus it was not until 19 September 1918 that Allenby launched his large but heterogeneous force of 12,000 cavalry, 57,000 infantry and 540 guns against eleven Turkish divisions – numbering respectively 4,000, 40,000 and 430 – holding a front from Jaffa east to the river Jordan and down its eastern bank to the Dead Sea. Only twelve days later, after one of the war's most spectacular campaigns, his advance units entered Damascus. Beirut fell on 8 October, Tripoli on the 18th and Aleppo on the 25th. In just six weeks he had pushed forward some 350 miles, utterly destroyed the Turkish army in Syria, taken 75,000 prisoners, all 430 guns and huge quantities of arms, ammunition and supplies. British casualties numbered 5,666. 'Making all allowances for the British superiority in strength,' wrote the military historian Liddell Hart, '[the campaign] must rank as one of the masterpieces of military history, as perfect in execution as in design.'

The Ottoman Empire, which was to have been Germany's path to the Persian Gulf and central Asia, was now in ruins. Its Arab territories were lost, not only in Palestine and Syria but in Mesopotamia too, along with the Arabian peninsula. The collapse of Bulgaria in September had opened up the western approaches to Constantinople, while British and Indian forces were advancing from the south and east. Beyond the Black Sea towards the Caucasus, former subjects of the Sultan – Georgians and Armenians, Azerbaijanis and Kurds – were

---

[1] A statement made on 2 November 1917 by Arthur Balfour, British Foreign Secretary, in a letter to Lionel, 2nd Baron Rothschild, a leader of British Jewry, informing him of British support for 'the establishment in Palestine of a national home for the Jewish people, provided that nothing shall be done which may prejudice the civil and religious rights of existing non-Jewish communities in Palestine'.

struggling to form their own new nation-states. On 30 October, on board HMS *Agamemnon* – a not inappropriate name in the circumstances – off the Aegean island of Mudros, the empire's representatives sued for peace.

CHAPTER XXXIII

The Peace

On 18 January 1919 – two months and one week after the armistice – the Paris Peace Conference held its opening session. It was, rather surprisingly, a Saturday, but that was the date insisted upon, with a fine sense of irony, by the French Prime Minister Georges Clemenceau, as being the forty-eighth anniversary of the coronation of Wilhelm I as Kaiser of Germany. The primary task facing the delegates was to forge a new Europe; and so, after a fashion, they did. Their success can be measured by the fact that exactly twenty years later their new Europe began – just like the old one – to tear itself to shreds.

Where the Mediterranean was concerned, the countries lining its southern shore were still under foreign control: Morocco, Algeria and Tunisia looked to France, Libya to Italy, Egypt to Britain (which had proclaimed a protectorate in December 1914). All those along the northern – with the single exception of Spain, which had somehow succeeded in preserving its neutrality – had been to some degree involved in the hostilities; all had seen fighting on their soil; and all those that had ended on the winning side hoped that the Conference would provide them with substantial benefits of one kind or another in or on the Middle Sea. These hopes all centred on a single fact: the break-up of the Ottoman Empire. France – which had lost a quarter of her male population between the ages of eighteen and thirty, with twice as many again wounded – was naturally concerned above all else with Germany, but she was also keeping a covetous eye on Syria and Lebanon, on which she had long had political designs. Italy, delighted as she was by the demise of her old enemy Austria–Hungary, was always anxious about what went on across the Adriatic, and was distinctly worried by the prospect of a unified state of the southern Slavs – comprising Croatia, Slovenia, Serbia, Montenegro, Bosnia–Herzegovina and northeastern Macedonia – which seemed likely to replace the Sultan's Balkan dominions. How much better it would be if she could emerge from the Conference with the land 'from Trento to Trieste', the Dalmatian coast as far as Albania and finally the islands of the Dodecanese, with – just possibly – a little of the Anatolian mainland thrown in.

Greece, as we saw in the last chapter, was already in a state of extreme exuberance when the war ended, but Venizelos's ambitions were perhaps higher than those of any other statesman present in Paris. His mind was set, as it had been throughout his life, on the Great Idea: Byzantium revived, with a Greek Asia Minor, St Sophia returned to the Orthodox faith and a Greek *basileus* once more on the throne in Constantinople. Of course he could not voice such demands in so many words at the Conference; all he asked for was northern Epirus, Thrace, a few islands and a vast tract of Asia Minor from the Sea of Marmara to Smyrna (Izmir). He did not include Constantinople (although, as he laughingly suggested to his friends, once the Turks were dispossessed of it the city would inevitably fall into Greek hands sooner or later). Inside and outside the plenary sessions, Venizelos impressed everyone he met. The sheer impact of his personality made him one of the most dazzling stars of the Conference, and his conversation did the rest. Western Europe had never seen – or heard – anything like him. The young diplomat Harold Nicolson described him in wonderment as 'a strange medley of charm, brigandage, *weltpolitik*, patriotism, courage, literature . . . above all this large muscular smiling man, with his eyes glinting through spectacles, and on his head a square skull-cap of black silk'.

Great Britain for her part could not by any stretch of the imagination be described as a Mediterranean country. She possessed, however, the three still vitally important bases of Gibraltar, Malta and Cyprus, and her part ownership of the Suez Canal had, as we have seen, long given her an intense interest in Egypt and the Levant. Thus, since she had already got a good deal of what she wanted – the German navy and merchant marine now safely in her hands, the German colonies in Africa surrendered, the collapse of Russia spelling the end of that threat to northern India and what was known as the Great Game – she could now afford to concentrate her energies on the eastern Mediterranean. At its northeast corner, she was anxious to prevent hostile warships passing through the straits to and from the Black Sea. She was also increasingly concerned about her allies, the French. The two countries had stuck together throughout the war, but the peace would bring new stresses and strains – not the least of which would be caused by the need to safeguard the increasingly important oil supplies from Mosul in northern Iraq and from Persia. As early as 1916 Sir Mark Sykes and M. Georges Picot had secretly agreed that when the time came to slice up the Sultan's Levantine dominions France would take Syria, the

Lebanon and a good deal of southern Anatolia while Britain would acquire, along with most of modern Iraq, the Mediterranean ports of Acre and Haifa. Outside these two ports an area corresponding roughly to the present state of Israel would – thanks to its special, delicate status as the Holy Land – be reserved for a special international regime of its own. Already, however, it was clear that the partitioning was not going to be so easy, and Allenby's recent entry into Jerusalem had done little to reassure Catholic France. In short, the two major European powers in the Middle East did not trust each other an inch – and both were perfectly right not to do so.

On the other hand, they had both made the same mistake: they had reckoned without the Arabs. The arrival at the Conference of the Emir Feisal, proudly introduced by Lawrence (also in full Arab dress), soon changed all that. Feisal was a Hashemite, a member of the noblest of all Arab families, since it traced its descent in the male line back to the daughter of the Prophet. In 1915 Feisal's father, the Sherif of Mecca, had been promised by the High Commissioner for Egypt, Sir Henry McMahon, that if the Arabs were to rise up against the Turks they would be given all assistance by the British and, after the war, gain their independence.[1] With the help of Lawrence – who had repeated these promises, though on no authority but his own – Feisal had performed his part of the bargain; he had now come to Paris to claim his reward.

He got it, in a way. In that same year Allenby installed him as head of a military administration in Damascus. The French assumed responsibility for the coast, with Beirut as their centre, while the British took over Palestine. But these proved to be only interim measures. In March 1920 a Syrian Congress met in Damascus and proclaimed Feisal king of a united Syria, including Palestine; only a month later, however, the Allied Conference of San Remo decided that both should be put under a new mandate system, with France taking on the mandate for Syria. The French began as they meant to continue. In June they issued an ultimatum demanding Syrian recognition of their new authority, after which they marched in and expelled Feisal; finally, in July 1922, the League of Nations approved the mandate for Syria and Lebanon, which had declared itself a separate state. Feisal had meanwhile been made King of Iraq, while his older brother Abdullah assumed the crown of Transjordan – since 1949 known as the Hashemite Kingdom of Jordan.

---

[1] How this promise accorded with the Sykes–Picot Agreement – or, later, with the Balfour Declaration – was never made entirely clear.

Jordan and Iraq are no concern of ours; Palestine, however, is. The last visitor to the Peace Conference who deserves special mention here is Dr Chaim Weizmann – shortly to be appointed president of the World Zionist Organisation. Weizmann, who had already been largely responsible for the Balfour Declaration, addressed the Supreme Council on 27 February with an energetic appeal for the establishment of a Jewish home in Palestine. As an observer, he was also present at the San Remo conference which confirmed the Declaration and awarded the Palestine mandate to Great Britain. Later, during the 1920s and 1930s, his negotiating skills were to be severely tested as Britain – confronted by increasing civil disorder resulting from nascent Arab nationalism – lost her early enthusiasm for Zionism and tried to retreat from her commitments. But he won through in the end, and lived to become, in 1948, the first President of the state of Israel.

The Paris Peace Conference of 1919, and the Treaty of Versailles which followed it, marked the end of the old world and the beginning of the new. In 1914 five great empires were centred on European capitals. Five years later three – the German, the Austro-Hungarian and the Russian – were gone, and one – the Ottoman – was on its deathbed. Only the last – the British – survived. The world, henceforth, was to be a very different place.

And so our story is told – so far, at least, as this book is concerned. Obviously, the history of the Middle Sea will never be over until that sea itself runs dry; but whereas an account of a specific period can be rounded to an elegant close, one which takes as its subject merely a given region of the world can be brought only to an arbitrary termination, and this particular example of the latter genre is more than long enough already. With every day that passes, life becomes more eventful. History not only becomes longer; it moves at a faster pace. In the early chapters of this book, a century could be covered in a page or two; towards the end of it, an entire chapter may barely accommodate a decade. To have continued through the Second World War and its consequences to the end of the second millennium would probably have resulted in a volume at least twice as long as this, and would have constituted a penance for author and reader alike.

Some six or seven thousand years ago the Mediterranean gave birth to Western civilisation as we know it. Its relatively small size, its confined shape, the gentleness of its climate, the blessed fertility and the manifold indentations of its European and Asiatic shores, all combined to provide a uniquely protective environment in which its various peoples could develop and flourish. Even the light played its part, giving those peoples a clarity of outlook unmatched in less favoured regions. In gods they believed, as no less than three great religions attest, but in the sunlit Mediterranean world there was no place for the ghosts and the giants, the goblins and the trolls, that feature so prominently in the folklore of the misty and lugubrious north. For all this, and much else besides, we owe an immense and incalculable debt. One important question, however, remains to be answered: now that the contribution has been made, how important still is the contributor? Does the Middle Sea of today retain the significance that it enjoyed when the world was young?

Alas, the answer must be no. When the world was young it was limitless; now it has shrunk pitiably, and the Mediterranean has shrunk with it. Today it is easier to fight a war in Iraq or even Korea than it was a century ago to transport an army from England to Italy or Spain. The flight from Gibraltar to Istanbul takes little more than three hours. Trade routes no longer exist. Transport ships and tankers continue to ply to and from the pipeline terminals of the Middle East, but the sea itself is rapidly being taken over by a new and terrible phenomenon: the monster cruise ship, prowling ceaselessly from port to port, from island to island, vomiting out on to each more people than many of them would in former days have seen in a lifetime.

At the start of the third millennium, therefore, it is becoming increasingly clear that its old *raison d'être* is lost for ever, and that the prime purpose of today's Mediterranean is pleasure. This is not, perhaps, in every respect a bad thing; it could be argued that waters which were in the past all too often stained with blood are a good deal better off under a thin film of *ambre solaire*. One tends to forget, too, the miseries of former days at sea – days when the backs of galley slaves bled under the lash, when ships were stricken by plague and obliged to remain offshore until no man on board was left alive, when a sudden summer storm could be tantamount to a death-warrant for an entire crew. What is sad is the loss of dignity: that the world's most historic body of water should be so taken for granted, so polluted; that many of its shores should be so littered with old plastic as to be practically unvisitable; and that many others are maintained only through the efforts of thousands of sweepers, working all day to keep them clean.

Here, perhaps, is yet another reason for this book to end where it does. It has chronicled many disasters, and not a few tragedies. It has considered the Middle Sea by turns as a cradle and a grave, a bond and a barrier, a blessing and a battlefield. How sad to watch it decline into a playground, as the old harbours are converted into yacht marinas and the triremes are replaced by jet-skis. How much better to draw the curtain while it was still essentially the Mediterranean it had always been, of which every wave told a story, and every drop was noble.

Bibliography

ABULAFIA, D. *Frederick II: A Medieval Emperor*. London 1988.

——— (ed.) *The Mediterranean in History*. London 2003.

ABUN-NASR, J. M. *A History of the Maghrib in the Islamic Period*. Cambridge 1987.

ACTON, H. *The Bourbons of Naples (1734–1825)*. London 1957.

———. *The Last Bourbons of Naples (1825–1861)*. London 1961.

ALSOP, J. *From the Silent Earth: A Report on the Greek Bronze Age*. London 1965.

ANCELL, S. *A Circumstantial Journal of the Long and Tedious Blockade and Siege of Gibraltar*. Liverpool 1785.

ANTONIUS, G. *The Arab Awakening: The Story of the Arab National Movement*. London 1938.

ARMSTRONG, K. *Islam: A Short History*. London 2000.

ARONSON, T. *Royal Vendetta: The Crown of Spain 1829–1965*. London 1967.

ASPREY, R. B. *The Rise and Fall of Napoleon Bonaparte*. 2 vols. London 2000.

ATKINSON, W. C. *Spain: A Brief History*. London 1934.

BALBI DI CORREGGIO, F. *The Siege of Malta, 1565*. Trans. H. A. Balbi. Copenhagen 1961.

BARBER, M. *The New Knighthood: A History of the Order of the Temple*. Cambridge 1994.

BARKER, E. *Macedonia: Its Place in Balkan Power Politics*. London 1950.

BARNETT, C. *Bonaparte*. London 1978.

BARRACLOUGH, G. *From Agadir to Armageddon: Anatomy of a Crisis*. London 1982.

BERTRAND, L. *The History of Spain. Part I: From the Visigoths to the Death of Philip II*. Trans. W. B. Wells. London 1952.

BOWMAN, J. *Crete*. London 1970.

BRADFORD, E. *Mediterranean*. London 1971.

———. *The Sultan's Admiral: The Life of Barbarossa*. London 1969.

———. *The Shield and the Sword: The Knights of St John*. London 1972.

BRANTÔME, ABBÉ DE. *Oeuvres du Seigneur de Brantôme*. Paris 1740.

BRAUDEL, F. *La Méditerranée et le monde méditerranéen à l'époque de Philippe II*. 2nd edn. Paris 1966.

———. *Autour de la Méditerranée*. Paris 1996.

BREWER, D. *The Flame of Freedom: The Greek War of Independence 1821–33*. London 2001.

BRIGHT, J. F. *Maria Theresa*. London 1897.

BURN, A. R. *Minoans, Philistines and Greeks, BC 1400–900*. London 1930.

BUSH, CAPT. E. W. *Gallipoli*. London 1975.

CAMBON, H. *Histoire du Maroc*. Paris 1952.

The Cambridge Illustrated History of the Middle Ages. Ed. R. Fossier. Cambridge 1989.

The Cambridge Medieval History. Planned by J. B. Bury. 8 vols. Cambridge 1911–32.

The Cambridge Modern History. Planned by Lord Acton. 13 vols. Cambridge 1902–12.

CARR, R. *Spain, 1808–1939*. Oxford 1966.

CARR, R. (ed.) *Spain: A History*. Oxford 2000.

CHAMBERLIN, E. R. *The World of the Italian Renaissance*. London 1982.

CHEYNE, A. G. *Muslim Spain: Its History and Culture*. Minneapolis 1974.

CHURCHILL, W. S. *World Crisis, 1911–1918*. 4 vols. London 1923.

COLLISON-MORLEY, L. *Naples Through the Centuries*. London 1925.

CONN, S. *Gibraltar in British Diplomacy in the Eighteenth Century*. New Haven 1942.

CORBETT, J. S. *England in the Mediterranean, 1603–1713*. 2 vols. London 1904.

DAKIN, D. *The Greek Struggle for Independence 1821–33*. London 1973.

Dizionario biografico degli Italiani. Rome, 1960–.

DODWELL, H. *The Founder of Modern Egypt: A Study of Muhammad 'Ali*. Cambridge 1931.

DRINKWATER, J. *A History of the Siege of Gibraltar*. London 1846.

DUFAYARD, C. *Histoire de Savoie*. Paris 1922.

EGGENBERGER, D. *A Dictionary of Battles*. London 1967.

ELGOOD, P. G. *Bonaparte's Adventure in Egypt*. London 1931.

Enciclopedia universal ilustrada Europeo-Americana. 70 vols. with appendices and annual supplements. Barcelona, Bilbao, Madrid 1909–.

The Encyclopedia of Islam. 4 vols. London and Leyden 1913–38.

EULALIA, HRH THE INFANTA OF SPAIN. *Court Life from Within.* London 1915.

———. *Memoirs.* London 1936.

EUSEBIUS, BISHOP OF CAESAREA. *A History of the Church from Christ to Constantine.* Trans. G. A. Williamson. London 1965.

FERMOR, P. LEIGH. *A Time of Gifts.* London 1977.

FINLAY, G. *A History of Greece from its Conquest by the Romans to the Present Time, B.C.146–A.D. 1864.* 7 vols. Oxford, 1851–77.

FINLEY, M. and MACK SMITH, D. *A History of Sicily.* 3 vols. London 1968.

FISHER, SIR G. *Barbary Legend: War, Trade and Piracy in North Africa, 1415–1830.* London 1957.

FISHER, H. A. L. *A History of Europe.* London 1936.

FORSTER, E. M. *Alexandria: A History and a Guide.* Alexandria 1922.

FOSS, A. *Ibiza and Minorca.* London 1975.

GARDNER, B. *Allenby.* London 1965.

GEORGE, H. B. *Genealogical Tables Illustrative of Modern History.* 5th edn. Oxford 1916.

GHORBAL, S. *The Beginnings of the Egyptian Question and the Rise of Mehemet Ali.* London 1928.

GIBBON, E. *The History of the Decline and Fall of the Roman Empire.* Ed. B. Radice. London 1983.

GILLINGHAM, J. *The Life and Times of Richard I.* London 1973.

GRANT, M. *Cleopatra.* London 1972.

———. *History of Rome.* London 1978.

———. *Julius Caesar.* London 1969.

GREEN, P. *A Concise History of Ancient Greece to the Close of the Classical Era.* London 1973.

GREGORY, D. *Minorca, the Illusory Prize: A History of the British Occupations of Minorca between 1708 and 1802.* London and Toronto 1990.

GSELL, S., Marçais, G. and Yver, G. *Histoire d'Algérie.* Paris 1927.

GUNN, P. *Naples: A Palimpsest.* London 1961.

HAMILTON, I. *Gallipoli Diary.* London 1920.

HARDEN, D. *The Phoenicians.* London 1962.

HASLIP, J. *The Sultan: The Life of Abdul Hamid.* London 1958.

HAZEL, J. *Who's Who in the Greek World.* London 2000.

HEARDER, H. and WALEY, D. P. (eds.) *A Short History of Italy.* Cambridge 1963.

HILLS, G. *Rock of Contention: A History of Gibraltar*. London 1974.

HOOK, J. *The Sack of Rome*. London 1972.

HORDEN, P. and PURCELL, N. *The Corrupting Sea: A Study of Mediterranean History*. London 2000.

INALCIK, H. *The Ottoman Empire: The Classical Age 1300–1600*. Trans. N. Itzkowitz and C. Imber. London 1973.

JACKSON, G. *The Making of Medieval Spain*. London 1972.

JAMES, L. *Imperial Warrior: The Life and Times of Field-Marshal Viscount Allenby, 1861–1936*. London 1993.

JAMES, R. R. *Gallipoli*. London 1965.

JENKINS, R. *Churchill*. London 2001.

JOINVILLE, SIEUR DE. *Histoire de Saint Louis*. Ed. N. de Wailly. Paris 1874.

JULIEN, C.-A. *Histoire de l'Afrique du Nord*. Paris 1961.

JURIEN DE LA GRAVIÈRE, ADMIRAL. *Les derniers jours de la marine à rames*. Paris 1885.

——. *Doria et Barberousse*. Paris 1886.

——. *Les chevaliers de Malte et la marine de Philippe II*. 2 vols. Paris 1887.

——. *Les corsaires barbaresques et la marine de Soliman*. Paris 1887.

——. *La guerre de Chypre et la bataille de Lepante*. 2 vols. Paris 1888.

KANTOROWICZ, E. *Frederick the Second, 1194–1250*. Trans. E. O. Lorimer. London 1931.

KEYES, R. *The Naval Memoirs of Admiral of the Fleet Sir Roger Keyes*. London 1934.

KING, R. *Sardinia*. London 1975.

KINROSS, LORD. *Atatürk: The Rebirth of a Nation*. London 1964.

——. *Between Two Seas: The Creation of the Suez Canal*. London 1968.

——. *The Ottoman Centuries: The Rise and Fall of the Turkish Empire*. London 1977.

KNIGHT, W. S. M. *The History of the Great European War: Its Causes and Effects*. 10 vols. London 1914–20.

LANE, F. C. *Venetian Ships and Shipbuilders of the Renaissance*. Baltimore 1934.

——. *Venice and History*. Baltimore 1966.

——. *Venice, a Maritime Republic*. Baltimore 1973.

LANE FOX, R. *Alexander the Great*. London 1973.

LANE-POOLE, S. *The Barbary Corsairs*. London 1890.

LAVERY, B. *Nelson and the Nile*. London 1998.

LAWRENCE, T. E. *Revolt in the Desert*. London 1927.

LEO AFRICANUS. *The History and Description of Africa, and of the Notable Things therein Contained*. Trans. J. Pory, ed. R. Brown. 3 vols. London 1896.

LEWIS, B. *The Muslim Discovery of Europe*. London 1982.

LIVERMORE, H. V. *A New History of Portugal*. Cambridge 1976.

LLOYD, C. *The Nile Campaign*. Newton Abbot and New York 1973.

LUKE, SIR H. *Malta: An Account and an Appreciation*. London 1949.

MACBRIDE, M. (ed.) *With Napoleon at Waterloo, and other unpublished documents of the Waterloo and Peninsular Campaigns*. (Includes extracts from the diary of Sgt. D. Nicol, *With Abercrombie [sic] and Moore in Egypt*.) London 1911.

MACKAY, A. *Spain in the Middle Ages: From Frontier to Empire, 1000–1500*. London 1977.

MACKESY, P. *British Victory in Egypt, 1801*. London 1995.

MACMILLAN, M. *The Peacemakers: The Paris Conference of 1919 and its Attempt to End War*. London 2001.

MADELIN, L. *Histoire du Consulat et de l'Empire*. 16 vols. Paris 1937–52.

MANSEL, P. *Constantinople: City of the World's Desire, 1453–1924*. London 1995.

MARKHAM, F. *Napoleon*. London 1963.

MARKOE, G. *Phoenicians*. London 2000.

MASEFIELD, J. *Gallipoli*. London 1916.

MASSON, G. *Frederick II of Hohenstaufen: A Life*. London 1957.

MAUROIS, A. *A History of France*. London 1949.

MAZOWER, M. *Salonica, City of Ghosts: Christians, Muslims and Jews 1430–1950*. London 2004.

MELLERSH, H. E. L. *Chronology of the Ancient World*. Oxford 1994.

MILLER, W. *The Latins in the Levant: A History of Frankish Greece, 1204–1566*. London 1908.

———. *Essays on the Latin Orient*. Cambridge 1921.

MOOREHEAD, A. *Gallipoli*. London 1956.

MOUSSET, A. *Histoire d'Espagne*. Paris 1947.

The New Encyclopedia Britannica. 15th edn. Chicago 1998.

NICOLSON, H. *Peacemaking 1919*. London 1933.

NORWICH, J. J. *The Normans in the South*. London 1967.

———. *The Kingdom in the Sun*. London 1970.

———. *Venice: The Rise to Empire*. London 1977.

———. *Venice: The Greatness and the Fall*. London 1981.

——. *Byzantium: The Early Centuries*. London 1988.

——. *Byzantium: The Apogee*. London 1991.

——. *Byzantium: The Decline and Fall*. London 1995.

——. *Paradise of Cities: Nineteenth-Century Venice Seen through Foreign Eyes*. London 2003.

OMAN, C. *Nelson*. London 1947.

The Oxford Classical Dictionary. Oxford 1996.

The Oxford Dictionary of National Biography. 61 vols. Oxford 2004.

PALMER, A. *The Kaiser: Warlord of the Second Reich*. New York 1978.

——. *The Decline and Fall of the Ottoman Empire*. London 1992.

PARRY, J. H. *The Discovery of the Sea*. London 1975.

PASTOR, L. *The History of the Popes from the Close of the Middle Ages*. Trans. F. I. Antrobus and R. F. Kerr. London 1891–1953.

PETTIFER, J. (ed.) *The New Macedonian Question*. London 1999.

PICK, ROBERT. *Empress Maria Theresa*. London 1966.

PRESCOTT, W. H. *History of the Reign of Ferdinand and Isabella the Catholic*. 3 vols. Philadelphia 1864.

PRICE, W. H. C. *The Balkan Cockpit: The Political and Military Story of the Balkan Wars in Macedonia*. London 1915.

PROCOPIUS. *The Secret History*. Trans. G. A. Williamson. London 1966.

PRYOR, J. H. *Geography, Technology and War: Studies in the Maritime History of the Mediterranean, 649–1571*. Cambridge 1988.

READ, J. *The Moors in Spain and Portugal*. London 1974.

READ, P. P. *The Templars*. London 1999.

RICO, E. *Maria Cristina, la reina burguesa*. Barcelona 1994.

RODD, SIR R. *The Princes of Achaia and the Chronicles of Morea: A Study of Greece in the Middle Ages*. 2 vols. London 1907.

ROSSITER, S. *Crete* (Blue Guide). London 1974.

RUNCIMAN, S. *A History of the Crusades*. 3 vols. Cambridge 1951–4.

——. *The Sicilian Vespers*. Cambridge 1958.

RUSSELL, J. *Gibraltar Besieged*. London 1965.

RUSSELL, P. E. *San Pedro de Cardena and the Heroic History of the Cid*. *Medium Aevum*, vol. xxvii, no. 2 (1958).

SCHLIEMANN, H. *Troy and its Remains*. London 1875.

SHEPHERD, W. R. *Historical Atlas*. 8th edn. London 1956.

SPILSBURY, J. *A Journal of the Siege of Gibraltar, 1779–1783*. Gibraltar 1908.

SUETONIUS. *History of Twelve Caesars*. Trans. P. Holland. London 1930.

SWIRE, J. *Bulgarian Conspiracy*. London 1939.

TENENTI, A. *Piracy and the Decline of Venice, 1580–1615*. Trans. J. and B. Pullan, London 1967.

THIRY, BARON. *Les Années de jeunesse de Napoléon Bonaparte*. Paris 1975.

———. *Bonaparte en Egypte*. Paris 1973.

THUCYDIDES. *History of the Peloponnesian War*. Trans. and introd. R. Warner. London 1962.

TRAILL, D. A. *Schliemann of Troy: Treasure and Deceit*. London 1995.

TURNER, W. *Journal of a Tour in the Levant*. London 1820.

VAN DEN MEER. *Atlas of European Civilisation*. Eng. version by T. A. Birrell. Amsterdam 1954.

VILLARI, L. *The Republic of Ragusa: An Episode of the Turkish Conquest*. London 1904.

VILLEHARDOUIN, GEOFFREY OF. *La Conquête de Constantinople*. Ed. E. Faral. 2 vols. Paris 1938–9.

WARNER, R. *Men of Athens*. London 1972.

WAVELL, COL. A. P. *The Palestine Campaigns*. London 1929.

WHITMAN, C. H. *Homer and the Heroic Tradition*. Cambridge, MA 1958.

WILSON, SIR R. *History of the British Expedition to Egypt*. London 1803.

WRIGHT, J. *The Jesuits: Missions, Myths and Histories*. London 2004.

YOUNG, K. *The Greek Passion: A Study in People and Politics*. London 1969.

YOUNG, M. *Corfu and the other Ionian Islands* (Travellers' Guide). London 1977.

ZIEGLER, P. *The Black Death*. London 1969.

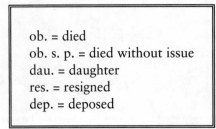

ob. = died
ob. s. p. = died without issue
dau. = daughter
res. = resigned
dep. = deposed

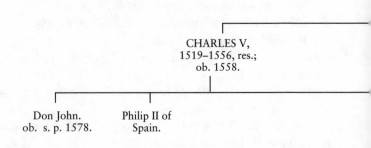

CHARLES V,
1519–1556, res.;
ob. 1558.

Don John.   Philip II of
ob. s. p. 1578.   Spain.

JOSEPH I,
1705–1711.

1. JOSEPH II   2. LEOPOLD II = Maria Louisa, dau. of
1765–1790, ob. s. p.   1790–1792.   Charles III of Spain.

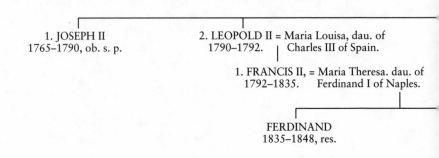

                            1. FRANCIS II, = Maria Theresa. dau. of
                               1792–1835.   Ferdinand I of Naples.

                            FERDINAND
                            1835–1848, res.

MAXIMILIAN I = Mary, dau. of Charles the Bold.
1493–1519.

Philip, ob. 1506. = Joanna (the mad), heiress of Spain, ob.1555.

Ferdinand I, = Anne, heiress of Hungary and Bohemia.
1556–1564.

Mary = MAXIMILIAN II
1564–1576.

Mary = Charles D. of
Styria.

Mary Anne = FERDINAND II,
1619–1637.

FERDINAND III, 1637–1657. = Mary, dau. of Philip III of Spain.

LEOPOLD I = Margaret Theresa, dau. of Philip IV of Spain.
1658–1705.

CHARLES VI = Elizabeth Christina, dau. of Lewis Rudolf,
1711–1740.   D. of Brunswick-Wolfenbüttel.

FRANCIS I, D. of Lorraine, = MARIA THERESA,
1745–1765.   ob. 1780.

3. Maria Carolina = Ferdinand I
of Naples.

5. Marie Antoinette, = Louis XVI of
executed 1793.   France.

Francis = Sophia, dau. of Maximilian I
of Bavaria.

FRANCIS JOSEPH = Elizabeth of Bavaria
1848–1916.   (assassinated 1898)

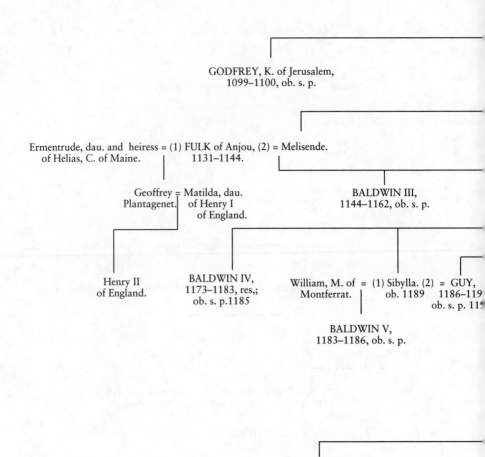

GODFREY, K. of Jerusalem,
1099–1100, ob. s. p.

Ermentrude, dau. and heiress = (1) FULK of Anjou, (2) = Melisende.
of Helias, C. of Maine.   1131–1144.

Geoffrey = Matilda, dau.   BALDWIN III,
Plantagenet. of Henry I   1144–1162, ob. s. p.
              of England.

Henry II   BALDWIN IV,   William, M. of = (1) Sibylla. (2) = GUY,
of England.   1173–1183, res,;   Montferrat.   ob. 1189   1186–119
                ob. s. p.1185   ob. s. p. 11

                              BALDWIN V,
                              1183–1186, ob. s. p.

HENRY, ob. 1253.

HUGH II, ob. s. p. 1267.

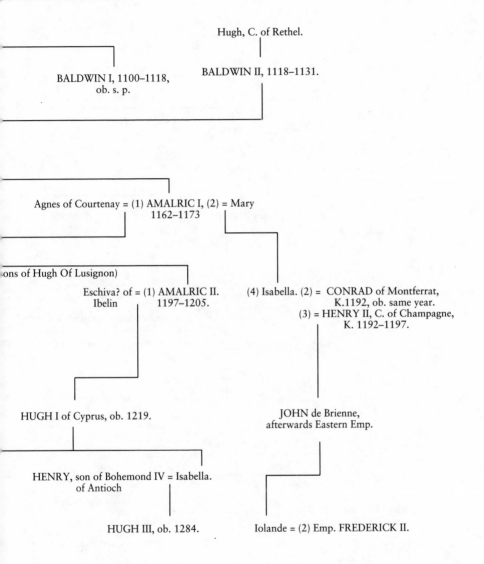

Hugh, C. of Rethel.

BALDWIN I, 1100–1118,
ob. s. p.

BALDWIN II, 1118–1131.

Agnes of Courtenay = (1) AMALRIC I, (2) = Mary
1162–1173

ons of Hugh Of Lusignon)

Eschiva? of = (1) AMALRIC II.
Ibelin   1197–1205.

(4) Isabella. (2) = CONRAD of Montferrat,
K.1192, ob. same year.
(3) = HENRY II, C. of Champagne,
K. 1192–1197.

HUGH I of Cyprus, ob. 1219.

JOHN de Brienne,
afterwards Eastern Emp.

HENRY, son of Bohemond IV = Isabella.
of Antioch

HUGH III, ob. 1284.

Iolande = (2) Emp. FREDERICK II.

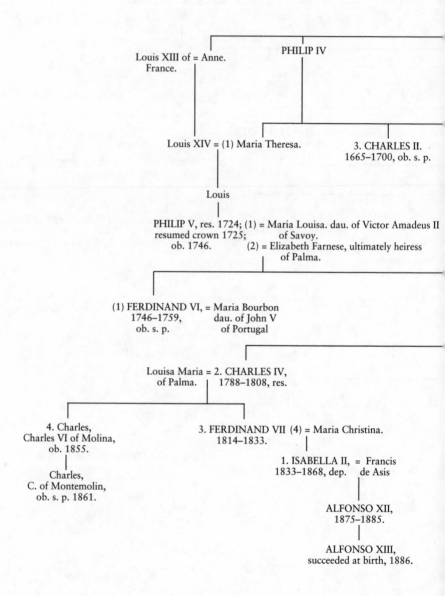

Louis XIII of = Anne.
France.

PHILIP IV

Louis XIV = (1) Maria Theresa.

3. CHARLES II.
1665–1700, ob. s. p.

Louis

PHILIP V, res. 1724; (1) = Maria Louisa. dau. of Victor Amadeus II
resumed crown 1725;   of Savoy.
    ob. 1746.   (2) = Elizabeth Farnese, ultimately heiress
                  of Palma.

(1) FERDINAND VI, = Maria Bourbon
    1746–1759,   dau. of John V
     ob. s. p.   of Portugal

Louisa Maria = 2. CHARLES IV,
  of Palma.   1788–1808, res.

4. Charles,
Charles VI of Molina,
ob. 1855.

Charles,
C. of Montemolin,
ob. s. p. 1861.

3. FERDINAND VII (4) = Maria Christina.
    1814–1833.

1. ISABELLA II, = Francis
1833–1868, dep.   de Asis

ALFONSO XII,
1875–1885.

ALFONSO XIII,
succeeded at birth, 1886.

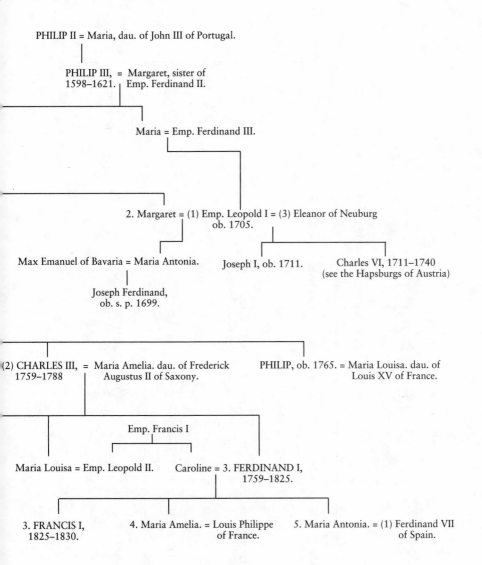

PHILIP II = Maria, dau. of John III of Portugal.

PHILIP III, = Margaret, sister of
1598–1621. Emp. Ferdinand II.

Maria = Emp. Ferdinand III.

2. Margaret = (1) Emp. Leopold I = (3) Eleanor of Neuburg
ob. 1705.

Max Emanuel of Bavaria = Maria Antonia.

Joseph I, ob. 1711.

Charles VI, 1711–1740
(see the Hapsburgs of Austria)

Joseph Ferdinand,
ob. s. p. 1699.

(2) CHARLES III, = Maria Amelia. dau. of Frederick
1759–1788 Augustus II of Saxony.

PHILIP, ob. 1765. = Maria Louisa. dau. of
Louis XV of France.

Emp. Francis I

Maria Louisa = Emp. Leopold II.

Caroline = 3. FERDINAND I,
1759–1825.

3. FRANCIS I,
1825–1830.

4. Maria Amelia. = Louis Philippe
of France.

5. Maria Antonia. = (1) Ferdinand VII
of Spain.

THE HOUSE OF SAVOY

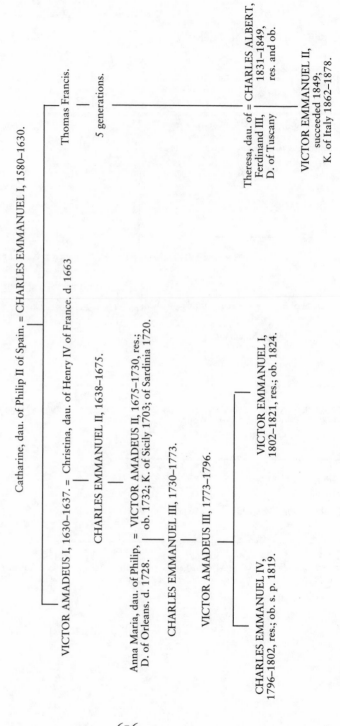

Catharine, dau. of Philip II of Spain. = CHARLES EMMANUEL I, 1580–1630.

VICTOR AMADEUS I, 1630–1637. = Christina, dau. of Henry IV of France. d. 1663

Thomas Francis.

5 generations.

CHARLES EMMANUEL II, 1638–1675.

Anna Maria, dau. of Philip, = VICTOR AMADEUS II, 1675–1730, res.;
D. of Orleans. d. 1728.   ob. 1732; K. of Sicily 1703; of Sardinia 1720.

CHARLES EMMANUEL III, 1730–1773.

VICTOR AMADEUS III, 1773–1796.

VICTOR EMMANUEL I,
1802–1821, res.; ob. 1824.

CHARLES EMMANUEL IV,
1796–1802, res.; ob. s. p. 1819.

Theresa, dau. of = CHARLES ALBERT,
Ferdinand III,   1831–1849,
D. of Tuscany   res. and ob.

VICTOR EMMANUEL II,
succeeded 1849;
K. of Italy 1862–1878.

616

THE HOUSE OF HAUTEVILLE

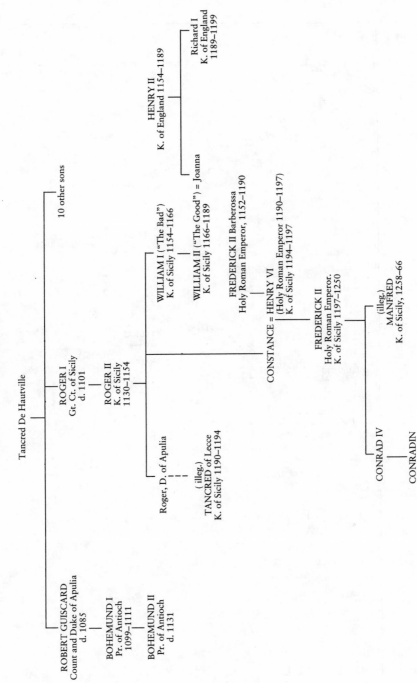

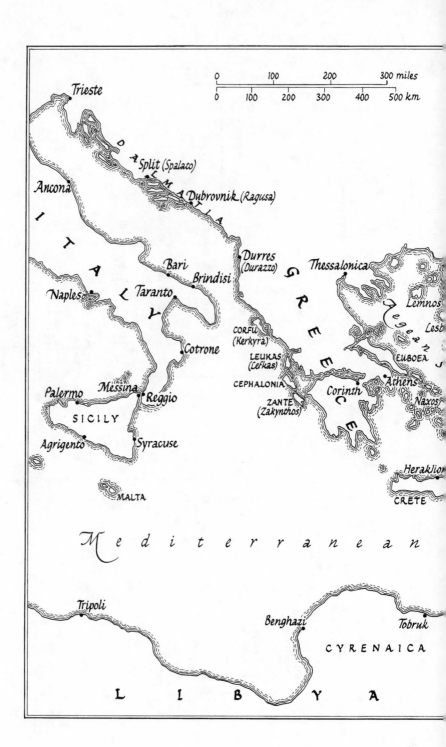

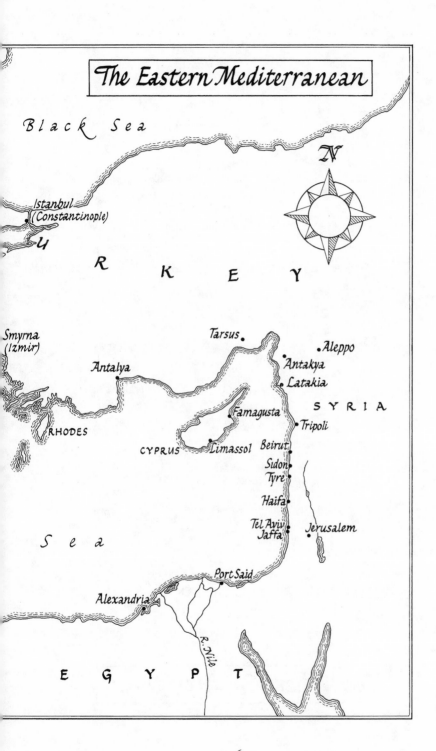

The Eastern Mediterranean

Black Sea

Istanbul
(Constantinople)

T U R K E Y

Smyrna
(Izmir)

Antalya

Tarsus

Aleppo

Antakya

Latakia

SYRIA

Famagusta

Tripoli

RHODES

CYPRUS   Limassol   Beirut

Sidon

Tyre

Haifa

Tel Aviv
Jaffa

Jerusalem

Sea

Port Said

Alexandria

R. Nile

E G Y P T

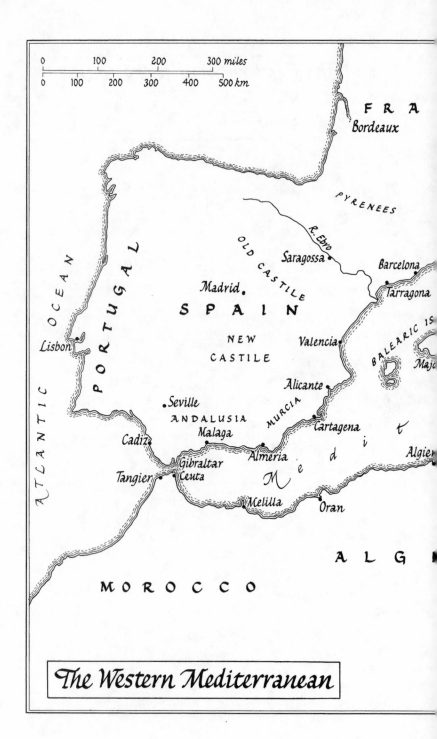

The Western Mediterranean

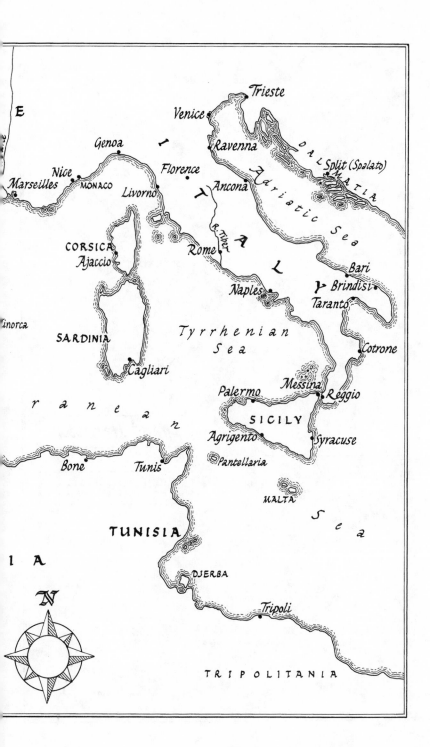

E

Trieste

Venice

I *Genoa*

Nice *Florence* *Ravenna*

Marseilles MONACO

Livorno T *Ancona*

CORSICA A *Rome* R. *Tiber* *Ancona*

Ajaccio L

inorca SARDINIA

Cagliari

r a n e a n

Bone *Tunis*

TUNISIA

N

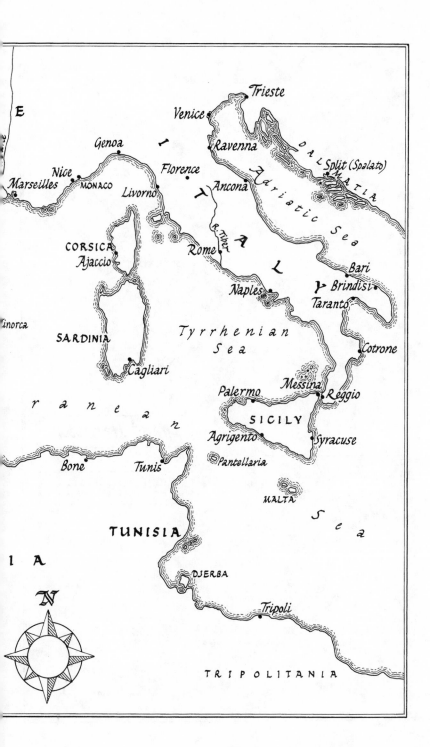

DAL *Split (Spalato)*

MATIA

Adriatic Sea

Bari

Brindisi

Naples *Taranto*

Cotrone

Tyrrhenian Sea

Palermo *Messina* *Reggio*

SICILY

Agrigento *Syracuse*

Pantellaria

MALTA

S e a

DJERBA

Tripoli

TRIPOLITANIA

I A

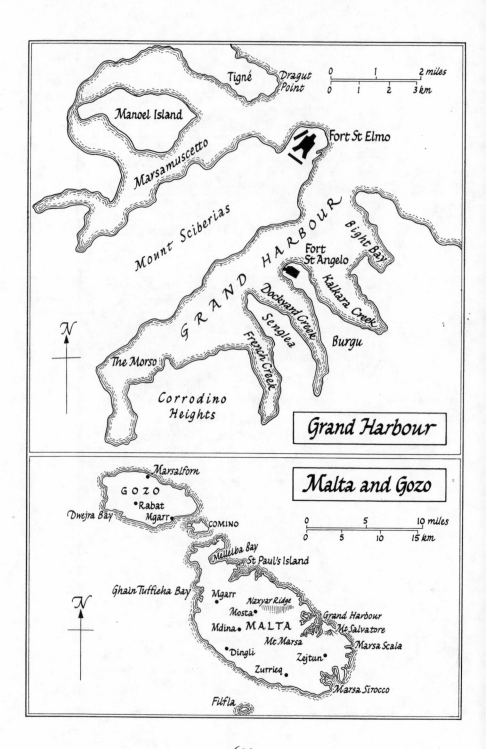

Tigné

Dragut
Point

Manoel Island

Marsamuscetto

Fort St Elmo

Mount Sciberias

GRAND HARBOUR

Fort
St Angelo

Bight Bay

Kalkara Creek

Dockyard Creek

Senglea

Burgu

French Creek

The Morso

Corrodino
Heights

N

Grand Harbour

0   1   2 miles
0   1   2   3 km

Malta and Gozo

Marsalforn

GOZO

Dwejra Bay

Rabat

Mgarr

COMINO

Melleiba Bay

St Paul's Island

Ghain Tuffieha Bay

Mgarr

Naxyar Ridge

Grand Harbour

Mosta

Mt Salvatore

Mdina

MALTA

Marsa Scala

Dingli

Mt Marsa

Zejtun

Zurrieq

Marsa Sirocco

Filfla

N

0   5   10 miles
0   5   10   15 km

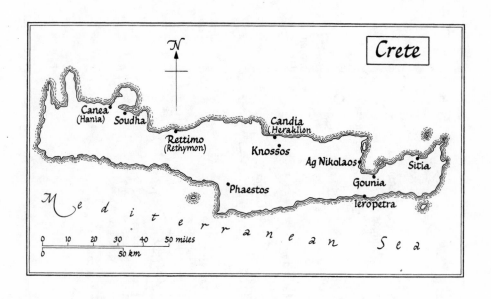

N

Crete

Canea
(Hania)
Soudha

Candia
(Heraklion)

Rettimo
(Rethymon)

Knossos

Ag Nikolaos

Sitia

Gounia

Phaestos

Ieropetra

Mediterranean Sea

0   10   20   30   40   50 miles
0   50 km

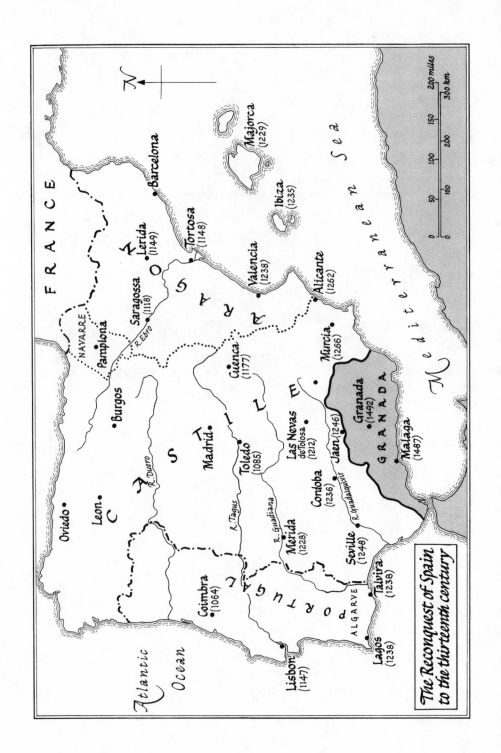

The Reconquest of Spain
to the thirteenth century

FRANCE

NAVARRE

Oviedo •

Leon •

Burgos •

Pamplona •

Saragossa (1118)

R. Ebro

Lerida (1149)

Barcelona

Tortosa (1148)

Majorca (1229)

Ibiza (1235)

Valencia (1238)

Alicante (1252)

A R A G O N

C A S T I L E

R. Duero

Madrid •

Cuenca (1177)

Toledo (1085)

R. Tagus

Las Navas de Tolosa (1212)

Murcia (1266)

Jaen (1246)

Granada (1492)

G R A N A D A

Malaga (1487)

Cordoba (1236)

R. Guadalquivir

R. Guadiana

Mérida (1228)

Seville (1248)

Coimbra (1064)

P O R T U G A L

ALGARVE

Tavira (1238)

Lagos (1238)

Lisbon (1147)

Atlantic Ocean

Mediterranean Sea

200 miles
300 km.

150

100

50

0

Southern Italy and Sicily

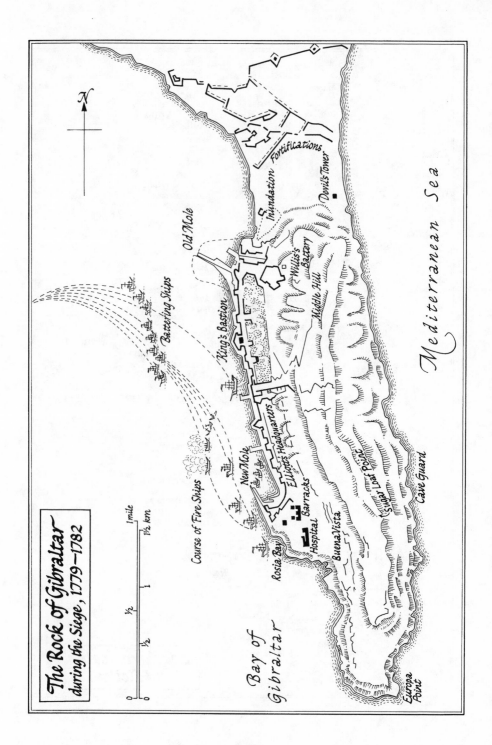

The Rock of Gibraltar
during the Siege, 1779–1782

N

Mediterranean Sea

Bay of
Gibraltar

Battering Ships

Course of Fire Ships

Old Mole

Inundation

Fortifications

Devil's Tower

Willis's

Middle Hill

Battery

King's Bastion

New Mole

Elliot's Headquarters

Barracks

Hospital

Buena Vista

Sugar Loaf Point

Cave Guard

Rosia Bay

Europa
Point

1 mile

½ km

½

1

½

626

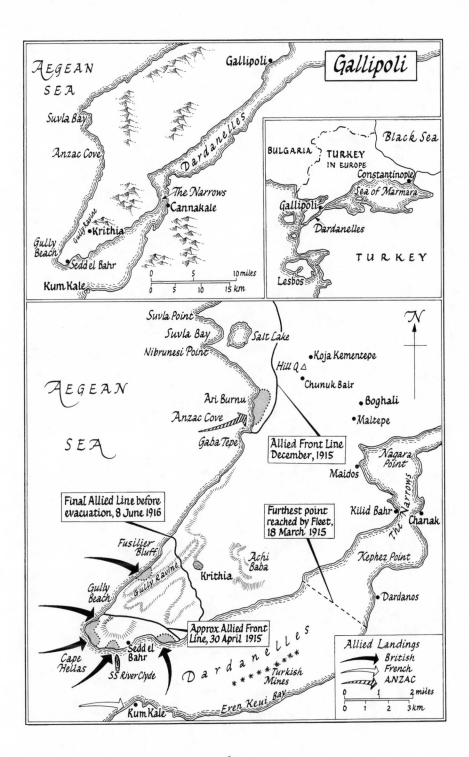

Gallipoli

Aegean Sea

Gallipoli

Suvla Bay

Anzac Cove

The Narrows
Cannakale

Gully Ravine
Krithia

Gully Beach
Sedd el Bahr

Kum Kale

0 ___ 5 ___ 10 miles
0 ___ 5 ___ 10 ___ 15 km

BULGARIA

TURKEY IN EUROPE

Black Sea

Constantinople

Sea of Marmara

Gallipoli

Dardanelles

TURKEY

Lesbos

Suvla Point
Suvla Bay
Nibrunesi Point

Salt Lake

Koja Kementepe

Hill Q △

Chunuk Bair

Ari Burnu

Anzac Cove

Gaba Tepe

Boghali

Maltepe

Allied Front Line
December, 1915

Nagara Point

Maidos

AEGEAN

SEA

Final Allied Line before
evacuation, 8 June 1916

Fusilier Bluff

Gully Ravine

Gully Beach

Cape Hellas

Sedd el Bahr

SS River Clyde

Kum Kale

Furthest point
reached by Fleet,
18 March 1915

Achi Baba

Krithia

Kilid Bahr

The Narrows

Chanak

Kephez Point

Dardanos

Approx. Allied Front
Line, 30 April 1915

Dardanelles

Turkish Mines

Eren Keui Bay

Allied Landings
British
French
ANZAC

0 ___ 1 ___ 2 miles
0 ___ 1 ___ 2 ___ 3 km

Index

Visconti, Valentina, Duchess of Milan, 247
Visigoths, 56, 68–9
Vitellius, Roman Emperor, 48
Vivaldi, Ugolino and Guido, 242
Vladimirescu, Theodore, 464–5
Volturno river, battle of (1860), 532–3
Vrionis, Omer, 474

Walewska, Marie, 456
Walpole, Sir Robert, 384n
Walsh, Robert, 468
Ward, Captain John, 332
Waterloo, battle of (1815), 456–7
Waugh, Evelyn, 50
Wavell, Lieut.-Colonel Archibald P. (*later* Field Marshal Earl), 592, 594
Weizmann, Chaim, 600
Wellington, Arthur Wellesley, 1st Duke of, 455
Western Empire *see* Holy Roman Empire
Whitaker, Samuel, 397
Wilhelm I, Kaiser of Germany, 597
Wilhelm II, Kaiser of Germany, 500, 554n, 575, 594
William III (of Orange), King of England, 365–6, 368
William IV, King of Great Britain (*earlier* Prince), 394n
William I (the Silent), Prince of Orange, 329, 364n

William I ('the Bad'), King of Sicily, 106–7, 109
William II ('the Good'), King of Sicily, 109–10, 126, 157
William of Champlitte, 144, 146–8
Wilson, Lieut.-Colonel Robert, 448
Wolseley, General Sir Garnet (*later* Viscount), 556
Worms, Council of (1048), 99
Worms, Diet of (1521), 272

Xanthos, Emmanuel, 462–3
Xerxes, Persian Emperor, 17–18
Ximenes, Cardinal Francisco, Archbishop of Toledo, 263, 283–4

Yolande de Brienne, wife of Emperor Frederick II, 160–4
Young Arab movement, 573
Young Italy movement (*La Giovine Italia*), 513, 515
Young Turks movement, 570–1
Yussif Pasha, 466

Zama, battle of (203 BC), 30–1
Zane, Girolamo, 312–14
Zara (Zadar), Dalmatia, 134–5, 312
Zedekiah, King of Judah, 14
Zen, Antonio, 358–60
Zeno, Byzantine Emperor, 60
Zorzi family (of Venice), 145n
Zulian, Biagio, 344